FORENSIC SCIENCE

Third Edition

From the CRIME SCENE to the CRIME LAB

RICHARD SAFERSTEIN, Ph.D.

Forensic Science Consultant, Mt. Laurel, New Jersey

PEARSON

Boston   Columbus   Indianapolis   New York   San Francisco   Hoboken
Amsterdam   Cape Town   Dubai   London   Madrid   Milan   Munich   Paris   Montréal   Toronto
Delhi   Mexico City   São Paulo   Sydney   Hong Kong   Seoul   Singapore   Taipei   Tokyo

Editorial Director: Andrew Gilfillan
Product Manager: Gary Bauer
Program Manager: Tara Horton
Editorial Assistant: Lynda Cramer
Director of Marketing: David Gesell
Senior Marketing Manager: Mary Salzman
Senior Marketing Coordinator: Alicia Wozniak
Senior Marketing Assistant: Les Roberts
Project Management Team Lead: JoEllen Gohr
Project Manager: Jessica H. Sykes
Procurement Specialist: Deidra Skahill

Senior Art Director: Diane Ernsberger
Cover Designer: Cenveo
Cover Art: Medical RF.com/Corbis
Media Project Manager: April Cleland
Full-Service Project Management: Lori Bradshaw/S4Carlisle
Publishing Services
Composition: S4Carlisle Publishing Services
Printer/Binder: Courier/Kendallville
Cover Printer: Courier/Kendallville
Text Font: Versailles LT Std

Library of Congress Cataloging-in-Publication Data
Saferstein, Richard
   Forensic science: from the crime scene to the crime lab / Richard Saferstein, PhD, Forensic Science Consultant, Mt. Laurel, New Jersey.—Third Edition.
     pages cm
   ISBN 978-0-13-359128-6—ISBN 0-13-359128-X 1. Criminal investigation. 2. Crime scene searches. 3. Forensic sciences. 4. Evidence, Criminal. I. Title.
   HV8073.S214 2014
   363.25—dc23

2014030568

10 9 8 7 6 5 4 3 2 1

ISBN 10:   0-13-359128-X
ISBN 13: 978-0-13-359128-6

For Mom (1917–2010)
and to
Zave and Gabrielle

BRIEF CONTENTS

:: CONTENTS

6 Death Investigation   123

7 Crime-Scene Reconstruction   152

8 Fingerprints   163

9 Firearms, Tool Marks, and Other Impressions 191

10 Bloodstain Pattern Analysis 230

11 Drugs 251

15 Biological Stain Analysis: DNA 369

16 Forensic Aspects of Fire and Explosion Investigation 410

19 Mobile Device Forensics 490

by Peter Stephenson

:: PREFACE

New to This Edition

- **New!** Chapter 19 "Mobile Device Forensics" is completely new to the text. Forensics on mobile devices, like cell phones, can provide an overlay to physical evidence and forensic timelines to give a clearer picture of the events preceding and following a crime event.
- Chapter 3, "Recording the Crime Scene," has been revised to emphasize the almost exclusive use of digital cameras for photographing the crime scene.
- Chapter 4, "Collection of Crime-Scene Evidence," has been expanded to emphasize the proper collection of DNA evidence to preserve its integrity.
- Chapter 15, "Biological Stain Analysis: DNA," has been expanded to emphasize safety considerations in the collection of DNA evidence and the avoidance of potential sources of contamination.
- Information throughout the text has been updated and many new figures have been added to illustrate concepts discussed in the chapters.

Purpose of This Book

When one sets out to write a textbook on the current state of forensic science, the first things that come to mind are all the sophisticated high-tech devices at the disposal of the forensic analyst. A textbook devoted to this topic can quickly overwhelm the student who has little or no prior coursework in the basic sciences and who is averse to correcting this deficiency. Although a study of forensic science must include coverage of some basic scientific principles, the coverage must be presented in a fashion that will not "turn off" the student. Like the second edition, *Forensic Science: From the Crime Scene to the Crime Lab*, Third Edition, is designed to accomplish this objective by presenting the science of forensics in a straightforward and student-friendly format.

Topics are arranged to integrate scientific methodology with actual forensic applications. Discussions of the scientific topics focus on state-of-the-art technology without delving into extraneous theories that may bore or overwhelm the nonscience student. Only the most relevant scientific and technological concepts are presented. A major portion of the text centers on the role of the crime-scene investigator in preserving, recording, and collecting physical evidence at the crime scene. Chapter 3, describing the application of photography to the crime scene, has been updated to emphasize the dominant role of the digital camera at the crime scene. One key concern during the collection of a DNA-containing specimen is contamination. Appropriate insights have been added to the text for minimizing this type of occurrence during the collection and packaging of biological evidence. The third edition also includes a new chapter (Chapter 19), "Mobile Device Forensic." Mobile devices, like cell phones, can provide an overlay to physical evidence and forensic timelines to give a clearer picture of the events preceding and following a crime event.

Descriptions and pertinent forensic facts about cases of notoriety are provided for the reader. The intent is to demonstrate to the reader actual applications of forensic science to real-life case investigations.

The reader is offered the option of delving into the more difficult technical aspects of the subject by reading the Closer Analysis features. This option can be bypassed without detracting from a basic comprehension of the subject of forensic science.

Within and at the end of each chapter, the reader will encounter Quick Reviews and a Chapter Review that recap all of the major points of the chapter. The end-of-chapter Summary is followed by Review Questions, as well as Application and Critical Thinking exercises designed to enhance the reader's learning experience.

Acknowledgments

I am most appreciative of the contribution that retired Lieutenant Andrew (Drew) Donofrio of New Jersey's Bergen County Prosecutor's Office and now a leading private computer forensic examiner made to this new edition. I was fortunate to find in Drew a contributor who not only possesses extraordinary skill, knowledge, and hands-on experience with computer forensics, but was able to combine those attributes with sophisticated communication skills. Likewise, I was fortunate to have Dr. Peter Stephenson contribute to this book on the subject of mobile forensics. He brings skills as a cybercriminologist, author, and educator in digital forensics.

Likewise, I was very fortunate to engage the services of Michelle Tetrault as my research assistant during the preparation of the first and second editions of *Forensic Science: From the Crime Scene to the Crime Lab*. Michelle is an extraordinarily gifted student out of Cedar Crest College in Allentown, Pennsylvania, and George Washington University. She was instrumental in helping me write and organize a number of the chapters in this text. Her skills and tenacity in carrying out her tasks are acknowledged and greatly appreciated. Likewise, Jacque Campbell, a graduate student in forensic science from Arcadia University, provided valuable assistance in preparing chapter updates and examination questions for the new edition.

Many people provided assistance and advice in the preparation of this book. Many faculty members, colleagues, and friends have read and commented on various portions of the text. I would like to acknowledge the contributions of Anita Wonder, Robert J. Phillips, Norman H. Reeves, Jeffrey C. Kercheval, Robert Thompson, Roger Ely, Jose R. Almirall, Michael Malone, Ronald Welsh, Joshua Wilborne, David Pauly, Jan Johnson, Natalie Borgan, Dr. Barbara Needell, Robin D. Williams, Peter Diaczuk, Ken Radwill, Randi Dubnick, and Jacqueline E. Joseph. I'm appreciative of the contributions, reviews, and comments that Dr. Claus Speth, Dr. Mark Taff, Dr. Elizabeth Laposata, Thomas P. Mauriello, and Michelle D. Miranda provided during the preparation of Chapter 6, "Death Investigation."

Finally, I thank the following reviewers of this edition: Charles Kocher, Cumberland County College; Jill Shelley, Northern Kentucky University; Sam Thomas, Hawaii Community

College; Ronald Thrasher, Oklahoma State University; Robert Wardle, Youngstown State University; and Ted Yeshion, Edinboro University.

Instructor Supplements

Instructor's Manual with Test Bank includes content outlines for classroom discussion, teaching suggestions, and answers to selected end-of-chapter questions from the text. This also contains a Word document version of the test bank.

TestGen. This computerized test generation system gives you maximum flexibility in creating and administering tests on paper, electronically, or online. It provides state-of-the-art features for viewing and editing test bank questions, dragging a selected question into a test you are creating, and printing sleek, formatted tests in a variety of layouts. Select test items from test banks included with TestGen for quick test creation, or write your own questions from scratch. TestGen's random generator provides the option to display different text or calculated number values each time questions are used.

PowerPoint Presentations. Our presentations offer clear, straightforward outlines and notes to use for class lectures or study materials. Photos, illustrations, charts, and tables from the book are included in the presentations when applicable.

To access supplementary materials online, instructors need to request an instructor access code. Go to **www.pearsonhighered.com/irc**, where you can register for an instructor access code. Within 48 hours after registering, you will receive a confirming e-mail, including an instructor access code. Once you have received your code, go to the site and log on for full instructions on downloading the materials you wish to use.

Pearson Online Course Solutions

Forensic Science: From the Crime Scene to the Crime Lab, Third Edition, is supported by online course solutions that include interactive learning modules, a variety of assessment tools, videos, simulations, and current event features. Go to www.pearsonhighered.com or contact your local representative for the latest information.

Alternate Versions

eBooks. This text is also available in multiple eBook formats including Adobe Reader and CourseSmart. *CourseSmart* is an exciting new choice for students looking to save money. As an alternative to purchasing the printed textbook, students can purchase an electronic version of the same content. With a *CourseSmart* eTextbook, students can search the text, make notes online, print out reading assignments that incorporate lecture notes, and bookmark important passages for later review. For more information, or to purchase access to the *CourseSmart* eTextbook, visit **www.coursesmart.com**.

:: ABOUT THE AUTHOR

RICHARD SAFERSTEIN, Ph.D., retired in 1991 after serving for twenty-one years as the chief forensic scientist of the New Jersey State Police Laboratory, one of the largest crime laboratories in the United States. He currently acts as a consultant for attorneys and the media in the area of forensic science. During the O. J. Simpson criminal trial, Dr. Saferstein provided extensive commentary on forensic aspects of the case for the *Rivera Live* show, the E! television network, ABC radio, and various radio talk shows. Dr. Saferstein holds degrees from the City College of New York and earned his doctorate degree in chemistry in 1970 from the City University of New York. From 1972 to 1991, he taught an introductory forensic science course in the criminal justice programs at the College of New Jersey and Ocean County College. These teaching experiences played an influential role in Dr. Saferstein's authorship in 1977 of the widely used introductory textbook *Criminalistics: An Introduction to Forensic Science,* currently in its eleventh edition. Dr. Saferstein's basic philosophy in writing *Forensic Science: From the Crime Scene to the Crime Lab*, Third Edition, is to make forensic science understandable and meaningful to the non-science reader while giving the reader an appreciation for the scientific principles that underlie the subject.

Dr. Saferstein has authored or coauthored more than forty-five technical papers covering a variety of forensic topics. He authored *Basic Laboratory Exercises for Forensic Science,* Second Edition (Prentice Hall, 2011) and coauthored *Lab Manual for Criminalistics,* Eleventh Edition (Prentice Hall, 2015). He has also edited the widely used professional reference books *Forensic Science Handbook,* Volume 1, Second Edition (Prentice Hall, 2002), *Forensic Science Handbook,* Volume 2, Second Edition (Prentice Hall, 2005), and *Forensic Science Handbook,* Volume 3, Second Edition (Prentice Hall, 2010). Dr. Saferstein is a member of the American Chemical Society, American Academy of Forensic Sciences, Canadian Society of Forensic Scientists, International Association for Identification, Northeastern Association of Forensic Scientists, and Society of Forensic Toxicologists.

In 2006, Dr. Saferstein received the American Academy of Forensic Sciences Paul L. Kirk award for distinguished service and contributions to the field of criminalistics.

Introduction

Red Huber-Pool/Getty Images

LEARNING OBJECTIVES

After studying this chapter, you should be able to:

- Define forensic science and list the major disciplines forensic science encompasses.
- Recognize the major contributors to the development of forensic science.
- Account for the rapid growth of forensic laboratories in the past forty years.
- Describe the services of a typical comprehensive crime laboratory in the criminal justice system.
- List the functions of a forensic scientist as it relates to the crime laboratory.
- Compare and contrast the Frye and Daubert decisions relating to the admissibility of scientific evidence in the courtroom.
- Explain the role and responsibilities of the expert witness.
- List the specialized forensic services, aside from the crime laboratory, that are generally available to law enforcement personnel.

CASEY ANTHONY: THE CSI EFFECT?

Few criminal proceedings have captured the attention of the American public or have invoked stronger emotions than the Casey Anthony murder trial. How could a defendant who failed to report her two-year-old child missing for thirty-one days walk away scot-free from a murder conviction? This case had all the makings of a strong circumstantial case for the state.

The state's theory was that Casey used chloroform to render her daughter unconscious, placed duct tape over Caylee's mouth and nose, and kept the body in the trunk for several days before disposing of it. Caylee's decomposed remains were discovered more than five months after she was reported missing.

Have TV forensic dramas created an environment in the courtroom that necessitates the existence of physical evidence to directly link a defendant to a crime scene? The closest the state came to a direct link was a hair found in the trunk of Casey's car. However, the DNA test on the hair could link the hair only to Caylee's maternal relatives: Casey, Casey's mother (Caylee's maternal grandmother), and Casey's brother (Caylee's uncle). And Caylee herself. No unique characteristics were found to link the duct tape on the body with that found in the Anthony home.

No DNA, no fingerprints, no conviction.

Definition and Scope of Forensic Science

Forensic science, in its broadest definition, is the application of science to law. As our society has grown more complex, it has become more dependent on rules of law to regulate the activities of its members. Forensic science applies the knowledge and technology of science to the definition and enforcement of such laws.

Each year, as government finds it increasingly necessary to regulate the activities that most intimately influence our daily lives, science merges more closely with civil and criminal law. Consider, for example, the laws and agencies that regulate the quality of our food, the nature and potency of drugs, the extent of automobile emissions, the kind of fuel oil we burn, the purity of our drinking water, and the pesticides we use on our crops and plants. It would be difficult to conceive of a food or drug regulation or environmental protection act that could be effectively monitored and enforced without the assistance of scientific technology and the skill of the scientific community.

Laws are continually being broadened and revised to counter the alarming increase in crime rates. In response to public concern, law enforcement agencies have expanded their patrol and investigative functions, hoping to stem the rising tide of crime. At the same time, they are looking more to the scientific community for advice and technical support for their efforts. Can the technology that put astronauts on the moon, split the atom, and eradicated most dreaded diseases be enlisted in this critical battle?

Unfortunately, science cannot offer final and authoritative solutions to problems that stem from a maze of social and psychological factors. However, as the content of this book attests, science occupies an important and unique role in the criminal justice system—a role that relates to the scientist's ability to supply accurate and objective information about the events that have occurred at a crime scene. A good deal of work remains to be done if the full potential of science as applied to criminal investigations is to be realized.

Because of the vast array of civil and criminal laws that regulate society, forensic science, in its broadest sense, has become so comprehensive a subject that a meaningful introductory textbook treating its role and techniques would be difficult to create and probably overwhelming to read. For this reason, we have narrowed the scope of the subject according to the most common definition: **Forensic science is the application of science to the criminal and civil laws that are enforced by police agencies in a criminal justice system.** "Forensic science" is an umbrella term encompassing a myriad of professions that use their skills to aid law enforcement officials in conducting their investigations.

The diversity of professions practicing forensic science is illustrated by the eleven sections of the American Academy of Forensic Science, the largest forensic science organization in the world:

1. Criminalistics
2. Digital and Multimedia Sciences
3. Engineering Science
4. General
5. Jurisprudence
6. Odontology
7. Pathology/Biology
8. Physical Anthropology
9. Psychiatry/Behavioral Science
10. Questioned Documents
11. Toxicology

Even this list of professions is not exclusive. It does not encompass skills such as fingerprint examination, firearm and tool mark examination, and photography.

Obviously, to author a book covering all of the major activities of forensic science as they apply to the enforcement of criminal and civil laws by police agencies would be a major undertaking. Thus, this book will further restrict itself to discussions of the subjects of chemistry, biology, physics, geology, and computer technology, which are useful for determining the evidential value of crime-scene and related evidence. Forensic pathology, psychology, anthropology, and odontology also encompass important and relevant areas of knowledge and practice in law enforcement, each being an integral part of the total forensic science service that is provided to any up-to-date criminal justice system. However, these subjects go beyond the intended scope of this book, and except for brief discussions, along with pointing the reader to relevant websites, the reader is referred elsewhere for discussions of their applications and techniques. Instead, this book focuses on the services of what has popularly become known as the crime laboratory, where the principles and techniques of the physical and natural sciences are practiced and applied to the analysis of crime-scene evidence.

For many, the term "criminalistics" seems more descriptive than "forensic science" for describing the services of a crime laboratory. Regardless of his or her title—"criminalist" or "forensic scientist"—the trend of events has made the scientist in the crime laboratory an active participant in the criminal justice system.

Prime-time television shows like *CSI: Crime Scene Investigation* have greatly increased the public's awareness of the use of science in criminal and civil investigations (see Figure 1-1). However, by simplifying scientific procedures to fit the allotted airtime, these shows have created within both the public and the legal community unrealistic expectations of forensic science. In these shows, members of the CSI team collect evidence at the crime scene, process all evidence, question witnesses, interrogate suspects, carry out search warrants, and testify in court. In the real world, these tasks are almost always

FIGURE 1-1 A scene from *CSI*, a forensic science television show. *SUN/Newscom*

delegated to different people in different parts of the criminal justice system. Procedures that in reality could take days, weeks, months, or years appear on these shows to take mere minutes. This false image is significantly responsible for the public's high interest in and expectations for DNA evidence.

The dramatization of forensic science on television has led the public to believe that every crime scene will yield forensic evidence, and it produces unrealistic expectations that a prosecutor's case should always be bolstered and supported by forensic evidence. This phenomenon is known as the "CSI effect." Some jurists believe that this phenomenon ultimately detracts from the search for truth and justice in the courtroom.

History and Development of Forensic Science

Forensic science owes its origins, first, to the individuals who developed the principles and techniques needed to identify or compare physical evidence and, second, to those who recognized the need to merge these principles into a coherent discipline that could be practically applied to a criminal justice system.

The roots of forensic science reach back many centuries, and history records a number of instances in which individuals closely observed evidence and applied basic scientific principles to solve crimes. Not until relatively recently, however, did forensic science take on the more careful and systematic approach that characterizes the modern discipline.

EARLY DEVELOPMENTS

One of the earliest records of applying forensics to solve criminal cases comes from third-century China. A manuscript titled *Yi Yu Ji* ("A Collection of Criminal Cases") reports how a coroner solved a case in which a woman was suspected of murdering her husband and burning the body, claiming that he died in an accidental fire. Noticing that the husband's corpse had no ashes in its mouth, the coroner performed an experiment to test the woman's story. He burned two pigs—one alive and one dead—and then checked for ashes inside the mouth of each. He found ashes in the mouth of the pig that was alive before it was burned, but none in the mouth of the pig that was dead beforehand. The coroner thus concluded that the husband, too, was dead before his body was burned. Confronted with this evidence, the woman admitted her guilt. The Chinese were also among the first to recognize the potential of fingerprints as a means of identification.

Although cases such as that of the Chinese coroner are noteworthy, this kind of scientific approach to criminal investigation was for many years the exception rather than the rule. Limited knowledge of anatomy and pathology hampered the development of forensic science until the late seventeenth and early eighteenth centuries. For example, the first recorded notes about fingerprint characteristics were prepared in 1686 by Marcello Malpighi, a professor of anatomy at the University of Bologna in Italy. Malpighi, however, did not acknowledge the value of fingerprints as a method of identification. The first scientific paper about the nature of fingerprints did not appear until more than a century later, but it also did not recognize their potential as a form of identification.

INITIAL SCIENTIFIC ADVANCES

As physicians gained a greater understanding of the workings of the body, the first scientific treatises on forensic science began to appear, such as the 1798 work "A Treatise on Forensic Medicine and Public Health" by the French physician

François-Emanuel Fodéré. Breakthroughs in chemistry at this time also helped forensic science take significant strides forward. In 1775, the Swedish chemist Carl Wilhelm Scheele devised the first successful test for detecting the poison arsenic in corpses. By 1806, the German chemist Valentin Ross had discovered a more precise method for detecting small amounts of arsenic in the walls of a victim's stomach. The most significant early figure in this area was Mathieu Orfila (see Figure 1-2), a Spaniard who is considered the father of forensic toxicology. In 1814, Orfila published the first scientific treatise on the detection of poisons and their effects on animals. This treatise established forensic toxicology as a legitimate scientific endeavor.

The mid-1800s saw a spate of advances in several scientific disciplines that furthered the field of forensic science. In 1828, William Nichol invented the polarizing microscope. Eleven years later, Henri-Louis Bayard formulated the first procedures for microscopic detection of sperm. Other developments during this time included the first microcrystalline test for hemoglobin (1853) and the first presumptive test for blood (1863). Such tests soon found practical applications in criminal trials. Toxicological evidence at trial was first used in 1839, when a Scottish chemist named James Marsh testified that he had detected arsenic in a victim's body. During the 1850s and 1860s, the new science of photography was also used in forensics to record images of prisoners and crime scenes.

FIGURE 1-2 Mathieu Orfila. *Matthieu Orfila/The Granger Collection*

LATE NINETEENTH-CENTURY PROGRESS

By the late nineteenth century, public officials were beginning to apply knowledge from virtually all scientific disciplines to the study of crime. Anthropology and morphology (the study of the structure of living organisms) were applied to the first system of personal identification, devised by the French scientist Alphonse Bertillon in 1879. Bertillon's system, which he dubbed "anthropometry," was a procedure that involved taking a series of bodily measurements as a means of distinguishing one individual from another (see Figure 1-3). For nearly two decades, this system was considered the most accurate method of personal identification. Bertillon's early efforts earned him the distinction of being known as the "father of criminal identification."

Bertillon's anthropometry, however, would soon be supplanted by a more reliable method of identification: fingerprinting. Two years before the publication of Bertillon's system, U.S. microscopist Thomas Taylor had suggested that fingerprints could be used as a means of identification, but his ideas were not immediately followed up. Three years later, the Scottish physician Henry Faulds made a similar assertion in a paper published in the journal *Nature*. However, it was the Englishman Francis Henry Galton who undertook the first definitive study of fingerprints and developed a methodology of classifying them for filing. In 1892, Galton published a book titled *Finger Prints* that contained the first statistical proof supporting the uniqueness of fingerprints and the effectiveness of his method. His book went on to describe the basic principles that would form our present system of identification by fingerprints.

The first treatise describing the application of scientific disciplines to the field of criminal investigation was written by Hans Gross in 1893. Gross,

FIGURE 1-3   Bertillon's system of bodily measurements used for the identification of an individual. *Sirchie Finger Print Laboratories, Youngsville, NC, www.sirchie.com*

a public prosecutor and judge in Graz, Austria, spent many years studying and developing principles of criminal investigation. In his classic book *Handbuch für Untersuchungsrichter als System der Kriminalistik* (later published in English under the title *Criminal Investigation*), he detailed the assistance that investigators could expect from the fields of microscopy, chemistry, physics, mineralogy, zoology, botany, anthropometry, and fingerprinting. He later introduced the forensic journal *Archiv für Kriminal Anthropologie und Kriminalistik,* which still reports improved methods of scientific crime detection.

Ironically, the best-known figure in nineteenth-century forensics is not a real person but a fictional character: the legendary detective Sherlock Holmes (see Figure 1-4). Many people today believe that Holmes's creator, Sir Arthur Conan Doyle, had a considerable influence on popularizing scientific crime-detection methods. In adventures with his partner and biographer, Dr. John Watson, Holmes was the first to apply the newly developing principles of serology (the study of blood and bodily fluids), fingerprinting, firearms identification, and questioned-document examination long before their value was recognized and accepted by real-life criminal investigators. Holmes's feats excited the imagination of an emerging generation of forensic scientists and criminal investigators. Even in the first Sherlock Holmes novel, *A Study in Scarlet,* published in 1887, we find examples of Doyle's uncanny ability to describe scientific methods of detection years before they were actually discovered and implemented. For instance, here Holmes explains the potential usefulness of forensic serology to criminal investigation:

FIGURE 1-4 Sir Arthur Conan Doyle's legendary detective Sherlock Holmes applied many of the principles of modern forensic science long before they were adopted widely by real-life police. *Paul C. Chauncey/Corbis*

> "I've found it. I've found it," he shouted to my companion, running toward us with a test tube in his hand. "I have found a reagent which is precipitated by hemoglobin and by nothing else. . . . Why, man, it is the most practical medico-legal discovery for years. Don't you see that it gives us an infallible test for bloodstains? . . . The old guaiacum test was very clumsy and uncertain. So is the microscopic examination for blood corpuscles. The latter is valueless if the stains are a few hours old. Now, this appears to act as well whether the blood is old or new. Had this test been invented, there are hundreds of men now walking the earth who would long ago have paid the penalty of their crimes. . . . Criminal cases are continually hinging upon that one point. A man is suspected of a crime months perhaps after it has been committed. His linen or clothes are examined and brownish stains discovered upon them. Are they bloodstains, or rust stains, or fruit stains, or what are they? That is a question which has puzzled many an expert, and why? Because there was no reliable test. Now we have the Sherlock Holmes test, and there will no longer be any difficulty."

TWENTIETH-CENTURY BREAKTHROUGHS

The pace of technological change quickened considerably in the twentieth century, and with it the rate of advancements in forensic science. In 1901, Dr. Karl Landsteiner discovered that blood can be grouped into different categories, now recognized as the blood types A, B, AB, and O. The possibility that blood grouping could be useful in identifying an individual intrigued Dr. Leone Lattes, a professor at the Institute of Forensic Medicine at the University of Turin in Italy. In 1915, Lattes devised a relatively simple procedure for determining the blood group of the dried blood in a bloodstain, a technique that he immediately applied to criminal investigations.

At around the same time, Albert S. Osborn was conducting pioneering work in document examination. In 1910, Osborn wrote the first significant text in this field, *Questioned Documents*. This book is still a primary reference for document examiners. Osborn's development of fundamental principles of document examination was responsible for the acceptance of documents as scientific evidence by the courts.

One of the most important contributors to the field in the early twentieth century was the Frenchman Edmond Locard (see Figure 1-5). Although Hans Gross was a pioneering advocate for the use of the scientific method in criminal investigations, Locard first demonstrated how the principles enunciated by Gross could be incorporated within a workable crime laboratory. Locard's formal education was in both medicine and law. In 1910, he persuaded the Lyons Police Department to give him two attic rooms and two assistants to start a police laboratory. During Locard's first years of work, the instruments available to him were a microscope and a rudimentary spectrometer. However, his enthusiasm quickly overcame the technical and budgetary deficiencies he encountered, and from these modest beginnings, Locard conducted research and made discoveries that became known throughout the world by forensic scientists and criminal investigators. Eventually he became the founder and director of the Institute of Criminalistics at the University of Lyons, which quickly developed into a leading international center for study and research in forensic science.

Locard's exchange principle
Whenever two objects come into contact with one another, materials are exchanged between them.

Locard asserted that when two objects come into contact with each other a cross-transfer of materials occurs (**Locard's exchange principle**). He strongly believed that every criminal can be connected to a crime by dust particles carried from the crime scene. This concept was reinforced by a series of successful and well-publicized investigations. In one case, presented with counterfeit coins and the names of three suspects, Locard urged the police to bring the suspects' clothing to his laboratory. On careful examination, he located small metallic particles in all the garments. Chemical analysis revealed that the particles and coins were composed of exactly the same metallic elements. Confronted with this evidence, the suspects were arrested and soon confessed to the crime. After World War I, Locard's successes inspired the formation of police laboratories in Vienna, Berlin, Sweden, Finland, and Holland.

The microscope came into widespread use in forensic science during the twentieth century, and its applications grew dramatically. Perhaps the leading figure in the field of microscopy was Dr. Walter C. McCrone. During his lifetime, McCrone became the world's preeminent microscopist. Through his books, journal publications, and research institute, he was a tireless advocate for applying microscopy to analytical problems, particularly forensic science cases. McCrone's exceptional communication skills made him a much-sought-after instructor, and he educated thousands of forensic scientists throughout the world in the application of microscopic techniques. Dr. McCrone used microscopy, often in conjunction with other analytical methodologies, to examine evidence in thousands of criminal and civil cases throughout his long and illustrious career.

Another trailblazer in forensic applications of microscopy was U.S. Army Colonel Calvin Goddard, who refined the techniques of firearms examination by using the comparison microscope. Goddard's work allows investigators to determine whether a particular gun has fired a bullet by comparing the bullet with another that is test-fired from the suspect's weapon. From the mid-1920s on, his expertise established the comparison microscope as the indispensable tool of the modern firearms examiner.

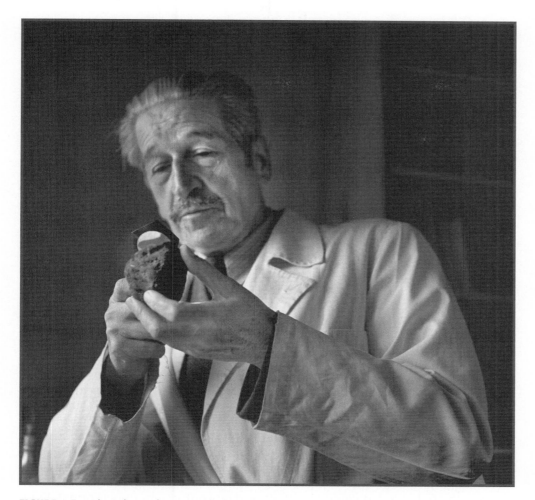

FIGURE 1-5 Edmond Locard. *Roger Viollet/The Image Works*

MODERN SCIENTIFIC ADVANCES

Since the mid-twentieth century, a revolution in computer technology has made possible a quantum leap forward in human knowledge. The resulting explosion of scientific advances has had a dramatic impact on the field of forensic science by introducing a wide array of sophisticated techniques for analyzing evidence related to a crime. Procedures such as chromatography, spectrophotometry, and electrophoresis (all discussed in later chapters) allow the modern forensic scientist to determine with astounding accuracy the identity of a substance and to connect even tiny fragments of evidence to a particular person and place.

Undoubtedly the most significant modern advance in forensic science has been the discovery and refinement of DNA typing in the late twentieth and early twenty-first centuries. Sir Alec Jeffreys developed the first DNA profiling test in 1984, and two years later he applied it for the first time to solve a crime, identifying Colin Pitchfork as the murderer of two young English girls. The same case also marked the first time DNA profiling established the innocence of a criminal suspect. Made possible by scientific breakthroughs in the 1950s and 1960s, DNA typing offers law enforcement officials a powerful tool for establishing the precise identity of a suspect, even when only a small amount of physical evidence is available. Combined with the modern analytical tools mentioned earlier, DNA typing has revolutionized the practice of forensic science (see Figure 1-6).

Another significant recent development in forensics is the establishment of computerized databases to store information on physical evidence such as

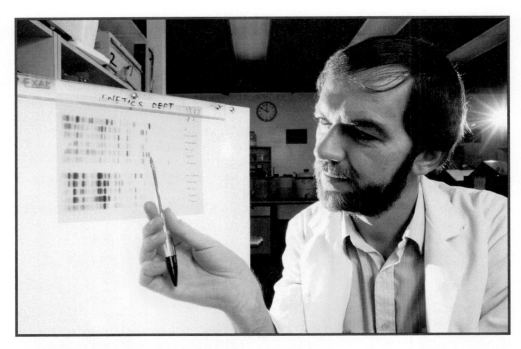

FIGURE 1-6 Sir Alec Jeffreys. *Homer Sykes/Alamy*

fingerprints, markings on bullets and shell casings, and DNA. These databases have proved to be invaluable, enabling law enforcement officials to compare evidence found at crime scenes to thousands of pieces of similar information. This has significantly reduced the time required to analyze evidence and increased the accuracy of the work done by police and forensic investigators.

Although this brief narrative is by no means a complete summary of historical advances in forensics, it provides an idea of the progress that has been made in the field by dedicated scientists and law enforcement personnel. Even Sherlock Holmes probably couldn't have imagined the extent to which science is applied in the service of criminal investigation today.

Quick Review

- Forensic science is the application of science to criminal and civil laws that are enforced by police agencies in a criminal justice system.
- The first system of personal identification was called "anthropometry." It distinguished one individual from another based on a series of bodily measurements.
- Forensic science owes its origins to individuals such as Bertillon, Galton, Lattes, Goddard, Osborn, and Locard, who developed the principles and techniques needed to identify and compare physical evidence.
- Locard's exchange principle states that, when two objects come into contact with each other, a cross-transfer of materials occurs that can connect a criminal suspect to his or her victim.

Crime Laboratories

The steady advance of forensic science technologies during the twentieth century led to the establishment of the first facilities specifically dedicated to forensic analysis of criminal evidence. These crime laboratories are now the centers for both forensic investigation of ongoing criminal cases and research into new techniques and procedures to aid investigators in the future.

HISTORY OF CRIME LABS IN THE UNITED STATES

The oldest forensic laboratory in the United States is the Los Angeles Police Department, created in 1923 by August Vollmer, a police chief from Berkeley, California. In the 1930s, Vollmer headed the first U.S. university institute for criminology and criminalistics at the University of California at Berkeley. However, this institute lacked any official status in the university until 1948, when a school of criminology was formed. The famous criminalist Paul Kirk was selected to head the school's criminalistics department. Many graduates of this school have gone on to develop forensic laboratories in other parts of the state and country.

In 1932, the Federal Bureau of Investigation (FBI), under the directorship of J. Edgar Hoover, organized a national laboratory that offered forensic services to all law enforcement agencies in the country. During its formative stages, Hoover consulted extensively with business executives, manufacturers, and scientists, whose knowledge and experience guided the new facility through its infancy. The FBI Laboratory is now the world's largest forensic laboratory, performing more than one million examinations every year (see Figure 1-7). Its accomplishments have earned it worldwide recognition, and its structure and organization have served as a model for forensic laboratories formed at the state and local levels in the United States as well as in other countries. Furthermore, the opening of the FBI's Forensic Science Research and Training Center in 1981 gave the United States, for the first time, a facility dedicated to conducting research toward new and reliable scientific methods that can be applied to forensic science. This facility is also used to train crime laboratory personnel in the latest forensic science techniques and methods.

Despite the existence of the FBI Laboratory, the United States has no national system of forensic laboratories. Instead, many local law enforcement jurisdictions—city, county, and state—each operate their own independent crime labs. California, for example, has numerous federal, state, county, and city crime laboratories, many of which operate independently. However, in 1972 the California Department of Justice created a network of integrated state-operated crime laboratories consisting of regional and satellite facilities. An informal exchange of information and expertise occurs within California's criminalist community through a regional professional society, the California Association of Criminalists. This organization is the forerunner of a number of regional organizations that have developed throughout the United States to foster cooperation among the nation's growing community of criminalists.

(a)

(b)

FIGURE 1-7 (a) Exterior and (b) interior views of the FBI crime laboratory in Quantico, Virginia. *Charles Dharapak/AP Images*

ORGANIZATION OF A CRIME LABORATORY

The development of crime laboratories in the United States has been characterized by rapid growth accompanied by an unfortunate lack of national and regional planning and coordination. It is estimated that more than 411 public crime laboratories currently operate at various levels of government—federal, state, county, and municipal. The size and diversity of crime laboratories make it impossible to select any one model that best describes a typical crime laboratory. Although most of these facilities function as part of a police department, others operate under the direction of the prosecutor's or district attorney's office, and some work with the laboratories of the medical examiner or coroner. Far fewer are affiliated with universities or exist as independent agencies in government. Laboratory staff sizes range from one person to more than one hundred, and services offered may be quite diverse or very specialized, depending on the responsibilities of the agency that houses the laboratory.

THE GROWTH OF CRIME LABORATORIES

Most existing crime laboratories have been organized by agencies that either foresaw their potential application to criminal investigations or were pressed by the increasing demands of casework. Several reasons explain the unparalleled growth of crime laboratories during the past forty years: Supreme Court decisions in the 1960s compelled police to place greater emphasis on securing scientifically evaluated evidence. The requirement to advise criminal suspects of their constitutional rights and their right of immediate access to counsel has all but eliminated confessions as a routine investigative tool; successful prosecution of criminal cases requires a thorough and professional police investigation, frequently incorporating the skills of forensic science experts. Modern technology has provided forensic scientists with many new skills and techniques to meet the challenges accompanying their increased participation in the criminal justice system.

Coinciding with changing judicial requirements has been the staggering increase in crime rates in the United States over the past forty years. Although it seems that this factor alone could account for the increased use of crime laboratory services by police agencies, only a small percentage of police investigations generate evidence requiring scientific examination. There is one important exception, however: drug-related arrests. All illicit-drug seizures must be sent to a forensic laboratory for confirmatory chemical analysis before the case can be adjudicated. Since the mid-1960s, drug abuse has accelerated to nearly uncontrollable levels and has resulted in crime laboratories being inundated with drug specimens.

A more recent contributor to the growth and maturation of crime laboratories has been the advent of DNA profiling. Since the early 1990s, this technology has progressed to the point of individualization or near-individualization of biological evidence. That is, traces of blood, semen stains, hair, and saliva residues left behind on stamps, cups, bite marks, and so on, can be positively linked to a criminal. To meet the demands of DNA technology, crime labs have expanded staff and in many cases modernized their physical plants. The labor-intensive demands and sophisticated requirements of DNA technology have affected the structure of the forensic laboratory as has no other technology in the past fifty years. Likewise, DNA profiling has become the dominant factor in the general public's perception of the workings and capabilities of the modern crime laboratory.

In coming years an estimated ten thousand forensic scientists will be added to the rolls of both public and private forensic laboratories to process crime-scene evidence for DNA and to acquire DNA profiles, as mandated by state laws, from the hundreds of thousands of individuals convicted of crimes.

This endeavor has already added many new scientists to the field and will eventually more than double the number of scientists employed by forensic laboratories in the United States.

A major problem facing the forensic DNA community is the substantial backlog of unanalyzed DNA samples from crime scenes. The number of unanalyzed casework DNA samples reported by state and national agencies is more than 57,000. The estimated number of untested convicted offender samples is more than 500,000. In an attempt to eliminate the backlog of convicted offender or arrestee samples to be analyzed and entered into the Combined DNA Index System (CODIS), the federal government has initiated funding for in-house analysis of samples at the crime laboratory or outsourcing samples to private laboratories for analysis.

Beginning in 2008, California began collecting DNA samples from all people arrested on suspicion of a felony, not waiting until a person is convicted. The state's database, with approximately one million DNA profiles, is already the third largest in the world, behind those maintained by the United Kingdom and the FBI. The federal government plans to begin doing the same.

CRIME LABORATORIES IN THE UNITED STATES Historically, our federal system of government, combined with a desire to retain local control, has produced a variety of independent laboratories in the United States, precluding the creation of a national system. Crime laboratories to a large extent mirror the fragmented law enforcement structure that exists on the national, state, and local levels. The federal government has no single law enforcement or investigative agency with unlimited jurisdiction.

Four major federal crime laboratories have been created to help investigate and enforce criminal laws that extend beyond the jurisdictional boundaries of state and local forces. The FBI (Department of Justice) maintains the largest crime laboratory in the world. An ultramodern facility housing the FBI's forensic science services is located in Quantico, Virginia. Its expertise and technology support its broad investigative powers. The Drug Enforcement Administration laboratories (Department of Justice) analyze drugs seized in violation of federal laws regulating the production, sale, and transportation of drugs. The laboratories of the Bureau of Alcohol, Tobacco, Firearms, and Explosives (Department of Justice) analyze alcoholic beverages and documents relating to alcohol and firearm excise-tax enforcement and examine weapons, explosive devices, and related evidence to enforce the Gun Control Act of 1968 and the Organized Crime Control Act of 1970. The U.S. Postal Inspection Service maintains laboratories concerned with criminal investigations relating to the postal service. Each of these federal facilities offers its expertise to any local agency that requests assistance in relevant investigative matters.

Most state governments maintain a crime laboratory to service state and local law enforcement agencies that do not have ready access to a laboratory. Some states, such as Alabama, California, Illinois, Michigan, New Jersey, Texas, Washington, Oregon, Virginia, and Florida, have developed a comprehensive statewide system of regional or satellite laboratories. These operate under the direction of a central facility and provide forensic services to most areas of the state. Having a regional laboratory that operates as part of a statewide system has increased the accessibility of many local law enforcement agencies to a crime laboratory, while minimizing duplication of services and ensuring maximum interlaboratory cooperation through the sharing of expertise and equipment.

Local laboratories provide services to county and municipal agencies. Generally, these facilities operate independent of the state crime laboratory and are financed directly by local government. However, as costs have risen, some counties have combined resources and created multicounty laboratories to service their jurisdictions. Many of the larger cities in the United States maintain their own crime laboratories, usually under the direction of the local police department. Frequently, a large population and high crime rates combine to make a municipal facility, such as that of New York City, the largest crime laboratory in the state.

CRIME LABORATORIES ABROAD   Like the United States, most countries in the world have created and now maintain forensic facilities. In contrast to the American system of independent local laboratories, Great Britain had developed a national system of regional laboratories under the direction of the government's Home Office. In the early 1990s, the British Home Office reorganized the country's forensic laboratories into the Forensic Science Service and instituted a system in which police agencies are charged a fee for services rendered by the laboratory. The fee-for-service concept encouraged the creation of a number of private laboratories that provide services to both police and criminal defense attorneys. One such organization is LGC. In 2010, the British government announced the closure of the Forensic Science Service, citing financial losses. The laboratories closed in 2012, and forensic work in England and Wales is now contracted out to the private sector. Since privatization, LGC has grown to be the largest forensic science provider in the United Kingdom, employing more than 700 forensic scientists servicing both police agencies and the private sector.

In Canada, forensic services are provided by three government-funded institutes: (1) six Royal Canadian Mounted Police regional laboratories, (2) the Centre of Forensic Sciences in Toronto, and (3) the Institute of Legal Medicine and Police Science in Montreal. The Royal Canadian Mounted Police opened its first laboratory in Regina, Saskatchewan, in 1937. Altogether, more than a hundred countries throughout the world have at least one laboratory facility offering services in the field of forensic science.

SERVICES OF THE CRIME LABORATORY

Bearing in mind the independent development of crime laboratories in the United States, the wide variation in the services offered to different communities is not surprising. There are many reasons for this, including (1) variations in local laws, (2) the different capabilities and functions of the organization to which a laboratory is attached, and (3) budgetary and staffing limitations.

In recent years, many local crime laboratories have been created solely to process drug specimens. Often these facilities were staffed with few personnel and operated under limited budgets. Although many have expanded their forensic services, some still primarily perform drug analyses. Among crime laboratories providing services beyond drug identification, the diversity and quality of services rendered varies significantly. The following forensic science units might be found in a "full-service" crime laboratory.

BASIC SERVICES PROVIDED BY FULL-SERVICE CRIME LABORATORIES

PHYSICAL SCIENCE UNIT   The physical science unit applies principles and techniques of chemistry, physics, and geology to the identification and comparison of crime-scene evidence. It is staffed by criminalists who have the expertise to use chemical tests and modern analytical instrumentation to examine items as diverse as drugs, glass, paint, explosives, and soil. In a laboratory that has a staff large enough to permit specialization, the responsibilities of this unit may be further subdivided into drug identification, soil and mineral analyses, and examination of a variety of trace physical evidence.

BIOLOGY UNIT The biology unit is staffed with biologists and biochemists who identify and perform DNA profiling on bloodstains and other dried body fluids, compare hairs and fibers, and identify and compare botanical materials such as wood and plants (see Figure 1-8).

FIREARMS UNIT The firearms unit examines firearms, discharged bullets, cartridge cases, shotgun shells, and ammunition of all types. Garments and other objects are also examined to detect firearm discharge residues and to approximate how far from a target a weapon was fired. The basic principles of firearms examination are also applied to comparing marks made by tools (see Figure 1-9).

DOCUMENT EXAMINATION UNIT The document examination unit studies the handwriting and type-writing on documents in question to ascertain their authenticity and/or source. Related responsibilities include analyzing paper and ink and examining indented writings (i.e., the partially visible depressions that appear on the sheet of paper that was underneath the one that was written on), obliterations, erasures, and burned or charred documents.

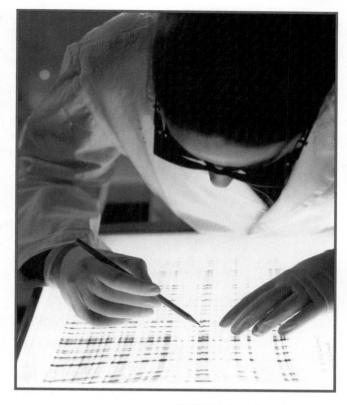

FIGURE 1-8 A forensic scientist performing DNA analysis. *Mauro Fermariello/Photo Researchers, Inc.*

PHOTOGRAPHY UNIT A complete photographic laboratory examines and records physical evidence. Its procedures may require the use of highly specialized photographic techniques, such as digital imaging and infrared, ultraviolet, and X-ray photography, to make invisible information visible to the naked eye. This unit also prepares photographic exhibits for courtroom presentation.

FIGURE 1-9 A forensic analyst examining a firearm. *Mediacolor's/Alamy*

OPTIONAL SERVICES PROVIDED BY FULL-SERVICE CRIME LABORATORIES

TOXICOLOGY UNIT   The toxicology group examines body fluids and organs to determine the presence or absence of drugs and poisons. Frequently, such functions are shared with or may be the sole responsibility of a separate laboratory facility placed under the direction of the medical examiner's or coroner's office. In most jurisdictions, field instruments such as the intoxilyzer are used to determine how much alcohol an individual has consumed. Often the toxicology unit also trains operators of these instruments and maintains and services them.

LATENT FINGERPRINT UNIT   The latent fingerprint unit processes and examines evidence for latent fingerprints when they are submitted in conjunction with other laboratory examinations.

POLYGRAPH UNIT   The polygraph, or lie detector, has become an essential tool of the criminal investigator rather than the forensic scientist. However, during the formative years of polygraph technology, many police agencies incorporated this unit into the laboratory's administrative structure, where it sometimes remains today. In any case, its functions are handled by people trained in the techniques of criminal investigation and interrogation (see Figure 1-10).

VOICEPRINT ANALYSIS UNIT   In cases involving telephoned threats or tape-recorded messages, investigators may require the skills of the voiceprint analysis unit to tie the voice to a particular suspect. To this end, a good deal of casework has been performed with the sound spectrograph, an instrument that transforms speech into a visual graphic display called a "voiceprint." The validity of this technique as a means of personal identification rests on the premise that the sound patterns produced in speech are unique to the individual and that the voiceprint displays this uniqueness.

CRIME-SCENE INVESTIGATION UNIT   The concept of incorporating crime-scene evidence collection into the services forensic laboratories offer is slowly gaining ground in the United States. This unit dispatches specially trained

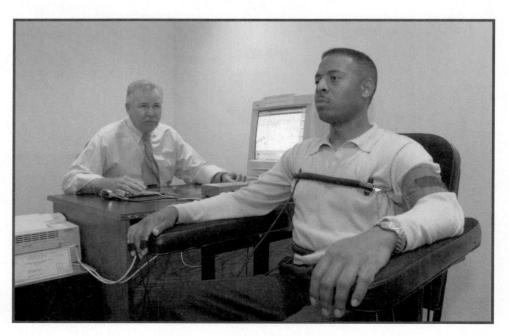

FIGURE 1-10   An individual undergoing a polygraph test. *Sandy Schaeffer/Getty Images*

personnel (civilian and/or police) to the crime scene to collect and preserve physical evidence that will be processed at the crime laboratory.

Whatever the organizational structure of a forensic science laboratory may be, specialization must not impede the overall coordination of services demanded by today's criminal investigator. Laboratory administrators need to keep open the lines of communication between analysts (civilian and uniformed), crime-scene investigators, and police personnel. Inevitably, forensic investigations require the skills of many individuals. One notoriously high-profile investigation illustrates this process: the search for the source of the anthrax letters mailed shortly after September 11, 2001. Figure 1-11 shows one of the letters and illustrates the multitude of skills required in the investigation—skills possessed by forensic chemists and biologists, fingerprint examiners, and forensic document examiners.

WebExtra 1.1

Take a Virtual Tour of a Forensic Laboratory

OTHER FORENSIC SCIENCE SERVICES

Even though this textbook is devoted to describing the services normally provided by a crime laboratory, the field of forensic science is by no means limited to the areas covered in this book. A number of specialized forensic science services outside the crime laboratory are routinely available to law enforcement personnel. These services are important aids to a criminal investigation and require the involvement of individuals who have highly specialized skills.

Three specialized forensic services—forensic pathology, forensic anthropology, and forensic entomology—are frequently employed at a murder scene and will be discussed at greater length when we examine crime-scene procedures in Chapter 6. Other services, such as those discussed next, are used in a wide variety of criminal investigations.

FORENSIC PSYCHIATRY Forensic psychiatry is a specialized area that examines the relationship between human behavior and legal proceedings. Forensic psychiatrists are retained for both civil and criminal litigations. In civil cases, they typically perform tasks such as determining whether an individual is competent to make decisions about preparing a will, settling property, or refusing medical treatment. In criminal cases, forensic psychologists evaluate behavioral disorders and determine whether defendants are competent to stand trial. Forensic psychiatrists also examine behavior patterns of criminals as an aid in developing a suspect's behavioral profile.

FORENSIC ODONTOLOGY Practitioners of forensic odontology help identify victims based on dental evidence when the body is in an unrecognizable state. Teeth are composed of enamel, the hardest substance in the body. Because of enamel's resilience, the teeth outlast tissues and organs during decomposition. The characteristics of teeth, their alignment, and the overall structure of the mouth provide individual evidence for identifying a specific person. Based on dental records such as X-rays and dental casts, even a photograph of the person's smile, a set of dental remains can be matched to a suspected victim. Another application of forensic odontology to criminal investigations is bite mark analysis. Bite marks are sometimes left on a victim of assault. A forensic odontologist can compare the marks left on a victim to the tooth structure of the suspect (see Figure 1-12).

FORENSIC ENGINEERING Forensic engineers are concerned with failure analysis, accident reconstruction, and causes and origins of fires and explosions. Forensic engineers answer questions such as these: How did an accident or structural failure occur? Were the parties involved responsible? If so, how were they responsible? Accident scenes are examined, photographs are reviewed, and any mechanical objects involved are inspected.

Photocopier toner may reveal its manufacturer through chemical and physical properties (p. 447).

Fingerprints may be detectable on paper using a variety of chemical developing techniques (pp. 172–80).

Paper examination may identify a manufacturer. General appearance, watermarks, fiber analysis, and chemical analysis of pigments, additives, and fillers may reveal a paper's origin (p. 455).

DNA may be recovered from saliva residues on the back of a stamp (p. 399). However, in this case, the stamp is printed onto the envelope.

Ink analysis may reveal a pen's manufacturer (pp. 454–55).

Trace evidence, such as hairs and fibers, may be present within the contents of the envelope.

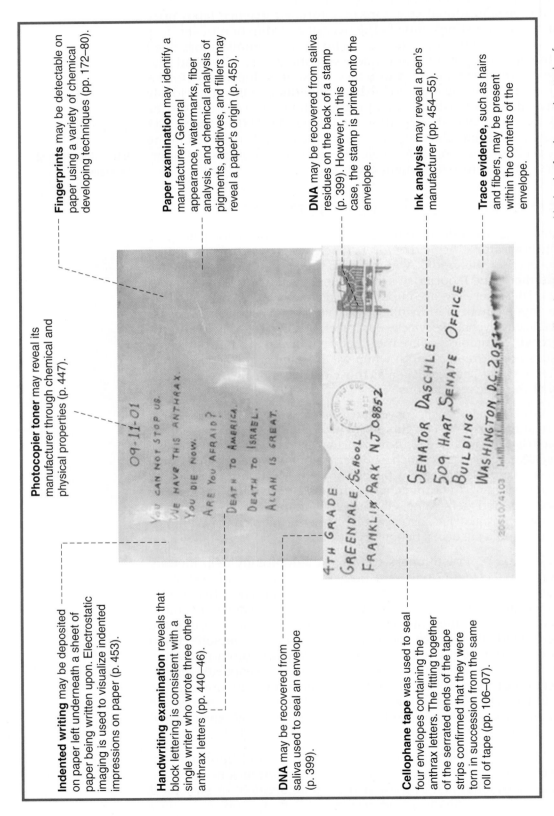

09-11-01

YOU CAN NOT STOP US.
WE HAVE THIS ANTHRAX.
YOU DIE NOW.
ARE YOU AFRAID?

DEATH TO AMERICA.
DEATH TO ISRAEL.
ALLAH IS GREAT.

4TH GRADE
GREENDALE SCHOOL
FRANKLIN PARK NJ 08852

SENATOR DASCHLE
509 HART SENATE OFFICE
BUILDING
WASHINGTON D.C. 20510

Indented writing may be deposited on paper left underneath a sheet of paper being written upon. Electrostatic imaging is used to visualize indented impressions on paper (p. 453).

Handwriting examination reveals that block lettering is consistent with a single writer who wrote three other anthrax letters (pp. 440–46).

DNA may be recovered from saliva used to seal an envelope (p. 399).

Cellophane tape was used to seal four envelopes containing the anthrax letters. The fitting together of the serrated ends of the tape strips confirmed that they were torn in succession from the same roll of tape (pp. 106–07).

FIGURE 1-11 An envelope containing anthrax spores along with an anonymous letter was sent to the office of Senator Tom Daschle shortly after the terrorist attacks of September 11, 2001. A variety of forensic skills were used to examine the envelope and letter. Also, bar codes placed on the front and back of the envelope by mail-sorting machines contain address information and information about where the envelope was first processed. *FBI/Getty Images*

FIGURE 1-12   (a) A bite mark on a victim's body. (b) Comparison to a suspect's teeth. *Barbara Needell*

FORENSIC COMPUTER AND DIGITAL ANALYSIS   Forensic computer science is a new and fast-growing field that involves identifying, collecting, preserving, and examining information derived from computers and other digital devices, such as cell phones. Law enforcement aspects of this work normally involve recovering deleted or overwritten data from a computer's hard drive and tracking hacking activities within a compromised system. The fields of forensic computer analysis and recovery of data from mobile devices will be addressed in detail in Chapters 18 and 19.

Quick Review

- The development of crime laboratories in the United States has been characterized by rapid growth accompanied by a lack of national and regional planning and coordination.
- Four major reasons for the increase in the number of crime laboratories in the United States since the 1960s are as follows: (1) The requirement to advise criminal suspects of their constitutional rights and their right of immediate access to counsel has all but eliminated confessions as a routine investigative tool. (2) There has been a staggering increase in crime rates in the United States. (3) All illicit-drug seizures must be sent to a forensic laboratory for confirmatory chemical analysis before the case can be adjudicated in court. (4) DNA profiling was developed and is now often required.
- The technical support provided by crime laboratories can be assigned to five basic services: the physical science unit, the biology unit, the firearms unit, the document examination unit, and the photography unit.
- Some crime laboratories offer optional services such as toxicology, fingerprint analysis, polygraph administration, voiceprint analysis, and crime-scene investigation.
- Special forensic science services available to the law enforcement community include forensic pathology, forensic anthropology, forensic entomology, forensic psychiatry, forensic odontology, forensic engineering, and forensic computer and digital analysis.

Functions of the Forensic Scientist

Although a forensic scientist relies primarily on scientific knowledge and skill, only half of the job is performed in the laboratory. The other half takes place in the courtroom, where the ultimate significance of the evidence is determined. The forensic scientist must not only analyze physical evidence but also persuade a jury to accept the conclusions derived from that analysis.

ANALYZING PHYSICAL EVIDENCE

First and foremost, the forensic scientist must be skilled in applying the principles and techniques of the physical and natural sciences to analyze the many types of physical evidence that may be recovered during a criminal investigation. Of the three major avenues available to police investigators for assistance in solving a crime—confessions, eyewitness accounts by victims or witnesses, and the evaluation of physical evidence retrieved from the crime scene—only physical evidence is free of inherent error or bias.

Criminal cases are replete with examples of individuals who were incorrectly charged with and convicted of committing a crime because of faulty memories or lapses in judgment. For example, investigators may be led astray during their preliminary evaluation of the events and circumstances surrounding the commission of a crime. These errors might be compounded by misleading eyewitness statements and inappropriate confessions. These same concerns don't apply to physical evidence.

What is it about physical evidence that allows investigators to sort out facts as they are and not as they want them to be? The hallmark of physical evidence is that it must undergo scientific inquiry. Science derives its integrity from adherence to strict guidelines that ensure the careful and systematic collection, organization, and analysis of information—a process known as the **scientific method**. The underlying principles of the scientific method provide a safety net to ensure that the outcome of an investigation is not tainted by human emotion or compromised by distorting, belittling, or ignoring contrary evidence.

The scientific method begins by formulating a question worthy of investigation, such as who committed a particular crime. The investigator next formulates a hypothesis, a reasonable explanation proposed to answer the question. What follows is the basic foundation of scientific inquiry: the testing of the hypothesis through experimentation. The testing process must be thorough and recognized by other scientists as valid. Scientists and investigators must accept the experimental findings even when they wish they were different. Finally, when the hypothesis is validated by experimentation, it becomes suitable as scientific evidence, appropriate for use in a criminal investigation and, ultimately, available for admission in a court of law.

scientific method
A process that uses strict guidelines to ensure careful and systematic collection, organization, and analysis of information.

DETERMINING ADMISSIBILITY OF EVIDENCE   In rejecting the scientific validity of the lie detector (polygraph), the District of Columbia Circuit Court in 1923 set forth what has since become a standard guideline for determining the judicial admissibility of scientific examinations. In *Frye* v. *United States,*[1] the court ruled that, in order to be admitted as evidence at trial, the questioned procedure, technique, or principles must be "generally accepted" by a meaningful segment of the relevant scientific community. In practice, this approach requires the proponent of a scientific test to present to the court a collection of experts who can testify that the scientific issue before the court is generally accepted by the relevant members of the scientific community. Furthermore, in determining whether a novel technique meets criteria associated with "general acceptance," courts have frequently taken note of books and papers written on the subject, as well as prior judicial decisions relating to the reliability and general acceptance of the technique. In recent years many observers have questioned whether this approach is flexible enough to deal with new scientific issues that may not have gained widespread support within the scientific community.

The Federal Rules of Evidence offer an alternative to the *Frye* standard, one that some courts believe espouses a more flexible guideline for admitting scientific evidence. Part of the Federal Rules of Evidence governs the admissibility of all evidence, including expert testimony, in federal courts, and many states have adopted codes similar to those of the Federal Rules. Specifically, Rule 702 of the Federal Rules of Evidence sets a different standard from "general acceptance" for admissibility of expert testimony. Under this standard, a witness "qualified as an expert by knowledge, skill, experience, training, or education" may offer expert testimony on a scientific or technical matter if "(1) the testimony is based on sufficient facts or data, (2) the testimony is the product of reliable principles and methods, and (3) the witness has applied the principles and methods reliably to the facts of the case."

In a landmark ruling in the 1993 case of *Daubert* v. *Merrell Dow Pharmaceuticals, Inc.,*[2] the U.S. Supreme Court (see Figure 1-13) asserted that "general acceptance," or the *Frye* standard, is not an absolute prerequisite to the admissibility of scientific evidence under the Federal Rules of Evidence. According to the Court, the Rules of Evidence—especially Rule 702—assign to the trial judge the task of ensuring that an expert's testimony rests on a reliable foundation and is relevant to the case. Although this ruling applies only to federal courts, many state courts are expected to use this decision as a guideline in setting standards for the admissibility of scientific evidence.

JUDGING SCIENTIFIC EVIDENCE   In *Daubert,* the Court advocates that trial judges assume the ultimate responsibility for acting as a "gatekeeper" who determines the admissibility and reliability of scientific evidence presented in their courts. The Court offered some guidelines as to how a judge can gauge the veracity of scientific evidence, emphasizing that the inquiry should be flexible. Suggested areas of inquiry include the following:

1. Whether the scientific technique or theory can be (and has been) tested
2. Whether the technique or theory has been subject to peer review and publication

FIGURE 1-13   A sketch of a U.S. Supreme Court hearing. *Art Lien*

3. The technique's potential rate of error
4. The existence and maintenance of standards controlling the technique's operation
5. Whether the scientific theory or method has attracted widespread acceptance within a relevant scientific community

Some legal experts have expressed concern that abandoning *Frye*'s general-acceptance test will result in the introduction of absurd and irrational pseudoscientific claims in the courtroom. The Supreme Court rejected these concerns, pointing out the inherent strengths of the U.S. judicial process in identifying unreliable evidence:

> In this regard the respondent seems to us to be overly pessimistic about the capabilities of the jury and of the adversary system generally. Vigorous cross-examination, presentation of contrary evidence, and careful instruction on the burden of proof are the traditional and appropriate means of attacking shaky but admissible evidence.

In a 1999 decision, *Kumho Tire Co., Ltd.* v. *Carmichael,*[3] the Court unanimously ruled that the "gatekeeping" role of the trial judge applied not only to scientific testimony but to all expert testimony:

> We conclude that *Daubert*'s general holding—setting forth the trial judge's general "gatekeeping" obligation—applies not only to testimony based on "scientific" knowledge, but also to testimony based on "technical" and "other specialized" knowledge. . . . We also conclude that a trial court may consider one or more of the more specific factors that *Daubert* mentioned when doing so will help determine that testimony's reliability. But, as the Court stated in *Daubert,* the test of reliability is "flexible," and *Daubert*'s list of specific factors neither necessarily nor exclusively applies to all experts in every case.

The case of *Coppolino* v. *State*[4] (examined more closely in the Case Files feature on page 23) exemplifies the flexibility and wide discretion that the *Daubert* ruling, twenty-five years later, apparently gave to trial judges in matters of scientific inquiry. The issue in question was whether the results of a new procedure that has not been widely accepted in the scientific community are necessarily inadmissible as evidence. The court rejected this argument, recognizing that researchers must devise new scientific tests to solve the special problems that continually arise in the forensic laboratory.

The *Coppolino* ruling acknowledged that even well-established scientific procedures were once new and unproved and noted the court's duty to protect the public when weighing the admissibility of a new test. In the words of the concurring opinion, "Society need not tolerate homicide until there develops a body of medical literature about some particular lethal agent." The court emphasized, however, that although these tests may be new and unique, they are admissible only if they are based on scientifically valid principles and techniques.

PROVIDING EXPERT TESTIMONY

Because the results of their work may be a factor in determining a person's ultimate guilt or innocence, forensic scientists may be required to testify about their methods and conclusions at a trial or hearing.

Trial courts have broad discretion in accepting an individual as an **expert witness** on any particular subject. Generally, if a witness can establish to the satisfaction of a trial judge that he or she possesses a particular skill or has knowledge in a trade or profession that will aid the court in determining the truth of the matter at issue, that individual will be accepted as an expert witness. Depending on the subject area in question, the court will usually consider knowledge acquired through experience, training, education, or a combination of these as sufficient grounds for qualification as an expert witness.

expert witness
An individual whom the court determines to possess knowledge relevant to the trial that is not expected of the average layperson.

■■■■ CASEFILES ■■■■

DR. COPPOLINO'S DEADLY HOUSE CALLS

A frantic late-night telephone call brought a local physician to the Florida home of Drs. Carl and Carmela Coppolino. The physician arrived to find Carmela beyond help. Carmela Coppolino's body, unexamined by anyone, was then buried in her family's plot in her home state of New Jersey.

A little more than a month later, Carl married a moneyed socialite, Mary Gibson. News of Carl's marriage infuriated Marjorie Farber, a former New Jersey neighbor of Dr. Coppolino who had been having an affair with the good doctor. Soon Marjorie had an interesting story to recount to investigators: Her husband's death two years before, although ruled to be from natural causes, had actually been murder! Carl, an anesthesiologist, had given Marjorie a syringe containing some medication and told her to inject her husband, William, while he was sleeping. Ultimately, Marjorie claimed, she was unable to inject the full dose and called Carl, who finished the job by suffocating William with a pillow.

Marjorie Farber's astonishing story was supported in part by Carl's having recently increased his wife's life insurance. Carmela's $65,000 policy, along with his new wife's fortune, would keep Dr. Coppolino in high society for the rest of his life. Based on this information, authorities in New Jersey and Florida obtained exhumation orders for both William Farber and Carmela Coppolino. After both bodies were examined, Dr. Coppolino was charged with the murders of William and Carmela.

Officials decided to try Dr. Coppolino first in New Jersey for the murder of William Farber. The Farber autopsy did not reveal any evidence of poisoning but seemed to show strong evidence of strangulation. The absence of toxicological findings left the jury to deliberate the conflicting medical expert testimony versus the sensational story told by a scorned and embittered woman. In the end, Dr. Coppolino was acquitted.

The Florida trial presented another chance to bring Carl Coppolino to justice. Recalling Dr. Coppolino's career as an anesthesiologist, the prosecution theorized that to commit these murders Coppolino had exploited his access to the many potent drugs used during surgery, specifically an injectable paralytic agent, succinylcholine chloride.

Carmela's body was exhumed, and it was found that Carmela had been injected in her left buttock shortly before her death. Ultimately, a completely novel procedure for detecting succinylcholine chloride was devised. With this procedure, elevated levels of succinic acid were found in Carmela's brain, which proved that she had received a large dose of the paralytic drug shortly before her death. This evidence, along with evidence of the same drug residues in the injection site on her buttock, was presented in the Florida murder trial of Carl Coppolino, who was convicted of second-degree murder.

In court, an expert witness may be asked questions intended to demonstrate his or her ability and competence pertaining to the matter at hand. Competency may be established by having the witness cite educational degrees, participation in special courses, membership in professional societies, and any professional articles or books published. Also important is the number of years of occupational experience the witness has had in areas related to the matter before the court.

Unfortunately, few schools confer degrees in forensic science. Most chemists, biologists, geologists, and physicists prepare themselves for careers in forensic science by combining training under an experienced examiner with independent study. Of course, formal education in the physical sciences provides a firm foundation for learning and understanding the principles and techniques of forensic science. Nevertheless, for the most part, courts must rely on training and years of experience as a measurement of the knowledge and ability of the expert.

Before the judge rules on the witness's qualifications, the opposing attorney may cross-examine the witness and point out weaknesses in training and knowledge. Most courts are reluctant to disqualify an individual as an expert even when presented with someone whose background is only remotely associated with the issue at hand. The question of what credentials are suitable for qualification as an expert is ambiguous and highly subjective and one that the courts wisely try to avoid.

The weight that a judge or jury assigns to "expert" testimony in subsequent deliberations is, however, quite another matter. Undoubtedly, education and experience have considerable bearing on what value should be assigned to the expert's opinions. Just as important may be his or her demeanor and ability to explain scientific data and conclusions clearly, concisely, and logically to a judge and jury composed of nonscientists. The problem of sorting out the strengths and weaknesses of expert testimony falls to prosecution and defense counsel.

The ordinary or lay witness must testify on events or observations that arise from personal knowledge. This testimony must be factual and, with few exceptions, cannot contain the personal opinions of the witness. On the other hand, the expert witness is called on to evaluate evidence when the court lacks the expertise to do so. This expert then expresses an opinion as to the significance of the findings. The views expressed are accepted only as representing the expert's opinion and may later be accepted or ignored in jury deliberations (see Figure 1-14).

The expert cannot render any view with absolute certainty. At best, he or she may be able to offer an opinion based only on a reasonable scientific certainty derived from training and experience. Obviously, the expert is expected to defend vigorously the techniques and conclusions of the analysis, but at the same time he or she must not be reluctant to discuss impartially any findings that could minimize the significance of the analysis. The forensic scientist should not be an advocate of one party's cause but an advocate of truth only. An adversary system of justice must give the prosecutor and defense ample opportunity to offer expert opinions and to argue the merits of such testimony. Ultimately, the duty of the judge or jury is to weigh the pros and cons of all the information presented when deciding guilt or innocence.

The necessity for the forensic scientist to appear in court has been imposed on the criminal justice system by a 2009 U.S. Supreme Court case, *Melendez-Diaz* v. *Massachusetts*.[5] The *Melendez-Diaz* decision addressed the practice of using evidence affidavits or laboratory certificates in lieu of in-person testimony by forensic analysts. In its reasoning, the Court relied on a previous ruling, *Crawford* v. *Washington*,[6] where it explored the meaning of the Confrontation Clause of the Sixth Amendment. In the *Crawford* case, a recorded statement by a spouse was used against her husband in his prosecution. Crawford argued that this was a violation of his right to confront witnesses against him under the Sixth Amendment, and the Court agreed. Using

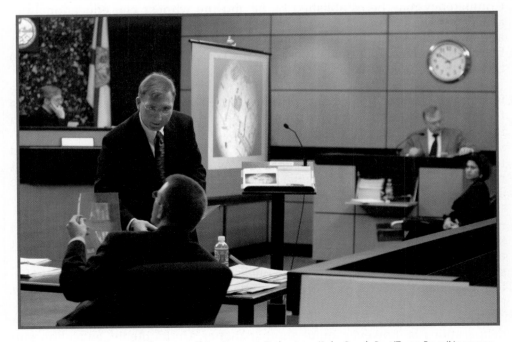

FIGURE 1-14   An expert witness testifying in court. *Taylor Jones/Palm Beach Post/Zuma Press/Newscom*

the same logic in *Melendez-Diaz,* the Court reasoned that introducing forensic science evidence via an affidavit or a certificate denied a defendant the opportunity to cross-examine the analyst. In 2011, the Supreme Court reaffirmed the *Melendez-Diaz* decision in the case of *Bullcoming v. New Mexico*[7] by rejecting a substitute expert witness in lieu of the original analyst:

> The question presented is whether the Confrontation Clause permits the prosecution to introduce a forensic laboratory report containing a testimonial certification—made for the purpose of proving a particular fact—through the in-court testimony of a scientist who did not sign the certification or perform or observe the test reported in the certification. We hold that surrogate testimony of that order does not meet the constitutional requirement. The accused's right is to be confronted with the analyst who made the certification, unless that analyst is unavailable at trial, and the accused had an opportunity, pretrial, to cross-examine that particular scientist.

WebExtra 1.2

Watch a Forensic Expert Witness Testify—I

WebExtra 1.3

Watch a Forensic Expert Witness Testify—II

FURNISHING TRAINING IN THE PROPER RECOGNITION, COLLECTION, AND PRESERVATION OF PHYSICAL EVIDENCE

The competence of a laboratory staff and the sophistication of its analytical equipment have little or no value if relevant evidence cannot be properly recognized, collected, and preserved at the site of a crime. For this reason, the forensic staff must have responsibilities that will influence the conduct of the crime-scene investigation.

The most direct and effective response to this problem has been to dispatch specially trained evidence-collection technicians to the crime scene. A growing number of crime laboratories and the police agencies they service keep trained "evidence technicians" on 24-hour call to help criminal investigators retrieve evidence. These technicians are trained by the laboratory staff to recognize and gather pertinent physical evidence at the crime scene. They are assigned to the laboratory full-time for continued exposure to forensic techniques and procedures. They have at their disposal all the proper tools and supplies for proper collection and packaging of evidence for future scientific examination.

Unfortunately, many police forces still have not adopted this approach. Often a patrol officer or detective collects the evidence. The individual's effectiveness in this role depends on the extent of his or her training and working relationship with the laboratory. For maximum use of the skills of the crime laboratory, training of the crime-scene investigator must go beyond superficial classroom lectures to involve extensive personal contact with the forensic scientist. Each must become aware of the other's problems, techniques, and limitations.

The training of police officers in evidence collection and their familiarization with the capabilities of a crime laboratory should not be restricted to a select group of personnel on the force. Every officer engaged in fieldwork, whether it be traffic, patrol, investigation, or juvenile control, often must process evidence for laboratory examination. Obviously, it would be difficult and time consuming to give everyone the in-depth training and attention that a qualified criminal investigator requires. However, familiarity with crime laboratory services and capabilities can be gained through periodic lectures, laboratory tours, and dissemination of manuals prepared by the laboratory staff that outline the proper methods for collecting and submitting physical evidence to the laboratory (see Figure 1-15).

A brief outline describing the proper collection and packaging of common types of physical evidence is found in Appendix I. The procedures and information summarized in this appendix are discussed in greater detail in forthcoming chapters.

FIGURE 1-15 Representative evidence-collection guides prepared by various governmental agencies. *Richard Saferstein, Ph.D.*

Quick Review

- A forensic scientist must be skilled in applying the principles and techniques of the physical and natural sciences to analyzing evidence that may be recovered during a criminal investigation.
- The cases *Frye* v. *United States* and *Daubert* v. *Merrell Dow Pharmaceuticals, Inc.* set guidelines for determining the admissibility of scientific evidence into the courtroom.
- An expert witness evaluates evidence based on specialized training and experience.
- Forensic scientists participate in training law enforcement personnel in the proper recognition, collection, and preservation of physical evidence.

EXPLORING FORENSIC SCIENCE ON THE INTERNET

There are no limits to the amount or type of information that can be found on the Internet. The fields of law enforcement and forensic science have not been left behind by advancing computer technology. Extensive information about forensic science is available on the Internet. The types of information available on websites range from simple explanations of the various fields of forensics to intricate details of crime-scene reconstruction. People can also find information on which colleges offer degree programs in forensics and webpages posted by law enforcement agencies that detail their activities as well as employment opportunities.

GENERAL FORENSICS SITES

Reddy's Forensic Home Page (www.forensicpage.com) is a valuable starting point. This site is a collection of forensic webpages in categories such as new links in forensics; general forensic information sources; associations, colleges, and societies; literature and journals; forensic laboratories; general webpages; forensic-related mailing lists and newsgroups; universities; conferences; and various forensic fields of expertise.

Another website offering a multitude of information related to forensic science is Zeno's Forensic Site (www.forensic.to/forensic.html). Here users can find links related to forensic education and expert consultation, as well as a wealth of information concerning specific fields of forensic science.

A comprehensive and useful website for those interested in law enforcement is Officer.com (www.officer.com). This comprehensive collection of criminal justice resources is organized into easy-to-read subdirectories that relate to topics such as law enforcement agencies, police association and organization sites, criminal justice organizations, law research pages, and police mailing-list directories.

WEBSITES ON SPECIFIC TOPICS

AN INTRODUCTION TO FORENSIC FIREARM IDENTIFICATION This website contains an extensive collection of information relating to the identification of firearms. An individual can explore in detail how to examine bullets, cartridge cases, and clothing for gunshot residues and suspect shooters' hands for primer residues. Information on the latest technology involving the automated firearms search system National Integrated Ballistic Identification Network (NIBIN) can also be found on this site.

WebExtra 1.4

An Introduction to Forensic Firearm Identification

CARPENTER'S FORENSIC SCIENCE RESOURCES This site provides a bibliography involving forensic evidence. For example, the user can find references about DNA, fingerprints, hairs, fibers, and questioned documents as they relate to crime scenes and assist investigations. This website is an excellent place to start a research project in forensic science.

WebExtra 1.5

Carpenter's Forensic Science Resources

CRIME SCENE INVESTIGATOR NETWORK For those who are interested in learning the process of crime-scene investigation, this site provides detailed guidelines and information regarding crime-scene response and the collection and preservation of evidence. For example, information concerning the packaging and analysis of bloodstains, seminal fluids, hairs, fibers, paint, glass, firearms, documents, and fingerprints can be found through this website. It explains the importance of inspecting the crime scene and the impact forensic evidence has on the investigation.

WebExtra 1.6

Crime Scene Investigator Network

CRIMES AND CLUES Users interested in learning about the forensic aspects of fingerprinting will find this to be a useful and informative website. The site covers the history of fingerprints, as well as subjects pertaining to the development of latent fingerprints. The user will also find links to other websites covering a variety of subjects pertaining to crime-scene investigation, documentation of the crime scene, and expert testimony.

WebExtra 1.7

Crimes and Clues

QUESTIONED-DOCUMENT EXAMINATION This basic, informative webpage answers frequently asked questions concerning document examination, explains the application of typical document examinations, and details the basic facts and theory of handwriting and signatures. There are also links to noted document examination cases that present the user with real-life applications of forensic document examination.

WebExtra 1.8

Questioned-Document Examination

CHAPTER REVIEW

- Forensic science is the application of science to criminal and civil laws that are enforced by police agencies in a criminal justice system.
- The first system of personal identification was called "anthropometry." It distinguished one individual from another based on a series of bodily measurements.
- Forensic science owes its origins to individuals such as Bertillon, Galton, Lattes, Goddard, Osborn, and Locard, who developed the principles and techniques needed to identify and compare physical evidence.
- Locard's exchange principle states that, when two objects come into contact with each other, a cross-transfer of materials occurs that can connect a criminal suspect to his or her victim.
- The development of crime laboratories in the United States has been characterized by rapid growth accompanied by a lack of national and regional planning and coordination.
- Four major reasons for the increase in the number of crime laboratories in the United States since the 1960s are as follows: (1) The requirement to advise criminal suspects of their constitutional rights and their right of immediate access to counsel has all but eliminated confessions as a routine investigative tool. (2) There has been a staggering increase in crime rates in the United States. (3) All illicit-drug seizures must be sent to a forensic laboratory for confirmatory chemical analysis before the case can be adjudicated in court. (4) DNA profiling was developed and is now often required.
- The technical support provided by crime laboratories can be assigned to five basic services: the physical science unit, the biology unit, the firearms unit, the document examination unit, and the photography unit.
- Some crime laboratories offer optional services such as toxicology, fingerprint analysis, polygraph administration, voiceprint analysis, and crime-scene investigation.
- Special forensic science services available to the law enforcement community include forensic pathology, forensic anthropology, forensic entomology, forensic psychiatry, forensic odontology, forensic engineering, and forensic computer and digital analysis.
- A forensic scientist must be skilled in applying the principles and techniques of the physical and natural sciences to analyzing evidence that may be recovered during a criminal investigation.
- The cases *Frye* v. *United States* and *Daubert* v. *Merrell Dow Pharmaceuticals, Inc.* set guidelines for determining the admissibility of scientific evidence into the courtroom.
- An expert witness evaluates evidence based on specialized training and experience.
- Forensic scientists participate in training law enforcement personnel in the proper recognition, collection, and preservation of physical evidence.

KEY TERMS

expert witness, 22   Locard's exchange principle, 8   scientific method, 20

REVIEW QUESTIONS

1. The application of science to law describes _____.
2. The Spaniard _____ published the first writings about the detection of poisons and the effects of poisons on animals, and he is considered the "father of forensic toxicology."
3. A system of personal identification using a series of bodily measurements was first devised by _____, and he called it _____.
4. The fictional exploits of _____ excited the imagination of an emerging generation of forensic scientists and criminal investigators.
5. One of the first functional crime laboratories was formed in Lyons, France, in 1910 under the direction of _____, who developed _____, a theory stating that there is mutual transfer of material when two objects make contact with each other.
6. The application of science to criminal investigation was advocated by the Austrian magistrate _____.
7. True or False: The important advancement in the fields of blood typing and document examination were made in the early part of the twentieth century. _____
8. The Italian scientist _____ devised the first workable procedure for typing dried bloodstains.
9. Early efforts at applying scientific principles to document examination are associated with _____.
10. The first DNA profiling test was developed by _____ in 1984, and it was first used in 1986 to identify the murderer of two young English girls.

11. True or False: Computerized databases exist for fingerprints, bullets, cartridge cases, and DNA. _____

12. The first forensic laboratory in the United States was created in 1923 by the _____ Police Department.

13. Although no national system of forensic laboratories exists in the United States, the state of _____ is an excellent example of a geographical area in the United States that has created a system of integrated regional and satellite laboratories.

14. A decentralized system of crime laboratories currently exists in the United States under the auspices of various governmental agencies at the _____, _____, _____, and _____ levels of government.

15. In contrast to the United States, Britain has a crime laboratory system characterized by a national system of _____ laboratories.

16. Four important federal agencies offering forensic services are _____, _____, _____, and _____.

17. The application of chemistry, physics, and geology to the identification and comparison of crime-scene evidence is the function of the _____ unit of a crime laboratory.

18. The examination of blood, hairs, fibers, and botanical materials is conducted in the _____ unit of a crime laboratory.

19. The examination of bullets, cartridge cases, shotgun shells, and ammunition of all types is the responsibility of the _____ unit.

20. The study of handwriting and typewriting on questioned documents is carried out by the _____ unit to ascertain authenticity and/or source.

21. The examination of body fluids and organs for drugs and poisons is a function of the _____ unit.

22. The _____ unit dispatches trained personnel to the scene of a crime to retrieve evidence for laboratory examination.

23. True or False: Special forensic science services available to the law enforcement community include forensic pathology, forensic anthropology, and forensic astronomy. _____

24. The "general acceptance" principle, which serves as a criterion for the judicial admissibility of scientific evidence, was set forth in the case of _____.

25. In the case of _____, the Supreme Court ruled that, in assessing the admissibility of new and unique scientific tests, the trial judge did not have to rely solely on the concept of "general acceptance."

26. True or False: The U.S. Supreme Court decision in *Kumho Tire Co., Ltd.* v. *Carmichael* restricted the "gatekeeping" role of a trial judge to scientific testimony only. _____

27. A Florida case that exemplifies the flexibility and wide discretion that the trial judge has in matters of scientific inquiry is _____.

28. A(n) _____ is a person who can demonstrate a particular skill or has knowledge in a trade or profession that will help the court determine the truth of the matter at issue.

29. True or False: The expert witness's courtroom demeanor may play an important role in deciding what weight the court will assign to his or her testimony. _____

30. True or False: The testimony of an expert witness incorporates his or her personal opinion relating to a matter he or she has either studied or examined. _____

31. True or False: In 2004, the U.S. Supreme Court addressed issues relating to the Confrontation Clause of the Sixth Amendment in the case of *Crawford* v. *Washington*. _____

32. The 2009 U.S. Supreme Court decision _____ addressed the practice of using affidavits in lieu of in-person testimony by forensic examiners.

33. The ability of the investigator to recognize and collect crime-scene evidence properly depends on the amount of _____ received from the crime laboratory.

APPLICATION AND CRITICAL THINKING

1. Most crime labs in the United States are funded and operated by the government and provide services free to police and prosecutors. Great Britain, however, relies on private laboratories that charge fees for their services and keep any profits they make. Suggest potential strengths and weaknesses of each system.

2. Police investigating an apparent suicide collect the following items at the scene: a note purportedly written by the victim, a revolver bearing very faint fingerprints, and traces of skin and blood under the victim's fingernails. What units of the crime laboratory will examine each piece of evidence?

3. List at least three advantages of having an evidence-collection unit process a crime scene instead of a patrol officer or detective.

4. What legal issue was raised on appeal by the defense in Carl Coppolino's Florida murder trial? What court ruling is most relevant to the decision to reject the appeal? Explain your answer.

5. **A Timeline of Forensic Science** The following images depict different types of evidence or techniques for analyzing evidence. Place the images in order pertaining to the time in history (least recent to most recent) at which each type of evidence or technique was first introduced. Do this using the letters assigned to the images.

(A)

(B)

(C)

(D)

(E)

(F)

(G)

(A), (B) *Dorling Kindersley Ltd.;* (B) *Dorling Kindersley Ltd.;* (C) *Richard Megna/Fundamental Photographs;* (D) *James Steidl/Shutterstock;* (E) *George Whitely/Getty Images;* (F) *Orlando/Three Lions/Getty Images;* (G) *Alan Abramowitz/Getty Images*

6. **Evidence Processing at the Crime Laboratory** You are the evidence technician at the front desk of the state crime lab. You receive the following items of evidence to check in on a very busy day. You must indicate to which unit each piece of evidence must be sent for analysis. Your crime lab has a criminalistics (physical science) unit, a drug unit, a biology unit, a firearms unit, a document examination unit, a toxicology unit, a latent fingerprinting unit, an anthropology unit, and a forensic computer and digital analysis unit.

A. _____

B. _____

C. _____

D. _____

E. _____

F. _____

G. _____

H. _____

I. _____

J. _____

K. _____

L. _____

M. _____

(A) Keith Brofsky/Getty Images; (B) Michael P. Gadomski/Science Source; (C) Saivann/Shutterstock; (D) Haemin Rapp/Shutterstock; (E) George Whitely/Getty Images; (F) Jack Hollingsworth/Photodisc/Getty Images; (G) Horacio Villalobos/Corbis; (H) Andy Crawford/ Dorling Kindersley, Ltd.; (I) Hugh Threlfall/Alamy; (J) Gary Ombler/Dorling Kindersley, Ltd.; (K) Danilo Calilung/Corbis; (L) Peter Anderson/Dorling Kindersley Ltd.; (M) Matthew Ward/Dorling Kindersley, Ltd.

ENDNOTES

1. 293 Fed. 1013 (D.C. Cir. 1923).

2. 509 U.S. 579 (1993).

3. 526 U.S. 137 (1999).

4. 223 So. 2d 68 (Fla. App. 1968), app. dismissed, 234 So. 2d (Fla. 1969), cert. denied, 399 U.S. 927 (1970).

5. 557 U.S. 305 (2009).

6. 541 U.S. 36 (2004).

7. 131 S. Ct. 2705 (2011).

2 Securing and Searching the Crime Scene

Karl Gehring/Getty Images

LEARNING OBJECTIVES

After studying this chapter, you should be able to:

- Discuss the responsibilities of the first police officer who arrives at the crime scene.
- Describe the role of the lead investigator in coordinating the crime-scene search.
- Describe the conditions at the crime scene that should be given particular notice.
- Understand the various search patterns investigators can use to systematically search the crime scene for evidence.
- Appreciate the necessity of documenting all initial observations and evidence collected.

JONBENET RAMSEY: WHO DID IT?

Patsy and John Ramsey were in the upper crust of Boulder, Colorado, society. In the span of five short years, John had built his computer company into a billion-dollar corporation. In addition to financial success, the Ramseys also had a beautiful six-year-old daughter, JonBenet.

Just after 5:00 a.m. on December 26, 1996, Patsy Ramsey awoke and walked downstairs to her kitchen. At the foot of the staircase, she found a two-and-a-half-page note saying that JonBenet had been kidnapped. The note contained a ransom demand of $118,000. When the police arrived to investigate, it was quite apparent that JonBenet was missing.

In retrospect, some serious mistakes were made in securing the crime scene, the Ramsey household. Initially, the police conducted a cursory search of the house but failed to find JonBenet. They did not seal the house off; in fact, four of the Ramseys' friends along with their pastor were let into the home and allowed to move about at will. John was permitted to leave the premises unattended for one and a half hours. One hour after his return, John and two of his friends searched the house again. This time John went down into the basement, where he discovered JonBenet's body. He removed a white blanket from JonBenet and carried her upstairs, placing the body on the living room floor.

The murder of JonBenet Ramsey remains as baffling a mystery today as it was on the first day of its investigation. Ample physical evidence supports both the theory that the crime was committed by an outsider and the competing theory that JonBenet was murdered by someone who resided in the Ramsey household. Perhaps better care at securing and processing the crime scene would have resolved some of the crime's outstanding questions.

Forensic science begins at the crime scene. To be useful to investigators, evidence at a crime scene must be preserved and recorded in its original condition as much as possible. Failure to protect a crime scene properly may result in the destruction or altering of evidence, which can hinder the search for the perpetrator by misleading investigators about the facts of the incident.

Securing the Crime Scene

The first officer to arrive at the scene of a crime is responsible for taking steps to preserve and protect the area to the greatest extent possible. The officer should not let his or her guard down; the scene should always be treated as though the crime were still occurring until it is proved otherwise. Arriving officers should immediately ascertain that the perpetrator is no longer in the immediate area of the crime scene and is not a threat to anyone at or near the crime scene. Special note should be taken of any vehicles or people leaving the scene.

Of course, first priority should be given to obtaining medical assistance for individuals in need of it. If medical assistance is needed, the officer should direct medical workers to approach the body by an indirect route to minimize the possibility of disturbing evidence. This pathway should later be used by investigative personnel for the same reason. The first responding officer must quickly evaluate the victim's condition before the victim is taken to a medical facility. The officer must also record any statements made by the victim and instruct the emergency medical personnel to record any statements the victim makes on the way to the hospital. This information should later be included in notes.

The officer should call for any backup or investigative personnel required and, as soon as possible, detain all potential suspects or witnesses still at the scene. The officer must identify all individuals at the scene, including bystanders and medical personnel. At the same time, he or she should exclude all unauthorized personnel from the scene. This includes family and friends of the victim, who should be shown as much compassion as possible.

The first responder(s) are responsible for establishing the boundaries of the scene to be protected. The boundaries should encompass the center of the scene where the crime occurred, any paths of entry or exit, and any areas where evidence may have been discarded or moved. For indoor scenes this may include anything from a single room to an entire house and yard. The center of the crime scene is usually apparent, and a sufficient area around this spot should be closed off. The boundaries of an outdoor crime scene are more difficult to determine and can span miles, especially if a vehicle is involved. The officer should initially denote the boundaries of the scene using crime-scene tape, ropes, or traffic cones (see Figure 2-1). As additional officers arrive, investigators should immediately take measures to isolate the area around the taped-off section. Police barricades, along with the strategic positioning of guards, will prevent unauthorized access to the area. Only investigative personnel assigned to the scene should be admitted. The responding officers must keep an accurate log of who enters and exits the scene and the time at which they do so.

Sometimes the exclusion of unauthorized personnel proves to be more difficult than expected. Crimes of violence are especially susceptible to attention by higher-level police officials and members of the media, as well as by emotionally charged neighbors and curiosity seekers. Every individual who enters the scene has the potential to destroy physical evidence, even if by unintentional carelessness. To exercise proper control over the crime scene, the officer charged with the responsibility for protecting it must have the authority to exclude everyone, including fellow police officers not directly involved in processing the site or in conducting the investigation. Seasoned criminal investigators are always prepared to relate horror stories about crime scenes where physical evidence was rendered totally valueless by hordes of people who, for one reason or another, tramped through the site. Securing and isolating the crime scene are critical steps in an investigation, the accomplishment

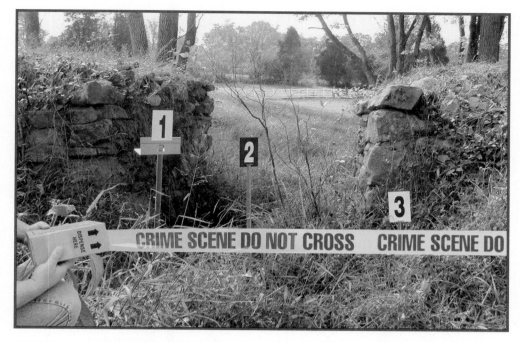

FIGURE 2-1   The first investigators to arrive must secure the crime scene and establish a perimeter. This perimeter may be delineated by crime-scene tape, ropes, or barricades. *Sirchie Finger Print Laboratories*

of which is the mark of a trained and professional crime-scene investigative team. It is also important to park the crime-scene vehicle where it will not destroy evidence but also be secure and easily accessible.

It is worth noting that personnel should *never* do anything while at the crime scene—including smoking, eating, drinking, or littering—that might alter the scene. No aspects of the scene, including a body at a death scene, should be moved or disturbed unless they pose a serious threat to investigating officers or bystanders. This means that no one should open or close faucets or flush toilets at the scene. Also, officers should avoid altering temperature conditions at the scene by adjusting windows, doors, or the heat or air-conditioning.

Quick Review

- The first officer arriving on the scene of a crime has the responsibility to preserve and protect the area to the greatest extent possible.
- First priority should be given to obtaining medical assistance for individuals in need of it.
- Steps must be taken by the first responder to exclude all unauthorized personnel from the scene and keep an accurate log of who enters and exits the scene and the time at which they do so.

Surveying the Crime Scene

Once the scene has been secured, with the help of others, a lead investigator will start the process of evaluating the area. The lead investigator will immediately gain an overview of the situation and develop a strategy for the systematic examination and documentation of the entire crime scene.

THE WALK-THROUGH

walk-through

The initial survey of the crime scene carried out by the lead investigator to gain an overview of the scene in order to formulate a plan for processing the scene.

The initial survey of the scene is typically called the **walk-through**. First, the perpetrator's path of entry and exit should be established. The investigators should then follow an indirect path to the center of the scene, possibly one already established by the first responding officer to allow for medical attention. Some investigators attempt to follow the path of the suspect, but this may destroy possible evidence.

Logic dictates that obvious items of crime-scene evidence will first come to the attention of the crime-scene investigator. The investigator must document and photograph these items. Any fragile evidence, such as shoe and tire impressions, may be secured by the investigator or tagged for the search team. Investigators conducting the first walk-through should carry reflective numbered markers and place a marker near each item of evidence they locate. These markers will alert other crime-scene personnel to the location of difficult-to-observe evidence. The investigators should remember that the crime scene is three-dimensional; evidence may be found on the walls or ceilings as well as on the floor and other surfaces. It may also be practical to have one or two individuals canvas the area outside the barricaded scene.

The investigator should ask the following questions:

- Is the scene indoors or outdoors?
- What is the location of the scene (street address if applicable)?
- What are the weather or temperature conditions?
- In what type of building and neighborhood is the scene located?
- Was there any odor detected by the first responder upon arrival?
- Are doors and windows open or closed, locked or unlocked?
- Given the states of windows and doors, what are possible points of entry and exit?
- Is anything damaged, out of place, or missing? Are there objects that do not appear to belong there?
- Does an object's condition suggest that a struggle took place?
- Are lights and electrical appliances on or off?
- Is food present? Is it in the middle of being prepared, partially eaten, and so on?
- Does this scene appear to involve violence?
- What are the contents of any ashtrays and trash cans at the crime site? Are there tooth marks or lipstick on cigarette butts?
- What is the state of the bathroom? Are towels wet or dry? Is the toilet seat up or down?
- Are there any places where the suspect could have easily and quickly hidden a weapon?
- Is there a vehicle nearby? If so, is the engine hot or cold?

Investigators should take particular note of aspects of the scene that suggest the timing of the incident. For example, if today's newspaper is on the table, it suggests that the incident occurred after the paper was delivered. The investigator's notes should include answers to basic questions and descriptions of everything observed at the scene. These simple observations may prove significant in the later investigation.

The presence or absence of certain evidence can offer key clues to the investigator. For example, objects that appear out of place, such as a child's toy in the house of a couple without children or relatives without children, may be very important. It is also important to observe whether objects that should be at the scene, such as a television or computer, are missing or displaced.

The presence or absence of evidence may also suggest whether the scene is a primary or secondary scene. A **primary scene** is one at which the original incident occurred. The **secondary scene** is a location that became part of the crime by activities after the initial incident, such as using a car to transport a body. If a victim suffered severe injury involving heavy loss of blood but little or no blood is present where the body is found, it is likely to be a secondary scene.

ASSIGNING TASKS

Investigators must establish a center of operations, or **command center**, at the scene. Here, members of the investigative team receive their assignments, store their equipment, and meet to discuss aspects of the case. The command center must be located outside the taped-off boundary of the scene and contain the basic equipment needed to photograph, sketch, process, and collect evidence. An equipped crime-scene vehicle usually serves the purpose well. If multiple scenes are involved, the command center should also be a center for communicating with investigators at the other scenes.

At the command center, the lead investigator assigns tasks after the initial walk-through. Basic tasks include locating possible evidence, assessing the evidence, processing evidence (e.g., dusting for fingerprints and casting footprints or tire impressions), and photographing and sketching the scene. The tasks should be carried out in this exact order to properly process the scene. The number of personnel assigned to each task depends on the scene and the discretion of the lead investigator. In some cases, a single crime-scene investigator might be required to handle all these tasks.

primary scene
A crime scene at which the original criminal act was perpetrated.

secondary scene
A crime scene separate from the primary scene that became part of the crime by its involvement in activities after the initial criminal act was perpetrated.

command center
A secure site outside the boundaries of a crime scene where equipment is stored, tasks are assigned, and communication occurs.

Quick Review

- The lead investigator is responsible for developing a strategy for the systematic examination and documentation of the entire crime scene.
- The lead investigator must gain an overview of the general setting of the scene. Of particular importance are objects that do not appear to belong or aspects of the scene that may suggest the timing of the incident.
- The presence or absence of evidence may also suggest whether the scene is a primary or secondary scene.
- At the command center, members of the investigative team receive their assignments, store their equipment, congregate to talk about aspects of the case, and communicate with personnel at other crime scenes.

Searching the Crime Scene

There are many methods for searching the scene in a logical and systematic fashion to locate evidence. How one carries out a crime-scene search depends on the locale and size of the area, as well as on the actions of the suspect(s) and victim(s) at the scene. When possible, it is advisable to have one person supervising and coordinating the collection of evidence. Without proper control, the search may be conducted in an atmosphere of confusion with needless duplication of effort. The areas searched must include all probable points of entry and exit used by the criminals. The search team may want to use a simple flashlight to illuminate surfaces at an oblique angle to reveal latent (hidden) fingerprints, handprints, footwear imprints, and other residues.

TYPES OF SEARCH PATTERNS

line/strip search pattern
A search method used by one or two investigators who walk in straight lines across the crime scene.

LINE/STRIP SEARCH PATTERN In the line/strip search pattern, one or two investigators start at the boundary at one end of the scene and walk straight across to the other side. They then move a little farther along the border and walk straight back to the other side (see Figure 2-2[a]). This method is best used in scenes where the boundaries are well established because the boundaries dictate the beginning and end of the search lines. If the boundary is incorrectly chosen, important evidence may remain undiscovered outside the search area.

grid search pattern
A search method employed by two or more people who perform overlapping line searches forming a grid.

GRID SEARCH PATTERN The grid search pattern employs two people performing line searches that originate from adjacent corners and form perpendicular lines (see Figure 2-2[b]). One searcher will move in a north-south direction while a simultaneous search is conducted in an east-west direction. Both move back and forth as in the line/strip search pattern. This method is very thorough, but the boundaries must be well established.

spiral search pattern
A search method in which the investigator moves in an inward spiral from the boundary to the center of the scene or in an outward spiral from the center to the boundary of a scene.

SPIRAL SEARCH PATTERN The spiral search pattern usually employs one person. The investigator moves in an inward spiral from the boundary to the center of the scene or in an outward spiral from the center to the boundary (see Figure 2-2[c]). The inward spiral method is helpful because the searcher is moving from an area light with evidence to an area where more evidence will most likely be found. Either spiral approach facilitates the location of footprints leading away from the scene in any direction. However, it is often difficult for a searcher to complete a perfect spiral, and evidence could be missed.

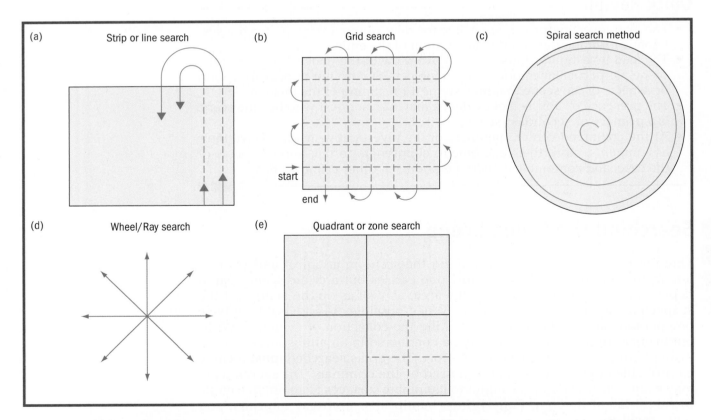

FIGURE 2-2 (a) Line/strip search pattern; (b) grid search pattern; (c) spiral search pattern; (d) wheel/ray search pattern; (e) quadrant/zone search pattern. *Richard Saferstein, Ph.D., CRIMINALISTICS: AN INTRODUCTION TO FORENSIC SCIENCE, 11e, ©2015. Printed and Electronically reproduced by permission of Pearson Education, Inc., Upper Saddle River, New Jersey.*

WHEEL/RAY SEARCH PATTERN   The wheel/ray search pattern employs several people moving from the boundary straight toward the center of the scene (inward) or from the center straight to the boundary (outward). This method is not preferred because the areas between the "rays" are not searched (see Figure 2-2[d]).

QUADRANT/ZONE SEARCH PATTERN   The quadrant/zone search pattern involves dividing the scene into zones or quadrants, and team members are assigned to search each section. Each of these sections can be subdivided into smaller sections for smaller teams to search thoroughly (see Figure 2-2[e]). This method is best suited for scenes that cover a large area.

VEHICLE SEARCHES   If the scene includes a vehicle, the vehicle search must be carefully planned and systematically carried out. The nature of the case determines how detailed the search must be. At all times investigators must be careful to avoid contact with surfaces that may contain fingerprints such as a steering wheel or door handle. In hit-and-run cases, the outside and undercarriage of the car must be examined with care. In this case the vehicle itself is the "weapon." Particular attention is paid to looking for any evidence resulting from a cross-transfer of evidence between the car and the victim; this includes blood, tissue, hair, fibers, and fabric impressions. Traces of paint or broken glass may be located on the victim or roadway. In a vehicle burglary or theft, the search focuses on the place of entry. Tool marks and fingerprints usually are important in these cases. If the car was used for transportation, more attention may be given to the interior of the car. However, all areas of the vehicle, inside and outside, should be searched with equal care for physical evidence at the scene, or the vehicle may be towed to a police department garage.

NIGHT SEARCHES   Searches during the night are especially difficult. Indoors, artificial lights frequently can be used. However, it can be very difficult outdoors even to determine the boundaries of the scene. When possible, the scene should be taped off, left undisturbed, and guarded until daylight. If impending weather or other circumstances do not allow for waiting until daylight, a perimeter must be estimated and floodlights should be set up for the search.

LOCATING EVIDENCE

The purpose of the crime-scene search is to locate physical evidence. What to search for will be determined by the particular circumstances of the crime. This may include footprints, weapons, blood spatter, objects possibly touched by the suspect, trace fibers, or hairs. For example, in the case of homicide, the search will be centered on the weapon and any type of evidence left as a result of contact between the victim and the assailant. The cross-transfer of evidence, such as hairs, fibers, and blood, between individuals involved in the crime is particularly useful for linking suspects to the crime site and for corroborating events that transpired during the commission of the crime. Special attention should be paid to the body and the area surrounding it. During the investigation of a burglary, officers should attempt to locate tool marks at the point of entry. In most crimes, a thorough and systematic search for latent fingerprints is required. When an investigator finds an object of possible evidentiary value, he or she should record its location in notes, sketches, and photographs and then mark its location with an evidence marker (see Figure 2-3).

The search ends when the team or lead investigator determines that all pertinent evidence has been located to the best of the team's ability. When this determination is made, the team carries out a final survey of the scene. This should include a visual overview of all parts of the scene. Investigators should take an inventory of all evidence collected so nothing is lost or left behind.

wheel/ray search pattern
A search method employed by several people who move from the boundary straight toward the center of the scene (inward) or from the center straight to the boundary (outward).

quadrant/zone search pattern
A search method in which the crime scene is divided into smaller sections (zones or quadrants) and team members are assigned to search each section. (Each of these sections can be subdivided into smaller sections for smaller teams to search thoroughly.)

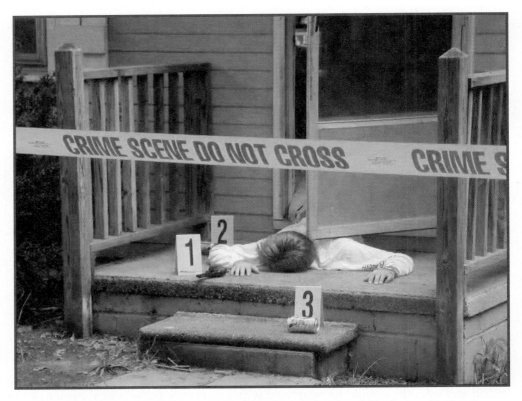

FIGURE 2-3 Numbered evidence markers are used to show the location of (1) a firearm, (2) a beverage can, and (3) another beverage can at a crime scene. *Sirchie Finger Print Laboratories*

The team members should be sure to retrieve all equipment. They should also verify that any threats to health or safety at the scene have been or will be dealt with properly. Once all of these measures have been taken, the scene can be released to the proper authorities.

Obviously, the skill of crime-scene investigators at recognizing evidence and searching relevant locations is paramount to successfully processing the crime scene. Although training can impart general knowledge about conducting a proper crime-scene investigation, ultimately the investigator must rely on experience gained from numerous investigations to formulate a successful strategy for recovering relevant physical evidence at crime scenes. If the investigator cannot recognize physical evidence or cannot properly preserve it for laboratory examination, no amount of sophisticated laboratory instrumentation or technical expertise can salvage the situation.

The know-how for conducting a proper crime-scene search for physical evidence is not beyond the grasp of any police department, regardless of its size. With proper training, police agencies can ensure they competently process crime scenes. In many jurisdictions, however, police agencies have delegated this task to a specialized team of technicians known as crime-scene investigators.

WebExtra 2.1

Autopsy of a Murder
Search for clues at the scene of a murder. Once you've located the relevant evidence, you will need to collect the evidence for laboratory testing.

Quick Review

- How one carries out a crime-scene search will depend on the locale and size of the area, as well as on the actions of the suspect(s) and victim(s) at the scene.
- The purpose of the crime-scene search is to locate physical evidence. The particular circumstances of the crime determine what to search for first.

- When evidence is found, the location is documented in notes, photographs, and sketches.
- When the search is deemed complete, the investigating team conducts a final survey that includes a visual overview of all parts of the scene, an inventory of all evidence collected, the retrieval of all equipment, and the neutralization of all health or safety threats. Once all of these measures have been taken, the scene can be released to the proper authorities.

CHAPTER REVIEW

- The first officer arriving on the scene of a crime has the responsibility to preserve and protect the area to the greatest extent possible.

- First priority should be given to obtaining medical assistance for individuals in need of it.

- Steps must be taken by the first responder to exclude all unauthorized personnel from the scene and keep an accurate log of who enters and exits the scene and the time at which they do so.

- The lead investigator is responsible for developing a strategy for the systematic examination and documentation of the entire crime scene.

- The lead investigator must gain an overview of the general setting of the scene. Of particular importance are objects that do not appear to belong or aspects of the scene that may suggest the timing of the incident.

- The presence or absence of evidence may also suggest whether the scene is a primary or secondary scene.

- At the command center, members of the investigative team receive their assignments, store their equipment, congregate to talk about aspects of the case, and communicate with personnel at other crime scenes.

- How one carries out a crime-scene search will depend on the locale and size of the area, as well as on the actions of the suspect(s) and victim(s) at the scene.

- The purpose of the crime-scene search is to locate physical evidence. The particular circumstances of the crime determine what to search for first.

- When evidence is found, the location is documented in notes, photographs, and sketches.

- When the search is deemed complete, the investigating team conducts a final survey that includes a visual overview of all parts of the scene, an inventory of all evidence collected, the retrieval of all equipment, and the neutralization of all health or safety threats. Once all of these measures have been taken, the scene can be released to the proper authorities.

KEY TERMS

command center, 37

grid search pattern, 38

line/strip search pattern, 38

primary scene, 37

quadrant/zone search pattern, 39

secondary scene, 37

spiral search pattern, 38

walk-through, 36

wheel/ray search pattern, 39

REVIEW QUESTIONS

1. True or False: Failure to protect a crime scene properly may result in the destruction or altering of evidence. _____

2. The _____ arriving on the scene of a crime is responsible for taking steps to preserve and protect the area to the greatest extent possible, and he or she must rely on his or her training to deal with any violent or hazardous circumstances.

3. At a crime scene, first priority should be given to obtaining _____ for individuals in need of it and attempting to minimize the disturbance of evidence.

4. All unauthorized personnel must be _____ from crime scenes.

5. True or False: The boundaries of the crime scene, denoted by crime-scene tape, rope, or traffic cones, should encompass only the center of the scene where the crime occurred. _____

6. Even though all unauthorized personnel are not admitted to the scene, a very accurate _____ must be kept of those who do enter and exit the scene and the time at which they do so.

7. True or False: The lead investigator immediately proceeds to gain an overview of the situation and develop a strategy for the systematic examination of the crime scene during the final survey. _____

8. A(n) _____ crime scene is one at which the original incident, such as a beating or rape, occurred. A(n) _____ crime scene became part of the crime as a result of activities that occurred after the initial incident.

9. The investigative team receives assignments, stores equipment, and congregates to talk about aspects of the case at the _____.

10. A detailed search of the crime scene must be conducted in a(n) _____ fashion.

11. The crime-scene search is undertaken to locate _____.

12. True or False: The search patterns that may be used to search a crime scene for evidence include the line pattern, grid pattern, polar coordinate pattern, and spiral pattern. _____

13. When carrying out vehicle searches, investigators must be careful to avoid contact with surfaces that may contain _____ such as steering wheels or door handles.

14. True or False: During nighttime, outdoor scenes should be taped off, left undisturbed, and guarded until daylight. _____

15. True or False: The search is concluded when the district attorney determines that all pertinent evidence has been located to the best of the team's ability. _____

16. Once a(n) _____ of the scene has been carried out, the scene can be released to the proper authorities.

17. True or False: If the investigator does not recognize physical evidence or does not properly preserve it for laboratory examination, sophisticated laboratory instrumentation or technical expertise can salvage the situation and attain the desired results. _____

APPLICATION AND CRITICAL THINKING

1. You are the first officer at the scene of an outdoor assault. You find the victim bleeding but conscious, with two of the victim's friends and several onlookers standing nearby. You call for backup and quickly glance around but see no one fleeing the scene. Describe the steps you would take while you wait for backup to arrive.

2. What kind of search pattern(s) would investigators be most likely to employ in each of the following situations:

   a) Two people searching a small area with well-defined boundaries

   b) Several people searching a large area

   c) A single person searching a large area

3. Officer Bill Walter arrives at the scene of an apparent murder: a body bearing several gunshot wounds lies on the floor of a small, un-air-conditioned house in late July. A pungent odor almost overwhelms him when he enters the house, so he opens a window to allow him to breathe so he can investigate the scene. While airing out the house, he secures the scene and interviews bystanders. When he inspects the scene, he discovers very little blood in the room and little evidence of a struggle. What mistake did Officer Walter make in his investigation? What conclusion did he draw about the scene from his observations?

CASE ANALYSIS

Investigators looking into the kidnapping and murder of Drug Enforcement Administration (DEA) special agent Enrique Camarena and DEA source Alfredo Zavala faced several hurdles that threatened to derail their efforts to collect evidence in the case. These hurdles almost prevented forensics experts from determining the facts of the case and threatened to undermine the investigation of the crime. However, despite these obstacles, use of standard forensic techniques eventually enabled investigators to solve the case. Read about the Camarena case in the following Case Reading; then answer the following questions:

1. What were the main challenges facing investigators who were collecting evidence in the case? Give specific examples.

2. Explain how investigators used reference samples to determine that the victims had been held at the residence located at 881 Lope De Vega.

3. Explain how investigators used soil evidence to determine that the victims' bodies had been buried and later moved to the site where they were discovered.

CASE READING

THE ENRIQUE CAMARENA CASE: A FORENSIC NIGHTMARE

MICHAEL P. MALONE
SPECIAL AGENT, LABORATORY DIVISION
FEDERAL BUREAU OF INVESTIGATION, WASHINGTON, D.C.

On February 7, 1985, US Drug Enforcement Agency (DEA) Special Agent (SA) Enrique Camarena was abducted near the US Consulate in Guadalajara, Mexico. A short time later, Capt. Alfredo Zavala, a DEA source, was also abducted from a car near the Guadalajara Airport. These two abductions would trigger a series of events leading to one of the largest investigations ever conducted by the DEA and would result in one of the most extensive cases ever received by the FBI Laboratory. . . .

THE ABDUCTION

On February 7, 1985, SA Camarena left the DEA resident office to meet his wife for lunch. On this day, a witness observed a man being forced into the rear seat of a light-colored compact car in front of the Camelot Restaurant and provided descriptions of several of the assailants. After some initial reluctance, Primer Comandante Pavon-Reyes of the Mexican Federal Judicial Police (MFJP) was put in charge of the investigation, and Mexican investigators were assigned to the case. Two known drug traffickers, Rafael Caro-Quintero and Ernesto Fonseca, were quickly developed as suspects. . . .

THE INVESTIGATION

During February 1985, searches of several residences and ranches throughout Mexico proved fruitless, despite the efforts of the DEA task force assigned to investigate this matter and the tremendous pressure being applied by the US government to accelerate the investigation. High-level US government officials, as well as their Mexican counterparts, were becoming directly involved in the case. It is believed that, because of this "heat," the Mexican drug traffickers and certain Mexican law enforcement officials fabricated a plan. According to the plan, the MFJP would receive an anonymous letter indicating that SA Camarena and Captain Zavala were being held at the Bravo drug gang's ranch in La Angostura, Michoacan, approximately 60 miles southeast of Guadalajara. The MFJP was supposed to raid the ranch, eliminate the drug gang, and eventually discover the bodies of SA Camarena and Captain Zavala buried on the ranch. The DEA would then be notified and the case would be closed. Thus, the Bravo gang would make an easy scapegoat.

During early March, MFJP officers raided the Bravo ranch before the DEA agents arrived. In the resulting shootout, all of the gang members, as well as one MFJP officer, were killed. However, due to a mix-up, the bodies of SA Camarena and Captain Zavala were not buried on the Bravo ranch in time to be discovered as planned. Shortly after this shootout, a passerby on a road near the Bravo ranch found two partially decomposed bodies wrapped in plastic bags. The bodies were removed and transported to a local morgue, where they were autopsied. The DEA was then advised of the discovery of the bodies and their subsequent removal to another morgue in Guadalajara, where a second autopsy was performed.

Cadaver number 1 was quickly identified by the fingerprint expert as SA Camarena. Although Mexican officials would not allow the second body to be identified at this time, it was later identified through dental records as Captain Zavala.

Undated photo of Enrique Camarena. *Associated Press*

The FBI forensic team requested permission to process the clothing, cordage, and burial sheet found with the bodies, but the request was denied. However, they were allowed to cut small "known" samples from these items and obtain hair samples from both bodies. Soil samples were also removed from the bodies and the clothing items. FBI and DEA personnel proceeded to the Bravo ranch, where the bodies were initially found. Because this site had been a completely uncontrolled crime scene, contaminated by both police personnel and onlookers, only a limited crime scene search was conducted. It was immediately noted that there was no gravesite in the area and that the color of the soil where the bodies had been deposited differed from the soil that had been removed from the bodies. Therefore, "known" soil samples from the drop site were taken to compare with soil removed from the victims. It was also noted that there were no significant body fluids at the "burial" site. This led the forensic team to conclude that the bodies had been buried elsewhere, exhumed, and transported to this site.

In late March 1985, DEA agents located a black Mercury Grand Marquis that they believed was used in the kidnapping or transportation of SA Camarena. The vehicle had been stored in a garage in Guadalajara, and a brick wall had been constructed at the entrance to conceal it. The vehicle was traced to a Ford dealership owned by Caro-Quintero. Under the watchful eye of the MFJP at the Guadalajara Airport, the FBI forensic team processed the vehicle for any hair, fiber, blood, and/or fingerprint evidence it might contain.

During April 1985, the MFJP informed the DEA that they believed they had located the residence where SA Camarena and Captain Zavala had been held. The FBI forensic team was immediately dispatched to Guadalajara; however, they were not allowed to proceed to the residence, located at 881 Lope De Vega, until an MFJP forensic team had processed the residence and had removed all of the obvious evidence.

On the first day after their arrival, the FBI forensic team surveyed and began a crime-scene search of the residence and surrounding grounds (see Figure 1). The residence consisted of a large, two-story structure with a swimming pool, covered patio, aviary, and tennis court surrounded by a common wall. The most logical place to hold a prisoner at this location would be in the small outbuilding located to the rear of the main residence. This outbuilding, designated as the "guest house" by investigators, consisted of a small room with a beige rug and an adjoining bathroom. The entire room and bathroom were processed for hairs, fibers, and latent fingerprints. The single door into this room was made of steel and reinforced by iron bars. It was ultimately determined by means of testimony and forensic evidence that several individuals interrogated and tortured SA Camarena

in this room. In addition, a locked bedroom, located on the second floor of the main house, was also processed, and the bed linens were removed from a single bed. Known carpet samples were taken from every room in the residence.

A beige Volkswagen Atlantic parked under a carport at the rear of the residence fit the general description of the smaller vehicle noted by the witness to SA Camarena's abduction. The VW Atlantic was also processed for hairs, fibers, and fingerprints.

On the second day, a thorough grounds search was conducted. As FBI forensic team members were walking around the tennis court, they caught a glimpse of something blue in one of the drains. On closer inspection, there appeared to be a folded license plate at the bottom of the drain. The license plate was retrieved, unfolded, and photographed. The MFJP officers, all of whom were now at the tennis court, became upset at this discovery, and one of them immediately contacted his superior at MFJP headquarters, who ordered them to secure the license plate until the assistant primer comandante arrived on the scene. Upon his arrival approximately 20 minutes later, he seized the license plate and would not allow the Americans to conduct any further searches.

In September 1985, DEA personnel went to La Primavera Park and recovered a soil sample. This sample matched the soil samples from SA Camarena and Captain Zavala's cadavers almost grain for grain, which indicated that this site was almost certainly their burial site before they were relocated to the Bravo ranch.

Later that fall, after further negotiations between the US and the Mexican governments, permission was finally granted for an FBI forensic team to process the evidence seized by the MFJP forensic team from 881 Lope De Vega the previous April. The evidence consisted of small samples the MFJP had taken of SA Camarena's burial sheet, a piece of rope used to bind SA Camarena, a portion of a pillowcase removed from bedroom number 3, a piece of unsoiled rope removed from the covered patio, and a laboratory report prepared by the MFJP Crime Laboratory. The remainder of the evidence had been destroyed for "health reasons."

In January 1986, a drug trafficker named Rene Verdugo, who was considered to be a high-ranking member of the Caro-Quintero gang, was apprehended and taken to San Diego, where he was arrested by the DEA. He was then transported to Washington, D.C., where samples of his hair were taken. He refused to testify before the federal grand jury investigating the Camarena case. Later that year, DEA personnel obtained hair samples in Mexico City from Sergio Espino-Verdin, a former federal comandante who is believed to have been SA Camarena's primary interrogator during his ordeal at 881 Lope De Vega.

FIGURE 1   A diagram of the 881 Lope De Vega grounds. Camarena was held prisoner in the guest house. *Federal Bureau of Investigation*

THE TRIAL

In July 1988, the main trial for the murder, interrogation, and abduction of SA Camarena began in US District Court in Los Angeles, California. The forensic evidence presented in this trial identified 881 Lope De Vega as the site where SA Camarena had been held. The evidence also strongly associated two Mexican citizens, Rene Verdugo and Sergio Espino-Verdin, with the "guest house" at 881 Lope De Vega. Several types of forensic evidence were used to associate SA Camarena with 881 Lope De Vega: forcibly removed head hairs found in the "guest house"

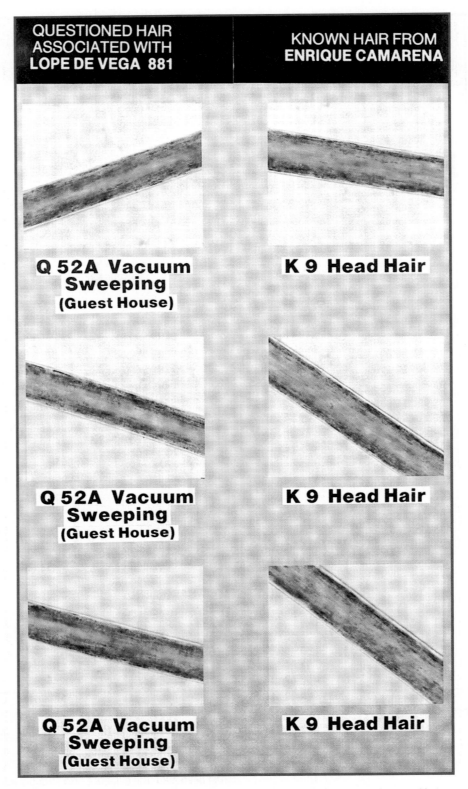

FIGURE 2   A trial chart showing hair comparisons between known Camarena hairs and hairs recovered from 881 Lope De Vega. *Federal Bureau of Investigation*

FIGURE 3 A trial chart showing hair comparisons between known Camarena hairs and hairs recovered from the Mercury Grand Marquis. *Federal Bureau of Investigation*

and bedroom number 4, in the VW Atlantic, and in the Mercury Grand Marquis, and two types of polyester rug fibers: a dark, rose-colored fiber and a light-colored fiber (see Figures 2 and 3). Fabric evidence was also presented, which demonstrated the similarities of color, composition, construction, and design between SA Camarena's burial sheet and the two pillowcases recovered from bedrooms number 3 and 5.

Based on this evidence associating SA Camarena and 881 Lope De Vega, the FBI Laboratory examiner was able to testify that SA Camarena was at this residence, as well as in the VW Atlantic and the Mercury Grand Marquis, and that he had been in a position such that his head hairs were forcibly removed. Captain Alfredo Zavala was also found to be associated with the "guest house" at 881 Lope De Vega. Light-colored nylon rug fibers found on samples of his clothing taken at

the second autopsy matched the fibers from the "guest house" carpet.

A detailed model of the residence at 881 Lope De Vega was prepared by the Special Projects Section of the FBI Laboratory for the trial (see Figure 4). Over twenty trial charts were also prepared to explain the various types of forensic evidence. These charts proved invaluable in clarifying the complicated techniques and characteristics used in the examination of the hair, fiber, fabric, and cordage evidence (see Figure 5).

CONCLUSION

After an eight-week trial, conducted under tight security and involving hundreds of witnesses, all of the defendants were found guilty and convicted on all counts, and are currently serving lengthy sentences.

FIGURE 4   A model of 881 Lope De Vega prepared as a trial exhibit. *Federal Bureau of Investigation*

CATEGORIES OF FORENSIC EVIDENCE
IN CAMARENA CASE

LOCATION	TYPE OF EVIDENCE					
	Hair	Carpet Fibers	Fabric Match	Cordage Match	Tape Match	Misc.
Mercury	Camarena Head Hair					Blood on Floor Mat
VW Atlantic	Camarena Head Hair					Blood on Tissue
Guest House	Camarena Head Hair	Zavala Clothes Nylon				
Bedroom #3		Camarena Blindfold Polyester	Pillow Case Camarena Burial Sheet			
Bedroom #4	Camarena Head Hair	Camarena Blindfold & Burial Sheet Polyester				
Bedroom #5			Pillow Case Camarena Burial Sheet			
Tennis Court						License Plate VW/Merc.
Camarena Burial Sheet	Camarena Head Hair	Bedroom #4 Polyester	Pillow Case Bedrooms #3 and #5			Soil La Primavera
Source — Blindfold/ Rope	Camarena Head Hair	Bedrooms #3 and #4 Polyester			Camarena Blindfold Tape	
Camarena Burial Cordage				Burial Rope from Covered Patio		
Zavala Clothing	Zavala Head Hair	Guest House Nylon				Soil La Primavera

FIGURE 5   A trial chart used to show the association of Camarena and Zavala with various locations. *Federal Bureau of Investigation*

3

Recording the Crime Scene

LEARNING OBJECTIVES

After studying this chapter, you should be able to:

- Explain the steps to be taken to fully record the crime scene.
- Describe the proper format and content of crime-scene notes.
- Understand the basic features of digital cameras in order to produce examination-quality photographs.
- Understand the basic guideline requirements for creating acceptable crime-scene photographs.
- Explain the importance of compositional requirements in capturing crime-scene images.
- Describe the process and importance of creating a rough and a finished crime-scene sketch.

THE LINDBERGH BABY CASE

On the evening of March 1, 1932, a kidnapper crept up his homemade ladder and stole the baby of Charles and Anne Lindbergh directly from the second-floor nursery of their house in Hopewell, New Jersey. The only evidence of his coming was a ransom note, the ladder, a chisel, and the tragic absence of the infant. Although the $50,000 ransom had been paid, the baby turned up dead in the woods a mile away a couple of months later. There was no additional sign of the killer. Fortunately, when it was finally studied by wood technologist Arthur Koehler, the abandoned ladder yielded some important investigative clues.

By studying the types of wood used and the cutter marks on the wood, Koehler ascertained where the materials might have come from and what specific equipment was used to create them. Koehler traced the wood from a South Carolina mill to a lumberyard in the Bronx, New York. Unfortunately, the trail went cold because the lumberyard did not keep sales records. The break in the case came in 1934, when Bruno Richard Hauptmann paid for gasoline with a bill that matched a serial number on the ransom money. Koehler was able to show that microscopic markings on the wood were made by a tool in Hauptmann's possession. A ladder rail recovered from the homemade ladder had characteristics consistent with wood present in Hauptmann's attic. Ultimately, handwriting analysis of the ransom note clearly showed it had been written by Hauptmann.

Notes

Investigators have only a limited amount of time to work a crime scene in its untouched state. They must not lose the opportunity to permanently record the scene in its original condition. Such records not only will prove useful during the subsequent investigation but also must be presented at a trial in order to document the condition of the crime scene and the location of physical evidence. Notes, photographs, and sketches are the three methods of crime-scene recording (see Figure 3-1).

The note-taking process begins with the call to a crime-scene investigator to report to a scene. The first notes should identify the person who contacted the investigator and record the time of the contact and any preliminary information disclosed, including the case number. When the lead investigator arrives, the note taker should record the date and time of arrival, who is present, and the identities of any other personnel who are being contacted. If additional personnel are contacted, their names, titles, and times of arrival should be recorded.

A crime scene should be off-limits to any people who are not directly involved with the processing. Investigators must keep very precise records of personnel movements in and out of the scene, beginning with the movements of the first responding officer. It is also important to record the tasks assigned to each member of a team, as well as the beginning and ending times of the processing of the scene.

Before the scene is sketched, photographed, or searched, the lead investigator carries out the initial walk-through. During this walk-through, the investigator should take notes on many aspects of the crime scene in its original condition. Notes taken by an investigator should be uniform in format for all cases. The notes should be in ink (preferably black or blue) and written in a bound notebook. Most important, notes should be written at the time of the crime-scene investigation, not left to record from memory at a later time. At this time, the investigator may need to interview the first responding officer. The officer should supply information on any events at the crime scene that the officer or others witnessed. When the walk-through is complete, the lead investigator assigns specific tasks or areas to members of the crime-scene team. The notes should also record these assignments, as well as the times at which each task was started and completed.

Once a search for evidence has taken place, the team members mark the location of all evidence. The investigator should note whether any evidence was disturbed by emergency medical personnel, a suspect, or investigative personnel. Before the team collects items of evidence, the investigator must fully describe each item in his or her notes. The person who collects a piece of evidence should note who found it, where it was located, how it was packaged, who packaged it, and when it was packaged. The notes should also mention whether the evidence underwent any field tests or processing.

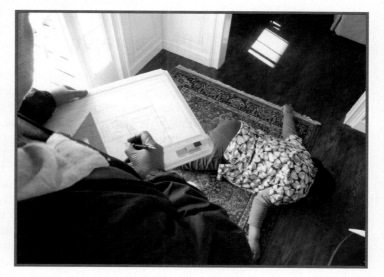

FIGURE 3-1 Sketching a victim at the crime scene and the victim's relation to the crime scene. *Evident*

If a victim is present at a homicide scene, the investigator should observe and record the state of the body before the medical examiner or coroner moves it. The notes should describe the victim's appearance and record the position of the body and any visible wounds or blood spatter. The investigator should make note of any identifying features or marks on the body, such as tattoos. He or she should also make a list of objects found on the body, such as a wallet or jewelry, before collecting those items. Moving the body may reveal previously unseen injuries and physical evidence that the investigator should record. The notes should indicate when the medical examiner or coroner moved the body and whether the victim was moved or affected in some way by emergency medical procedures. Any preliminary identification of a victim or suspect should be recorded.

Audio recording of notes at a scene can be advantageous because detailed notes can be spoken much faster than they can be written. This may also leave the investigators' hands free to carry out other tasks while recording the notes. However, care must be taken to avoid embarrassing conversation in recordings that will be used as evidence in a trial. Digital voice recordings are easily uploaded to a computer, but they must be copied to a disk or flash drive to produce a hard copy. Another method of recording notes is by narrating a digital video of the crime scene. This has the advantage of combining note taking with photography. However, at some point the recording must be transcribed into a written document.

The note taker must keep in mind that this written record may be his or her only way of refreshing his or her memory months, perhaps years, after a crime has been processed. The notes must be sufficiently detailed to anticipate this need.

Quick Review

- Because investigators have only a limited amount of time to work a crime site in its untouched state, the opportunity must not be lost.
- Crime-scene notes should include contact information, personnel information and movements, task assignments, observations of the victim and scene, and information about the evidence before and after it is processed.
- Recording notes on digital voice recorders is advantageous, but investigators should take care to speak clearly and avoid including side conversations.

Photography

All jurisdictions commonly accept photographs of crime scenes as visual evidence in criminal investigations. Investigators should therefore understand the procedures and principles of good crime-scene photography in order to best illustrate aspects of the scene. The goal of photography at crime scenes is to produce examination-quality photographs that document the crime scene and provide evidence. This means that everyone involved in the case, from the investigators to the judge and jury, must be able to interpret the photographs easily.

Forensic photography documents and preserves the original crime scene intact for future investigation and shows the layout of the scene, the position and dimensions of evidence to be collected, and the physical relationship of objects at the scene to one another. Photographs taken from many angles can show possible lines of sight of victims, suspects, and witnesses. Photography is also important for documenting biological evidence in its original condition because this kind of evidence is often altered during testing.

In order to be admissible as evidence within the justice system, photographs must meet the following criteria: (1) they must represent the crime scene as found, without manipulation or bias; (2) any re-creations of scenes or manipulation must be documented; (3) they must have bearing on the case in question; and (4) they must not engage in emotional manipulation of the jury.

Photographs cannot stand alone, however, they are complementary to notes and sketches and are an important part of the forensic documentation process. This process involves the collection, the organization, and the investigation of visual information through digital photography, digital videography, note taking, manual sketching, **computer-aided drafting (CAD)**, and three-dimensional imaging systems.

DIGITAL PHOTOGRAPHY

Currently **digital photography** is the preferred approach to crime-scene photography. A digital photograph is made when a light-sensitive microchip inside a digital camera is exposed to light coming from an object or scene. A digital camera captures light on each of millions of tiny picture elements called "pixels." The light is recorded on each pixel as a specific electric charge using a charged coupled device (CCD) or complementary metal oxide semiconductor (CMOS). The camera reads this charge number as image information, and then stores the image as a file on a memory card.

The number of pixels used to capture light is directly related to the resolution of the picture. Resolution is defined as the minimum distance that must separate two objects in order for them to be viewed as distinct objects. The lower the distance needed, the greater the resolution of the photograph. Photographs of increasingly higher resolution show more and more detail and sharpness. The greater the number of pixels featured on the digital camera, the better the resolution will be.

Because the number of pixels on a digital camera is in the millions, it is usually referred to in terms of **megapixels**. A camera that has four million pixels is a four-megapixel camera. A standard four-megapixel camera can create a clear image on a photographic print of up to 8 by 10 inches. As the number of megapixels increases, the clarity increases, allowing photographers to create bigger prints. Crime-scene photographers usually use cameras that feature as many as twelve megapixels or more. The Scientific Working Group on Image Technology (SWGIT) recommends using a single-lens reflex (SLR) camera with at least eight-megapixel resolution.

Digital photography of crime scenes has many advantages. Digital imaging technologies can increase the pace of investigation, aid in the provision of evidence, as well as the identification of suspects. Investigators can observe the images immediately after taking them to ensure that important photographs are clear and show the best possible detail. As technology advances, digital photography provides other advantages over traditional film. For example, photographers can electronically stitch together individual images of a crime scene that were captured with a digital camera to create a nearly three-dimensional panoramic view of the crime scene (see Figure 3-2). With the aid of a computer, any area of the scene captured digitally can be enhanced and examined in fine detail.

However, the effectiveness and utility of such technologies depend on the quality of image and the reliability of the process. The very nature of digital images opens digital photography up to important criticisms within forensic science casework. Because the photographs are digital, they can be easily manipulated by using computer software. This manipulation goes beyond traditional photograph enhancement such as adjusting brightness and contrast or color balancing. Computer software allows a person to crop a photo, remove repeating patterns such as window screens, superimpose images, and alter photos significantly in many other ways. Because the primary function of crime-scene photography is to provide an accurate depiction, this is a major

computer-aided drafting (CAD)
The process of creating a scaled drawing using specially designed computer software.

digital photography
The use of electronic means to capture light and save an image on a microchip.

megapixel
One million pixels; used to describe a digital camera in terms of sensor resolution (i.e., four megapixels equals four million pixels).

FIGURE 3-2 Individual images (top) are shown before being electronically stitched together into a single panoramic image (bottom). Individual photographs should be taken with approximately 30% overlap. *Imaging Forensics Inc.*

concern, and care must be taken to maintain an original version of the image without modification.

Law enforcement agencies should establish guidelines or standard operating procedures (SOPs) to ensure the quality of digital images and the integrity of the digital imaging process. Digital images must meet a number of criteria in order to be admissible in the justice system: (1) they must be reliable; (2) they must be reproducible; (3) they must be secured and their integrity must be assured; and (4) both original and altered images and their metadata must be made available within the judicial process. To ensure that their digital images are admissible, many jurisdictions have developed or are developing SOPs for the use of digital photography. Sometimes admissibility requirements dictate that a detailed and accurate photography log be kept by the crime-scene photographer to be submitted along with the testimony of the photographer as to the accuracy of the photographs. The goal is to set guidelines for determining the circumstances under which digital photography may be used and to establish and enforce strict protocols for image security and chain of custody. For example, digital photographs should be copied only to writable disks. They should never be placed on rewritable disks that can be altered or erased. If an image is to be enhanced in some way, the new image must be saved separately, not written over the original image.

The crime-scene photographer using digital photography also has to be conscious of the kind of file format in which the crime-scene images are saved. Digital images are preserved by either lossy or lossless compression. Lossy compression condenses files by discarding some image information. The information lost during this compression is irretrievable. An example of this type of file is the Joint Photographic Experts Group (JPEG) format. This format is usually available in low-cost consumer digital cameras. A JPEG may be suitable for general crime-scene overview photographs; however, any photograph to be used for in-depth evaluation of an object or subject, such as a comparison analysis or analysis of body wounds, requires images without compression loss. **Lossless compression** condenses files without discarding information so no important image information is lost. A tagged image file format (TIFF) or a raw image (RAW) format satisfies this requirement. RAW stores the highest quality image but requires special software for viewing. High-end digital cameras generally offer the option of capturing an image in a number of formats.

The digital era promises new and elegant approaches to documenting the crime scene. Cameras such as that shown in Figure 3-3 are capable of taking dozens of digital images while scanning the crime scene. Photographic and laser data from multiple scan locations are combined to produce three-dimensional models of the scene in full color that can be viewed from any vantage point, measured, and used for analysis and courtroom presentations.

PHOTOGRAPHIC EQUIPMENT AND PRINCIPLES

Forensic photography requires, at minimum, a **digital single-lens reflex (DSLR) camera** with at minimum eight-megapixel resolution, interchangeable macro, zoom, and other lenses, and manual override; an external flash with a six-foot extension cord and a ring flash attachment; a remote shutter release cable; lighting slaves and towers; barrier and bypass filters; as well as polarizing filters, tripods, reflectors, tape measure, scales, and storage media.

CAMERAS The most commonly used camera for crime-scene photography is the digital single-lens reflex camera, or DSLR (see Figure 3-4). Digital imaging technology is now dominant in all aspects of photography.

Although the general public is more familiar with digital "point-and-shoot" cameras, DSLR cameras are required for photographing a crime scene. DSLR cameras allow for the use of a wide range of lenses, flashes, and filters. Further, DSLR cameras give photographers the option of manually selecting f-stop, shutter speed, and other variables associated with photography. These settings are discussed in further detail in the following sections. DSLRs also have a large imaging microchip that produces higher-quality images and prints than the traditional "point-and-shoot" digital cameras can produce. Most DSLRs can also be modified to take infrared (IR) and ultraviolet (UV) photographs.

LENSES The lens of the camera is the mechanism that bends light to focus an image on the digital microchip. In general, the thicker the lens, the greater its ability to bend light. Each lens has a specific focal length, which is the distance between the lens and the image projected on the film or microchip. As the thickness and bending ability of the lens increases, the focal length decreases because the lens can bend light onto a surface closer to it. Photographers generally use lenses with long focal lengths to capture in more detail objects far from the camera. The kind of lens one uses, therefore, has a great impact on the quality of the photographs a camera produces.

Focal lengths for digital cameras are based on the size of the charge-coupled device (CCD) or complementary metal-oxide-semiconductor (CMOS) digital sensor, and lenses for digital cameras are marketed as analogous to those for 35 mm film cameras, though in reality digital focal lengths are not equivalent to 35 mm camera focal lengths. Most DSLR cameras have a

WebExtra 3.1

Creating a Three-Dimensional Model of a Crime Scene with the Ability to Measure Relevant Areas of the Scene
www.mycrimekit.com

lossless compression
A compression method for digital files that decreases the file size without discarding digital data.

digital single lens reflex (DSLR) camera
A type of camera that uses the same lens for viewing and for taking the picture. The image seen in the viewfinder or on the LCD monitor is how the photo will turn out.

FIGURE 3-3 A computer-controlled scanner has both a high-resolution, professional digital camera and a long-range laser rangefinder. The tripod-mounted device rotates a full 360 degrees, taking dozens of photographs and measuring millions of individual points. Photographic and laser data from multiple scan locations are combined to produce three-dimensional models of the scene. *3rd Tech, Inc.*

FIGURE 3-4 An example of a digital single lens reflex (DSLR) camera. *White Rabbit83/ Shutterstock*

aperture
The size of the diaphragm opening through which light enters the camera.

f-stop
A setting on a camera that controls the aperture diameter to determine the amount of light transmitted through the lens to the film or microchip.

fixed normal or multipurpose lens, typically in the range of 14 to 55 mm, and accept a variety of other lenses. Some digital cameras have specific settings to mimic the effects of special lenses. For example, the macro setting on a digital camera, usually represented by a flower symbol, offers the attributes of a macro lens by making the foreground appear larger and the background appear smaller. DSLR cameras open and close the aperture of the lens electronically based on the subject being photographed.

Normal Lens   The normal lens has a 50 to 55 mm focal length. It can be used for most photographs that need to be taken at a crime scene because it can capture as much area as half a wall. It can also take satisfactory photographs of pieces of evidence at standard distances.

Telephoto Lens   The telephoto lens is like a telescope attachment for the camera, capturing a close-up image of a distant object or subject. This lens has a focal length of 100 mm or greater. This means that a 200 mm telephoto lens, for example, produces an image that is four times the magnification of the normal 50 mm lens.

Wide-Angle Lens   A photographer who needs to capture a wider area uses a wide-angle lens with a focal length of less than 50 mm. The typical focal length of the wide-angle lens is 35 mm, and it can show much more area in one photograph than can a normal lens. For example, this lens is useful in photographing wide objects such as the facade of a building; it will capture more detail to the left and right of the center of the structure than will a normal lens.

Macro Lens   When very close photographs and good detail are required, the photographer might use a macro lens. The macro lens has a focal length of less than 50 mm and a 1:1 or 1:2 magnification ratio. It is especially useful for close-ups of fiber or tool mark evidence.

Multipurpose Lens   A multipurpose lens, commonly called a "zoom" lens, can also be used for crime-scene photography. These lenses have a range of focal lengths, usually from 28 to 80 mm. This type of lens allows the photographer to take normal, wide-angle, and telephoto photographs without changing lenses.

APERTURE AND SHUTTER SPEED   The amount of light gathered by the camera is regulated by the aperture and shutter speed of the camera. The camera **aperture** is the diameter of the opening of the mechanism, called the "diaphragm," which allows in light. One adjusts the aperture by setting the f-number, which is equal to the focal length of the lens divided by the diameter of the aperture. Thus, the f-number and aperture are inversely related. The lower the f-number setting, the wider the aperture and the more light it allows in. Standard f-number settings have come to be known as **f-stops**, ranging along a continuum of possible aperture sizes. For example, the lowest f-number (1.0) is arbitrarily designated as f-stop zero (f-0). Each f-stop represents a twofold difference in the amount of light entering the camera. Because f-stop and aperture are inversely related, f-2 thus would have a larger aperture than f-22. Newer digital cameras have f-stops in one-third and one-half increments, allowing more control over the light entering through the aperture. Some digital cameras, called "aperture priority cameras," allow the user to control the f-stop manually, but not the shutter speed.

The shutter of a camera is the mechanism that controls the exposure of the film or microchip to light. The **shutter speed** is the length of time that the microchip is exposed to light. This is measured in fractions of a second by factors of 1/2 (i.e., 1/2, 1/4, 1/8, etc.). DSLR cameras have a wide range of options for adjusting f-stop and shutter speed. The green "auto" mode automatically selects an appropriate f-stop and shutter speed for the conditions. Alternately, digital cameras may have a setting known as "sports mode" to capture subjects in motion by using a higher (faster) shutter speed. This setting is usually represented by a symbol of a figure running or a foot kicking a ball. A digital camera's "night mode," denoted by a moon or star, is set for a lower (slower) shutter speed. This allows the shutter to be open longer to gather as much light as possible to create the image. DSLR cameras allow the user to change shutter speed by adjusting a control knob on the camera, although the photographer can operate the camera in a fully manual mode. DSLR cameras may also provide an antishake function.

shutter speed
The length of time that the film or microchip is exposed to light.

DEPTH OF FIELD   An important trait of a photograph is the **depth of field** shown. Depth of field is the amount of area in the foreground and background of an in-focus object that is also relatively in focus. Crime-scene photographers should strive to maximize depth of field—that is, make sure that every element of the composition is in focus. This is especially important in photographs of an entire scene and of three-dimensional objects.

Several variables determine depth of field: aperture size, f-stop selection, lens selection, and distance between camera and subject. The smaller the aperture is, the greater the depth of field will be. It is important to remember that the aperture is measured on a camera by the f-stop number, which is inversely related to the aperture diameter. This means that higher f-stops will yield higher depths of field. The "landscape mode" on a digital camera (generally represented by a mountain symbol) automatically selects higher f-stops to improve the depth of field when the background and foreground are important, such as in scenery photographs. The "portrait mode" of a digital camera, on the other hand, selects lower f-stops to decrease the depth of field and make the subject stand out clearly against a blurred background. Wide-angle lenses are generally preferred.

depth of field
The amount of area in the foreground and background of an in-focus photographic subject that is also relatively in focus.

ILLUMINATION   "Illumination" refers to the light falling on an object in a photograph. An important photographic aspect of light is its **color temperature**. This is the measurement of the difference in hue between a light source and a theoretical source of perfect white light. On the color temperature scale, a "hot" light source has a bluer hue, whereas a "cold" light source has a red–orange hue. Different light sources exhibit different color temperatures. Similarly, sunlight will exhibit varying color temperatures during different times of the day and in different weather conditions.

Most digital cameras have automatic "white balance" settings that allow them to automatically compensate for color temperatures that deviate from white. Some digital cameras feature additional white balance modes for specific light sources, including incandescent lighting, fluorescent lighting, direct sunlight, and overcast sunlight. White balance can be corrected only by using software if the original photo was taken using the RAW setting. Additionally, some digital cameras provide white balance bracketing with a series of three photographs, each with a different temperature, from which to choose. Photo-editing software can also be used to alter white balance.

color temperature
The measure of the "degree of whiteness" of a light source compared to a hypothetical source of perfect white light.

Measuring and Manipulating. "Illumination lighting" of a scene can be natural or artificial. Natural lighting, also called "ambient" lighting, requires the photographer to work with the light as he or she finds it at the scene. Artificial lighting employs flashes and other tactics to supplement and enhance the lighting at the scene. A photographer must be able to recognize and manipulate the amount of light and the angle of illumination in a photograph.

Metering. Light meters are devices that allow photographers to measure the amount of light in a shot. Most digital cameras feature through-the-lens (TTL) metering systems that measure the light reaching the camera. The photographer may have to choose a function from the menu to activate the light meter. Digital cameras designed for the casual user rely on preprogrammed settings and computer technology to determine the optimal settings (such as shutter speed and f-stop) for each photograph taken. In place of manual f-stop operation, a digital camera may allow exposure compensation—adjusted with a function button and displayed in the viewfinder—that the photographer can adjust to capture an extremely bright or dark image. Most digital cameras offer the values −2, −1, 0, 1, and 2. The "0" setting refers to the starting point—that is, the conditions the camera's autofocus feature determines to be optimal. Adjusting toward negative numbers will reduce the exposure, thereby darkening a bright (overexposed) shot.

To compensate for backlighting, a camera may have a center-weighted or spot-metering setting. Center-weighted metering directs the camera to determine the optimal settings based on the light conditions present in the center of the field. Spot metering directs the camera to calculate the best settings for the light conditions at the spot on the center of the viewfinder. The default setting, called "matrix" or "evaluative metering," is based on the average light intensity across the entire field of view. Some manufacturers have preprogrammed settings named for specific light conditions and composition. Some of the more expensive digital cameras show a graph of the light present in the photograph to help suggest exposure settings.

Flashes. A photographer uses a flash when ambient lighting is insufficient— that is, not bright enough to allow proper exposure at an f/8 or smaller aperture. Flash lighting can replace sunlight or can function as supplemental light to minimize shadow. Photographers should ensure that the flash strikes in concert with camera perspective and lens focal length.

Most commercially available digital cameras have mounted electronic strobe flashes. This integrated flash can illuminate subjects only up to ten feet away. Many digital cameras have a flash bracket for using a supplementary flash when one is necessary. Digital cameras also have a feature called "fill flash." This narrows the range of the flash to concentrate illumination on only a dark, backlit subject or object. This is used to eliminate undesirable shadows that may obscure the subject. Fill flash can be used to eliminate shadows under trees and vehicles.

A flash unit is an electronic flash that is not mounted to the camera. It is either separately operated or connected to the camera by a cord. In either case, the user must time the flash with the correct shutter speed for flash photography (usually 1/60). The flash unit, also called a slave flash or lighting slave, is very important to crime-scene photography because it can illuminate dark areas or create lighting at various angles to show greater detail. "Ring flash attachments" are circular flashes attached to the circumference of the camera lens that can produce photographs with even lighting and minimal shadows.

A flash can produce direct reflective, direct, and oblique lighting, depending on the photographer's needs. Direct reflective lighting occurs when the flash is attached to the camera or placed at 90 degrees to the plane of view. It provides high contrast, but may show light reflectance in the photograph. Direct lighting is aimed 45 degrees to the plane of view to minimize reflectance. Oblique lighting involves placing the flash at an angle to the plane of view that is lower than 45 degrees to show greater detail by creating a shadowing effect. Some patterns and textures, particularly in impression evidence such as fingerprints, benefit from side lighting. Reflectors can help to ease the effect of harsh shadows, as can bouncing light off of a reflective surface already present at the scene.

Regardless of what kind of flash is used, it may be necessary to manually increase or decrease the flash power. For example, decreasing the flash power can help avoid overexposing a close subject.

Filters. By manipulating light with filters, photographers can help enhance specific elements of a picture or show elements of the picture that are not usually visible. The spectrum of light comprises the visible spectrum as well as ultraviolet and infrared light. Filters allow only specific wavelengths (colors) of light to reach the film.

The most common types of filters are barrier and bypass filters. "Barrier filters" block one specific wavelength of light (i.e., color) from reaching the film or microchip, making areas of that color appear lighter in the photograph. This is helpful when a fingerprint or other feature on a piece of evidence is difficult to see against a surface of a specific color. A "bypass filter" allows only a small range of wavelengths of light to reach the microchip and blocks all others. Ultraviolet (UV) photography uses a bypass filter that allows only ultraviolet light to reach the microchip. Objects that fluoresce, or glow, under ultraviolet light—such as semen, components of some fibers, and fluorescent fingerprint powder—appear more readily using this technique. It is also sometimes used when photographing wounds to show greater contrast. Other filters can be used for infrared (IR) photography.

By using a filter of a complementary color, a photographer can make certain areas of an object appear darker. A red filter, for example, will darken blue/green areas, and an orange/yellow filter will darken blue/violet areas. A polarizer filter may be used to eliminate reflections from windows and water and to eliminate glare. A photographer may also employ a filter when the light source used at the scene is a laser.

"Polarizing filters" are attached to the front of the camera lens to avoid glare.

TRIPODS Using a tripod can improve the quality of a photograph by eliminating the possibility of blurred photos resulting from unsteady hands. Any photograph taken at a shutter speed of less than 60 (1/60 second) must be taken from a tripod. A tripod with independently adjustable legs is a superior choice because it is suitable for uneven terrain. A ball-head mount tripod should be used to assure that photographs are in sharp focus. The tripod should also have a bubble level on it to help ensure 90-degree images of evidence (see Figure 3-5).

FIGURE 3-5 A tripod used for crime-scene photography should have adjustable legs that are sturdy to ensure 90-degree photographs. *Sirchie Finger Print Laboratories*

SCALES Photographers use scales to allow measurement of objects at the crime scenes. Some scales, such as adhesive photo scales and rulers available for purchase, are specifically designed for length measurement at crime scenes, but other objects at the crime scene with known dimensions can also be used for reference. Scales should be flat, rigid, and labeled with the case number, the date and time the photograph was taken, the address and location of the shot, and the photographer's name, initials, badge number, or other identification number.

During shooting, the scale should be placed on the same plane as the evidence being photographed. This placement is important in order to avoid distortions of the relative size of scale units from the camera's perspective, as well as to maintain the sharpness of the scale in the photograph.

Quick Review

- Digital cameras feature a light-sensitive microchip that captures light on each of millions of tiny picture elements, called "pixels." The light is recorded on each pixel as a specific charge that will later be electronically translated to an image. The number of pixels on a camera is measured in the millions, called "megapixels," and directly affects an image's resolution.
- Digital images are preserved by either lossy or lossless compression.
- DSLR cameras allow for the use of a wide range of lenses, including normal lenses, telephoto lenses, wide-angle lenses, macro lenses, and multipurpose lenses. The kind of lens used affects the appearance of the image.
- The aperture and shutter speed regulate the amount of light gathered by the camera. These settings can be manually adjusted on DSLR cameras.
- The "f-stop" determines depth of field, or the amount of area in the foreground and background that is in focus. The higher the f-stop, the smaller the aperture and the greater the depth of field. Landscape and portrait settings on a digital camera adjust for higher and lower f-stops, respectively.
- The color temperature of the light source used will make a photographic image appear orangish or bluish. Many digital cameras combat this with "white balance" capability. Exposure compensation and electronic flashes can be used to capture images of dark or light subjects. Flash units, or slave flashes, are helpful to provide oblique or versatile illumination.
- Filters are used with DSLR cameras to block certain wavelengths of light (barrier filters) or allow in only certain wavelengths of light (bypass filters). Filters can be used to show greater detail in photographs by adjusting the appearance of specific colors.
- Tripods can greatly improve the quality of a photograph by preventing blurriness caused by the movement of the photographer's hand. They also help ensure 90-degree close-up photographs of evidence.

Crime-Scene Photography

BASIC GUIDELINES

Photograph the crime scene in an unaltered condition Except for injured parties, subjects and objects must not be moved until they have been photographed from all necessary angles. If objects are removed, positions changed, or items added, the photographs may not be admissible as evidence at a trial. In that case, their intended value will be lost. Evidence should not be reintroduced into the scene in order to take photographs. If a body is found at the crime scene, it should be photographed before it is moved. The

photography log
The form on which the investigator records the details of each photograph taken at a crime scene.

body must be photographed at various angles so the body's position is well documented.

Fill the frame The object being photographed should not be difficult to distinguish from a background that is not vital to the overall image. Filling the frame may require physically moving the camera closer to the subject and into a position that does not show undesirable objects in view. Sometimes important details can be gathered from photographing down on the subject's level. These details might not otherwise be apparent.

Avoid shadows in the photograph A photographer might not think to use a flash when outdoors. However, doing so can help fill in shadows.

Maximize depth of field A crime scene's depth of field can be very small or very large. In either case, it is important to have all items of significance in focus.

Photograph the scene in a logical sequence This means that the crime scene should include the area in which the crime actually took place and all adjacent areas where important acts occurred immediately before or after the commission of the crime. The photographer commonly will work from the perimeter to the center of a scene. The sequence used must be kept consistent for all crime scenes. This will show the external overall scene first, then the internal overall scene, and then work down to individual pieces of evidence, making sure to establish the relationship between pieces of evidence and fixed features of the scene so that jurors in the trial can easily relate them back to the larger scene (see Figure 3-6).

Keep a log A **photography log** or "photo identifier form" should be recorded as the first image of the series if a digital camera is used. The top of the photography log form should include the case number, the type of scene, the date, the location of the scene, a description of the camera and lenses being used, the film type and speed (if applicable) being used, and the photographer's name and title. The log should also contain a table where each photograph will be logged. Each photograph's log should show the date and time the photograph was taken, the location of the picture, the f-stop and shutter speed settings, the lighting used and the lighting angle (if applicable), the angle of the camera, and a description of the subject of the picture. Some digital cameras produce an electronic photography log, but this metadata should be recorded on a photo memo form as well in case the electronic log is lost. This log must be submitted along with notes and the written photography log form, as well as the testimony of the investigator, for the digital photographs to be considered for admissibility.

(a)

(b)

(c)

FIGURE 3-6 This sequence of crime-scene photographs shows the proper progression of photographing the scene. (a) The sequence begins with an overview photograph of the entry to the victim's bedroom showing evidence markers in place. (b) The medium-range photograph shows the evidence marker next to the door denoting a cartridge case. (c) The close-up photograph shows the cartridge in detail with a scale in the photograph. *Richard Saferstein, Ph.D.*

Crime-Scene Images

COMPOSITIONAL CONSIDERATIONS

Crime-scene photographers bear responsibility for making sure their composition provides a complete picture of the scene and evidence. Composition includes the establishment of viewpoint and the selection of which elements of the scene to include (or emphasize) and which elements to exclude (or de-emphasize). As much as possible, crime-scene photographers should eliminate anything from the composition that is not the primary subject of the photograph.

Among the strategies that crime-scene photographers use to establish proper composition are tilting the camera up or down in order to avoid distracting elements in the foreground or background; widening or narrowing the view in order to eliminate distracting elements along the periphery of the scene; controlling shadows cast by the sun or by the photographer herself, as well as anticipating and minimizing shadows caused by the flash; and blocking lens flare from the sun by using a "lens hood" or her hand.

OVERVIEW PHOTOGRAPHS   The first pictures the photographer takes are overview photographs of the entire scene and surrounding area, including points of exit and entry. These photographs provide information about the general area where the crime took place, the specific scene of the crime, about the relation of items of evidence to each other and to fixed features of the crime scene, and about the actual items of evidence. Overview photos are generally shot from a natural perspective (although aerial shots are also possible).

Overview photos begin from a distance and gradually zone in on the specific crime scene. At times, crime-scene photographs may find it difficult or impossible to take external overview photos at an active crime scene. Overview photos should be taken from the outside borders of the scene from various angles. If the crime took place indoors, the entire room should be photographed to show each wall area. Rooms adjacent to the actual crime site must be similarly photographed. If the crime scene includes a body, photographs must show the body's position and location relative to the entire scene. When taking overview photographs, the crime-scene photographer should include at least one object in multiple overview photographs to help visually piece the scene together. This object is called a "visual tag." Although one generally should avoid having individuals present in photographs, it may be helpful to photograph witnesses in the locations from which they viewed the crime. This can help the jury determine what a witness could or could not have seen from these locations. One may also wish to photograph the sight lines of suspects and victims. If a camera boom is available, the photographer should take pictures from overhead.

MEDIUM-RANGE PHOTOGRAPHS   The next set of pictures should be medium-range photographs that show the layout of smaller significant areas of the crime scene. Medium-range shots should be taken with evidence markers in place to show the spatial relationships between and among pieces of evidence in greater detail than in the overview photographs. A key medium-range photograph standard to all crime scenes is one that includes the "center" of the scene. In violent crimes, this usually includes the site where the victim was found and the surrounding area.

CLOSE-UP PHOTOGRAPHS   Close-up photographs, taken last, show the greatest detail of individual objects or evidence. Macro lenses should be used when taking close-ups in order to fill the frame. A supplemental lens called an "extension tube" as well as close-up filter sets for magnification may also be used. At a minimum, there are four photographs required at a crime scene: an overview photograph, a medium-range photograph, a close-up photograph, and a close-up photograph with a scale. These photographs create an adequate visual record of the position and appearance of an item of evidence at a crime scene.

The pictures must be taken at a 90-degree angle to the object, with and without evidence markers and scales. Scales should be placed as close to the evidence as possible without affecting it in any way. After the 90-degree photographs have been taken, photographs from other angles may be taken. For three-dimensional objects, oblique lighting may be needed. It is also important to bracket close-up photographs. This means that the same photograph should be taken at varying f-stops and shutter speeds to ensure the best detail possible. Filters may also be important for close-up photographs.

PHOTOGRAPHING BODIES AND WOUNDS   Important photographs are those depicting injuries and weapons lying near a body. As with crime-scene photography in general, the photographer progresses from a general to a more specific viewpoint when documenting bodies and wounds. A full-body shot can be taken using a tripod to raise the camera over the body.

When photographing bodies, the photographer begins with a full-body panorama, using the same compositional principles outlined above. The most difficult part of this process may be taking the full-face photograph. The optimal focal length for filling the frame when photographing faces is 100 to 120 mm. Photographs taken from too near or in too much shadow may distort the face and render it unrecognizable, which could affect witnesses' ability to identify the person in the photo. Wounds should be photographed in clear relation to fixed features of the body. The photographer should also document any elements that may assist in the identification of the body or in establishing the post-mortem interval (PMI) (the length of time the body has been deceased). Finally, after the body is removed from the scene, the surface beneath the body should be photographed.

PHOTOGRAPHY AT NIGHT   Photography at night can be very challenging. It is best to wait until morning, but there are a few methods to use if this is not possible. Firefighters or police officers commonly bring floodlights to outdoor crime scenes at night. Photographers often use reflectors to focus flash illumination on both indoor and outdoor scenes. A technique called "painting with light" allows photographers to illuminate long distances at night. This involves mounting a camera on a tripod and locking the shutter open in complete darkness. The photographer then proceeds around the crime scene, firing off a flash to illuminate all areas of the crime scene—usually about three to four flashes in total. The shutter is then closed to capture the image. In place of painting with light, one may use multiple flash units that are placed strategically around the crime scene. The units are synchronized to flash simultaneously when the shutter is released.

All photographs of the crime scene should be repeated during daylight hours. Although many items of evidence may have been removed in the interim, it is advantageous to have overall views of the area in daylight.

INDOOR SCENES   Typically, the earliest photographs of an indoor crime scene are overview photographs of the exterior of the building that locate the scene and any evidence present on the exterior. The next photographs are of the entrance itself, then photographs are taken of the scene as viewed from the entrance. The photographer then moves around the interior of the scene in a clockwise or counterclockwise direction, taking photographs from each corner and possibly the middle of each wall to provide a complete 360-degree view of the scene. Medium-range photographs must then be taken of each wall, the floor, and the ceiling, as well as of the relative locations of groups of evidence from different angles. The crime-scene photographer should be conscious of other rooms that may contain evidence and photograph them thoroughly as well. Close-up photographs should be taken of all located evidence (with and without scales) and of injuries on a victim. Investigators should give special attention to locating and photographing any impressions made by footwear going into or out of an indoor scene.

OUTDOOR SCENES At outdoor crime scenes, especially those involving vehicles, the earliest photographs may be of the street signs closest to the scene. Overview photographs are then taken from the defined borders of the scene. Investigators note the positions from which these pictures were taken on the photography log using global positioning system (GPS) coordinates or by measuring the distance to the positions from the nearest roadways. Medium-range photographs are taken of groups of evidence or of zones of a scene that are too large to photograph as a whole. Close-up photographs must be taken correctly, because evidence at an outdoor scene rarely remains undisturbed for very long. If a vehicle is included in the scene or is the scene, overview photographs should be taken of the front and left side and then the back and right side. Particular attention should be paid to capturing license plates and vehicle identification numbers (VINs) images in the series of photographs taken. If the vehicle was stolen or burglarized, pictures should show where on the vehicle the culprit gained access. Aerial photography may be required for large outdoor scenes or to show the relationship of multiple scenes. It may also be useful to show weather conditions and traffic patterns near an outdoor site.

ACCIDENT PHOTOGRAPHY The site of the accident is not simply where the wrecked cars are resting. The scene also includes the approach. As with other crime scenes, the objective in investigating an accident scene is to determine how and why the events took place. This could lead an investigator to retrace the path of the vehicle several blocks from the crash site. It is important to note any local traffic-control devices such as speed-limit signs and traffic lights. Anything that should control a driver's and/or pedestrian's behavior must be documented.

The accident-scene photographer must get shots at various points along the approach to the impact site. This makes it possible for a reconstructionist to determine what a driver might have seen and when. It is important to establish possible obstructions a driver might have encountered. Another important task for the photographer is to verify witnesses' viewpoints. It must be confirmed that what the witnesses say they saw could actually have been seen from their positions at the time of the accident.

One of the most helpful pieces of evidence for determining how the accident occurred is the tire tracks. The photographer is not responsible for reading these marks, but he or she is expected to document them so that someone can. Several views should be taken of each mark to better determine directionality and length. Other marks may be present at the scene, such as marks on guardrails, poles, trees, buildings, and other vehicles.

The entire vehicle, not only the damaged portions, should be photographed (see Figure 3-7). This information can be useful in court if the driver claims he or she was struck by another car that caused the accident. If this alibi is accurate, there will be evidence of it in the photographs. Photographs should also be taken of the license plate, pedals,

FIGURE 3-7 Photograph of the scene of an automobile accident.
Richard Saferstein, Ph.D.

airbags, seat belts, speedometer, and lamp filaments. Sometimes it is possible to verify which pedal the driver was pressing at the time of the accident. This may be possible if the driver's shoes or bare feet took on the impression of the pedal, or if the pedal took on the impression of the sole of the shoe. An impression can also confirm the identity of the driver when there is more than one occupant and no one admits to having been in the driver's seat.

ARSON PHOTOGRAPHY   Overview photographs of an arson scene should show the relative location of the scene, with the aid of street signs if possible. The arson scene also requires specific medium-range and close-up photographs of the likely point of entry, point of origin, and any areas of fire activity. Close-up photographs are also required for all located evidence. Photographers may use special lighting techniques or filters to show the maximum contrast between dark-colored arson debris and dark-colored backgrounds. Because perpetrators of arson crimes frequently return to the scene, it may be especially important to photograph the crowd outside an arson scene.

SEXUAL ASSAULT VICTIM PHOTOGRAPHY   In cases involving sexual assault, overview photographs also should be taken of the scene and surrounding area. Medium-range photographs of the position of the victim in relation to the scene may be important. Medium-range and close-up photographs should be taken of any wounds the victim may have sustained. These may include cuts, bruises, or blunt-force-trauma wounds. However, given the nature of the crime and probable locations of wounds on the victim's body, it is important that photographing be respectful. It is also important to photograph the clothing the victim was wearing during the attack.

IMPRESSION PHOTOGRAPHY   If tire or footwear impressions are found at a crime scene, overview and medium-range photographs should be taken to show the relative position and direction of the impressions. Close-up photographs of tire and footwear impressions must be taken before the impression is cast. A tripod must be used to ensure the film is arranged 90 degrees to the plane of view (see Figure 3-8). Lighting from the side of the impression (oblique lighting) should be utilized to provide the best detail and maximum contrast through shadowing. It is helpful to use a flashlight to determine the best angle light to photograph the impression. A scale must be included in the photograph so that a 1:1 ratio print can later be created for comparison to exemplar tires or footwear (see Figure 3-9). It may also be wise to include an identifying tag in the photograph to indicate where the impression was found and which part of the impression is represented in the photograph. A tire impression must be photographed using an overlapping photograph sequence, and a minimum of eight feet of the tire impression should be photographed.

BLOODSTAIN PHOTOGRAPHY   Overview and medium-range photographs should show the orientation and location of bloodstain evidence. Overview photographs are taken of the entire crime scene, including overviews of the bloodstain patterns within the scene. If multiple bloodstain patterns cover a large surface area, the area can be subdivided into zones or a grid. Close-up photographs, with a scale in place, should be taken of each pertinent stain or group of stains. If analysis of a blood spatter pattern (see Chapter 10) is done at the scene, photographs should be taken of the drawn area of convergence and area of origin. Bloodstains detected with luminol (see Chapter 15) must be photographed in complete darkness. The camera's shutter is locked open for approximately 3 minutes at an f-stop of 22, and a flash at 1/16 power is fired at the beginning of the three minutes.

LATENT FINGERPRINT PHOTOGRAPHY   Close-up photographs of latent (hidden) fingerprints must show the ridge details of the fingerprints for

FIGURE 3-8 A tripod and scale are used to take a close-up photograph of a tire impression marked with an evidence marker at 90 degrees. *Sirchie Finger Print Laboratories*

FIGURE 3-9 This photograph of a tire impression includes a scale so that a 1:1 image can later be produced. *Sirchie Finger Print Laboratories*

(a)

(b)

FIGURE 3-10 A specialized camera is used to photograph latent fingerprints on a cereal box (a) and creates a 1:1 photograph (b). *Sirchie Finger Print Laboratories*

possible identification of their source. Any developed fingerprints should be photographed before they are retrieved. Photographs can be taken by a special latent fingerprint camera that is designed to create a 1:1 photograph of fingerprint evidence (see Figure 3-10) or by a digital camera fitted with an adapter. Commonly, black-and-white photography is used to show greater contrast. An item label should be included in the photograph in order to identify the location of the fingerprint. The picture must be taken at 90 degrees using a high f-stop and oblique lighting for maximum detail. A fingerprint should be photographed using a standard digital camera, and a scale should be included in the photograph. If the pattern is enhanced with a blood reagent, photographs should be taken as the pattern develops.

SHOOTING INCIDENT PHOTOGRAPHY As with any other type of crime scene, the first step in photographing shooting incidents is capturing the overall setting. Before any specific attention can be paid to bullets or cartridge cases, a complete 360-degree view of the site should be photographed. In addition to pictures of the scene itself, photographs must also be taken from the viewpoints that involved parties or witnesses might have had. One of the most difficult parts of photographing a shooting scene is finding the bullet. Bullets have the ability to ricochet, infiltrate, and embed themselves into various surfaces. They also might fragment on impact, or their shape may become distorted. The damage done by a fired bullet must be photographed as well as the bullet itself.

VIDEO DOCUMENTATION

The use of digital video recording at crime scenes is becoming increasingly popular because the cost of this equipment is decreasing. Video recording of crime scenes is even required in some jurisdictions as a preliminary "tour" of the scene.

The same principles used in crime-scene photographs apply to video recording. As with conventional photography, video recording should include the entire scene and the immediately surrounding area. Long shots as well as close-ups should be taken in a slow and systematic manner. The way the investigator moves through the scene should be logical and should illustrate potential paths of entry, exit, and movement. Furthermore, it is desirable to have one crime-scene investigator narrate the events and scenes being recorded while another does the actual shooting. Only the narrator's voice should be heard, and no personnel should be in the shots.

Video recording can have advantages over still photography in certain situations. For example, modern video cameras allow the user to play back a scene and check it for completeness. Video can be especially helpful in arson scenes, where still photographs have trouble showing detail, and where determining the path of the fire is very important. In addition, many video cameras can also take still photographs, and on a computer stills can be created from the video recordings. Video essentially combines notes and photography. Some cameras even have a "night vision" feature, which is similar to infrared photography.

However, there are some disadvantages to video recording crime scenes. First, although some cameras have a stabilization feature, most cameras will inevitably shake during filming. Also, zooming and panning can be very sloppy; these techniques should be used only occasionally and should be done very slowly. Extra noise, such as wind or other investigators talking, can obscure narration or may be inappropriate and damaging. Because of the "on the spot" nature of the narration, investigators may stumble over words, which can be confusing when a video is used in court. To avoid this, some investigators record the video with the sound off and dub notes over it later.

Although video recording can capture the sounds and scenes of the crime site with relative ease, the technique cannot be used in place of still photography at this time. The still photograph remains unsurpassed in defining details for the human eye.

Quick Review

- Digital photography is used widely for documenting crime scenes.
- The crime scene should be recorded in a minimum of four photographs: an overview photograph, a medium-range photograph, a close-up photograph, and a close-up photograph with a scale.
- Special techniques and unique considerations apply when photographing indoor scenes, outdoor scenes, night scenes, accident scenes, arson scenes, sexual assault victims, impression evidence, bloodstain evidence, latent fingerprint evidence, and shooting incidents.
- Video documentation is helpful for showing possible paths and for combining note narration with photography. However, still pictures are still required for their ability to show detail and especially for close-up views of evidence.

Sketching the Crime Scene

Once the crime-scene investigator has taken sufficient notes and photographs, he or she sketches the scene. The sketch serves many important functions in the legal investigation of a crime. If done correctly, a sketch can clearly show the layout of an indoor or outdoor crime scene and the relationship in space of all the items and features significant to the investigation. Sketches are especially important to illustrate the location of collected evidence. A sketch can clarify objects and features already described in notes or shown in photographs. Sketches can also show measurements over long distances and the topography of outdoor scenes. Possible paths of entry, exit, and movement through the scene may be speculated from a good sketch. Additionally, the state of the scene illustrated by the sketch may help to demonstrate the feasibility of a witness's testimony. To be effective, a sketch must be clear enough to be used in reconstruction by other investigative personnel and to illustrate aspects of the crime scene to a jury.

THE ROUGH SKETCH

The investigator may have neither the skill nor the time to make a polished sketch of the scene. However, this is not required during the early phase of the investigation. What is necessary is a **rough sketch** containing an accurate depiction of the dimensions of the scene and showing the location of all objects having a bearing on the case. It shows all recovered items of physical evidence, as well as other important features of the crime scene (see Figure 3-11).

rough sketch
The rudimentary first sketch created at the crime scene with care for accuracy in depicting dimensions and locations but no concern for aesthetic appearance.

The following tools are required to create the sketch (see Figure 3-12):

- Graph paper or drawing paper
- Two measuring tapes
- Clipboard or drawing surface
- Pencils
- Straightedge ruler
- Erasers
- Compass or GPS device
- Optional tools including drawing compasses, protractors (half- or full-circle), architect scales, French curves, drafting triangles, and rolling measuring devices

All sketches must include the following features:

- The "title block" contains the case number, the agency number (if applicable), the name and title of the artist, the location of the scene, and the date and time at which the sketch was created. It may also state the victim's name, the names of any suspects, or the type of crime. The title block should appear in the lower-right corner of the sketch paper.
- The "legend" should contain the key to the identity and dimensions of objects or evidence and may be represented by symbols, letters, or numbers.
- The "compass" should show an arrow to denote north in relation to the scene.
- The "body" of the sketch contains the drawing itself and all dimensions and objects located within it.

CREATING THE SKETCH

1. Define the boundaries of the sketch. These may be walls for an indoor sketch. Make sure that the area within these boundaries includes all the pertinent objects and evidence.
2. Establish known points from which to measure the locations of objects and evidence. These points should be fixed. These can be walls or doors in indoor scenes. Trees, telephone poles, street signs, or natural features (e.g., boulders) can be used for outdoor scenes.
3. The walls or boundaries should be drawn in first, leaving as much room as possible for the contents. If walls are used, their dimensions should be recorded.

FIGURE 3-11 A rough sketch of a crime scene. *Courtesy Sirchie Finger Print Laboratories, Youngsville, NC, www.sirchie.com*

FIGURE 3-12   A basic kit for sketching the crime scene. *Sirchie Finger Print Laboratories*

4. Measurements should be taken from the fixed points to pieces of evidence first. There are three methods of measurement from the two points of reference.

- The "rectangular" method measures two distances to an object that make a right angle with each other and to two fixed, flat surfaces. These surfaces are usually walls (see Figure 3-13 [a]).
- The "triangulation" method measures the distance of the object from two fixed points of known distance from each other. This forms a triangle. In an indoor scene these points are usually the corners of a room (see Figure 3-13 [b]).
- The "baseline" method is especially useful for outdoor scenes. First, two fixed objects on opposite sides of the scene are located (designated A and B). A line is then made between them and measured. Each object or piece of evidence has a line drawn from it to the baseline to make a 90-degree angle with the baseline. The distance of the line from the object to the baseline is then measured, along with its point of intersection with the baseline (see Figure 3-13 [c]).
- The "polar coordinates" method uses only one reference point. The sketch in Figure 3-13 [d] shows the distance and angle at which an object is located in the scene relative to the reference point.

Distances shown on the sketch must be accurate and not the result of a guess or estimate. For this reason, all measurements should be made with a tape measure and confirmed by two people. The simplest way to label the location of an item in a sketch is to assign it a number or letter. A legend will then correlate the number or letter to the item's description and dimensions. Symbols for objects should be consistent. Typically, items of evidence are assigned

FIGURE 3-13 (a) The rectangular measurement method; (b) the triangulation measurement method; (c) the baseline measurement method; and (d) the polar coordinates measurement method.

numbers (possibly correlating to their evidence marker number), and nonevidentiary objects are assigned letters. The distances and dimensions of these objects not considered to be evidence are measured, recorded, and drawn last. Distances between objects also can be measured and drawn. It is very important that units of measure are kept the same throughout the sketch. Usually inches and feet are used in the United States because those measurements are easily understood by the investigative personnel and the jury.

THE FINISHED SKETCH

finished sketch
The perfected final sketch that is constructed with care and concern for aesthetic appearance and drawn to scale.

Unlike the rough sketch, the **finished sketch** is constructed with care and concern for aesthetic appearance. The finished sketch must be drawn to scale. The legend should contain the scale (e.g., 1/2″ = 1′). When the finished sketch is completed, it must reflect information contained within the rough sketch to be admissible evidence in a courtroom. An indoor overview sketch shows the floors of one or more rooms, doors and windows, and any evidence or objects on the floor (see Figures 3-14 and 3-15). An outdoor overview sketch is like an aerial view of a small or large outdoor scene. A final sketch can be done by an investigator or a hired professional. It can be done by hand in pen or by computer (see Figure 3-16).

The process of computer-aided drafting (CAD) has become the standard method for reconstructing crime scenes from rough sketches (see Figure 3-17). The software, ranging from simple, low-cost programs to complex, expensive

CASE 10-789-90
301 N. CENTRE ST.
March 15, 2007 11: 40 PM
HOMICIDE

VICTIM: LESTER W. BROWN
INVESTIGATOR: SGT. L.A. DUFFY
ASS'T BY: PTLM. R.W. HICKS

BOOKCASE

DESK

COUCH

TABLE

FIREPLACE

LAMP TABLE

CHAIR

BOOKCASE

LEGEND:
A. COCKTAIL GLASS
B. TELEPHONE
C. VICTIM
D. BULLET HOLE
E. BLOOD STAINS
F. SHELL CASING
△ CAMERA LOCATIONS

'D - 3' 4¾" FROM FLOOR

SCALE: ¼" = 1 FOOT

FIGURE 3-14 An overview finished sketch of a room interior. *Courtesy Sirchie Finger Print Laboratories, Youngsville, NC, www.sirchie.com*

FIGURE 3-15 An overview finished sketch of an office scene. *Sirchie Finger Print Laboratories*

ones, contains predrawn objects, such as intersections, roadways, buildings, and rooms, onto which information can be added. A generous symbol library provides a variety of images that can be used to add intricate details, such as blood spatters, to a crime-scene sketch. Equipped with a zoom function, computerized sketching programs can enlarge a specific area for a more detailed picture. These sketches may also be able to show bullet trajectories in scenes where a gun was involved. CAD programs allow users to select a scale size so that the final product can be produced in a size suitable for courtroom presentation.

Three-dimensional CAD sketches can also be created. These sketches show the nature of the crime scene from many angles. This can be helpful in crime reconstruction and in the trial setting. Some can also be animated to show how the events suggested in the reconstruction would lead to the final state of the scene.

Case 176-96
S. Maple Ave.
August 28, 1996
Fatal Accident
(Hit & Run)
Victim—
  George Wilson

Invest.: C. Lewis
Ass't.: R. Daniels

Legend:
A. Debris
B. Body of Victim
C. Utility Pole No.
   60645
D. Wilson Residence
E. Jones Residence
F. Sidewalk
G. Skid Marks
▲ Camera Locations

Scale: 1/8" = 1 foot

TB03-175ENG-REV2

S. MAPLE AVE.

E. OAK BLVD.

25 MPH SIGN

STOP SIGN

N

D

E

F

FIGURE 3-16 A finished sketch of an outdoor crime scene. *Sirchie Finger Print Laboratories*

Quick Review

- The crime-scene sketch plays an important role in the legal investigation of a crime by clearly showing possible points of entry and/or exit, evidence locations, and the general layout of the crime scene. It will also refresh the investigator's memories about the case after time has passed.
- The rough sketch is made at the scene to show basic measurements of the scene and spatial relationships between items.
- The finished sketch is created from the rough sketch with care and concern for appearance. It must include a scale, and it may be created using a computer-aided drafting program.

FIGURE 3-17 Construction of a crime-scene diagram with the aid of a computer-aided drafting program. *Sirchie Finger Print Laboratories*

CHAPTER REVIEW

- Because investigators have only a limited amount of time to work a crime site in its untouched state, the opportunity must not be lost.

- Crime-scene notes should include contact information, personnel information and movements, task assignments, observations of the victim and scene, and information about the evidence before and after it is processed.

- Recording notes on digital voice recorders is advantageous, but investigators should take care to speak clearly and avoid including side conversations.

- Digital cameras feature a light-sensitive microchip that captures light on each of millions of tiny picture elements, called "pixels." The light is recorded on each pixel as a specific charge that will later be electronically translated to an image. The number of pixels on a camera is measured in the millions, called "megapixels," and directly affects an image's resolution.

- Digital images are preserved by either lossy or lossless compression.

- DSLR cameras allow for the use of a wide range of lenses including normal lenses, telephoto lenses, wide-angle lenses, macro lenses, and multipurpose lenses. The kind of lens used affects the appearance of the image.

- The aperture and shutter speed regulate the amount of light gathered by the camera. These settings can be manually adjusted on DSLR cameras.

- The f-stop determines depth of field, or the amount of area in the foreground and background that is in focus. The higher the f-stop, the smaller the aperture and the greater the depth of field. Landscape and portrait settings on a digital camera adjust for higher and lower f-stops, respectively.

- The color temperature of the light source used will make a photographic image appear orangish or bluish. Many digital cameras combat this with "white balance" capability. Exposure compensation and electronic flashes can be used to capture images of dark or light subjects. Flash units, or slave flashes, are helpful to provide oblique or versatile illumination.

- Filters are used with DSLR cameras to block certain wavelengths of light (barrier filters) or allow in only certain wavelengths of light (bypass filters). Filters can be used to show greater detail in photographs by adjusting the appearance of specific colors.

- Tripods can greatly improve the quality of a photograph by preventing blurriness caused by the movement of the photographer's hand. They also help ensure 90-degree close-up photographs of evidence.

- Digital photography is used widely for documenting crime scenes.

- The crime scene should be recorded with a minimum of four photographs: an overview photograph, a medium-range photograph, a close-up photograph, and a close-up photograph with a scale.

- Special techniques and unique considerations apply when photographing indoor scenes, outdoor scenes, night scenes, accident scenes, arson scenes, sexual assault victims, impression evidence, bloodstain evidence, latent fingerprint evidence, and shooting incidents.

- Video documentation is helpful for showing possible paths and for combining note narration with photography. However, still pictures are still required for their ability to show detail and especially for close-up views of evidence.

- The crime scene sketch plays an important role in the legal investigation of a crime by clearly showing possible points of entry and/or exit, evidence locations, and the general layout of the crime scene. It will also refresh the investigator's memories about the case after time has passed.

- The rough sketch is made at the scene to show basic measurements of the scene and spatial relationships between items.

- The finished sketch is created from the rough sketch with care and concern for appearance. It must include a scale, and it may be created using a computer-aided drafting (CAD) program.

KEY TERMS

aperture, 56
color temperature, 57
computer-aided drafting (CAD), 53
depth of field, 57

digital photography, 53
digital single lens reflex (DSLR) camera, 55
finished sketch, 72
f-stop, 56

lossless compression, 55
megapixel, 53
photography log, 61
rough sketch, 69
shutter speed, 57

REVIEW QUESTIONS

1. Three methods for recording the crime scene are _____, _____, and _____.

2. True or False: The note-taking process begins with the call to a crime-scene investigator to report to a scene. _____

3. The crime-scene notes should include a precise record of personnel movements in and out of the scene, starting with the _____.

4. True or False: Crime-scene notes should be written from memory back at the laboratory. _____

5. Before evidence is collected, it must be fully described in the investigator's _____.

6. True or False: When an injured or deceased victim is present at the scene, the state of the body before being moved should be observed but not recorded. _____

7. True or False: The value of crime-scene photographs lies in their ability to show the layout of the scene, the position of witnesses, and the physical relationship of people to one another in the scene. _____

8. The most commonly used camera for crime-scene photography is the _____ camera.

9. True or False: The lens of the camera is the mechanism for bending light to focus the image on the digital microchip, and the kind of lens is determined by the lens's focal length. _____

10. To ensure that their digital images will be admissible, many jurisdictions have developed or are developing _____ for the use of digital photography to avoid the possibility of enhancement or doctoring of crime-scene photographs.

11. The camera _____ is the measurement of the diameter of the opening of the diaphragm, and it is adjusted on a digital camera by adjusting the f-stop.

12. The _____, measured in fractions of a second, is the length of time the microchip is exposed to light.

13. The _____ of a photograph is the amount of area in the foreground and background of an in-focus object that is also relatively in focus.

14. True or False: On the color temperature scale, a "hot" light source has a red–orange hue, whereas a "cold" light source has a blue hue. _____

15. The _____ is the most commonly used type of flash in photography. This type of flash is usually on the top or front of a camera.

16. A digital camera captures light on a light-sensitive _____.

17. True or False: Crime-scene photographers generally use simple "point and shoot" digital cameras. _____

18. A(n) _____ filter blocks one wavelength of light bouncing off the subject and allows all others to reach the camera's microchip.

19. The _____, filled out by the crime-scene photographer, should include the case and scene information and the parameters of each photograph.

20. The most important prerequisite for photographing a crime scene is to have it in a(n) _____ condition.

21. True or False: Each crime scene should be photographed as completely as possible in a logical sequence that includes the area in which the crime actually took place and all adjacent areas where important acts occurred. _____

22. The succession of photographs taken at a crime scene is _____ photographs first, _____ photographs second, and _____ photographs last.

23. True or False: Overview photographs should include only points of entry and points of exit. _____

24. To show the greatest detail of individual objects or evidence, close-up photographs must be taken at an angle of _____ and with and without evidence markers and scales.

25. A technique called _____ may be used to illuminate long distances in total darkness in night photography.

26. True or False: In indoor or outdoor scenes, the crime-scene photographer moves around the boundary of the scene in a clockwise or counterclockwise direction, taking photographs from many vantage points and angles to provide a complete 360-degree view of the scene. _____

27. In _____ cases it may be especially important to photograph the crowd outside the scene because perpetrators of these crimes frequently return to the scene.

28. True or False: Victims of violent crimes may have wounds that should be photographed, but this should be done respectfully. _____

29. True or False: Close-up photographs of tire and footwear impressions at a crime scene must be taken after the impression is cast. _____

30. The process of _____ the crime scene essentially combines note taking and photography.

31. An investigator need draw only a(n) _____ sketch at the crime scene to show its dimensions and pertinent objects.

32. When creating a rough sketch, one should take measurements from fixed points to pieces of evidence by using either the _____, _____, _____, or _____ method.

33. True or False: The distances and dimensions shown on the sketch can be a guess or estimate, and the use of a tape measure is not required. _____

34. Unlike the rough sketch, the _____ is constructed with care and concern for aesthetic appearance and must be drawn to scale.

35. _____ programs provide an extensive symbol library and may create a three-dimensional sketch.

APPLICATION AND CRITICAL THINKING

1. What type of lens would a photographer likely use to create each of the following photos?
   a) An extreme close-up photo of a fiber found at a crime scene
   b) A medium-range shot of part of a wall
   c) A photo showing the entire length of a wall

2. What kind of filter would a photographer probably use for the following shots?
   a) A photo of a fingerprint imaged with a fluorescent powder
   b) A photo in which the investigator wishes to highlight an area of a particular color
   c) A piece of evidence that is difficult to see against a specific background color

3. The digital camera offers a wide range of options for optimizing the photograph of a subject. What setting would be used in each of the following situations?
   a) Capturing subjects in motion
   b) Reducing exposure time
   c) Increasing depth of field
   d) Shooting in a particular type of light, such as fluorescent
   e) Calculating the best setting for light conditions at the center of a field

4. What important elements are missing from the following crime-scene sketch?

2741 Aragon St.
9/6/06

Sketch by Officer
John Smith

N

DOOR

DINING ROOM

WINDOW

WINDOW

A—Dining room table
B—Chair
C—Overturned chair
D—0.38 Revolver
E—Male body
F—Table
G—Chair

4 Collection of Crime-Scene Evidence

© Pietro Crocchioni/epa european pressphoto agency b.v/Alamy

LEARNING OBJECTIVES

After studying this chapter, you should be able to:
- Define physical evidence.
- Review the common types of physical evidence encountered at crime scenes.
- Describe proper techniques for handling evidence to avoid damage or contamination.
- Understand collecting and packaging procedures for common types of physical evidence.
- Define and understand the concept of "chain of custody."
- List the steps that are typically required to maintain appropriate health and safety standards at the crime scene.
- Discuss the implications of the Mincey and Tyler cases.

AMANDA KNOX: A FLAWED CASE OF MURDER

In September 2007, Amanda Knox moved to Parugia, Italy, as a foreign exchange student attending language classes at the University for Foreigners. Knox shared an upstairs flat in a cottage with Meredith Kercher and two other women. Within weeks of her arrival, Knox became romantically linked to an Italian student, Raffaele Sollecito, and began spending nights at his home.

On November 1, Kercher was brutally murdered. Early that afternoon, Kercher's naked body was found inside her bedroom covered by a bedspread soaked in blood and with stab wounds to her throat. As the investigation proceeded, police matched fingerprints found in Kercher's bedroom to Rudy Guede, whom Knox and Kercher had met weeks earlier when he was playing guitar on the downstairs floor of their cottage flat. Guede was subsequently arrested and charged with the Kercher murder. His DNA was later found at the crime scene, on and inside Kercher's body. The prosecution also charged Knox and Sollecito with murder and sexual assault.

According to the prosecution's theory, Knox was part of a satanic ritual sex game that went out of control. The Knox case became the subject of intense media scrutiny, focusing in part on Knox's alleged romantic escapades. The prosecution alleged that the murder weapon was a kitchen knife found in Sollecito's kitchen that had Kercher's DNA on the blade and Knox's DNA on the handle. The DNA on the handle could have arisen from Knox's handling of the knife while cooking for Sollecito. Experts questioned the veracity of the DNA protocols conducted on the knife blade. Expert analysis concluded that the knife wounds were inconsistent with the knife recovered from Sollecito's residence. Guede was convicted of Kercher's murder. Knox was convicted of slander, sexual violence, and murder and sentenced to twenty-six years in prison. Four years later her conviction was set aside by the Italian supreme court and a new trial was ordered. The retrial held in 2013–14 again resulted in a verdict of guilty for murder. Knox remains in her hometown of Seattle awaiting her fate.

Common Types of Physical Evidence

It would be impossible to list all the objects that could conceivably be important to a crime. Every crime scene has to be treated on an individual basis, having its own peculiar history, circumstances, and problems. However, it is practical to be aware of types of items whose scientific examination is likely to yield significant results in ascertaining the nature and circumstances of a crime. The investigator who is thoroughly familiar with the recognition, collection, and analysis of these items, as well as with laboratory procedures and capabilities, can make logical decisions when faced with uncommon and unexpected circumstances at the crime scene. Equally important, a qualified evidence collector cannot rely on collection procedures memorized from a pamphlet but must be able to make innovative, on-the-spot decisions at the crime scene.

Blood, Semen, and Saliva   All suspected blood, semen, or saliva—liquid or dried, animal or human—present in a form that suggests a relationship to the offense or people involved in a crime. This category includes blood or semen dried onto fabrics or other objects, as well as cigarette butts that may contain saliva residues. These substances are subjected to serological and biochemical analysis to determine identity and possible origin.

Documents   Any handwriting and typewriting submitted so that authenticity or source can be determined. Related items include paper, ink, indented writings, obliterations, and burned or charred documents.

Drugs   Any substance in violation of laws regulating the sale, manufacture, distribution, and use of drugs.

Explosives   Any device containing an explosive charge, as well as all objects removed from the scene of an explosion that are suspected to contain the residues of an explosive.

Fibers   Any natural or synthetic fiber whose transfer may be useful in establishing a relationship between objects and/or people.

Fingerprints   All prints of this nature, hidden (latent) and visible.

Firearms and Ammunition   Any firearm, as well as discharged or intact ammunition, suspected of being involved in a criminal offense.

Glass   Any glass particle or fragment that may have been transferred to a person or object involved in a crime. This category includes windowpanes containing holes made by a bullet or other projectile.

Hair   Any animal or human hair present that could link a person with a crime.

Impressions   Tire markings, shoe prints, depressions in soft soils, and all other forms of tracks. Glove and other fabric impressions, as well as bite marks in skin or foodstuffs, are also included in this category.

Organs and Physiological Fluids   Body organs and fluids submitted for analysis to detect the possible existence of drugs and poisons. This category includes blood to be analyzed for the presence of alcohol and other drugs.

Paint   Any paint, liquid or dried, that may have been transferred from the surface of one object to another during the commission of a crime. A common example is the transfer of paint from one vehicle to another during an automobile collision.

Petroleum Products   Any petroleum product removed from a suspect or recovered from a crime scene. The most common examples are gasoline residues removed from the scene of an arson and grease or oil stains whose presence may suggest involvement in a crime.

FIGURE 4-1 The gun is fired at a set distance from the target, and the gun-powder left on the target is compared to powder stains on a victim's clothing. The density and shape of the powder stains vary with the distance from which the gun was fired. *Mikael Karlsson/ Arresting Images*

Plastic Bags A disposable polyethylene bag such as a garbage bag that may be evidential in a homicide or drug case. Examinations are conducted to associate a bag with a similar bag in the possession of a suspect.

Plastic, Rubber, and Other Polymers Remnants of these manufactured materials recovered at crime scenes may be linked to objects recovered in the possession of a criminal suspect.

Powder Residues Any item suspected of containing powder residues resulting from the discharge of a firearm (see Figure 4-1).

Serial Numbers This category includes all stolen property submitted to the laboratory for the restoration of erased identification numbers.

Soil and Minerals All items containing soil or minerals that could link a person or object to a particular location. Common examples are soil imbedded in shoes and insulation found on garments.

Tool Marks This category includes any object suspected of containing the impression of another object that served as a tool in a crime. For example, a screwdriver or crowbar could produce tool marks by being impressed into or scraped along a wall.

Vehicle Lights The examination of vehicle headlights and taillights is normally conducted to determine whether a light was on or off at the time of impact.

Wood and Other Vegetative Matter Any fragments of wood, sawdust, shavings, or vegetative matter discovered on clothing, shoes, or tools that could link a person or object to a crime location.

Quick Review

- Biological crime-scene evidence includes blood, saliva, semen, DNA, hair, organs, and physiological fluids.
- Impression crime-scene evidence includes tire markings, shoe prints, depressions in soft soils, all other forms of tracks, glove and other fabric impressions, tool marks, and bite marks.
- Manufactured items considered common items of crime-scene evidence include firearms, ammunition, fibers, paint, glass, petroleum products, plastic bags, rubber, polymers, and vehicle headlights.

Evidence-Collection Tools

The well-prepared evidence collector arrives at a crime scene with a large assortment of packaging materials and tools ready to encounter any type of situation. These tools are usually kept in an evidence-collection kit (see Figure 4-2).

- Notebook
- Pen (black or blue ink)
- Ruler
- Chalk or crayons
- Magnifying glass
- Flashlight
- Disposable forceps and similar tools that may be needed to pick up small items
- Scalpels or razor blades

FIGURE 4-2 A typical evidence-collection kit. *Sirchie Finger Print Laboratories*

- Swabs and medicine droppers for presumptive testing
- Gauze or sterile cloth
- Unbreakable plastic pill bottles with pressure lids
- Evidence sealing tape
- Evidence tags (indoor) or flags (outdoor) (see Figure 4-3)
- Various sizes of paper bags, boxes, and manila envelopes
- Red "biohazard" labels
- Paper for wrapping or for creating "druggist folds"
- Alternate light source (see Figure 4-4)
- Lifting tape for gathering hair or trace evidence
- Vacuum collector with filters
- Fingerprint powders, brushes, and lifters
- Disposable gloves, face masks, and shoe covers

MOBILE CRIME LABORATORIES

In recent years, many police departments have gone to the expense of purchasing and equipping "mobile crime laboratories" for their evidence technicians. However, the term "mobile crime laboratory" is a misnomer. These vehicles carry the necessary supplies to protect the crime scene; to photograph, collect, and package physical evidence; and to perform latent print development. They are not designed to carry out the functions of a chemical laboratory. "Crime-scene search vehicle" would be a more appropriate but perhaps less dramatic name for such a vehicle (see Figure 4-5).

FIGURE 4-3 Evidence flags are used for outdoor crime scenes. *Sirchie Finger Print Laboratories*

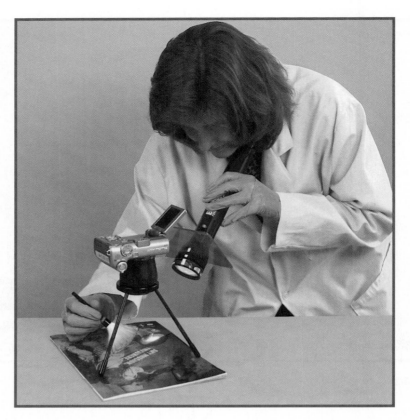

FIGURE 4-4 An example of an alternate light source in use. This can be used to visually enhance many types of evidence. *Sirchie Finger Print Laboratories*

■ Procedures for Collecting and Packaging
■ Physical Evidence

physical evidence
Any object that can establish that a crime has or has not been committed or can link a crime and its victim or perpetrator.

Physical evidence can be anything from massive objects to microscopic traces. Many items of evidence are obvious when present, but others may be detected only through examination in the crime laboratory. For example, minute traces of blood may be discovered on garments only after a thorough search in the laboratory, or the presence of hairs and fibers may be revealed in vacuum sweepings or on garments only after close laboratory scrutiny. For this reason, investigators should collect possible carriers of trace evidence in addition to more discernible items. This may include vacuum sweepings, fingernail scrapings, clothing, and vehicles.

The investigator should vacuum critical areas of the crime scene and submit the sweepings to the laboratory for analysis. The sweepings from different areas must be collected and packaged separately. A portable vacuum cleaner equipped with a special filter attachment is suitable for this purpose (see Figure 4-6). Fingernail scrapings from individuals who were in contact with other individuals may contain minute fragments of evidence capable of providing a link between assailant and victim. The investigator should scrape the undersurface of each nail with a dull object such as a toothpick to avoid cutting the skin. These scrapings will be subjected to microscopic examination in the laboratory. All clothing from the victim and suspect(s) should be collected and packaged separately. These objects will be further examined at the laboratory for trace, fiber, and hair evidence.

FIGURE 4-5   An inside view of a mobile crime-scene van: (a) driver's side and (b) passenger's side. *Sirchie Finger Print Laboratories*

FIGURE 4-6   A vacuum sweeper attachment, constructed of clear plastic in two pieces that are joined by a threaded joint. A metal screen is mounted in one half to support a filter paper to collect debris. The unit attaches to the hose of the vacuum sweeper. After a designated area of the crime scene is vacuumed, the filter paper is removed and retained for laboratory examination. *Sirchie Finger Print Laboratories*

When a vehicle is involved in a crime, investigators should pay particular attention to signs of a cross-transfer of evidence between the car and the victim—this includes blood, tissue, hair, fibers, and fabric impressions. Traces of paint or broken glass may be located on the victim or roadway. The entire car should be processed for fingerprints. In cases in which the car was used for transportation, more attention may be given to the interior of the car. However, all areas of the vehicle, inside and outside, should be searched with equal care for physical evidence.

The search for physical evidence must extend beyond the crime scene to the autopsy room of a deceased victim. Here, the medical examiner or coroner carefully examines the victim to establish a cause and manner of death. Tissues and organs are routinely retained for pathological and toxicological examination. At the same time, arrangements must be made between the examiner and investigator to secure a variety of items that may be obtainable from the body for laboratory examination.

HANDLING EVIDENCE

contamination
The transfer of extraneous matter between the collector and the evidence or multiple pieces of evidence, producing tainted evidence that cannot be used in the subsequent investigation.

Investigators must handle and process physical evidence in a way that prevents any changes in it between the time the evidence is removed from the crime scene and the time it is received by the crime laboratory. Changes can arise through **contamination**, breakage, evaporation, accidental scratching or bending, or improper or careless packaging. The use of latex gloves or disposable forceps when touching evidence can often prevent such problems. Any equipment that is not disposable should be cleaned and/or sanitized between collections of each piece of evidence. Evidence should remain unmoved until investigators have documented its location and appearance in notes, sketches, and photographs.

Evidence best maintains its integrity when kept in its original condition as it was found at the crime site. Whenever possible, one should submit intact evidence to the laboratory. The investigator normally should not remove blood, hairs, fibers, soil particles, or other types of trace evidence from garments, weapons, or any other articles that bear them. Instead, he or she should send the entire object to the laboratory for processing.

Of course, if evidence is adhering to an object in a precarious manner, good judgment dictates removing and packaging the item. Investigators must use common sense when handling evidence adhering to a large structure, such as a door, wall, or floor; they should remove the specimen with a forceps or other appropriate tool. In the case of a bloodstain, the investigator may either scrape the stain off the surface, transfer the stain to a moistened swab, or cut out the area of the object bearing the stain.

PACKAGING EVIDENCE

The well-prepared evidence collector arrives at a crime scene with a large assortment of packaging materials and tools, ready to encounter any type of situation. Forceps and similar tools may be used to pick up small items. Unbreakable plastic pill bottles with pressure lids are excellent containers for hairs, glass, fibers, and various other kinds of small or trace evidence. Alternatively, manila envelopes, screw-cap glass vials, sealable plastic bags, and metal pillboxes are adequate containers for most trace evidence encountered at crime scenes (see Figure 4-7). Charred debris recovered from the scene of a suspicious fire must be sealed in an airtight container to prevent the evaporation of volatile petroleum residues. New paint cans or tightly sealed jars are recommended in such situations (see Figure 4-8).

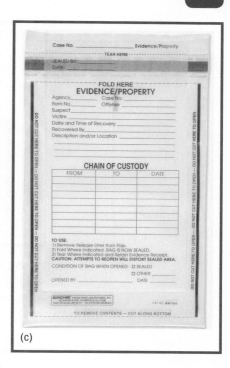

FIGURE 4-7 (a) A manila evidence envelope, (b) metal pillboxes, and (c) a sealable plastic evidence bag. *Sirchie Finger Print Laboratories*

FIGURE 4-8 Airtight metal cans used to package arson evidence. *Sirchie Finger Print Laboratories*

FIGURE 4-9 A druggist fold is used to package paint transfer evidence. *Sirchie Finger Print Laboratories*

Ordinary mailing envelopes should not be used as evidence containers, because powders and fine particles will leak out of their corners. Instead, small amounts of trace evidence can be conveniently packaged in a carefully folded paper, using what is known as a "druggist fold" (see Figure 4-9). This method consists of placing the evidence in the center of a piece of paper, folding one-third of the piece of paper over the middle third (and the evidence), folding the opposite end (one-third) over that, then repeating the process on the other two sides. After folding the paper in this manner, one should tuck the outside two flaps into each other to produce a closed container that keeps the specimen from falling out.

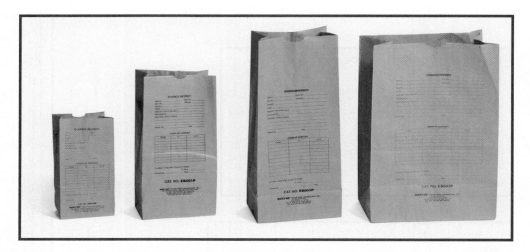

FIGURE 4-10   Paper bags and manila envelopes are recommended evidence containers for biological evidence, especially objects suspected of containing blood and semen stains. Each object should be packaged in a separate bag or envelope. *Sirchie Finger Print Laboratories*

Each individual item, or items that are similar and collected at different locations, should be placed in separate containers. Packaging evidence separately prevents damage through contact and prevents cross-contamination.

BIOLOGICAL MATERIALS   Use only disposable tools to collect biological materials for packaging. If biological materials such as blood are stored in airtight containers, the accumulation of moisture may encourage the growth of mold, which can destroy their evidential value. In these instances, wrapping paper, manila envelopes, or paper bags are the recommended packaging materials (see Figure 4-10). As a matter of routine, all items possibly containing biological fluid evidence should be air-dried and placed individually in separate paper bags to ensure a constant circulation of air around them. This will prevent the formation of mold and mildew. Paper packaging is easily written on, but seals may not be sturdy. Finally, place a red biohazard sticker on both the secured evidence bag and the property receipt to ensure all handlers will be aware the item is contaminated with biological fluids, such as blood, saliva, or semen (see Table 4.1).

The evidence collector must handle all body fluids and biologically stained materials as little as possible. All body fluids must be assumed to be infectious, so investigators must wear disposable latex gloves while handling the evidence. Latex gloves also significantly reduce the possibility that the evidence collector will contaminate the evidence. Investigators should change gloves frequently during the evidence-collection phase of the investigation. Safety and contamination considerations also dictate that evidence collectors wear face masks and shoe covers.

DNA Evidence.   The advent of DNA analysis brought one of the most significant recent advances in crime-scene investigation. This technique is valuable for making it possible to identify suspects through detecting and analyzing minute quantities of DNA deposited on evidence as a result of contact with saliva, sweat, or skin cells. The search for DNA evidence should include any and all objects with which the suspect or victim may have come into bodily contact. Likely sources of DNA evidence include stamps and envelopes that have been licked, a cup or can that has touched a person's lips, chewing gum, the sweatband of a hat, and a bed sheet containing dead skin cells.

TABLE 4.1 Best Practices in Biological Evidence Packaging

Containers
- Use paper bags, manila envelopes, cardboard boxes, and similar porous materials for all biological evidence.
- Use butcher paper or art paper for wrapping evidence, for padding in the evidence container, and/or as a general drop cloth to collect trace evidence.
- Package evidence and seal the container to protect it from loss, cross-transfer, contamination, and/or deleterious change.
- For security purposes, seal the package in such a manner that opening it causes obvious damage or alteration to the container or its seal.

Item Packaging
- Package each item separately; avoid commingling items to prevent cross-contamination.
- Use a biohazard label to indicate that a potential biohazard is present.
- Plastic bags are not preferred for storage because of the possibility of bacterial growth or mold.
- If drying wet evidence is not possible, place the evidence in an impermeable, nonporous container and place the container in a refrigerator that maintains a temperature of 2–8°C (approximately 35–46°F) and that is located away from direct sunlight until the evidence can be air-dried or submitted to the laboratory.
- Seal each package with evidence tape or other seals, such as heat seals and gum seals; if possible, do not use staples. Mark across the seal with the sealer's identification or initials and the date.

Source: Reprinted in part from *The Biological Evidence Preservation Handbook: Best Practices for Evidence Handlers,* http://nvlpubs.nist.gov/nistpubs/ir/2013/NIST.IR.7928.pdf

One key concern during the collection of a DNA-containing specimen is contamination. Contamination—in this case, introducing foreign DNA—can occur from coughing or sneezing onto evidence during the collection process. Transfer of DNA can also occur when items of evidence are incorrectly placed in contact with each other during packaging. To prevent contamination, the evidence collector must wear a face mask and lab coat, use disposable latex gloves, and work with disposable forceps. The evidence collector must also take into consideration that biological materials, such as dried blood, should be considered potentially infectious. It's recommended practice that the biological evidence collector wear disposable coveralls, shoe covers, and eye protection as an extra precaution to avoid contaminating DNA evidence and being exposed to infectious diseases.

Blood analysis has great evidential value when it allows the investigator to demonstrate a transfer between a victim and a suspect. For this reason, all clothing from both the victim and suspect should be collected and sent to the laboratory for examination, even when the presence of blood on a garment does not appear obvious to the investigator. Laboratory search procedures are far more revealing and sensitive than any that can be conducted at the crime scene. A detailed description of the proper collection and packaging of various types of physical evidence will be discussed in forthcoming chapters.

MAINTAINING THE CHAIN OF CUSTODY

Whenever evidence is presented in court as an exhibit, the investigator must establish continuity of possession, or the **chain of custody**. This means that he or she must account for every person who handled or examined the evidence. Failure to substantiate the evidence's chain of custody may lead to serious

chain of custody
A list of all people who came into possession of an item of evidence.

FIGURE 4-11   Proper evidence tape seals on evidence in various packages. *Sirchie Finger Print Laboratories*

questions regarding the authenticity and integrity of the evidence and the examinations of it. Adhering to standard procedures in recording the location of evidence, marking it for identification, and properly completing evidence-submission forms for laboratory analysis are the best guarantee that the evidence will withstand inquiries about what happened to it from the time it was found to its presentation in court.

Once an investigator selects an evidence container, he or she must mark it for identification. All evidence packages must be labeled, and their openings must be sealed with evidence tape (see Figure 4-11). Evidence containers often have a preprinted identification form for the evidence collector to fill out; otherwise, the collector must attach an evidence tag to the container (see Figure 4-12). The investigator who packaged the evidence must write his or her initials and the date on the evidence tape seal. Anyone who removes the evidence for further testing or observation at a later time should try to avoid breaking the original seal if possible so that the information on the seal will not be lost. The person who reseals the packaging should record his or her initials and the date on the new seal.

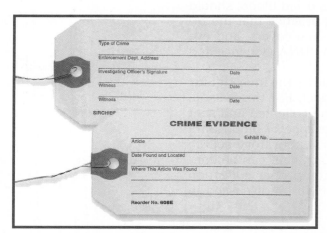

FIGURE 4-12   Examples of evidence tags that may be attached directly to the evidence. *Sirchie Finger Print Laboratories*

At a minimum, the record of the evidence that is used to demonstrate chain of custody shows the collector's initials, the location of the evidence, and the date of collection. Transfer of evidence to another individual or delivery to the laboratory must be recorded in notes and other appropriate forms (see Figure 4-13). In fact, every individual who possesses the evidence must maintain a written record of its acquisition and disposition.

Frequently, all of the individuals involved in the collection and transportation of the evidence must testify in court. Thus, to avoid confusion and to retain complete control of the evidence at all times, the transfer of custody should be kept to a minimum.

If a delay occurs between the time evidence is collected and the time it is submitted to the forensic laboratory, the investigator must store the evidence in a secured area with only limited access by police personnel (see Figure 4-14).

OBTAINING STANDARD/ REFERENCE SAMPLES

To examine evidence, whether soil, blood, glass, hair, or fibers, often the forensic scientist must compare it with a sample of similar material whose origin is known. This is known as a **standard** or **reference sample**. Although most investigators have little difficulty recognizing and collecting relevant crime-scene evidence, few seem aware of the necessity and importance of providing the crime lab with a thorough sampling of standard/reference materials. Such materials may be obtained from the victim, a suspect, or other known sources. For instance, investigation of a hit-and-run incident might require the removal of standard/reference paint from a suspect vehicle. This will permit its comparison to paint recovered at the scene.

The presence of standard/reference samples greatly facilitates the work of the forensic scientist. For example, hair found at a crime scene will be of optimum value only when compared to standard/reference hairs removed from the suspect and victim. Likewise, bloodstained evidence must be accompanied by a whole-blood or **buccal swab** standard/reference sample obtained from all relevant crime-scene participants. The quality and quantity of standard/reference specimens often determines the evidential value of crime-scene evidence, and so must be treated with equal care.

CHAIN OF CUSTODY

Received From: _____
Received By: _____
Date: _____ Time: _____ am/pm

Received From: _____
Received By: _____
Date: _____ Time: _____ am/pm

Received From: _____
Received By: _____
Date: _____ Time: _____ am/pm

Received From: _____
Received By: _____
Date: _____ Time: _____ am/pm

Received From: _____
Received By: _____
Date: _____ Time: _____ am/pm

Received From: _____
Received By: _____
Date: _____ Time: _____ am/pm

CAT. NO. COC2100

FIGURE 4-13 A chain of custody form is used to record the name of every person who handled or examined the collected evidence. *Sirchie Finger Print Laboratories*

standard/reference sample
Physical evidence whose origin is known, such as blood or hair from a suspect, that can be compared to crime-scene evidence.

buccal swab
A swab of the inner portion of the cheek; performed to collect cells for use in determining the DNA profile of an individual.

FIGURE 4-14   An example of a secure evidence locker. *Sirchie Finger Print Laboratories*

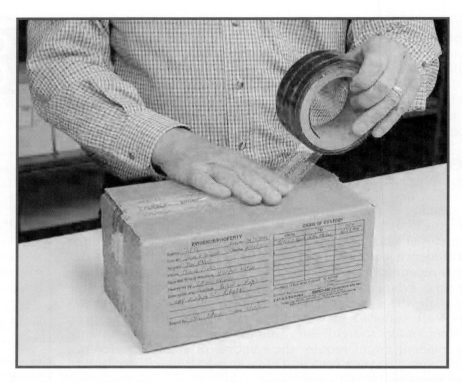

FIGURE 4-15 Evidence that has been correctly packaged and labeled can be sent through the mail. *Sirchie Finger Print Laboratories*

substrate controls

Surface material close to areas where physical evidence has been deposited.

Some types of evidence must also be accompanied by **substrate controls**. These are materials close to areas where physical evidence has been deposited. For example, an arson investigator who suspects that a surface has been exposed to an accelerant, such as gasoline, should collect a piece of the same surface material that he or she believes was *not* exposed to the accelerant. At the laboratory, forensic scientists will first test the substrate control to see whether the nature of the surface itself will interfere with the procedures used to detect and identify accelerants. Another common example of a substrate control is a material containing a bloodstain. Unstained areas close to the stain may be sampled to determine whether this material can interfere with the interpretation of laboratory results. Thorough collection and proper packaging of standard/reference specimens and substrate controls are marks of a skilled investigator.

SUBMITTING EVIDENCE

Evidence is usually submitted to the laboratory either personally or by mail. Although most evidence can be shipped by mail, postal regulations restrict the shipment of certain chemicals and live ammunition and prohibit the mailing of explosives. In such situations, one should consult the laboratory to determine the disposition of these substances. One must also exercise care when packaging evidence in order to prevent breakage or other accidental destruction during transit to the laboratory (see Figure 4-15). If the evidence is delivered personally, the deliverer should be familiar with the case to facilitate any discussions with laboratory personnel concerning specific aspects of the case.

Most laboratories require that an evidence-submission form accompany all submitted evidence (see Figure 4-16). The information on this form enables the laboratory analyst to make an intelligent and complete examination of the

CRIME:					COUNTY OF:		
Homicide; Aggravated Sexual Assault					Mercer		

VICTIM:	Age	Sex	Race	SUSPECT:	Age	Sex	Race
Jane Doe (v)	25	F	C	John Doe(s)	30	M	C

SUBMITTING AGENCY: (Address)
Trenton P.D. Central Evidence 225 N. Clinton Avenue, Trenton, N.J. 08609

FORWARD REPLIES TO:	(Name)	(Address)	Telephone Number:
Capt. John Smith, Chief of Detectives	Same as above		609 555-5555

INVESTIGATED BY:	DELIVERED BY: (Signature of Person Delivering Evidence)
Detective John Jones	

BRIEF HISTORY OF CASE: (Include Date and Location, if Applicable)
On March 1st, 2001 the victim was found dead in her bedroom. Victim was partially clothed and autopsy revealed that victim was stabbed numerous times and medical examiner stated that there was evidence of sexual assault. Victim was last seen drinking with suspect at a local tavern. Suspect was arrested and item # 23, a folding knife, was found in his pocket.

* Note* Suspect is HIV+

EXAMINATION REQUESTED ON SPECIMENS LISTED BELOW:

Examine items 2, 5, 8-11, 13-15, 18 and 19 for seminal material and compare to controls #'s 12 and 26. Examine #1, 2, 4, 7, 13, 14, 15, 18, 20, 21, 22 and 23 for trace evidence transfer. Examine #3 for saliva from suspect. Examine #6 for skin, blood and trace evidence. Examine #'s 20-23 for transfer blood evidence and compare to control #'s 12 and 26.

Item #	* Code	LIST OF SPECIMENS *SOURCE OF EVIDENCE CODE (V-Victim, S-Suspect, SC-Scene)
1	V	Debris collection
2	V	Clothing, white panties
3	V	Dried Secretions/bite marks
4	V	Head Hair Combings
5	V	Oral Specimens
6	V	Fingernail Specimens
7	V	Pubic Hair Combings
8	V	External Genital Specimen
9	V	Vaginal Specimens
10	V	Cervical Specimens

(LABORATORY USE ONLY)
DRUG ☐
TRACE ☐
BIO/CHEM ☐
TOX ☐
ABC ☐
EQUINE ☐
BALLISTICS ☐

FOR ADDITIONAL INFORMATION USE FORM 631A AND ATTACH

Page 1 of 2 pages

FIGURE 4-16   An example of a properly completed evidence-submission form. *Sirchie Finger Print Laboratories*

evidence. Providing a brief description of the case history is particularly important. This information allows the examiner to analyze the specimens in a logical sequence and make the proper comparisons; it also facilitates the search for trace quantities of evidence.

The submission form should specify the particular kind of examination requested for each type of evidence. However, the analyst is not bound to adhere strictly to the specific tests requested by the investigator. The discovery of new evidence may dictate changes in the tests required, or the analyst may find the initial requests incomplete or not totally relevant to the case. Items submitted for examination should be packaged separately and each item should be assigned a number or letter. The evidence-submission form should list the items and their identifying numbers or letters in an orderly and logical sequence.

Once evidence is received, it will undergo the requested tests and examinations. When a piece of evidence has been fully examined and tested, it must be submitted to long-term storage. The storage area and containers should be secure to prevent tampering and maintain the chain of custody.

Quick Review

- Physical evidence includes any and all objects that can establish that a crime has been committed or can link the crime and its victim or perpetrator.
- Many items of evidence may be detected only through examination of crime-scene materials at the crime laboratory. For this reason, it is important to collect possible carriers of trace evidence, such as clothing, vacuum sweepings, and fingernail scrapings, in addition to more discernable items.
- Each item of physical evidence collected at a crime scene must be placed in a separate, appropriate container to prevent damage through contact and cross-contamination.
- Investigators must maintain the chain of custody, a record for denoting the location of the evidence.
- Proper standard/reference samples must be collected at the crime scene and from appropriate subjects for comparison purposes in the laboratory. Substrate controls must also be collected.
- Typically, an evidence-submission form accompanies all evidence submitted to the crime laboratory. The form lists each item submitted for examination.

Ensuring Crime-Scene Safety*

Safety is one of the most important responsibilities of an employee because it can affect one's personal health. The employer can implement rules and regulations; educate employees about the standard operating procedures, also known as SOPs; and supply the proper equipment and resources, but it is the responsibility of the employee to enforce these safety standards in the field. Standard operating procedures should be reviewed annually by all crime-scene employees, and the agency should retain a record of reviews, which documents the date at which each employee reviewed the standard operating procedures. Updates of current crime-scene safety regulations and education should be provided annually by a designated crime-scene safety coordinator. Health inspections should also be included in the job requirements of personnel who operate certain safety equipment used at the crime scenes. For example, before an employee can wear a respirator at crime scenes, a physical health examination is required, and a proper fit must be ensured.

PERSONAL PROTECTIVE EQUIPMENT (PPE)

RESPIRATORY PROTECTION   Respiratory protection is one of the most important types of personal protective equipment (PPE). Respiratory protection can range from a disposable filter mask to a self-contained breathing apparatus,

*This section was contributed by and is used with the permission of Jan Johnson, Forensic Specialist; Certified IAI CSCSA; Retired State of Florida; Forensic Pieces, Inc., and Natalie M. Borgan, MS; Certified IAI CCSI; Crime Scene Technician, Coral Gables Police Department.

also known as SCBA. Every crime-scene unit should have a training program that teaches employees about the different types of respiratory protection so they will be able to choose the mask that is most appropriate for each crime scene. The most important thing to remember when using a mask is to make sure it is properly sealed, which is the perfect fit. A proper seal between the face and the respiratory mask prevents any chemicals or irritants from entering.

Crime-scene technicians or investigators should know the differences between the respiratory protections available for use at different crime-scene environments. Dust particle masks or N-95 masks are used for routine crime scenes. They are considered the most common type of respiratory protection. These masks are considered to be disposable and should be discarded after one use. The half-face cartridge respirator can be a disposable model with a mechanical filter or a reusable model with disposable filters. It is called a "half-face cartridge respirator" because it protects only the bottom half of the face, including the mouth and nose. A power-assisted air-purifying respirator is a positive-pressure system, which means that the air on the inside of the mask is at a higher pressure than the outside air pressure. This type of respirator allows the wearer to control the air that passes through the respirator to reduce or increase the amount of air that is filtered. Full-face respirators cover the entire face to protect the face and eyes from contaminants while filtering the air. This type of mask works well to filter contaminants, such as chemicals, dust, and spores, from the air the wearer breathes. First responders and firefighters especially benefit from these masks because they are in contact with hazardous chemicals on a daily basis.

A self-contained breathing apparatus has a tank, a regulator, and inhalation piece. If someone is claustrophobic, he or she would have a problem utilizing one of these respirators. Not all crime-scene personnel will be able to wear an SCBA. Investigators must first undergo a health screening to detect possible lung issues.

EYE PROTECTION   Eye protection is extremely important when a crime-scene worker is processing a crime scene where contaminants or chemicals could get into his or her eyes. The crime-scene technician must wear goggles even if he or she is wearing prescription glasses or contacts; glasses or contacts do not replace proper eye protection. If your eye comes into contact with a chemical, rinse your eye with water for a minimum of 15 minutes. Chemical goggles are the best type of goggles. Face shields are also considered eye protection, and goggles must be worn with them. If any type of laser is being used at the crime scene, workers should wear the appropriate eye protection.

CHEMICAL PROTECTIVE CLOTHING   Tyvek protective clothing is inexpensive, chemical resistant, and disposable. Tyvek is difficult to tear but easy to cut. In extreme temperatures, Tyvek should not be worn for longer than 15 minutes at a time: Because the material traps heat, the wearer must take a break from the Tyvek to allow his or her body to readjust to the ambient temperature. If the rest period is not provided, heat stroke and possible death may occur. Nomex brand protective clothing is fire retardant but not fireproof; it can only resist flames of up to approximately 220 degrees Celsius. Neoprene protective clothing has good chemical stability and is chemical resistant and waterproof. It is widely used and inexpensive. Butyl rubber is a synthetic rubber that is a harder and less porous material than natural rubber, and, although it is expensive, it is used in boots, aprons, and gloves. Saranex material is chemical resistant and disposable. However, workers need to be careful in hot conditions because heat stress can quickly become a serious problem when wearing this material.

Hand protection helps the crime-scene worker to avoid destroying and/ or contaminating evidence while protecting him or her from safety hazards. Gloves are essential when processing crime scenes. However, a crime-scene technician or investigator needs to know the different types of gloves available and, after assessing the situation, which will be the best for processing the scene. Gloves should be changed on a frequent basis during crime-scene processing, especially when a glove has become soiled or, to avoid cross-contamination, when the investigator is about to collect a different piece of evidence. Because gloves degrade over time, when gloves are purchased, the box should be dated and the box with the oldest date should be used up first. Gloves will also degrade in extreme temperatures.

Polyvinyl gloves are thin, clear gloves that don't provide any protection against chemicals or acids. These gloves are fine for processing crime scenes with black powder and biological fluids. Latex gloves are especially good for processing scenes with black powder and biological fluids. Because this type of glove is thin, gloves must be discarded after a single use. Latex is a relatively weak material, and the wearer must be alert for any pinholes, which can undermine the integrity of the glove. It is not a bad idea to "double glove" when using latex gloves, but this will not resolve the pinhole problem. There are individuals who are latex sensitive and therefore need to use a different type of glove to avoid an allergic reaction. Allergic reactions should be taken seriously; they can result in serious injury or even be fatal. Even exposure to another crime-scene investigator who is wearing latex can cause an allergic response in those allergic to latex.

Nitrile gloves are better than latex gloves and provide more protection. These gloves are inexpensive and resistant to some chemicals. Neoprene gloves are chemical resistant and must be worn when processing scenes with chemicals, such as acids and alcohol. At the crime scene, gloves should be changed often, and all contaminated protective gear should be removed and disposed of in biohazard bags.

By wearing shoe covers, the investigator will avoid creating new foot tracks at the crime scene. It should be a standard rule for investigators responding to crime scenes with a substantial amount of blood or biological fluids to wear foot protection, such as shoe covers or booties. The different types of foot protection include disposable Tyvek shoe covers with vinyl soles, disposable Tyvek high-top boots with vinyl soles, and disposable rubber shoe covers. Tyvek shoe covers are made to be strong and tear resistant. However, rubber shoe covers would be necessary at chemical crime scenes, such as clandestine labs. The benefits of rubber shoe covers are that they won't conduct electricity and are excellent to wear in wet environments. Alternatively, an investigator or technician can purchase and wear inexpensive new shoes and dispose of the contaminated shoes after processing the crime scene.

An investigator may expose children and pets to diseases by walking in biological fluids at a crime scene and then walking around in his or her residence with the same contaminated shoes. A crime-scene worker must have personal rules such as always leaving work shoes at the front door of his or her residence. If you set personal rules from the beginning, you can prevent contaminates from coming home with you. All nondisposable items such as lab coats, towels, and personal clothing that may be contaminated with potentially infectious material should be placed in a yellow plastic bag labeled "Infectious Linen" and laundered, at the expense of the employer, by a qualified laundry service. Personal clothing that may have been contaminated should never be taken home for cleaning. If a qualified laundry service for "Infectious Linen" is *not* available to the agency, these nondisposable items should be placed in a red plastic bag and labeled "Biohazard Material." These items will need to be destroyed because they may contain infectious material.

BIOLOGICAL HAZARDS

UNIVERSAL PRECAUTIONS AND BLOOD-BORNE PATHOGENS It is extremely important for every crime-scene technician to comprehend and apply the Universal Precaution Rule, which states that when an individual responds to a crime scene that has blood or tissue, he or she must assume the blood or tissue sample is infected and treat the sample as if it contains an infectious disease such as hepatitis B, hepatitis C, human immunodeficiency virus (HIV), or any number of other infectious agents. Make sure you wear your appropriate PPE, such as a mask and gloves, when working at a bloody crime scene or one involving biological fluids or tissue.

In general, all of the infectious viruses (hepatitis B, hepatitis C, and HIV) are composed of either DNA or RNA viruses that have the ability to infect humans by a number of different exposure routes. Whether the exposure is by an accidental stick from a needle or knife or broken glass or some other hazard at the crime scene or the laboratory, there is the possibility of acquiring an infection. Even indirect exposures caused by sloppy techniques such as talking on a cell phone while working in the hot zone may introduce the virus to the mucus membranes of your mouth or eyes. To prevent possible health hazards, a clean mask and gloves should be worn in the event a cell phone must be used at the scene.

It is not uncommon for both hepatic viruses to be present in a contaminating source, along with the HIV virus. There are numerous stages and clinical presentations that an individual with hepatitis can exhibit, and the ultimate outcome of hepatitis is quite variable and beyond the scope of this chapter. It is important to remember that the best treatment regarding exposure to blood-borne pathogens is prevention. Every crime scene technician should be vaccinated for hepatitis to avoid contracting these diseases in the event of an accidental exposure. The hepatitis immunization consists of three shots over a nine- to twelve-month period and should be effective for fifteen to twenty years.

In general, not every exposure to infected blood or bodily fluid will result in your acquiring an infection and the disease. Numerous factors, including the viral load of the infected material or fluid, the promptness and thoroughness of cleaning the site of the exposure (cuts or scrapes or splashes), the route of exposure, and the immune system of the exposed individual, all play a vital role in whether or not one will become infected.

If a piece of physical evidence is wet from blood, place the piece of evidence in a paper bag—even consider double-bagging the item with two brown paper bags to keep the outside bag free of contamination—and then place it in a red biohazard bag for transportation to the crime lab. Then, you can use the appropriate drying cabinet to let your evidence air dry before putting it in the property room. Remember to place a piece of butcher paper on the bottom of the drying cabinet in case any evidence falls off the item onto the butcher paper during the drying process. The original paper bag and the butcher paper should be kept and stored for possible analysis. After the contaminated bloody evidence has completely dried, use butcher paper to fold the item to avoid creating new patterns on the item, then place it in a new paper bag. Always remember to place a red biohazard sticker both on the final, secured evidence bag and the property receipt to ensure all handlers will know the item is contaminated with biological fluids.

DIFFERENT TYPES OF EXPOSURE AT CRIME SCENES

When an investigator responds to a crime scene, there are several different ways in which he or she can be exposed to toxins. If crime-scene personnel are trained and educated to identify these means of exposure, they can protect themselves with the proper personal protection equipment. Among the contaminants that can be present at a crime scene are various chemicals, gas, fumes, dust, and powders, and the only way to avoid exposure is by using the proper PPE.

ABSORPTION Absorption occurs when contaminants make contact with skin or absorb through mucus membrane areas, such as nostrils, mouth, and eyes. Also, contaminants can absorb readily through an unprotected cut on the skin, which is an easy point of entry. If contaminants come into contact with your eyes, rinse your eyes with water for a minimum of 15 minutes. Portable eyewash stations should be part of the crime-scene safety equipment.

INGESTION Ingestion occurs when contaminants enter the body through the mouth. An individual must be careful when considering drinking or eating at a crime scene to prevent ingestion of chemicals. The "cold zone," a work area described in detail in the following section, should be the only area within the crime scene where drinking and eating take place. Chewing gum is another way to ingest such toxins at the crime scene and should be considered taboo.

INHALATION Inhalation occurs when contaminants enter the body through the respiratory system. When an investigator or technician responds to a crime scene, he or she must assess the scene to determine which respiratory mask will offer the best protection from the contaminants present.

INJECTION An injection can enter the body in the form of a needle or sharp object. When working with needles or sharp objects, such as pieces of glass, an individual should wear proper gloves for protection and use special care to prevent being poked by sharp objects. Crime-scene personnel should take their time to be safe when processing all sharp objects, especially needles. They must also be mindful of how they package such objects for others who will receive the evidence and may not know of the inherent risks of handling it.

WORK ZONES

The "hot zone" is the active crime-scene area, which means contaminates and probable evidence exist in this region. In the hot zone, all crime-scene technicians should be suited up with PPE, such as masks, foot protection, eye protection, and gloves. There should be no food or drinks allowed in the hot zone. Also, the employees who are actively working the crime scene should be the only ones allowed in this area. The "warm zone" is the transition area between the cold and hot zones. This is the area where the crime-scene technicians will suit up with their PPE, and it is the staging area for the equipment. After the crime-scene processing is complete, the warm zone should also be the decontamination area used to prevent spreading any contamination. When potentially infectious materials are present at a crime scene, personnel should maintain a red biohazard plastic bag for the disposal of contaminated gloves, clothing, masks, pencils, wrapping paper, and so on. On departure from the scene, the biohazard bag must be taped shut and transported to an approved biohazardous waste pickup site. The "cold zone" is the safe area for all personnel who were not actively processing the scene. The first officer on the scene should be using this area to write down the names of the individuals entering and exiting the actual crime scene, or hot zone. The cold zone is also the area where employees can take breaks, eat, and drink. Every crime-scene technician should understand the importance of establishing and maintaining these separate work zones in scenes where contaminants are present. When traveling from the hot zone to the cold zone, decontaminating in the warm zone is essential.

Not every crime scene requires that work zones be established for safety. Simple cases such as burglaries and car thefts do not require zone assignments. Obviously, homicides and other crime scenes that contain bodily fluids and/or contaminants do require the establishment of work zones. The normal precautions of wearing gloves and masks and the like are more than sufficient for low-risk crime scenes. When responding to crime scenes that are contaminated, personnel need to know which zones are active, such as hot zone, warm zone, and cold zone, and therefore these zones need to be clearly delineated by the investigator so that personnel do not cross them in an unprotected state.

Quick Review

- Updates of current crime-scene safety regulations and education should be made annually by a designated crime-scene safety coordinator. Health inspections should also be included in the job requirements of personnel who operate certain safety equipment used at the crime scenes.
- Law enforcement officers and crime-scene technicians at a crime scene must use caution and protect themselves at all times from contracting AIDS or hepatitis. Bodily fluids must always be treated as though they were infectious.
- Crime-scene technicians most often use dust particle masks or N-95 masks at routine crime scenes. They are considered the most common type of respiratory protection. These masks are considered to be disposable and should be discarded after one use.
- It is recommended that personnel always wear doubled-up latex gloves and possibly wear chemical-resistant clothing, Tyvek-type shoe covers, a particle mask/respirator, goggles, and possibly face shields when potentially infectious material is present. Gloves should be changed often while processing the scene.
- When processing and collecting evidence at a crime scene, personnel should be alert to sharp objects, knives, hypodermic syringes, razor blades, and similar items.
- Eating, drinking, smoking, and chewing gum are prohibited at the immediate crime scene.
- The hot zone is the active crime-scene area, which means contaminates and probable evidence exist in this region. In the hot zone, all crime-scene technicians or investigators should be suited up with personal protection equipment, also known as PPE, such as masks, foot protection, eye protection, and gloves. No food or drinks should be allowed in the hot zone.

Legal Considerations at the Crime Scene

In police work, there is perhaps no experience more exasperating or demoralizing than to watch valuable evidence excluded from use against the accused because of legal considerations. This situation most often arises from what is deemed an "unreasonable" search and seizure of evidence. Therefore, the removal of any evidence from a person or from the scene of a crime must be done in conformity with the Fourth Amendment: "The right of the people to be secure in their persons, houses, papers, and effects, against unreasonable searches and seizures, shall not be violated, and no warrants shall issue, but upon probable cause, supported by oath or affirmation, and particularly describing the place to be searched, and the persons or things to be seized."

Since the 1960s, the Supreme Court of the United States has been particularly concerned with defining the circumstances under which the police can search for evidence in the absence of a court-approved search warrant. The Court has made a number of allowances to justify a warrantless search: (1) the existence of emergency circumstances, (2) the need to prevent the immediate loss or destruction of evidence, (3) a search of a person and property within the immediate control of the person provided it is made incident to a lawful arrest, and (4) a search made by consent of the parties involved. In cases other than these, police must be particularly cautious about processing a crime scene without a search warrant. In 1978, the Supreme Court addressed this very issue, and in doing so it set forth guidelines for investigators to follow in determining the propriety of conducting a warrantless search at a crime scene. Significantly, the two cases decided on this issue related to homicide and arson crime scenes, both of which are normally subjected to the most intensive forms of physical evidence searches by police.

In the case of *Mincey* v. *Arizona*,[1] the Court dealt with the legality of a four-day search at a homicide scene. The case involved a police raid on the home of Rufus Mincey, who had been suspected of dealing drugs. Under the pretext of buying drugs, an undercover police officer forced entry into Mincey's apartment and was killed in the scuffle that ensued. Without a search warrant, the police spent four days searching the apartment, recovering, among other things, bullets, drugs, and drug paraphernalia. These items were subsequently introduced as evidence at the trial. Mincey was convicted and on appeal contended that the evidence gathered from his apartment, without a warrant and without his consent, was illegally seized. The Court unanimously upheld Mincey's position, stating:

> We do not question the right of the police to respond to emergency situations. Numerous state and federal cases have recognized that the Fourth Amendment does not bar police officers from making warrantless entries and searches when they reasonably believe that a person within is in need of immediate aid. Similarly, when the police come upon the scene of a homicide they may make a prompt warrantless search of the area to see if there are other victims or if a killer is still on the premises. . . . Except for the fact that the offense under investigation was a homicide, there were no exigent circumstances in this case. . . . There was no indication that evidence would be lost, destroyed or removed during the time required to obtain a search warrant. Indeed, the police guard at the apartment minimized that possibility. And there is no suggestion that a search warrant could not easily and conveniently have been obtained. We decline to hold that the seriousness of the offense under investigation itself creates exigent circumstances of the kind that under the Fourth Amendment justify a warrantless search.

In *Michigan* v. *Tyler*,[2] fire destroyed a business establishment leased by Loren Tyler and a business partner. The fire was finally extinguished in the early hours of the morning; smoke, steam, and darkness, however, prevented fire and police officials from thoroughly examining the scene for evidence of arson. Officials then left the building unattended until 8:00 a.m., when they returned and began an inspection of the burned premises. During the morning, searchers recovered and removed assorted items of evidence from the building. On three other occasions—four days, seven days, and twenty-five days after the fire—investigators reentered the premises and removed additional items of evidence with neither a warrant nor consent. The evidence seized was used to convict Tyler and his partner of conspiracy to burn real property and related offenses. The Supreme Court upheld the reversal of the conviction, holding that the initial morning search had been proper but contending that evidence obtained from subsequent reentries to the scene was inadmissible: "We hold that an entry to fight a fire requires no warrant, and that once in the building, officials may remain there for a reasonable time to investigate the cause of a blaze. Thereafter, additional entries to investigate the cause of the fire must be made pursuant to the warrant procedures."

The message from the Supreme Court is clear: When time and circumstances permit, obtain a search warrant before investigating and retrieving physical evidence at the crime scene.

Quick Review

- The removal of any evidence from a person or from the scene of a crime must be in accordance with proper search and seizure procedure.
- Warrantless searches are allowed in situations including (1) the existence of emergency circumstances, (2) the need to prevent the immediate loss or destruction of evidence, (3) a search of a person and property within the immediate control of the person provided it is made incident to a lawful arrest, and (4) a search made with the consent of the parties involved.

CHAPTER REVIEW

- Biological crime-scene evidence includes blood, saliva, semen, DNA, hair, organs, and physiological fluids.

- Impression crime-scene evidence includes tire markings, shoe prints, depressions in soft soils, all other forms of tracks, glove and other fabric impressions, tool marks, and bite marks.

- Manufactured items considered common items of crime-scene evidence include firearms, ammunition, fibers, paint, glass, petroleum products, plastic bags, rubber, polymers, and vehicle headlights.

- Physical evidence includes any and all objects that can establish that a crime has been committed or can link the crime and its victim or perpetrator.

- Many items of evidence may be detected only through examination of crime-scene materials at the crime laboratory. For this reason, it is important to collect possible carriers of trace evidence, such as clothing, vacuum sweepings, and fingernail scrapings, in addition to more discernable items.

- Each item of physical evidence collected at a crime scene must be placed in a separate, appropriate container to prevent damage through contact and cross-contamination.

- Investigators must maintain the chain of custody, a record for denoting the location of the evidence.

- Proper standard/reference samples must be collected at the crime scene and from appropriate subjects for comparison purposes in the laboratory. Substrate controls must also be collected.

- Typically, an evidence-submission form accompanies all evidence submitted to the crime laboratory. The form lists each item submitted for examination.

- Updates of current crime-scene safety regulations and education should be made annually by a designated crime-scene safety coordinator. Health inspections should also be included in the job requirements of personnel who operate certain safety equipment used at the crime scenes.

- Law enforcement officers and crime-scene technicians must use caution and protect themselves at all times from contracting AIDS or hepatitis. Bodily fluids must always be treated as though they were infectious.

- Crime-scene technicians most often use dust particle masks or N-95 masks at routine crime scenes. They are considered the most common type of respiratory protection. These masks are considered to be disposable and should be discarded after one use.

- It is recommended that personnel always wear doubled-up latex gloves and possibly wear chemical-resistant clothing, Tyvek-type shoe covers, a particle mask/respirator, goggles, and possibly face shields when potentially infectious material is present. Gloves should be changed often while processing the scene.

- When processing and collecting evidence at a crime scene, personnel should be alert to sharp objects, knives, hypodermic syringes, razor blades, and similar items.

- Eating, drinking, smoking, and chewing gum are prohibited at the immediate crime scene.
- The hot zone is the active crime-scene area, which means contaminates and probable evidence exist in this region. In the hot zone, all crime-scene technicians or investigators should be suited up with personal protection equipment, also known as PPE, such as masks, foot protection, eye protection, and gloves. No food or drinks should be allowed in the hot zone.
- The removal of any evidence from a person or from the scene of a crime must be in accordance with the proper search and seizure procedure.
- Warrantless searches are allowed in situations including (1) the existence of emergency circumstances, (2) the need to prevent the immediate loss or destruction of evidence, (3) a search of a person and property within the immediate control of the person provided it is made incident to a lawful arrest, and (4) a search made with the consent of the parties involved.

KEY TERMS

buccal swab, 91

chain of custody, 89

contamination, 86

physical evidence, 84

standard/reference sample, 91

substrate control, 92

REVIEW QUESTIONS

1. The term _____ encompasses all objects that can establish whether a crime has been committed or can link a crime and its victim or perpetrator.

2. True or False: The well-prepared evidence collector arrives at a crime scene with a large assortment of packaging materials and tools ready to encounter any type of situation. _____

3. The _____ purchased by some police departments for evidence collection carry the necessary supplies to protect the crime scene; photograph, collect, and package physical evidence; and perform latent-print development.

4. Because some items of evidence may be detected only through examination of crime-scene materials in the crime laboratory, it is important to collect all potential _____ of physical evidence.

5. True or False: Critical areas of the crime scene should be vacuumed and the sweepings submitted to the laboratory for analysis. _____

6. An individual may have hand contact with the skin of another individual during the commission of a crime, so _____ scrapings should be collected because they may contain minute fragments of evidence capable of providing a link between assailant and victim.

7. True or False: The problems of contamination can often be avoided through the use of latex gloves or disposable forceps when touching evidence. _____

8. True or False: Whenever possible, trace evidence is to be removed from the object that bears it. _____

9. Each item collected at the crime scene must be placed in a(n) _____ container.

10. True or False: Unbreakable plastic pill bottles, manila envelopes, screw-cap glass vials, sealable plastic bags, and metal pillboxes with pressure lids are excellent containers for blood or arson evidence. _____

11. True or False: An ordinary mailing envelope is considered a good general-purpose evidence container. _____

12. True or False: Charred debris recovered from the scene of an arson is best placed in a porous container. _____

13. Small amounts of trace evidence can also be conveniently packaged in a(n) _____, a carefully folded paper packet.

14. Only _____ tools should be used to collect biological materials for packaging.

15. Packaging material for biological evidence, including blood-stained evidence, should be made of _____ to ensure a constant circulation of air through them.

16. _____ of DNA-containing evidence can easily occur by coughing or sneezing onto a stain during the collection process or by contact caused by improper packaging.

17. As a matter of routine, all moist biological stains are to be _____ before packaging.

18. The possibility of future legal proceedings requires that a(n) _____ be established with respect to the possession and location of all physical evidence.

19. True or False: The investigator who packaged the evidence must write his or her initials and the date on the evidence tape seal, and the evidence should be opened at a different location on the packaging for further testing. _____

20. Most physical evidence collected at the crime site will require the accompanying submission of _____ material for comparison purposes.

21. Blood evidence should be accompanied by known controls in the form of whole blood or _____ from victims or suspects.

22. Uncontaminated areas close to where bloodstains were deposited are called _____ and should be collected from the crime scene.

23. True or False: Evidence is usually submitted to the laboratory either personally or by mail depending on the distance the submitting agency must travel to the laboratory and the urgency of the case. _____

24. A(n) _____ form accompanies all evidence submitted to the laboratory and delineates the examination requested for each item of evidence.

25. Although the chance of law enforcement officers contracting AIDS or hepatitis at the crime scene is low, bodily fluids must always be treated as though they are _____.

26. At the crime scene, latex gloves should be changed often, and all contaminated protective gear should be removed and disposed of in _____ bags.

27. True or False: The removal of any evidence from a person must be done in accordance with the proper search and seizure procedure, but it is not required for removal of crime-scene evidence. _____

28. In the case of *Mincey* v. *Arizona*, the Supreme Court restricted the practice of conducting a(n) _____ search at a homicide scene.

29. In the case of *Michigan* v. *Tyler*, the Supreme Court dealt with search and seizure procedures at a(n) _____ scene.

APPLICATION AND CRITICAL THINKING

1. Officer Martin Guajardo is the first responder at an apparent homicide scene. After securing the area, interviewing the sole witness, and calling for backup, he begins to search for evidence. He makes note of a bloody knife lying next to the body. A small scrap of bloody cloth is clinging precariously to the knife. Because it is a very windy day, Officer Guajardo removes the scrap of fabric and seals it in a plastic bag. A few moments later, the crime-scene team, including a photographer, arrives to take over the investigation. What mistakes, if any, did Officer Guajardo make prior to the arrival of the crime-scene team?

2. During his search of a homicide scene, Investigator David Gurney collects evidence that includes a bloody shirt. After the crime-scene team has completely processed the scene, Investigator Gurney packages the shirt in a paper bag, seals the bag, and labels it to indicate the contents. He then delivers the shirt to the laboratory with an evidence-submission form. There, a forensic scientist breaks the seal, removes the shirt, and performs a series of tests on it. He replaces the shirt, discards the old seal, and places a new seal on the package containing his initials and the date on which it was resealed. What mistakes, if any, were made in handling the shirt?

ENDNOTES

1. 437 U.S. 385 (1978).

2. 436 U.S. 499 (1978).

Physical Evidence

LEARNING OBJECTIVES

After studying this chapter, you should be able to:

- Explain the difference between the identification and comparison of physical evidence.
- Define and contrast individual and class characteristics of physical evidence.
- Appreciate the value of class evidence as it relates to a criminal investigation.
- List and explain the function of national databases available to forensic scientists.

THE GRIM SLEEPER

The killing spree began in 1985 in Los Angeles, California, and apparently ended in 1988. All but one of the serial killer's eight victims were black females. Many of his victims were prostitutes with whom he would have sexual contact before strangling or shooting them. In 2002, the killing resumed. The attacker was dubbed the "Grim Sleeper" because he appeared to have taken a fourteen-year hiatus from his crimes. By 2007, three more females were added to his list of victims. What proved particularly frustrating to investigators was that, even though this killer left behind DNA evidence at many of his crime scenes, a search of the DNA databases proved fruitless in establishing an identification. If the killer had been convicted of criminal activities in the past, they never resulted in the collection of his DNA and its placement in the California database. Finally, in 2010, police arrested and identified Lonnie David Franklin, Jr. as the Grim Sleeper. The arrest of Franklin came about through a familial DNA search, which trolls through the DNA database looking for partial DNA matches that could be linked to a close relative in the file. One prisoner—Franklin's son Christopher—shared a strong familial pattern with the serial killer. Investigators used DNA collected off a discarded pizza crust eaten by Lonnie Franklin to link his DNA to the Grim Sleeper's victims.

Examination of Physical Evidence

Physical evidence is usually examined by a forensic scientist for identification or comparison.

IDENTIFICATION

The purpose of **identification** is to determine the physical or chemical identity of a substance with the most certainty that existing analytical techniques will permit. For example, the crime laboratory is frequently asked to identify the chemical composition of preparations that may contain illicit drugs such as heroin, cocaine, or barbiturates. It may be asked to identify gasoline in residues recovered from the debris of a fire, or it may have to identify the nature of explosive residues—for example, dynamite or TNT. Also, the identification of blood, semen, hair, or wood would, as a matter of routine, include a determination of species origin. For example, did a bloodstain originate from a human or a dog or cat? Each of these requests requires the analysis and ultimate identification of a specific physical or chemical substance to the exclusion of all other possible substances.

The process of identification first requires adopting testing procedures that give characteristic results for specific standard materials. Once these test results have been established, they may be permanently recorded and used repeatedly to prove the identity of suspect materials. For example, to ascertain that a particular suspect powder is heroin, the test results on the powder must be identical to those that have been previously obtained from a known heroin sample.

Second, identification requires that the number and type of tests used to identify a substance be sufficient to exclude all other substances. This means that the examiner must devise a specific analytical scheme that will eliminate all but one substance from consideration. Hence, if the examiner concludes that a white powder contains heroin, the test results must have been comprehensive enough to have excluded all other drugs—or, for that matter, all other substances—from consideration.

Simple rules cannot be devised for defining what constitutes a thorough and foolproof analytical scheme. Obviously, each type of evidence requires a unique test, and each test has a different degree of specificity. Thus, one substance could conceivably be identified by one test, whereas another may require the combination of five or six different tests to arrive at an identification. Because the forensic scientist has little or no control over the quality and quantity of the specimens received, a standard series of tests cannot prevent all possible problems and pitfalls. So the forensic scientist must determine at what point the analysis can be concluded and when the criteria for positive identification has been satisfied; for this, he or she must rely on knowledge gained through education and experience. Ultimately, the conclusion will have to be substantiated beyond any reasonable doubt in a court of law.

COMPARISON

A **comparison** analysis subjects a suspect specimen and a standard, or reference, specimen to the same tests and examinations to ultimately determine whether they have a common origin. For example, the forensic scientist may link a suspect to a particular location by noting the similarities of a hair found at the crime scene to hairs removed from the suspect's head (see Figure 5-1). Or a paint chip found on a hit-and-run victim's garment may be compared with paint removed from a vehicle suspected of being involved in the incident.

identification
The process of determining a substance's physical or chemical identity.

comparison
The process of ascertaining whether two or more objects have a common origin.

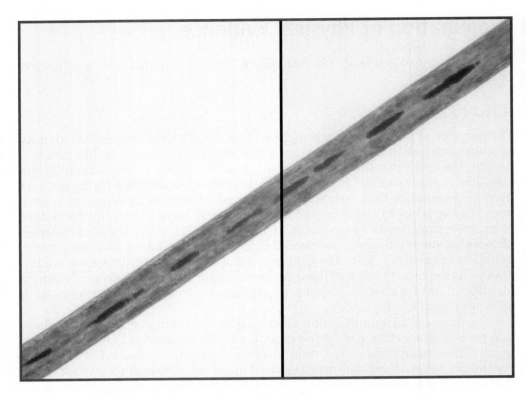

FIGURE 5-1   A side-by-side comparison of hairs. *Chris Palenik*

The forensic comparison is actually a two-step procedure. First, combinations of select properties are chosen from the suspect and the standard/reference specimen for comparison. The question of which and how many properties are selected depends on the type of materials being examined. (This subject will receive a good deal of discussion in forthcoming chapters.) The overriding consideration must be the ultimate evidential value the conclusion will have.

Once the examination has been completed, the forensic scientist must draw a conclusion about the origins of the specimens. Reaching this conclusion is the second objective. Do they come from the same source or not? Certainly, if one or more of the properties selected for comparison do not agree, the analyst will conclude that the specimens are not the same and therefore could not have originated from the same source. Suppose, on the other hand, that all the properties do compare and the specimens, as far as the examiner can determine, are indistinguishable. Does it logically follow that they came from the same source? Not necessarily.

To comprehend the evidential value of a comparison, one must appreciate the role that probability has in ascertaining the origins of two or more specimens. Simply defined, "probability" is the frequency of occurrences of an event. If a coin is flipped a hundred times, in theory we can expect heads to come up fifty times. Hence, the probability of the event (heads) occurring is fifty in one hundred. In this case, probability is the odds that a certain match will occur when two specimens are compared.

individual characteristics
Properties of evidence that can be attributed to a particular source with an extremely high degree of certainty.

INDIVIDUAL CHARACTERISTICS   Evidence that can be associated with a unique common source with an extremely high degree of probability is said to possess **individual characteristics**. Examples of such associations are the matching ridge characteristics of two fingerprints, matching random striations (markings) on bullets or tool marks, matching irregular and random

FIGURE 5-2 The body of a woman was found with evidence of a stablike wound in the neck. A pathologist found a knife blade tip in the wound in the neck. The knife blade tip was compared with the broken blade of a knife found in the trousers pocket of the accused. A close examination reveals the fit of the indentations on the edges and individual characteristics of stria from the sharpening procedure. *Center of Forensic Sciences*

wear patterns in tire or footwear impressions, consistent handwriting characteristics, the fitting together of the irregular edges of broken objects in the manner of a jigsaw puzzle (see Figure 5-2), or matching striation marks running across plastic bags that were made sequentially (see Figure 5-3).

In all of these cases, it is not possible to state with mathematical exactness the probability that the specimens are of common origin; it can be concluded only that the probability is so high as to defy mathematical calculations or human comprehension. Furthermore, the conclusion of common origin must be substantiated by the practical experience of the examiner. For example, the French scientist Victor Balthazard determined mathematically that the probability of two individuals having the same fingerprints is one out of 1×10^{60}, or 1 followed by sixty zeros. This probability is so small as to exclude the possibility of any two individuals having the same fingerprints. This contention is supported by the experience of fingerprint examiners who, after classifying millions of prints over the past hundred years, have never found any two to be exactly alike.

CLASS CHARACTERISTICS One disappointment awaiting the investigator unfamiliar with the limitations of forensic science is the frequent inability of the laboratory to relate physical evidence to a common origin with a high degree of certainty. Evidence is said to possess **class characteristics** when it can

class characteristics
Properties of evidence that can be associated only with a group and not with a single source.

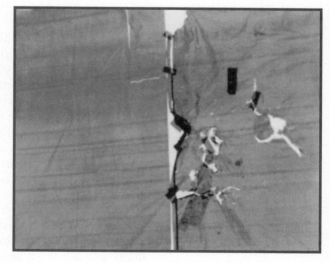

FIGURE 5-3 The bound body of a young woman was recovered from a river. Her head was covered with a black polyethylene trash bag (shown on the right). Among the items recovered from one of several suspects was another black polyethylene trash bag (shown on the left). A side-by-side comparison of the two bags' extrusion marks and pigment bands showed them to be consecutively manufactured. This information allowed investigators to focus their attention on one suspect, who ultimately was convicted of the homicide. *Richard Saferstein, Ph.D.*

be associated only with a group and not with a single source. Here again, probability is a determining factor. For example, if we compare two single-layer automobile paint chips of a similar color, their chance of originating from the same car is not nearly as great as when we compare two paint chips with seven similar layers of paint, not all of which were part of the car's original color. The former will have class characteristics and can be associated with, at the most specific, one car model (which may number in the thousands); the latter may be judged to have individual characteristics and thus has a high probability of originating from one specific car.

Blood offers another good example of evidence that can have class characteristics. For example, suppose that two blood specimens are compared and both are found to be of human origin, type A. The frequency of occurrence of type A blood in the U.S. population is approximately 26 percent—hardly a basis for establishing the common origin of the specimens. However, if other blood factors are also determined and are found to compare, the probability that the two blood specimens originated from a common source increases. Thus, if one uses a series of blood factors that occur independently of each other, then one can apply the **product rule** to calculate the overall frequency of occurrence of the blood in a population. In this case, the product rule states that multiplying together the frequency of each factor present and occurring independently in a blood sample will determine how common blood containing that combination of factors is in the general population.

For example, in the O. J. Simpson murder case, a bloodstain located at the crime scene was found to contain a number of factors that compared to O. J.'s blood:

product rule

A formula for determining how frequently a certain combination of characteristics occurs in a population. The product rule states that one must first determine the probability of each characteristic's occurring separately and independently, then multiply together the frequencies of all these independently occurring characteristics. The result is the overall frequency of occurrence for that particular combination of characteristics.

Blood Factors	Frequency
A	26%
EsD	85%
PGM 2+2−	2%

The product of all the frequencies shown in the table determines the probability that any one individual possesses such a combination of blood factors. In this instance, applying the product rule, $0.26 \times 0.85 \times 0.02$ equals 0.0044. Thus, only 0.44 percent, or less than 1 in 200 people, would be expected to have this particular combination of blood factors. These bloodstain factors did not match either of the two victims, Nicole Brown Simpson or Ronald Goldman, thus eliminating them as possible sources of the blood. Although the forensic scientist did not definitively link the bloodstains to one person (in this case, O. J. Simpson), this analysis provided data that permitted investigators and the courts to better assess the evidential value of the crime-scene stain.

As we will discuss in Chapter 15, the product rule is used to determine the frequency of occurrence of DNA profiles developed from blood and other biological materials. Importantly, modern DNA technology provides enough factors to allow an analyst to individualize blood, semen, and other biological materials to a single person.

Quick Review

- Two methods used by forensic scientists when examining physical evidence are identification and comparison.
- Identification is the process of determining a substance's chemical or physical identity to the exclusion of all other substances (e.g., drugs, explosives, petroleum products, blood, semen, and hair species).

- A comparison analysis determines whether a suspect specimen and a standard/reference specimen have a common origin.
- Evidence that can be linked to a common source with an extremely high degree of probability is said to possess individual characteristics.
- Evidence that is associated with an entire group is said to have class characteristics.
- The overall frequency of occurrence of an event, such as a match between two substances, can be determined by multiplying together the frequencies of all independently occurring instances related to that event. This is known as the product rule.

Significance of Physical Evidence

One of the current weaknesses of forensic science is the inability of the examiner to assign exact or even approximate probability values when comparing most class physical evidence. For example, what is the probability that a nylon fiber originated from a particular sweater, or that a hair came from a particular person's head, or that a paint chip came from a car suspected to have been involved in a hit-and-run accident? Very few statistical data are available from which to derive this information, and in a society that is increasingly dependent on mass-produced products, the gathering of such data is becoming an increasingly elusive goal.

One of the primary endeavors of forensic scientists must be to create and update statistical databases for evaluating the significance of class physical evidence. Of course, when such information—for example, the population frequency of blood factors—is available, it is used; but, for the most part, the forensic scientist must rely on personal experience when interpreting the significance of class physical evidence.

People who are unfamiliar with the realities of modern criminalistics are often disappointed to learn that most items of physical evidence retrieved at crime scenes cannot be linked definitively to a single person or object (Figure 5-4). Although investigators always try to uncover physical evidence with individual characteristics—such as fingerprints, tool marks, and bullets—the chances of finding class physical evidence are far greater. To deny or belittle the value of such evidence is to reject the potential role that criminalistics can play in a criminal investigation.

In practice, criminal cases are fashioned for the courtroom around a collection of diverse elements, each pointing to the guilt or involvement of a party in the criminal act. Often, most of the evidence gathered is subjective, prone to human error and bias. The believability of eyewitness accounts, confessions, and informant testimony can all be disputed, maligned, and subjected to severe attack and skepticism in the courtroom. Under these circumstances, errors in human judgment are often magnified by the defense to detract from the credibility of the witness.

FIGURE 5-4 A computer-generated image of DNA superimposed on a fingerprint, representing two of the most frequently found individualized items of evidence at crime scenes. *Alfred Pasieka/Photo Researchers, Inc.*

ASSESSING THE VALUE OF EVIDENCE

The value of class physical evidence hinges on its ability to corroborate events with data in a manner that is, as nearly as possible, free of human error and bias. It is the thread that binds together other investigative findings that are

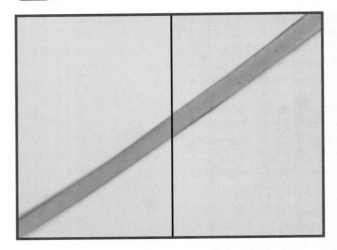

FIGURE 5-5 A side-by-side comparison of fibers. *Chris Palenik*

more dependent on human judgments and, therefore, more prone to human failings. The fact that scientists have not yet learned to individualize many kinds of physical evidence means that criminal investigators should not abdicate or falter in their pursuit of all investigative leads. However, the ability of scientists to achieve a high degree of success in evaluating class physical evidence means that criminal investigators can pursue their work with a much greater chance of success.

Again, defining the significance of an item of class evidence in exact mathematical terms is usually a difficult if not impossible goal. Although class evidence is by its very nature not unique, meaningful items of physical evidence, such as those listed at the beginning of this chapter, are extremely variable in reality. Select, for example, a colored fiber from an article of clothing and try to locate that exact color on the clothing of random individuals you meet, or select a car color and try to match it to that of other cars you see on local streets. It will be difficult to find a match. Furthermore, keep in mind that a forensic comparison goes beyond a mere color comparison and involves examining and comparing a variety of chemical and/or physical properties (see Figure 5-5). The chances are low of encountering two indistinguishable items of physical evidence at a crime scene that actually originated from different sources. Obviously, given these circumstances, only objects that exhibit significant variability are appropriate for classification as physical evidence.

In the same way, when one is dealing with more than one type of class evidence, their collective presence may lead to an extremely high certainty that they originated from the same source. As the number of objects linking an individual to a crime increases, the probability of involvement increases dramatically. A classic example of this situation can be found in the evidence presented at the trial of Wayne Williams. Williams was charged with the murders of two individuals in the Atlanta, Georgia, metropolitan area; he was also linked to the murders of ten other boys and young men. An essential element of the state's case involved the association of Williams with the victims through a variety of fiber evidence. Actually, twenty-eight types of fibers linked Williams to the murder victims, evidence that the forensic examiner characterized as "overwhelming."

CAUTIONS AND LIMITATIONS IN DEALING WITH PHYSICAL EVIDENCE

In further evaluating the contribution of physical evidence, one cannot overlook one important reality in the courtroom: The weight or significance accorded physical evidence is a determination left entirely to the "trier of fact," usually a jury of laypeople. Given the high esteem in which scientists are generally held by society and the infallible image of forensic science created by books and television, scientifically evaluated evidence often takes on an aura of special reliability and trustworthiness in the courtroom. Often, physical evidence, whether individual or class, is accorded great weight during jury deliberations and becomes a primary factor in reinforcing or overcoming lingering doubts about guilt or innocence. In fact, a number of jurists have already cautioned against giving carte blanche approval for admitting scientific testimony without first considering its relevance to the case. Given the potential weight of scientific evidence, failure to take proper safeguards may unfairly prejudice a case against the accused.

Physical evidence may serve also to exclude or exonerate a person from suspicion. For instance, if type A blood is linked to the suspect, all individuals who have types B, AB, and O blood can be eliminated from consideration. Because it is not possible to assess at the crime scene what value, if any, the scientist will find in the evidence collected or what significance such findings will ultimately have to a jury, the thorough collection and scientific evaluation of physical evidence must become a routine part of all criminal investigations.

Just when an item of physical evidence crosses the line that distinguishes class from individual is difficult to determine and is often the source of heated debate and honest disagreement among forensic scientists. How many striations are necessary to individualize a mark to a single tool and no other? How many color layers individualize a paint chip to a single car? How many ridge characteristics individualize a fingerprint, and how many handwriting characteristics tie a person to a signature? These questions defy simple answers. The task of the forensic scientist is to find as many characteristics as possible to compare one substance with another. The significance attached to the findings is decided by the quality and composition of the evidence, the case history, and the examiner's experience. Ultimately, the conclusion can range from mere speculation to near certainty.

There are practical limits to the properties and characteristics the forensic scientist can select for comparison. Carried to the extreme, no two things in this world are alike in every detail. Modern analytical techniques have become so sophisticated and sensitive that the criminalist must define the limits of natural variation among materials when interpreting the data gathered from a comparative analysis. For example, we will learn in Chapter 14 that two properties, density and refractive index, are best suited for comparing two pieces of glass. But the latest techniques that have been developed to measure these properties are so sensitive that they can even distinguish glass originating from a single pane of glass. Certainly this goes beyond the desires of a criminalist trying to determine only whether two glass particles originated from the same window. Similarly, if the surface of a paint chip is magnified 1,600 times with a powerful scanning electron microscope, fine details are revealed that could not be duplicated in any other paint chip from the very same painted surface. Under these circumstances, no two paint chips, even those coming from the same surface, could ever compare in the truest sense of the word. Therefore, practicality dictates that such examinations be conducted at a less revealing, but more meaningful, magnification (see Figure 5-6).

Distinguishing evidential variations from natural variations is not always an easy task. Learning how to use the microscope and all the other modern instruments in a crime laboratory properly is one thing; gaining the proficiency needed to interpret the observations and data is another. As new crime laboratories are created and others expand to meet the requirements of the law enforcement community, many individuals are starting new careers in forensic science. They must be cautioned that merely reading relevant textbooks and journals is no substitute for experience in this most practical of sciences.

Quick Review

- The value of class physical evidence lies in its ability to corroborate events with data in a manner that is, as nearly as possible, free of human error and bias.
- As the number of objects linking an individual to a crime scene increases, so does the likelihood of that individual's involvement with the crime.
- A person may be exonerated or excluded from suspicion if physical evidence collected at a crime scene is found to be different from standard/reference samples collected from that subject.

(a)

(b)

FIGURE 5-6   (a) A two-layer paint chip magnified 244 times with a scanning electron microscope. (b) The same paint chip viewed at a magnification of 1,600 times. *Richard Saferstein, Ph.D.*

Forensic Databases

In a criminal investigation, the ultimate contribution a criminalist can make is to link a suspect to a crime through comparative analysis. This comparison defines the unique role of the criminalist in a criminal investigation. Of course, a one-on-one comparison requires a suspect. Little or nothing of evidential value can be accomplished if crime-scene investigators acquire fingerprints, hairs, fibers, paint, blood, and semen without the ability to link these items to a suspect. In this respect, computer technology has dramatically altered the role of the crime laboratory in the investigative process.

No longer is the crime laboratory a passive bystander waiting for investigators to uncover clues about who may have committed a crime. Today, the crime laboratory is on the forefront of the investigation seeking to identify perpetrators. This dramatic enhancement of the role of forensic science in criminal investigation has come about with the creation of computerized databases that not only link data from all fifty states but also tie together data from police agencies throughout the world.

FINGERPRINT DATABASES

The premier model of all forensic database systems is the Integrated Automated Fingerprint Identification System (IAFIS), a national fingerprint and criminal history system maintained by the FBI and launched in 1999. IAFIS contains the fingerprints and corresponding criminal history information of nearly 75 million subjects (i.e., 750 million fingerprint images), which are submitted voluntarily to the FBI by state, local, and federal law enforcement agencies.

FIGURE 5-7   A forensic scientist using the IAFIS database. *Ulrich Baumgarten/Getty Images*

A crime-scene fingerprint or latent fingerprint is a dramatic find for the criminal investigator. Once the quality of the print has been deemed suitable for the IAFIS search, the latent-print examiner creates a digital image of the print with either a digital camera or a scanner. Next, the examiner, with the aid of a coder, marks points on the print to guide the computerized search (see Figure 5-7). The print is then electronically submitted to IAFIS, and within minutes the search of all fingerprint images in IAFIS is completed; the examiner may receive a list of potential candidates and their corresponding fingerprints for comparison and verification (see Figure 5-8).

Many countries throughout the world have created "national automated fingerprint identification systems" that are comparable to the FBI's model. For example, a computerized fingerprint database containing nearly nine million ten-print records connects the Home Office and forty-three police forces throughout England and Wales.

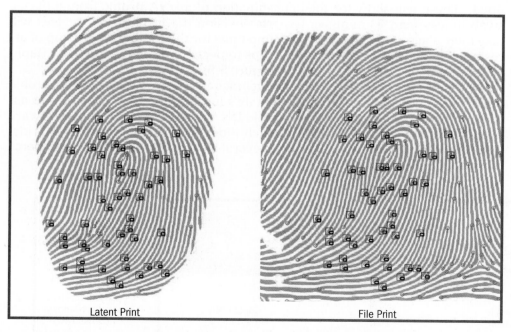

Latent Print   File Print

FIGURE 5-8   The computerized search of a fingerprint database first requires that selected ridge characteristics be designated by a coder. The positions of these ridge characteristics serve as a basis for comparing the print against fingerprints on file. *Sirchie Finger Print Laboratories*

DNA DATABASES

In 1998, the FBI's Combined DNA Index System (CODIS) became fully operational. CODIS enables federal, state, and local crime laboratories to electronically exchange and compare DNA profiles, thereby linking crimes to each other and to convicted offenders. All fifty states have enacted legislation to establish a data bank containing DNA profiles of individuals convicted of felony sexual offenses (and other crimes, depending on each state's statute). CODIS creates investigative leads from three indexes: the "forensic," "offender," and "arrestee" indices. The forensic index currently contains about 470,000 DNA profiles from unsolved crime-scene evidence. Based on a match, police in multiple jurisdictions can identify serial crimes, allowing coordination of investigations and sharing of leads developed independently. The offender index contains the profiles of more than ten million convicted individuals. The FBI has joined numerous states that collect DNA samples from those awaiting trial and will collect DNA from detained immigrants. This information will be entered into the arrestee index database, presently at 1.5 million.[1]

Constitutional issues regarding the appropriateness of collecting DNA from arrestees not convicted of any crime, but who nevertheless were the subject of a CODIS search against DNA collected from unsolved crimes, was decided in the case of *Maryland* v. *King*.[2]

> When officers make an arrest supported by probable cause to hold for a serious offense and bring the suspect to a station to be detained in custody, taking and analyzing a cheek swab of the arrestee's DNA is, like fingerprinting and photographing, a legitimate police booking procedure that is reasonable under the Fourth Amendment.

rapid DNA
A process for developing DNA profiles from a buccal swab in 90 minutes or less that are compatible with a CODIS search.

With the Supreme Court sanctioning the collection of cheek or buccal swabs from arrestees, the necessity for the analysis of a swab as close to the time of arrest as possible becomes apparent. The term **rapid DNA** has become part of the lingo of forensic science and describes approaches for rapidly obtaining a DNA profile from a buccal swab. A number of compact instruments are already commercially available and others are being developed.[3] These will allow for the determination of a DNA profile from a buccal swab in less than 90 minutes. Experts envision that rapid DNA devices will take their place alongside fingerprinting units for the routine processing of arrestees. Recently the FBI has taken steps to permit profiles collected by Rapid DNA into the CODIS data base (see Figure 5-9).

Another approach is to maintain an independent data base of DNA profile information gathered from within a state's local region (county, cities) to assist in the generation of leads from rapid DNA profiles. SmallPond, a software product, allows for the creation of such independent data bases. In Florida, SmallPond is allowing Palm Bay, and several local agencies to form a cooperative alliance using rapid DNA profiles.

CODIS database — DNA profile evaluation — DNA Profile — Rapid DNA Instrument — Buccal swab or swab containing evidential DNA

FIGURE 5-9 A Rapid DNA Instrument is used to create a DNA profile that is compatible with the CODIS data base.

Unfortunately, hundreds of thousands of samples are backlogged, still awaiting DNA analysis and entry into the offender index. Law enforcement agencies search this index against DNA profiles recovered from biological evidence found at unsolved crime scenes. This approach has proven to be tremendously successful in identifying perpetrators because most crimes involving biological evidence are committed by repeat offenders.

Several countries throughout the world have initiated national DNA data banks. The United Kingdom's National DNA Database, established in 1995, was the world's first national database. Currently it holds more than four million profiles, and DNA can be taken for entry into the database from anyone arrested for an offense likely to involve a prison term. In a typical month, matches are found linking suspects to 26 murders; 57 rapes and other sexual offenses; and 3,000 motor vehicle, property, and drug crimes. The National DNA Data Bank, housed in Ottawa, Canada, contains more than 250,000 DNA profiles from convicted individuals and has assisted in more than 24,000 cases including 1,740 murders and more than 3,000 sexual assaults.

OTHER DATABASES

It has been estimated that there are approximately 40,000 unidentified human remains that have been buried or cremated by law enforcement authorities in the United States. In a typical year, medical examiners and coroners handle approximately 4,000 unidentified human decedent cases, 1,000 of which remain unidentified after one year.

The National Missing and Unidentified Persons System (NamUs) was created in 2007 as a national centralized repository and resource center for missing persons and unidentified decedent records. NamUs is a free online system that can be searched by medical examiners, coroners, law enforcement officials, and the general public from all over the country in hopes of resolving these cases. NameUs comprises three databases, all of which are open to the general public. Total cases reported to NameUs is nearly 16,000 with nearly 10,000 open cases.

CASEFILES

In 1975, police found Gerald Wallace's body on his living room couch. He had been savagely beaten, his hands bound with an electric cord. Detectives searched his ransacked house, cataloging every piece of evidence they could find. None of it led to the murderer. They had no witnesses. Sixteen years after the fact, a lone fingerprint, lifted from a cigarette pack found in Wallace's house and kept for sixteen years in the police files, was entered into the Pennsylvania State Police AFIS database. Within minutes, it hit on a match. That print, police say, gave investigators the identity of a man who had been at the house the night of the murder. Police talked to him. He led them to other witnesses, who led police to the man who was ultimately charged with the murder of Gerald Wallace.

CASEFILES

Fort Collins, Colorado, and Philadelphia, Pennsylvania, are separated by nearly 1,800 miles, but in 2001 they were tragically linked though DNA. Troy Graves left the Philadelphia area in 1999, joined the air force, and settled down with his wife in Colorado. Subsequently, a frenzied string of eight sexual assaults around the Colorado University campus set off a manhunt that ultimately resulted in the arrest of Graves. However, his DNA profile inextricably identified him as Philadelphia's notorious "Center City rapist." This assailant had attacked four women in 1997 and brutally murdered Shannon Schieber, a Wharton School graduate student, in 1998. His last known attack in Philadelphia was the rape of an eighteen-year-old student in August 1999, shortly before Graves left the city. In 2002, Graves was returned to Philadelphia, where he was sentenced to life in prison without parole.

The Missing Persons Database contains information about missing persons that can be entered by anyone; however, before a person appears as a case on NamUs, there must be verification by law enforcement. When a new missing person is entered into NameUs, the system automatically performs cross-matching with links to state clearinghouses, medical examiners' and coroners' offices, law enforcement agencies, and victim assistance groups to check potential matches between cases.

The Unidentified Persons Database contains information entered by medical examiners and coroners. Unidentified persons are people who have died and whose bodies have not been identified. Anyone can search this database using characteristics such as sex, race, tattoos, and other distinctive body features, as well as dental information. However, sensitive case data is restricted and can be viewed only by select agencies.

The Unclaimed Persons Database contains information about deceased persons who have been identified by name, but for whom no next of kin or family member has been identified or located to claim the body for burial or other disposition. Only medical examiners and coroners may enter cases in this database. However, the database is searchable by the public using a missing person's name and year of birth.

In 2011, the NamUs database was awarded to the University of North Texas Health Science Center for system management and ongoing development.

The National Integrated Ballistics Information Network (NIBIN), maintained by the Bureau of Alcohol, Tobacco, Firearms and Explosives, allows firearms analysts to acquire, digitize, and compare markings made by firearms on bullets and cartridge casings recovered from crime scenes. The NIBIN program currently has 236 sites that are electronically joined to sixteen multistate regions.

The heart of NIBIN is the Integrated Ballistic Identification System (IBIS), comprising a microscope and a computer unit that can capture an image of a bullet or cartridge casing. The images are then forwarded to a regional server, where they are stored and correlated to other images in the regional database. IBIS does not positively match bullets or casings fired from the same weapon; this must be done by a firearms examiner. IBIS does, however, facilitate the work of the firearms examiner by producing a short list of candidates for the examiner to manually compare. Nearly 1.6 million pieces of crime-scene evidence have been entered in NIBIN, and more than 47,000 "hits" have been recorded, many of them yielding investigative information not obtainable by other means.

The International Forensic Automotive Paint Data Query Database contains chemical and color information pertaining to original automotive paints. This database, developed and maintained by the Forensic Laboratory Services of the Royal Canadian Mounted Police (RCMP), contains information about the make, model, year, and assembly plant of more than 13,000 vehicles, with a library of more than 50,000 layers of paint. Contributors to the PDQ include the RCMP and forensic laboratories in Ontario and Quebec, as well as forty U.S. forensic laboratories and police agencies in twenty-one other countries. Accredited users of PDQ are required to submit sixty new automotive paint samples per year to be added to the database. The PDQ database has found its greatest utility in the investigation of hit-and-runs by providing police with possible make, model, and year information to aid in the search for the unknown vehicles.

The previously described databases are maintained and controlled by government agencies. There is one exception: a commercially available computer retrieval system for comparing and identifying crime-scene shoe prints, known as "shoeprint image capture and retrieval (SICAR)."[4] SICAR's pattern-coding system enables an analyst to create a simple description of a shoe print by assigning codes to individual pattern features (see Figure 5-10). Shoe print images can be entered into SICAR via either a scanner or a digital camera. This product has a comprehensive shoe sole database (SoleMate®) that includes

■■■■ CASEFILES ■■■■

After a series of armed robberies in which suspects fired shots, the sheriff's office of Broward County, Florida, entered the cartridge casings from the crime scenes into NIBIN. Through NIBIN, four of the armed robberies were linked to the same .40-caliber handgun. A short time later, sheriff's deputies noticed suspicious activity around a local business. When they attempted to interview the suspects, the suspects fled in a vehicle. During the chase, the suspects attempted to dispose of a handgun; deputies recovered the gun after making the arrests. The gun was test-fired, and the resulting evidence was entered into NIBIN, which indicated a possible link between this handgun and the four previous armed robberies. Firearms examiners confirmed the link by examining the original evidence. The suspects were arrested and charged with four prior armed robbery offenses.

■■■■ CASEFILES ■■■■

A fifty-three-year-old man was walking his dog in the early morning hours. He was struck and killed by an unknown vehicle and later found lying in the roadway. No witnesses were present, and the police had no leads regarding the suspect vehicle. A metallic-gold-painted plastic fragment recovered from the scene and the victim's clothing were submitted to the Virginia Department of Forensic Science for analysis.

The victim's clothing was scraped, and several minute, metallic gold paint particles were recovered. The majority of these particles contained only topcoats, but one very minute particle contained two primer layers and a very limited amount of topcoat. The color of the primer surface layer was similar to that typically associated with some Fords. Subsequent spectral searches in the Paint Data Query (PDQ) database indicated that the paint probably originated from a 1990 or newer Ford.

The most discriminating aspect of this paint was the unusual-looking metallic gold topcoat. A search of automotive repaint books yielded only one color that closely matched the paint recovered in this case. The color, aztec gold metallic, was determined to have been used only on 1997 Ford Mustangs.

The results of the examination were relayed via telephone to the investigating detective. The investigating detective quickly determined that only 11,000 1997 Ford Mustangs were produced in aztec gold metallic. Only two of these vehicles were registered and had been previously stopped in the jurisdiction of the offense. Ninety minutes after the make/model/year information was relayed to the investigator, he called back to say he had located a suspect vehicle. Molding from the vehicle and known paint samples were submitted for comparison. Subsequent laboratory comparisons showed that the painted plastic piece recovered from the scene physically fitted together with the molding on the car, and the paint recovered from the victim's clothing was consistent with paint samples taken from the suspect's vehicle.

Source of data: Based on information obtained from Brenda Christy, Virginia Department of Forensic Science

more than 22,000 footwear entries providing investigators with a means for linking a crime-scene footwear impression to a particular shoe manufacturer. A second database, TreadMate®, has been created to house tire tread patterns. Currently, it contains 6,000 records.

Quick Review

- The creation of computerized databases for fingerprints, criminal histories, DNA profiles, markings on bullets and cartridges, automotive paints, and shoe prints has dramatically enhanced the role of forensic science in criminal investigation.
- IAFIS is the Integrated Automated Fingerprint Identification System, a national fingerprint and criminal history database maintained by the FBI. IAFIS allows criminal investigators to compare fingerprints at a crime scene to an index of 680 million known prints. CODIS is the FBI's Combined DNA Index System. It enables federal, state, and local crime laboratories to electronically exchange and compare DNA profiles, linking crimes to each other and to convicted offenders.

FIGURE 5-10   The crime-scene footwear print on the right is being searched against 8,000 eight thousand sole patterns to determine its brand and style. *Foster and Freeman*

Forensic Palynology: Pollen and Spores as Evidence

Of the many plant species on earth, more than half a million produce pollen or spores. The pollen or spores produced by each species has a unique type of ornamentation and morphology. This means that pollen or spores can be identified and used to provide links between a crime scene and a person or object if examined by a trained analyst. This technique is called "forensic palynology" and includes the collection and examination of pollen and spores connected with crime scenes, illegal activities, or terrorism. Microscopy is the principal tool used in the field of forensic palynology.

CHARACTERISTICS OF SPORES AND POLLEN

In nature, pollen grains are the single-celled male gametophytes (reproductive cells) of seed-bearing plants. The pollen grain wall ("exine") is durable because it protects and carries the "sperms" needed for plant reproduction. Spores consist of both the male and female gametes of plants such as algae, fungi, mosses, and ferns. Pollen-producing plants are either "anemophilous" (their pollen is dispersed by wind) or "entomophilous" (their pollen is carried and dispersed by insects or small animals). Fairly precise geographical locations can often be identified by the presence of different mixtures of airborne pollens produced by anemophilous plants. For example, it may be possible to identify a geographical origin using a profile of the pollen samples retrieved from a suspect's clothing by analyzing the type and percentages of airborne pollen grains. Entomophilous plants usually produce a small amount of pollen that is very sticky in nature. Therefore, this type of pollen is very rarely deposited on clothing or other objects except by direct contact with the plant. This information is useful when reconstructing the events of a crime because it may indicate that the clothing, a vehicle, or other objects on which this pollen is found came into direct contact with plant types found at a crime scene.

ANALYSIS OF SPORES AND POLLEN

Both spores and pollen are microscopic in size and are produced by adult plants, then dispersed by the millions, and both can be analyzed using similar methods that use a variety of microscopic techniques. Using a compound light microscope with magnification capabilities up to $1,000\times$, analysts usually can identify pollen and spores as having come from a specific plant family or genus, and sometime even the unique species. However, often the pollen or spores of related species may look so similar that identification of the species is possible only by careful analysis using a scanning electron microscope (SEM) (see pp. 212–213 and Figure 5-11).

Unique shapes, aperture type, and surface ornamentation are typically used to identify spore samples. Useful features for characterizing pollen grains include shape, apertures, and wall and surface sculpturing. Shapes of pollen grains include spheres, triangles, ellipses, hexagons, pentagons, and many other geometric variations. "Apertures" are the openings on pollen grains from which the pollen tube grows and carries the sperms to the egg to complete fertilization. "Sculpturing" of the pollen refers to the pattern of the pollen grain surface.

To avoid destruction or contamination of pollen evidence, early collection of forensic pollen samples for analysis is important and should be completed as soon as possible at a crime scene by a trained palynologist. This expert's first task is to calculate the estimated production and dispersal patterns of spores and pollen (called the "pollen rain") for the crime scene or area of interest and, using that information, to produce a kind of "pollen fingerprint" of that location.

The information gained from the analysis of pollen and spore evidence has many possible uses. It can link a suspect or object to the crime scene or the victim, prove or disprove a suspect's alibi, include or exclude suspects, track the previous whereabouts of some item or suspect, or indicate the geographical origin of some item. In the past, pollen and spore evidence has been used to locate human remains and concealed burial sites, establish the season or time of death of a victim, locate the source areas of illegal drugs and fake pharmaceuticals, identify terrorists, and prove the perpetration of illegal poaching and the adulteration of commercial foods.

FIGURE 5-11 Scanning electron micrograph of ragweed pollen at a magnification of 11703 if the image is printed 10 cm wide.
Mediscan/Alamy

A case exemplifying the application of forensic palynology to a criminal investigation occurred when a victim was kidnapped, robbed, and then murdered in the eastern part of the American Midwest.[5] The victim's car was stolen but later abandoned when it got stuck in mud near a busy highway. The next night a drifter was arrested in a nearby town for breaking into a closed store. While in jail awaiting trial, the drifter told a fellow inmate about his car being stuck in the mud, stating that he would not be in jail but for that mishap. The other prisoner, hoping to work a deal for a lighter sentence, told this story to the sheriff.

During the investigation of the crime scene, one of the law enforcement agents noticed that there was a large field of mature corn growing between the dirt road where the stolen car had been abandoned in the mud and the nearby highway leading to the next town. The investigator wondered if traces of torn corn leaves on the suspect's clothing might link him to the crime scene. Fortunately, the drifter's shirt and pants had been removed and stored in sterile paper bags when he was arrested. As were all prisoners in that region, he had been given a pair of orange overalls to wear while in jail.

The shirt and pants were sent to a botanist, who was asked to search for traces of corn leaves on the clothing. The botanist was also a palynologist, and thus also collected samples and searched for traces of pollen. The pollen samples yielded the best results. The samples collected from the suspect's shirt revealed that the neck and shoulder region of the shirt had high concentrations of fresh corn pollen. The forensic sample collected from the pants also contained corn pollen but in lower numbers. The forensic pollen data indicated that the drifter had recently walked through a corn field similar to the one between the abandoned car and the highway. As he walked through the field, he had brushed against the blooming male tassels on the corn plants, which are about head high. This accounted for the large amount of corn pollen found on the shoulder and neck area of the shirt. Lesser amounts of corn pollen also fell on the drifter's pants as he walked through the field. While the suspect awaited trial, additional evidence and several fingerprints from the victim's farm also linked him to the murder.

Quick Review

- Forensic palynology involves the collection and examination of pollen and spores connected with crime scenes, illegal activities, or terrorism. The microscope is the principal tool used in the field of forensic palynology.
- The information gained from the analysis of pollen and spore evidence has many possible uses. It can link a suspect or object to the crime scene or the victim, prove or disprove a suspect's alibi, include or exclude suspects, track the previous whereabouts of some item or suspect, or indicate the geographical origin of some item.

CASEFILES

MURDER AND THE HORSE CHESTNUT TREE

Roger Severs was the son of a wealthy English couple, Eileen and Derek Severs, who were reported missing in 1983. Police investigators were greeted at the Severs home by Roger, who at first explained that his parents had decided to spend some time in London. Suspicion of foul play quickly arose when investigators located traces of blood in the residence. More blood was found in Derek's car and there were signs of blood spatter on the garage door. Curiously, a number of green fibers were located throughout the house, as well as in the trunk of Derek's car.

A thorough geological examination of soil and vegetation caked onto Severs's car wheel rims seemed to indicate that the car had been in a location at the edge of a wooded area. Closer examination of the debris also revealed the presence of horse chestnut pollen. Horse chestnut is an exceptionally rare tree in the region of the Severs residence.

Using land maps, a geologist located possible areas where horse chestnut pollen might be found. In one of the locations, investigators found a shallow grave that contained the bludgeoned bodies of the elder Severses. Not surprisingly, they were wrapped in a green blanket. A jury rejected Roger's defense of diminished capacity and found him guilty of murder.

CHAPTER REVIEW

- Two methods used by forensic scientists when examining physical evidence are identification and comparison.

- Identification is the process of determining a substance's chemical or physical identity to the exclusion of all other substances (e.g., drugs, explosives, petroleum products, blood, semen, and hair species).

- A comparison analysis determines whether a suspect specimen and a standard/reference specimen have a common origin.

- Evidence that can be associated with a common source with an extremely high degree of probability is said to possess individual characteristics.

- Evidence associated with only a group is said to have class characteristics.

- The overall frequency of occurrence of an event, such as a match between two substances, can be obtained by multiplying together the frequencies of all independently occurring instances related to that event. This is known as the "product rule."

- The value of class physical evidence lies in its ability to corroborate events with data in a manner that is, as nearly as possible, free of human error and bias.

- As the number of objects linking an individual to a crime scene increases, so does the likelihood of that individual's involvement with the crime.

- A person may be exonerated or excluded from suspicion if physical evidence collected at a crime scene is found to be different from standard/reference samples collected from that subject.

- The creation of computerized databases for fingerprints, criminal histories, DNA profiles, markings on bullets and cartridges, automotive paints, and shoe prints has dramatically enhanced the role of forensic science in criminal investigation.

- IAFIS is the Integrated Automated Fingerprint Identification System, a national fingerprint and criminal history database maintained by the FBI. IAFIS allows criminal investigators to compare fingerprints at a crime scene to an index of 680 million known prints. CODIS is the FBI's Combined DNA Index System. It enables federal, state, and local crime laboratories to electronically exchange and compare DNA profiles, linking crimes to each other and to convicted offenders.

- Forensic palynology involves the collection and examination of pollen and spores connected with crime scenes, illegal activities, or terrorism. The microscope is the principal tool used in the field of forensic palynology.

KEY TERMS

class characteristics, 107

comparison, 105

identification, 105

individual characteristics, 106

product rule, 108

rapid DNA, 114

REVIEW QUESTIONS

1. The process of _____ determines a substance's physical or chemical identity with the most certainty that existing analytical techniques will permit.

2. The number and type of tests needed to identify a substance must be sufficient to _____ all other substances from consideration.

3. A(n) _____ analysis subjects a suspect and a standard/reference specimen to the same tests and examination for the ultimate purpose of determining whether they have a common origin.

4. _____ is the frequency of occurrence of an event.

5. Evidence that can be traced to a common source with an extremely high degree of probability is said to possess _____ characteristics.

6. Evidence associated with a group, not a single source, is said to possess _____ characteristics.

7. True or False: One of the major deficiencies of forensic science is the inability of the examiner to assign exact or approximate probability values to the comparison of most class physical evidence. _____

8. Although databases are consistently updated so that scientists can assign probabilities to class evidence, for the most part forensic scientists must rely on _____ when interpreting the significance of class physical evidence.

9. The believability of _____ accounts, confessions, and informant testimony can all be disputed, maligned, and subjected to severe attack and skepticism in the courtroom.

10. The value of class physical evidence lies in its ability to _____ events with data in a manner that is, as nearly as possible, free of human error and bias.

11. The _____ accorded physical evidence during a trial is left entirely to the trier of fact.

12. True or False: Given the potential weight of scientific evidence in a trial setting, failure to take proper safeguards may unfairly prejudice a case against the suspect. _____

13. True or False: Physical evidence cannot be used to exclude or exonerate a person from suspicion of committing a crime. _____

14. True or False: The distinction between individual and class evidence is always easy to make. _____

15. Modern analytical techniques have become so sensitive that the forensic examiner must be aware of the _____ among materials when interpreting the significance of comparative data.

16. Students studying forensic science must be cautioned that merely reading relevant textbooks and journals is no substitute for _____ in this most practical of sciences.

17. True or False: A fingerprint can be positively identified through the IAFIS database. _____

18. A database applicable to DNA profiling is the FBI's _____.

19. True or False: Both spores and pollen can be identified and used to link a crime scene to an individual. _____

20. True or False: Spores can be characterized by shape and surface characteristics through a simple visual examination. _____

APPLICATION AND CRITICAL THINKING

1. Arrange the following tasks in order, from the one that would require the least extensive testing procedure to the one that would require the most extensive. Explain your answer.
   a) Determining whether an unknown substance contains an illicit drug
   b) Determining the composition of an unknown substance
   c) Determining whether an unknown substance contains heroin

2. The following are three possible combinations of DNA characteristics that might be found in an individual's genetic profile. Using the probability rule, rank each of these combinations from most common to least common. The number in parentheses after each characteristic indicates its percentage distribution in the population.
   a) FGA 24,24 (3.6%), TH01 6,8 (8.1%), and D16S539 11,12 (8.9%)
   b) vWA 14,19 (6.2%), D21S11 30,30 (3.9%), and D13S317 12,12 (8.5%)
   c) CSF1PO 9,10 (11.2%), D18S51 14,17 (2.8%), and D8S1179 17,18 (6.7%)

3. For each of the following pieces of evidence, indicate whether the item is more likely to possess class or individual characteristics. Explain your answers.
   a) An impression from a new automobile tire
   b) A fingerprint
   c) A spent bullet cartridge
   d) A mass-produced synthetic fiber
   e) Pieces of a shredded document
   f) Commercial potting soil
   g) Skin and hair scrapings
   h) Fragments of a multilayer custom automobile paint

4. Which of the forensic databases described in the text contain information that relates primarily to evidence exhibiting class characteristics? Which ones contain information that relates primarily to evidence exhibiting individual characteristics? Explain your answers.

5. An investigator at a murder scene notes signs of a prolonged struggle between the attacker and victim. Name at least three types of physical evidence for which the investigator would probably collect standard/reference samples, and explain why he or she would collect them.

ENDNOTES

1. *Collecting DNA at Arrest: Policies, Practices, and Implications,* https://www.ncjrs.gov/pdffiles1/nij/grants/242812.pdf

2. 133 S.Ct. 1236 (2013).

3. J. A. Lounsbury and J. P. Landers, "Ultrafast Amplification of DNA on Plastic Microdevices for Forensic Short Tandem Repeat Analysis," *Journal of Forensic Sciences,* 58 (2013): 866.

4. Foster & Freeman Limited, http://www.fosterfreeman.co.uk.

5. V. M. Bryant and G. D. Jones, "Forensic Palynology: Current Status of a Rarely Used Technique in the United States of America," *Forensic Science International,* 163 (2006): 183–197.

6

Death Investigation

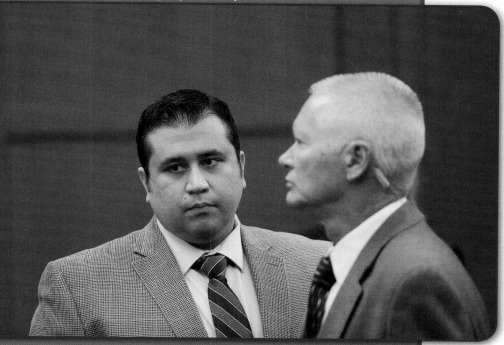

LEARNING OBJECTIVES

After studying this chapter, you should be able to:
- Describe the role of the forensic pathologist.
- Distinguish cause and manner of death.
- Describe common causes of death.
- Describe the external, internal, and toxicology phases of an autopsy.
- List various categories associated with the manner of death.
- Describe chemical and physical changes helpful for estimating time of death.
- Discuss the role of the forensic anthropologist in death investigation.
- Describe the role of the forensic entomologist in death investigation.

THE GEORGE ZIMMERMAN CASE: SELF-DEFENSE OR MURDER?

The setting was Sanford, Florida, when during a rainy night Trayvon Martin, a 17-year-old African American high school student, was returning to the Twin Lakes housing complex after walking to a local convenience store to purchase candy and a beverage. George Zimmerman, a local neighborhood watch volunteer noticed Martin walking around the community and proceeded to call 911 dispatch. As Martin realized Zimmerman was following him, he began to run with Zimmerman in pursuit behind him. The dispatcher, still on the phone with Zimmerman, can be heard telling him that he should not follow Martin. After the call is disconnected, a violent struggle ensued and Martin suffered a single gunshot wound to his chest. Police reported to the scene not long after, finding Martin dead on the ground, and Zimmerman bloodied and bruised with a broken nose.

At trial George Zimmerman faced charges of manslaughter and murder in the second degree. The trial engendered intense media discussions revolving around racial bias that had not been seen since the days of the O.J. Simpson trial. The prosecution claimed that Zimmerman was an overzealous watch volunteer when he chased after Martin and provoked a confrontation. Zimmerman's defense countered these accusations by citing Florida's "Stand Your Ground" law, and suggested that Martin's death was a product of self-defense. According to Zimmerman's testimony, Martin had him pinned down on the sidewalk, and was punching and beating his head. During the altercation, Zimmerman alleged that his gun was exposed and as Martin reached for the weapon, Zimmerman grabbed and fired his weapon, killing Martin. During the trial, expert witness Anthony Di Maio, a forensic pathologist, claimed that the angle of the gunshot wound and the area in which Martin was shot proved to be consistent with Martin straddling Zimmerman while beating his face. Di Maio went one step further by explaining the significance of a "powder tattooing" on Martin's body. Di Maio's testimony revealed that the gunshot powder residue found on Trayvon Martin was evidence that he was shot at close range, further supporting Zimmerman's account

Zimmerman was found not guilty of all charges and released amid cries of social and legal injustice and racial prejudice.

Role of the Forensic Pathologist

forensic pathologists
Investigative personnel, typically medical examiners or coroners, who investigate the cause, manner, and time of death of a victim in a crime. A physician who has been trained to conduct autopsies.

Few investigations bring with them the intense focus of community interest and news media coverage as that of a suspicious death. Generally, **forensic pathologists** associated with the medical examiner's or coroner's office are responsible for determining the cause of an undetermined or unexpected death. These officers coordinate their response with that of law enforcement in the ensuing investigation. The titles "coroner" and "medical examiner" are often used interchangeably, but there are significant differences in their job descriptions. In the United States, there's a mix of state medical examiner systems, county medical examiner offices, and county coroner systems. The coroner is an elected official and may or may not possess a medical degree. (The term "coroner" dates back hundreds of years to the rule of King Henry II of England, who created the office of the coroner to collect money and personal possessions from people who had died.) The medical examiner, on the other hand, is almost always an appointed official and is usually a physician who generally is a board-certified forensic pathologist and is responsible for certifying the manner and the cause of a death.

The tasks of examining the case for the cause and manner of death and recording the results in a death certificate are the responsibilities of both offices. However, although both the coroner's office and the medical examiner's office are charged with investigating suspicious deaths, only the pathologist is trained to perform an autopsy. Ideally, the coroner's or medical examiner's office should be staffed with physicians who are board certified in forensic pathology and should charge them with determining the cause of death by autopsy. The cause-of-death determination, however, involves not just an autopsy but also the history of death, witness statements, relevant medical records, and any scene investigation, all of which constitute the surrounding circumstances of death.

From a practical point of view, it is often not feasible for the forensic pathologist to personally solicit information regarding the circumstances surrounding a death or to respond in-person to every death scene. Thus, the gathering of vital information and the scene investigation can be delegated to trained coroner/medical examiner investigators who, when a crime scene is involved, coordinate their efforts with those of crime-scene and criminal investigators. The forensic pathologist's work is also aided by the skills of specialists including forensic anthropologists, forensic entomologists, and forensic odontologists.

SCENE INVESTIGATION

With regard to any scene investigation, protection of the overall scene and the body are of paramount importance, as is the ultimate removal of the body in a medically acceptable manner. The death investigation involves documenting and photographing the undisturbed scene; collecting relevant physical evidence; attempting to determine time of death, which must be done in a timely fashion at the scene; and, among other things, ascertaining premortem locations of the body and whether any postmortem movement of the body occurred. Examples of observations that can be made of the body at the scene include bruises along the upper lip, which may be evidence of smothering; a black eye limited to the eyelids, which implies an injury from inside the head; or bleeding from the ear, which implies a basal skull fracture.

A critical phase of the death investigation will be a preliminary reconstruction of events that preceded the onset of death, so all significant details of the scene must be recorded. Blood spatter and blood flow patterns must be documented. Blood should be sampled for testing in case some of the blood was cast off by a perpetrator. Any tire marks or shoe prints must be documented. Fingerprints must be processed and collected. Of particular importance is the search for any evidence discarded, dropped, or cast off by a perpetrator. When a weapon is involved, there must be a concerted effort to locate and recover the suspect weapon. In the case of firearm deaths, fired bullets or casings must be found and their locations documented. In such firearm deaths, before the body is moved or clothing is removed, blood spatter directionality and trace evidence (such as hairs) on the hands must be documented. Paper bags then should be placed over the hands and secured around the wrist or arm (paper prevents moisture condensation) to preserve any additional evidence.

Photographs must always be taken before the scene is altered in any way (except from life-saving efforts). This includes moving the body or anything on the body, such as clothing or jewelry. A particularly violent scene can carry with it a large amount of blood and disorder. Blood may be found at different locations throughout the scene. This could prove to be important in shaping the events that led to the final outcome; it may be possible to determine the initial location of the injury, as well as victim and assailant movements throughout the course of events. Initially it may be difficult to properly infer the source of the wounds and the order in which they were received at the scene. Photographs then will play a very large role when reconstructing the events later. As always, photographs should be taken with a scale, always first overall, then at medium range, then close up. The photographer must also be careful not to get caught up in capturing the injuries exclusively. Negative findings can also be significant. This means photographs should also be taken of areas on the body where injuries are not apparent.

Protection of the body and the overall scene is of paramount importance, as is the ultimate removal of the body in a medically acceptable manner. Often the initial phase of the investigation will focus on determining the identity of the deceased, often called the "decedent." Although this task may be relatively simple to accomplish through a visual examination, complications can arise. Body decomposition and the existence of extensive trauma can complicate the identification. This may necessitate the application of more sophisticated technology, such as DNA, fingerprinting, dental examination, and facial reconstruction.

Quick Review

- Forensic pathologists associated with the medical examiner's or coroner's office are responsible for determining the cause of an undetermined or unexpected death.
- Although both the coroner's office and the medical examiner's office are charged with investigating suspicious deaths, only the pathologist is trained to perform an autopsy. The tasks of examining a body for the cause and manner of death and recording the results in the death certificate are the responsibilities of both offices.
- Protection of the body and the overall scene is of paramount importance, as is the ultimate removal of the body in a medically acceptable manner.

CAUSE OF DEATH

A primary objective of the autopsy is to determine the cause of death. The **cause of death** is that which initiates the series of events ending in death. The most important determination in a violent death is the character of the injury that started the chain of events that resulted in death. However, if the sequence of events leading to death is sufficiently prolonged, then the decedent may actually suffer from adverse medical conditions brought about by the initial injury and

cause of death
Identifies the injury or disease that led to the chain of events resulting in death.

then die as a result of those conditions. In that case, it will be up to the forensic pathologist to make the determination that the original injury inflicted on the victim was the underlying cause of death. Some of the more common causes of death are discussed here.

BLUNT-FORCE INJURY A blunt-force injury is caused by a nonsharpened object such as a bat or pipe. A blunt-force injury can abrade, or scrape, tissue. If tissue is crushed by a blunt force to the point of causing skin to overstretch, a laceration will form, characterized by the skin splitting and tearing. Lacerations exhibit abrasions around the open wound, tissue bridging within the open wound, and torn or disturbed tissue beneath the skin surrounding the open portion of the wound. Blunt-force injury can also crush tissue. This will cause bleeding from tiny ruptured blood vessels within and beneath the skin, known as a "contusion," or bruise (see Figure 6-1). Much has been written about determining the age of bruises, but forensic pathologists have become keenly aware that attempting to "age" bruises based on color and changes in color over time is fraught with difficulty, and contusions must be interpreted with great care and reserve. Some contusions become visible externally only over time, and frequently, bruises will not be visible externally but become eminently visible internally within soft tissues (e.g., in the abdomen and on the back, arms, and legs).

A contusion can sometimes exhibit the pattern of the weapon used. For example, if a person wearing a ring strikes another person, the ring may imprint its pattern onto the skin. A person who stomps on another may leave the impression of his or her shoe heel. Over time, however, the bruise will lose its original shape and pattern and undergo color changes. Some objects will produce a characteristic bruised perimeter and a white center.

FIGURE 6-1 Bruising (contusions) on the skin.
mundoview/Shutterstock

The outward appearance of the injuries does not always coincide with the injuries sustained inside the body. This is something the pathologist must keep in mind when examining blunt-force injuries. A single blow to certain parts of the body can cause instantaneous death with little visible damage. Likewise, a blow to the head can cause a concussion that can be instantly fatal.

SHARP-FORCE INJURIES Sharp-force injuries occur from weapons with sharp edges, such as knives or blades. These weapons are capable of cutting or stabbing. A "cut" is formed when the weapon produces an injury that is longer than it is deep. In contrast, a "stab" is deeper than its length. As shown in Figure 6-2, the tissue associated with these types of wounds is not crushed or torn but sliced.

A scene that involves a sharp-force injury is usually especially bloody and unruly. Blood may be found at different locations throughout the scene. Again, this information may make it possible to determine the initial location of the injury as well as where the body was moved throughout the course of events. It is particularly important in sharp-force cases to examine the victim for defensive wounds. A victim's forearm that exhibits wounds may indicate defense wounds. These occur when the victim attempts to fight off the attacker or block assaults. Though defense wounds are more typical on the outer forearms, they can also be evident on the lower extremities if the victim tries to protect him- or herself by kicking. A lack of any defense wounds can lead a pathologist to conclude that the victim was either unconscious or somehow tied up during the assault.

FIGURE 6-2 A stab wound.
Elizabeth Laposata

ASPHYXIA   Asphyxia encompasses a variety of conditions that involve interference with the intake of oxygen. For example, death at a fire scene is caused primarily by the extremely toxic gas carbon monoxide. When carbon monoxide is present, hemoglobin, the protein in red blood cells that transports oxygen, will bind to the carbon monoxide instead of oxygen. This is carbon monoxide poisoning, and this deadly complex of hemoglobin and carbon monoxide is known as "carboxyhemoglobin." Bound up with carbon monoxide, the hemoglobin is prevented from transporting oxygen throughout the body, causing asphyxia. High levels of carbon monoxide in the blood will cause death. Low levels of carbon monoxide can cause a victim to become disoriented and lose consciousness.

Carbon monoxide will not continue to build up in the body after death. The levels found in a fire victim then can be used to determine whether the individual was breathing at the time of the fire. The presence of soot is another indicator that the victim was alive during the fire. These black particles are often seen in the airway of fire victims who inhaled smoke before death. During the autopsy, soot can be observed especially in the larynx and trachea and even in the lungs. Sometimes the victim will actually swallow the soot. In these cases, traces can be found in the esophagus and the lining of the stomach.

The ultimate cause of a death from hanging is typically the cessation of blood flow to or from the brain. Victims of hangings may show signs of petechiae on the eyelids, along with a swollen and a blue/purplish appearance of the face. **Petechiae** are very small and are caused by blood having escaped into the tissues as a result of capillaries bursting (see Figure 6-3). Although petechiae are witnessed in hanging cases, they are more common in strangulation deaths. Typically the hyoid bone (the bone on which the tongue rests) and thyroid cartilage (located below the hyoid) are not fractured in cases of hanging. A break of the thyroid cartilage is common, however, in manual strangulation cases.

In hangings it is vitally important to document exactly how the victim was initially found and the position of the encircling noose, as shown in Figure 6-4. The type of knot used may strongly support the notion that another person was involved in the hanging. This means that the knot should always be preserved for later examination. Either the noose should be slipped off the victim's head intact, or the noose should be cut distant from the knot. Defense wounds are

petechiae
Pinpoint hemorrhaging often observed in the white area of the victim's eyes; often observed in strangulation cases.

FIGURE 6-3   Petechial hemorrhages in a victim's eye. *Elizabeth Laposata*

FIGURE 6-4   A ligature pattern on a neck with corresponding ligature. *Elizabeth Laposata*

FIGURE 6-5   A contact gunshot wound to the temple of a suicide victim. *D. Willough/Custom Medical Stock Photo*

FIGURE 6-6   A gunshot entrance wound to the head from a weapon fired several inches from the target. *Elizabeth Laposata*

common on strangulation victims. Often the marks found on the neck of a victim are the victim's own, made in the attempt to loosen whatever was constricting his or her neck. Even in cases of hanging by suicide, there can be defensive wounds on the neck.

Smothering can occur by various materials that block the mouth, nose, and internal airway. Pillows or a hand can inhibit breathing. Gags that are used to silence a victim can be sucked into the airway and block oxygen flow. Typically a death by smothering is homicidal in nature. Accidental smothering usually occurs only in infants or in cases where a victim is trapped under an obstruction.

GUNSHOT WOUNDS   When evaluating a gunshot wound, the estimated range of fire is one of the most important characteristics to analyze. The appearance of the wound can be of help in estimating whether the firearm used to inflict the wound was discharged while in contact with the victim's body (Figure 6-5) or from a distance of only inches to many feet away. The investigator will compare powder residue distribution around the wound to test fires collected from the inflicting firearm to make this estimate. Obviously, if the firearm was fired at a distance of several feet, suicide is a highly unlikely cause of death because the wound could not have been self-inflicted (Figure 6-6). Gunpowder residue on the victim's hand is a possible indicator of suicide, but this is not always the case. Evidence of contact shots, that is, shots fired with the gun held against the body of the victim, typically indicates that the death was not an accident. The autopsy must include a determination of the path or "wound track" of the projectile. The wound track is determined by observing the wound from the outside of the body, following the track of the projectile through the body, and documenting its terminus. The pathologist will recover any and all projectiles from the body, carefully protecting their forensic markings. The autopsy of gunshot victims should include several facts in addition to the general autopsy facts: Scene investigation and the results of toxicological and serological analyses are important. All findings regarding the bullet wounds should be noted, as well as descriptions of the clothing. The police report with a thorough description of the scene is also important.

A gunshot wound may not necessarily explain why a victim died. A person who sustains a gunshot wound can bleed to death in a matter of minutes or up to several hours. Infection can also be a contributory cause of death, especially in cases where the victim was shot in the abdomen: He or she might live several days but eventually succumb to infection. In cases where the victim was shot in the head but survives in a comatose state, pneumonia often develops. These intervening factors are considered contributory causes of death, but the gunshot wound is still considered the underlying cause of death.

SUBSTANCE ABUSE   Drug abuse continues to be an enormous problem in the United States. Drug enforcement is a multibillion-dollar industry. Many of the abused drugs in the country are illegal, but not all are. Deaths as a result of substance abuse are common cases that a forensic pathologist must face. Because drug abuse is so common, the forensic pathologist will routinely test for the presence of drugs in nearly all investigations, and routine tests are available for many commonly abused drugs. As technology has improved, many drugs can be detected at very low levels. These factors have helped considerably in making substance abuse testing easier and less expensive.

Drug abuse can directly cause death, or it can cause complications that can serve as a contributing factor to death. An abuser can misuse a drug or a number of drugs for years, accumulating detrimental effects in that time. Death as a result of those effects is typically labeled a natural death by the pathologist. Drugs can also alter a person's judgment and psychomotor skills to the point that a fatal accident occurs. Drugs are also often at the source of acts of violence that result in death.

Quick Review

- A primary objective of the autopsy is to determine the cause of death. The cause of death is that which initiates the series of events ending in death.
- The most important determination in a violent death is the character of the injury that started the chain of events that resulted in death.
- Some of the more common causes of death are blunt-force injury, sharp-force injury, asphyxia, gunshot wound, and substance abuse.
- A blunt-force injury is caused by a nonsharpened object such as a bat or pipe. A blunt-force injury can abrade tissue or can cause a contusion arising from bleeding from tiny ruptured blood vessels within and beneath the skin.
- Sharp-force injuries occur from weapons with sharp edges, such as knives or blades.
- Asphyxia encompasses a variety of conditions that involve interference with the intake of oxygen. For example, death at a fire scene is caused primarily by the extremely toxic gas, carbon monoxide.
- Gunshot wounds originate from projectiles fired by a firearm. The distance a weapon was fired from a target is one of the most important factors in characterizing a gunshot wound.
- Because drug abuse is so common, a forensic pathologist will routinely order toxicological tests for the presence of drugs in nearly all autopsies.

THE AUTOPSY

autopsy
A surgical procedure performed by a pathologist on a dead body to ascertain—from the body, organs, and bodily fluids—the cause of death.

An **autopsy**, in its broadest definition, is simply the examination of a body after death (i.e., a postmortem examination). The autopsy can be further described as one of two types: a clinical/hospital autopsy or a forensic/medicolegal autopsy. The clinical/hospital autopsy focuses on the internal organ findings and medical conditions. Its purpose is to confirm the clinical diagnoses, the presence and extent of disease, any medical conditions that were overlooked, and the appropriateness and outcome of therapy. In contrast, the goal of a forensic/medicolegal autopsy is to determine the cause of death and confirm the manner of death, often to be used in criminal proceedings. The forensic autopsy usually emphasizes external and internal findings while developing meaningful forensic correlations between sustained injuries and the crime scene (see Figures 6-7 and 6-8).

All the steps of the forensic autopsy must be carefully documented and photographed. The documentation should include date, time, place, by whom the autopsy was

FIGURE 6-7 An autopsy suite. *Robert Seeberg/Caro/Alamy*

FIGURE 6-8   Tools used for an autopsy. *Robert Seeberg/Caro/Alamy*

performed, and who attended the autopsy. Photographs of the injuries, complete with a scale, and descriptions of each photograph's location are important when correlating external wounds with internal damage. Negative photographs—photographs of uninjured parts of the body—are also important. The autopsy report and photographs are so important because, once the body is buried, no further evidence can be collected and no additional findings can occur.

EVIDENCE FROM THE AUTOPSY   The search for physical evidence must extend beyond the crime scene to the autopsy room of a deceased victim. Here, the medical examiner or pathologist carefully examines the victim to establish the cause and manner of death. As a matter of routine, tissues and organs are retained for pathological and toxicological examination. At the same time, arrangements must be made between the examiner and investigator to secure a variety of items that may be obtainable from the body for laboratory examination. The following are among the items to be collected and sent to the forensic laboratory:

- Victim's clothing
- Fingernail scrapings
- Combings from head and pubic areas
- Buccal swab (for DNA-typing purposes)
- Vaginal, anal, and oral swabs (in sex-related crimes)
- Bullets recovered from the body
- Swabs of body areas suspected of being in contact with DNA arising from touching or saliva
- Hand swabs from shooting victims (for gunshot residue analysis)

These items of evidence should be properly packaged and labeled like all other evidence. Once the body is buried, efforts at obtaining these items may prove difficult or futile. Furthermore, a lengthy time delay in obtaining many of these items will diminish or destroy their forensic value.

EXTERNAL EXAMINATION   The forensic autopsy consists of an external examination and an internal examination. The first steps taken for the external examination include a broad overview of the condition of the body and the clothing. Obvious damage to the clothing should be matched up to injuries on the body. General characteristics of the body should be noted, including sex, height, weight, approximate age, color of hair, and physical condition. The presence of tattoos and scars, as well as puncture and track marks, are noted. All evidence of apparent medical intervention must be carefully noted, described, and photographed because occasionally these may be misinterpreted, especially chest tube insertions and emergency cardiac punctures. The mouth and nose are examined for the presence of vomit and/or blood and trace evidence, and the ears are examined for blood. Any irritations in the nasal cavity can be indicative of drug sniffing.

Often, paper bags are placed over the hands at the crime scene until it is time to examine them. This prevents contamination and possible loss of trace evidence, such as hairs and fibers. This preservation of evidence can play an important role in identifying a suspect. A victim will sometimes have skin and DNA under his or her fingernails from fighting with the assailant.

The external examination also consists of classifying the injuries. This includes distinguishing between different types of wounds, such as a stab wound versus a gunshot wound. The injuries that are examined may include abrasions, contusions, lacerations, and sharp injury wounds. Hemorrhages in the eyelids (petechiae) are also essential to note, as they can indicate strangulation. Attention is also paid to the genitalia, especially in cases where sexual abuse is suspected. In these cases, vaginal, oral, and rectal samples are taken.

The discharge from a firearm will produce characteristic markings on the skin. This discharge is a combination of soot and gunpowder. It will leave markings called "stippling" or "tattooing" around the bullet hole. The stippling can be analyzed in terms of its span and density in order to approximate the range of fire. The range of fire may prove to be the most important factor in distinguishing a homicide from a suicide.

X-ray examinations can be very useful in the autopsy process. They are most commonly performed in gunshot wound cases and stab wound cases. Even if the bullet, knife, or other piercing weapon is recovered outside the body, an X-ray will identify any fragments still inside the body. An X-ray will also help determine the path of the projectile or sharp utensil. X-rays can also be very helpful in cases where the victim was beaten, especially situations in which the victim is a child: An X-ray can show past bone fractures and a possible pattern of abuse.

INTERNAL EXAMINATION   The dissection of the human body generally entails the removal of all internal organs through a Y-shaped incision beginning at the top of each shoulder and extending down to the pubic bone. Performing the internal examination entails weighing, dissecting, and sectioning each organ of the body. When required and in accordance with jurisdictional rules, microscopic examination of the sectioned organs is conducted, which can help in determining the cause of death. For example, microscopic examination of lungs and liver can confirm chronic intravenous drug abuse. Examination of the cranium requires cutting an incision from behind one ear to the other, peeling the scalp upward and backward, and sawing of the skull in a circular cut; then the skull cap is removed to reveal the brain, as shown in Figure 6-9.

Special care is taken to identify any preexisting conditions or malformations in the organs that might have contributed to the death of the victim. Pulmonary edema (fluid accumulation in the lungs) is frequently found in victims of chronic cocaine and amphetamine abuse. Heart malformations may cause suspicious death in an otherwise healthy individual.

Special attention is paid to the digestive tract if poisoning is suspected. The stomach can show partially digested or dissolved pills. Chemical analyses can also be carried out to show signs of poisoning. The amount of pills or tablets in the stomach can aid in the determination of manner of death as well. It is not always a sure sign, but typically it is unlikely that a person will accidentally swallow a large number of pills. This would suggest suicide rather than an accidental overdose. Stomach contents may reveal the deceased's last meal. The extent of digestion can help with determining the time of death.

FIGURE 6-9   A brain during autopsy. *SPL/Science Source*

Toxicology.   The internal examination is also where toxicological specimens are taken. These include samples of blood, stomach content, bile, and urine. All bile in the gallbladder and all stomach content are collected. In addition to these, brain matter, liver, and vitreous humor are gathered. These specimens can play especially large roles in cases where poisoning or drug abuse is suspected.

Blood is often tested to determine the presence and levels of alcohol and drugs. Blood should be taken from areas of the body where there is the least chance of contamination. Blood should never be collected from body cavities, where it may be contaminated from adjacent structures. Many changes occur in the body after death, and these changes can alter the drugs present in the system at the time of death. This can make interpreting how much of a drug was present, if any at all, a very challenging task. Some drugs redistribute or reenter the blood after death and thus may complicate the interpretation of postmortem blood levels of these drugs. This phenomenon is known as "postmortem redistribution." For this reason, it is best to collect blood at distant areas of the body to allow the toxicologist to compare the agreement of the drug concentrations found. The ideal location to retrieve the blood is internally, directly from the inferior vena cava (the large vein inside the lower abdominal region, which receives its blood from the femoral veins) using a syringe. Where postmortem redistribution of drugs may have occurred, blood should also be collected at autopsy from the superior venous system directly above the heart.

For illicit as well as legal substances, it is necessary to know what levels are indicative of therapeutic use and what levels indicate toxicity of a given substance. Much information regarding therapeutic versus toxic drug levels has been published. This data can help pathologists and toxicologists ascertain the cause of death. Most drug-related deaths are quite apparent from the blood concentrations of alcohol and/or a drug found in the postmortem toxicological report. (Note that depressant drugs will act in concert with alcohol.) However, in some cases of drug-induced death, drug levels may not always provide evidence. Cocaine is a prime example of this. Cocaine-induced sudden death is an event with an incubation period. Structural alterations of the cardiovascular system are required, and such alterations take months, or perhaps years, of chronic cocaine use. In these individuals, death and toxicity may occur after the use of even a trivial amount of the drug.

WebExtra 6.1

See How an Autopsy Is Performed

Unlike drug analyses, general testing for poisons is not a routine procedure carried out by the pathologist. However, if a specific poison is suspected, a particular test must be performed. A body that displays a cherry-red discoloration often leads a pathologist to suspect carbon monoxide poisoning. The pathologist would then perform a toxicological test of the blood. Poisoning by cyanide could also produce a pinkish discoloration. Often, cyanide toxicity will show additional signs, such as a distinct smell of burnt almonds. Corrosion around the lips of a victim may lead to a suspicion of ingesting an acid or alkaline substance.

Quick Review

- An autopsy, in its broadest definition, is simply the examination of a body after death.
- The forensic autopsy consists of an external examination and an internal examination.
- The first steps taken for the external examination include a broad overview of the condition of the body and the clothing.
- The external examination also consists of classifying the injuries. This includes distinguishing between different types of wounds, such as a stab wound versus a gunshot wound.

■■■■ CASEFILES ■■■■

HAROLD SHIPMAN, DR. DEATH

Kathleen Grundy's sudden death in 1998 was shocking news to her daughter, Angela Woodruff. Mrs. Grundy, an eighty-one-year-old widow, was believed to be in good health when her physician, Dr. Harold Shipman, visited her a few hours before her demise. Some hours later, when friends came to her home to check on her whereabouts, they found Mrs. Grundy lying on a sofa fully dressed and dead.

Dr. Shipman pronounced her dead and informed her daughter that an autopsy was not necessary. A few days later, Mrs. Woodruff was surprised to learn that a will had surfaced leaving all of Mrs. Grundy's money to Dr. Shipman. The will was immediately recognized as a forgery and led to the exhumation of Mrs. Grundy's body. A toxicological analysis of the remains revealed a lethal quantity of morphine.

In retrospect, there was good reason to suspect that Dr. Shipman was capable of foul play. In the 1970s, he was asked to leave a medical practice because of a drug abuse problem and charges that he obtained drugs by forgery and deception. However, Dr. Shipman was quickly back to practicing medicine. By 1998, local undertakers became suspicious because of the number of his patients who were dying. What is more, all the patients who had died were elderly women who were found sitting in a chair or lying fully clothed on a bed. As police investigated, the horror of Dr. Shipman's deeds became apparent. One clinical audit estimated that Dr. Shipman had killed at least 236 of his patients over a 24-year period. Most of the deaths were attributed to fatal doses of heroin or morphine. Toxicological analysis on seven exhumed bodies clearly showed significant quantities of morphine. Convicted of murder, Dr. Shipman hanged himself in his jail cell in 2004.

- The dissection of the human body generally entails the removal of all internal organs through a Y-shaped incision beginning at the top of each shoulder and extending down to the pubic bone.
- The internal examination entails weighing, dissecting, and sectioning each organ of the body.
- Blood is often routinely tested to determine the presence and levels of alcohol and drugs.
- Some drugs redistribute or reenter the blood after death and thus may complicate the interpretation of postmortem blood levels of these drugs.

■■■■

MANNER OF DEATH

The **manner of death** relates to the circumstances that led to the fatal result and is the culmination of the complete investigation, including the determination of cause of death. The certification of the circumstances and manner of death is the responsibility of the coroner's and medical examiner's offices. The manner in which death occurred is classified in death certifications as one of five categories: homicide, suicide, accidental, natural, or undetermined.

HOMICIDE Although there is no universal agreement on its definition, generally the term "homicide," as certified by coroners' and medical examiners' offices, is defined as a nonaccidental death resulting from grossly negligent, reckless, or intentional actions of another person. Both the cause and manner of death, as certified by the coroners'/medical examiners' offices, can become the subject of expert debate during any subsequent judicial proceedings. However, this does not result in a revision of the death certification unless there has been negligence on the part of the certifying offices.

If the pathologist was unable to go to the scene, he or she should receive adequate information detailing the conditions of the scene from coroner/medical examiner investigators and law enforcement personnel. This information should include how the body was discovered as well as when and where. It is also an

manner of death
A determination made by a forensic pathologist of the cause of death. Five broad categories are homicide, suicide, accidental, natural, and undetermined.

important first step for investigators to make note of the algor mortis, livor mortis, and/or rigor mortis of the body at the scene. These will help to determine time of death.

SUICIDE   Suicide is the result of an individual taking his or her own life with lethal intention. For a determination of suicide, it must be demonstrated that the individual carried out the act alone. If there is any doubt about the intentions of the victim, the death is not classified as a suicide; the death is ruled as an accident or even as undetermined. The most common methods of suicide include self-inflicted gunshot wounds, hanging, and drug overdosing. Although drug abuse is deliberately committed by a victim, it is not considered suicide unless it was clearly intended as a lethal act.

Various challenges are associated with discriminating suicide from an accident or even homicide. The victim's personal history, including his or her psychiatric history, becomes relevant. Suicidal threats or past attempts would give obvious evidence of a suicide as opposed to an accident. In all cases of suspected suicide, a thorough search of the victim's possessions should be made to locate a suicide note.

Multiple gunshot wounds might lead one to suspect homicide. However, a person who is committed to ending his or her own life may take several shots if the wounds are not instantly fatal. It is imperative to confirm that it is physically possible that the victim could inflict the wounds. There are a few areas of the body that strongly point toward homicide. These are areas that are not easily accessible to the victim's own reach. For example, anywhere on the back of a victim is difficult and sometimes impossible for the victim to have shot by his or her own hand. This is especially true if the wound was made in the back of the head. For suicides, the most common shot is to the temple of the head. The mouth, forehead, and chest are also common.

Also, if the wound was immediately incapacitating, the weapon should be present. Blood spatter analysis should be consistent with the proposed order of events. All victims involved in gunshot cases should have their hands swabbed for gunshot residue.

ACCIDENTAL   In all deaths that are ruled accidental, there must not be intent to cause harm through gross negligence on the part of a perpetrator or the victim. Traffic accidents make up a large percentage of accidental deaths, followed by drug overdoses and drownings. The surviving driver may have vehicular homicide charges brought against him or her, especially if the driver is determined to have been driving under the influence of drugs or alcohol. In this case, the official manner of death certified on the death certificate in many jurisdictions would be "vehicular homicide."

All cases that have the possibility of being ruled an accident should have toxicological analyses carried out. The presence of drugs and/or alcohol in the victim's system can potentially affect the determination. Also, the pathologist should be aware that some events might be disguised as accidents to cover up a homicide or suicide. For example, bodies recovered from a house fire might show evidence that the victims were dead before the fire started. This evidence might include a lack of soot in the victim's airways or no indication of elevated levels of carbon monoxide. This scenario, although not common, illustrates how the autopsy and scene can apparently not correlate with each other. No matter how obvious a scene may appear, the two should always correspond with one another. Cases of electrocution are generally ruled as accidents, but this may be difficult to prove. High-voltage electrocutions will usually leave burns on the body. Low-voltage electrocutions, however, may show few to no signs of trauma. The scene then becomes crucial in ascertaining the events surrounding the death.

The determination of manner of death in drownings (accidental, suicidal, or homicidal), falls (accidental, pushed, or deliberate), and asphyxiations can be exceedingly difficult, and therefore the investigation in all of its components becomes much more important than the autopsy.

NATURAL CAUSES   The differentiation between the categories of manner of death can be difficult to make. The distinction between natural and accidental deaths can pose challenges. The classification of natural death includes disease and continual environmental abuse. This abuse can encompass various events, such as chronic drug and alcohol abuse or longtime exposure to natural toxins or asbestos. Again, although drug abuse is deliberately committed by the victim, a death caused by drug use is not considered suicide unless it is clear that drugs were taken as an intentionally lethal act. Acute ethanol intoxication can be ruled as either natural or accidental depending on the circumstances. If the victim suffers from chronic alcoholism, the death is ruled to be natural. If the victim is a teenager experimenting with alcohol for the first time, the death is ruled an accident.

UNDETERMINED   A death is ruled to be undetermined only when a rational classification cannot be established. This can happen when the mechanism that caused the death cannot be determined by a physical finding at the autopsy or because of the absence of meaningful findings in the subsequent toxicological and microscopic examinations.

Quick Review

- The manner in which death occurred is classified in death certificates as one of five categories: homicide, suicide, accidental, natural, or undetermined.
- Homicide is generally defined as a nonaccidental death resulting from grossly negligent, reckless, or intentional actions of another person.
- Suicide is the result of an individual taking his or her own life with lethal intention. Although drug abuse is deliberately committed by a victim, it is not considered the cause of suicide unless it was clearly intended as a lethal act.
- In all deaths that are ruled accidental, there must not be intent to cause harm through gross negligence on the part of a perpetrator or the victim. Traffic accidents make up a large percentage of accidental deaths, followed by drug overdoses and drownings.
- The classification of natural death includes disease and continual environmental abuse. This abuse can encompass various events, such as chronic drug and alcohol abuse or longtime exposure to natural toxins or asbestos.
- An undetermined cause of death arises when the cause of death cannot be determined by a physical finding at the autopsy or because of the absence of meaningful findings in the subsequent toxicological and microscopic examinations.

ESTIMATING TIME OF DEATH

A pathologist can never give an exact time of death. However, there are many characteristics that the examiner can analyze in order to arrive at an approximate time of death. Some features can give a very probable time of death, but others are extremely variable. Witnesses can serve to reconstruct the events leading up to the death and the incidents that occurred after the death, along with the times when they occurred, but a single witness's account alone is not enough to make an accurate determination. The chemical and physical changes that occur after death must also be examined.

ALGOR MORTIS   After death, the body undergoes a process in which it continually adjusts to equalize with the environmental temperature. This process is known as **algor mortis**. An algor mortis determination must be performed at the scene as early as possible. The first step is to determine as best as possible

algor mortis
A process that occurs after death in which the body temperature continually cools until it reaches the ambient or room temperature.

FIGURE 6-10 Livor mortis.
Elizabeth Laposata

livor mortis
A medical condition that occurs after death and results in the settling of blood in areas of the body closest to the ground.

what the environmental temperatures may have been prior to discovering the body. Then the environmental temperature and the bilateral axillary and/or ear canal temperatures are recorded at the crime scene (rectal temperatures are usually too disruptive at the scene). The cooling rate of a typical body can be used to estimate the time of death. At average ambient temperatures of 70°F to 72°F, the body loses heat at a rate of approximately 1.0°F to 1.5°F per hour until the body reaches the ambient or room temperature. However, the rate of heat loss is influenced by factors such as ambient temperature, the size of the body, and the victim's clothing. Because of such factors, this method can only approximate the amount of time that has elapsed since death.

LIVOR MORTIS   Another condition that begins when circulation ceases is **livor mortis**. When the human heart stops pumping, the blood begins to settle in the parts of the body closest to the ground. As shown in Figure 6-10, the skin becomes a bluish-purple color in these areas. The onset of this condition begins 20 minutes to 3 hours after death and under average conditions continues for up to 16 hours after death, at which point all lividity, or coloring, is fixed. Initially, lividity can be pressed out of the vessels when the skin is pressed, that is, lividity can be "blanched." With time, coloring becomes "fixed" in the vessels, beginning in the most dependent (lowest) areas and progressing to the least dependent areas, then finally no blanching can be elicited anywhere. In any case, levels of lividity are tested at the scene with regard to whether it is completely fixed, blanches when subjected to light pressure, or blanches when subjected to significant pressure. A range of time of death can be estimated if at least some of the lividity is still blanching. However, the environmental temperature and the rate of body temperature decline (i.e., algor mortis) directly affect the rate of fixation of lividity and therefore must be taken into account when attempting to estimate time of death from lividity.

Different lividity patterns in a body may indicate that the body was moved after death, but before livor mortis had fully fixed. The skin does not become discolored in areas where the body is restricted by either clothing or an object pressing against the body. This information can be useful in determining whether the victim's position was changed after death. Livor mortis that is a deep purple is often seen in cases where the victim suffered asphyxia or heart failure.

rigor mortis
A medical condition that occurs after death and results in the stiffening of muscle mass. The rigidity of the body begins within 24 hours of death and disappears within 36 hours of death.

RIGOR MORTIS   Immediately following death, a chemical change occurs in the muscles that causes them to become rigid, as shown in Figure 6-11. This condition, **rigor mortis**, evolves over the first 24 hours under average temperature and body conditions. This rigidity subsides as time goes on, however, and disappears after about 36 hours under average conditions. Rigor will develop in the position that the body was in at the time of death, essentially freezing the body in that pose. Discovering a body in a position that defies gravity is a likely indicator that the body was moved after death.

Although rigor mortis can roughly indicate a time of death, there are factors that can alter this determination. An environment that is hot can speed up the process significantly. Conditions that affected the body before death, such as exercise or physical activity, can also speed up the process. Because rigor mortis occurs as a result of the muscles stiffening, individuals with decreased muscle mass may not develop rigor completely. Examples of these individuals may be infants or elderly or obese persons.

POTASSIUM EYE LEVELS   Another approach helpful for estimating the time of death is to determine potassium levels in the decedent's ocular fluid, that is, the fluid within the eye, also known as the "vitreous humor." It is important to draw a clean, bloodless vitreous sample from one eye with a syringe as soon as possible at the scene, then draw a second sample from the other eye an hour or two later.

FIGURE 6-11 Rigor mortis in the arms of a decedent. *Elizabeth Laposata*

After death, cells within the inner surface of the eyeball release potassium into the ocular fluid. By analyzing the amount of potassium present at various intervals after death, the forensic pathologist can determine the rate at which potassium is released into the vitreous humor and use it to approximate the time of death. However, the rate of potassium release also is dependent on ambient temperatures.

STOMACH CONTENTS Special attention must be paid to the digestive tract. The identification of food items in the stomach may help to determine the location of the decedent prior to death (during his or her last meal). The quantity, consistency, and color of bile, and the degree of digestion of food in the stomach and its passage into the small intestine can help to determine the time of death. The stomach also can contain partially digested or dissolved pills. Chemical analyses can be carried out to identify and analyze substances found in the stomach. These can aid in the determination of cause, and manner of death.

DECOMPOSITION Once decomposition has set in, the preceding methods of determining time of death are no longer of any use. After death, two decomposition processes take place: autolysis and putrefaction. Autolysis is fundamentally self-digestion by cells' own enzymes, and its rate varies from organ to organ depending on the mechanism of death, the enzyme content of the respective organs, the position of the body, and environmental factors. Putrefaction is decomposition carried out by microorganisms such as bacteria. Putrefaction is accompanied by bloating, discoloration, and a foul smell caused by accumulating gases. Again, the rate of putrefaction is dependent on the mechanism of death (e.g., congestive respiratory versus sudden cardiac death) allowing bacteria to spread from the bowel, presence or absence of infection, environmental temperatures and humidity, degree of obesity, extent of clothing, and so on. Green discoloration often begins in the abdomen. Darker green or purple discoloration follows on the face. The skin begins to blister with gas and then peel (called "slippage"). The skin of the hands and feet can actually detach and come off the body like a glove. This stage is also accompanied by bloating, which causes the eyes to bulge and the tongue to protrude. The chest and extremities will then turn a green/purple discoloration and bloat.

In the postmortem period of decomposition, a waxy substance called "adipocere" may form. Adipocere adds a white or gray waxlike consistency to fatty tissues in the face and extremities that can take on a yellow to tan color. Typically, adipocere takes about three months to develop.

Quick Review

- After death, the body undergoes a process known as algor mortis in which it will continually adjust to equalize with the environmental temperature.
- Another condition beginning when circulation ceases is livor mortis. When the human heart stops pumping, the blood begins to settle in the parts of the body closest to the ground. The skin becomes a bluish-purple color in these areas.
- Immediately following death, a chemical change known as rigor mortis occurs in the muscles, causing them to become rigid.
- Another approach helpful for estimating the time of death is to measure potassium levels in the ocular fluid.
- The identification of food items in the stomach may help to determine the location of the decedent prior to death, during his or her last meal.

Role of the Forensic Anthropologist

forensic anthropology
The use of anthropological knowledge of humans and skeletal structure to examine and identify human skeletal remains.

Forensic anthropology is concerned primarily with the identification and examination of human skeletal remains. Skeletal bones are remarkably durable and undergo an extremely slow breakdown process that lasts decades or centuries. Because of their resistance to decomposition, skeletal remains can provide a multitude of individual characteristics long after a victim's death. An examination of bones may reveal a victim's sex, approximate age, race, height, and the nature of a physical injury.

RECOVERING AND PROCESSING REMAINS

Thorough documentation is required throughout the processes of recovery and examination of human remains. A site where human remains are found must be treated as a crime scene (see Figure 6-12). These sites are usually located

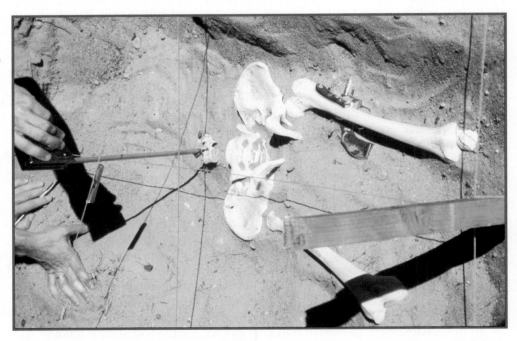

FIGURE 6-12   Crime-scene site showing a pelvis partly buried in sand and a femur lying across a revolver.
Paul Sledzik/National Transportation Safety Board

by civilians who then contact law enforcement personnel. The scene should be secured as soon as possible to prevent any further alteration of the scene. The scene should then be searched to locate all bones, if they are scattered, and any other items of evidence such as footwear impressions or discarded items. Many tools can be useful when searching for evidence at a "tomb" site, including aerial photography, metal detectors, ground-penetrating radar, infrared photography, apparatuses that detect the gases produced by biological decomposition, and so-called cadaver dogs that detect the odors caused by biological decomposition. All items that are found must be tagged, photographed, sketched, and documented in notes. Once all bones and other evidence are found, a scene sketch should be made to show the exact location of each item (preferably using global positioning system [GPS] coordinates), and the spatial relationship of all evidence. Once the skeletal remains have been recovered, they can be examined to deduce information about the identity of the decedent.

DETERMINING VICTIM CHARACTERISTICS

The sex of the decedent can be determined by the size and shape of various skeletal features, especially those of the pelvis and skull, or cranium. Female pelvic bones tend to form a wider, more circular opening than those in a male pelvis because of a woman's child-bearing capabilities. The female sacrum (flat bone above the tailbone) is wider and shorter (see Figure 6-13[a]) than a male's; the length and width of the male sacrum are roughly equal (see Figure 6-13[b]). The angle formed at the bottom of the pelvis (i.e., subpubic angle) is approximately a right angle (90 degrees) in females, but it is acute (less than 90 degrees) in males. In general, male craniums are larger in overall size than those of females. A male cranium tends to have a more pronounced brow bone and mastoid process (a bony protrusion behind the jaw) than a female cranium (see Figure 6-14). See Table 6.1 for a summary of the differing features of female and male skeletons from head to toe. These are typical cases; not all skeletons may display the given characteristics to clearly indicate the sex of the decedent.

The method for determining the age of a decedent varies depending on the victim's growth stage. For infants and toddlers, age can be estimated by

(a)   (b)

FIGURE 6-13   (a) Frontal shot of female pelvis and hips. This view shows the wide, circular nature of the pelvic opening and the short, wide nature of the sacrum. (b) Human male pelvis. This view shows the narrow pelvic opening and long, narrow sacrum. (a) *Geoff Brightling/Dorling Kindersley, Ltd.*

FIGURE 6-14   Male (left) and female (right) human skulls showing male skull's larger size and more pronounced brow bone. *Robert Marien/Corbis*

TABLE 6.1   Summary of Skeletal Features by Gender

	FEMALE	MALE
Cranium (skull)	Medium to large in size	Large in size
Forehead	High in height, vaulted, rounded	Low in height, sloped, backward
Brow bone	Diminished	Pronounced
Mastoid process	Diminished or absent	Pronounced
Mandible (jaw) angle	Obtuse (>90 degrees)	Approximately right (90 degrees)
Pelvis opening	Wide, circular	Narrow, noncircular
Sacrum	Short, wide, turned outward	Approximately equal width/length, turned inward
Subpubic angle	Approximately right (90 degrees)	Acute (<90 degrees)
Femur	Narrow, angled inward from pelvis	Thick, relatively straight from pelvis
Overall skeleton	Slender	Robust

the length of the long bones (e.g., femur and humerus) when compared to a known growth curve. Different sections of the skull also fuse together at different stages during early development, and the appearance of fused or divided sections can be used to estimate the age of bones still in early developmental stages (see Figure 6-15). In infant skeletons, formation of teeth can be used in age determination; this is based on the fact that permanent teeth start to form

FIGURE 6-15   A lateral view of a fetal skull showing the separated bones of the skull before they have had a chance to fuse. *Dave King/Dorling Kindersley, Ltd.*

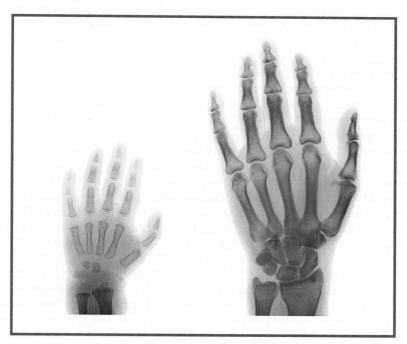

FIGURE 6-16   Colored X-rays of healthy human hands at 3 years (left) and at 20 years. Bones display in red, and flesh is in blue. The child's hand has areas of cartilage in the joints between the finger bones (i.e., epiphyseal areas), where bone growth and fusion will occur. In the adult hand, all the bones are present, and the joints have closed. *SPL/Science Source*

at birth. If the skeletal remains belong to a child, the age of the decedent may be determined by observing the fusion or lack of fusion of epiphyseal regions of bones such as those of the mandible (i.e., lower jaw), fingers, wrist, long bones, and clavicle (see Figure 6-16). The average age at which each of these

FIGURE 6-17 The skull of an adult, with part of the jaw cut away to show the developing teeth.
John Watney/Science Source

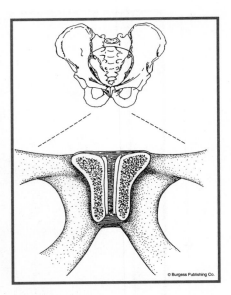

FIGURE 6-18 The symphysis pubis shown magnified beneath human pelvic bones.
Pearson Education Custom Publishing

regions fuses is known and can be compared against the state of the remains to provide a range of possible ages for the decedent. A child's cranium may also be identified by its smaller size and the presence of developing teeth as contrasted with the skull of an adult showing developing teeth (see Figure 6-17). After age 21, age is estimated by the level of change the surfaces of the bones have undergone, especially in areas of common wear such as the pubic symphysis. The pubic symphyseal face shown in Figure 6-18 is a raised platform that slowly changes over the years from a rough, rugged surface to a smooth, well-defined area. See Table 6.2 for a summary of the skeletal closures by age. It is important to note that these are average ages for closures; not all skeletons display closures at the given ages.

Although the categorization "race" has come under scrutiny and is difficult to define, forensic anthropologists use broad classes to characterize the likely (but not definite) ancestry of skeletal remains. The possible racial ancestry of the decedent can be assessed by the appearance of various cranial features on the skeletal remains. For example, eye orbits tend to be circular in Mongoloid skeletons (i.e., of Asian descent), oval in Caucasoid skeletons (i.e., of European descent), and square in Negroid skeletons (i.e., of African descent). The frontal plane of the cranium may also vary. The frontal plane of Mongoloid craniums may be flat or projected outward; that of Caucasoid craniums is flat; and that of Negroid craniums is projected outward. The nasal cavity tends to be small and rounded in Mongoloids, long and narrow in Caucasoids, and wide in Negroids. Skeletal remains of decedents of Asian ancestry, including those of Native American descent, also tend to have "scooped-out" or shovel-shaped incisor teeth. See Table 6.3 for a summary of the differing features of skeletons that can indicate ancestry. These are typical cases; not all skeletons may display the given characteristics to indicate the ancestry of the decedent.

The height of the victim, when alive, can be estimated by measuring the long bones of the skeleton, especially in the lower limbs. Even partial bones can yield useful results. However, meaningful stature calculations from known equations must be based on the determined sex and race of the remains. See Table 6.4 for examples of equations used to calculate the height of the decedent from skeletal remains. These equations should yield estimations within 5 cm of actual height.

TABLE 6.2 Summary of Skeletal Closures by Age

AGE (MONTHS)	CLOSURE
6–9	Mandible (jaw) fused
4–6	Humerus head bones fused
7–8	Pelvis frontal bones fused
4–16	Femur shaft sections built
9–13	Elbow bones fused
10	Finger bones fused
16–18	Femur head bones fused to shaft bones
18	Wrist bones fused
18–21	Humerus head bones fused to shaft bones
18–24	Sternum fused to clavicle
20–25	Pelvic bones fully formed
21–22	Clavicle fused
21–30	Labodial suture (rear of cranium) fused
24–30	Sacrum bones fused
30–32	Sagittal suture (center of cranium) fused
48–50	Coronal suture (front of cranium) fused

TABLE 6.3 Summary of Skeletal Characteristics Indicating Racial Ancestry

	EYE ORBITALS	NASAL CAVITY	INCISORS	CRANIUM FRONTAL PLANE
Caucasoid	Oval	Long, narrow	Smooth	Flat
Mongoloid	Circular	Small, rounded	Shoveled interior	Flat or projected outward
Negroid	Square	Wide	Smooth	Projected outward

OTHER CONTRIBUTIONS OF FORENSIC ANTHROPOLOGY

A forensic anthropologist may create facial reconstructions to help identify skeletal remains. Facial reconstruction clay is placed and shaped over the victim's actual cranium, and it takes into account the decedent's estimated age, ancestry, and sex (see Figure 6-19). With the help of this technique, a composite of the victim can be drawn and advertised in an attempt to identify the victim.

Forensic anthropologists are also helpful in identifying victims of a mass disaster such as a plane crash. When such a tragedy occurs, forensic

■■■■ CASEFILES ■■■■
IDENTIFYING A SERIAL KILLER'S VICTIMS

The worst serial killer in the United States calmly admitted his guilt as he led investigators to a crawl space under his house. There, John Wayne Gacy had buried 28 young men, after brutally raping and murdering them in cold blood. Because no forms of identification were found with the bodies, the police were forced to examine missing-person reports for leads. However, these boys and men were so alike in age, race, and stature that police were unable to individually identify most of the victims. Clyde Snow, the world-renowned forensic anthropologist from Oklahoma, was asked to help the investigators make these difficult identifications.

Snow began by making a 35-point examination of each skull for comparison to known individuals. By examining each skeleton, he made sure each bone was correctly attributed to an individual. This was crucial to later efforts because some of the victims had been buried on top of older graves, mingling their remains. Once Snow was sure all the bones were sorted properly, he began his in-depth study. Long bones such as the femur (thigh bone) were used to estimate each individual's height. This helped narrow the search in the attempt to match the victims with the descriptions of missing people.

After narrowing the list of missing people to those fitting the general description, investigators consulted missing persons' hospital and dental records. Evidence of injury, illness, or surgery and other unique skeletal defects of the victims were matched to information in the records to make identifications. Snow also pointed out features that gave useful clues to the victim's behavior and medical history. For example, he discovered that one of Gacy's victims had a healed fracture on his left arm, and that his left scapula (shoulder blade) and arm bore the telltale signs of a left-handed individual. These details were matched to a missing-person report, and another young victim was identified.

For the most difficult cases, Snow called in the help of forensic sculptor and facial reconstructionist Betty Pat Gatliff. She used clay and depth markers to put the "flesh" back on the faces of these forgotten boys in the hopes that someone would recognize them after the photographs of the reconstructed faces were released to the media. Her efforts were successful, but investigators found some families unwilling to accept the idea that their loved one was among Gacy's victims. Even with Gatliff's help, nine of Gacy's victims remain unidentified.

TABLE 6.4   Equations for Height Calculation from Skeletal Remains

	CAUCASOID	NEGROID	UNKNOWN ANCESTRY
Female	Height (cm) = femur length (cm) × 2.47 + 54.10	Height (cm) = femur length (cm) × 2.28 + 59.76	Height (cm) = femur length (cm) × 3.01 + 32.52
	Height (cm) = humerus length (cm) × 3.36 + 57.97	Height (cm) = humerus length (cm) × 3.08 + 64.67	Height (cm) = humerus length (cm) × 4.62 + 19.00
Male	Height (cm) = femur length (cm) × 2.32 + 65.53	Height (cm) = femur length (cm) × 2.10 + 72.22	Height (cm) = femur length (cm) × 2.71 + 45.86
	Height (cm) = humerus length (cm) × 2.89 + 78.10	Height (cm) = humerus length (cm) × 2.88 + 75.48	Height (cm) = humerus length (cm) × 4.62 + 19.00

anthropologists can help identify victims using the collection of bone fragments. Usually, the identification of the remains will depend on medical records, especially dental records of the individuals. However, definite identification of remains can be made only by analyzing the decedent's DNA profile, fingerprints, or medical records. Recovered remains may still contain some soft tissue material, such as the tissue of the hand, which may yield a DNA profile for identification purposes. If the tissue is dried out, it may be possible to rehydrate it to recover fingerprints also.

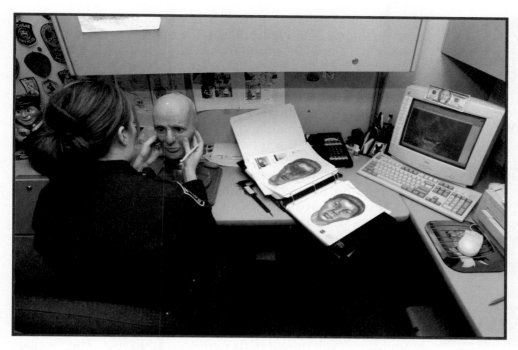

FIGURE 6-19   Trooper Sarah Foster, a Michigan State Police forensic artist, works on a three-dimensional facial reconstruction from an unidentified human skull at Richmond Post in Richmond, MI. *Paul Sancya/ AP Images*

Quick Review

- Forensic anthropology is concerned primarily with the identification and examination of human skeletal remains.
- The gender of the decedent can be determined by the size and shape of various skeletal features, especially those of the pelvis and skull, or cranium.
- The height of the victim when alive can be estimated by measuring the long bones of the skeleton, especially those in the lower limbs.

Role of the Forensic Entomologist

The study of insects and their relation to a criminal investigation is known as forensic entomology. In practice, **forensic entomology** is commonly used to estimate the time of death when the circumstances surrounding the crime are unknown. This determination can be carried out by observing the stage of development of maggots or insects' sequence of arrival.

DETERMINING TIME OF DEATH

After decomposition begins, necrophilious insects, or insects that feed on dead tissue, are the first to infest the body, usually within 24 hours. The most common and important of these is the blowfly, recognized by its green or blue color. Blowfly eggs are laid in human remains and ultimately hatch into maggots, or fly larvae, that consume human organs and tissues (see Figure 6-20). Typically, a single blowfly can lay up to 2,000 eggs during its lifetime. The resulting larvae gather and feed as a "maggot mass" on the

forensic entomology
The study of insect matter, growth patterns, and succession of arrival at a crime scene to determine the time since death.

FIGURE 6-20 A scanning electron micrograph of 2-hour-old blowfly maggots. *Jeremy Burgess/ Science Source*

postmortem interval (PMI)
The length of time that has elapsed since a person has died. If the time is not known, a number of medical or scientific techniques may be used to estimate it.

decomposing remains. Forensic entomologists can approximate how long a body has been left exposed by examining the stage of development of the fly larvae. This kind of determination is best for a timeline of hours to approximately one month because the blowfly goes through the stages of its life cycle at a known sequence and in known time intervals that span this period. By determining the most developed stage of fly found on the body, entomologists can approximate the **postmortem interval (PMI)**, or the time that has elapsed since death (see Figure 6-21). Newly emerged flies are of important forensic interest, as they indicate that an entire blowfly cycle has been completed on the decomposing body. Likewise, empty pupal cases indicate that a fly has completed its entire life cycle on the body. Flies known as "cheese skippers" are primarily found on human corpses in the later stages of decomposition, long after the blowflies have left the corpse.

Time determinations based on the blowfly cycle are not always straightforward, however. The time required for each stage of development is affected by environmental influences such as geographical location, climate, weather conditions, and the presence of drugs. For example, cold temperatures hinder the development of fly eggs into adult flies. The forensic entomologist must consider these conditions when estimating the PMI.

Information about the arrival of other species of insects may also help determine the PMI. The sequence of arrival of these groups depends mostly on the body's natural decomposition process. Predator insects generally arrive and prey on the necrophilious insects. Several kinds of beetles will be found, either feeding directly on the corpse's tissues or as predators feeding on blowfly eggs and maggots present on the corpse. Next, omnivore insects arrive at the body. These insects feed on the body, on other insects, and on any surrounding vegetation. Ants and wasps are an example of omnivore insects. Last comes the arrival of indigenous insects, such as spiders, whose presence on or near the body is coincidental as they move about their environment.

OTHER CONTRIBUTIONS OF FORENSIC ENTOMOLOGY

Entomological evidence can also provide other pertinent information. In general, insects first colonize the body's naturally moist orifices. However, if open wounds are present, they will colonize there first. Although the decomposition processes may conceal wounds, colonization away from natural orifices may indicate the locations of wounds on the body. If maggots are found extensively on the hands and forearms, for example, this suggests the presence of defensive wounds on the victim. Insects that have fed on the body may also have accumulated any drugs present in the flesh, and analyzing these insects can yield the identity of these drugs.

If resources allow, all insect evidence should be carefully collected by a forensic entomology expert. When this is not possible, collection should be carried out by an investigator with experience in death investigation. The entire body and the area where insect evidence was found must be photographed and documented before collection. Insect specimens should be taken from each area on the body where they are found and labeled to show from where they were collected.

■ ■ ■ ■ CASEFILES ■ ■ ■ ■
THE DANIELLE VAN DAM MURDER CASE

Sometime during the night of February 1, 2002, seven-year-old Danielle Van Dam disappeared from her bedroom in the Sabre Springs suburb of San Diego, California. On February 27, three and a half weeks later, searchers found her naked body in a trash-covered lot about 25 miles from her home. Because of the high degree of decomposition of the girl's remains, the medical examiner could not pinpoint the exact time of the girl's death. Her neighbor, fifty-year-old engineer David Westerfield, was accused of kidnapping Danielle, killing her, and dumping her body in the desert. During the subsequent investigation, Danielle's blood was found on Westerfield's clothes, her fingerprints and blood were found in his RV, and child pornography was found on his home computer.

The actual time of the seven-year-old's death became a central issue during the murder trial. Westerfield had been under constant police surveillance since February 4. Any suggestion that Danielle was placed at the dump site after that date would have eliminated him as a suspect. Conflicting expert testimony was elicited from forensic entomologists who were called on to estimate when the body was dumped. The forensic entomologist who went to the dump site, witnessed the autopsy, and collected and analyzed insects from both locations estimated that Danielle died between February 16 and 18. A forensic entomologist and a forensic anthropologist both called to testify on behalf of the prosecution noted that the very hot, very dry weather at the dump site might have mummified Danielle's body almost immediately, thus causing a delay in the flies colonizing the body.

The jurors convicted Westerfield of the kidnapping and murder of Danielle Van Dam, and a San Diego judge sentenced David Westerfield to death. Danielle Van Dam's parents filed and settled a wrongful death suit against Westerfield, requiring his automotive and homeowners' insurance carriers to pay the Van Dams an undisclosed amount, reported to be between $400,000 and $1 million.

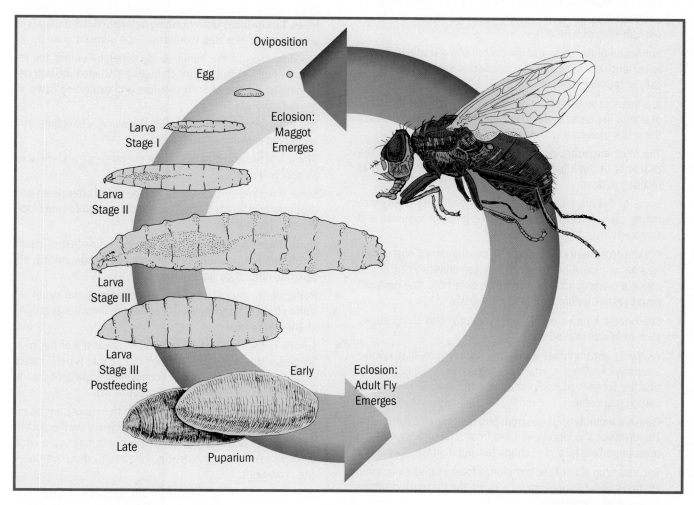

FIGURE 6-21   Typical blowfly life cycle from egg deposition to adult fly emergence. This cycle is representative of any one of nearly ninety species of blowflies in North America. *Based on E.P. Catts, Entomology and Death: A Procedural Guide. 1990, 2008*

Quick Review

- Forensic entomologists can approximate how long a body has been left exposed by examining the stage of development of fly larvae on the body.
- Information about the arrival of other species of insects may also help determine the postmortem interval. The sequence of arrival of these groups depends mostly on the body's natural decomposition process.
- In general, insects first colonize the body's naturally moist orifices. However, if open wounds are present, they will colonize there first.

CHAPTER REVIEW

- Forensic pathologists associated with the medical examiner's or coroner's office are responsible for determining the cause of an undetermined or unexpected death.
- Although both the coroner's office and the medical examiner's office are charged with investigating suspicious deaths, only the pathologist is trained to perform an autopsy. The tasks of examining the body for cause and manner of death and recording the results in the death certificate are all responsibilities of both offices.
- Protection of the body and the overall scene is of paramount importance, as is the ultimate removal of the body in a medically acceptable manner.
- A primary objective of the autopsy is to determine the cause of death. The cause of death is defined as that which initiates the series of events ending in death.
- The most important determination in a violent death is the character of the injury that started the chain of events that resulted in death.
- Some of the more common causes of death are blunt-force injury, sharp-force injuries, asphyxia, gunshot wounds, and substance abuse.
- A blunt-force injury is caused by a nonsharpened object such as a bat or pipe. A blunt-force injury can abrade tissue or can cause a contusion arising from bleeding from tiny ruptured blood vessels within and beneath the skin.
- Sharp-force injuries occur from weapons with sharp edges, such as knives or blades.
- Asphyxia encompasses a variety of conditions that involve interference with the intake of oxygen. For example, death at a fire scene is caused primarily by the extremely toxic gas carbon monoxide.
- Gunshot wounds originate from projectiles fired by a firearm. The distance a weapon was fired from a target is one of the most important factors in characterizing a gunshot wound.
- Because drug abuse is so common, a forensic pathologist will routinely order toxicological tests for the presence of drugs in nearly all autopsies.

- An autopsy, in its broadest definition, is simply the examination of a body after death.
- The forensic autopsy consists of an external examination and an internal examination.
- The first steps taken for the external examination include a broad overview of the condition of the body and the clothing.
- The external examination also consists of classifying the injuries. This includes distinguishing between different types of wounds, such as a stab wound versus a gunshot wound.
- The dissection of the human body generally entails the removal of all internal organs through a Y-shaped incision beginning at the top of each shoulder and extending down to the pubic bone.
- The internal examination entails weighing, dissecting, and sectioning each organ of the body.
- Blood is often tested to determine the presence and levels of alcohol and drugs.
- Some drugs redistribute or reenter the blood after death and thus may complicate the interpretation of postmortem blood levels of these drugs.
- The manner in which death occurred is classified in death certifications as one of five categories: homicide, suicide, accidental, natural, or undetermined.
- Homicide is generally defined as a nonaccidental death resulting from grossly negligent, reckless, or intentional actions of another person.
- Suicide is the result of an individual taking his or her own life with lethal intention. Although drug abuse is deliberately committed by a victim, it is not considered a cause of suicide unless it was clearly intended as a lethal act.
- In all deaths that are ruled accidental, there must not be intent to cause harm through gross negligence on the part of a perpetrator or the victim. Traffic accidents make up a large percentage of accidental deaths, followed by drug overdoses and drownings.
- The classification of natural death includes disease and continual environmental abuse. This abuse can encompass

various events, such as chronic drug and alcohol abuse or longtime exposure to natural toxins or asbestos.

- An undetermined cause of death arises when the cause of death cannot be determined by a physical finding at the autopsy or because of the absence of meaningful findings in the subsequent toxicological and microscopic examinations.

- After death, the body undergoes a process known as algor mortis in which it will continually adjust to equalize with the environmental temperature.

- Another condition beginning when circulation ceases is livor mortis. When the human heart stops pumping, the blood begins to settle in the parts of the body closest to the ground. The skin appears bluish-purple in these areas.

- Immediately following death, a chemical change known as rigor mortis occurs in the muscles, causing them to become rigid.

- Another approach helpful for estimating the time of death is to measure potassium levels in the ocular fluid.

- The identification of food items in the stomach may help to determine the location of the decedent prior to death (i.e., during his or her last meal).

- Forensic anthropology is concerned primarily with the identification and examination of human skeletal remains.

- The gender of the decedent can be determined by the size and shape of various skeletal features, especially those in the pelvis and skull, or cranium.

- The height of the victim when alive can be estimated by measuring the long bones of the skeleton, especially those in the lower limbs.

- Forensic entomologists can approximate how long a body has been left exposed by examining the stage of development of the fly larvae on the body.

- Information about the arrival of other species of insects may also help determine the postmortem interval. The sequence of arrival of these groups depends mostly on the body's natural decomposition process.

- In general, insects first colonize the body's naturally moist orifices. However, if open wounds are present, they will colonize there first.

KEY TERMS

algor mortis, 135

autopsy, 129

cause of death, 125

forensic anthropology, 138

forensic entomology, 145

forensic pathologist, 124

livor mortis, 136

manner of death, 133

petechiae, 127

postmortem interval (PMI), 146

rigor mortis, 136

REVIEW QUESTIONS

1. The titles of _____ and _____ are often used interchangeably, but there are significant differences in their job descriptions.

2. True or False: The medical examiner is an elected official and is not required to possess a medical degree. _____

3. Although both a coroner and a forensic pathologist are charged with investigating a suspicious death, only the _____ is trained to perform an autopsy.

4. True or False: If it appears that a victim did not shoot him- or herself or anyone else, the victim's hands should not be swabbed. _____

5. The primary objective of the autopsy is to determine the _____.

6. True or False: The manner of death is defined as that which initiates the series of events ending in death. _____

7. A(n) _____ force injury can abrade and crush tissue.

8. True or False: The outward appearance of the injuries will always match the injuries sustained inside the body. _____

9. Wounds on a victim's forearm may be _____ wounds.

10. True or False: A lack of any defense wounds can lead a pathologist to believe that the victim was either unconscious or somehow tied up during the assault. _____

11. Asphyxia encompasses a variety of conditions that involve interference with the intake of _____.

12. True or False: Death at a fire scene is primarily caused by the extremely toxic gas carbon monoxide. _____

13. The protein in red blood cells that transports oxygen is known as _____.

14. True or False: High levels of carbon monoxide must be present for a victim to become disoriented and lose consciousness. _____

15. True or False: Carbon monoxide will continue to build up in the body after death. _____

16. Carbon monoxide levels and the presence of soot can be used to determine whether the individual was _____ at the time of the fire.

17. Victims of hangings often show signs of _____ on the eyelids, cheeks, and forehead.

18. Petechiae are caused by the escaping of blood into the tissue as a result of _____ bursting.

19. True or False: Petechiae are more common in hangings than strangulation deaths. _____

20. True or False: Typically the hyoid bone and thyroid cartilage are not fractured in hanging cases. _____

21. True or False: For gunshot victims, the cause of death can be listed as a gunshot wound. _____

22. True or False: Because drug abuse is so common, the forensic pathologist will routinely test for the presence of drugs in nearly all investigations. _____

23. A(n) _____ in its broadest definition is simply the examination of a body after death.

24. True or False: There are two types of autopsies: a forensic/medicolegal autopsy and a clinical/hospital autopsy. _____

25. The autopsy consists of a(n) _____ examination and a(n) _____ examination.

26. The discharge from a firearm will produce characteristic markings on the skin known as _____.

27. True or False: X-ray examinations are most commonly performed in gunshot wound cases and stab wound cases. _____

28. Pulmonary _____, or fluid accumulation in the lungs, is frequently found in victims of chronic cocaine and amphetamine abuse.

29. True or False: The liver can contain partially digested or dissolved pills. _____

30. True or False: The ideal location to take a blood sample is from the heart. _____

31. _____ is the redistribution of drugs after death.

32. True or False: General testing for poisons is not a routine procedure carried out by the pathologist. _____

33. A body that displays a cherry-red discoloration often leads a pathologist to suspect poisoning by _____.

34. True or False: A pathologist can often give an exact time of death. _____

35. The process of the body's continually decreasing in temperature after death until it reaches the environmental temperature is known as _____.

36. The process of the blood settling in parts of the body closest to the ground after death is known as _____.

37. True or False: Different lividity patterns on a body may indicate that the body was moved after death but before livor mortis had fully fixed. _____

38. Levels of _____ in the ocular fluid can help indicate the time of death.

39. After death, two decomposition processes take place: _____ and _____.

40. The female bone structure differs from the male structure within the _____ area because of a woman's childbearing capabilities.

41. True or False: A definite identification of remains cannot be made through the analysis of the decedent's DNA profile, fingerprints, or medical records. _____

42. True or False: A site where human remains are found must be treated as a crime scene, and the site and surrounding area should be secured, searched, and carefully processed. _____

43. The field of _____ takes advantage of the durable nature of bones over a long period of time to examine and identify human skeletal remains through a multitude of individual characteristics.

44. The study of insects and their relation to a criminal investigation, known as _____, is commonly used to estimate the time of death when the circumstances surrounding the crime are unknown.

45. By determining the oldest stage of fly found on the body and taking environmental factors into consideration, entomologists can approximate the _____ interval.

46. True or False: Another method to determine PMI is by observing the schedule of arrival of different species of insects on the body. _____

■■■■ APPLICATION AND CRITICAL THINKING

1. Rigor mortis, livor mortis, and algor mortis are all used to help determine time of death. However, each method has its limitations. For each method, describe at least one condition that would render that method unsuitable or inaccurate for determining time of death.

2. What kind of forensic expert would most likely be asked to help identify human remains in each of the following conditions?
   a) A body that has been decomposing for a day or two
   b) Fragmentary remains of a few arm bones and part of a jaw
   c) A skeleton that is missing its skull

3. Identify a reasonable manner of death for each of the following situations:
   a) A contact wound to the back of the head
   b) An elevated carboxyhemoglobin blood level in a fire victim
   c) A fractured hyoid bone
   d) Death by overdose of a first-time user of alcohol
   e) A gunshot wound to the chest from a distance of 3 feet
   f) Sudden death of a young chronic user of cocaine

4. Creating a Forensic Anthropology Victim Profile

A nearly complete human skeleton has been found. The skeleton has the features shown in the accompanying table and image. Approximate the gender, ancestry, age range, and height of the individual based on this information.

Geoff Brightling/Dorling Kindersley, Ltd.

Cranium	
Size	Medium
Forehead	Rounded, projected outward
Mastoid process	Absent
Jaw	Angle = 110 degrees
Teeth	All permanent
Sagittal suture	Not fused
Coronal suture	Not fused
Eye orbits	Squared
Nasal cavity	Large, wide
Incisors	Smooth
Pelvis	
Opening	*See figure*
Sacrum	*See figure*
Subpubic angle	90–100 degrees
Long Bones	
Femur	Fully fused, 44.1 cm long
Clavicle	Fully fused

Gender _____   Ancestry _____

Age Range _____   Height _____

5. Sequence of Insect Arrival in Forensic Entomology

The following images depict the sequence of events at the site of a decomposing body. Place the arrival events in order of occurrence from earliest to latest.

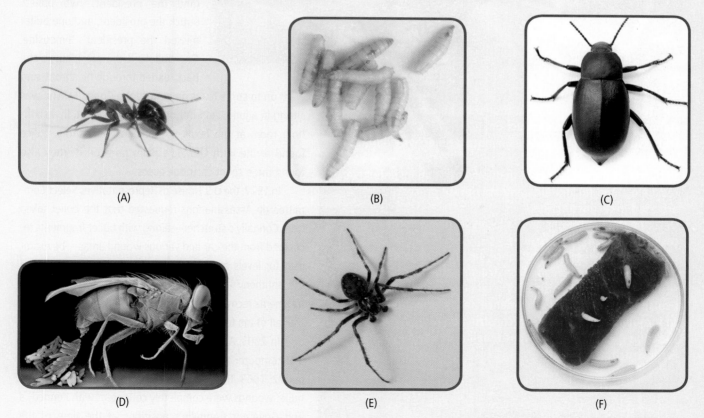

(A)   (B)   (C)

(D)   (E)   (F)

(A) *Tim Ridley/Dorling Kindersley, Ltd.;* (B) *Kim Taylor/Dorling Kindersley, Ltd.;* (C) *irin-k/Shutterstock;* (D) *Volker Steger/Science Source;* (E) *Jerry Young/Dorling Kindersley, Ltd.;* (F) *Andy Crawford/Dorling Kindersley, Ltd.*

7 Crime-Scene Reconstruction

LEARNING OBJECTIVES

After studying this chapter, you should be able to:

- Define crime-scene reconstruction.
- Discuss the ways investigators maintain objectivity during reconstruction.
- Understand the processes of deductive reasoning, inductive reasoning, and falsifiability and how these processes are used in reconstruction.
- Describe the limitations and fallacies involved in the reconstruction of crime scenes.
- Explain the role physical evidence, testimonial evidence, and reenactments play in reconstructing the events surrounding the commission of a crime.
- Explain the assessment of evidence and information to formulate a crime-scene reconstruction.
- Describe the utility of an event timeline in a crime-scene reconstruction.

THE ASSASSINATION OF PRESIDENT KENNEDY

Ever since President John F. Kennedy was killed in 1963, questions have lingered about whether Lee Harvey Oswald was part of a conspiracy to assassinate the president or a lone assassin. The Warren Commission, the official government body appointed to investigate the shooting, concluded that Oswald acted alone. However, over the years, eyewitness accounts and acoustical data interpreted by some experts have been used to contend that a second shooter fired at the president from a region in front of the limousine (the so-called "grassy knoll").

In arriving at its conclusions, the Warren Commission reconstructed the crime as follows: From a hidden position on the sixth floor of the Texas School Book Depository building where he worked, Oswald fired three shots from behind the president. Two bullets struck the president, and one bullet missed the president's limousine. One bullet hit the president in the back, exited through his throat, and went on to strike Texas governor John Connally, who was sitting in a jump seat in front of the president. In a sixth-floor room at the Texas School Book Depository, police found a rifle with Oswald's palm print on it. They also found three spent cartridge cases.

In 1977, the U.S. House of Representatives Select Committee on Assassinations requested that the bullet taken from Connally's stretcher—along with bullet fragments recovered from the car and various wound areas—be examined for levels of trace elements. Investigators compared the antimony and silver content of the bullet and bullet fragments recovered after the assassination and concluded that all of the fragments probably came from two bullets.

In 2003, ABC TV broadcast the results of a ten-year 3-D computer animation study of the events of November 22, 1963. The animation graphically showed that the bullet wounds were completely consistent with Kennedy's and Governor Connally's positions at the time of the shooting, and that by following the bullets' trajectories backward they could have originated only from a narrow region including a few windows on the sixth floor of the School Book Depository.

Fundamentals of Crime-Scene Reconstruction

Previous discussions dealing with the processes of identification and comparison have stressed laboratory work routinely performed by forensic scientists. However, there is another dimension to the role that forensic scientists play during the course of a criminal investigation: participating in a team effort to reconstruct events that occurred prior to, during, and subsequent to the commission of a crime.

Reconstructing the circumstances of a crime scene entails a collaborative effort that includes experienced law enforcement personnel, medical examiners, and criminalists. All of these professionals contribute unique perspectives to develop the crime-scene reconstruction. Was more than one person involved? How was the victim killed? Were actions taken to cover up what took place? To answer these questions, all personnel involved with the investigation must pay careful attention and think logically.

Crime-scene reconstruction is the method used to develop a likely sequence of events at a crime scene by observing and evaluating physical evidence and statements made by individuals involved with the incident. The evidence may also include information obtained from reenactments. Therefore, reconstructions have the best chance of being accurate when investigators use proper documentation and collection methods for all types of evidence.

STRIVING FOR OBJECTIVITY

One of the most important features of a logical and systematic inquiry is objectivity. **Objectivity** is professional detachment practiced by individuals to avoid letting personal beliefs or biases affect the conclusions they reach through observations. Even trained scientists come to their jobs with some expectations or biases. These can have a negative effect on the process of reconstruction by leading to the incorrect analysis or interpretation of the information provided by the evidence. For that reason, all data and evidence must be continually reevaluated throughout the process of crime-scene reconstruction. It may also be wise to have several individuals analyze the evidence and present independent interpretations.

Investigators should approach each case free of previous theories or expectations. For example, if a victim is found dead from a gunshot wound to the temple and he is holding a gun, the investigator should not assume his death was a suicide. Surmising that the death was a suicide may cause the investigator to create a "self-fulfilling prophecy" by considering only information that supports this theory in the reconstruction. Crime-scene reconstruction personnel should never try to *prove* any theory or hypothesis. Instead, they should use the processes of deductive reasoning, inductive reasoning, and falsifiability to create a logical reconstruction of crime-scene events.

DEDUCTIVE REASONING **Deductive reasoning** is the process of drawing a conclusion based on known facts or premises. Using deductive reasoning allows an investigator to come to a definitive conclusion. For example, if an investigator finds a fingerprint from the victim on a table, then the victim *definitely* touched the table with whatever finger the print came from. This conclusion makes no assumptions about how, when, or why the victim touched the table, but it establishes a concrete event. Another example is locating a muddy footprint outside the door of a burglary scene. Laboratory examination shows the impression to have individual markings belonging to a sneaker owned by a suspect. Linking the footprint to a particular suspect strongly suggests the presence of the suspect's footwear at the crime scene. This observation becomes particularly relevant in identifying the suspect as the perpetrator if it can be shown that the suspect has no prior association with the locale of the crime.

crime-scene reconstruction
The method used to develop a likely sequence of events at a crime scene by the observation and evaluation of physical evidence and statements made by individuals involved with the incident.

objectivity
A manner of professional detachment practiced by individuals to avoid letting personal beliefs or biases affect the conclusions reached through observations.

deductive reasoning
The process of drawing a conclusion based on known facts or premises.

inductive reasoning
The process of drawing a conclusion from premises one does not know are correct.

INDUCTIVE REASONING   When using **inductive reasoning**, one attempts to draw a conclusion based on premises one does not know are correct. This process leads to a conclusion that is probable but not definitive. Here the danger is overgeneralization—making an observation about an event and assuming the observation is always or nearly always applicable to events of the same kind. For example, if a large amount of a victim's blood is found at a crime scene, then the victim *probably* was present and injured at the crime scene. It is also possible that the victim was injured somewhere else and large amounts of the victim's blood were transported to the scene, but this scenario is not *probable*. One must be careful using conclusions drawn from inductive reasoning, and never confuse them with conclusions drawn from deductive reasoning.

falsifiability
The ability of a theory to be disproved by being tested against known information.

FALSIFIABILITY   It is very easy for an investigator to locate and include evidence that supports a theory. To avoid causing a self-fulfilling prophecy, investigators should test the **falsifiability** of a theory. This means that they should try to *disprove* the theory. Those involved in reconstructing the crime scene must always be aware of all *plausible alternatives* that could have led to the state of any piece of evidence. They must keep an open mind to avoid narrowing their view to one or a few possibilities, potentially excluding more plausible scenarios. Once they have identified all possibilities, the investigators should set about prioritizing their reconstruction theories. They may do this by examining each alternative explanation and determining how consistent it is with the physical evidence, eyewitness accounts, and general dynamics of the crime scene.

The crime-scene reconstruction typically produces the *most probable* conclusion. However, being mindful of plausible alternate explanations will help provide other leads if an aspect of a reconstruction theory does not appear to fit all the facts of the case. No evidence or data should ever be excluded. A crime-scene reconstruction theory must be supported by *all* interpreted evidence or it cannot be accepted.

LIMITATIONS TO RECONSTRUCTION

Crime-scene investigators apply systematic reasoning to bolster their reconstructions, but certain fallacies of reasoning can undermine their conclusions. Each inquiry must be accompanied by an attitude of skepticism and knowledge of fallacies that can impede a search for the truth.

BIFURCATION   The fallacy of bifurcation happens when investigators or attorneys try to apply a simple "yes or no" answer to a complex question. Not all information gained from the crime scene leads to a clear-cut solution or conclusion, and asking for a simple answer to a complex question may be an attempt to cloud the truth.

GENERALIZATION   Generalizing about aspects of evidence can be both helpful and harmful to an investigation. Generalizations about the shape of bloodstains can help determine the direction and approximate angle of the deposition of a droplet. This is helpful to the investigation and reconstruction. However, generalizations about the kind of force that creates a pattern may send the investigation in the wrong direction. For example, fine droplets, called "high-velocity spatter," are usually found when a victim suffers a gunshot wound. However, sometimes blunt force beatings also produce fine droplets that look like high-velocity spatter. If an investigator generalizes that high-velocity spatter always comes from gunshot wounds, this may divert the investigation toward looking for a weapon that doesn't exist.

FALSE LINKAGE   False linkage occurs when an investigator assumes a link between two or more objects of evidence that starts the investigation down the wrong path. For example, suppose that investigators find footwear impressions at a crime scene in a high-traffic area of a park. The investigators may assume the impressions are linked to the perpetrator when in truth they may belong to an unrelated person who walked there earlier in the day.

The biggest limitation associated with reconstruction is that investigators can use only what is left behind to theorize what occurred in the past. The information available to make these theories is often much less than would be needed to create a full timeline of events. The reconstruction team can only strive to make optimum use of all the available evidence, witness statements, and appropriate investigative leads to define what events occurred at specific moments and the order in which they happened. Reconstruction also relies on information from toxicology tests, DNA typing, autopsies, interrogations, and many other sources. However, the results of these tests and processes may take quite a bit of time. This means that the reconstructing team may not receive all relevant information for days, weeks, or months after the incident. It is important to remember that crime-scene reconstruction does not provide instant gratification for all the effort it requires.

Quick Review

- Because crime-scene reconstruction develops a likely sequence of events at a crime scene with physical evidence, testimony, and reenactments, proper documentation and collection methods must be used for all types of evidence.
- Investigative personnel bring some expectations or biases to reconstruction, and these can have a negative effect on the process. It is, therefore, very important for personnel to practice objectivity, or professional distance.
- The processes of deductive reasoning, inductive reasoning, and falsifiability are very important to the reconstruction process, but they must be differentiated and used properly.
- Investigators must be aware that the fallacies of bifurcation, generalization, and false linkage can impede a search for the truth. Avoiding these fallacies will help investigators maintain objectivity throughout the reconstruction.

Requirements for Crime-Scene Reconstruction

PERSONNEL INVOLVED IN RECONSTRUCTION

Because investigators consider many types of evidence when reconstructing a crime scene, reconstruction is a team effort that involves various professionals putting together many pieces of a puzzle. The team as a whole works to answer the typical "who, what, when, where, why, and how" of a crime scene. Often, reconstruction requires the involvement of a medical examiner and at least one criminalist. For example, an investigator might call on a trained medical examiner to determine whether a body has been moved after death by evaluating the livor distribution within the body. A criminalist or trained crime-scene investigator can also bring special skills to the reconstruction of events that occurred during the commission of a crime. For example, a criminalist using a laser beam to plot the approximate trajectory of a bullet can help determine the probable position of the shooter relative to that of the victim (see Figure 7-1).

Other skills that a criminalist or expert may employ during a crime-scene reconstruction analysis include blood spatter analysis (discussed more fully in Chapter 10), determining the direction of impact of projectiles penetrating glass objects (discussed in Chapter 14), locating gunshot residues deposited on victims' clothing for the purpose of estimating the distance of a shooter from a target (discussed in Chapter 9), and searching for primer residues deposited on the hands of a suspect shooter (discussed in Chapter 9).

■■■■■ CASEFILES

PISTORIUS: VALENTINE'S DAY MURDER

Oscar Pistorius overcame leaps and bounds many others in his position have failed to achieve. Pistorius was a double amputee from the time he was a child; both of his legs had to be removed due to a medical condition he had from birth. Despite his physical disability, Pistorius chased the dream of becoming an Olympic runner. This dream became a reality in 2012, when Pistorius faced able-bodied opponents in the Summer Olympics. Oscar Pistorius has received endless notoriety for his athletic achievement, and has been dubbed by the media as the "blade runner".

Pistorius and his super model girlfriend Reeva Steenkamp had been dating for over three months, and according to security logs from Pistorius's gated South African neighborhood, Steenkamp had been staying with him for multiple days. On Valentine's day, 2013, Steenkamp was found lying motionless on the ground, suffering multiple 9 mm pistol wounds to her body and head. Reeva Steenkamp had been shot multiple times through a locked wooden bathroom door by Pistorius. Pistorius claimed that he had fired the shots because he thought there was an intruder in the house. The Olympic runner appeared to be distraught and grieving heavily over his deceased girlfriend. Local South African prosecutors ultimately charged Pistorius with murder due to the circumstances of the event.

During the trial, the prosecution painted a picture of Pistorius as a violent and angry lover. Prosecutors claimed that Steenkamp ran into the bathroom and locked the door to seek protection from a spiteful Pistorius during a heated argument. Detectives placed Steenkamp in a defensive position, crouched behind the bathroom door with her arms and hands crossed in front of her face; as to protect herself from Pistorius. The prosecution also questioned why Pistorius would engage the intruder, rather than grabbing his girlfriend and leaving the residence. The defense called upon the support of Wollie Wolmarans, a ballistics expert, to support Pistorius's account of the incident. According to Wolmaran's expert testimony, wood splinter marks around Steenkamp's arm proved that she was reaching out to open the door when the incident occurred contrary to the prosecution's account of Steenkamp being crouched and protecting herself in the bathroom.

Oscar Pistorius was found guilty on a charge of culpable homicide, equivalent to manslaughter, after being acquitted of murder in the killing of his girlfriend. The presiding judge ruled that there was not enough evidence to support the contention that Pistorius knew that Steenkamp was behind the toilet door.

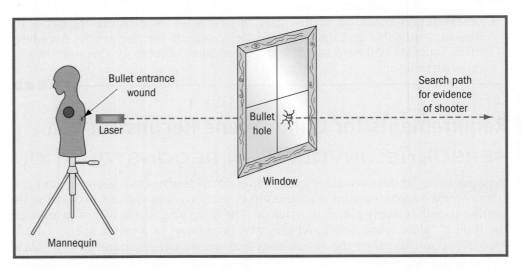

FIGURE 7-1 A laser beam is used to determine the search area for the position of a shooter who has fired a bullet through a window and wounded a victim. The bullet's path is determined by lining up the victim's bullet wound with the bullet hole in the pane of glass.

GATHERING EVIDENCE AND DATA FROM THE CRIME SCENE

Physical evidence left behind at a crime scene plays a crucial role in reconstructing the sequence of events surrounding the crime. Although the evidence alone may not describe everything that happened, it can support or contradict accounts given by witnesses and/or suspects. Information obtained from physical evidence can also generate leads and confirm the reconstruction of a crime to a jury. The collection, documentation, and interpretation of physical evidence is the foundation of a reconstruction. Reconstruction develops a likely sequence of events by the observation and evaluation of physical evidence as well as statements made by witnesses and input from those involved with the investigation of the incident. Analysis of all available data will help to create a workable model for reconstruction.

DIRECT PHYSICAL EVIDENCE Information from **direct physical evidence** provides a definite conclusion or direction. The analysis of direct physical evidence employs deductive reasoning to state a fact that can be understood by everyone. For example, if a transfer bloodstain on the clothing of a homicide victim has a DNA type consistent with that of the suspect, the victim must have had contact with the suspect after the suspect was injured and began bleeding. However, this assumes no prior contact or relationship existed between the victim and the suspect.

direct physical evidence
An item of evidence from which an indisputable fact or detail of the events at the crime scene can be concluded.

CIRCUMSTANTIAL EVIDENCE Information from **circumstantial evidence** provides a lead but no definite conclusion. With the use of inductive reasoning, an investigator can identify many possible causes for the state of the evidence. For example, the presence of semen in the DNA analysis of a female victim can be consistent with either forcible rape or consensual sex. Individual hair or fiber evidence found at the scene is considered highly circumstantial. It may suggest that an individual was present during the commission of the crime, but there are also other probable explanations for how it got there. Circumstantial evidence, when examined in the context of a crime scene, has only a few possible explanations, and one of these may be more probable than the others.

circumstantial evidence
An item of evidence that suggests the occurrence of one of several possible events at the crime scene.

TESTIMONIAL EVIDENCE An investigator should carefully scrutinize eyewitness testimony about what occurred at a crime scene. Eyewitness accounts, also called **testimonial evidence**, are sometimes highly subjective and heavily biased. Unfortunately, people lie or misinterpret the facts. Fortunately, physical evidence does not lie. Therefore, crime-scene reconstruction should include only testimonial evidence that is corroborated by aspects of physical evidence.

testimonial evidence
Informational evidence gained from statements from witnesses, suspects, and others who have some knowledge of the crime scene.

REENACTMENTS Some events at the crime scene lend themselves to a **reenactment** by live personnel, mannequins, or computer-generated models. Individuals used in live reenactments should be as close as possible in size and strength to the actual participants at the crime scene. The information gained from reenactments can show whether a theory of how an event occurred is physically possible and whether physical evidence is consistent with that theory.

reenactment
The process by which investigators attempt to re-create the circumstances surrounding a particular event at the crime scene in order to observe the result and gain information.

CONFIRMING CHAIN OF CUSTODY

As mentioned previously, a great deal of time may pass before all pertinent evidence and information can be gathered in order to begin reconstruction. Once all the evidence has been gathered, investigators must establish the chain of custody of items and the integrity of testimonial evidence. A missing link in the chain of custody of an item means that it was unaccounted for during a period of time. During this time, the evidence could have been tampered with, contaminated, or damaged. Evidence without a confirmed chain of custody cannot and should not be included in reconstruction. If there is any question about the legality or authenticity of testimonial evidence, it should be excluded from reconstruction.

Quick Review

- Crime-scene reconstruction is a team effort that requires the expertise of various professionals, depending on the kind of case.
- Information gathered from direct physical evidence provides a definite conclusion or direction, whereas circumstantial evidence provides a lead but no definite conclusion for reconstructing the crime.

- Testimonial evidence from eyewitnesses is sometimes highly subjective and heavily biased and must be used in reconstruction only if it is corroborated by physical evidence.
- Reenactments of events at a crime scene can be carried out by live personnel, mannequins, or computer-generated models.
- Evidence used in a crime-scene reconstruction must have a complete and valid chain of custody.

Assessment of Evidence and Information to Form Theories

One of the pitfalls of crime-scene reconstruction is generalizing the assessment and processing of evidence. Different categories or types of crime-scene evidence must be studied with very specific techniques and considerations during the investigation. The kinds of evidence that may be found at a crime scene are highly diverse. In forthcoming chapters, we will discuss the reconstructive properties of specific groups of crime-scene evidence.

ASSESSMENT OF EVIDENCE

Each item of evidence should first be analyzed and tested separately from all other evidence. To maintain objectivity and avoid the fallacy of false linkage, items of evidence should not be linked or grouped together during the initial phase of the investigation. Once all possible information has been recovered from each item, this information can be coupled with information about other items of evidence. It is important at this step to observe whether separate items of evidence make sense together or verify an event. For example, suppose an investigator finds that a trail of blood leading down the back stairs of a house stops abruptly at a patch of dirt. This might seem unusual but would make perfect sense if tire impressions were found in the dirt at the location where the trail stops. The investigator seeks to use evidence to link the crime scene, victims, suspects, and witnesses. These links provide the foundation for theories about specific events at the crime scene. Missing links may help to suggest what further data need to be recovered from available evidence or witnesses.

Studying the pattern formed by cartridges ejected from a firearm provides an excellent illustration of the process and difficulty of gaining information from a specific type of evidence. The location of a cartridge casing at a crime scene may suggest the position of the shooter, but the investigator must take into consideration the type of firearm used, the type of ammunition used, the position of the gun with respect to the shooter's body, the height of the firearm from the ground, and the terrain and layout of the scene. Investigators study the effect of these conditions through reenactments that must be as authentic as possible. The reenactment should involve the same firearm and ammunition used in the crime. Even the amount of lubrication of the firearm may affect cartridge ejection characteristics. The firing position of the firearm—whether sideways, upright, or otherwise—can affect where a cartridge will fall.

As with many kinds of evidence, so with cartridge case ejection, investigators must take substrate conditions into consideration. That is, the type and topography of the surface onto which the cartridge falls may affect its position. For example, a cartridge may travel farther after landing on an angled surface or a hard surface, such as concrete, than it would after landing on a level or soft surface. Cartridge cases may also contain trace evidence of damage if they contacted an intermediate surface before landing. A matching mark on the surface the cartridge contacted may also help to determine the shooter's position.

The cartridge itself can provide clues about the firearm that ejected it. The cartridge may bear marks on the base from the breechblock, firing pin, and ejector mechanism of the gun. The shaft of the cartridge may show chambering marks, gouge marks, and drag marks imparted by the firing chamber of the firearm. The collection of marks, their position, and any striations (i.e., fine grooves) within the marks will probably be unique to one firearm. Cartridge cases represent only one example of many types of evidentiary items that may be found at a crime scene. However, this example clearly demonstrates that a complex set of techniques and considerations is involved in studying each piece of evidence.

The example of cartridge case ejection patterns also raises the specter that an attempt at reconstruction can fail. That is, the movement of the shooter, the number of shooters, and the number of bullets discharged will produce multiple cartridge cases in various locations, introducing complexities into the analysis. These complexities may not be as easy to resolve as they would in a reconstruction involving a single cartridge case. When such complexities arise, some investigators fall into the trap of reading too much into evidence that may not provide resolution. The fact is, reconstruction may not be able to answer all of the questions. The complexities of the analysis may overwhelm the reconstruction team and prevent them from coming up with plausible answers.

FORMING THEORIES FOR RECONSTRUCTION

The final steps of crime-scene reconstruction require the reconstruction team to bring together all the evidence and information to form plausible theories and a plausible sequence of individual events. Theories can suggest how a group of linked items was created by individual events at a crime scene.

Often the beginning and end of the sequence of events at a crime scene are obvious to the investigators. For example, a tool mark or a footwear impression can mark the site of forced entry into a house, beginning the sequence of events at the crime scene. Footwear impressions or tire impressions leading away from the house may show the exit of the suspect from the crime scene and thus the end of the sequence of events. However, the sequence and timeline of the remaining events may be much more difficult to determine. Sometimes the evidence that signifies the start or end of events provides clues to the missing events in the middle. For example, suppose an investigator finds bloody footwear imprints exiting a crime scene. Logic dictates that blood was present at the crime scene, and that it somehow became deposited on the shoes of an individual who subsequently left the crime scene. These clues can provide suggestions about where the reconstruction should focus its attention.

All available information and evidence must fit into the overall picture. When creating a crime-scene reconstruction, the team must focus on the issues at hand and use all the information that is not in dispute to create a framework in which to explore definitive events.

An **event timeline** will list each event or "moment" that occurred at a crime scene in various probable orders within a known or estimated time frame. Some reconstruction teams develop an event timeline chart (see Figure 7-2). Investigators should chart each sequence and include information on evidence to illustrate how each event could have occurred and the timeline in which they occurred. Once the various orders have been identified, each sequence should be tested against the evidence.

event timeline
The end product of crime-scene reconstruction that shows the possible sequence of occurrences at the crime scene and the known or estimated time period in which they took place.

Quick Review

- In order for physical or testimonial evidence to be used in reconstruction theories, the chain of custody of items and the integrity of testimonial evidence must be established.

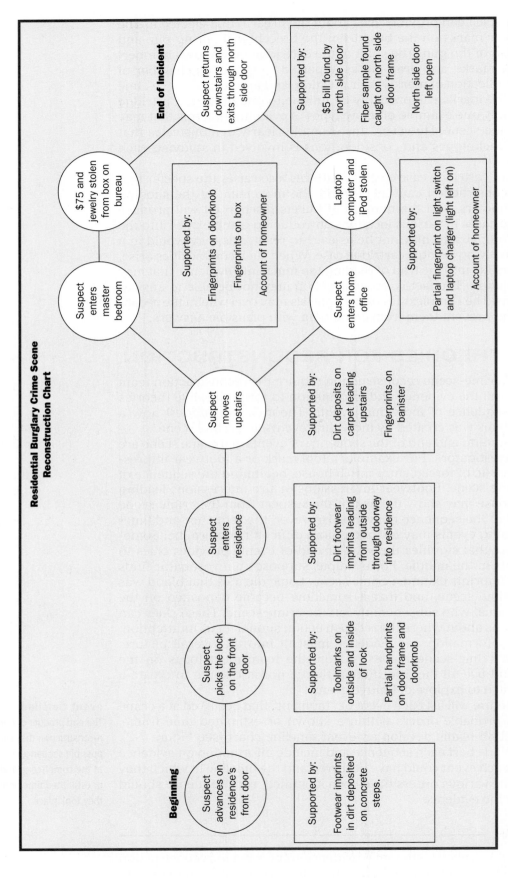

FIGURE 7-2 An example of an event timeline chart for a residential burglary. At one point two possible sequences of events are shown. Each event contains a list of evidence that supports the event's occurrence and sequence.

- Individual items of evidence are first analyzed and tested separate from all other evidence; items should not be linked or grouped together during the initial phase of the investigation. Once all items have been evaluated this way, they may be coupled with other items of evidence that are clearly linked.
- Different categories or types of crime-scene evidence have to be studied with very specific techniques and considerations during the investigation. The kinds of evidence that may be found at a crime scene are highly diverse, and knowledge of techniques for processing each is needed to recover all pertinent information.
- The reconstruction team must bring together all the linked groups of evidence and information to form theories about how each group of linked items was created by individual events at a crime scene.

CHAPTER REVIEW

- Because crime-scene reconstruction develops a likely sequence of events at a crime scene with physical evidence, testimony, and reenactments, proper documentation and collection methods must be used for all types of evidence.
- Investigative personnel may bring some expectations or biases to reconstruction, and these can have a negative effect on the process. It is, therefore, very important for personnel to practice objectivity, or professional distance.
- The processes of deductive reasoning, inductive reasoning, and falsifiability are very important to the reconstruction process, but they must be differentiated and used properly.
- Investigators must be aware that the fallacies of bifurcation, generalization, and false linkage can impede a search for the truth. Avoiding these fallacies will help investigators maintain objectivity throughout the reconstruction.
- Crime-scene reconstruction is a team effort that requires the expertise of various professionals, depending on the kind of case.
- Information gathered from direct physical evidence provides a definite conclusion or direction, whereas circumstantial evidence provides a lead but no definite conclusion for reconstructing the crime.
- Testimonial evidence from eyewitnesses is sometimes highly subjective and heavily biased and must be used in reconstruction only if it is corroborated by physical evidence.

- Reenactments of events at a crime scene can be carried out by live personnel, mannequins, or computer-generated models.
- Evidence used in a crime-scene reconstruction must have a complete and valid chain of custody.
- In order for physical or testimonial evidence to be used in reconstruction theories, the chain of custody of items and the integrity of testimonial evidence must be established.
- Individual items of evidence are first analyzed and tested separate from all other evidence; items should not be linked or grouped together during the initial phase of the investigation. Once all items have been evaluated this way, they may be coupled with other items of evidence that are clearly linked.
- Different categories or types of crime-scene evidence have to be studied with very specific techniques and considerations during the investigation. The kinds of evidence that may be found at a crime scene are highly diverse, and knowledge of techniques for processing each is needed to recover all pertinent information.
- The reconstruction team must bring together all the linked groups of evidence and information to form theories about how each group of linked items was created by individual events at a crime scene.

KEY TERMS

circumstantial evidence, 157
crime-scene reconstruction, 153
deductive reasoning, 153
direct physical evidence, 157

event timeline, 159
falsifiability, 154
inductive reasoning, 154

objectivity, 153
reenactment, 157
testimonial evidence, 157

REVIEW QUESTIONS

1. _____ is the method used to develop a likely sequence of events at a crime scene by the observation and evaluation of physical evidence and statements made by individuals involved with the incident.

2. Reconstructing the circumstances of a crime scene is a team effort that may include the help of law enforcement personnel, medical examiners, and _____.

3. To avoid letting personal beliefs or biases affect the conclusions reached through observations, crime-scene reconstruction teams must practice _____.

4. True or False: Expectations or biases can have a positive effect on the process of reconstruction by leading to correct analysis or interpretation of the information provided by the evidence. _____

5. True or False: Members of the crime-scene reconstruction team should design the examination and theory formation process to prove a theory or hypothesis that they believe to be true. _____

6. _____ reasoning is being used when a given fact or finding leads to a conclusion that is probable but not definitive. _____ reasoning is being used when a given fact or finding leads to a definitive conclusion.

7. Inductive reasoning is used to analyze _____ that provides a lead but no definite conclusion.

8. Another way to avoid bias is to test the _____ of all theories of how a crime occurred and all plausible alternatives against the evidence.

9. The inherent fallacy of _____ exists when investigators or attorneys try to apply a simple "yes or no" answer to a complex question.

10. True or False: Generalizing about aspects of evidence is always helpful to an investigation. _____

11. When a link is prematurely assumed between two or more objects of evidence, this is the fallacy of _____.

12. True or False: The biggest limitation to crime-scene reconstruction is the fact that what is left behind at a crime scene is often much less than is needed to create a full timeline of events that occurred in the past. _____

13. _____ left behind at the crime scene is helpful in reconstruction to support or contradict accounts given by witnesses and/or suspects.

14. The analysis of _____ employs deductive reasoning and provides a definite conclusion or direction.

15. Eyewitness accounts, called _____, are sometimes highly subjective and heavily biased because people may lie or misinterpret the facts.

16. The re-creation of events at a crime scene, called a _____, may be performed by live personnel, mannequins, or computer-generated models.

17. For an item of physical evidence to be used in a reconstruction, it must have a confirmed and intact _____.

18. True or False: Each item of evidence should first be analyzed and tested separate from all other evidence to avoid false linkage of evidence. _____

19. True or False: The kinds of evidence that may be found at a crime scene are few, and similar categories or types of crime-scene evidence have to be studied with similar techniques and considerations. _____

20. Once all evidence has been evaluated, the reconstruction team must bring together all the evidence and information to form plausible _____.

21. True or False: The beginning and end of the sequence of events at a crime scene are usually obvious to the investigators and may suggest what events occurred in between. _____

22. A(n) _____ created for the reconstruction defines each event that occurred at a crime scene in various probable orders within a known or estimated time frame.

APPLICATION AND CRITICAL THINKING

1. Which logical fallacy is described in each of the following situations?
   a) An investigator finds a body wrapped in a bloody sheet and assumes that all the blood came from the victim.
   b) An officer investigating a hit-and-run accident spots a car with a dented bumper near the scene and assumes it was involved.
   c) The district attorney asks an investigator whether highly suggestive circumstantial evidence leads to a particular conclusion.

2. While investigating a murder scene, police gather evidence that includes a dead body riddled with stab wounds, fingerprints on a bloody knife found near the body, and a ticket stub from a theater several miles away from the scene. Investigators determine that the knife belonged to the victim, but matched the prints on the knife to an acquaintance of the victim. When questioned, the acquaintance claims he was at the movies at the time of the murder—the same movie shown on the stub found at the scene. What direct physical evidence connects the acquaintance to the crime scene? What circumstantial evidence connects him to the scene? What can you conclude about the acquaintance's involvement solely from direct physical evidence and deductive reasoning? What might you conclude, considering circumstantial evidence and inductive reasoning as well?

8 Fingerprints

Joseph Louw/Time & Life Pictures/Getty Images

LEARNING OBJECTIVES

After studying this chapter, you should be able to:

- Describe important historical milestones in the history of fingerprinting.
- Identify the common ridge characteristics of a fingerprint.
- List the three major fingerprint patterns and their respective subclasses.
- Distinguish visible, plastic, and latent fingerprints.
- Describe the primary classification system for fingerprints.
- Describe the concept of an automated fingerprint identification system (AFIS).
- List the techniques for developing latent fingerprints on porous and nonporous objects.
- Describe the proper procedures for preserving a developed latent fingerprint.

JAMES EARL RAY: CONSPIRATOR OR LONE GUNMAN?

Since his arrest in 1968 for the assassination of Dr. Martin Luther King Jr., endless speculation has swirled around the motives and connections of James Earl Ray. Ray was a career criminal who was serving time for armed robbery when he escaped from the Missouri State Prison almost one year before the assassination. On April 3, 1968, Ray arrived in Memphis, Tennessee. The next day he rented a room at Bessie Brewer's Rooming House, across the street from the Lorraine Motel, where Dr. King was staying.

At 6:00 p.m., Dr. King left his second-story motel room and stepped onto the balcony. As King turned toward his room, a shot rang out, striking the civil rights activist. Nothing could be done to revive him, and Dr. King was pronounced dead at 7:05 p.m. The assailant ran on foot from Bessie Brewer's, stopping to leave a blanket-covered package in front of a nearby building, and then drove off in a white Mustang. The package contained a high-powered rifle equipped with a scope, a radio, some clothes, a pair of binoculars, a couple of beer cans, and a receipt for the binoculars. Almost a week after the shooting, the white Mustang was found abandoned in Atlanta, Georgia.

Fingerprints later identified as James Earl Ray's were found in the Mustang, on the rifle, on the binoculars, and on a beer can. In 1969, Ray entered a guilty plea in return for a sentence of ninety-nine years. Although a variety of conspiracy theories surround this crime, it is an indisputable fact that a fingerprint on the rifle that killed Martin Luther King Jr. was from the hands of James Earl Ray.

History of Fingerprinting

Since the beginnings of criminal investigation, police have sought an infallible means of human identification. The first systematic attempt at personal identification was devised and introduced by a French police expert, Alphonse Bertillon, in 1883. The Bertillon system relied on a detailed description (**portrait parlé**) of the subject, combined with full-length and profile photographs and a system of precise body measurements known as **anthropometry**.

The use of anthropometry as a method of identification rested on the premise that the dimensions of the human bone system remain fixed from age 20 until death. Skeleton sizes were thought to be so extremely diverse that no two individuals could have exactly the same measurements. Bertillon recommended the routine taking of eleven measurements of the human anatomy, including height, reach, width of head, and length of the left foot.

For two decades, this system was considered the most accurate method of identification. But in the early years of the twentieth century, police began to appreciate and accept a system of identification based on the classification of finger ridge patterns known as "fingerprints." Today, the fingerprint is the pillar of modern criminal identification.

portrait parlé
A verbal description of a perpetrator's physical characteristics and dress provided by an eyewitness.

anthropometry
A system of identification of individuals by measurement of parts of the body, developed by Alphonse Bertillon.

EARLY USE OF FINGERPRINTS

In China, fingerprints were used as far back as three thousand years ago to sign legal documents. Whether this practice was performed as a ceremonial custom or as a means of proving personal identity remains a point of conjecture; the answer is lost to history. The examples of fingerprinting in ancient history are ambiguous, and the few prints that remain did not in fact contribute to the development of fingerprinting techniques as we know them today.

Several years before Bertillon began work on his system, William Herschel, an English civil servant stationed in India, started requiring Indian citizens to sign contracts with the imprint of their right hand, which was pressed against a stamp pad for the purpose. The motives for Herschel's requirement remain unclear: He may have envisioned fingerprinting as a means of personal identification, or he may have been adapting for his purposes the Hindu custom that a trace of bodily contact is more binding than a signature on a contract. In any case, he did not publish anything about his activities until after Henry Fauld, a Scottish physician working in a hospital in Japan, published his own views on the potential application of fingerprinting to personal identification.

In 1880, Fauld suggested that skin ridge patterns could be important for the identification of criminals. He told about a thief who left his fingerprint on a whitewashed wall, and how in comparing these prints with those of a suspect, he found that they were quite different. A few days later, another suspect was found whose fingerprints compared with those on the wall. When confronted with this evidence, the individual confessed to the crime.

Fauld was convinced that fingerprints furnished infallible proof of identification. He even offered to set up, at his own expense, a fingerprint bureau at Scotland Yard to test the practicality of the method. But his offer was rejected in favor of the Bertillon system. This decision was reversed less than two decades later.

EARLY CLASSIFICATION OF FINGERPRINTS

The extensive research into fingerprinting conducted by another Englishman, Francis Galton, finally made police agencies aware of its potential application.

In 1892, Galton published his classic textbook *Finger Prints,* the first book of its kind on the subject. In *Finger Prints,* Galton discussed the anatomy of fingerprints and suggested methods for recording them. He also proposed assigning fingerprints one of three pattern types: loops, arches, or whorls. Most important, the book demonstrated that no two prints are identical and that an individual's prints remain unchanged from year to year. At Galton's insistence, the British government adopted fingerprinting as a supplement to the Bertillon system.

The next step in the development of fingerprint technology was the creation of classification systems capable of filing thousands of prints in a logical and searchable sequence. Dr. Juan Vucetich, an Argentinian police officer fascinated by Galton's work, devised a workable concept in 1891. His classification system has been refined over the years and is still widely used today in most Spanish-speaking countries. In 1897, another classification system was proposed by an Englishman, Sir Edward Richard Henry. Four years later, Henry's system was adopted by Scotland Yard. Today, most English-speaking countries, including the United States, use some version of Henry's classification system to file fingerprints.

ADOPTION OF FINGERPRINTING

Early in the twentieth century, Bertillon's measurement system began to fall into disfavor. Its results were highly susceptible to error, particularly when the measurements were taken by people who were not thoroughly trained. The method was dealt its most severe and notable setback in 1903 when a convict named Will West arrived at Fort Leavenworth prison. Startlingly, a routine check of the prison files revealed that a William West, already in the prison, could not be distinguished from the new prisoner by body measurements or even by photographs. In fact, the two men looked just like twins, and their measurements were practically the same. Subsequently, fingerprints of the prisoners clearly distinguished them.

In the United States, the first systematic and official use of fingerprints for personal identification was adopted by the New York City Civil Service Commission in 1901. The method was used for certifying all civil service applications. Several U.S. police officials received instruction in fingerprint identification from representatives of Scotland Yard at the 1904 World's Fair in St. Louis. After the fair and the Will West incident, fingerprinting began to be used in earnest in all major cities of the United States.

In 1924, the fingerprint records of the Bureau of Investigation and Leavenworth were merged to form the nucleus of the identification records of the new Federal Bureau of Investigation. The FBI has the largest collection of fingerprints in the world. By the beginning of World War I, England and practically all of Europe had also adopted fingerprinting as their primary method of identifying criminals.

Fundamental Principles of Fingerprints

Since Galton's time, and as a result of his efforts, fingerprints have become an integral part of policing and forensic science. The principal reason for this is that fingerprints constitute a unique and unchanging means of personal identification. In fact, fingerprint analysts have formulated three basic principles of fingerprints that encompass these notions of their uniqueness, stability, and appropriateness as a means of identification.

FIRST PRINCIPLE: A FINGERPRINT IS AN INDIVIDUAL CHARACTERISTIC; NO TWO FINGERS HAVE YET BEEN FOUND TO POSSESS IDENTICAL RIDGE CHARACTERISTICS

The acceptance of fingerprint evidence by the courts has always been predicated on the assumption that no two individuals have identical fingerprints. Early fingerprint experts consistently referred to Galton's calculation, showing the possible existence of 64 billion different fingerprints, to support this contention. Later, researchers questioned the validity of Galton's figures and attempted to devise mathematical models to better approximate this value. However, no matter what mathematical model one refers to, the conclusions are always the same: The probability for the existence of two identical fingerprint patterns in the world's population is extremely small.

Not only is this principle supported by theoretical calculations, but just as important, it is verified by the millions of individuals who have had their prints classified during the past 110 years—no two have ever been found to be identical. The FBI has nearly 50 million fingerprint records in its computer database and has yet to find an identical image belonging to two different people.

The individuality of a fingerprint is not determined by its general shape or pattern but by a careful study of its **ridge characteristics** (also known as **minutiae**). The identity, number, and relative location of characteristics such as those illustrated in Figure 8-1 impart individuality to a fingerprint. If two prints are to match, they must reveal characteristics that not only are identical but also have the same relative location to one another in the print. In a judicial proceeding, a point-by-point comparison must be demonstrated by an expert, using charts similar to the one shown in Figure 8-2, in order to prove the identity of an individual.

An expert can easily compare the characteristics of two complete fingerprints; the average fingerprint has as many as 150 individual ridge characteristics. However, most prints recovered at crime scenes are partial impressions, showing only a segment of the entire print. Under these circumstances, the expert can compare only a small number of ridge characteristics from the recovered print to a known recorded print.

ridge characteristics (minutiae)
Ridge endings, bifurcations, enclosures, and other ridge details that must match in two fingerprints to establish their common origin.

FIGURE 8-1 Fingerprint ridge characteristics. *Sirchie Finger Print Laboratories*

1. Bifurcation
2. Ridge ending
3. Enclosure
4. Ridge ending
5. Bifurcation
6. Bifurcation
7. Bifurcation
8. Ridge ending
9. Ridge ending
10. Short ridge
11. Bifurcation
12. Ridge ending

FIGURE 8-2 A fingerprint exhibit illustrating the matching ridge characteristics between the crime-scene print and an inked impression of one of the suspect's fingers. *Richard Saferstein, Ph.D.*

For years, experts have debated how many ridge comparisons are necessary to identify two fingerprints as the same. Numbers that range from eight to sixteen have been suggested as being sufficient to meet the criteria of individuality. However, the difficulty in establishing such a minimum is that no comprehensive statistical study has ever determined the frequency of occurrence of different ridge characteristics and their relative locations. Until such a study is undertaken and completed, no meaningful guidelines can be established for defining the uniqueness of a fingerprint.

In 1973, after a three-year study of this question, the International Association for Identification concluded that "no valid basis exists for requiring a predetermined minimum number of friction ridge characters which must be present in two impressions in order to establish positive identification." Hence, the final determination must be based on the experience and knowledge of the expert, with the understanding that others may profess honest differences of opinion on the uniqueness of a fingerprint when the question of minimal number of ridge characteristics is involved. In 1995, members of the international fingerprint community at a conference in Israel issued the Ne'urim Declaration, which supported the 1973 International Association for Identification resolution.

SECOND PRINCIPLE: A FINGERPRINT REMAINS UNCHANGED DURING AN INDIVIDUAL'S LIFETIME

Fingerprints are a reproduction of friction skin ridges found on the palm side of the fingers and thumbs. Similar friction skin can also be found on the surface of the palms and soles of the feet. Apparently, these skin surfaces have been designed by nature to provide our bodies with a firmer grasp and a resistance to slipping. A visual inspection of friction skin reveals a series of lines corresponding to hills (ridges) and valleys (grooves). The shape and form of the skin ridges are what one sees as the black lines of an inked fingerprint impression.

Actually, skin is composed of layers of cells. Those nearest the surface make up the outer portion of the skin known as the "epidermis," and the inner skin is known as the "dermis." A cross-section of skin (see Figure 8-3) reveals a boundary of cells separating the epidermis and dermis. The shape of this boundary, made up of "dermal papillae," determines the form and pattern of the ridges on the surface of the skin. Once the dermal papillae develop in the human fetus, the ridge patterns remain unchanged throughout life, except for enlarging during growth.

Each skin ridge is populated by a single row of pores that are the openings for ducts leading from the sweat glands. Through these pores, perspiration is discharged and deposited on the surface of the skin. Once the finger touches a surface, perspiration, along with oils that may have been picked up by touching the hairy portions of the body, is transferred onto that surface, thereby leaving an impression of the finger's ridge pattern (i.e., a fingerprint). Prints deposited in this manner are invisible to the eye and are commonly referred to as **latent fingerprints.**

latent fingerprint
A fingerprint made by the deposit of oils and/or perspiration; it is invisible to the naked eye.

Although it is impossible to change one's fingerprints, some criminals have tried to obscure them. If an injury reaches deeply enough into the skin and damages the dermal papillae, a permanent scar forms. However, for this to happen, such a wound would have to penetrate 1 to 2 millimeters beneath the skin's surface. Indeed, efforts at intentionally scarring the skin can only be self-defeating, for it is totally impossible to obliterate all of the ridge characteristics on the hand, and the presence of permanent scars merely provides new characteristics for identification.

Perhaps the most publicized attempt at obliterating fingerprints was that of the notorious gangster John Dillinger, who tried to destroy his own fingerprints by applying a corrosive acid to them. Prints taken at the morgue after

Ridge island
Sweat pores
Epidermis
Papillae
Dermis
Duct of sweat gland
Sweat gland
Nerves of touch

FIGURE 8-3 Cross-section of human skin.

FIGURE 8-4 The right index finger impression of John Dillinger, before scarification on the left and afterward on the right. Comparison is proved by the fourteen matching ridge characteristics. *Sirchie Finger Print Laboratories*

he was shot to death, when compared to fingerprints recorded at the time of a previous arrest, proved that his efforts had been fruitless (see Figure 8-4).

THIRD PRINCIPLE: FINGERPRINTS HAVE GENERAL RIDGE PATTERNS THAT PERMIT THEM TO BE CLASSIFIED SYSTEMATICALLY

All fingerprints are divided into three classes on the basis of their general pattern: **loops, whorls,** and **arches**. Sixty to 65 percent of the population have loops, 30 to 35 percent have whorls, and about 5 percent have arches. These three classes form the basis for all ten-finger classification systems presently in use.

A loop must have one or more ridges entering from one side of the print, recurving, and exiting from the same side. If the loop opens toward the little finger, it is called an "ulnar loop"; if it opens toward the thumb, it is a "radial loop." A typical loop pattern is illustrated in Figure 8-5.

Whorls are actually divided into four distinct groups, as shown in Figure 8-6: plain, central pocket loop, double loop, and accidental. A plain whorl and a central pocket loop have at least one ridge that makes a complete circuit. This ridge may be in the form of a spiral, oval, or any variant of a circle. As the name implies, the double loop is made up of two loops combined in one fingerprint. Any whorl classified as an accidental either contains two or more patterns (not including the plain arch) or is a pattern not covered by other categories. Hence, an accidental may consist of a combination of a loop and a plain whorl or a loop and a tented arch.

Arches, the least common of the three general patterns, are subdivided into two distinct groups: plain arches and tented arches, as shown in Figure 8-7. The plain arch is the simplest of all fingerprint patterns; it is formed by ridges entering from one side of the print and exiting on the opposite side. Generally, these ridges tend to rise in the center of the print, forming a wavelike pattern. The tented arch is similar to the plain arch except that instead of rising smoothly at the center, there is a sharp upthrust or spike, or the ridges meet at an angle that is less than 90 degrees.[1]

loop

A class of fingerprints characterized by ridge lines that enter from one side of the pattern and curve around to exit from the same side of the pattern.

whorl

A class of fingerprints that includes ridge patterns that are generally rounded or circular.

arch

A class of fingerprints characterized by ridge lines that enter the print from one side and exit the other side.

FIGURE 8-5 Loop-type pattern has ridges entering from one side of the print, recurving, and exiting from the same side. These patterns resemble a lake. *Anthony Smith and Erika DiPalma*

PLAIN WHORL CENTRAL POCKET LOOP DOUBLE LOOP ACCIDENTAL

FIGURE 8-6 Whorl types. (a) Plain whorl. One or more ridges form a complete circlelike pattern around the center. These often look like a bull's eye. (b) Central pocket loop. Ridges form a loop pattern which go around the circlelike pattern in the center. These often look like a peacock eye. (c) Double loop whorl. Two separate loops are present in one impression. These often look like the symbol of the yin and the yang. (d) Accidental whorl. A mixture of two different types of patterns. These often look like an accident since several patterns are occupying the same space. *Anthony Smith and Erika DiPalma*

PLAIN ARCH TENTED ARCH

FIGURE 8-7 Arch patterns. (a) Plain arch. Ridges enter the impression rise to the center and exit the opposite side of the impression. These often resemble hills. (b) Tented arch. Ridges enter the impression, spike towards the center, and exit the opposite side of the impression. These often resemble a tent. *Anthony Smith and Erika DiPalma*

THE ACE-V PROCESS

ACE-V is an acronym for the four-step process—analysis, comparison, evaluation, and verification—used to identify and individualize a fingerprint. The first step requires the examiner to identify any distortions associated with the friction ridges, as well as any external factors, such as surface or deposition factors or processing techniques, that may impinge on the print's appearance. If the examiner determines the latent print adequate, he or she will declare the print to be of value for the comparison stage.

The comparison step requires the examiner to compare the questioned print to the known print at three levels. Level 1 looks at the general ridge flow and pattern configuration. Level 2 includes locating and comparing ridge characteristics, or minutiae. Level 2 details can individualize a print. Level 3 includes the examination and location of ridge pores, breaks, creases, scars, and other permanent minutiae. During the comparison phase, the examiner compares the latent print side by side with an exemplar print in their totality.

The evaluation stage requires one of three decisions to be arrived at. The decisions that can be reported are: identification (the latent print and exemplar came from the same source); exclusion (the latent print and exemplar did not come from the same source); inconclusive (one cannot determine that the latent print and exemplar came from the same source, or not, to a sufficiently strong level of certainty).

The final step in the process involves verification of the examiner's result. It requires an independent examination of the questioned and known prints by a second examiner. Ultimately, a consensus between the two examiners must be arrived at before a final conclusion is drawn.

Quick Review

- Fingerprints are a reproduction of friction skin ridges found on the palm side of the fingers and thumbs.
- The basic principles underlying the use of fingerprints in criminal investigations are as follows: (1) A fingerprint is an individual characteristic because no two fingers have yet been found to possess identical ridge characteristics, (2) a fingerprint remains unchanged during an individual's lifetime, and (3) fingerprints have general ridge patterns that permit them to be systematically classified.
- All fingerprints are divided into three classes on the basis of their general pattern: loops, whorls, and arches.
- The individuality of a fingerprint is determined not by its general shape or pattern but by a careful study of its ridge characteristics. The expert must demonstrate a point-by-point comparison in order to prove the identity of an individual.
- A four-step process known as ACE-V (analysis, comparison, evaluation, and verification) is used to identify and individualize a fingerprint.
- The final step in the process involves verification of the examiner's conclusion by a second examiner.
- When a finger touches a surface, perspiration and oils are transferred onto that surface, leaving a fingerprint. Prints deposited in this manner are invisible to the eye and are commonly referred to as "latent" or "invisible" fingerprints.

Classification of Fingerprints

The original Henry system, as adopted by Scotland Yard in 1901, converted ridge patterns on all ten fingers into a series of letters and numbers arranged in the form of a fraction. However, the system as it was originally designed could accommodate files of up to only 100,000 sets of prints. Thus, as collections grew in size, it became necessary to expand the capacity of the classification system. In the United States, the FBI, faced with the problem of filing ever-increasing numbers of prints, expanded its classification capacity by modifying the original Henry system and adding additional extensions. These modifications are collectively known as the "FBI system" and are used by most agencies in the United States today. Although we will not discuss all of the divisions of the FBI system, a description of just one part—the primary classification—will provide an interesting insight into the process of fingerprint classification.

The "primary classification" is part of the original Henry system and provides the first classification step in the FBI system. Using this classification alone, all of the fingerprint cards in the world could be divided into 1,024 groups. The first step in obtaining the primary classification is to pair up fingers, placing one finger in the numerator of a fraction, the other in the denominator. The fingers are paired in the following sequence:

$$\frac{\text{R. Index}}{\text{R. Thumb}} \quad \frac{\text{R. Ring}}{\text{R. Middle}} \quad \frac{\text{L. Thumb}}{\text{R. Little}} \quad \frac{\text{L. Middle}}{\text{L. Index}} \quad \frac{\text{L. Little}}{\text{L. Ring}}$$

The presence or absence of the whorl pattern is the basis for the determination of the primary classification. If a whorl pattern is found on any finger of the first pair, it is assigned a value of 16; on the second pair, a value of 8; on the third pair, a value of 4; on the fourth pair, a value of 2; and on the last pair, a value of 1. Any finger with an arch or loop pattern is assigned a value of 0. Approximately 25 percent of the population falls into the 1/1 category; that is, all their fingers have either loops or arches.

After values for all ten fingers are obtained in this manner, they are totaled, and 1 is added to both the numerator and denominator. The fraction thus obtained is the primary classification. For example, if the right index and right middle fingers are whorls and all the others are loops, the primary classification is

$$\frac{16 + 0 + 0 + 0 + 0 + 1}{0 + 8 + 0 + 0 + 0 + 1} = \frac{17}{9}$$

A fingerprint classification system cannot in itself unequivocally identify an individual; it merely provides the fingerprint examiner with a number of candidates, all of whom have a set of prints in the system's file. The identification must always be made by a final visual comparison of the ridge characteristics of the suspect print and the file print; only these features can impart individuality to a fingerprint. Although ridge patterns impart class characteristics to the print, the type and position of ridge characteristics give the print individual character.

Quick Review

- The primary classification is the first step in classifying fingerprints under the FBI system. The presence or absence of the whorl pattern is the basis for the determination of the primary classification.

Automated Fingerprint Identification Systems

The Henry system and its subclassifications have proved to be a cumbersome system for storing, retrieving, and searching for fingerprints, particularly as fingerprint collections grow in size. Nevertheless, until the emergence of fingerprint computer technology, this manual approach was the only viable method for maintaining fingerprint collections. Since 1970, technological advances have made it possible to classify and retrieve fingerprints by computer. Automated fingerprint identification systems (AFISs) have proliferated throughout the law enforcement community.

In 1999, the FBI initiated full operation of the Integrated Automated Fingerprint Identification System (IAFIS), the largest AFIS in the United States, which links state AFIS computers with the FBI database. This system contains nearly 68 million fingerprint records. However, an AFIS can come in all sizes ranging from the FBI's IAFIS to independent systems operated by cities, counties, and other agencies of local government (see Figure 8-8). Unfortunately, these local systems often cannot be linked to the state's AFIS system because of differences in software configurations.

HOW AFIS WORKS

The heart of AFIS technology is the ability of a computer to scan and digitally encode fingerprints so they can be subjected to high-speed computer processing. The AFIS uses automatic scanning devices that convert the image of a fingerprint into digital minutiae that contain data about points of termination (i.e., ridge endings) and the branching of ridges into two ridges (i.e., bifurcations). The relative position and orientation of the minutiae are also recorded, allowing the computer to store each fingerprint in the form of a digitally recorded geometric pattern.

The computer's search algorithm determines the degree of correlation between the location and relationship of the minutiae in the search print and those in the file prints. In this manner, a computer can make thousands of fingerprint comparisons in a second. For example, a set of ten fingerprints can be searched against a file of 500,000 ten-finger prints (i.e., "ten-prints") in about eight-tenths of a second. During the search for a match, the computer uses a scoring system that assigns prints to each of the criteria set by an operator. When the search is complete, the computer produces a list of file prints that have the closest correlation to the search prints. All of the selected prints are then examined by a fingerprint expert, who makes the final verification of the print's identity. Thus, the AFIS makes no final conclusions about the identity of a fingerprint; this function is left to the eyes of a trained examiner.

The speed and accuracy of ten-print processing by AFIS systems have made it possible to search a single latent crime-scene fingerprint against an entire file's print collection. Before AFIS, police were usually restricted to comparing crime-scene fingerprints against those of known suspects. The impact of the AFIS on no-suspect cases has been dramatic. In its first year of operation, San Francisco's AFIS computer conducted 5,514 latent fingerprint searches and achieved 1,001 identifications—a hit rate of 18 percent. Contrast this with the previous year's success rate of 8 percent for manual latent-print searches.

Using a single system, an AFIS computer automatically filters out imperfections in a latent print, enhances its image, and creates a graphic representation of the fingerprint's ridge endings and bifurcations and their directions. The computer then searches file prints for a match. The image of the latent print and a matching file print are then displayed side by side on a high-resolution video monitor, as shown in Figure 8-9. The matching latent and file prints are then verified and charted by a fingerprint examiner at a video workstation.

The stereotypical booking officer rolling inked fingers onto a standard ten-print card for ultimate transmission to a database has, for the most part, been replaced with digital-capture devices (**Live Scan**) that eliminate ink and paper (see Figure 8-10). The Live Scan captures an image of each finger and the palms as they are lightly pressed against a glass plate. Within minutes the booking agency can enter the fingerprint record into the AFIS database and then search the database for previous records of the same individual.

FIGURE 8-8 An AFIS system designed for use by local law enforcement agencies. *AFIX Technologies Inc.*

Live Scan
An inkless device that captures digital images of fingerprints and palm prints and electronically transmits them to an AFIS.

CONSIDERATIONS WITH AFIS

AFIS has fundamentally changed the way criminal investigators operate, allowing them to spend less time developing suspect lists and more time investigating the suspects located by the computer. However, investigators must be cautioned against overreliance on a computer. Sometimes a latent print does not generate a hit because of the poor quality of the file print. To avoid potential problems, investigators must still fingerprint all known suspects in a case and then manually search these prints against the crime-scene prints.

FIGURE 8-9 A side-by-side comparison of a latent print against a file fingerprint is conducted in seconds, and their similarity rating (SIM) is displayed on the upper-left portion of the screen. *Sirchie Finger Print Laboratories, Youngsville, NC, www.sirchie.com*

FIGURE 8-10 Live Scan technology enables law enforcement personnel to print and compare a subject's fingerprints rapidly, without inking the fingerprints. *MorphoTrak, Inc.*

AFIS computers are available from several suppliers. Each system scans fingerprint images and detects and records information about minutiae (e.g., ridge endings and bifurcations); however, they do not all incorporate the same features, coordinate systems, or units of measure to record fingerprint information. These software incompatibilities often mean that, although state systems can communicate with the FBI's IAFIS, they do not communicate with each other directly. Likewise, local and state systems frequently cannot share information with each other. Many of these technical problems will be resolved as more agencies follow transmission standards developed by the National Institute of Standards and Technology and the FBI.

Quick Review

- The fingerprint database known as AFIS converts an image of a fingerprint into digital minutiae that contain data showing ridges at their points of termination (i.e., ridge endings) and of branching into two ridges (i.e., bifurcations).
- AFIS makes no final decisions on the identification of a fingerprint, instead leaving this function to a trained examiner.
- Live Scan is an inkless device that captures digital images of fingerprints and palm prints and electronically transmits them to an AFIS.

Methods of Detecting Fingerprints

Through common usage, the term "latent fingerprint" has become associated with any fingerprint discovered at a crime scene. Sometimes, however, prints found at the scene of a crime are quite visible to the eye, and the word "latent" is a misnomer.

Actually, there are three kinds of crime-scene prints. **Visible prints** are made by fingers touching a surface after the ridges have been in contact with a colored material such as blood, paint, grease, or ink; **plastic prints** are ridge impressions left on a soft material such as putty, wax, soap, or dust; and "latent" or "invisible prints" are impressions caused by the transfer of body perspiration or oils from finger ridges to the surface of an object.

LOCATING FINGERPRINTS

Locating visible or plastic prints at the crime scene normally presents little problem to the investigator because these prints are usually distinct and visible to the eye. Obviously, locating latent or invisible prints is much more difficult and requires the use of techniques that make the print visible. The investigator can choose from several methods for visualizing a latent print, and his or her choice depends on the type of surface being examined.

Hard and nonabsorbent surfaces (e.g., glass, mirror, tile, and painted wood) require different development procedures than do surfaces that are soft and porous (e.g., paper, cardboard, and cloth). Prints on the former surfaces are developed preferably by the application of a powder or by treatment with Super Glue, whereas prints on the latter generally require treatment with one or more chemicals.

Sometimes the most difficult aspect of fingerprint examination is the location of prints. Recent advances in fingerprint technology have led to the development of an ultraviolet image converter for the purpose of detecting latent fingerprints. This device, called the "reflected ultraviolet imaging system" (RUVIS), can locate prints on most nonabsorbent surfaces without the aid of chemical or powder treatments (see Figure 8-11).

RUVIS detects the print in its natural state by aiming UV light at the surface suspected of containing prints. When the UV light strikes a fingerprint, the light is reflected back to the viewer, differentiating the print from its background surface. The transmitted UV light is then converted into visible light by an image

visible print
A fingerprint made when the finger deposits a visible material such as ink, dirt, or blood onto a surface.

plastic print
A fingerprint impressed in a soft surface.

FIGURE 8-11 A Reflected Ultraviolet Imaging System allows an investigator to directly view surfaces for the presence of untreated latent fingerprints. *Sirchie Finger Print Laboratories*

▪▪▪▪ CASEFILES ▪▪▪▪
THE NIGHT STALKER

Richard Ramirez, the Night Stalker. *Bettmann/Corbis*

Richard Ramirez committed his first murder in June 1984. His victim was a seventy-nine-year-old woman who was stabbed repeatedly and sexually assaulted, and then her throat was slashed. It was eight months before Ramirez killed again: In the spring of 1985, he began a murderous rampage that resulted in thirteen additional killings and five rapes.

Ramirez's modus operandi was to enter a home through an open window, shoot the male residents, and savagely rape female victims. He scribed a pentagram and the words "Jack the Knife" on a wall in the home of one of his victims and was reported by another to have forced her to "swear to Satan" during the assault. His identity yet unknown, the news media dubbed him the "Night Stalker." As the body count continued to rise, public hysteria and a media frenzy prevailed.

The break in the case came when the license plate of what seemed to be a car related to a sighting of the Night Stalker was reported to the police. The police determined from the plate number that the car had been stolen and eventually located it, abandoned in a parking lot. After processing the car for prints, police found one usable partial fingerprint. This fingerprint was entered into the Los Angeles Police Department's brand-new AFIS computerized fingerprint system.

Without AFIS, it would have taken a single technician, manually searching Los Angeles's 1.7 million print cards, sixty-seven years to come up with the perpetrator's prints. Thanks to AFIS, it took only a few seconds to match and identify them. The Night Stalker was identified as Richard Ramirez, who had been fingerprinted following a traffic violation some years before. Police searching the home of one of his friends found the gun used to commit the murders, and jewelry belonging to his victims was found in the possession of Ramirez's sister. Ramirez was convicted of murder and sentenced to death in 1989. He died of natural causes in prison in 2013.

---

intensifier. Once the print is located in this manner, the crime-scene investigator can develop it in the most appropriate fashion (see Figure 8-12).

DEVELOPING LATENT PRINTS

Several techniques are available to the criminalist for developing latent prints on a variety of surfaces. These range from chemical methods such as using powders and iodine fuming to the use of laser light.

iodine fuming
A technique for visualizing latent fingerprints by exposing them to iodine vapors.

sublimation
A physical change from a solid directly into a gaseous state.

FINGERPRINT POWDERS Fingerprint powders are commercially available in a variety of compositions and colors. These powders, when applied lightly to a nonabsorbent surface with a camel's-hair or fiberglass brush, readily adhere to perspiration residues and/or deposits of body oils left on the surface (see Figure 8-13).

Experienced examiners find that gray and black powders are adequate for most latent-print work; the examiner selects the powder that affords the best color contrast with the surface being dusted. Therefore, the gray powder,

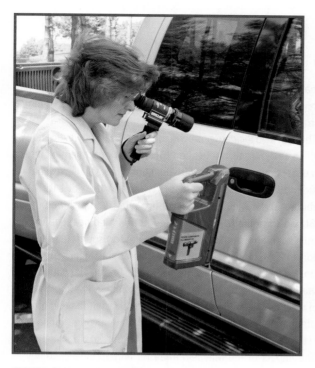

FIGURE 8-12   Using a Reflected Ultraviolet Imaging System with the aid of a UV lamp to search for latent fingerprints. *Sirchie Finger Print Laboratories*

FIGURE 8-13   Developing a latent fingerprint on a surface by applying a fingerprint powder with a fiberglass brush. *Sirchie Finger Print Laboratories*

composed of an aluminum dust, is used on dark-colored surfaces. It is also applied to mirrors and metal surfaces that are polished to a mirrorlike finish because these surfaces photograph as black. The black powder, composed basically of black carbon or charcoal, is applied to white or light-colored surfaces.

Other types of powders are available for developing latent prints. A magnetic-sensitive powder can be spread over a surface using a magnet in the form of a Magna Brush. A Magna Brush does not have any bristles to come into contact with the surface, so there is less chance that the print will be destroyed or damaged. The magnet-sensitive powder comes in black and gray and is especially useful on such items as finished leather and rough plastics, on which the texture of the surface tends to hold particles of ordinary powder. Fluorescent powders are also used to develop latent fingerprints. These powders fluoresce under ultraviolet light. By photographing the fluorescence pattern of the developing print under UV light, it is possible to see the print clearly in situations in which the color of the surface might otherwise obscure the print.

IODINE FUMING   Of the several chemical methods used for visualizing latent prints, **iodine fuming** is the oldest. Iodine is a solid crystal that, when heated, converts into a vapor without passing through a liquid phase; such a transformation is called **sublimation**. Most often, the suspect material is placed in an enclosed cabinet along with iodine crystals (see Figure 8-14). As the crystals are

FIGURE 8-14   A heated fuming cabinet. *Sirchie Finger Print Laboratories*

■■■■ **CASE**FILES ■■■■
THE MAYFIELD AFFAIR

On March 11, 2004, a series of ten explosions at four sites occurred on commuter trains traveling to or near the Atocha train station in Madrid, Spain. The death toll from these explosions was nearly 200, with more than 1,500 injured. On the day of the attack, a plastic bag was found in a van previously reported as stolen. The bag contained copper detonators like those used in the train bombs.

On March 17, the FBI received electronic images of latent fingerprints that were recovered from the plastic bag, and a search was initiated on the FBI's IAFIS. A senior fingerprint examiner encoded seven minutiae points from the high-resolution image of one suspect latent fingerprint and initiated an IAFIS search, eventually matching the print to Brandon Mayfield. Mayfield's prints were in the FBI's central database because they had been taken when he joined the military, where he served for eight years before being honorably discharged as a second lieutenant.

After a visual comparison of the suspect print and file prints, the examiner concluded a "100 percent match." The identification was verified by a retired FBI fingerprint examiner with more than thirty years of experience who was working under contract with the bureau, as well as by a court-appointed independent fingerprint examiner (see the photos).

Mayfield, age 37, a Muslim convert, was arrested on May 6 on a material witness warrant. The U.S. Attorney's Office came up with a list of Mayfield's potential ties to Muslim terrorists that they included in the affidavit they presented to the federal judge who ordered his arrest and detention. The document also said that, although no travel records were found for Mayfield, "It is believed that Mayfield may have traveled under a false or fictitious name." On May 24, Spanish investigators linked the print from the plastic bag to an Algerian national, and Mayfield's case was thrown out. The FBI issued him a highly unusual official apology, and his ordeal became a stunning embarrassment to the U.S. government.

The Mayfield incident has been the subject of an investigation by the Office of the Inspector General (OIG), U.S. Department of Justice (www.usdoj.gov/oig/special/s0601/final.pdf). The OIG investigation concluded that a "series of systemic issues" in the FBI Laboratory contributed to the Mayfield misidentification. The report noted that the FBI had since made significant procedural modifications to help prevent similar errors in the future, and it strongly supported the FBI's decision to develop more objective standards for fingerprint identification. An internal review of the FBI Latent Print Unit conducted in the aftermath of the Mayfield affair has resulted in the implementation of revisions in training as well as in the decision-making process for determining the comparative value of a latent print, along with more stringent verification policies and procedures.[2]

The impact of the Mayfield affair on fingerprint technology as currently practiced and the weight courts will assign to fingerprint matches in the future remain open questions.

(a)   (b)

(a) Questioned print recovered in connection with the Madrid bombing investigation. *Sirchie Finger Print Laboratories* (b) File print of Brandon Mayfield. *Department of Justice*

heated, the resultant vapors fill the chamber and combine with constituents of the latent print to make it visible.

Unfortunately, iodine prints are not permanent and begin to fade once the fuming process is stopped. Therefore, the examiner must photograph the prints immediately upon development in order to retain a permanent record.

Alternatively, iodine-developed prints can be fixed by spraying them with a 1 percent solution of starch in water. The print then turns blue and lasts for several weeks to several months.

The reasons latent prints are visualized by iodine vapors are not yet fully understood. Many believe that the iodine fumes combine with fatty oils; however, there is also convincing evidence that the iodine may actually interact with residual water left on a print from perspiration.[3]

NINHYDRIN Another chemical used for visualizing latent prints is **ninhydrin**. The development of latent prints with ninhydrin results from its chemical reaction with amino acids present in trace amounts in perspiration, creating a purple-blue color. A ninhydrin (triketohydrindene hydrate) solution is commonly sprayed onto a porous surface from an aerosol can. The solution is prepared by mixing the ninhydrin powder with a suitable solvent, such as acetone or ethyl alcohol; a 0.6 percent solution appears to be effective for most applications.

Generally, prints begin to appear within an hour or two after ninhydrin application; however, weaker prints may be visualized after 24 to 48 hours. The development can be hastened if the treated specimen is heated in an oven or on a hot plate at a temperature of 80°C to 100°C. The ninhydrin method has developed latent prints on old paper after as long as fifteen years.

PHYSICAL DEVELOPER Physical Developer is a third chemical mixture used for visualizing latent prints. Physical Developer is a silver nitrate-based liquid reagent. This method has gained wide acceptance by fingerprint examiners who have found it effective for visualizing latent prints that remain undetected by the previously described methods. Also, this technique is very effective for developing latent fingerprints on porous articles that may have been wet at one time.

For most fingerprint examiners, the chemical method of choice is ninhydrin. Its extreme sensitivity and ease of application have all but eliminated the use of iodine for latent-print visualization. However, when ninhydrin fails, development with Physical Developer may provide identifiable results. Application of Physical Developer washes away any traces of proteins from an object's surface; hence, if one wishes to use all of the previously mentioned chemical development methods on the same surface, it is necessary to first fume with iodine, follow this treatment with ninhydrin, and then apply Physical Developer to the object.

SUPER GLUE FUMING In the past, chemical treatment for fingerprint development was reserved for porous surfaces such as paper and cardboard. However, since 1982, a chemical technique known as **Super Glue fuming** has gained wide popularity for developing latent prints on nonporous surfaces such as metals, electrical tape, leather, and plastic bags (see Figure 8-15).[4]

Super Glue is approximately 98 to 99 percent cyanoacrylate ester, a chemical that interacts with and visualizes a latent fingerprint. Cyanoacrylate ester fumes can be created when Super Glue is placed on absorbent cotton treated with sodium hydroxide. The fumes can also be created by heating the glue. The fumes and the evidential object are contained within an enclosed chamber for up to 6 hours. Development occurs when fumes from the glue adhere to the latent print, usually producing a

ninhydrin
A chemical reagent used to develop latent fingerprints on porous materials by reacting with the amino acids in perspiration.

Physical Developer
A silver nitrate–based reagent formulated to develop latent fingerprints on porous surfaces.

Super Glue fuming
A technique for visualizing latent fingerprints on nonporous surfaces by exposing them to cyanoacrylate vapors; named for the commercial product Super Glue.

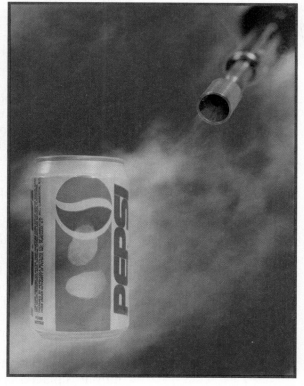

FIGURE 8-15 Super Glue fuming a nonporous metallic surface in the search for latent fingerprints. *Sirchie Finger Print Laboratories*

(a)   (b)

FIGURE 8-16 (a) A handheld fuming wand uses disposable cartridges containing cyanoacrylate. The wand is used to develop prints at the crime scene and (b) in the laboratory. *Sirchie Finger Print Laboratories*

white-appearing latent print. Interestingly, small enclosed areas, such as the interior of an automobile, have been successfully processed for latent prints with fumes from Super Glue.

Through the use of a small, handheld wand, cyanoacrylate fuming is now easily done at a crime scene or in a laboratory setting. The wand heats a small cartridge containing cyanoacrylate. Once heated, the cyanoacrylate vaporizes, allowing the operator to direct the fumes onto the suspect area (see Figure 8-16).

OTHER TECHNIQUES FOR VISUALIZATION In recent years, researchers have explored a variety of new processes applicable to the visualization of latent fingerprints. However, for many years progress in this field was minimal. Fingerprint specialists traditionally relied on three chemical techniques—iodine, ninhydrin, and silver nitrate—to reveal a hidden fingerprint. Then, Super Glue fuming extended chemical development to prints deposited on nonporous surfaces.

Another hint of things to come emerged with the discovery that latent fingerprints could be visualized by exposure to laser light. This laser method took advantage of the fact that perspiration contains a variety of components that **fluoresce** when illuminated by the light of a laser.

The next advancement in latent-fingerprint development occurred with the discovery that fingerprints could be treated with chemicals that would induce fluorescence when exposed to laser illumination. For example, application of zinc chloride after ninhydrin treatment or application of the dye rhodamine 6G after Super Glue fuming causes fluorescence and increases the sensitivity of detection on exposure to laser illumination. The discovery of numerous chemical developers for visualizing fingerprints through fluorescence quickly followed. This knowledge set the stage for the next advance in latent-fingerprint development: the "alternate light source."

With the advent of chemically induced fluorescence, lasers were no longer needed to induce fingerprints to fluoresce through perspiration residues. High-intensity light sources, or alternate light sources, have proliferated and all but replaced laser lights (see Figure 8-17). High-intensity quartz halogen or xenon-arc light sources can be focused on a suspect area through a fiber-optic cable. This light can be passed through several filters, giving the user

fluoresce
To emit visible light when exposed to light of a shorter wavelength.

FIGURE 8-17 An alternate light source system incorporating a high-intensity light source. *Foster and Freeman USA, Inc.*

more flexibility in selecting the wavelength of light to be aimed at the latent print. Alternatively, lightweight, portable alternate light sources that use light-emitting diodes (LEDs) are also commercially available (see Figure 8-18).

In most cases, these light sources have proved as effective as laser light in developing latent prints, and they are commercially available at costs significantly below those of laser illuminators. Furthermore, these light sources are portable and can be readily taken to any crime scene.

A large number of chemical treatment processes are available to the fingerprint examiner, and the field is in a constant state of flux. Selection of an appropriate procedure is best left to technicians who have developed their skills through casework experience. Newer chemical processes include a substitute for ninhydrin called DFO (1,8-diazafluoren-9-one). This chemical visualizes latent prints on porous materials when exposed to an alternate light source. DFO has been shown to develop two and a half times more latent prints on paper than ninhydrin. Also, 1,2-indanedione is emerging as a potential reagent for the development of latent fingerprints on porous surfaces. It gives both good initial color and strong fluorescence when reacting with amino acids derived from prints, and thus it has the potential to provide in one process what ninhydrin and DFO can do in two steps. Dye combinations known as RAM, RAY, and MRM 10, when used in conjunction with Super Glue fuming, have been effective in visualizing latent fingerprints by fluorescence. A number of chemical formulas useful for latent-print development are listed in Appendix III.

Studies have demonstrated that common fingerprint-developing agents do not interfere

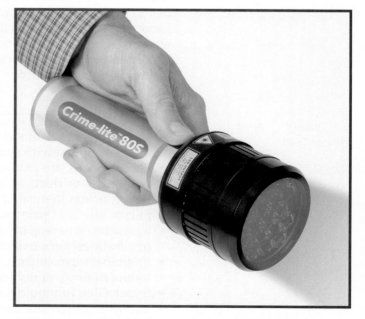

FIGURE 8-18 A lightweight handheld alternate light source that uses LEDs. *Foster and Freeman USA, Inc.*

CLOSER ANALYSIS
FLUORESCENCE

Fluorescence occurs when a substance absorbs light and reemits the light in wavelengths longer than that of the illuminating source. Importantly, substances that emit light or fluoresce are more readily seen either with the naked eye or through photography than are non-light-emitting materials. The high sensitivity of fluorescence serves as the underlying principle of many of the new chemical techniques used to visualize latent fingerprints.

The earliest use of fluorescence to visualize fingerprints came with the direct illumination of a fingerprint with argon-ion lasers. This laser type was chosen because its blue-green light induced some of the perspiration components of a fingerprint to fluoresce (see Figure UA 8.3). The major drawback of this approach is that the perspiration components of a fingerprint are often present in quantities too minute to observe even with the aid of fluorescence.

The fingerprint examiner, wearing safety goggles containing optical filters, visually examines the specimen being exposed to the laser light. The filters absorb the laser light and permit the wavelengths at which latent-print residues fluoresce to pass through to the eyes of the wearer. The filter also protects the operator against eye damage from scattered or reflected laser light. Likewise, latent-print residue producing sufficient fluorescence can be photographed by placing this same filter across the lens of the camera. Examination of specimens and photography of the fluorescing latent prints are carried out in a darkened room.

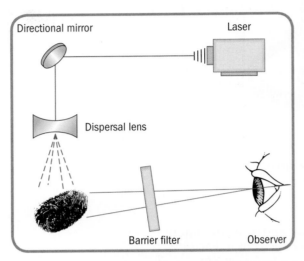

A schematic depicting latent-print detection with the aid of a laser. *Federal Bureau of Investigation*

---

with DNA-testing methods used for characterizing bloodstains.[5] Nonetheless, in cases involving items with material adhering to their surfaces and/or items that will require further laboratory examinations, fingerprint processing should not be performed at the crime scene. Rather, the items should be submitted to the laboratory, where they can be processed for fingerprints in conjunction with other necessary examinations.

Quick Review

- Visible prints are made when fingers touch a surface after the ridges have been in contact with a colored material such as blood, paint, grease, or ink.
- Plastic prints are ridge impressions left on a soft material, such as putty, wax, soap, or dust.
- Latent prints deposited on hard and nonabsorbent surfaces (e.g., glass, a mirror, tile, and painted wood) are usually developed by the application of a powder, whereas prints on porous surfaces (e.g., papers and cardboard) generally require treatment with a chemical.
- Examiners use various chemical methods to visualize latent prints, such as iodine fuming, ninhydrin, and Physical Developer.
- Super Glue fuming develops latent prints on nonporous surfaces.
- Latent fingerprints can also be treated with chemicals that induce fluorescence when exposed to a high-intensity light or an alternate light source.

Preservation of Developed Prints

Once the latent print has been visualized, it must be permanently preserved for future comparison and possible use in court as evidence. A photograph must be taken before any further attempts at preservation. Any camera equipped with a close-up lens will do; however, many investigators prefer to use a camera specially designed for fingerprint photography. Such a camera comes equipped with a fixed focus to take photographs on a 1:1 scale when the camera's open eye is held exactly flush against the print's surface (see Figure 8-19). In addition, photographs must be taken to provide an overall view of the print's location with respect to other evidential items at the crime scene.

Once photographs have been secured, one of two procedures is followed. If the object is small enough to be transported without destroying the print, it should be preserved in its entirety. The print should be covered with cellophane so it will be protected from damage. On the other hand, prints on large immovable objects that have been developed with a powder can best be preserved by "lifting." The most popular type of lifter is a broad adhesive tape similar to Scotch tape. Fingerprint powder is applied to the print, and the surface containing the print is covered with the adhesive side of the tape. When the tape is pulled up, the powder is transferred to the tape. Then the tape is placed on a properly labeled card that provides a good background contrast with the powder.

A variation of this procedure is the use of an adhesive-backed clear plastic sheet attached to a colored cardboard backing. Before it is applied to the print, a celluloid separator is peeled from the plastic sheet to expose the adhesive lifting surface. The tape is then pressed evenly and firmly over the powdered print and pulled up (see Figure 8-20). The sheet containing the adhering

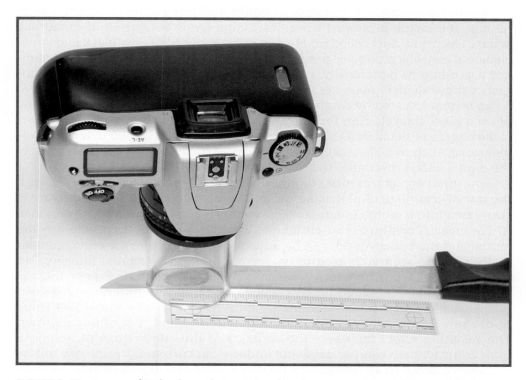

FIGURE 8-19   A camera fitted with an adapter designed to give an approximate 1:1 photograph of a fingerprint. *Sirchie Finger Print Laboratories*

FIGURE 8-20 "Lifting" a fingerprint. *Sirchie Finger Print Laboratories*

powder is then pressed against the cardboard backing to provide a permanent record of the fingerprint.

■ Digital Imaging for Fingerprint Enhancement

When fingerprints are lifted from a crime scene, they are not usually in perfect condition, which can make analysis difficult. As computers have advanced technology in most fields, fingerprint imaging has not been left behind. With the help of digital-imaging software, fingerprints can now be enhanced for the most accurate and comprehensive analysis.

digital imaging
A process through which a picture is converted into a series of square electronic dots known as pixels.

pixel
A square electronic dot that is used to compose a digital image.

Digital imaging is the process by which a picture is converted into a digital file. The image produced from this digital file is composed of numerous square electronic dots called **pixels**. Images composed of only black and white elements are referred to as "grayscale images." Each pixel is assigned a number according to its intensity, ranging from 0 (black) to 255 (white), and together these shaded pixels create an image. Once an image is digitally stored, it can be manipulated by computer software that changes the numerical value of each pixel, thus altering the image as directed by the user. The "resolution" is the degree of detail that can be seen in an image. It is defined in terms of dimensions, such as 800 × 600 pixels. The larger the numbers, the more closely the digital image resembles the real-world image.

The input of pictures into a digital-imaging system is usually done through the use of scanners, digital cameras, and video cameras. After the picture is converted into a digital image, several methods can be employed to enhance it. The overall brightness of an image, as well as the contrast between the image and the background, can be adjusted through contrast-enhancement methods. One approach used to enhance an image is "spatial filtering," in which several types of filters produce various effects. A low-pass filter is used to eliminate harsh edges by reducing the intensity difference between pixels. A high-pass filter operates by modifying a pixel's numerical value to exaggerate the difference between its intensity and that of its neighbor. The resulting effect increases the contrast of the edges, thus providing a high contrast between the elements and the background. Frequency analysis, also referred to as "frequency Fourier transform" (FFT), is used to identify periodic or repetitive patterns such as lines or dots that interfere with the interpretation of the image. These patterns are diminished or eliminated

FIGURE 8-21 A fingerprint being enhanced in Adobe Photoshop. In this example, on the left is the original scan of an inked fingerprint on a check. On the right is the same image after eliminating the green security background using Adobe Photoshop's Channel Mixer. *Imaging Forensics*

to enhance the appearance of the image. Interestingly, the spaces between fingerprint ridges are themselves periodic. Therefore, the fingerprint can be identified apart from its background in FFT mode and then enhanced. Likewise, if ridges from overlapping prints are positioned in different directions, their corresponding frequency information is at different locations in FFT mode. The ridges of one latent print can then be enhanced while the ridges of the other are suppressed.

Color interferences can pose a problem when analyzing an image. For example, a latent fingerprint found on paper currency or a check may be difficult to analyze because of the distracting colored background. With the imaging software, the colored background can simply be removed to make the image stand out (see Figure 8-21). If the image itself is a particular color, such as a ninhydrin-developed print, the color can be isolated and enhanced to distinguish it from the background.

Digital-imaging software also provides functions in which portions of the image can be examined individually. With a scaling and resizing tool, the user can select a part of an image and resize it for a closer look. This function operates much like a magnifying glass, helping the examiner view the fine details of an image.

An important and useful tool, especially for fingerprint identification, is the "compare" function. This specialized feature places two images side by side and allows the examiner to chart the common features in both images simultaneously (see Figure 8-22). The "zoom" function is used in conjunction with the compare tool. As the examiner viewing the image on the screen zooms in to a portion of one image, the software automatically zooms in to the second image for comparison.

Digital imaging is undoubtedly an effective tool for enhancing and analyzing images, and the benefits of digital enhancement methods are apparent when weak images are made more distinguishable. However, the tools are only as useful as the images they have to work with. If the details do not exist on the original images, the enhancement procedures are not going to work.

Case # 05-01234

Latent Print
Inside of bathroom window

John Smith
Finger #7

VIRTUAL LAB
FINGERPRINTING
To perform a virtual fingerprinting analysis, go to *www.pearsoncustom .com/us/vlm/*.

FIGURE 8-22 Current imaging software allows fingerprint analysts to prepare a fingerprint comparison chart. The fingerprint examiner can compare prints side by side and display important features that are consistent between the fingerprints. This sort of digital display can be created in about thirty to sixty minutes. *Imaging Forensics*

Quick Review

- Once a latent print has been visualized, it must be permanently preserved for future comparison and for possible use as court evidence. A photograph must be taken before any further attempts at preservation are made.
- A common method for preserving a print developed with a powder is lifting the print with an adhesive tape.
- Digital imaging is a process in which a picture is converted into a series of square electronic dots known as "pixels." Fingerprints can be enhanced with digital imaging.

CHAPTER REVIEW

- Fingerprints are a reproduction of friction skin ridges found on the palm side of fingers and thumbs.

- The basic principles underlying the use of fingerprints in criminal investigations are as follows: (1) A fingerprint is an individual characteristic because no two fingers have yet been found to possess identical ridge characteristics; (2) a fingerprint remains unchanged during an individual's lifetime; and (3) fingerprints have general ridge patterns that permit them to be systematically classified.

- All fingerprints are divided into three classes on the basis of their general pattern: loops, whorls, and arches.

- The individuality of a fingerprint is determined not by its general shape or pattern but by a careful study of its ridge characteristics. The expert must demonstrate a point-by-point comparison in order to prove the identity of an individual.

- A four-step process known as ACE-V (analysis, comparison, evaluation, and verification) is used to identify and individualize a fingerprint.

- The final step in the process involves verification of the examiner's conclusion by a second examiner.

- When a finger touches a surface, perspiration and oils are transferred onto that surface, leaving a fingerprint. Prints deposited in this manner are invisible to the eye and are commonly referred to as "latent" or "invisible" fingerprints.

- The primary classification is the first step in classifying fingerprints under the FBI system. The presence or absence of the whorl pattern is the basis for the determination of the primary classification.

- The fingerprint database known as AFIS converts an image of a fingerprint into digital minutiae that contain data showing ridges at their points of termination (i.e., ridge endings) and of branching into two ridges (i.e., bifurcations).

- AFIS makes no final decisions on the identification of a fingerprint, instead leaving this function to a trained examiner.

- Live Scan is an inkless device that captures digital images of fingerprints and palm prints and electronically transmits them to an AFIS.

- Visible prints are made when fingers touch a surface after the ridges have been in contact with a colored material such as blood, paint, grease, or ink.

- Plastic prints are ridge impressions left on a soft material, such as putty, wax, soap, or dust.

- Latent prints deposited on hard and nonabsorbent surfaces (e.g., glass, a mirror, tile, and painted wood) are usually developed by the application of a powder, whereas prints on porous surfaces (e.g., papers and cardboard) generally require treatment with a chemical.

- Examiners use various chemical methods to visualize latent prints, such as iodine fuming, ninhydrin, and Physical Developer.

- Super Glue fuming develops latent prints on nonporous surfaces.

- Latent fingerprints can also be treated with chemicals that induce fluorescence when exposed to a high-intensity light or an alternate light source.

- Once a latent print has been visualized, it must be permanently preserved for future comparison and for possible use as court evidence. A photograph must be taken before any further attempts at preservation are made.

- A common method for preserving a print developed with a powder is lifting the print with an adhesive tape.

- Digital imaging is a process in which a picture is converted into a series of square electronic dots known as "pixels." Fingerprints can be enhanced with digital imaging.

KEY TERMS

anthropometry, 164
arch, 169
digital imaging, 184
fluoresce, 180
iodine fuming, 177
latent fingerprint, 168

Live Scan, 173
loop, 169
ninhydrin, 179
Physical Developer, 179
pixel, 184
plastic print, 175

portrait parlé, 164
ridge characteristics (minutiae), 166
sublimation, 177
Super Glue fuming, 179
visible print, 175
whorl, 169

REVIEW QUESTIONS

1. The first systematic attempt at personal identification was devised and introduced by _____.

2. A system of identification relying on precise body measurements is known as _____.

3. The first book written on the subject of fingerprints, called *Finger Prints*, was written in 1892 by _____ and discussed the anatomy of fingerprints and suggested methods for recording them.

4. The fingerprint classification system used in most English-speaking countries was devised by _____.

5. True or False: The first systematic and official use of fingerprints for personal identification in the United States was adopted by the New York City Civil Service Commission. _____

6. The _____ has the largest collection of fingerprints in the world.

7. Galton calculated that approximately _____ different fingerprints could exist, and current figures are similarly high.

8. True or False: The individuality of a fingerprint is determined by its pattern. _____

9. A point-by-point comparison of a fingerprint's _____ must be demonstrated in order to prove identity.

10. _____ are a reproduction of friction skin ridges.

11. The form and pattern of skin ridges are determined by the skin layer called the _____.

12. Fingerprints deposited on a surface when oils and sweat are excreted from pores on the friction ridges are called _____ fingerprints.

13. A permanent scar forms in the skin only when an injury damages the _____.

14. True or False: Fingerprints cannot be changed during a person's lifetime. _____

15. The three general patterns into which fingerprints are divided are _____, _____, and _____.

16. The most common fingerprint pattern is the _____.

17. Approximately 5 percent of the population has the _____ fingerprint pattern.

18. A loop pattern that opens toward the thumb is known as a(n) _____ loop.

19. The simplest of all fingerprint patterns is the _____.

20. ACE-V is an acronym for a four-step process: _____, _____, _____, and _____.

21. True or False: Level 2 details cannot individualize a fingerprint. _____

22. The presence or absence of the _____ pattern is used as a basis for determining the primary classification in the Henry system.

23. The largest category (25 percent) of the population has a _____ primary classification, meaning all their fingers have loops or arches.

24. True or False: A fingerprint classification system can unequivocally identify an individual. _____

25. True or False: Computerized fingerprint search systems match prints by comparing the positions of bifurcations and ridge endings. _____

26. By determining the degree of correlation between the location and relationship of the _____ for both the search and file fingerprints, a computer can make thousands of fingerprint comparisons in a second.

27. The digital-capture device called _____ has eliminated ink and paper for the collection of file fingerprints.

28. A fingerprint left by a person with soiled or stained fingertips is called a(n) _____.

29. _____ fingerprints are impressions left on a soft material.

30. Fingerprints on hard and nonabsorbent surfaces are best developed by the application of a(n) _____.

31. Fingerprints on porous surfaces are best developed with _____ treatment.

32. _____ vapors chemically combine with fatty oils or residual water to visualize a fingerprint.

33. The chemical _____ visualizes fingerprints by its reaction with amino acids.

34. Chemical treatment with _____ visualizes fingerprints on porous articles that may have been wet at one time.

35. True or False: A latent fingerprint is first treated with Physical Developer followed by ninhydrin. _____

36. A chemical technique known as _____ is used to develop latent prints on nonporous surfaces such as metal and plastic.

37. _____ occurs when a substance absorbs light and reemits the light in wavelengths longer than the illuminating source.

38. High-intensity light sources, known as _____, are effective in developing latent fingerprints.

39. Once a fingerprint has been visualized, it must first be preserved by _____.

40. Fingerprints on large immovable objects that have been developed with a powder can best be preserved by _____ with a broad adhesive tape similar to Scotch tape.

APPLICATION AND CRITICAL THINKING

1. Classify each of the following prints as loop, whorl, or arch.

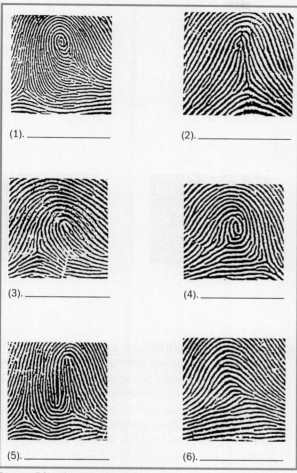

(1). _____

(2). _____

(3). _____

(4). _____

(5). _____

(6). _____

Pearson Education, Inc.

2. Following is a description of the types of prints from the fingers of a criminal suspect. Using the FBI system, determine the primary classification of this individual.

Finger	Right Hand	Left Hand
Thumb	Whorl	Whorl
Index	Loop	Whorl
Middle	Whorl	Arch
Ring	Whorl	Whorl
Little	Arch	Whorl

3. While searching a murder scene, you find the following items that you believe may contain latent fingerprints. Indicate whether prints on each item should be developed using fingerprint powder or chemicals.

a) A leather sofa

b) A mirror

c) A painted wooden knife handle

d) Blood-soaked newspapers

e) A revolver

4. Criminalist Frank Mortimer is using digital imaging to enhance latent fingerprints. Indicate which features of digital imaging he would most likely use for each of the following tasks:

a) Isolating part of a print and enlarging it for closer examination

b) Increasing the contrast between a print and the background surface on which it is located

c) Examining two prints that overlap each other

5. The following are fingerprint patterns of three men and a woman with criminal records for robbery. Identify the following fingerprints according to the three groups and the subgroups of fingerprints.

KJ *Pearson Education, Inc.*

Ivan *Pearson Education, Inc.*

Lisa *Pearson Education, Inc.*

Charlie *Pearson Education, Inc.*

6. Count the number of bifurcations in the following prints. Choose between 9, 11, and 13.

Pearson Education, Inc.

Number of bifurcations: _____

7. At the Museum of Culture Studies, a diary that belonged to Martin Luther King Jr. has been stolen and replaced by a fake. The only evidence is a fingerprint impression left by the thief on the fake diary. The police suspect four individuals who have had previous criminal records for similar crimes. Their fingerprints already exist in the police database. KJ, Ivan, Lisa, and Charlie are the four suspects. Carefully examine the criminal's fingerprint impression and identify which of any suspect matches with it.

Pearson Education, Inc.

Crime Scene Fingerprint

KJ

Ivan

Lisa

Charlie

Pearson Education, Inc.

ENDNOTES

1. A tented arch is also any pattern that resembles a loop but lacks one of the essential requirements for classification as a loop.

2. M. A. Smrz et al., "Review of FBI Latent Print Unit Processes and Recommendations to Improve Practices and Quality," *Journal of Forensic Identification* 56 (2006): 402–433.

3. J. Almag, Y. Sasson, and A. Anati, "Chemical Reagents for the Development of Latent Fingerprints II: Controlled Addition of Water Vapor to Iodine Fumes—A Solution to the Aging Problem," *Journal of Forensic Sciences* 24 (1979): 431.

4. F. G. Kendall and B. W. Rehn, "Rapid Method of Super Glue Fuming Application for the Development of Latent Fingerprints," *Journal of Forensic Sciences* 28 (1983): 777.

5. C. Roux et al., "A Further Study to Investigate the Effect of Fingerprint Enhancement Techniques on the DNA Analysis of Bloodstains," *Journal of Forensic Identification* 49 (1999): 357; C. J. Frégeau et al., "Fingerprint Enhancement Revisited and the Effects of Blood Enhancement Chemicals on Subsequent Profiler Plus™ Fluorescent Short Tandem Repeat DNA Analysis of Fresh and Aged Bloody Fingerprints," *Journal of Forensic Sciences* 45 (2000): 354; P. Grubwieser et al., "Systematic Study on STR Profiling on Blood and Saliva Traces after Visualization of Fingerprints," *Journal of Forensic Sciences* 48 (2003): 733.

9

Firearms, Tool Marks, and Other Impressions

Tracy A. Woodward/The Washington Post/Getty Images

LEARNING OBJECTIVES

After studying this chapter, you should be able to:

- Describe the categories and various types of firearms.
- Describe techniques for rifling a barrel.
- Recognize the class and individual characteristics of bullets and cartridge cases.
- Understand the use of the comparison microscope to compare bullets and cartridge cases.
- Explain the concept of the NIBIN database.
- Explain the procedure for determining how far from a target a weapon was fired.
- Identify the laboratory tests for determining whether an individual has fired a weapon.
- Understand the proper collection and preservation of firearm evidence.
- Explain the forensic significance of class and individual characteristics to the comparison of tool mark, footwear, and tire impressions.
- List some common field reagents used to enhance bloody footprints.

THE BELTWAY SNIPERS

During a three-week period in October 2002, ten people were killed and three others wounded as two snipers terrorized the region in and around the Baltimore/ Washington metropolitan area. The arrest of John Allen Muhammad, 41, and Lee Boyd Malvo, 17, ended the ordeal. The semiautomatic .223-caliber rifle seized from them was ultimately linked by firearm tests to eight of the ten killings. The car that Muhammad and Malvo were driving had been specially adapted with one hole in the trunk through which a rifle barrel could protrude, so that a sniper could shoot from inside the slightly ajar trunk.

The major break in the case came when a friend of Muhammad's called police suggesting that Muhammad and his friend Malvo were the likely snipers. Muhammad's automobile records revealed numerous traffic stops in the Beltway area during the time of the shootings. Another break in the case came when Malvo called a priest to boast of a killing that had occurred weeks before, in Montgomery, Alabama. Investigators traced the claim to a recent liquor store holdup that left one person dead. Fortunately, the perpetrator of this crime left a latent fingerprint at the murder scene. Authorities quickly tracked the print to Malvo, a Jamaican citizen, through his fingerprints on file with the Immigration and Naturalization Service. A description of Muhammad's car was released to the media, leading to tips from alert citizens who noticed the car parked in a rest area with both occupants asleep.

The motive for the shooting spree was believed to be a plot to extort $10 million from local and state governments. Muhammad was sentenced to death, and Malvo is currently serving life imprisonment without parole.

Just as natural variations in skin ridge patterns and characteristics provide a key to human identification, minute random markings on surfaces can impart individuality to inanimate objects. Structural variations and irregularities caused by scratches, nicks, breaks, and wear permit the criminalist to relate a bullet to a gun, a scratch or abrasion mark to a single tool, or a tire track to a particular automobile. Individualization, so vigorously pursued in all other areas of criminalistics, is frequently attainable in firearms and tool mark examination.

Although a portion of this chapter will be devoted to the comparison of surface features for the purpose of bullet identification, a complete description of the services and capabilities of the modern forensic firearms laboratory cannot be restricted to just this one subject, important as it may be. The high frequency of shooting cases means that the science of **firearms identification** must extend beyond mere comparison of bullets to include knowledge of the operation of all types of weapons, restoration of obliterated serial numbers on weapons, detection and characterization of gunpowder residues on garments and around wounds, estimation of muzzle-to-target distances, and detection of powder residues on hands. Each of these functions will be covered in this chapter.

firearms identification
A discipline primarily concerned with determining whether a bullet or cartridge was fired by a particular weapon.

Types of Firearms

Generally, firearms can be divided into two categories: handguns and long guns. "Handguns," or pistols, are firearms that are designed to be held and fired with one hand. The three most common types of handguns are single-shot handguns, revolvers, and semiautomatics. All handguns can be classified as single-action or double-action firearms. Single-action firearms require the hammer to be manually cocked backward each time before the trigger is pulled in order to fire. Double-action firearms cock the hammer when the trigger is pulled and then reload the firing chamber after the round is fired.

Single-shot pistols can fire only one round, or shot, at a time. Each round must be manually loaded into the chamber before firing.

The revolver features several firing chambers located within a revolving cylinder. As the revolver is fired, the cylinder can rotate clockwise or counterclockwise. Each firing chamber holds one cartridge, which is lined up with the barrel mechanically when the round is fired. The cartridge cases have to be manually ejected to reload the firing chambers. "Swing-out revolvers" feature a cylinder that swings out to the side of the weapon to be loaded (see Figure 9-1). "Break-top revolvers" are hinged so that both the barrel and the cylinder flip downward for loading. "Solid-frame revolvers" have no mechanism to uncover all the firing chambers at once. Instead a small "gate" at the back of the gun allows one chamber to be loaded at a time; the cylinder is then rotated, and the next chamber is loaded with a cartridge.

FIGURE 9-1 A swing-out revolver features a cylinder that swings out to the side of the weapon to be loaded. *Dorling Kindersley LLC*

Semiautomatic pistols feature a removable magazine that is most often contained within the grip of the firearm. Once the magazine is loaded, the hammer is cocked by pulling the slide on the top of the gun rearward and then releasing it to load the first round. The firing of the cartridge generates gases that are used to eject the cartridge case, cock the hammer, and load the next round. A semiautomatic pistol (see Figure 9-2) fires one shot per trigger pull. An automatic firearm, such as a machine gun, fires as long as the trigger is pressed or until the ammunition is depleted.

"Long guns" are either rifles or shotguns. Rifles and shotguns are designed to be fired while resting on the shoulder. The two principal differences between rifled firearms and shotguns are found in the ammunition and the barrel. Shotgun ammunition, called a "shell," contains numerous ball-shaped projectiles, called shot. The barrel of a shotgun is smooth without the grooves and lands found in rifles. A shotgun barrel can also be narrowed toward the muzzle in order to concentrate shot when fired. This narrowing of the barrel is called the "choke" of the shotgun. A shotgun may be single or double barreled. The two barrels of a double-barreled shotgun may be arranged horizontally (side by side) or vertically (one over another). The barrels may also have different choke diameters.

The various types of rifles and shotguns have different reloading mechanisms. The single-shot gun can chamber and fire only one round at a time. Just as with single-shot pistols, the round has to be loaded manually each time. Repeating long guns use a mechanical instrument of some sort to eject spent cartridges, load a new round, and cock the hammer after a round is fired. These include lever-action, pump or slide-action, bolt-action (see Figure 9-3), and semiautomatic (see Figure 9-4) long guns, the names of which refer to the loading mechanism used on each. Semiautomatic rifles use the force of the gas produced during firing to eject the spent cartridge, load a new round, and cock the hammer. Semiautomatic firearms use a disconnector mechanism to fire one shot per trigger pull, whereas fully automatic firearms do not have such a mechanism and fire multiple consecutive shots with a single pull of the trigger.

FIGURE 9-2   A semiautomatic pistol. *Dorling Kindersley Limited*

Bullet and Cartridge Comparisons

The inner surface of the rifled barrel of a gun leaves its markings on a bullet passing through it. These markings are particular to each gun. Hence, if one bullet found at the scene of a crime and another test-fired from a suspect's gun exhibit the same markings, the suspect is linked to the crime. Because these inner surface markings, or striations, are so important for bullet comparison, it is important to know why and how they originate.

FIGURE 9-3   A bolt-action long gun uses the movement of a bolt mechanism to expel the spent cartridge case, load the next round, and cock the hammer. *George Pickow/Getty Images*

FIGURE 9-4 A semiautomatic long gun uses the energy from the firing reaction to expel the spent cartridge case, load the next round, and cock the hammer. *Tim Ridley/Dorling Kindersley Limited, LTD.*

grooves
The cut or low-lying portions between the lands in a rifled bore.

rifling
The spiral grooves formed in the bore of a firearm barrel that impart spin to the projectile when it is fired.

bore
The interior of a firearm barrel.

lands
The raised portion between the grooves in a rifled bore.

caliber
The diameter of the bore of a rifled firearm, usually expressed in hundredths of an inch or millimeters—for example, .22 caliber and 9 millimeter.

THE GUN BARREL

The gun barrel is produced from a solid bar of steel that has been hollowed out by drilling. The microscopic drill marks left on the barrel's inner surface are randomly irregular and in themselves impart a uniqueness to each barrel. However, the manufacture of a barrel requires the additional step of impressing its inner surface with spiral **grooves**, a step known as **rifling**. The surfaces of the original **bore** remaining between the grooves are called **lands** (see Figure 9-5).

As a fired bullet travels through a barrel, it engages the rifling grooves. These grooves then guide the bullet through the barrel, giving it a rapid spin. This is done because a spinning bullet does not tumble end over end on leaving the barrel, but instead remains on a true and accurate course.

The diameter of the gun barrel, shown in Figure 9-6, is measured between opposite lands and is known as the **caliber** of the weapon. Caliber is normally recorded in hundredths of an inch or in millimeters—for example, .22 caliber and 9 millimeter. Actually, the term "caliber," as it is commonly applied, is not an exact measurement of the barrel's diameter; for example, a .38-caliber weapon might actually have a bore diameter that ranges from 0.345 to 0.365 inch.

RIFLING METHODS Before 1940, barrels were rifled by having one or two grooves at a time cut into the surface with steel hook cutters. The cutting tool was rotated as it passed down the barrel, so that the final results were grooves spiraling to either the right or left. However, as the need for increased speed and efficiency in methods of weapons manufacture became apparent, newer techniques were developed that were far more suitable for mass production.

The broach cutter consists of a series of concentric steel rings, with each ring slightly larger than the preceding one. As the broach passes through the barrel, it simultaneously cuts all grooves into the barrel at the required depth. The broach rotates as it passes through the barrel, giving the grooves their desired direction and rate of twist. A broach cutter ring is shown in Figure 9-7.

FIGURE 9-5 Interior view of a gun barrel, showing the presence of lands and grooves. *SAFERSTEIN, RICHARD, Ph.D., CRIMINALISTICS: AN INTRODUCTION TO FORENSIC SCIENCE, 11th Ed., ©2015. Reprinted and Electronically reproduced by permission of Pearson Education, Inc., Upper Saddle River, New Jersey.*

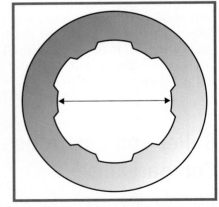

FIGURE 9-6 A cross-section of a barrel with six grooves. The diameter of the bore is the caliber. *SAFERSTEIN, RICHARD, Ph.D., CRIMINALISTICS: AN INTRODUCTION TO FORENSIC SCIENCE, 11th Ed., ©2015. Reprinted and Electronically reproduced by permission of Pearson Education, Inc., Upper Saddle River, New Jersey.*

In contrast to the broach, the button process involves no cuttings. A steel plug or "button" impressed with the desired number of grooves is forced under extremely high pressure through the barrel. A single pass of the button down the barrel compresses the metal to create lands and grooves on the barrel walls that are negative forms of those on the button. The button rotates to produce the desired direction and rate of twist (see Figure 9-8).

Like the button process, the mandrel-rifling hammer-forging process involves no cutting of metal. A "mandrel" is a rod of hardened steel machined so its form is the reverse impression of the rifling it is intended to produce. The mandrel is inserted into a slightly oversized bore, and the barrel is compressed with hammering or heavy rollers into the mandrel's form.

Every firearms manufacturer chooses a rifling process that is best suited to meet the production standards and requirements of its product. Once the choice is made, however, the class characteristics of the weapon's barrel remain consistent; each has the same number of lands and grooves, with the same approximate width and direction of twist. For example, .32-caliber Smith & Wesson revolvers have five lands and grooves twisting to the right. On the other hand, Colt .32-caliber revolvers exhibit six lands and grooves twisting to the left. Although these class characteristics permit the examiner to distinguish one type or brand name of weapon from another, they do not impart individuality to any one barrel; no class characteristic can do this.

If one could cut a barrel open lengthwise, careful examination of the interior would reveal the existence of fine lines, or "striations," running the length of the barrel's lands and grooves. These striations are impressed into the metal as the negatives of minute imperfections found on the rifling cutter's surface, or they are produced by minute chips of steel pushed against the barrel's inner surface by a moving broach cutter. The random distribution and irregularities of these markings are impossible to duplicate exactly in any two barrels. No two rifled barrels, even those manufactured in succession, have identical striation markings. These striations form the individual characteristics of the barrel.

COMPARING BULLET MARKINGS   As the bullet passes through the barrel, its surface is impressed with the rifled markings of the barrel. The bullet emerges from the barrel carrying the impressions of the bore's interior surface (see Figure 9-9). Because there is no practical way to directly compare the markings

FIGURE 9-7   A segment of a broach cutter. *Susan Walsh/ Associated Press*

FIGURE 9-8   (*top*) Cross-section of a .22-caliber rifled barrel. (*bottom*) A button used to produce the lands and grooves in the barrel. *Richard Saferstein, Ph.D.*

FIGURE 9-9 A bullet is impressed with the rifling markings of the barrel when it emerges from the weapon. *Richard Saferstein, Ph.D.*

WebExtra 9.1

Practice Matching Bullets with the Aid of a 3-D Interactive Illustration

on the fired bullet and those within a barrel, the examiner must obtain test bullets fired through the suspect barrel for comparison. To prevent damage to the test bullet's markings and to facilitate the bullet's recovery, test firings are normally made into a recovery box filled with cotton or into a water tank (see Figure 9-10).

The number of lands and grooves and their direction of twist are obvious points of comparison during the initial stages of the examination. Any differences in these class characteristics immediately eliminate the possibility that both bullets traveled through the same barrel. A bullet with five lands and grooves could not possibly have been fired from a weapon of like caliber with six lands and grooves, nor could one having a right twist have come through a barrel impressed with a left twist. If both bullets carry the same class characteristics, the analyst must then begin to match the striated markings on both bullets. This can be done only with the assistance of a comparison microscope.

Modern firearms identification began with the development and use of the comparison microscope. This instrument is the firearms examiner's most important tool. The test and evidence bullets are mounted on cylindrical adjustable holders beneath the objective lenses of the microscope, each pointing in the same direction (see Figure 9-11). Both bullets are observed simultaneously within the same field of view, and the examiner rotates one bullet until a well-defined land or groove comes into view.

Once the striation markings are located, the other bullet is rotated until a matching region is found. Not only must the

FIGURE 9-10 In ballistics testing, a suspect firearm is fired into a water tank. The bullet is slowed and stopped by the water, fished out undamaged, and compared to bullets from the crime scene. *Courtesy Mikael Karlsson/Arresting Images*

lands and grooves of the test and evidence bullet have identical widths, but the longitudinal striations on each must coincide. When a matching area is located, the two bullets are simultaneously rotated to obtain additional matching areas around the periphery of the bullets. Figure 9-12 shows a typical photomicrograph of a bullet match as viewed under a comparison microscope.

CONSIDERATIONS IN BULLET COMPARISON Unfortunately, the firearms examiner rarely encounters a perfect match all around the bullet's periphery. The presence of grit and rust can alter the markings on bullets fired through the same barrel. More commonly, recovered evidence bullets become so mutilated and distorted on impact that they yield only a small area with intact markings.

Furthermore, striation markings on a barrel are not permanent structures; they are subject to continuing alteration through wear as succeeding bullets traverse the length of the barrel. Fortunately, these changes are usually not dramatic and do not prevent the matching of two bullets fired by the same weapon. As with fingerprint comparison, there are no hard-and-fast rules governing the minimum number of points required for a bullet comparison. The final opinion must be based on the judgment, experience, and knowledge of the expert.

Frequently, the firearms examiner receives a spent bullet without an accompanying suspect weapon and is asked to determine the caliber and possible make of the weapon. If a bullet appears not to have lost any metal, its weight may be one factor in determining its caliber. In some instances, the number of lands and grooves, the direction of twist, and the widths of lands and grooves are useful class characteristics for eliminating certain makes of weapons from consideration.

FIGURE 9-11 A bullet holder beneath the objective lens of a comparison microscope. *Leica Microsystems Inc.*

FIGURE 9-12 A photomicrograph of two bullets through a comparison microscope. The test bullet is on the right; the questioned bullet is on the left. *Diaczuk, Peter*

For example, a bullet that has five lands and grooves and twists to the right could not have come from a weapon manufactured by Colt because Colts are not manufactured with these class characteristics.

Sometimes a bullet has rifling marks that set the weapon from which it was fired apart from most other manufactured weapons, as is the case with Marlin rifles. These weapons are rifled by a technique known as "microgrooving" and may have eight to twenty-four grooves impressed into their barrels; few other weapons are manufactured in this fashion. For this reason, the FBI maintains a record known as the General Rifling Characteristics File. This file contains listings of class characteristics, such as land- and groove-width measurements, for known weapons. It is periodically updated and distributed to the law enforcement community to help identify rifled weapons from retrieved bullets.

Unlike rifled firearms, a shotgun has a smooth barrel, so projectiles passing through a shotgun barrel are not impressed with any characteristic markings that can be related back to the weapon later. Shotguns generally fire small lead balls or pellets contained within a shotgun shell (see Figure 9-13). A paper or plastic wad pushes the pellets through the barrel when the shell's powder charge is ignited. By weighing and measuring the diameter of the shot recovered at a crime scene, the examiner can usually determine the size of shot used in the shell. The size and shape of the recovered wad may also reveal the gauge of the shotgun used and, in some instances, may indicate the manufacturer of the fired shell.

The diameter of the shotgun barrel is expressed in terms of its **gauge**.[1] The higher the gauge number, the smaller the barrel's diameter. For example, a 12-gauge shotgun has a bore diameter of 0.730 inch, and a 16-gauge shotgun has an interior diameter of 0.670 inch. The exception to this rule is the .410-gauge shotgun, whose gauge number refers directly to the barrel's bore measurement of 0.41 inch in diameter.

CARTRIDGE CASES

The act of pulling a trigger releases the weapon's firing pin, causing it to strike the primer, which in turn ignites the powder. The expanding gases generated by the burning gunpowder propel the bullet forward through the barrel, simultaneously pushing the spent cartridge case or shell back with equal force against the **breech face mark**. As the bullet is marked by its passage through the barrel, the shell is also impressed with markings by its contact with the

gauge
The size designation of a shotgun; originally the number of lead balls with the same diameter as the barrel that would make a pound. The only exception is the .410 shotgun, in which bore size is 0.41 inch.

breech face mark
The rear part of a firearm barrel.

FIGURE 9-13 A cross-section of a loaded shotgun shell. *SAFERSTEIN, RICHARD, Ph.D., CRIMINALISTICS: AN INTRODUCTION TO FORENSIC SCIENCE, 11th Ed., ©2015. Reprinted and Electronically reproduced by permission of Pearson Education, Inc., Upper Saddle River, New Jersey.*

CLOSER ANALYSIS
THE COMPARISON MICROSCOPE

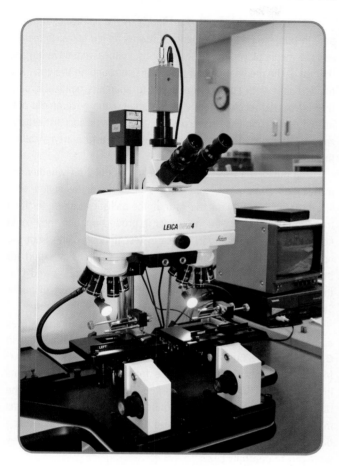

The comparison microscope—two independent objective lenses joined together by an optical bridge. *Leica Microsystems, Inc.*

Forensic microscopy often requires a side-by-side comparison of specimens. This kind of examination can best be performed with a comparison microscope, such as the one pictured in the figure.

Basically, the comparison microscope is two compound microscopes combined into one unit. The unique feature of its design is that it uses a bridge incorporating a series of mirrors and lenses to join two independent objective lenses into a single binocular unit. A viewer looking through the eyepiece lenses of the comparison microscope observes a circular field equally divided into two parts by a fine line. The specimen mounted under the left-hand objective appears in the left half of the field, and the specimen under the right-hand objective appears in the right half of the field. It is important to closely match the optical characteristics of the objective lenses to ensure that both specimens are seen at equal magnification and with minimal but identical lens distortions. Comparison microscopes designed to compare opaque objects, such as bullets and cartridges, are equipped with vertical or reflected illumination. Comparison microscopes used to compare hairs or fibers use transmitted illumination.

Figure 9-12 shows the striation markings on two bullets that have been placed under the objective lenses of a comparison microscope. Modern firearms examination began with the introduction of the comparison microscope, which gives the firearms examiner a side-by-side, magnified view of two bullets. Bullets that are fired through the same rifle barrel display comparable rifling markings on their surfaces. Matching the majority of striations present on each bullet justifies a conclusion that both bullets traveled through the same barrel.

---

metal surfaces of the weapon's firing and loading mechanisms. As with bullets, these markings can be reproduced in test-fired cartridges to provide distinctive points of comparison for individualizing a spent shell to a rifled weapon or shotgun.

The cup of the firing pin is impressed into the relatively soft metal of the primer on the cartridge case, revealing the minute distortions of the firing pin. These imperfections may be sufficiently random to individualize the pin impression to a single weapon. Similarly, the cartridge case, in its rearward thrust, is impressed with the surface markings of the breech face mark. The breech face mark, like any machined surface, is populated with random striation markings that become a highly distinctive signature for individualizing its surface.

Other distinctive markings that may appear on the brass portions of shells as a result of metal-to-metal contact are caused by the **extractor** and **ejector** mechanism and the magazine, or clip, as well as by imperfections on the firing

WebExtra 9.2

3-D Shotgun Shell Illustrations

WebExtra 9.3

3-D Revolver Cartridge Illustrations

extractor
The mechanism in a firearm that withdraws a cartridge or fired case from the chamber.

ejector
The mechanism in a firearm that throws the cartridge or fired case from the firearm.

■■■■ CASEFILES ■■■■

SACCO AND VANZETTI

In 1920, two security guards were viciously gunned down by unidentified assailants. The security guards were transporting shoe factory payrolls, nearly $16,000 in cash, at the time of the robbery-murder. Eyewitnesses described the assailants as "Italian-looking," one with a full handlebar moustache. The robbers had used two firearms that left behind three different brands of shells.

Two suspects were identified and arrested: Nicola Sacco and his friend, the amply mustachioed Bartolomeo Vanzetti. After denying owning any firearms, each was found to be in possession of a loaded pistol. In fact, Sacco's pistol was .32 caliber, the same caliber as the crime-scene bullets. In Sacco's pockets were found twenty-three bullets matching the brands of the empty shells found at the murder scene.

Sacco and Vanzetti. *Corbis*

This case coincided with the "Red Scare," a politically turbulent time in post–World War I America. Citizens feared socialist zealots, and the media played up these emotions. Political maneuvering and the use of the media muddied the waters surrounding the case, and the fact that both suspects belonged to anarchist political groups that advocated revolutionary violence against the government only incited public animosity toward them. Sympathetic socialist organizations attempted to turn Sacco and Vanzetti into martyrs, calling their prosecution a "witch hunt."

The outcome of the trial ultimately depended on whether the prosecution could prove that Sacco's pistol fired the bullets that killed the two security guards. At trial, the ballistics experts testified that the bullets used were no longer in production, and they could not find similar ammunition to use in test firings—aside from the unused cartridges found in Sacco's pockets. A forensics expert for the prosecution concluded that a visual examination showed that the bullets matched, leading the jury to return a verdict of guilty. Sacco and Vanzetti were sentenced to death.

Because of continued public protests, a committee was appointed in 1927 to review the case. Around this time, Calvin Goddard, at the Bureau of Forensic Ballistics in New York, perfected the comparison microscope for use in forensic firearms investigations. The committee asked Goddard to examine the bullets in question. A test-fired bullet from Sacco's weapon was matched conclusively by Goddard to one of the crime-scene bullets. The fates of Sacco and Vanzetti were sealed, and they were put to death in 1927.

WebExtra 9.4

3-D Pistol Cartridge Illustrations

WebExtra 9.5

3-D Rifle Cartridge Illustrations

WebExtra 9.6

View Animations to Illustrate the Firing Process and the Extraction/Ejection Process of a Semiautomatic Pistol

www.mycrimekit.com

chamber walls. The photomicrographs in Figure 9-14 reveal a comparison of the firing pin and breech face mark impressions on evidence and test-fired shells.

These impressions provide points for individualizing the shell to a weapon that are just as valuable as cartridge cases discharged from a rifled firearm. Furthermore, in the absence of a suspect weapon, the size and shape of a firing pin impression and/or the position of ejector marks in relationship to extractor and other markings may provide some clue to the type or make of the weapon that fired the questioned shell, or at least eliminate a large number of possibilities.

Quick Review

- The manufacture of a gun barrel requires impressing its inner surface with spiral grooves, a step known as "rifling." Rifling imparts spin to the projectile when it is fired, which keeps it on an accurate course.
- No two rifled barrels have identical striation markings. These striations form the individual characteristics of the barrel. The inner surface of the barrel of a gun transfers its striation markings to bullets that pass through it.

(a)   (b)

FIGURE 9-14   A comparison microscope photomicrograph showing a match between (a) firing pin impressions and (b) the breech face mark on two shells. *Ronald Welsh*

- The class characteristics of a rifled barrel include the number of lands and grooves and the width and direction of twist.
- The comparison microscope is a firearms examiner's most important tool because it allows two bullets to be compared simultaneously.
- The firing pin, breech face mark, and ejector and extractor mechanism also offer a highly distinctive signature for individualization of cartridge cases.
- Unlike handguns, a shotgun is not rifled—it has a smooth barrel. Because of this, shotgun shells are not impressed with any characteristic rifling striation markings that can be used to compare two shotgun shells to determine whether they were fired from the same weapon.

Automated Firearms Search Systems

The use of firearms, especially semiautomatic weapons, during the commission of a crime has significantly increased throughout the United States. Because of the expense of such firearms, the likelihood that a specific weapon will be used in multiple crimes has risen. The advent of computerized imaging technology has made it possible to store bullet and cartridge surface characteristics in a manner analogous to automated fingerprint files. Using this concept, crime laboratories can be networked, allowing them to share information on bullets and cartridges retrieved from several jurisdictions.

EARLY SYSTEMS

The effort to build a national computerized database for firearms evidence in the United States had a rather confusing and inefficient start in the early 1990s. Two major federal law enforcement agencies, the FBI and the Bureau of Alcohol, Tobacco, Firearms, and Explosives (ATF), offered the law enforcement community competing and incompatible computerized systems.

The automated search system developed for the FBI was known as "DRUGFIRE." This system emphasized the examination of unique markings on the cartridge casings expended by the weapon. The specimen was analyzed through a microscope attached to a video camera. The magnification allowed for a close-up view to identify individual characteristics. The image was captured by the video camera, digitized, and stored in a database. Although

DRUGFIRE emphasized cartridge-case imagery, the images of highly charac-teristic bullet striations could also be stored in a like manner for conducting comparisons.

The Integrated Ballistic Identification System (IBIS), developed for the Bureau of Alcohol, Tobacco, Firearms, and Explosives, processed digital mi-croscopic images of identifying features found on both expended bullets and cartridge casings. IBIS incorporated two software programs: Bulletproof, a bullet-analyzing module, and Brasscatcher, a cartridge-case-analyzing mod-ule. A schematic diagram of Bulletproof's operation is depicted in Figure 9-15.

NIBIN   In 1999, members of the FBI and ATF joined forces to introduce the National Integrated Ballistics Information Network (NIBIN) program to the discipline of firearms examination. The new, unified system incorporates both DRUGFIRE and IBIS technologies. ATF has overall responsibility for the system sites, and the FBI is responsible for the communications network.

Agencies using the new NIBIN technology produce database files from bullets and cartridge casings retrieved from crime scenes or test fires from retrieved firearms. More than two hundred law enforcement agencies world-wide have adopted this technology. The success of the system has been proved: With more than 1.6 million images compiled nationwide, law enforcement

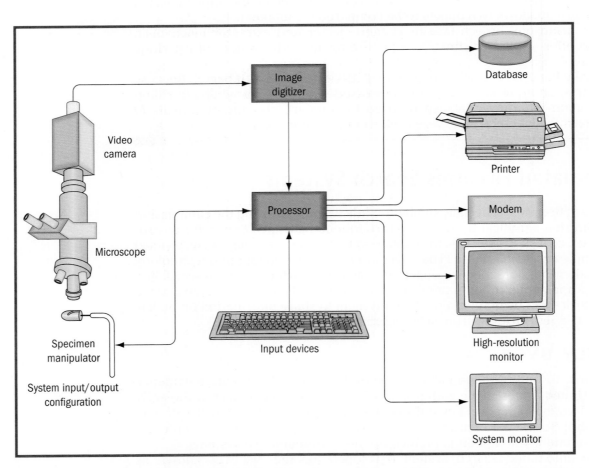

FIGURE 9-15   Bulletproof configuration. The sample is mounted on the specimen manipulator and illuminated by the light source from a microscope. The image is captured by a video camera and digitized. This digital image is then stored in a database, available for retrieval and comparison. The search for a match includes analyzing the width of land and groove impressions along with both rifling and individual characteristics. The Brasscatcher software uses the same system configuration but emphasizes the analysis of expended cartridge casings rather than the expended bullets. *Forensic Technologies, Inc.*

agencies have connected more than 34,000 bullets and casings to more than one crime (see Figure 9-16).

For example, in a recent case, a robbery-turned-double-homicide left two store clerks dead. Two bullets and two .40-caliber Smith & Wesson cartridge casings were recovered. Later that day, a Houston security guard was shot and killed during a botched armed robbery. A bullet and .40-caliber Smith & Wesson cartridge casing were recovered and entered into NIBIN. Once these were processed, a correlation was found between the murder of the security officer and a separate aggravated robbery that had occurred two weeks earlier. All three crimes were linked with a firearm believed to be a .40-caliber Smith & Wesson pistol.

FIGURE 9-16   Bullets A, B, C, and D were acquired by the IBIS database at different times from different crime scenes. D is a fragmented bullet that had only three land impressions available for acquisition. On entering bullet D, IBIS found a potential matching candidate in the database: B. On the far right, bullet D is compared to bullet B using the IBIS imaging software. Finally, a forensic firearms examiner using the actual evidence under a conventional comparison microscope will confirm the match between B and D. *Forensic Technology WAI Inc.*

Further investigation into the use of a victim's credit card helped police locate two suspects. In the possession of one suspect was a .40-caliber Smith & Wesson pistol. The gun was test-fired and imaged into NIBIN. The casing from the test-fired weapon matched the evidence obtained in the robbery and the aggravated robbery-homicides. A firearms examiner verified the associations by traditional comparisons. Before this computerized technology existed, it would have taken years—or it may have been impossible—to link all of these shootings to a single firearm.

In another example, the ATF laboratory in Rockville, Maryland, received 1,466 cartridge casings from the Ovcara mass burial site in Bosnia. After processing and imaging profiles for all casings, the examiners determined that eighteen different firearms had been used at the site. With the help of NIBIN technology and competent examiners, jurists attempted to convict an individual for war crimes.

NIBIN serves only as a screening tool for firearms evidence. A computerized system does not replace the skills of the firearms examiner. NIBIN can screen hundreds of unsolved firearms cases and may narrow the possibilities to several firearms. However, the final comparison will be made by a forensic examiner through traditional microscopic methods.

BALLISTIC FINGERPRINTING

Participating crime laboratories in the United States are building databases of bullet and cartridge cases found at crime scenes and those fired in tests of guns seized from criminals. As these databases prove their usefulness in solving crimes, law enforcement officials and the political community are scrutinizing the feasibility of scaling this concept up to create a system of "ballistic fingerprinting." This system would entail the capture and storage of appropriate markings on bullets and cartridges test-fired from handguns and rifles before they are sold to the public. Questions regarding who will be responsible for collecting the images and details of how will they be stored are but two of many issues to be decided. The concept of ballistic fingerprinting is an intriguing one for the law enforcement community and promises to be explored and debated intensely in the future.

Quick Review

- The advent of computerized imaging technology has made possible the storage of bullet and cartridge surface characteristics in a manner analogous to automated fingerprint files.
- Two automated firearms search systems are DRUGFIRE, developed by the FBI, and IBIS, developed by the ATF.
- NIBIN is the National Integrated Ballistics Information Network, a unified firearms search system that incorporates both DRUGFIRE and IBIS technologies.

Gunpowder Residues

Modern ammunition is propelled toward a target by the expanding gases created by the ignition of smokeless powder or nitrocellulose in a cartridge. Under ideal circumstances, all of the powder is consumed in the process and converted into the rapidly expanding gases. However, in practice the powder is never totally burned. When a firearm is discharged, unburned and partially burned particles of gunpowder in addition to smoke are propelled out of the barrel, along with the bullet, toward the target. If the muzzle of the weapon is sufficiently close, these products are deposited onto the target. The distribution of gunpowder particles and other discharge residues around the bullet hole permits a **distance determination**, an assessment of the distance from which a handgun or rifle was fired.

DISTANCE DETERMINATION

In incidents involving gunshot wounds, it is often necessary to determine the distance from which the weapon was fired. For example, in incidents involving a shooting death, the suspect often pleads self-defense as the motive for the attack. Such claims are fertile grounds for distance determinations because finding the proximity of the people involved is necessary to establish the facts of the incident. Similarly, careful examination of the gunshot wounds of suicide victims usually reveals characteristics associated with a very close-range shot. The absence of such characteristics strongly indicates that the wound was not self-inflicted and signals the possibility of foul play.

The accuracy of a distance determination varies according to the circumstances of the case. When the investigator is unable to recover a suspect weapon, the best the examiner can do is to state whether a shot could have been fired a given distance from the target. More exact opinions are possible only when the examiner has the suspect weapon in hand and knows the type of ammunition used in the shooting.

HANDGUNS AND RIFLES   The precise distance from which a handgun or rifle has been fired must be determined by carefully comparing the powder residue pattern on the victim's clothing or skin to test patterns made by firing the suspect weapon at varying distances from a target. A white cloth or a fabric comparable to the victim's clothing may be used as a test target (see Figure 9-17). Because the spread and density of the residue pattern vary widely among weapons and ammunition, such a comparison is significant only when it is made with the suspect weapon and suspect ammunition, or with ammunition of the same type and make. By comparing the test and evidence patterns, the examiner may find enough similarity in shape and density by which to judge the distance from which the shot was fired.

Without the weapon, the examiner is restricted to looking for recognizable characteristics around the bullet hole. Such findings are at best approximations made as a result of general observations and based on the examiner's experience. However, some noticeable characteristics should be sought. For instance, when the weapon is held in contact with or less than 1 inch from the target, a heavy concentration of residue from smokelike vaporous lead usually surrounds the bullet's entrance hole. Often, loose fibers surrounding a contact hole show scorch marks from the flame discharge of the weapon, and some synthetic fibers may show signs of being melted as a result of the heat from the discharge. Furthermore, the blowback of muzzle gases may produce a stellate (i.e., star-shaped) tear pattern around the hole. Such a hole is invariably surrounded by a rim of a smokelike deposit of vaporous lead (see Figure 9-18).

A halo of vaporous lead deposited around a bullet hole normally indicates the bullet was discharged 18 inches or less from the target. The presence of scattered specks of unburned and partially burned powder grains without any accompanying soot can often be observed at distances up to approximately 25 inches. Occasionally, however, scattered gunpowder particles are noted at a firing distance as far out as 36 inches. A weapon that has been fired more

distance determination
The process of determining the distance between the firearm and a target, usually based on the distribution of powder patterns or the spread of a shot pattern.

(a) (b) (c) (d)

FIGURE 9-17 Test powder patterns made with a Glock 9mm luger fired at the following distances: (a) contact, (b) 6 inches, (c) 12 inches, and (d) 18 inches. *Michelle D. Miranda*

FIGURE 9-18 A contact shot. *Michelle D. Miranda*

than 3 feet from a target usually does not deposit any powder residues on the target's surface. (However, with ball powder ammunition, this distance may be extended to 8 feet.)

When a weapon has been fired from 3 feet or more away, the only visual indication that the hole was made by a bullet is a dark ring, known as "bullet wipe," around the perimeter of the entrance hole. Bullet wipe consists of a mixture of carbon, dirt, lubricant, primer residue, and lead wiped off the bullet's surface as it passes through the target. Again, in the absence of a suspect weapon, these observations are only general guidelines for estimating target distances. Numerous factors—barrel length, caliber, type of ammunition, and type and condition of the weapon fired—influence the amount of gunpowder residue deposited on a target.

SHOTGUNS The determination of firing distances involving shotguns must also be related to test firings performed with the suspect weapon using the same type of ammunition known to be used in the crime. In the absence of a weapon, the muzzle-to-target distance can be estimated by measuring the spread of the discharged shot. With close-range shots varying in distance up to 5 feet, the shot charge enters the target as a concentrated mass, producing a hole somewhat larger than the bore of the barrel. As the distance increases, the pellets progressively separate and spread out. Generally speaking, the spread in the pattern made by a 12-gauge shotgun increases 1 inch for each yard of distance. Thus, a 10-inch pattern would be produced at approximately 10 yards. Of course, this is only a rule of thumb; normally, many variables can affect the shot pattern.

Other factors include the barrel length, the size and quantity of the pellets fired, the quantity of powder charge used to propel the pellets, and the choke of the gun under examination. **Choke** is the degree of constriction placed at the muzzle end of the barrel. The greater the choke, the narrower the shotgun pattern and the faster and farther the pellets will travel.

choke
An interior constriction placed at or near the muzzle end of a shotgun's barrel to control shot dispersion.

POWDER RESIDUES ON GARMENTS

When garments or other evidence relevant to a shooting are received in the crime laboratory, the surfaces of all items are first examined microscopically for gunpowder residue. These particles may be identifiable by their characteristic colors, sizes, and shapes. However, the absence of visual indications does not preclude the possibility that gunpowder residue is present. Sometimes the lack of color contrast between the powder and garment or the presence of heavily encrusted deposits of blood can obscure the visual detection of gunpowder. Often, an infrared photograph of the suspect area overcomes the problem. Such a photograph may enhance the visual color contrast, thus revealing vaporous lead and powder particles deposited around the hole (see Figure 9-19). In other situations, this may not help, and the analyst must use chemical tests to detect gunpowder residues.

(a)　　　　　(b)

FIGURE 9-19 (a) A shirt bearing a powder stain, photographed under normal light. (b) An infrared photograph of the same shirt. *Richard Saferstein, Ph.D.*

Greiss test
A chemical test used to examine patterns of gunpowder residues around bullet holes.

Nitrites are one type of chemical product that results from the incomplete combustion of smokeless (nitrocellulose) powder. One test method for locating powder residues involves transferring particles embedded on the target surface to chemically treated gelatin-coated photographic paper. This procedure is known as the **Greiss test**. The examiner presses the photographic paper onto the target with a hot iron; once the nitrite particles are on the paper, they are made easily visible through chemical treatment. In addition, comparing the developed nitrite pattern to nitrite patterns obtained from test firings at known distances can be useful in determining the shooting distance from the target. A second chemical test is then performed to detect any trace of lead residue around the bullet hole. The questioned surface is sprayed with a solution of sodium rhodizonate, followed by a series of oversprays of acid solutions. This treatment turns lead particles pink, then blue-violet.

Quick Review

- The distribution of gunpowder particles and other discharge residues around a bullet hole permits an assessment of the distance from which a handgun or rifle was fired.
- The precise distance from which a handgun or rifle was fired is determined by carefully comparing the powder residue pattern on the victim's clothing to test patterns made when the suspect weapon is fired at varying distances from a target.
- The Greiss test is a chemical test used to examine patterns of gunpowder residues around bullet holes. It tests for the presence of nitrites.

Primer Residues on the Hands

The firing of a weapon not only propels residues toward the target, but it also blows gunpowder and primer residues back toward the shooter (see Figure 9-20). As a result, traces of these residues are often deposited on the firing hand of the shooter, and their detection can provide valuable information about whether an individual has recently fired a weapon.

DETECTING PRIMER RESIDUES

Early efforts at demonstrating powder residues on the hands centered on chemical tests that could detect unburned gunpowder or nitrates. For many years, the "dermal nitrate test" was popular. It required the application of hot paraffin or wax to the suspect's hand with a paintbrush. After drying into a solid crust, the paraffin was removed and tested with diphenylamine. A blue color indicated a positive reaction for nitrates. However, the dermal nitrate test has fallen into disfavor with law enforcement agencies, owing mainly to its lack of specificity. Common materials such as fertilizers, cosmetics, urine, and tobacco all give positive reactions that are indistinguishable from that obtained for gunpowder by this test.

Efforts to identify a shooter now center on the detection of primer residues deposited on the hand of a shooter at the time of firing. With the exception of those in most .22-caliber ammunition, primers currently manufactured contain a blend of lead styphnate, barium nitrate, and antimony sulfide. Residues from these materials are most likely to be deposited on the thumb web and the back of the firing hand of a shooter because these areas are closest to gases escaping along the side or back of the gun during discharge. In addition, individuals who handle a gun without firing it may have primer residues deposited on the palm of the hand where it has been in contact with the weapon.

FIGURE 9-20   When a handgun is fired, gunpowder and primer residues are normally blown back toward the hand of the shooter. *Forensic Technology WAI, Inc.*

However, with the handling of a used firearm, the passage of time, and the resumption of normal activities following a shooting, gunshot residues from the back of the hand are frequently redistributed to other areas, including the palms. Therefore, it is not unusual to find higher levels of barium and antimony on the palms than on the backs of the hands of known shooters. Another possibility is the deposition of significant levels of barium and antimony on the hands of an individual who is near a firearm when it is discharged.

TESTS FOR PRIMER RESIDUES

The determination of whether a person has fired or handled a weapon or has been near a discharged firearm is normally made by measuring the presence and possibly the amount of barium and antimony on the relevant portions of the suspect's hands. A variety of materials and techniques are used for removing these residues. The most popular approach, and certainly the most convenient for the field investigator, is to apply an adhesive tape or adhesive to the hand's surface to remove any adhering residue particles.

SWABBING   Another approach is to remove any residues present by swabbing both the firing and nonfiring hands with cotton that has been moistened with 5 percent nitric acid. The front and back of each hand are swabbed separately. All four swabs, along with a moistened control, are then forwarded to the crime laboratory for analysis.

In any case, once the hands are treated for the collection of barium and antimony, the collection medium must be analyzed for the presence of these elements. High barium and antimony levels on the suspect's hand(s) strongly indicate that the person fired or handled a weapon or was near a firearm when it was discharged. Because these elements are normally present in small quantities (e.g., less than 10 micrograms) after a firing, only the most sensitive analytical techniques can be used to detect them.

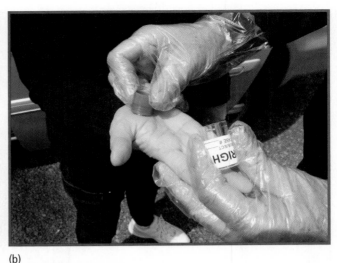

(a)

(b)

FIGURE 9-21 (a) Adhesive stubs used to sample a suspect shooter's hands. (b) Sampling a suspect's hand for gunshot residue with an adhesive stub. *Evident*

Unfortunately, even though most specimens submitted for this type of analysis have been obtained from individuals strongly suspected of having fired a gun, there has been a low rate of positive findings. The major difficulty appears to be the short time that primer residues remain on the hands. These residues are readily removed by intentional or unintentional washing, rubbing, or wiping of the hands. In fact, one study demonstrated that it is very difficult to detect primer residues on cotton hand swabs taken just two hours after firing a weapon.[2] Hence, some laboratories do not accept cotton hand swabs taken from living people six or more hours after a firing has occurred.

In cases that involve suicide victims, a higher rate of positive findings for the presence of gunshot residue is obtained when the hand swabbing is conducted before the person's body is moved or when the hands are protected by paper bags.[3] However, hand swabbing or the application of an adhesive cannot be used to detect firings of most .22-caliber rim-fire ammunition. Such ammunition's primer may contain only barium or neither barium nor antimony.

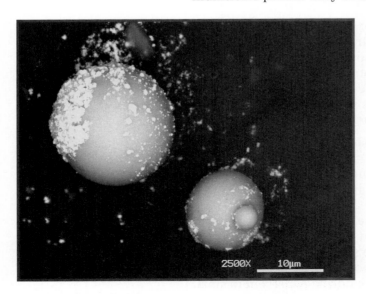

2500X   10μm

FIGURE 9-22 An SEM view of gunshot residue particles. *JEOL USA Inc.*

SEM TESTING Most laboratories that can detect gunshot residue require application of an adhesive to the shooter's hands (see Figure 9-21). Adhesive containing stubs is applied against the surface to be sampled by repeatedly dabbing. A minimum of 20–30 dabs should be applied to the surface. Microscopic primer and gunpowder particles on the adhesive are then found with a scanning electron microscope (SEM). The characteristic size and shape of these particles distinguishes them from other contaminants on the hands (see Figure 9-22). When the SEM is linked to an X-ray analyzer, an elemental analysis of the particles can be conducted. A finding of a select combination of elements (i.e., lead, barium, and antimony) confirms that the particles are indeed primer residue (see Figure 9-23).

The major advantage of the SEM approach for primer residue detection is its enhanced specificity over hand swabbing. The SEM characterizes primer particles by their size and shape as well as by their chemical composition. Unfortunately, the

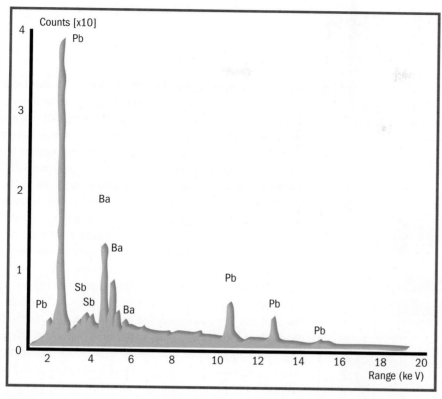

FIGURE 9-23   A spectrum showing the presence of lead, barium, and antimony in gunshot residue. *Image courtesy of JEOL USA. Used by permission of JEOL Ltd.*

excessive operator time required to find and characterize gunshot residue has discouraged the use of this technique. The availability of automated particle search and identification systems for use with scanning electron microscopes may overcome this problem. Results of work performed with automated systems show that it is significantly faster than a manual approach for finding gunshot residue particles.[4] Appendix II contains a detailed description of primer residue collection procedures.

Quick Review

- Firing a weapon propels residues toward the target and blows gunpowder and primer residues back toward the shooter. Traces of these residues are often deposited on the firing hand of the shooter, providing valuable information about whether an individual has recently fired a weapon.
- Examiners measure the amount of barium and antimony on the relevant portion of the suspect's hands or characterize the morphology of particles containing these elements to determine whether a person has fired or handled a weapon or was near a discharged firearm.

Serial Number Restoration

Today, many manufactured items, including automobile engine blocks and firearms, are impressed with serial numbers for identification. Increasingly, the criminalist must restore such numbers when they have been removed or obliterated by grinding, rifling, or punching.

Serial numbers are usually stamped on a metal body or frame or on a metal plate with hard steel dies. These dies strike the metal surface with a force that

CLOSER ANALYSIS
THE SCANNING ELECTRON MICROSCOPE (SEM)

The scanning electron microscope (SEM) creates an image by aiming a beam of electrons at a specimen; then the electron emissions from the specimen are studied on a closed-circuit TV (see Figure 1). This is accomplished by using electromagnetic focusing to direct electrons emitted by a hot tungsten filament onto the surface of the specimen. This primary electron beam causes the elements that make up the upper layers of the specimen to emit electrons known as "secondary" electrons. About 20 to 30 percent of the primary electrons rebound off the surface of the specimen. These electrons are known as "back-scattered electrons." The emitted electrons (both secondary and backscattered) are collected, and the amplified signal is displayed on a cathode-ray, or TV, tube. By scanning the primary electron beam across the specimen's surface in synchronization with the cathode-ray tube, the SEM converts the emitted electrons into an image of the specimen that displays on the cathode-ray tube.

The major attractions of the SEM image are its high magnification, high resolution, and great depth of focus. In its usual mode, the SEM has a magnification that ranges from 10× to 100,000×. Its depth of focus is 300 times better than that of optical systems at similar magnifications, and the resultant picture is almost stereoscopic in appearance. Its great depth of field and magnification are exemplified in the magnified cystolithic hair on the marijuana leaf shown in Figure 2. A SEM image of a vehicle's headlight filaments may reveal whether the headlights were on or off at the time of a collision (see Figures 3 and 4).

FIGURE 1   A scanning electron microscope. *Image courtesy of JEOL USA*

FIGURE 2   The cystolithic hairs of the marijuana leaf, as viewed with a scanning electron microscope (800x). *Richard Saferstein, Ph.D.*

FIGURE 3   The melted ends of a hot filament break indicate that the headlights were on when an accident occurred. *Image courtesy of JEOL USA*

(continued)

CLOSER ANALYSIS (continued)

FIGURE 4   The sharp ends of a cold filament break indicate that the headlights were off when an accident occurred. *Foster & Freeman USA Inc.*

Another facet of scanning electron microscopy is the use of X-ray production to determine the elemental composition of a specimen. X-rays are generated when the electron beam of the scanning electron microscope strikes a target. When the SEM is coupled with an X-ray analyzer, the emitted X-rays can be sorted according to their energy values and used to build a picture of the elemental distribution in the specimen. Because each element emits X-rays of characteristic energy values, the X-ray analyzer can identify the elements present in a specimen. Furthermore, the elemental concentration can be determined by measuring the intensity of the X-ray emission.

As shown in Figure 5, when a sample of gunshot residue collected off the hands of a suspect shooter is exposed to a beam of electrons from the scanning electron microscope, X-rays are emitted. These X-rays are passed into a detector, where they are converted into electrical signals. These signals are sorted and displayed according to the energies of the emitted X-rays. Through the use of this technique, the elements lead, antimony, and barium, frequently found in most primers, can be rapidly detected and identified.

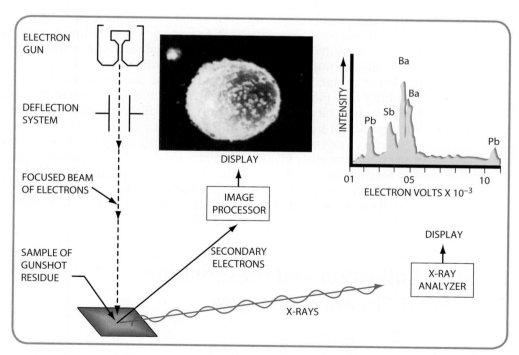

FIGURE 5   A schematic diagram of a scanning electron microscope displaying the image of a gunshot residue particle. Simultaneously, an X-ray analyzer detects and displays X-ray emissions from the elements lead (Pb), antimony (Sb), and barium (Ba) present in the particle. *Richard Saferstein, Ph.D.*

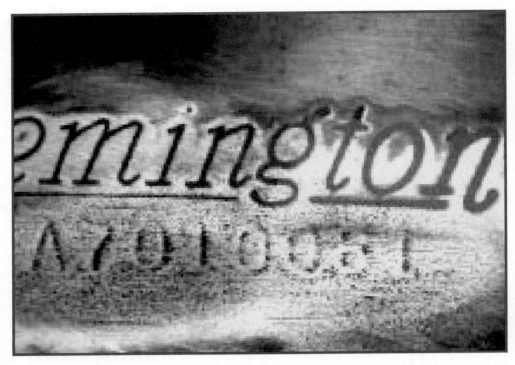

FIGURE 9-24 Obliterated or altered serial numbers on firearms can be restored by analysts using chemical means. *Federal Bureau of Investigation*

allows each digit to sink into the metal at a prescribed depth. Serial numbers can be restored because the metal crystals in the stamped zone are placed under a permanent strain that extends a bit beneath the original numbers. When a suitable etching agent is applied, the strained area dissolves faster than the unaltered metal, thus revealing the etched pattern in the form of the original numbers (see Figure 9-24). However, if the zone of strain has been removed, or if the area has been impressed with a different strain pattern, the number usually cannot be restored.

Before any treatment with the etching reagent, the obliterated surface must be thoroughly cleaned of dirt and oil and polished to a mirrorlike finish. The reagent is swabbed onto the surface with a cotton ball. The choice of etching reagent depends on the type of metal surface being worked on. A solution of hydrochloric acid (120 milliliters), copper chloride (90 grams), and water (100 milliliters) generally works well for steel surfaces.

Collection and Preservation of Firearms Evidence

FIREARMS

The Hollywood technique of picking up a weapon by its barrel with a pencil or stick in order to protect fingerprints must be avoided. This practice only disturbs powder deposits, rust, or dirt lodged in the barrel, and consequently may alter the striation markings on test-fired bullets. If recovery of latent fingerprints is a primary concern, the investigator should hold the weapon by the edge of the trigger guard or by the checkered portion of the grip, which usually does not retain identifiable fingerprints.

The most important consideration in handling a weapon is safety. Before any weapon is sent to the laboratory, all precautions must be taken to prevent an accidental discharge of a loaded weapon in transit. In most cases, it will be necessary to unload the weapon. If this is done, first a record should be made of the weapon's hammer and safety position; likewise, the location of all fired and unfired ammunition in the weapon must be recorded.

When a revolver is recovered, the chamber position should be indicated by a scratch mark on the cylinder where it aligns with the barrel. Each chamber is designated a number on a diagram, and as each cartridge or casing is removed, it should be marked to correspond to the number of its corresponding chamber in the diagram. Knowledge of the cylinder position of a cartridge casing may be useful for later determination of the sequence of events, particularly in shooting cases, when more than one shot was fired. Each round should be placed in a separate box or envelope. If the weapon is an automatic, the magazine must be removed and checked for prints and the chamber then emptied.

As with any other type of physical evidence recovered at a crime scene, firearms evidence must be marked for identification, and a chain of custody must be established. When a firearm is recovered, an identification tag should be attached to the trigger guard. The tag should include appropriate identifying data, including the weapon's serial number, make and model, and the investigator's initials.

When a weapon is recovered from an underwater location, no effort should be made to dry or clean it. Instead, the firearm should be transported to the laboratory in a receptacle containing enough of the same water to keep it submerged. This procedure prevents rust from developing during transport.

AMMUNITION

The protection of class and individual markings on bullets and cartridge cases must be the primary concern of the field investigator. Thus, extreme caution is needed when removing a lodged bullet from a wall or other object. If the bullet's surface is accidentally scratched during this operation, valuable striation markings could be obliterated. It is best to free bullets from their target by carefully breaking away the surrounding support material while avoiding direct contact with the projectile.

Bullets, cartridge casings, and discharged shells from shotguns should just be placed in a container that is appropriately marked for identification. It is recommended that the investigator not directly mark these items with a scribe. In any case, the investigator must protect the bullet by wrapping it in tissue paper before placing it in a pillbox or an evidence envelope for shipment to the crime laboratory. Minute traces of evidence such as paint and fibers may be adhering to the bullet; the investigator must take care to leave these trace materials intact.

When semiautomatic or automatic weapons have been fired, the ejection pattern of the casings can help establish the relationship of the suspect to the victim. For this reason, the investigator must note the exact location where a shell casing was recovered.

GUNPOWDER DEPOSITS

The clothing of a firearms victim must be carefully preserved to prevent damage or disruption to powder residues deposited around a bullet or shot hole. Cutting or tearing of clothing in the area of the holes must be avoided when removing the clothing. All wet clothing should be air-dried out of direct sunlight and then folded carefully to avoid disrupting the area around the bullet hole. Each item should be placed in a separate paper bag.

Quick Review

- Criminalists can restore serial numbers removed or obliterated by grinding, rifling, or punching.
- Because the metal crystals in the stamped zone are placed under a permanent strain that extends a bit beneath the original numbers, the serial number can sometimes be restored through chemical etching.
- A suspect firearm should never be picked up by inserting an object into its barrel because this practice may alter the striation markings on test-fired bullets.
- Before unloading a suspect weapon, the weapon's hammer and safety position should be recorded, as well as the locations of all fired and unfired ammunition in the weapon.
- The protection of class and individual markings on bullets and cartridge cases is the primary concern of the field investigator when recovering bullets and cartridge casings.

Tool Marks

A "tool mark" is any impression, cut, gouge, or abrasion caused by a tool coming into contact with another object. Most often, tool marks are encountered at burglary scenes that involve forcible entry into a building or safe. Generally, these marks occur as indented impressions into a softer surface or as abrasion marks caused by the tool cutting or sliding against another object.

FIGURE 9-25 A comparison of a tool mark with a suspect screwdriver. Note how the presence of nicks and breaks on the tool's edge helps individualize the tool to the mark. *Richard Saferstein, Ph.D.*

COMPARING TOOL MARKS

Typically, an indented impression is left on the frame of a door or window as a result of the prying action of a screwdriver or crowbar. Careful examination of these impressions can reveal important class characteristics—that is, the size and shape of the tool. However, they rarely reveal any significant individual characteristics that could permit the examiner to individualize the mark to a single tool. Such characteristics, when they do exist, usually take the form of discernible random nicks and breaks that the tool has acquired through wear and use (see Figure 9-25).

Just as the machined surfaces of a firearm are impressed with random striations during its manufacture, the edges of a pry bar, chisel, screwdriver, knife, or cutting tool likewise display a series of microscopic irregularities that look like ridges and valleys. Such markings are created as a result of the machining processes used to cut and finish tools. The shape and pattern of such minute imperfections are further modified by damage and wear during the life of the tool. Considering the variety of patterns that the hills and valleys can assume, it is highly unlikely that any two tools will be identical. Hence, these minute imperfections impart individuality to each tool.

If the edge of a tool is scraped against a softer surface, it may cut a series of striated lines that reflect the pattern of the tool's edge. With the aid of a comparison microscope, markings left in this manner can be compared in the laboratory with test tool marks made from the suspect tool. When a sufficient number of striations match between the evidence and test markings, the result can be a positive comparison, and hence a definitive association of the tool with the evidence mark can be made.

FIGURE 9-26   A photograph of a tool mark comparison seen under a comparison microscope.
Leica Microsystems, Inc.

A major problem of tool mark comparisons is the difficulty in duplicating in the laboratory the tool mark left at the crime scene. A thorough comparison requires preparing a series of test marks by applying the suspect tool at various angles and pressures to a soft metal surface (lead is commonly used). This approach gives the examiner ample opportunities to duplicate many of the details of the original evidence marking. A photomicrograph of a typical tool mark comparison is illustrated in Figure 9-26.

COLLECTING TOOL MARK EVIDENCE

Whenever practical, the entire object or the part of the object bearing a tool mark should be submitted to the crime laboratory for examination. When removal of the tool mark is impractical, the only recourse is to photograph the marked area to scale and then make a cast of the mark. Liquid silicone casting material is best for reproducing most of the fine details of a mark (see Figure 9-27). However, even under the best conditions, the clarity of many of the tool mark's minute details will be lost or obscured in a photograph or cast. Of course, this will reduce the chance of individualizing the mark to a single tool.

The crime-scene investigator must never attempt to fit the suspect tool into the tool mark. Any contact between the tool and the marked surface may alter the mark and will, at the very least, raise serious questions about the integrity of the evidence. The suspect tool and mark must be packaged in separate containers, and every precaution must be taken to avoid contact between the tool and mark and another hard surface. Failure to protect the tool and mark from damage could result in the destruction of their individual characteristics.

Furthermore, the tool or its impression may contain valuable trace evidence. Chips of paint adhering to the mark or tool provide perhaps the best example of how the transfer of trace physical evidence can occur as a result of using a tool to gain forcible entry into a building. Obviously, the presence of trace evidence greatly enhances the evidential value of a tool or its mark. Preserving such evidence requires special care in handling and packaging to avoid loss or destruction.

(a)   (b)

FIGURE 9-27   (a) Casting a tool mark impression with a silicone-based putty. (b) An impression alongside a suspect tool. *Sirchie Finger Print Laboratories*

Quick Review

- The presence of minute imperfections on a tool imparts individuality to that tool. The shape and pattern of such imperfections are further modified by damage and wear during the life of the tool.
- The comparison microscope is used to compare crime-scene tool marks with test impressions made with the suspect tool.

Other Impressions

From time to time, other types of impressions are left at a crime scene. This evidence may take the form of a shoe, tire, or fabric impression. It may be as varied as a shoe impression left at a crime scene (Figure 9-28), a hit-and-run victim's garment that has come into violent contact with an automobile (Figure 9-29), or the impression of a bloody shoe print left on a floor or carpet at a homicide scene (Figure 9-30).

PRESERVING IMPRESSIONS

The primary consideration in collecting impressions at the crime scene is the preservation of the impression or its reproduction for later examination in the crime laboratory. Before any impression is moved or otherwise handled, it must be photographed to show all the observable details of the impression (a scale should be included in the picture). Several shots should be taken directly over the impression as well as at various angles around the impression. Skillful use of side lighting for illumination will help highlight many ridge details that might otherwise remain obscured. Photographs should also be taken to show the position of the questioned impression in relation to the overall crime scene.

Although photography is an important first step in preserving an impression, it must be considered merely a backup procedure that is available to the

(a)   (b)

FIGURE 9-28 (a) An impression of a shoe found at a crime scene. (b) A test impression made with a suspect shoe. A sufficient number of points of comparison exist to support the conclusion that the suspect shoe left the impression at the crime scene. *Richard Saferstein, Ph.D.*

FIGURE 9-29 A pattern impression on a car bumper arising from a hit-and-run. Note rivets from the jeans are present in the impression. The writing from the rivet on the right side of the bumper is clearly visible. *Diaczuk, Peter*

examiner should the impression be damaged before it reaches the crime laboratory. Naturally, the examiner prefers to receive the original impression to compare to the suspect shoe, tire, garment, and so forth. In most cases, when the impression is on a readily recoverable item, such as glass, paper, or floor tile, the evidence is easily transported intact to the laboratory.

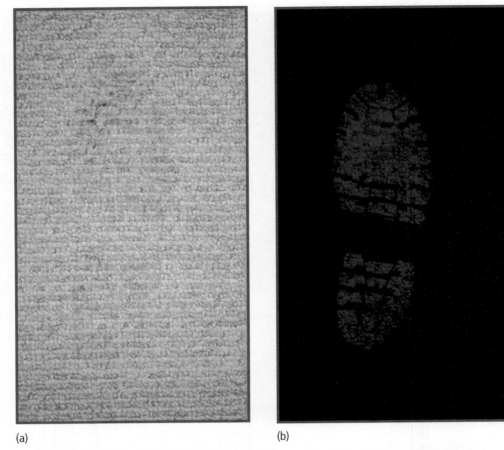

(a)   (b)

FIGURE 9-30   (a) A section of a carpet under normal light showing a faint footprint in blood. (b) Same section of the carpet after spraying with luminal. *Sirchie Finger Print Laboratories*

LIFTING IMPRESSIONS

If an impression on a surface that cannot be submitted to the laboratory is encountered, the investigator may be able to preserve the print in a manner that is analogous to lifting a fingerprint. This is especially true of impressions made in light deposits of dust or dirt. A lifting material large enough to lift the entire impression should be used. Carefully place the lifting material over the entire impression. Use a fingerprint roller to eliminate any air pockets before lifting the impression off the surface.

A more exotic approach to lifting and preserving dust impressions involves the use of a portable electrostatic lifting device. The principle is similar to that of creating an electrostatic charge on a comb and using the comb to lift small pieces of tissue paper. A sheet of Mylar film is placed on top of the dust mark, and the film is pressed against the impression with the aid of a roller. The high-voltage electrode of the electrostatic unit is then placed in contact with the film while the unit's earth electrodes are placed against a metal plate, or earth plate (see Figure 9-31). A charge difference develops between the Mylar film and the surface below the dust mark, so the dust attaches to the lifting film. In this manner, dust prints on chairs, walls, floors, and the like, can be transferred to Mylar film. Floor surfaces up to 40 feet long can be covered with a Mylar sheet and searched for dust impressions. The electrostatic lifting technique is particularly helpful in recovering barely visible dust prints on colored surfaces. Dust impressions can also be enhanced through chemical development (see Figure 9-32).

WebExtra 9.7

Bullet Standard Helps Tie Guns to Criminals

www.mycrimekit.com

FIGURE 9-31 Electrostatic lifting of a dust impression off a floor using an electrostatic unit. *Sirchie Finger Print Laboratories*

(a)

(b)

FIGURE 9-32 (a) A dust impression of a shoe print on cardboard before enhancement. (b) A shoe print after chemical enhancement with bromophenol blue and exposure to water vapor. *Israel Police Headquarters*

WebExtra 9.8

Casting a Footwear Impression

CASTING IMPRESSIONS

Shoe and tire marks impressed into soft earth at a crime scene are best preserved by photography and casting. Class I dental stone, a form of gypsum, is widely recommended for making casts of shoe and tire impressions. The cast should be allowed to air-dry for 24 to 48 hours before it is shipped to the forensic science laboratory for examination. Figure 9-33 illustrates a cast made from a shoe print in mud. The cast compares to the suspect shoe.

An aerosol product known as Snow Impression Wax is available for casting snow impressions. The recommended procedure is to spray three light coats of the wax at an interval of 1 to 2 minutes between layers, and then let it dry for 10 minutes. A viscous mixture of Class I dental stone is then poured into the wax-coated impression. After the casting material has hardened, the cast can be removed.

Several chemicals can be used to develop and enhance footwear impressions made with blood. In areas where a bloody footwear impression is very faint or where a subject has tracked through blood, leaving a trail of bloody impressions, chemical enhancement can visualize latent or nearly invisible footwear impressions. A number of chemical formulas useful for bloody footwear impression analysis are listed in Appendix IV.

Several blood enhancement chemicals have been examined for their impact on short tandem repeat (STR) DNA typing. (This particular method of DNA analysis will be discussed in Chapter 15.) None of the chemicals examined had a deleterious effect, on a short-term basis, on the ability to carry out STR DNA typing on the blood.[5]

COMPARING IMPRESSIONS

Whatever the circumstances, the laboratory procedures used to examine any type of impression remain the same. Of course, a comparison is possible only

(a)

(b)

(c)

FIGURE 9-33 (a) A shoe impression in mud. (b) A cast of a shoe impression. (c) A shoe suspected of leaving the muddy impression. *Sirchie Finger Print Laboratories*

CLOSER ANALYSIS
CASTING FOOTWEAR AND TIRE IMPRESSIONS

Footwear and tire impressions may be found at any type of crime scene and can provide a primary means to identify or exclude a suspect. The preferred method of collection for this type of evidence is casting the impression—that is, making a mold and preserving it for analysis in the lab. When a footwear or tire impression is found in dirt at the crime scene, the casting process is as follows:

MATERIALS

Ruler

One small can of aerosol hair spray

1-gallon zip-top bag

Paint stirrer or large, long-handled spoon

Carton of dental stone

Water

Camera

Plastic or metal casting frame (optional)

PROCEDURE

1. Retrieve any fragments or debris that are not imbedded within the impression. Photograph the impression before and after retrieving debris; include a ruler in the photograph. A frame for containing the dental stone may be installed around an impression that is shallow or located on an inclined surface.

2. To solidify the soil, a fixative such as hair spray is used (see [a]). Hold the can of hair spray about 18 inches from the soil within the impression. Very lightly, spray an even layer over the impression using a sweeping motion and taking care to avoid any damage to the impression.

3. Wait 10 minutes to allow the hair spray to dry.

4. Add an appropriate amount of water to a premeasured amount of dental stone (see [b]). Add water in increments. The usual amount is about 10 to 12 fluid ounces of water to about 1.5 to 2 pounds of dental stone. If using a zip-top bag, seal the bag and mix by working back and forth with your fingers for at least 3 minutes (see [c]). Mix until a pancake-batter-like consistency is reached.

(a) (b) (c)

(d) (e)

Casting a footwear impression at a crime scene: (a) The impression is hardened using aerosol hair spray. (b) The correct amount of water is added to a known amount of dental stone. (c) The mixture is kneaded by hand until the desired (pancake-batter-like) consistency is reached. (d) The dental stone is poured into the impression using a spoon as a medium to disperse the flow. (e) The impression is filled with dental stone and allowed to dry before removal. *Courtesy Sirchie Finger Print Laboratories, Youngsville, NC, www.sirchie.com*

(continued)

CLOSER ANALYSIS (continued)

5. Open one corner of the bag. Pour the dental stone through the opening onto the ground beside the impression and allow it to carefully run into the impression. Use a paint stirrer, a spoon, or a gloved hand as a medium to disperse the stream so it does not destroy the fine details of the impression (see [d]). Continue pouring until the dental stone completely fills the impression (see [e]) and reaches at least 1/2 inch in thickness. If necessary, additional casting material may be poured over the top of the original cast to add thickness.

6. Label the wet plaster surface with the date, initials, and any other information required for evidence labeling.

7. When the cast no longer adheres to the soil and is relatively dry (usually about 1 hour), remove the cast. If necessary, the cast can be dug out from the sides.

8. Store the cast for 48 hours to allow it to dry completely. If a cast is not allowed to dry long enough, some ridge details may disappear.

9. Once the cast is dry, rinse any loose soil from it with softly running water. A soft-bristled brush may also be used. Do not scrub or pick off anything. Pat dry with paper towels.

FIGURE 9-34 Upper dental model from the teeth of the suspect matches the individual teeth characteristics of the bite marks.
Barbara Needell, DMD, DABFO

when the item suspected of having made the impression is recovered. Test impressions may be necessary to compare the characteristics of the suspect item with the evidence impression.

The evidential value of the impression is determined by the number of class and individual characteristics that the examiner finds. Agreement with respect to size, shape, or design may permit the conclusion that the impression could have been made by a particular shoe, tire, or garment, but one cannot entirely exclude other possible sources from having the same class characteristics. More significant is the existence of individual characteristics arising out of wear, cuts, gouges, or other damage. A sufficient number or the uniqueness of such points of comparison supports a finding that both the evidence and test impressions originated from only one source.

When a tire tread impression is left at a crime scene, the laboratory can examine the design of the impression and possibly determine the style and/or manufacturer of the tire. This may be particularly helpful to investigators when a suspect tire has not yet been located.

New computer software may help the forensic scientist compare shoe prints. For example, an automated shoe print identification system developed in England, called "shoeprint image capture and retrieval (SICAR)," incorporates multiple databases to search known and unknown footwear files for comparison against footwear specimens. With the system, an impression from a crime scene can be compared to a reference database to find out what type of shoe caused the imprint. That same impression can also be searched in the suspect and crime databases to reveal whether that shoe print matches the shoes of a person who has been in custody or the shoe prints left behind at another crime scene. When matches are made during the searching process, the images are displayed side by side on the computer screen (see Figure 5-9 in Chapter 5).

Human bite marks on skin and foodstuffs have been important items of evidence for convicting defendants in a number of homicide and rape cases in recent years. If a sufficient number of points of similarity between test and suspect bite marks are present, a forensic odontologist may conclude that a bite mark was made by a particular individual (see Figure 9-34).

▪▪▪▪ CASEFILES ▪▪▪▪

THE O. J. SIMPSON TRIAL:
WHO LEFT THE IMPRESSIONS AT THE CRIME SCENE?

On the night of June 12, 1994, Nicole Brown—ex-wife of football star O. J. Simpson—and her friend Ron Goldman were brutally murdered on the grounds outside her home in Brentwood, California. O. J. Simpson was arrested for their murders but professed his innocence. At the crime scene, investigators found bloody shoe impressions along the concrete walkway leading up to the front door of Brown's condominium. These shoe impressions were of extremely high quality and of intricate detail. The news media broadcast countless images of these bloody shoe prints on television, making it obvious to the killer that those shoes would surely link him to the crime.

Famed FBI shoe print examiner William J. Bodziak investigated the footwear evidence from the scene. His first task was to identify the brand of shoe that made the marks. Because the pattern was very clear and distinct, with complete toe-to-heel detail, this seemed like a simple task at first. Bodziak compared this pattern to the thousands of sole patterns in the FBI's database. None matched. He then went to his reference collection of books and trade show brochures, again with no success.

Bodziak's experience told him that these were expensive, Italian-made, casual dress shoes with a sole made from synthetic material. Using this knowledge, he shopped the high-end stores for a similar tread pattern but still was unable to identify the shoes. He then drew a composite sketch of the sole and faxed the image to law enforcement agencies and shoe manufacturers and distributors worldwide. The owner of the American distributing company for Bruno Magli shoes was the only one to respond.

Further exhaustive investigation revealed that these were extremely rare shoes. There were two styles of shoe bearing this exact sole design. They had been available for only 2 years at a mere forty stores in the United States and Puerto Rico. The Lorenzo style had a bootlike upper that came to the ankle. The Lyon style had a lower, more typical dress shoe shape. The impressions had been made by a size 12 shoe, and it was later determined that only 299 pairs of size 12 with this tread pattern were sold in the United States.

Simpson flatly denied ever owning these shoes, adding that he would never wear anything so ugly. However, he was known to wear a size 12, and photographs taken almost 9 months before the murders show Simpson wearing a pair of black leather Bruno Magli Lorenzo shoes. These shoes were available in several colors, so this narrows the number of shoes matching Simpson's pair of Lorenzos (this size, color, and style) sold in the United States to twenty-nine pairs.

Proving that Simpson owned a pair of shoes that had the exact pattern found printed in blood at the crime scene was an essential component of the case, but it was not done in time to be used during the criminal prosecution. The photographs of Simpson in his Bruno Magli shoes were released after the culmination of the criminal trial, so the jury never heard the direct evidence that Simpson owned these shoes. However, this proved to be an important link uniting Simpson with the crime scene in the civil trial. Although O. J. Simpson was acquitted of the murders of Nicole Brown and Ron Goldman in the criminal trial, he was judged responsible for their murders in the civil court case.

Quick Review

- Shoe and tire marks impressed into soft earth at a crime scene are best preserved by photography and casting.
- The electrostatic lifting technique is particularly helpful in recovering barely visible dust prints on floor surfaces.
- In areas where a bloody footwear impression is very faint or where the subject has tracked through blood and left a trail of bloody impressions, chemical enhancement can visualize latent or nearly invisible blood impressions.

VIRTUAL LAB
FOOTWEAR IMPRESSIONS
To perform a virtual footwear impression analysis, go to
www.pearsoncustom.com/us/vlm/

VIRTUAL LAB
TOOL MARK ANALYSIS
To perform a virtual tool mark analysis, go to *www.pearsoncustom.com/us/vlm/*

▪▪▪▪

CHAPTER REVIEW

- The manufacture of a gun barrel requires impressing its inner surface with spiral grooves, a step known as "rifling." Rifling imparts spin to the projectile when it is fired, which keeps it on an accurate course.

- No two rifled barrels have identical striation markings. These striations form the individual characteristics of the barrel. The inner surface of the barrel of a gun leaves its striation markings on a bullet passing through it.

- The class characteristics of a rifled barrel include the number of lands and grooves and the width and direction of twist.

- The comparison microscope is a firearms examiner's most important tool because it allows two bullets to be compared simultaneously.

- The firing pin, breech face mark, and ejector and extractor mechanism also offer a highly distinctive signature for individualization of cartridge cases.

- Unlike handguns, a shotgun is not rifled—it has a smooth barrel. Because of this, shotgun shells are not impressed with any characteristic rifling striation markings that can be used to compare two shotgun shells to determine whether they were fired from the same weapon.

- The advent of computerized imaging technology has made possible the storage of bullet and cartridge surface characteristics in a manner analogous to automated fingerprint files.

- Two automated firearms search systems are DRUGFIRE, developed by the FBI, and IBIS, developed by the ATF.

- NIBIN is the National Integrated Ballistics Information Network, a unified firearms search system that incorporates both DRUGFIRE and IBIS technologies.

- The distribution of gunpowder particles and other discharge residues around a bullet hole permits an assessment of the distance from which a handgun or rifle was fired.

- The precise distance from which a handgun or rifle was fired is determined by carefully comparing the powder residue pattern on the victim's clothing to test patterns made when the suspect weapon is fired at varying distances from a target.

- The Greiss test is a chemical test used to examine patterns of gunpowder residues around bullet holes. It tests for the presence of nitrates.

- Firing a weapon propels residues toward the target and blows gunpowder and primer residues back toward the shooter. Traces of these residues are often deposited on the firing hand of the shooter, providing valuable information about whether an individual has recently fired a weapon.

- Examiners measure the amount of barium and antimony on the relevant portion of the suspect's hands or characterize the morphology of particles containing these elements to determine whether a person has fired or handled a weapon or was near a discharged firearm.

- Criminalists can restore serial numbers removed or obliterated by grinding, rifling, or punching.

- Because the metal crystals in the stamped zone are placed under a permanent strain that extends a short distance beneath the original numbers, the serial number can be restored through chemical etching.

- A suspect firearm should never be picked up by inserting an object into its barrel because this practice may alter the striation markings on test-fired bullets.

- Before unloading a suspect weapon, the weapon's hammer and safety position should be recorded, as well as the location of all fired and unfired ammunition in the weapon.

- The protection of class and individual markings on bullets and cartridge cases is the primary concern of the field investigator when recovering bullets and cartridge casings.

- The presence of minute imperfections on a tool imparts individuality to that tool. The shape and pattern of such imperfections are further modified by damage and wear during the life of the tool.

- The comparison microscope is used to compare crime-scene tool marks with test impressions made with the suspect tool.

- Shoe and tire marks impressed into soft earth at a crime scene are best preserved by photography and casting.

- The electrostatic lifting technique is particularly helpful in recovering barely visible dust prints on floor surfaces.

- In areas where a bloody footwear impression is very faint or where the subject has tracked through blood and left a trail of bloody impressions, chemical enhancement can visualize latent or nearly invisible blood impressions.

■■■■ KEY TERMS

bore, 194

breech face mark, 198

caliber, 194

choke, 207

distance determination, 205

ejector, 199

extractor, 199

firearms identification, 192

gauge, 198

Greiss test, 208

grooves, 194

lands, 194

rifling, 194

■■■■ REVIEW QUESTIONS

1. Firearms can be divided into two categories: _____ and _____ guns.

2. Handguns, or pistols, are firearms that are designed to be held and fired with one hand, and the most common types of handguns are _____, _____, and _____.

3. The _____ features several firing chambers, each holding one cartridge, located within a revolving cylinder that lines the chamber up with the barrel mechanically when the round is fired.

4. A cartridge for a shotgun, called a "shell," contains numerous ball-shaped projectiles, called _____.

5. A shotgun barrel is not rifled and can also be narrowed toward the muzzle in order to concentrate shot when fired. The degree of narrowing of the barrel is called the _____ of the shotgun.

6. The _____ is the original part of the bore left after rifling grooves are formed.

7. The diameter of the gun barrel is known as its _____.

8. True or False: The number of lands and grooves is a class characteristic of a barrel. _____

9. The _____ characteristics of a rifled barrel are formed by striations impressed into the barrel's surface.

10. The most important instrument for comparing bullets is the _____.

11. To make a match between a test bullet and a recovered bullet, the lands and grooves of the test and evidence bullets must have identical widths, and the longitudinal _____ on each must coincide.

12. True or False: It is always possible to determine the make of a weapon by examining a bullet it fired. _____

13. A shotgun has a(n) _____ barrel.

14. The diameter of a shotgun barrel is expressed by the term _____.

15. True or False: Shotgun pellets can be individualized to a single weapon. _____

16. True or False: A cartridge case can be individualized to a single weapon. _____

17. The automated firearms search system developed by the FBI and ATF as a unified system incorporating both DRUGFIRE and IBIS technologies is known as _____.

18. True or False: The distribution of gunpowder particles and other discharge residues around a bullet hole permits an approximate determination of the distance from which the gun was fired. _____

19. True or False: Without the benefit of a weapon, an examiner can make an exact determination of firing distance. _____

20. A halo of vaporous lead deposited around a bullet hole normally indicates a discharge _____ to _____ inches from the target.

21. If a firearm has been fired more than 3 feet from a target, usually no residue is deposited, but a dark ring, known as _____, is observed.

22. As a rule of thumb, the spread in the pattern made by a 12-gauge shotgun increases 1 inch for every _____ of distance from the target.

23. A(n) _____ photograph may help visualize gunpowder deposits around a target.

24. True or False: One test method for locating powder residues involves transferring particles embedded on the target surface to chemically treated photographic paper. _____

25. Current methods for identifying a shooter rely on the detection of _____ residues on the hands.

26. Determining whether an individual has fired a weapon is done by measuring the elements _____ and _____ present on the hands.

27. True or False: Firings with all types of ammunition can be detected from hand swabbings with nitric acid. _____

28. Microscopic primer and gunpowder particles on the adhesives applied to a suspected shooter's hand can be detected with a(n) _____.

29. True or False: Restoration of serial numbers is possible because in the stamped zone the metal is placed under a permanent strain that extends beneath the original numbers. _____

30. True or False: It is proper to insert a pencil into the barrel when picking up a crime-scene gun. _____

31. Recovered bullets are initialed on either the _____ or _____ of the bullet.

32. True or False: Because minute traces of evidence such as paint and fibers may be adhering to a recovered bullet, the investigator must take care to remove these trace materials immediately. _____

33. True or False: Cartridge cases are best marked at the base of the shell. _____

34. The clothing of the victim of a shooting must be handled so as to prevent disruption of _____ around bullet holes.

35. A(n) _____ is any impression caused by a tool coming into contact with another object.

36. Tool marks compare only when a sufficient number of _____ match between the evidence and test markings.

37. Objects bearing tool marks either should be submitted intact to the crime lab, or a(n) _____ should be taken of the tool mark.

38. An imprint may be lifted using lifting sheets or a(n) _____.

39. Shoe and tire marks impressed into soft earth at a crime scene are best preserved by _____ and _____.

40. A wear pattern, cut, gouge, or other damage pattern can impart _____ characteristics to a shoe.

■■■■ APPLICATION AND CRITICAL THINKING

1. Name and briefly describe two popular approaches for collecting gunshot residue from a suspect's hands. What is the most specific method of analysis for gunshot residue?

2. You are investigating a shooting involving a 12-gauge shotgun with a moderately high choke. The spread of the pattern made by the pellets measures 12 inches. In your opinion, which of the following is probably closest to the distance from the target to the shooter? Explain your answer and explain why the other answers are likely to be incorrect.
   a) 18 yards
   b) 12 yards
   c) 6 yards
   d) 30 yards

3. Criminalist Ben Baldanza is collecting evidence from the scene of a shooting. After locating the revolver suspected of firing the shots, Ben picks the gun up by the grip, unloads it, and places the ammunition in an envelope. He then attaches an identification tag to the grip. Searching the scene, Ben finds a bullet lodged in the wall. He uses pliers to grab the bullet and pull it from the wall, and then inscribes the bullet with his initials and places it in an envelope. What mistakes, if any, did Ben make in collecting this evidence?

4. How would you go about collecting impressions in each of the following situations?
   a) You discover a shoe print in dry sand.
   b) You discover a tool mark on a windowsill.
   c) You discover tire marks in soft earth.
   d) You discover a shoe print on a loose piece of tile.
   e) You discover a very faint shoe print in dust on a colored linoleum floor.

5. Gunshot residue patterns (A) through (D) (contact, 1 inch, 6 inches, and 18 inches) from a 40-caliber pistol are shown below in the figures. Match the firing distance to each pattern.

(A) _____

(B) _____

(C) _____

(D) _____

Courtesy of Richard Saferstein, Ph.D.

ENDNOTES

1. Originally, the number of lead balls with the same diameter as the barrel would make a pound. For example, a 20-gauge shotgun has an inside diameter equal to the diameter of a lead ball that weighs 1/20 pound.

2. J. W. Kilty, "Activity after Shooting and Its Effect on the Retention of Primer Residues," *Journal of Forensic Sciences* 20 (1975): 219.

3. G. E. Reed et al., "Analysis of Gunshot Residue Test Results in 112 Suicides," *Journal of Forensic Sciences* 35 (1990): 62.

4. R. S. White and A. D. Owens, "Automation of Gunshot Residue Detection and Analysis by Scanning Electron Microscopy/Energy Dispersive X-Ray Analysis (SEM/EDX)," *Journal of Forensic Sciences* 32 (1987): 895; W. L. Tillman, "Automated Gunshot Residue Particle Search and Characterization," *Journal of Forensic Sciences* 32 (1987): 62.

5. C. J. Frégeau et al., "Fingerprint Enhancement Revisited and the Effects of Blood Enhancement Chemicals on Subsequent Profiler Plus™ Fluorescent Short Tandem Repeat DNA Analysis of Fresh and Aged Bloody Fingerprints," *Journal of Forensic Sciences* 45 (2000): 354.

10 Bloodstain Pattern Analysis

Bettmann/Corbis

LEARNING OBJECTIVES
After studying this chapter, you should be able to:
- Discuss the information that can be gained from bloodstain pattern analysis about the events involved in a violent crime.
- Explain how surface texture, directionality, and angle of impact affect the shape of individual bloodstains.
- Calculate the angle of impact of a bloodstain using its dimensions.
- Describe the classifications of low-, medium-, and high-velocity impact spatter and appreciate how these classifications should be used.
- Discuss the methods of determining the area of convergence and area of origin for impact spatter patterns.
- Understand how various blood pattern types are created and which features of each pattern can be used to aid in reconstructing events at a crime scene.
- Describe the methods for documenting bloodstain patterns at a crime scene.

THE SAM SHEPPARD CASE: A TRAIL OF BLOOD

Convicted in 1954 of bludgeoning his wife to death, Dr. Sam Sheppard achieved celebrity status when the storyline of TV's *The Fugitive* was apparently modeled on his efforts to seek vindication for the crime he professed not to have committed. Dr. Sheppard, a physician, claimed he was dozing on his living room couch when his pregnant wife, Marilyn, was attacked. Sheppard's story was that he quickly ran upstairs to stop the carnage but was knocked briefly unconscious by the intruder. The suspicion that fell on Dr. Sheppard was fueled by the revelation that he was having an adulterous affair. At trial, the local coroner testified that a pool of blood on Marilyn's pillow contained the impression of a "surgical instrument." After Sheppard had been imprisoned for ten years, the U.S. Supreme Court set aside his conviction because of the "massive, pervasive, and prejudicial publicity" that had attended his trial.

In 1966, the second Sheppard trial commenced. This time, the same coroner was forced to back off from his insistence that the bloody outline of a surgical instrument was present on Marilyn's pillow. However, a medical technician from the coroner's office now testified that blood on Dr. Sheppard's watch was from blood spatter, indicating that Dr. Sheppard was wearing the watch in the presence of the battering of his wife. The defense countered with the expert testimony of eminent criminalist Dr. Paul Kirk. Dr. Kirk concluded that blood spatter marks in the bedroom showed the killer to be left-handed. Dr. Sheppard was right-handed.

Dr. Kirk further testified that Sheppard stained his watch while attempting to obtain a pulse reading. After less than 12 hours of deliberation, the jury failed to convict Sheppard. But the ordeal had taken its toll. Four years later, Sheppard died, a victim of drug and alcohol abuse.

■ General Features of Bloodstain Formation

Crimes involving violent contact between individuals are frequently accompanied by bleeding and resultant bloodstain patterns. Crime-scene analysts have come to appreciate that bloodstain patterns deposited on floors, walls, ceilings, bedding, and other relevant objects can provide valuable insights into events that occurred during the commission of a violent crime. The information one is likely to uncover as a result of bloodstain pattern interpretation includes the following:

- The direction from which blood originated
- The angle at which a blood droplet struck a surface
- The location or position of a victim at the time a bloody wound was inflicted
- The movement of a bleeding individual at the crime scene
- The minimum number of blows that struck a bleeding victim
- The approximate location of an individual delivering blows that produced a bloodstain pattern

The crime-scene investigator must not overlook the fact that the location, distribution, and appearance of bloodstains and spatters may be useful for interpreting and reconstructing the events that accompanied the bleeding. A thorough analysis of the significance of the position and shape of blood patterns with respect to their origin and trajectory is exceedingly complex and requires the services of an examiner who is experienced in such determinations. Most important, the interpretation of bloodstain patterns necessitates a carefully planned control experiment using surface materials comparable to those found at the crime scene. This chapter presents the basic principles and common deductions behind bloodstain pattern analysis to give the reader general knowledge to use at the crime scene.

SURFACE TEXTURE

Surface texture is of paramount importance in the interpretation of bloodstain patterns; comparisons between standards and unknowns are valid only when identical surfaces are used. In general, harder and nonporous surfaces (e.g., glass or smooth tile) result in less spatter. Rough surfaces, such as a concrete floor or wood, usually result in irregularly shaped stains with serrated edges, possibly with **satellite spatter** (see Figure 10-1).

satellite spatter
Blood spatter around parent stain, with blood droplets whose pointed ends face against the direction of travel.

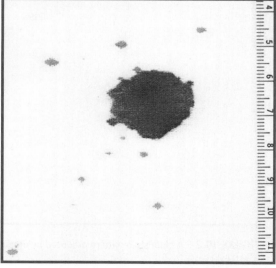

FIGURE 10-1 (a) A bloodstain from a single drop of blood that struck a glass surface after falling 24 inches. (b) A bloodstain from a single drop of blood that struck a cotton muslin sheet after falling 24 inches. *A Y, Wonder*

angle of impact
The angle of the source of the blood to the surface where it was deposited. It can be estimated from the width-to-length ratio of the stain to help determine the position of the victim or the weapon at the time when the bleeding wound was inflicted.

WebExtra 10.1

See How Bloodstain Spatter Patterns Are Formed

FIGURE 10-3 The higher pattern is of a single drop of human blood that fell 24 inches and struck hard, smooth cardboard at 50 degrees. On this drop the collection of blood shows the direction. The lower pattern is of a single drop of human blood that fell 24 inches and struck hard, smooth cardboard at 15 degrees. On this drop the tail shows the direction.
A Y, Wonder

DIRECTION AND ANGLE OF IMPACT

An investigator may discern the direction of travel of blood that struck an object by studying the stain's shape. As the stain becomes more elliptical in shape, its direction becomes more discernible because the pointed end of a bloodstain faces its direction of travel. The distorted or disrupted edge of an elongated stain indicates the direction of travel of the blood drop. Satellite spatter around parent stains will have the pointed end facing against the direction of travel. In Figure 10-2, the bloodstain pattern was produced by several droplets of blood that were traveling from left to right before striking a flat, level surface.

It is possible to determine the impact angle of blood on a flat surface by measuring the degree of circular distortion of the stain. A drop deposited at an **angle of impact** of about 90 degrees (directly vertical to the surface) will be approximately circular in shape with no tail or buildup of blood. However, as the angle of impact deviates from 90 degrees, the stain becomes elongated in shape. Buildup of blood will occur when the angles are larger, whereas longer and longer tails will appear as the angle of impact becomes smaller (see Figure 10-3).

Quick Review

- Individual bloodstains can convey to the bloodstain analyst the directionality and angle of impact of the blood when it impacted a surface. Bloodstain patterns may convey to the analyst the location of the victim (who was bleeding) or suspect (who was causing the bleeding), the movement of bleeding individuals, and the number of blows delivered.
- Surface texture is of paramount importance in the interpretation of bloodstain patterns; rounder drops generally are produced on smooth, nonporous surfaces, whereas rough surfaces result in irregular-edged drops. However, correlations between standards and unknowns are valid only when identical surfaces are used.
- The direction of travel of blood that struck an object may be discerned by the stain's shape. The pointed end of a bloodstain always faces its direction of travel.

FIGURE 10-2 A bloodstain pattern produced by droplets of blood that were traveling from left to right.
A Y, Wonder

CLOSER ANALYSIS
DETERMINING THE ANGLE OF IMPACT OF BLOODSTAINS

The distorted or disrupted edge of an elongated stain indicates the direction of travel of the blood drop. One may establish the location or origin of bloodshed by determining the directionality of the stain and the angle at which blood came into contact with the surface of impact. To determine the angle of impact, calculate the stain's length-to-width ratio and apply the formula

$$\text{Sin A} = \frac{\text{width of blood stain}}{\text{length of blood stain}}$$

Example: The width of a stain is 11 mm and the length is 22 mm.

$$\text{Then, sin A} = \frac{11 \text{ mm}}{22 \text{ mm}} = (11 \text{ mm} \div 22 \text{ mm}) = 0.50$$

A scientific calculator that has the trigonometry function will calculate that the inverse sine of 0.50 is equal to a 30-degree angle.

Note: The measurements for length and width should be made with a ruler, micrometer, or photographic loupe.

- The angle of impact of an individual bloodstain can be approximated by the degree of distortion or lengthening of the bloodstain, or it can be more effectively estimated using the width-to-length ratio of the stain.

Impact Bloodstain Spatter Patterns

The most common type of bloodstain pattern found at a crime scene is **impact spatter**. This pattern occurs when an object impacts the source of the blood. Spatter projected outward and away from the source, such as an exit wound, is called **forward spatter**. **Back spatter**, sometimes called "blow-back spatter," is blood projected backward from a source, such as an entrance wound, and potentially deposited on the object or person who created the impact. Impact spatter patterns consist of many droplets radiating in direct lines from the origin of blood to the stained surface (see Figure 10-4).

Investigators have derived a common classification system of impact spatter based on the velocity of the force impacting on a bloody object. In general, as the velocity of the force of the impact on the source of blood increases, so does the velocity of the blood droplets emanating from the source. It is also generally true that, as both the force and velocity of impact increase, the diameter of the resulting blood droplets decreases.

impact spatter
A bloodstain pattern produced when an object makes forceful contact with a source of blood, projecting droplets of blood outward from the source.

forward spatter
Blood that travels away from the source in the same direction as the force that caused the spatter.

back spatter
Blood directed back toward the source of the force that caused the spatter.

FIGURE 10-4 Impact spatter produced by an automatic weapon. The arrows show multiple direction of travel for skull fragments emanating from the gunshot. *A Y, Wonder*

CLASSIFYING IMPACT SPATTER

LOW-VELOCITY SPATTER An impact pattern consisting of a preponderance of large, separate, or compounded drops with diameters of 4 millimeters or more is known as **low-velocity spatter**. This kind of spatter is normally produced by gravity alone, by a minimal force, or by an object dropping into and splashing blood from a blood pool. Low-velocity stains can result from an applied force moving at up to 5 feet per second.

low-velocity spatter
An impact spatter pattern created by a force traveling at 5 feet per second or less and producing drops with diameters of greater than 4 millimeters.

medium-velocity spatter
An impact spatter pattern created by a force traveling at 5 to 25 feet per second and producing drops with diameters of between 1 and 4 millimeters.

MEDIUM-VELOCITY SPATTER   A pattern predominantly consisting of small drops with diameters of 1 to 4 millimeters is classified as **medium-velocity spatter**. This type of impact spatter is normally associated with blunt-force trauma to an individual or with other applied forces moving at between 5 to 25 feet per second.

HIGH-VELOCITY SPATTER   Very fine droplets with a preponderance of diameters of less than 1 millimeter are classified as **high-velocity spatter**. Here the spatter can result from an applied force of 100 feet per second or faster. Gunshot exit wounds or explosions commonly produce this type of spatter. However, because the droplets are very small, they may not travel far; they may fall to the floor or ground, where investigative personnel could overlook them.

Using droplet size to classify impact patterns by velocity is a useful tool that gives investigators insight into the general nature of a crime. However, the classifications of low, medium, and high velocity cannot illuminate the specific events that produced the stain pattern. For example, beatings can produce either high-velocity spatter or stain sizes that look more like low-velocity spatter. In general, one should use stain size categories very cautiously, and for descriptive purposes only, in evaluating impact spatter patterns. A more acceptable approach for classifying a bloodstain pattern should encompass observations of stain size, shape, location, and distribution.

Blood spatter patterns can arise from a number of distinctly different sources that will be discussed in this chapter. Illustrations of patterns emanating from impact, cast-off, and arterial spray are shown in Figure 10-5.

ORIGIN OF IMPACT PATTERNS

Impact spatter patterns can offer investigators clues about the origin of the blood spatter and, therefore, the position of the victim at the time of the impact.

(a)

(b)

(c)

FIGURE 10-5   (a) The action associated with producing impact spatter. (b) The action associated with producing cast-off spatter. (c) The action associated with producing arterial spray spatter. *A Y, Wonder*

AREA OF CONVERGENCE   The **area of convergence** is the point on a two-dimensional plane from which the drops originated. This can be established by drawing straight lines through the long axis of several individual bloodstains, following the line of their tails. The intersection of these lines is the area of convergence, and the approximate point of origin will be on a line straight out from this area. Figure 10-6 illustrates how to draw lines to find an area of convergence.

An object hitting a source of blood numerous times will never produce exactly the same pattern each time. One can therefore determine the number of impacts by drawing the area of convergence for groups of stains from separate impacts.

AREA OF ORIGIN   It may also be important to determine the **area of origin** of a bloodstain pattern, the area in a three-dimensional space from which the blood was projected. This will show the position of the victim or suspect in space when the stain-producing event took place. The distribution of the droplets in an impact pattern gives a general idea of the distance from the blood source to the bloodstained surface. Impact patterns produced at a distance close to the surface will appear as clustered stains. As the distance from the surface increases, so do the distribution and distance between droplets.

A common method for determining the area of origin at the crime scene is called the "string method." Figure 10-7 illustrates the steps in the string method:

1. Find the area of convergence for the stain pattern.
2. Place a pole or stand as an axis coming from the area of convergence.
3. Attach one end of a string next to each droplet. Place a protractor next to each droplet and lift the string until it lines up with the determined angle

high-velocity spatter
An impact spatter pattern created by a force traveling at 100 feet per second or faster and producing droplets with diameters of less than 1 millimeter.

area of convergence
The area on a two-dimensional plane where lines traced through the long axis of several individual bloodstains meet. This approximates the two-dimensional place from which the bloodstains were projected.

area of origin
The location in three-dimensional space from which blood that produced a bloodstain originated. The location of the area of convergence and the angle of impact for each bloodstain is used to approximate this area.

FIGURE 10-6   An illustration of stain convergence on a two-dimensional plane. Convergence represents the area from which the stains emanated. *The Institute of Applied Forensic Technology*

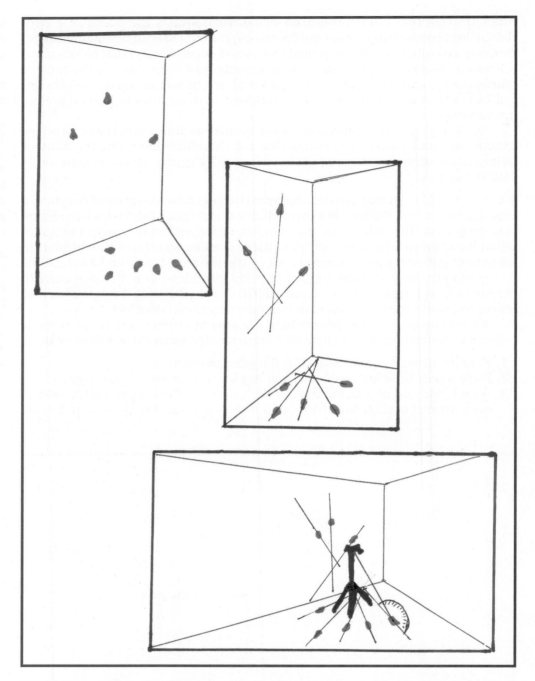

FIGURE 10-7 An illustration of the string method used at a crime scene to determine the area of origin of blood spatter. *A Y, Wonder*

of impact of the drop. Keeping the string in line with the angle, attach the other end of the string to the axis pole.

4. View the area of origin of the droplets where the strings appear to meet. Secure the strings at this area.

Quick Review

- An impact spatter pattern occurs when an object impacts a source of blood. This produces forward spatter projected forward from the source and back spatter projected backward from the source.

- Impact spatter patterns can be classified as low-velocity (>4 mm drops), medium-velocity (1–4 mm drops), or high-velocity (<1 mm drops) for descriptive purposes. These categories should not be used to make assumptions about what kind of force created the pattern.
- The area of convergence is the point on a two-dimensional plane from which the drops of an impact spatter pattern originated. This area can be estimated by drawing straight lines through the long axis of several individual bloodstains, following the line of their tails.
- The area of origin of a bloodstain pattern is the area in three-dimensional space from which blood was projected, showing the position of the victim or suspect when the stain-producing event took place. The string method is commonly used at a crime scene to approximate the area of origin.

More Bloodstain Spatter Patterns

GUNSHOT SPATTER

A shooting may leave a distinct gunshot spatter pattern. This may be characterized by both forward spatter from an exit wound and back spatter from an entrance wound. The presence of backspatter on a firearm or a shooter is dependent on the distance between the firearm and victim. Forward spatter generally leaves a pattern of very fine droplets characteristic of high-velocity spatter (see Figure 10-8). Medium- and large-sized drops may also be observed within the spatter pattern.

The location of injury, the size of the wound created, and the distance between the victim and the muzzle of the weapon all affect the amount of back spatter that occurs. Finding high-velocity spatter containing the victim's blood on a suspect can help investigators place the suspect in the vicinity when the gun was discharged. Back spatter created by a gunshot impact generally

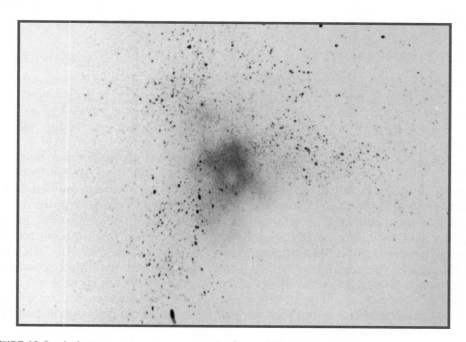

FIGURE 10-8 An impact spatter pattern emanating from a bullet striking a blood source (in this case a sponge) before passing through a cardboard target. Mist comes from the muzzle blast, not from the bullet impacting the blood source. *A Y, Wonder*

■■■■ CASEFILES ■■■■
BLOOD SPATTER EVIDENCE

Stephen Scher banged on the door of a cabin in the woods outside Montrose, Pennsylvania. According to Scher, his friend, Marty Dillon, had just shot himself while chasing after a porcupine. The two had been skeet shooting at Scher's cabin, enjoying a friendly sporting weekend, when Dillon spotted a porcupine and took off out of sight. Scher heard a single shot and waited to hear his friend's voice. After a few moments, he chased after Dillon and found him lying on the ground near a tree stump, bleeding from a wound in his chest. Scher administered CPR after locating his dying friend, but he was unable to save Dillon, who later died from his injuries. Police found that Dillon's untied boot had been the cause of his shotgun wound. They determined he had tripped while running with his loaded gun and shot himself. The grief-stricken Scher aroused no suspicion, so the shooting was ruled an accident.

Shortly thereafter, Scher moved away from Montrose, divorced his wife, and married Dillon's widow. This was too suspicious to be ignored; police reopened the case and decided to reconstruct the crime scene. The reconstruction provided investigators with several pieces of blood evidence that pointed to Scher as Dillon's murderer.

Police noticed that Scher's boots bore the unmistakable spray of high-velocity impact blood spatter, evidence that he was standing within an arm's length of Dillon when Dillon was shot. This pattern of bloodstains would not be expected to be created while administering CPR, as Scher claimed had happened. The spatter pattern also clearly refuted Scher's claim that he did not witness the incident. In addition, the tree stump near Dillon's body bore the same type of blood spatter, in a pattern that indicated Dillon was *seated on the stump*, not running, when he was shot. Finally, Dillon's ears were free of the high-velocity blood spatter that covered his face, but blood was on his hearing protectors found nearby. This is a clear indication that he was wearing his hearing protectors when he was shot and they were removed before investigators arrived. This and other evidence resulted in Scher's conviction for the murder of his long-time friend, Marty Dillon.

contains fewer and smaller, atomized stains than does forward spatter. Muzzle blast striking an entrance wound will cause the formation of atomized blood.

Depending on the distance from the victim that the gun was discharged, some back spatter may strike the gunman and enter the gun muzzle. This is called the "drawback effect." Blood within the muzzle of a gun can "place" the weapon in the vicinity of the gunshot wound. The presence of blow-back spatter on a weapon's muzzle is consistent with the weapon's having been close to the victim at the time of firing.

CAST-OFF SPATTER

cast-off
A bloodstain pattern that is created when blood is flung from a blood-bearing object in motion onto a surface.

A **cast-off** pattern is created when a blood-covered object flings blood in an arc onto a nearby surface. This kind of pattern commonly occurs when a person pulls a bloody fist or weapon back between delivering blows to a victim (see Figure 10-5[b]). The bloodstain tails will point in the direction that the object was moving.

The width of the cast-off pattern created by a bloody object may help suggest the kind of object produced by the pattern. The sizes of the drops are directly related to the size of the point from which they were propelled. Drops propelled from a small or pointed surface will be smaller and the pattern more linear; drops propelled from a large or blunt surface will be larger and the pattern wide. The volume of blood deposited on an object from the source also affects the size and number of droplets in the cast-off pattern. The less blood on the object, the smaller the stains produced. The pattern may also suggest whether the blow that caused the pattern was directed from right to left or left to right. The pattern will point in the direction of the backward thrust, which will be opposite the direction of the blow. This could suggest which hand the assailant used to deliver the blows.

Cast-off patterns may also show the *minimum* number of blows delivered to a victim. Each blow should be marked by an upward-and-downward or forward-and-backward arc pattern (see Figure 10-9). By counting and pairing

FIGURE 10-9 Swing was upper right to lower left. Return to position for the next blow was short swing at left. Cast-offs depend entirely on the weapon's ability to acquire and hold blood, how the swing is achieved, and where in space the victim is located for the blows to be struck. *A Y, Wonder*

the patterns, one can estimate the minimum number of blows. An investigator should take into consideration that the first blow would cause blood only to pool to the area; it would not produce a cast-off pattern. Also, some blows may not come into contact with blood and therefore will not produce a pattern. The medical examiner is in the best position to estimate the number of blows a victim received.

ARTERIAL SPRAY SPATTER

Arterial spray spatter is created when a victim suffers an injury to a main artery or the heart. The pressure of the continuing pumping of blood causes blood to spurt out of the injured area (see Figure 10-5[c]). Commonly, the pattern shows large spurted stains for each time the heart pumps. Some radial spikes, satellite spatter, or flow patterns may be evident because of the large volume of blood being expelled with each spurt. Drops may also be seen on the surface in fairly uniform size and shape and in parallel arrangement (see Figure 10-10).

The lineup of the stains shows the victim's movement. Any vertical arcs or waves in the line show fluctuations in blood pressure. The larger arterial stains are at the end of the overall pattern. The site of the initial injury to the artery can be found where the pattern begins with the biggest spurt. Arterial patterns can also be differentiated because the oxygenated blood spurting from the artery tends to be a brighter red color than blood expelled from impact wounds.

EXPIRATED BLOOD PATTERNS

A pattern created by blood that is expelled from the mouth or nose from an internal injury is called an **expirated blood pattern**. If the blood that creates such a pattern is under great pressure, it produces very fine high-velocity spatter. Expirated blood at very low velocities produces a stain cluster with irregular edges (see Figure 10-11). The presence of bubbles of oxygen in the drying drops can differentiate a pattern created by expirated

arterial spray
A characteristic bloodstain pattern caused by spurts that resulted from blood exiting under pressure from an arterial injury.

expirated blood pattern
A pattern created by blood that is expelled out of the nose, mouth, or respiratory system as a result of air pressure and/or airflow.

FIGURE 10-10 Arterial spray spatter found at a crime scene where a victim suffered injury to an artery. *Reeves, Norman*

FIGURE 10-11 An example of blood expelled with two wheezes from the mouth. *A Y, Wonder*

void
An area within a deposited spatter pattern that is clear of spatter, caused by an object or person's blocking the area at the time of the spatter's deposition.

blood from other types of bloodstains. Expirated blood also may be lighter in color than impact spatter as a result of being diluted by saliva. The presence of expirated blood gives an important clue to the injuries suffered and the events that took place at a crime scene.

VOID PATTERNS

A **void** is created when an object blocks the deposition of blood spatter onto a surface or object (see Figure 10-12). The spatter is deposited onto the object or person instead. The blank space on the surface or object may give a clue to the size and shape of the missing object or person. Once the object or person is found, the missing piece of the pattern should fit in, much like a puzzle piece, with the rest of the pattern. Voids may help establish the body position of the victim or assailant at the time of the incident.

Quick Review
- Gunshot spatter can consist of both forward spatter from an exit wound and back spatter from an entrance wound; however, only back spatter will be produced if the bullet does not exit the body.

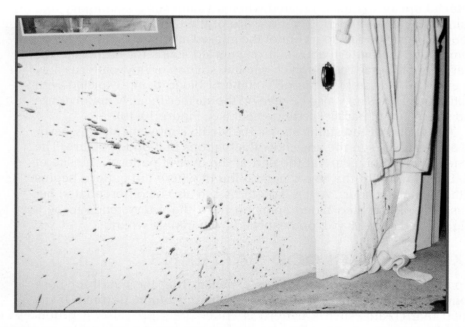

FIGURE 10-12 A void pattern is found behind a door where the surface of the door blocked the deposition of spatter on that area. This void, and the presence of spatter on the door, shows that the door was open when the spatter was deposited. *Reeves, Norman*

- A cast-off pattern is created when a blood-covered object flings blood in an arc onto a nearby surface. This kind of pattern commonly occurs when a person pulls a bloody fist or weapon back between delivering blows to a victim.
- The characteristic arterial spray spatter is created when a victim suffers an injury to a main artery or the heart, and the pressure of the continuing pumping of blood projects blood out of the injured area in spurts, which are apparent in the pattern.
- Expired blood is expelled from the mouth or nose and may appear as very fine high-velocity spatter or large low-velocity bloodstain clusters. This kind of pattern may contain bubbles of oxygen or be mixed with saliva.
- A void pattern is an area free of spatter where an object (or person) blocked the deposition of blood spatter onto a surface or object. Because the spatter was deposited onto the object or person instead, the shape of the void may give a clue about the size and shape of the missing object or person.

Other Bloodstain Patterns

Not all bloodstains at a crime scene appear as spatter patterns. The circumstances of the crime often create other types of stains that can be useful to investigators.

CONTACT/TRANSFER PATTERNS

When an object with blood on it touches another object that did not have blood on it, this produces a contact or **transfer pattern**. Examples of transfers with features include fingerprints (see Figure 10-13), handprints, footprints, footwear prints, tool prints, and fabric prints in blood. These may provide further leads by offering individual characteristics.

The size and general shape of a tool may be seen in a simple transfer. This can lead to narrowing the possible tools by class characteristics. A transfer that shows a very individualistic feature may help point to the tool that made the pattern.

Simple transfer patterns are produced when the bloody object makes contact with a surface and the object is removed without any further movement. Other transfers known as "swipe patterns" may be caused by movement of the bloody object across a surface. Generally, the pattern will lighten and "feather" as the pattern moves away from the initial contact point (see Figure 10-14). However, because "feathering" is also a function of the amount of pressure being applied to the surface, the analyst must interpret directionality with care. The direction of separate bloody transfers, such as footwear prints in blood, may show the movement of the suspect, victim, or others through the crime scene after the blood was present. The first transfer pattern will be dark and heavy with blood, whereas subsequent transfers will be increasingly lighter in color. The transfers get lighter as less and less blood is deposited from the transferring object's surface. Bloody shoe imprints may also suggest whether the wearer was running or walking. Running typically produces imprints with more space between them and more satellite or drop patterns between each imprint.

transfer pattern
A bloodstain pattern created when a surface that carries wet blood comes into contact with a second surface. Recognizable imprints of all or a portion of the original surface or the direction of movement may be observed.

FIGURE 10-13   A transfer pattern consisting of bloody fingerprints with apparent ridge detail. *Lawrence A Presley*

FIGURE 10-14 A series of swipe patterns moving from right to left. *A Y, Wonder*

FLOWS

Patterns made by drops or large amounts of blood flowing with the pull of gravity are called **flows**. Flows may be formed by single drops or large volumes of blood coming from an actively bleeding wound or blood deposited on a surface, from an arterial spurt, for example. Clotting of the blood's solid parts may occur when a flow extends onto an absorbent surface.

The flow direction may show movements of objects or bodies while the flow was still in progress or after the blood had dried. Figure 10-15 illustrates a situation in which movement of the surface while the flow was still in progress led to a specific pattern.

Interruption of a flow pattern may be helpful in assessing the sequence and passage of time between the flow and its interruption. If a flow found on an object or body does not appear to be consistent with the direction of gravity, one may surmise that the object or body was moved after the blood had dried.

POOLS

A pool of blood occurs when blood collects in a level (not sloped) and undisturbed place. Blood that pools on an absorbent surface may be absorbed throughout the surface and diffuse, creating a pattern larger than the original pool. This often occurs to pools on beds or sofas.

The approximate drying time of a pool of blood is related to the environmental condition of the scene. By experimentation, an analyst may be able to

flow

A bloodstain pattern formed by the movement of small or large amounts of blood as a result of gravity's pull.

FIGURE 10-15 The flow pattern suggests that the victim was upright and then fell while blood flowed. The assailant claimed the victim was stabbed while sleeping. *A Y, Wonder*

FIGURE 10-16 Skeletonization is shown in a bloodstain that was disturbed after the edges had time to dry. *A Y, Wonder*

FIGURE 10-17 A drop trail pattern leads away from the center of the mixed bloodstain pattern. *Reeves, Norman*

reasonably estimate the drying times of stains of different sizes. Small and large pools of blood can be helpful in reconstruction because they can be analyzed to estimate the amount of time that has elapsed since the blood was deposited. Considering the drying time of a blood pool can yield information about the timing of events that accompanied the incident.

The edges of a stain will dry to the surface, producing a phenomenon called **skeletonization** (see Figure 10-16). This usually occurs within 50 seconds of deposition for droplets, and it takes longer for larger volumes of blood. If the central area of the pooled bloodstain is then altered by wiping, the skeletonized perimeter will be left intact. This can be used to interpret whether movement or activity occurred shortly after the pool was deposited or later, after the perimeter had time to skeletonize first. This may be important for classifying the source of the original stain.

DROP TRAIL PATTERNS

A **drop trail pattern** is a series of drops that is separate from other patterns, and it is formed by blood dripping off an object or injury. The stains form a kind of line, usually the path made by the suspect after injuring or killing the victim. It may simply show movement, lead to a discarded weapon, or provide identification of the suspect if it is made from his or her own blood. Investigators often see this type of pattern in stabbings during which the criminal inadvertently cuts himself or herself as a result of using the force necessary to stab the victim. Figure 10-17 shows a drop trail pattern away from the center of action at a crime scene.

skeletonization
The process by which the edges of a bloodstain dry to the surface in a specific period of time (dependent on environmental and surface conditions). Skeletonization will remain apparent even after the rest of the bloodstain has been disturbed from its original position.

drop trail pattern
A pattern of bloodstains formed by the dripping of blood off a moving surface or person in a recognizable pathway separate from other patterns.

▪▪▪▪ CASEFILES ▪▪▪▪

BLOODSTAIN RECONSTRUCTION

An elderly male was found lying dead on his living room floor. He had been beaten about the face and head, stabbed in the chest, and robbed. The bloodstains found on the interior front door and the adjacent wall documented that the victim was beaten about the face with a fist and struck on the back of the head with his cane. A three-dimensional diagram and photograph illustrating the evidential bloodstain patterns are shown in Figures 1(a) and (b).

A detail photograph of bloodstains next to the interior door is shown in Figure 2. Arrow 1 in Figure 2 points to the cast-off pattern directed left to right as blood was flung from the perpetrator's fist while inflicting blows. Arrow 2 in Figure 2 points to three transfer impression patterns directed left to right as the perpetrator's bloodstained hand contacted the wall, as the fist blows were being inflicted on the victim. Arrow 3 in Figure 2 points to blood flow from the victim's wounds as he slumped against the wall.

Figure 3 contains a series of laboratory test patterns created to evaluate the patterns contained within Figure 2.

Figure 4 shows how the origin of individual impact spatter patterns located on the wall and door and emanating from the bleeding victim can be documented by the determination of separate areas of convergence.

A suspect was apprehended three days later, and he was found to have an acute fracture of the right hand. When he was confronted with the bloodstain evidence, the suspect admitted to striking the victim, first with his fist, then with a cane, and finally stabbing him with a kitchen knife. The suspect pleaded guilty to three first-degree felonies.

(a)

(b)

FIGURE 1 (a) A three-dimensional diagram illustrating bloodstain patterns that were located, documented, and reconstructed; (b) a crime-scene photograph of blood-stained areas. *A Three-Dimensional Diagram Illustrating Bloodstain Patterns That Were Located, Documented, And Reconstructed from The Institute of Applied Forensic Technology. Copyright © Institute of Applied Forensic Technology. Used by permission of The Institute of Applied Forensic Technology*

FIGURE 2 Positions of impact spatter from blows that were inflicted on the victim's face. *Institute of Applied Forensic Technology*

FIGURE 3   (a) A laboratory test pattern showing an impact spatter. The size and shape of the stains demonstrate a forceful impact 90 degrees to the target. (b) A laboratory test pattern illustrating a cast-off pattern directed left to right from an overhead swing. (c) A laboratory test pattern showing a repetitive transfer impression pattern produced by a bloodstained hand moving left to right across the target. (d) A laboratory test pattern illustrating vertical flow patterns. The left pattern represents a stationary source; the right pattern was produced by left-to-right motion. *Institute of Applied Forensic Technology*

FIGURE 4   (a) A convergence of impact spatter patterns associated with beating with a fist. (b) The convergence of impact spatter associated with the victim falling to the floor while bleeding from the nose. (c) The convergence of impact spatter associated with the victim being struck with a cane while lying face down at the door. *Institute of Applied Forensic Technology*

The shape of the stains in a drop trail pattern can help investigators determine the direction and speed at which a person was moving. The tails of the drops in a trail pattern point in the direction the person was moving. More circular stains are found where the person was moving slowly. This information may be helpful in reconstruction.

Quick Review

- Transfer patterns are created when an object with blood on it makes simple contact with a surface or moves along a surface. The direction of movement may be shown by a feathering of the pattern.
- Flows may originate from a single drop or a large amount of blood. Because the direction of the flow is caused by gravity, the direction of a pattern may suggest the original position of the surface when the flow was formed.
- A pool is formed where large amounts of blood collect. The pool may be absorbed into the surface of deposition over time.
- The presence of skeletonization on a feathered bloodstain suggests that the stain was disturbed after the perimeter had had sufficient time to dry.
- A drop trail pattern is separate from other patterns, and it is formed by a series of single blood droplets dripping off an object or injury.

Documenting Bloodstain Pattern Evidence

Blood spatter patterns of any kind can provide a great deal of information about the events that took place at a crime scene. For this reason, investigators should note, study, and photograph each pattern and drop. This must be done to accurately record the location of specific patterns and to distinguish the stains from which laboratory samples were taken. The photographs and sketches can also point out specific stains used in determining the direction of force, angle of impact, and area of origin.

Just as in general crime-scene photography, the investigator should create photographs and sketches of the overall pattern to show the orientation of the pattern to the scene. The medium-range documentation should include pictures and sketches of the whole pattern and the relationships between individual stains within the pattern. The close-up photographs and sketches should show the dimensions of each individual stain. Close-up photographs should be taken with a scale of some kind showing in the photograph.

Two common methods of documenting bloodstain patterns place attention on the scale of the patterns. The "grid method" involves setting up a grid of squares of known dimensions over the entire pattern using string and stakes (see Figure 10-18). All overall, medium-range, and close-up photographs are taken with and without the grid. The second method, called the "perimeter ruler method," involves setting up a rectangular border of rulers around the pattern and then placing a small ruler next to each stain. In this method, the large rulers show scale in the overall and medium-range photos, whereas the small rulers show scale in the close-up photographs (see Figure 10-19). Some investigation teams use tags in close-up photographs to show evidence numbers or other details.

An area-of-origin determination may be calculated at the discretion of the bloodstain analyst when the circumstances of the case warrant such a determination. All measurements of stains and calculations of angle of impact and point of origin should be recorded in crime-scene notes. Especially important stains can be roughly sketched within the notes.

Only some jurisdictions have a specialist on staff to decipher patterns either at the scene or from photographs at the lab. Therefore, it is important that all personnel be familiar with patterns to properly record and document them for use in reconstruction.

VIRTUAL LAB
BLOOD SPATTER EVIDENCE
To perform a virtual blood spatter analysis, go to *www.pearsoncustom.com/us/vlm/*

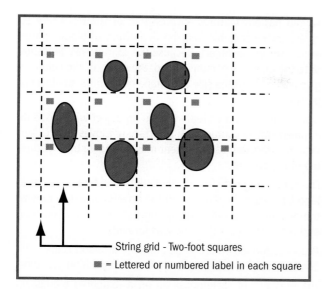

FIGURE 10-18 The grid method may be used for photographing bloodstain pattern evidence. *OGLE, ROBERT R., CRIME SCENE INVESTIGATION AND RECONSTRUCTION, 3rd Ed., © 2012, Reprinted and Electronically reproduced by permission of Pearson Education, Inc., Upper Saddle River, New Jersey.*

FIGURE 10-19 The perimeter ruler method may be used for photographing bloodstain pattern evidence. *Evident*

Quick Review

- Photographs and sketches should first be created of the overall bloodstain pattern to show the orientation of the pattern to the scene.
- Medium-range and close-up photographs may use the grid method or perimeter ruler method to show the orientation and relative size of the pattern and individual stains.

CHAPTER REVIEW

- Individual bloodstains can convey to the bloodstain analyst the directionality and angle of impact of the blood when it impacted a surface. Bloodstain patterns may convey to the analyst the location of victims (who was bleeding) or suspects (who was causing the bleeding), the movement of bleeding individuals, and the number of blows delivered.

- Surface texture is of paramount importance in the interpretation of bloodstain patterns; rounder drops generally are produced on smooth, nonporous surfaces, whereas rough surfaces result in irregular-edged drops. However, correlations between standards and unknowns are valid only when identical surfaces are used.

- The direction of travel of blood that struck an object may be discerned by the stain's shape. The pointed end of a bloodstain always faces its direction of travel.

- The angle of impact of an individual bloodstain can be approximated by the degree of distortion or lengthening of the bloodstain, or it can be more effectively estimated using the width-to-length ratio of the stain.

- An impact spatter pattern occurs when an object impacts a source of blood. This produces forward spatter projected forward from the source and back spatter projected backward from the source.

- Impact spatter patterns can be classified as low-velocity (>4 mm drops), medium-velocity (1–4 mm drops), or high-velocity (<1 mm drops) for descriptive purposes. These categories should not be used to assume what kind of force created the pattern.

- The area of convergence is the point on a two-dimensional plane from which the drops of an impact spatter pattern originated. This area can be estimated by drawing straight lines through the long axis of several individual bloodstains, following the line of their tails.

- The area of origin of a bloodstain pattern is the area in three-dimensional space from which blood was projected, showing the position of the victim or suspect when the stain-producing event took place. The string method is commonly used at a crime scene to approximate the position of the area of origin.

- Gunshot spatter can consist of both forward spatter from an exit wound and back spatter from an entrance wound; however, only back spatter will be produced if the bullet does not exit the body.

- A cast-off pattern is created when a blood-covered object flings blood in an arc onto a nearby surface. This kind of pattern commonly occurs when a person pulls a bloody fist or weapon back between delivering blows to a victim.

- The characteristic arterial spray spatter is created when a victim suffers an injury to a main artery or the heart, and the pressure of the continuing pumping of blood projects blood out of the injured area in spurts, which are apparent in the pattern.

- Expired blood is expelled from the mouth or nose and may appear as very fine high-velocity spatter or large low-velocity bloodstain clusters. This kind of pattern may contain bubbles of oxygen or be mixed with saliva.

- A void pattern features an area free of spatter where an object (or person) blocked the deposition of blood spatter onto a surface or object. Because the spatter was deposited onto the object or person instead, the shape of the void may give a clue about the size and shape of the missing object or person.

- Transfer patterns are created when an object with blood on it makes simple contact with a surface or moves along a surface. The direction of movement may be shown by a feathering of the pattern.

- Flows may originate from a single drop or a large amount of blood. Because the direction of the flow is caused by gravity, the direction of a pattern may suggest the original position of the surface when the flow was formed.

- A pool is formed where large amounts of blood collect. The pool may be absorbed into the surface of deposition over time.

- The presence of skeletonization on a feathered bloodstain suggests that the stain was disturbed after the perimeter had had sufficient time to dry.

- A drop trail pattern is separate from other patterns, and it is formed by a series of single blood droplets dripping off an object or injury.

- Photographs and sketches should first be created of the overall bloodstain pattern to show the orientation of the pattern to the scene.

- Medium-range and close-up photographs may use the grid method or perimeter ruler method to show the orientation and relative size of the pattern and individual stains.

▪▪▪▪ KEY TERMS

angle of impact, 232
area of convergence, 235
area of origin, 235
arterial spray, 239
back spatter, 233
cast-off, 238

drop trail pattern, 243
expired blood pattern, 239
flow, 242
forward spatter, 233
high-velocity spatter, 234
impact spatter, 233

low-velocity spatter, 233
medium-velocity spatter, 234
satellite spatter, 231
skeletonization, 243
transfer pattern, 241
void, 240

▪▪▪▪ REVIEW QUESTIONS

1. Violent contact between individuals at a crime scene frequently produces bleeding and results in the formation of _____.

2. The proper interpretation of bloodstain patterns necessitates carefully planned _____ using surface materials comparable to those found at the crime scene.

3. Bloodstain patterns may convey to the analyst the location and movements of _____ or _____ during the commission of a crime.

4. True or False: Harder and less porous surfaces result in less spatter, whereas rough surfaces result in stains with more spatter and serrated edges. _____

5. Generally, bloodstain diameter (increases/decreases) with height.

6. The _____ and _____ of blood striking an object may be discerned by the stain's shape.

7. A drop of blood that strikes a surface at an angle of impact of approximately 90 degrees will be close to (elliptical, circular) in shape.

8. The angle of impact of an individual bloodstain can be estimated using the ratio of _____ divided by _____.

9. _____ is the most common type of blood spatter found at a crime scene and is produced when an object forcefully contacts a source of blood.

10. True or False: Forward spatter consists of the blood projected backward from the source, and back spatter is projected outward and away from the source. _____

11. The classifications of impact spatter based on the size of droplets and from the velocity of an applied force are _____, _____, and _____ impact spatter.

12. True or False: The velocity of an applied force is a good way to classify impact patterns and to determine the kind of force that produced them. _____

13. The _____ is the point on a two-dimensional plane from which the drops originated.

14. The _____ of a bloodstain pattern in a three-dimensional space illustrates the position of the victim or suspect when the stain-producing event took place.

15. The _____ method is used at the crime scene to determine the area of origin.

16. A(n) _____ is created by contact between a bloody object and a surface.

17. The pattern made by a bloody object dragged across a surface (lightens, darkens) as the object moves away from the point of contact.

18. True or False: Footwear transfer patterns created by an individual who was running typically show imprints with more space between them than those of an individual who was walking. _____

19. True or False: The direction of a flow pattern may show movements of objects or bodies while the flow was still in progress or after the blood had dried. _____

20. The approximate drying time of a(n) _____ of blood determined by experimentation is related to the environmental conditions of the scene and may suggest how much time has elapsed since its deposition.

21. The edges of a bloodstain will generally _____ within 50 seconds of deposition and be left intact even if the central area of a bloodstain is altered by a wiping motion.

22. A(n) _____ pattern commonly originates from repeated strikes from weapons or fists and is characterized by an arc pattern of separate drops showing directionality.

23. True or False: Characteristics of a cast-off pattern arc cannot give clues about the kind of object that was used to produce the pattern. _____

24. When an injury to an artery is suffered, the pressure of the continuing pumping of blood projects blood out of the injured area in spurts, creating a pattern known as _____.

25. If a(n) _____ pattern is found at a scene, it may show movement, lead to a discarded weapon, or provide identification of the suspect by his or her own blood.

26. A bloodstain pattern created by _____ features bubbles of oxygen in the drying drops and may be lighter in color than impact spatter.

27. The shape and size of the blank space, or _____, created when an object blocks the deposition of spatter onto a surface and is then removed, may give a clue about the size and shape of the missing object or person.

28. True or False: Each bloodstain pattern found at a crime scene should be noted, studied, and photographed. _____

29. When documenting bloodstain patterns, the _____ involves setting up a grid of squares of known dimensions over the entire pattern and taking overview, medium-range, and close-up photographs with and without the grid.

30. The _____ method of bloodstain documentation involves setting up a border of rulers around the pattern and then placing a small ruler next to each stain to show relative position and size in photographs.

31. True or False: The pointed end of a bloodstain always faces toward its direction of travel. _____

■ ■ ■ ■ **APPLICATION AND CRITICAL THINKING**

1. After looking at the bloodstains in the figure, answer the following questions:

   a) Which three drops struck the surface closest to a 90-degree angle? Explain your answer.

   b) Which three drops struck the surface farthest from a 90-degree angle? Explain your answer.

   c) In what direction were drops 2 and 7 traveling when they struck the surface? Explain your answer.

2. Investigator Priscilla Wright arrives at a murder scene and finds the body of a victim who suffered a gunshot wound, but she doesn't see any blood spatter on the wall or floor behind it. What should she conclude from this observation?

3. Investigator Terry Martin arrives at an assault scene and finds a cast-off pattern consisting of tiny droplets of blood in a very linear arc pattern on a wall near the victim. What does this tell him about the weapon used in the crime?

Richard Saferstein, Ph.D.

11 Drugs

El Tiempo de Colombia/Newscom

LEARNING OBJECTIVES

After studying this chapter, you should be able to:
- Compare and contrast psychological and physical dependence.
- Name and classify the commonly abused drugs.
- Understand the proper collection and preservation of drug evidence.
- Describe the laboratory tests normally used in a routine drug identification analysis.
- Describe and explain the process of chromatography.
- Explain the difference between thin-layer chromatography and gas chromatography.
- Describe the utility of ultraviolet and infrared spectroscopy for the identification of organic compounds.
- Describe the technique of spectrophotometry and its application with respect to specific types of electromagnetic radiation,
- Describe the concept and utility of mass spectrometry for identification analysis.

PABLO ESCOBAR, DRUG LORD

In 1989, *Forbes* magazine listed Pablo Escobar as the seventh richest man in the world. Escobar began his climb to wealth as a teenage car thief in the streets of Medellin, Colombia, and eventually moved into the cocaine-smuggling business. At the peak of his power in the mid-1980s, he was shipping as much as eleven tons of cocaine per flight in jetliners to the United States. Law enforcement officials estimate that the Medellin cartel controlled 80 percent of the world's cocaine market and was taking in about $25 billion annually.

Escobar ruthlessly ruled by the gun: murdering, assassinating, and kidnapping. He was responsible for killing three presidential candidates in Colombia, as well as for the storming of the Colombian Supreme Court, which resulted in the murder of half the justices. All the while, Escobar curried favor with the Colombian general public by cultivating a Robin Hood image and distributing money to the poor.

In 1991, hoping to avoid extradition to the United States, Escobar turned himself in to the Colombian government and agreed to be sent to prison. However, the prison compound where he was sent could easily be mistaken for a country club. There he continued his high-flying lifestyle, trafficking by telephone and even murdering a few associates. When the Colombian government attempted to move Escobar to another jail, again fearing extradition to the United States, he escaped.

Pressured by the U.S. government, Colombia organized a task force dedicated to apprehending Escobar. The manhunt for Escobar ended on December 2, 1993, when he was cornered on the roof of one of his hideouts. A shootout ensued, and Escobar was fatally wounded by a bullet behind the ear.

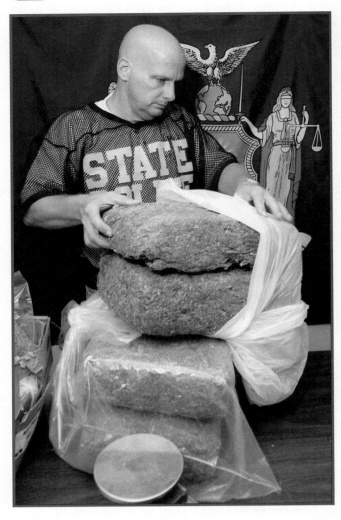

FIGURE 11-1 A drug bust.
*Syracuse Newspapers/
The Image Works*

A "drug" can be defined as a natural or synthetic substance that is used to produce physiological or psychological effects in humans or other animals. However, criminalists are concerned primarily with a small number of drugs—many of them illicit—that are commonly used for their intoxicating effects. These include marijuana, the most widely used illicit drug in the United States, and alcohol, which is consumed regularly by 90 million Americans. Drug abuse has grown from a problem generally associated with members of the lower end of the socioeconomic ladder to one that cuts across all social and ethnic classes of society. Today, approximately 23 million people in the United States use illicit drugs.

Because of the epidemic proportions of illegal drug use, more than 75 percent of the evidence evaluated by crime laboratories in the United States is drug related (see Figure 11-1). The deluge of drug specimens has necessitated the expansion of existing crime laboratories and the creation of new ones. For many concerned forensic scientists, the crime laboratory's preoccupation with drug evidence represents a serious distraction that takes time away from evaluating evidence related to homicides and other types of serious crimes. However, the increasing caseloads associated with drug evidence have justified the expansion of forensic laboratory services. This expansion has increased the overall analytical capabilities of crime laboratories.

Drug Dependence

In assessing the potential danger of drugs, society has become particularly conscious of their effects on human behavior. In fact, the first drugs to be regulated by law in the early years of the twentieth century were those deemed to have "habit-forming" properties. The early laws were aimed primarily at controlling opium and its derivatives; cocaine; and, later, marijuana. The ability of a drug to induce dependence after repeated use is submerged in a complex array of physiological and social factors.

Dependence on different drugs exists in numerous patterns and in all degrees of intensity, and depends on the nature of the drug, the route of administration, the dose, the frequency of administration, and the individual's rate of metabolism. Furthermore, nondrug factors play an equally crucial role in determining the behavioral patterns associated with drug use. The personal characteristics of the user, his or her expectations about the drug experience, society's attitudes toward and possible responses to the drug, and the setting in which the drug is used are all major determinants of drug dependence.

The questions of how to define and measure a given drug's influence on the individual and its danger to society are difficult to assess. The nature and significance of drug dependence must be considered from two overlapping points of view: the interaction of the drug with the individual, and the drug's impact on society. It will be useful to approach the problem from two distinctly different aspects of human behavior: **psychological dependence** and **physical dependence**.

psychological dependence
The conditioned use of a drug caused by underlying emotional needs.

physical dependence
The physiological need for a drug brought about by its regular use and characterized by withdrawal sickness when administration of the drug is abruptly stopped.

PSYCHOLOGICAL DEPENDENCE

The common denominator that characterizes all types of repeated drug use is psychological dependence on continued use of the drug. It is important to discard the unrealistic image that all drug users are hopeless "addicts" who are social dropouts. Most users present a quite normal appearance and remain both socially and economically integrated into the life of the community.

The reasons some people abstain from drugs while others become moderately or heavily involved are difficult if not impossible to delineate. Psychological needs arise from numerous personal and social factors that inevitably stem from the individual's desire to create a sense of well-being and to escape from reality. In some cases, the individual may seek relief from personal problems or stressful situations or may be trying to sustain a physical and emotional state that permits an improved level of performance. Whatever the reasons, the underlying psychological needs and the desire to fulfill them create a conditioned pattern of drug abuse (see Figure 11-2).

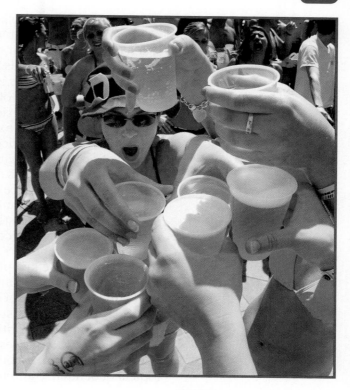

FIGURE 11-2 Young people drinking. *Jim Tiller/Associated Press*

The intensity of the psychological dependence associated with a drug's use is difficult to define and largely depends on the nature of the drug. For drugs such as alcohol, heroin, amphetamines, barbiturates, and cocaine, continued use will probably result in a high degree of involvement. Other drugs, such as marijuana and codeine, appear to have a considerably lower potential for the development of psychological dependence. However, this does not imply that repeated abuse of drugs deemed to have a low potential for psychological dependence is safe or will always produce low psychological dependence. We have no precise way to measure or predict the impact of drug abuse on the individual. Even if a system could be devised for controlling the many possible variables affecting a user's response, the unpredictability of the human personality would still come into play.

Our general knowledge of alcohol consumption should warn us of the fallacy of generalizing when attempting to describe the danger of drug abuse. Obviously, not all alcohol drinkers are psychologically addicted to the drug; most are "social" drinkers who drink in reasonable amounts and on an irregular basis. Many people have progressed beyond this stage and consider alcohol a necessary crutch for dealing with life's stresses and anxieties. However, a wide range of behavioral patterns exists among alcohol abusers, and to a large extent, the determination of the degree of psychological dependence must be made on an individual basis. Likewise, it would be fallacious to generalize that all users of marijuana can develop only a low degree of dependence on the drug. A wide range of factors also influences marijuana's effect, and heavy users of the drug expose themselves to the danger of developing a high degree of psychological dependence.

PHYSICAL DEPENDENCE

Although emotional well-being is the primary motive leading to repeated and intensive use of a drug, certain drugs, taken in sufficient dose and frequency, can produce physiological changes that encourage their continued use. Once the user abstains from such a drug, severe physical illness follows. The desire to avoid this "withdrawal sickness," or "abstinence syndrome," ultimately causes physical dependence, or addiction. Hence, for the addict who is accustomed to receiving large doses of heroin, the prospect of abstaining and encountering the resulting body chills, vomiting, stomach cramps, convulsions, insomnia, pain, and hallucinations is a powerful inducement for continuing to use.

Interestingly, some of the more widely abused drugs have little or no potential for creating physical dependence. Drugs such as marijuana, LSD, and cocaine create strong anxieties when their repeated use is discontinued; however, no medical evidence attributes these discomforts to physiological reactions that accompany withdrawal sickness. On the other hand, use of alcohol, heroin, and barbiturates can result in the development of physical dependence.

Physical dependence develops only when the drug user adheres to a regular schedule of drug intake; that is, the interval between doses must be short enough so that the effects of the drug never wear off completely. For example, the interval between injections of heroin for the drug addict probably does not exceed six to eight hours. Beyond this time the addict will begin to experience the uncomfortable symptoms of withdrawal. Many users of heroin avoid taking the drug on a regular basis for fear of becoming physically addicted to its use. Similarly, the risk of developing physical dependence on alcohol becomes greatest when the consumption is characterized by a continuing pattern of daily use in large quantities.

Table 11.1 categorizes some of the more commonly abused drugs according to their effects on the body and summarizes their tendency to produce psychological dependence and to induce physical dependence with repeated use.

SOCIETAL ASPECTS OF DRUG USE

The social impact of drug dependence is directly related to the extent to which the user has become preoccupied with the drug. Here, the most important element is the extent to which drug use has become interwoven in the fabric of the user's life. The more frequently the drug satisfies the person's need, the greater the likelihood that he or she will become preoccupied with its use, with a consequent neglect of individual and social responsibilities. Personal health, economic relationships, and family obligations may all suffer as the drug-seeking behavior increases in frequency and intensity and dominates the individual's life. The extreme of drug dependence may lead to behavior that has serious implications for the public's safety, health, and welfare.

Drug dependence in its broadest sense involves much of the world's population. As a result, a complex array of individual, social, cultural, legal, and medical factors ultimately influence society's decision to prohibit or impose strict controls on a drug's distribution and use. Invariably, society must weigh the beneficial aspects of the drug against the ultimate harm its abuse will do to the individual and to society as a whole. Obviously, many forms of drug dependence do not carry sufficient adverse social consequences to warrant their prohibition, as illustrated by the widespread use of such drug-containing substances as tobacco and coffee. Although the heavy and prolonged use of these drugs may eventually damage body organs and injure an individual's health, there is no evidence that they result in antisocial behavior, even with prolonged or excessive use. Hence, society is willing to accept the widespread use of these substances.

We are certainly all aware of the disastrous failure of the prohibition by the United States of alcohol use during the 1920s and also of the current debate on whether marijuana should be legalized. Each of these issues emphasizes the delicate balance between individual desires and needs and society's concern with the consequences of drug abuse; moreover, this balance is continuously subject to change and reevaluation.

TABLE 11.1 The Potential of Some Commonly Abused Drugs to Produce Dependence with Regular Use

DRUG	PSYCHOLOGICAL DEPENDENCE	PHYSICAL DEPENDENCE
Narcotics		
Morphine	High	Yes
Heroin	High	Yes
Methadone	High	Yes
Codeine	Low	Yes
Depressants		
Barbiturates (short-acting)	High	Yes
Barbiturates (long-acting)	Low	Yes
Alcohol	High	Yes
Methaqualone (Quaalude)	High	Yes
Meprobamate (Miltown, Equanil)	Moderate	Yes
Diazepam (Valium)	Moderate	Yes
Chlordiazepoxide (Librium)	Moderate	Yes
Stimulants		
Amphetamines	High	?
Cocaine	High	No
Caffeine	Low	No
Nicotine	High	Yes
Hallucinogens		
Marijuana	Low	No
LSD	Low	No
Phencyclidine (PCP)	High	No

Quick Review

- A drug is a natural or synthetic substance that is used to produce physiological or psychological effects in humans or other animals.
- Nondrug factors that play a part in drug dependence include the personal characteristics of the user, his or her expectations about the drug experience, society's attitudes toward and possible responses to the drug, and the setting in which the drug is used.
- Physical dependence is defined as a physiological need for a drug that has been brought about by its regular use. Psychological dependence is the conditioned use of a drug caused by underlying emotional needs.

Types of Drugs

NARCOTIC DRUGS

narcotic
A drug that induces sleep and depresses vital body functions such as blood pressure, pulse rate, and breathing rate.

The term **narcotic** is derived from the Greek word *narkotikos*, meaning "numbness" or "deadening." Although pharmacologists classify narcotic drugs as substances that relieve pain and produce sleep, the term "narcotic" has become popularly associated with any drug that is socially unacceptable. As a consequence of this incorrect perception, many drugs are improperly called "narcotics."

This confusion has produced legal definitions that differ from the pharmacological actions of many drugs. For example, until the early 1970s, most drug laws in the United States incorrectly designated marijuana as a narcotic. Even today, federal law classifies cocaine as a narcotic drug; however, pharmacologically speaking, cocaine is actually a powerful central nervous system stimulant, possessing properties opposite those normally associated with the depressant effects of a narcotic.

OPIATES Medical professionals apply the term "opiate" to most of the drugs properly classified as narcotics. Opiates behave pharmacologically like morphine, which is a painkiller derived from opium—the gummy, milky juice that exudes from cuts made on the unripe pods of the Asian poppy *(Papaver somniferum)*. Although morphine is readily extracted from opium, the most commonly used opium-based drug is heroin, which is produced by reacting morphine with acetic anhydride or acetyl chloride (see Figure 11-3). Heroin's high solubility in water makes its street preparation for intravenous administration rather simple, and only by injection are heroin's effects felt almost instantaneously and with maximum sensitivity. To prepare the drug for injection, the addict frequently dissolves it in a small quantity of water in a spoon. The process can be speeded up by heating the spoon over a candle or several matches. The solution is then drawn into a syringe or eyedropper and injected under the skin (see Figure 11-4).

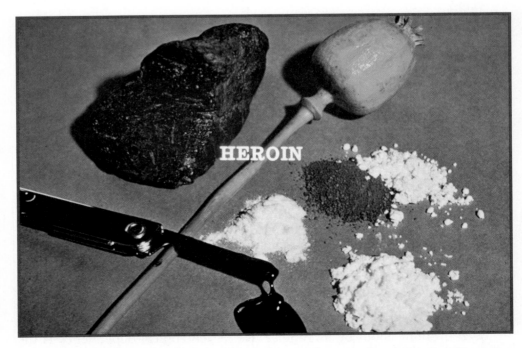

FIGURE 11-3 The opium poppy and its derivatives. Shown are the poppy plant, crude and smoking opium, codeine, heroin, and morphine. *Pearson Education, Inc.*

FIGURE 11-4   Heroin paraphernalia. *Drug Enforcement Administration*

Heroin and other narcotic drugs are **analgesics**—that is, they relieve pain by depressing the central nervous system. Besides being a powerful analgesic, heroin produces a "high" that is accompanied by drowsiness and a deep sense of well-being. The effect is short, generally lasting only 3 to 4 hours. Regular use of heroin—or any other narcotic drug—invariably leads to physical dependence, with all its dire consequences.

analgesic
A substance that lessens or eliminates pain.

Codeine is also present in opium, but it is usually prepared synthetically from morphine. It is commonly used as a cough suppressant in prescription cough syrup. Codeine, only one-sixth as strong as morphine, is not an attractive street drug for addicts.

SYNTHETIC OPIATES   A number of narcotic drugs are not naturally derived from opium. However, because they have physiological effects on the body that are similar to the opium narcotics, they are also commonly referred to as "opiates."

Methadone is perhaps the best-known synthetic opiate. In the 1960s, scientists discovered that a person who received periodic doses of methadone would not get high if he or she then took heroin or morphine. Although methadone is pharmacologically related to heroin, its administration appears to eliminate the addict's desire for heroin, with minimal side effects. These discoveries led to the establishment of controversial methadone maintenance programs in which heroin addicts receive methadone to reduce or prevent future heroin use. Physicians increasingly prescribe methadone for pain relief. Unfortunately, the wide availability of methadone for legitimate medical purposes has recently led to greater quantities of the drug being diverted into the illicit market.

In 1995, the U.S. Food and Drug Administration (FDA) approved the drug OxyContin for use as a painkiller. The active ingredient in OxyContin is oxycodone, a synthetic drug closely related to morphine and heroin in its chemical structure. OxyContin is an analgesic narcotic that has effects similar to those of heroin. It is prescribed for treatment of chronic pain, with doctors writing millions of OxyContin prescriptions each year. The drug has a time-release formula that the manufacturer initially believed would reduce the risk of abuse and addiction. This has not turned out to be the case. It is estimated that close to a quarter of a million individuals abuse the drug.

CLOSER ANALYSIS
WHAT'S IN THAT BAG?

The contents of a typical bag of heroin is an excellent example of the uncertainty attached to buying illicit drugs. For many years in the 1960s and into the early 1970s, the average bag contained 15 to 20 percent heroin. Currently, the average purity of heroin obtained in the illicit U.S. market is approximately 35 percent. The addict rarely knows or cares what composes the other 65 percent or so of the material. Traditionally, quinine has been the most common diluent of heroin. Like heroin, it has a bitter taste and was probably originally used to obscure the actual potency of a heroin preparation from those who wished to taste-test the material before buying it. Other diluents commonly added to heroin are starch, lactose, procaine (Novocain), and mannitol.

Because it is a legal drug that is diverted from legitimate sources, OxyContin is obtained very differently from illegal drugs. Pharmacy robberies, forged prescriptions, and theft of the drug from patients with a legitimate prescription are ways abusers access OxyContin. Some abusers visit numerous doctors and receive prescriptions even though their medical condition may not warrant it.

HALLUCINOGENS

hallucinogen
A substance that induces changes in normal thought processes, perceptions, and moods.

Hallucinogens are drugs that can cause marked alterations in normal thought processes, perceptions, and moods. Perhaps the most popular and controversial member of this class of drugs is marijuana.

MARIJUANA   Marijuana is the popular name of the plant *Cannabis sativa*, a weed that will grow wild in most climates. The *Cannabis* plant contains a chemical known as "tetrahydrocannabinol," or THC, which produces the psychoactive effects experienced by users. The THC content of *Cannabis* varies in different parts of the plant. The greatest concentration is usually found in a sticky resin produced by the plant, known as "hashish." Declining concentrations are typically found in the flowers and leaves, respectively. Little THC is found in the stem, roots, or seeds of the plant. The potency and resulting effect of the drug fluctuate, depending on the relative proportion of these plant parts in the marijuana mixture consumed by the user. The most common method of administration is by smoking either the dried flowers and leaves or various preparations of hashish (see Figure 11-5). Marijuana is also occasionally taken orally, typically baked in sweets such as brownies or cookies.

Any study of marijuana's effect on humans must consider the potency of the marijuana preparation. An interesting insight into the relationship between dosage level and marijuana's pharmacological effect was presented in the first report of the National Commission on Marijuana and Drug Abuse:

> At low, usual "social" doses the user may experience an increased sense of well-being; initial restlessness and hilarity followed by a dreamy, carefree state of relaxation; alteration of sensory perceptions including expansion of space and time; a more vivid sense of touch, sight, smell, taste and sound; a feeling of hunger, especially a craving for sweets; and subtle changes in thought formation and expression. To an unknowing observer, an individual in this state of consciousness would not appear noticeably different from his normal state.
>
> At higher, moderate doses these same reactions are intensified but the changes in the individual would still be scarcely noticeable to an observer. At very high doses, psychotomimetic phenomena may be experienced. These include distortion of body image, loss of personal identity, sensory and mental illusions, fantasies and hallucinations.[1]

FIGURE 11-5 Several rolled marijuana cigarettes lie on a pile of crushed, dried marijuana leaves next to a tobacco cigarette. *Drug Enforcement Administration*

Marijuana easily qualifies as the most widely used illicit drug in the United States. For instance, more than 43 million Americans have tried marijuana, according to the latest surveys, and almost half that number may be regular users. In addition to its widespread illegal use, accumulating evidence suggests that marijuana has potential medical uses. Two promising areas of research are marijuana's reduction of excessive eye pressure in sufferers of glaucoma and the lessening of nausea caused by powerful anticancer drugs. Marijuana may also be useful as a muscle relaxant.

No current evidence suggests that experimental or intermittent use of marijuana causes physical or psychological harm. Marijuana does not cause physical dependence. However, the risk of harm lies instead in heavy, long-term use, particularly of the more potent preparations. Heavy users can develop a strong psychological dependence on the drug. Some effects of marijuana use include increased heart rate, dry mouth, reddened eyes, impaired motor skills and concentration, and frequently hunger and an increased desire for sweets.

OTHER HALLUCINOGENS A substantial number of other substances with widely varying chemical compositions are also used recreationally because of their hallucinogenic properties. These include both naturally occurring substances such as mescaline and psilocybin and synthetically created drugs including lysergic acid diethylamide (LSD) and phencyclidine (PCP).

LSD is synthesized from lysergic acid, a substance derived from ergot, which is a type of fungus that attacks certain grasses and grains. The drug appears in a variety of forms—as a pill, added to a cube of sugar, or absorbed onto a small piece of paper—and is taken orally. Its hallucinogenic effects were first described by the Swiss chemist Albert Hofmann after he accidentally ingested some of the material in his laboratory in 1943. LSD produces marked changes in mood, leading to laughing or crying at the slightest provocation. Feelings of anxiety and tension almost always accompany LSD use. LSD is very potent; as little as 25 micrograms is enough to induce vivid visual hallucinations that can last for about 12 hours. Although physical dependence

CLOSER ANALYSIS
MARIJUANA AND HASHISH

Marijuana is a weed that will grow wild in most climates. The plant grows to a height of 5 to 15 feet and is characterized by an odd number of leaflets on each leaf. Normally each leaf contains five to nine leaflets, all with serrated or sawtooth edges.

The potency of marijuana depends on its form. Marijuana in the form of loose vegetation has an average THC content of about 3 to 4.5 percent. The more potent sinsemilla form averages about 6 to 12 percent in THC content. Sinsemilla is the unfertilized flowering tops of the female *Cannabis* plants, acquired by removing all male plants from the growing field at the first sign of their appearance. Production of sinsemilla requires a great deal of attention and care, and the plant is therefore cultivated on small plots.

Hashish preparations average about 2 to 8 percent THC. On the illicit drug market, hashish (see photo) usually appears in the form of compressed vegetation containing a high percentage of resin. A particularly potent form of hashish is known as "liquid hashish" or "hashish oil." Hashish in this form is normally a viscous substance, dark green with a tarry consistency. Liquid hashish is produced by efficiently extracting the THC-rich resin from the marijuana plant with an appropriate solvent, such as alcohol. The THC content of liquid hashish typically varies from 8 to 22 percent. Because of its extraordinary potency, one drop of the material can produce a "high."

The marijuana leaf. *SPL/Science Source Images*

Blocks of hashish in front of leaves and flowering tops of the marijuana plant. *James King-Holmes/Science Source Images*

does not develop with continued use, the individual user may be prone to flashbacks and psychotic reactions even after use is discontinued.

Abuse of the hallucinogen phencyclidine, commonly called "PCP," has recently grown to alarming proportions. Because this drug can be synthesized by simple chemical processes, it is manufactured surreptitiously for the illicit market in so-called clandestine laboratories (see Figure 11-6). These laboratories range from large, sophisticated operations to small labs located in garages or bathrooms. Small-time operators normally have little or no training in chemistry and employ "cookbook" methods to synthesize the drug. Some of the more knowledgeable and experienced operators have been able

CLOSER ANALYSIS
SYNTHETIC CANNABIS

Synthetic cannabinoids are chemicals designed to mimic the pharmacological effects of naturally occurring cannabinoids. These drugs are generally sold in retail establishments or over the Internet as herbal procedures, potpourri, or incense. Users generally spray the chemicals onto botanical materials and inhale the drug through burning or smoking.

Synthetic cannabinoids derive their pharmacological activity from their affinity toward cannabinoid (CB) receptor sites in the brain. Early in their availability, these synthetics went by the common names "K2" and "spice"; however, currently their chemical composition and names have become quite varied as clandestine laboratories have become adept and innovative in modifying their chemical structures seeking to circumvent control by drug laws. Because the chemical structure of synthetic cannabinoids do not resemble marijuana constituents, they cannot be detected by routine drug screening tests.

The symptomology associated with the use of synthetic cannabinoids can result in anxiety, agitation, and nausea. A federal law, the Food and Drug Administration Safety and Innovation Act, broadly covers any material that contains a synthetic cannabinoid.

---

to achieve clandestine production levels that approach a commercial level of operation.

Phencyclidine is often mixed with other drugs, such as LSD or amphetamines, and is sold as a powder (known as "angel dust"), capsule, or tablet, or as a liquid sprayed on plant leaves. The drug is smoked, ingested, or sniffed. Following oral intake of moderate doses (1 to 6 milligrams), the user first experiences feelings of strength and invulnerability, along with a dreamy sense of detachment. However, the user soon becomes unresponsive, confused, and agitated. Depression, irritability, feelings of isolation, audio and visual hallucinations, and sometimes paranoia accompany PCP use. Severe depression, tendencies toward violence, and suicide accompany long-term daily use of the drug. In some cases, the PCP user experiences sudden schizophrenic behavior days after the drug has been taken.

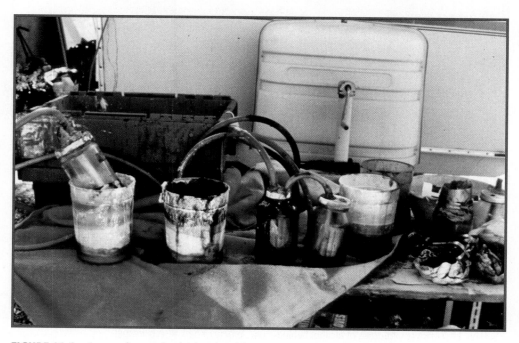

FIGURE 11-6   A scene from a clandestine drug laboratory. *Drug Enforcement Administration*

DEPRESSANTS

Depressants are drugs that slow down, or depress, the central nervous system. Several types of drugs fall into this category, including the most widely used drug in the United States: alcohol.

ALCOHOL (ETHYL ALCOHOL)   Many people overlook the fact that alcohol is a drug; however, it exerts a powerful **depressant** action on the central nervous system. When alcohol enters the bloodstream, it quickly travels to the brain, where it suppresses the brain's control of thought processes and muscle coordination. Low doses of alcohol tend to inhibit the mental processes of judgment, memory, and concentration. The drinker's personality becomes expansive, and he or she exudes confidence. When taken in moderate doses, alcohol reduces coordination substantially, inhibits orderly thought processes and speech patterns, and slows reaction times. Under these conditions, the ability to walk or drive becomes noticeably impaired. Higher doses of alcohol may cause the user to become highly irritable and emotional; displays of anger and crying are not uncommon. Extremely high doses may cause an individual to lapse into unconsciousness or even a comatose state that can precede a fatal depression of circulatory and respiratory functions. The behavioral patterns of alcohol intoxication vary and depend partly on such factors as the social setting, the amount consumed, and the personal expectation of the individual with regard to alcohol.

In the United States, the alcohol industry annually produces more than one billion gallons of spirits, wine, and beer for which 90 million consumers pay nearly $40 billion. Unquestionably, these and other statistics support the fact that alcohol is the most widely used and abused drug (see Figure 11-7).

BARBITURATES   Barbiturates are derivatives of barbituric acid, a substance first synthesized by a German chemist, Adolf Von Bayer, more than a hundred years ago. They are commonly referred to as "downers" because they relax the user, create a feeling of well-being, and produce sleep. Like alcohol,

depressant

A substance that slows down, or depresses, the functions of the central nervous system.

FIGURE 11-7   Rows of bottles of alcohol behind a bar. *Jeremy Liebman/Getty Images*

barbiturates suppress the vital functions of the central nervous system. Twenty-five barbiturate derivatives are currently used in medical practice in the United States; however, only five—amobarbital, secobarbital, phenobarbital, pentobarbital, and butabarbital—are used for most medical applications.

Normally, barbiturate users take these drugs orally. The average sedative dose is about 10 to 70 milligrams. When taken in this fashion, the drug enters the blood through the walls of the small intestine. Some barbiturates, such as phenobarbital, are classified as long-acting barbiturates. They are absorbed into the bloodstream more slowly than others and therefore produce less pronounced effects than faster-acting barbiturates. The slow action of phenobarbital accounts for its low incidence of abuse. Apparently, barbiturate abusers prefer the faster-acting varieties: secobarbital, pentobarbital, and amobarbital.

In the early 1970s, a nonbarbiturate depressant, methaqualone (brand name Quaalude), appeared on the illicit-drug scene. Methaqualone is a powerful sedative and muscle relaxant that possesses many of the depressant properties of barbiturates. When taken in prescribed amounts, barbiturates are relatively safe, but in instances of extensive and prolonged use, physical dependence can develop.

ANTIPSYCHOTIC AND ANTIANXIETY DRUGS Although antipsychotic and antianxiety drugs can be considered depressants, they differ from barbiturates in the extent of their effects on the central nervous system. Generally, these drugs produce a relaxing tranquility without impairing high-thinking faculties or inducing sleep. Antipsychotics, such as reserpine and chlorpromazine, have been used to reduce the anxieties and tension of mental patients. A group of antianxiety drugs are commonly prescribed to deal with the everyday tensions of many healthy people. These drugs include meprobamate (Miltown), chlordiazepoxide (Librium), diazepam (Valium), and Xanax.

In the past forty-five years, the use of these drugs—particularly antianxiety drugs—has grown dramatically. Medical evidence shows that these drugs produce psychological and physical dependence with repeated and high levels of usage. For this reason, the widespread prescribing of antianxiety drugs to overcome the pressures and tensions of life has worried many people who fear a legalized drug culture is being created.

"HUFFING" Since the early 1960s, "huffing," the practice of sniffing materials containing volatile solvents (e.g., airplane glue or model cement), has grown in popularity. Another dimension has more recently been added to the problem with the increasing popularity of sniffing aerosol gas propellants such as freon. All materials abused by huffing contain volatile or gaseous substances that are primarily central nervous system depressants. Although toluene (a solvent used in airplane glue) seems to be the most popular solvent to sniff, others can produce comparable physiological effects. These chemicals include naphtha, methyl ethyl ketone (i.e., antifreeze), gasoline, and trichloroethylene (a dry-cleaning solvent).

The usual immediate effects of huffing are a feeling of exhilaration and euphoria combined with slurred speech, impaired judgment, and double vision. Finally, the user may experience drowsiness and stupor, with these depressant effects slowly wearing off as the user returns to a normal state. Although most experts believe that users become psychologically dependent on the effects achieved by huffing, little evidence suggests that solvent inhalation is addictive. However, huffers expose themselves to the danger of liver, heart, and brain damage from the chemicals they have inhaled. Even worse, sniffing of some solvents, particularly halogenated hydrocarbons such as freon and related gases, is accompanied by a significant risk of immediate death.

FIGURE 11-8 Granular amphetamine beside a razor blade. *Cordelia Molloy/Photo Researchers,Inc.*

stimulant
A substance that speeds up, or stimulates, the activity of the central nervous system.

coca leaves and cocaine

FIGURE 11-9 Coca leaves and illicit forms of cocaine. *Drug Enforcement Administration*

STIMULANTS

The term **stimulants** refers to a range of drugs that stimulate, or speed up, the central nervous system.

AMPHETAMINES Amphetamines are a group of synthetic stimulants that share a similar chemical structure and are commonly referred to in the terminology of the drug culture as "uppers" or "speed." They are typically taken either orally or via intravenous injection and provide a feeling of well-being and increased alertness that is followed by a decrease in fatigue and a loss of appetite. However, these apparent benefits of the drug are accompanied by restlessness and instability or apprehensiveness, and once the stimulant effect wears off, depression may set in.

In the United States, the most serious form of amphetamine abuse stems from intravenous injection of amphetamine or its chemical derivative, methamphetamine (see Figure 11-8). The desire for a more intense amphetamine experience is the primary motive for this route of administration. The initial sensation of a "flash" or "rush," followed by an intense feeling of pleasure, constitutes the principal appeal of the intravenous route for the user. During a "speed binge," the individual may inject amphetamines every 2 to 3 hours. Users have reported experiencing a euphoria that produces hyperactivity, with a feeling of clarity of vision as well as hallucinations. As the effect of the amphetamines wears off, the individual lapses into a period of exhaustion and may sleep continuously for one or two days. Following this, the user often experiences a prolonged period of severe depression lasting from days to weeks.

A smokable form of methamphetamine, known as "ice," is reportedly in heavy demand in some areas of the United States. Ice is prepared by slowly evaporating a methamphetamine solution to produce large, crystal-clear "rocks." Like crack cocaine (discussed next), ice is smoked and produces effects similar to those of crack cocaine, but the effects last longer. Once the effects of ice wear off, users often become depressed and may sleep for days. Chronic users exhibit violent destructive behavior and acute psychosis similar to paranoid schizophrenia. Repeated use of amphetamines leads to a strong psychological dependence, which encourages their continued use.

COCAINE Between 1884 and 1887, pioneering psychologist Sigmund Freud created something of a sensation in European medical circles by describing his experiments with a new drug. He reported a substance of seemingly limitless potential as a source of "exhilaration and lasting euphoria" that permitted "intensive mental or physical work [to be] performed without fatigue." He wrote, "It is as though the need for food and sleep was completely banished."

The object of Freud's enthusiasm was cocaine, a stimulant extracted from the leaves of *Erythroxylon coca*, a plant grown in the Andes mountains of South America as well as in tropical Asia (see Figure 11-9). Most commonly, cocaine is sniffed or "snorted" and absorbed into the body through the mucous membranes of the nose, but it is sometimes injected. Cocaine is a powerful stimulant to the central nervous system, and its effects resemble those caused by amphetamines—namely, increased alertness and vigor accompanied by suppression of hunger, fatigue, and boredom. Cocaine produces a feeling of euphoria by stimulating a pleasure center in the base of the brain, in an area connected to nerves that are responsible for emotions. It stimulates this pleasure center to a far greater degree than it would ever normally be stimulated. Some regular users of cocaine report accompanying feelings of restlessness, irritability, and anxiety. Cocaine used chronically or at high doses can have toxic effects. Cocaine-related deaths result from cardiac arrest or seizures followed by respiratory arrest.

A particularly potent form of cocaine known as "crack" can be produced by mixing cocaine with baking soda and water and then heating the resulting solution. This material is then dried and broken into tiny chunks that dealers sell as crack "rocks" that are sufficiently volatile to be smoked. The faster the cocaine level rises in the brain, the greater the euphoria, and the fastest way to attain a rise in the brain's cocaine level is to smoke crack. Inhaling the cocaine vapor delivers the drug to the brain in less than 15 seconds—about as fast as injecting it and much faster than snorting it. The dark side of crack, however, is that the euphoria fades quickly as the cocaine levels rapidly drop, leaving the user feeling depressed, anxious, and pleasureless. The desire to return to the euphoric feeling is so intense that crack users quickly develop a habit for the drug that is almost impossible to overcome. Only a small percentage of crack abusers are ever cured of this drug habit. When a person uses large amounts of crack cocaine numerous times, he or she usually develops a sense of paranoia. Paronoid delusions cause the person to lose his or her sense of reality, leaving him or her trapped in a world full of voices, whispers, and suspicions. Sufferers come to believe that they are being followed and that their drug use is being watched.

In the United States, cocaine abuse is on the rise. Many people are using cocaine apparently to improve their ability to work and to keep going when tired. Although there is no evidence of physical dependency accompanying cocaine's repeated use, abstention from cocaine after prolonged use brings on severe bouts of mental depression that produce a very strong compulsion to resume using the drug. In fact, laboratory experiments with animals have demonstrated that, of all the commonly abused drugs, cocaine produces the strongest psychological compulsions for continued use.

The United States spends millions of dollars annually in attempting to control cultivation of the coca leaf in various South American countries and to prevent the trafficking of cocaine into the United States. Three-quarters of the cocaine smuggled into the United States was refined in clandestine laboratories in Colombia. The profits are astronomical. Peruvian farmers may be paid $200 for enough coca leaves to make one pound of cocaine. The refined cocaine is worth $1,000 when it leaves Colombia and sells at retail in the United States for up to $20,000.

CLUB DRUGS

The term "club drugs" refers to synthetic drugs that are often used at nightclubs, bars, and raves (i.e., all-night dance parties). Substances that are used as club drugs include, but are not limited to, methylenedioxymethamphetamine (MDMA) (also known as Ecstasy; see Figure 11-10), gamma hydroxybutyrate (GHB), Rohypnol ("roofies"), ketamine, and methamphetamine. These drugs have become popular on the dance scene as a way to induce the rave experience. A high incidence of use has been found among teens and young adults.

GHB and Rohypnol are central nervous system depressants that are often connected with drug-facilitated sexual assault, rape, and robbery. Effects accompanying the use of GHB include dizziness, sedation, headache, and

CLOSER ANALYSIS
BATH SALTS

It has become trendy in the drug culture to abuse a group of illicit substances known as "bath salts." These drugs are a mix of chemical derivatives derived from cathinone, a naturally occurring substance found in the khat plant. Cathinone is a stimulant having about half the potency of amphetamine. The allure of abusing cathinone and its chemical derivatives is to simulate the high associated with methamphetamine and cocaine abuse.

Synthetic derivatives of cathinone are commonly sold in powder, crystal, and liquid forms, but they are available also as tablets and capsules. They are sold in packages to be snorted, ingested, smoked, or injected. Like the side effects associated with methamphetamine or cocaine abuse, bath salts can induce agitation, violent behavior, and paranoia on the part of the user.

A federal law, the Food and Drug Administration Safety and Innovation Act, outlaws two synthetic cathinones, mephidrone and 3,4-methylenedioxypyrovalerone (MDPV), that are common constituents of bath salts.

---

nausea. Recreational users have reported euphoria, relaxation, disinhibition, and increased libido (i.e., sex drive). Rohypnol causes muscle relaxation, loss of consciousness, and an inability to remember what happened during the hours after ingesting the drug. Users of this drug are at particular risk of sexual assault because victims are physically unable to resist the attack. Effects are even stronger when the drug is combined with alcohol because the user experiences memory loss, blackouts, and disinhibition. Unsuspecting victims of intentional druggings become drowsy or dizzy. Drugs such as Rohypnol and GHB are odorless, colorless, and tasteless, and thus remain undetected when slipped into a drink.

MDMA, or Ecstasy, is a synthetic, mind-altering drug that exhibits many hallucinogenic and amphetamine-like effects. Ecstasy was originally patented as an appetite suppressant and was later discovered to induce feelings of happiness and relaxation. Recreational drug users find that Ecstasy enhances self-awareness and decreases inhibitions. However, seizures, muscle

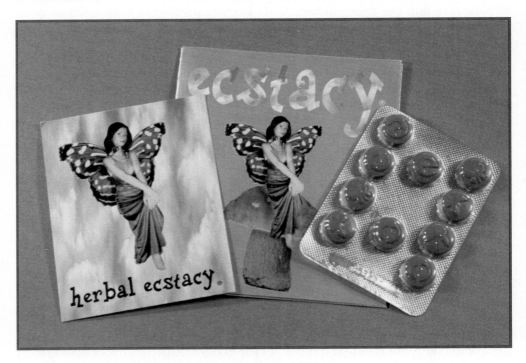

FIGURE 11-10 Ecstasy, a popular club drug. *Rusty Kennedy/AP Images*

breakdown, stroke, kidney failure, and cardiovascular system failure often accompany chronic abuse of Ecstasy. In addition, chronic use of Ecstasy leads to serious damage to the areas of the brain responsible for thought and memory. Ecstasy increases heart rate and blood pressure; produces muscle tension, teeth grinding, and nausea; and causes psychological difficulties such as confusion, severe anxiety, and paranoia. The drug can cause significant increases in body temperature from the combination of the drug's stimulant effect with the often hot, crowded atmosphere of a rave club.

Ketamine is primarily used in veterinary medicine as an animal anesthetic. When used by humans, the drug can cause euphoria and feelings of unreality accompanied by visual hallucinations. Ketamine can also cause impaired motor function, high blood pressure, amnesia, and mild respiratory depression.

FIGURE 11-11 Anabolic steroids: a vial of testosterone and a syringe. Testosterone, the male sex hormone, is sometimes abused by athletes for its protein-building (anabolic) effect. *SPL/Science Source Images*

ANABOLIC STEROIDS

Anabolic steroids are synthetic compounds that are chemically related to the male sex hormone testosterone. Testosterone has two effects on the body. It promotes the development of secondary male characteristics (i.e., androgenic effects), and it accelerates muscle growth (i.e., anabolic effects). Efforts to promote muscle growth and to minimize the hormone's androgenic effects have led to the synthesis of numerous anabolic steroids. However, a steroid free of the accompanying harmful side effects of an androgen drug has not yet been developed.

Incidence of steroid abuse first received widespread public attention when both amateur and professional athletes were discovered using these substances to enhance their performance. Interestingly, current research on male athletes given anabolic steroids has generally found little or, at best, marginal evidence of enhanced strength or performance. Although the full extent of anabolic steroid abuse by the general public is not fully known, the U.S. government is sufficiently concerned to regulate the availability of these drugs to the general population and to severely punish individuals for illegal possession and distribution of anabolic steroids. In 1991, anabolic steroids were classified as controlled dangerous substances, and the Drug Enforcement Administration was given enforcement power to prevent their illegal use and distribution (see Figure 11-11).

Anabolic steroids are usually taken by individuals who are unfamiliar with their harmful medical side effects. Liver cancer and other liver malfunctions have been linked to steroid use. These drugs also cause masculinizing effects in females, infertility, and diminished sex drive in males. For teenagers, anabolic steroids result in the premature halting of bone growth. Anabolic steroids can also cause unpredictable effects on mood and personality, leading to unprovoked acts of anger and destructive behavior. Depression is also a frequent side effect of anabolic steroid abuse.

anabolic steroids
Synthetic compounds, chemically related to the male sex hormone testosterone, that are used to promote muscle growth.

Quick Review

- Narcotic drugs are analgesics, meaning that they relieve pain by depressing the central nervous system.
- The most common source for narcotic drugs is opium. Morphine is extracted from opium and used to synthesize heroin.

- Opiates are not derived from opium or morphine, but they have the same physiological effects on the body. Examples of opiates are methadone and OxyContin (i.e., oxycodone).
- Hallucinogens cause marked changes in normal thought processes, perceptions, and moods. Marijuana is the most well-known drug in this class. Other hallucinogens include LSD, mescaline, PCP, psilocybin, and MDMA (or Ecstasy).
- Depressants decrease the activity of the central nervous system, calm irritability and excitability, and produce sleep. Depressants include alcohol (i.e., ethanol), barbiturates, tranquilizers, and various substances that can be sniffed such as airplane glue and model cement.
- Stimulants increase the activity of the central nervous system and are taken to increase alertness and activity. Stimulants include amphetamines, sometimes known as "uppers" or "speed," and cocaine, which in its free-base form is known as "crack."
- Club drugs are synthetic drugs that are used at nightclubs, bars, and raves (i.e., all-night dance parties). Some club drugs act as stimulants; others have depressant effects.
- Anabolic steroids are synthetic compounds that are chemically related to the male sex hormone testosterone. Anabolic steroids are often abused by individuals who are interested in accelerating muscle growth.

Drug-Control Laws

The provisions of drug laws are of particular interest to the criminalist, for they may impose specific analytical requirements on drug analysis. For example, the severity of a penalty associated with the manufacture, distribution, possession, and use of a drug may depend on the weight of the drug or its concentration in a mixture. In such cases, the chemist's report must contain all information that is needed to properly charge a suspect under the provisions of the existing law.

The provisions of any drug-control law are an outgrowth of national and local law enforcement requirements and customs, as well as the result of moral and political philosophies. These factors have produced a wide spectrum of national and local drug-control laws. Although their detailed discussion is beyond the intended scope of this book, a brief description of the U.S. federal law known as the Controlled Substances Act will illustrate a legal drug classification system that has been created to prevent and control drug abuse. Many states have modeled their own drug-control laws after this act, an important step in establishing uniform drug-control laws throughout the United States.

Collection and Preservation of Drug Evidence

Preparation of drug evidence for submission to the crime laboratory is normally relatively simple and accomplished with minimal precautions in the field. The field investigator must ensure that the evidence is properly packaged and labeled for delivery to the laboratory. Considering the countless forms and varieties of drug evidence that are seized, it is not practical to prescribe any single packaging procedure for fulfilling these requirements. Generally, common sense is the best guide in such situations, keeping in mind that the package must prevent loss and/or cross-contamination of the contents. Often, the original container in which the drug was seized will meet these requirements. Specimens suspected of containing volatile solvents, such as those involved in glue-sniffing cases, must be packaged in an airtight container to prevent evaporation of the solvent. All packages must be marked with sufficient information to ensure identification by the officer in future legal proceedings and to establish the chain of custody.

To aid the drug analyst, the investigator should supply any background information that may relate to a drug's identity. Analysis time can be markedly reduced when the chemist has this information. For the same reason, the results of drug-screening tests used in the field must also be transmitted to the laboratory. However, although these tests may indicate the presence of a drug and may help the officer establish probable cause to search and arrest a suspect, they do not offer conclusive evidence of a drug's identity.

Quick Review

- Federal law establishes five schedules of classification for controlled dangerous substances on the basis of a drug's potential for abuse, potential for physical and psychological dependence, and medical value.
- The packaging of drug evidence must prevent loss and/or cross-contamination of the contents, and often the original container in which the drug was seized is used. Specimens suspected of containing volatile solvents must be packaged in an airtight container to prevent evaporation.
- The investigator may help in the identification of the drug by supplying to the drug analyst any background information that may relate to the drug's identity.

Forensic Drug Analysis

One has only to look into the evidence vaults of crime laboratories to appreciate the assortment of drug specimens that confront the criminalist. The presence of a huge array of powders, tablets, capsules, vegetable matter, liquids, pipes, cigarettes, cookers, and syringes is testimony to the vitality and sophistication of the illicit-drug market. If outward appearance is not evidence enough of the difficult analytical chore facing the forensic chemist, consider the complexity of the drug preparations themselves. Usually these contain active drug ingredients of unknown origin and identity, as well as additives—for example, sugar, starch, and quinine—that dilute their potency and stretch their value on the illicit-drug market. Do not forget that illicit-drug dealers are not hampered by government regulations that ensure the quality and consistency of their product.

When a forensic chemist picks up a drug specimen for analysis, he or she can expect to find just about anything, so all contingencies must be prepared for. The analysis must leave no room for error because its results will have a direct bearing on the process of determining the guilt or innocence of a defendant. There is no middle ground in drug identification—either the specimen is a specific drug or it is not—and once a positive conclusion is drawn, the chemist must be prepared to support and defend the validity of the results in a court of law.

CLOSER ANALYSIS
CONTROLLED SUBSTANCES ACT

The federal Controlled Substances Act establishes five schedules of classification for controlled dangerous substances on the basis of a drug's potential for abuse, potential for physical and psychological dependence, and medical value. This classification system is extremely flexible in that the U.S. attorney general has the authority to add, delete, or reschedule a drug as more information becomes available.

Schedule I. Schedule I drugs have a high potential for abuse, have no currently accepted medical use in the United States, and/or lack accepted safety for use in treatment under medical supervision. Drugs controlled under this schedule include heroin, marijuana, methaqualone, and LSD.

Schedule II. Schedule II drugs have a high potential for abuse, a currently accepted medical use or a medical use with severe restrictions, and a potential for severe psychological or physical dependence. Schedule II drugs include opium and its derivatives not listed in schedule I, cocaine, methadone, phencyclidine (PCP), most amphetamine preparations, and most barbiturate preparations containing amobarbital, secobarbital, and pentobarbital. Dronabinol, the synthetic equivalent of the active ingredient in marijuana, has been placed in schedule II in recognition of its growing medical uses in treating glaucoma and chemotherapy patients.

Schedule III. Schedule III drugs have less potential for abuse than those in schedules I and II, a currently accepted medical use in the United States, and a potential for low or moderate physical dependence or high psychological dependence. Schedule III controls, among other substances, all barbiturate preparations (except phenobarbital) not covered under schedule II and certain codeine preparations. Anabolic steroids were added to this schedule in 1991.

Schedule IV. Schedule IV drugs have a low potential for abuse relative to schedule III drugs and have a current medical use in the United States; their abuse may lead to limited dependence relative to schedule III drugs. Drugs controlled in this schedule include propoxyphene (Darvon), phenobarbital, and tranquilizers such as meprobamate (Miltown), diazepam (Valium), and chlordiazepoxide (Librium).

Schedule V. Schedule V drugs must show low abuse potential, have medical use in the United States, and have less potential for producing dependence than schedule IV drugs. Schedule V controls certain opiate drug mixtures that contain nonnarcotic medicinal ingredients.

Controlled dangerous substances listed in schedules I and II are subject to manufacturing quotas set by the attorney general. For example, 8 billion doses of amphetamines were manufactured in

CONTROL MECHANISMS OF THE CONTROLLED SUBSTANCES ACT

Schedule	Registration	Record Keeping	Manufacturing Quotas	Distribution Restrictions	Dispensing Limits
I	Required	Separate	Yes	Order forms	Research use only
II	Required	Separate	Yes	Order forms	Rx: written; no refills
III	Required	Readily retrievable	No, but some drugs limited by schedule II quotas	Records required	Rx: written or oral; with medical authorization refills up to five times in 6 months
IV	Required	Readily retrievable	No, but some drugs limited by schedule II quotas	Records required	Rx: written or oral; with medical authorization refills up to five times in 6 months
V	Required	Readily retrievable	No, but some drugs limited by schedule II quotas	Records required	Over-the-counter (Rx drugs limited to MD's order) refills up to five times

SCREENING AND CONFIRMATION

The challenge or difficulty of forensic drug identification comes in selecting analytical procedures that will ensure a specific identification of a drug. Presented with a substance of unknown origin and composition, the forensic chemist must develop a plan of action that will ultimately yield the drug's identity. This plan, or scheme of analysis, is divided into two phases.

the United States in 1971. In 1972, production quotas were established reducing amphetamine production approximately 80 percent below 1971 levels.

The criminal penalties for the unauthorized manufacture, sale, or possession of controlled dangerous substances are related to the schedules as well. The most severe penalties are associated with drugs listed in schedules I and II. For example, for drugs included in schedules I and II, a first offense of individual trafficking is punishable by up to twenty years in prison and/or a fine of up to $1 million for an individual or up to $5 million for other than individuals. The table summarizes the control mechanisms and penalties for each schedule of the Controlled Substances Act.

The Controlled Substances Act also stipulates that an offense involving a controlled substance analog—a chemical substance substantially similar in chemical structure to a controlled substance—triggers penalties as if it were a controlled substance listed in schedule I. This section is designed to combat the proliferation of so-called designer drugs—substances that are chemically related to some controlled drugs and are pharmacologically very potent. These substances are manufactured by skilled individuals in clandestine laboratories with the knowledge that their products will not be covered by the schedules of the Controlled Substances Act. For instance, fentanyl is a powerful narcotic that is commercially marketed for

medical use and is also listed as a controlled dangerous substance. This drug is about a hundred times as potent as morphine. A number of substances chemically related to fentanyl have been synthesized by underground chemists and sold on the street. The first such substance we know of was sold under the street name China White. These drugs have been responsible for more than a hundred overdose deaths in California and nearly twenty deaths in western Pennsylvania. As designer drugs such as China White become identified by drug officials and linked to drug abuse, they are placed in appropriate schedules.

The Controlled Substances Act also reflects an effort to decrease the prevalence of clandestine drug laboratories designed to manufacture controlled substances. The act regulates the manufacture and distribution of precursors, the chemical compounds used by clandestine drug laboratories to synthesize abused drugs. Targeted precursor chemicals are listed in the definition section of the Controlled Substances Act. Severe penalties are assigned to a person who possesses a listed precursor chemical with the intent to manufacture a controlled substance or who possesses or distributes a listed chemical knowing, or having reasonable cause to believe, that the listed chemical will be used to manufacture a controlled substance. In addition, precursors to PCP, amphetamines, and methamphetamines are enumerated specifically in schedule II, making them subject to regulation in the same manner as other schedule II substances.

| IMPORT–EXPORT | | | | |
Narcotic	Nonnarcotic	Security	Manufacturer/Distributor Reports to Drug Enforcement Administration	Criminal Penalties for Individual Trafficking (First Offense)
Permit	Permit	Vault/safe	Yes	0–20 years/$1 million
Permit	Permit	Vault/safe	Yes	0–20 years/$1 million
Permit	Declaration	Secure storage area	Yes, narcotic; no, nonnarcotic	0–5 years/$250,000
Permit	Declaration	Secure storage area	Manufacturer only, narcotic; no, nonnarcotic	0–3 years/$250,000
Permit to import; declaration to export	Declaration	Secure storage area	Manufacturer only, narcotic; no, nonnarcotic	0–1 year/$100,000

Source: Drug Enforcement Administration, Washington, DC

First, faced with the prospect that the unknown substance may be any one of a thousand or more commonly encountered drugs, the analyst must employ **screening tests** to reduce these possibilities to a small and manageable number. This objective is often accomplished by subjecting the material to a series of color tests that produce characteristic colors for the more commonly encountered illicit drugs. Even if these tests produce negative results, their value lies in having excluded certain drugs from further consideration.

screening test
A preliminary test used to reduce the number of possible identities of an unknown substance.

Once the number of possibilities has been reduced substantially, the second phase of the analysis must be devoted to pinpointing and confirming the drug's identity. In an era in which crime laboratories receive voluminous quantities of drug evidence, it is impractical to subject a drug to all the chemical and instrumental tests available. Indeed, it is more realistic to look on these techniques as constituting a large analytical arsenal. The chemist, aided by training and experience, must choose tests that will most conveniently identify a particular drug.

confirmation

A single test that specifically identifies a substance.

Forensic chemists often use a specific test to identify a drug substance to the exclusion of all other known chemical substances. A single test that identifies a substance is known as a **confirmation**. The analytical scheme sometimes consists of a series of nonspecific or presumptive tests. Each test in itself is insufficient to prove the drug's identity; however, the proper analytical scheme encompasses a combination of test results that characterize one and only one chemical substance—the drug under investigation. Furthermore, experimental evidence must confirm that the probability of any other substance responding in an identical manner to the scheme selected is so small as to be beyond any reasonable scientific certainty.

Another consideration in selecting an analytical technique is the need for either a *qualitative* or a *quantitative* determination. The former relates just to the identity of the material, whereas the latter refers to the percentage of each component in the mixture. Hence, a qualitative identification of a powder may reveal the presence of heroin and quinine, whereas a quantitative analysis may conclude the presence of 10 percent heroin and 90 percent quinine.

Obviously, a qualitative identification must precede any attempt at quantitation; there is little value in attempting to quantitate a material without first determining its identity. Essentially, a qualitative analysis of a material requires the determination of numerous properties using a variety of analytical techniques. On the other hand, a quantitative measurement is usually accomplished by precise measurement of a single property of the material.

Forensic chemists normally rely on several tests for a routine drug-identification scheme: color tests, microcrystalline tests, chromatography, spectrophotometry, and mass spectrometry.

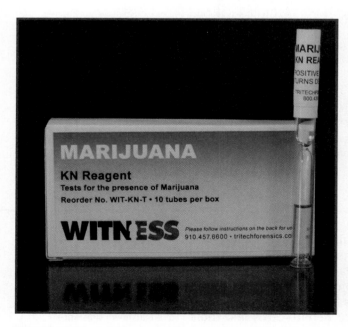

FIGURE 11-12 A field color-test kit for marijuana. *Tri-Tech, Inc.*

COLOR TESTS

Many drugs yield characteristic colors when brought into contact with specific chemical reagents. Not only do these tests provide a useful indicator of a drug's presence, but they are also used by investigators in the field to examine materials suspected of containing a drug (see Figure 11-12). However, color tests are useful for screening purposes only and are never taken as conclusive identification of unknown drugs.

Five primary color-test reagents are as follows:

1. *Marquis.* The reagent turns purple in the presence of heroin and morphine and most opium derivatives. Marquis becomes orange-brown when mixed with amphetamines and methamphetamines.
2. *Dillie-Koppanyi.* This is a valuable screening test for barbiturates, in whose presence the reagent turns a violet-blue color.
3. *Duquenois-Levine.* This is a valuable color test for marijuana, performed by adding a series

(a)

(b)

FIGURE 11-13 (a) A photomicrograph of a cocaine crystal formed in platinum chloride (400×). (b) A photomicrograph of a methamphetamine crystal formed in gold chloride (400×). *San Bernardino County Sheriff's Department*

of chemical solutions to the suspect vegetation. A positive result is shown by a purple color when chloroform is added.

4. ***Van Urk.*** The reagent turns blue-purple in the presence of LSD. However, owing to the extremely small quantities of LSD in illicit preparations, this test is difficult to conduct under field conditions.

5. ***Scott Test.*** This is a color test for cocaine. A powder containing cocaine turns a cobalt thiocyanate solution blue. Upon the addition of hydrochloric acid, the blue color is transformed to a clear pink color. Upon the addition of chloroform, if cocaine is present, the blue color reappears in the chloroform layer.

MICROCRYSTALLINE TESTS

A technique considerably more specific than color tests is the **microcrystalline test**. A drop of a chemical reagent is added to a small quantity of the drug on a microscopic slide. After a short time, a chemical reaction ensues, producing a crystalline precipitate. The size and shape of the crystals, examined under a compound microscope, reveal the identity of the drug. Crystal tests for cocaine and methamphetamine are illustrated in Figure 11-13.

Over the years, analysts have developed hundreds of crystal tests to characterize the most commonly abused drugs. These tests can be rapidly executed and often do not require the isolation of a drug from its diluents; however, because diluents can sometimes alter or modify the shape of the crystal, the examiner must develop experience in interpreting the results of the test.

Most color and crystal tests are largely empirical—that is, scientists do not fully understand why they produce the results they do. From the forensic chemist's point of view, this is not important. When the tests are properly chosen and used in proper combination, they reveal characteristics that identify the substance as a certain drug to the exclusion of all others.

microcrystalline test
A test that identifies a specific substance based on the color and shape of crystals formed when the substance is mixed with specific reagents.

Quick Review

- Analysts use screening tests to determine the identity of drugs present in a sample. These tests reduce the number of possible drugs to a small and manageable number.
- A series of color tests produce characteristic colors for the more commonly encountered illicit drugs. In a microcrystalline test, a drop of a chemical reagent added to a small quantity of drug on a microscope slide produces crystals highly characteristic of a drug.
- After preliminary testing, forensic chemists use more specific tests to identify a drug substance to the exclusion of all other known chemical substances.

CHROMATOGRAPHY

Chromatography is a means of separating and tentatively identifying the components of a mixture. It is particularly useful for analyzing drug specimens, which may be diluted with practically any material to increase the quantity of the product available to prospective customers. The task of identifying an illicit-drug preparation would be arduous without the aid of chromatographic methods to first separate the mixture into its components.

THIN-LAYER CHROMATOGRAPH Thin-layer chromatography (TLC) uses a solid stationary phase and a moving liquid phase to separate the constituents of a mixture. Thin-layer chromatography is a powerful tool for solving many of the analytical problems presented to the forensic scientist. The method is both rapid and sensitive; moreover, less than 100 micrograms of suspect material is required for the analysis. In addition, the equipment necessary for TLC work has minimal cost and space requirements. Importantly, numerous samples can be analyzed simultaneously on one thin-layer plate. This technique is principally used to detect and identify components in complex mixtures.

In TLC, the components of a suspect mixture are separated as they travel up a glass or plastic plate, eventually appearing as a series of dark or colored spots on the plate. This action is then compared to a standard sample separation of a specific drug, such as heroin. If both the standard and the suspect substances travel the same distance up the plate, they can tentatively be identified as being the same substance.

A thin-layer plate is prepared by coating a glass plate or plastic backing with a thin film of a granular material, usually silica gel or aluminum oxide. This granular material serves as the solid stationary phase and is usually held in place on the plate with a binding agent such as plaster of paris. If the sample to be analyzed is a solid, it must first be dissolved in a suitable solvent; then a few microliters of the solution are spotted with a capillary tube onto the granular surface near the lower edge of the plate. A liquid sample may be applied directly to the plate in the same manner. The plate is then placed upright in a closed chamber that contains a selected liquid, but the liquid must not touch the sample spot.

The liquid slowly rises up the plate by capillary action. This rising liquid is the moving phase in thin-layer chromatography. As the liquid moves past the sample spot, the components of the sample become distributed between the stationary solid phase and the moving liquid phase. The components with the greatest affinity for the moving phase travel up the plate faster than those that have greater affinity for the stationary phase. When the liquid front has moved a sufficient distance (usually 10 centimeters), the development is complete, and the plate is removed from the chamber and dried (see Figure 11-14). An example of the chromatographic separation of ink is shown in Figure 11-15.

Often the plate is sprayed with a chemical reagent that reacts with the separated substances and causes them to form colored spots. Figure 11-16 shows the chromatogram of a marijuana extract that has been separated into its components by TLC and visualized by having been sprayed with a chemical reagent.

Figure 11-17 shows a sample suspected of containing heroin and quinine that has been chromatographed alongside known heroin and quinine standards. The distance the unknown material migrated up the suspect plate is compared to the distances that heroin and quinine migrated up a standard sample plate. If the distances are the same, a tentative identification can be made. However, such an identification cannot be considered definitive because numerous other substances can migrate the same distance up the plate when chromatographed under similar conditions. Thus, thin-layer chromatography

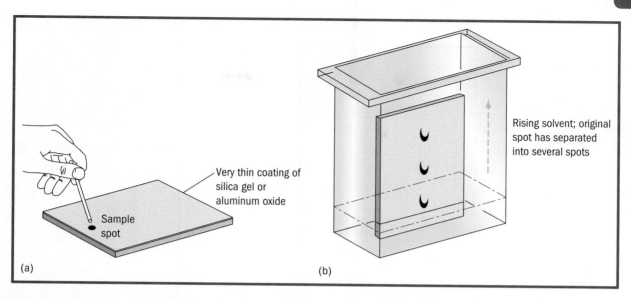

FIGURE 11-14 (a) In thin-layer chromatography, a liquid sample is spotted onto the granular surface of a gel-coated plate. (b) The plate is placed into a closed chamber that contains a liquid. As the liquid rises up the plate, the components of the sample distribute themselves between the coating and the moving liquid. The mixture is separated, with substances with a greater affinity for the moving liquid traveling up the plate at a faster speed. *SAFERSTEIN, RICHARD, Ph.D., CRIMINALISTICS: AN INTRODUCTION TO FORENSIC SCIENCE, 11th Ed., © 2015. Reprinted and Electronically reproduced by permission of Pearson Education, Inc., Upper Saddle River, New Jersey.*

alone cannot provide an absolute identification; it must be used in conjunction with other testing procedures to prove absolute identity.

GAS CHROMATOGRAPHY (GC) Gas chromatography (GC) separates mixtures based on their distribution between a stationary liquid phase and a moving gas phase. In gas chromatography, the moving phase is called the "carrier gas," which flows through a column constructed of glass. The stationary phase is a thin film of liquid within the column, which is known as a "capillary column."

Capillary columns are composed of glass and are 15 to 60 meters in length. These types of columns are very narrow, ranging from 0.25 to 0.75 millimeter in diameter. Capillary columns can be made narrow because their stationary liquid phase is actually a very thin film coating the column's inner wall.

As the carrier gas flows through the capillary column, it carries with it the components of a mixture that have been injected into the column. Components

FIGURE 11-15 (a) In thin-layer chromatography, the liquid phase begins to move up the stationary phase. (b) Liquid moves past the ink spot carrying the ink components up the stationary phase. (c) The moving liquid has separated the ink into its several components. *Richard Megna/ Fundamental Photographs*

FIGURE 11-16 A thin-layer chromatogram of a marijuana extract. *Sirchie Finger Print Laboratories*

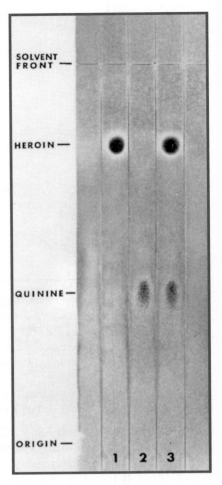

FIGURE 11-17 Chromatographs of known heroin (1) and quinine (2) standards alongside a suspect sample (3). *Richard Saferstein, Ph.D.*

with a greater affinity for the moving gas phase travel through the column more quickly than those with a greater affinity for the stationary liquid phase. Eventually, after the mixture has traversed the length of the column, it emerges separated into its components.

The time required for a component to emerge from the column after its injection into the column is known as the "retention time," which is a useful identifying characteristic. Figure 11-18(a) shows the chromatogram of two barbiturates; each barbiturate has tentatively been identified by comparing its retention time to those of known barbiturates, shown in Figure 11-18(b). However, because other substances may have comparable retention times under similar chromatographic conditions, gas chromatography cannot be considered an absolute means of identification. Conclusions derived from this technique must be confirmed with other testing procedures.

Gas chromatography is widely used because of its ability to resolve a highly complex mixture into its components, usually within minutes. It has the added advantages of being extremely sensitive and yielding quantitative results. Gas chromatography has sufficient sensitivity to detect and quantitate materials down to the nanogram (i.e., 0.000000001 gram).

WebExtra 11.1

Watch the Gas Chromatograph at Work

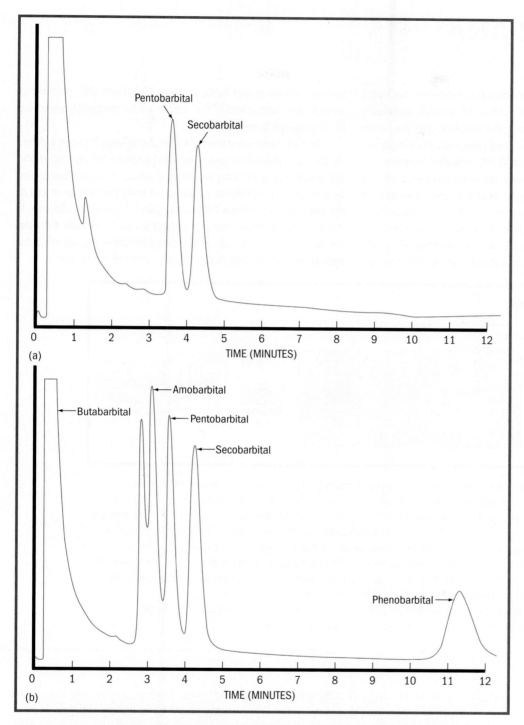

FIGURE 11-18 (a) An unknown mixture of barbiturates is identified by comparing its retention times to (b), a known mixture of barbiturates. *SAFERSTEIN, RICHARD, Ph.D., CRIMINALISTICS: AN INTRODUCTION TO FORENSIC SCIENCE, 11th Ed., © 2015. Reprinted and Electronically reproduced by permission of Pearson Education, Inc., Upper Saddle River, New Jersey.*

SPECTROPHOTOMETRY

The technique of chromatography is particularly suited for analyzing illicit drugs because it can separate a drug from other substances that may be present in the drug preparation. However, chromatography has the drawback of

CLOSER ANALYSIS
THE GAS CHROMATOGRAPH

A simplified scheme of the gas chromatograph is shown in the figure. The operation of the instrument can be summed up briefly as follows: The carrier gas is fed into the column at a constant rate. The carrier gas, generally nitrogen or helium, is chemically inert. The sample under investigation is injected as a liquid into a heated injection port with a syringe, where it is immediately vaporized and swept into the column by the carrier gas. The column itself is heated in an oven in order to keep the sample in a vapor state as it travels through the column. In the column, the components of the sample travel in the direction of the carrier gas flow at speeds that are determined by their distribution between the stationary and moving phases. If the analyst has selected the proper liquid phase and has made the column long enough, the components of the sample will be completely separated as they emerge from the column.

As each component emerges from the column, it enters a detector. One type of detector uses a flame to ionize the emerging chemical substance, thus generating an electrical signal. The signal is recorded on a strip-chart recorder as a function of time. This written record of the separation is called a "chromatogram." A gas chromatogram is a plot of the recorder response (on the vertical axis) over time (on the horizontal axis). A typical chromatogram shows a series of peaks, each of which corresponds to one component of the mixture.

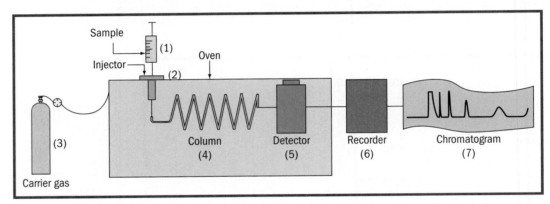

Basic gas chromatography. Gas chromatography permits rapid separation of complex mixtures into individual compounds and allows identification and quantitative determination of each compound. As shown, a sample is introduced by a syringe (1) into a heated injection chamber (2). A constant stream of nitrogen gas (3) flows through the injector, carrying the sample into the column (4), which contains a thin film of liquid. The sample is separated in the column, and the carrier gas and separated components emerge from the column and enter the detector (5). Signals developed by the detector activate the recorder (7), which makes a permanent record of the separation by tracing a series of peaks on the chromatograph (8). The time it takes a component to emerge from the column identifies the component present, and the peak area identifies the concentration. *SAFERSTEIN, RICHARD, Ph.D., CRIMINALISTICS: AN INTRODUCTION TO FORENSIC SCIENCE, 11th Ed., © 2015. Reprinted and Electronically reproduced by permission of Pearson Education, Inc., Upper Saddle River, New Jersey.*

spectrophotometry
An analytical method for identifying a substance by its selective absorption of different wavelengths of light.

dispersion
The separation of light into its component wavelengths.

refraction
The bending of a light wave caused by a change in its velocity.

not being able to specifically identify the material under investigation. For this reason, other analytical tools are frequently used to identify drugs. These include the technique of **spectrophotometry**, which can identify a substance by exposing it to a specific type of electromagnetic radiation.

ELECTROMAGNETIC SPECTRUM Many of us have held a glass prism up toward the sunlight and watched it transform light into the colors of the rainbow. The process of separating light into its component colors is called **dispersion**. Visible light usually travels at a constant velocity of nearly 300 million meters per second. However, on passing through the glass of a prism, each color component of light is slowed to a speed slightly different from those of the others, causing each component to bend at a different angle as it emerges from the prism (see Figure 11-19). This bending of light waves results in a change in velocity called **refraction**.

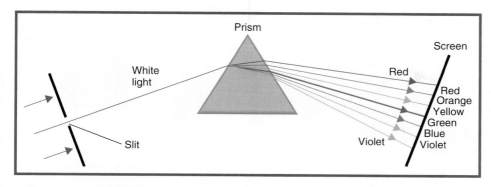

FIGURE 11-19 A representation of the dispersion of light by a glass prism. *SAFERSTEIN, RICHARD, Ph.D., CRIMINALISTICS: AN INTRODUCTION TO FORENSIC SCIENCE, 11th Ed., © 2015. Reprinted and Electronically reproduced by permission of Pearson Education, Inc., Upper Saddle River, New Jersey.*

The observation that a substance has a color is consistent with this description of white light. For example, when light passes through a red glass, the glass absorbs all the component colors of light except red, which passes through or is transmitted by the glass. Likewise, one can determine the color of an opaque object by observing its ability to absorb some of the component colors of light while reflecting others back to the eye. Color is thus a visual indication that objects absorb certain portions of **visible light** and transmit or reflect others. Scientists have long recognized this phenomenon and have learned to characterize chemical substances by the type and quantity of light they absorb. This has important implications for the identification and classification of forensic evidence.

Visible light is only a small part of a large family of radiation waves known as the **electromagnetic spectrum** (see Figure 11-20). All electromagnetic waves travel at the speed of light (*c*) and are distinguishable from one another only by their different wavelengths or frequencies. Hence, the only property that distinguishes **X-rays** from radio waves is the different frequencies the two types of waves possess.

Similarly, the range of colors that make up the visible spectrum can be correlated with frequency. For instance, the lowest frequencies of visible light are red; waves with a lower frequency fall into the invisible infrared (IR) region. The highest frequencies of visible light are violet; waves with a higher frequency extend into the invisible ultraviolet (UV) region. No definite boundaries exist between any colors or regions of the electromagnetic spectrum; instead, each region is composed of a continuous range of frequencies, each blending into the other.

visible light
Colored light ranging from red to violet in the electromagnetic spectrum.

electromagnetic spectrum
The entire range of radiation energy from the most energetic cosmic rays to the least energetic radio waves.

X-ray
A high-energy, short-wavelength form of electromagnetic radiation.

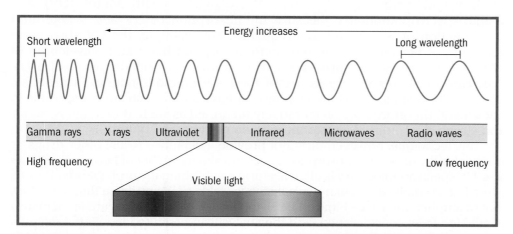

FIGURE 11-20 The electromagnetic spectrum. *SAFERSTEIN, RICHARD, Ph.D., CRIMINALISTICS: AN INTRODUCTION TO FORENSIC SCIENCE, 11th Ed., © 2015. Reprinted and Electronically reproduced by permission of Pearson Education, Inc., Upper Saddle River, New Jersey.*

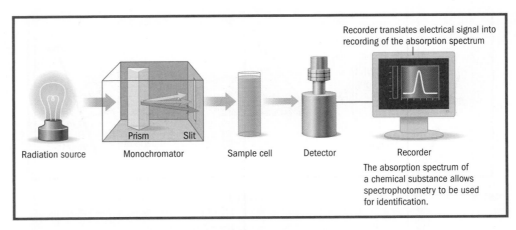

FIGURE 11-21 The parts of a simple spectrophotometer. *Richard Saferstein, Ph.D.*

Just as a substance can absorb visible light to produce color, many of the invisible radiations of the electromagnetic spectrum are likewise absorbed. This absorption phenomenon is the basis for spectrophotometry, an analytical technique that measures the quantity of radiation that a particular material absorbs as a function of **wavelength** or **frequency**.

THE SPECTROPHOTOMETER   An object does not absorb all the visible light it is exposed to; instead, it selectively absorbs some frequencies and reflects or transmits others. Similarly, the absorption of other types of electromagnetic radiation by chemical substances is also selective. Selective absorption of a substance is measured by an instrument called a "spectrophotometer," which produces a graph or "absorption spectrum" that depicts the absorption of light as a function of wavelength or frequency.

The spectrophotometer measures and records the absorption spectrum of a chemical. The basic components of a simple spectrophotometer are the same regardless of whether it is designed to measure the absorption of UV, visible, or IR radiation. These components are illustrated diagrammatically in Figure 11-21. They include (1) a radiation source, (2) a monochromator or frequency selector, (3) a sample holder, (4) a detector to convert electromagnetic radiation into an electrical signal, and (5) a recorder to produce a record of the signal.

The measuring absorption of UV, visible, and IR radiation is particularly applicable to obtaining qualitative data pertaining to the identification of drugs.

ULTRAVIOLET AND VISIBLE SPECTROPHOTOMETRY   Ultraviolet (UV) and visible spectrophotometry measure the absorption of UV and visible light as a function of wavelength or frequency. For example, the UV absorption spectrum of heroin shows a maximum absorption band at a wavelength of 278 nanometers (see Figure 11-22). This shows that the simplicity of a UV spectrum facilitates its use as a tool for determining a material's probable identity. For instance, a white powder may have a UV spectrum comparable to heroin and therefore may be tentatively identified as such. (Fortunately, sugar and starch, common diluents of heroin, do not absorb UV light.)

This technique, however, does not provide a definitive result; other drugs or materials may have a UV absorption spectrum similar to that of heroin. Nevertheless, UV spectrophotometry is often useful in establishing the *probable* identity of a drug. For example, if an unknown substance yields a UV spectrum that resembles that of amphetamine (see Figure 11-23), thousands of substances are immediately eliminated from consideration, and the analyst can begin to identify the material from a relatively small number of possibilities. A comprehensive collection of UV drug spectra provides an index that can rapidly be searched in order to tentatively identify a drug or, failing that, at least to exclude certain drugs from consideration.

wavelength
The distance between crests of adjacent waves.

frequency
The number of waves that pass a given point per unit of time.

ultraviolet
Invisible long frequencies of light beyond violet in the visible spectrum.

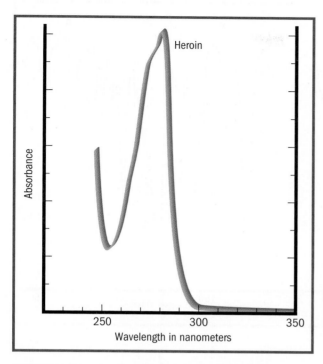

FIGURE 11-22 The ultraviolet spectrum of heroin. *SAFERSTEIN, RICHARD, Ph.D., CRIMINALISTICS: AN INTRODUCTION TO FORENSIC SCIENCE, 11th Ed., © 2015. Reprinted and Electronically reproduced by permission of Pearson Education, Inc., Upper Saddle River, New Jersey.*

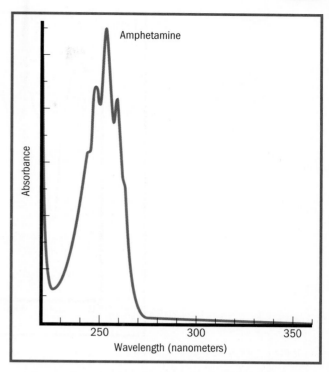

FIGURE 11-23 The ultraviolet spectrum of an amphetamine. *SAFERSTEIN, RICHARD, Ph.D., CRIMINALISTICS: AN INTRODUCTION TO FORENSIC SCIENCE, 11th Ed., © 2015. Reprinted and Electronically reproduced by permission of Pearson Education, Inc., Upper Saddle River, New Jersey.*

INFRARED SPECTROPHOTOMETRY In contrast to the simplicity of a UV spectrum, absorption in the **infrared (IR)** region provides a far more complex pattern. Figure 11-24 depicts the IR spectra of heroin and secobarbital. Here, the absorption bands are so numerous that each spectrum can provide enough characteristics to identify a substance specifically. **Different materials always have distinctively different infrared spectra; each IR spectrum is therefore equivalent to a "fingerprint" of that substance and no other.** This technique is one of the few tests available to the forensic scientist that can be considered specific in itself for identification. The IR spectra of thousands of organic compounds have been collected, indexed, and cataloged as invaluable references for identifying organic substances. The selective absorption of light by drugs in the UV and IR regions of the electromagnetic spectrum provides a valuable technique for characterizing drugs.

infrared

Invisible short frequencies of light before red in the visible spectrum.

MASS SPECTROMETRY

The "Gas Chromatography" section discussed the operation of the gas chromatograph. This instrument is one of the most important tools in a crime laboratory. Its ability to separate the components of a complex mixture is unsurpassed. However, gas chromatography has one important drawback: its inability to produce specific identification. A forensic chemist cannot unequivocally state the identity of a substance based solely on its retention time as determined by the gas chromatograph. Fortunately, by coupling the gas chromatograph to a mass spectrometer, forensic chemists have largely overcome this problem.

A mixture's components are first separated on the gas chromatograph. A direct connection between the gas chromatograph column and the mass spectrometer then allows each component to flow into the spectrometer as

(a)

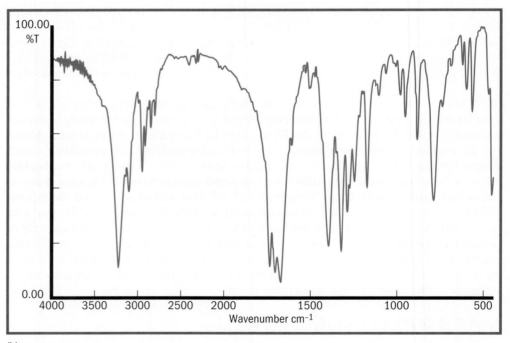

(b)

FIGURE 11-24 (a) The infrared spectrum of heroin. (b) The infrared spectrum of secobarbital. *SAFERSTEIN, RICHARD, Ph.D., CRIMINALISTICS: AN INTRODUCTION TO FORENSIC SCIENCE, 11th Ed., © 2015. Reprinted and Electronically reproduced by permission of Pearson Education, Inc., Upper Saddle River, New Jersey.*

ion
An atom or molecule bearing a positive or negative charge.

it emerges from the gas chromatograph. In the mass spectrometer, the material enters a high-vacuum chamber where a beam of high-energy electrons is aimed at the sample molecules. The electrons collide with the molecules, causing them to lose electrons and to acquire a positive charge. These positively charged molecules, or **ions**, are very unstable or are formed with excess energy and almost instantaneously decompose into numerous smaller fragments.

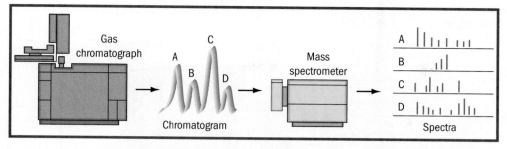

FIGURE 11-25 How GC/MS works. Left to right, the sample is separated into its components by the gas chromatograph, and then the components are ionized and identified by characteristic fragmentation patterns of the spectra produced by the mass spectrometer. *SAFERSTEIN, RICHARD, Ph.D., CRIMINALISTICS: AN INTRODUCTION TO FORENSIC SCIENCE, 11th Ed., © 2015. Reprinted and Electronically reproduced by permission of Pearson Education, Inc., Upper Saddle River, New Jersey.*

The fragments then pass through an electric or magnetic field, where they are separated according to their masses. The unique feature of mass spectrometry is that, under carefully controlled conditions, no two substances produce the same fragmentation pattern. In essence, one can think of this pattern as a "fingerprint" of the substance being examined (see Figure 11-25).

Mass spectrometry thus provides a specific means for identifying a chemical structure. It is also sensitive to minute concentrations. Mass spectrometry is widely used to identify drugs; however, further research is expected to yield significant applications for identifying other types of physical evidence. Figure 11-26 illustrates the mass spectra of heroin and cocaine; here, each

FIGURE 11-26 (a) The mass spectrum of heroin. (b) The mass spectrum of cocaine. *SAFERSTEIN, RICHARD, Ph.D., CRIMINALISTICS: AN INTRODUCTION TO FORENSIC SCIENCE, 11th Ed., © 2015. Reprinted and Electronically reproduced by permission of Pearson Education, Inc., Upper Saddle River, New Jersey.*

FIGURE 11-27   A tabletop mass spectrometer. (1) The sample is injected into a heated inlet port, and carrier gas sweeps it into the column. (2) The GC column separates the mixture into its components. (3) In the ion source, a filament wire emits electrons that strike the sample molecules, causing them to fragment as they leave the GC column. (4) The quadrupole, consisting of four rods, separates the fragments according to their mass. (5) The detector counts the fragments passing though the quadrupole. The signal is small and must be amplified. (6) The data system is responsible for total control of the entire GC/MS system. It detects and measures the abundance of each fragment and displays the mass spectrum. *Agilent Technologies, Inc. 2013*

WebExtra 11.2

Watch an Animation of a Mass Spectrometer

VIRTUAL LAB
DRUG IDENTIFICATION ANALYSIS
To perform a virtual drug identification analysis, go to
www.pearsoncustom.com/us/vlm/

VIRTUAL LAB
THIN-LAYER CHROMATOGRAPHY
OF INK
To perform a virtual thin-layer analysis, go to
www.pearsoncustom.com/us/vlm/

line represents a fragment of a different mass (actually the ratio of mass to charge), and the line height reflects the relative abundance of each fragment. Note how different the fragmentation patterns of heroin and cocaine are. Each mass spectrum is unique to each drug and therefore provides a specific test for identifying that substance.

The combination of the gas chromatograph and mass spectrometer (GC/MS) is further enhanced when a computer is added to the system. The integrated gas chromatograph/mass spectrometer/computer system provides the ultimate in speed, accuracy, and sensitivity. With the ability to record and store in its memory several hundred mass spectra, such a system can detect and identify substances present in quantities of only 1 millionth of a gram. Furthermore, the computer can be programmed to compare an unknown spectrum against a comprehensive library of mass spectra stored in its memory. The advent of personal computers and microcircuitry has enabled the design of mass spectrometer systems that can fit on small tables. Such a unit is pictured in Figure 11-27. With data obtained from a GC/MS determination, a forensic analyst can, with one instrument, separate the components of a complex drug mixture and then unequivocally identify each substance present in the mixture.

Research-grade mass spectrometers are found in laboratories as larger, floor-model units (see Figure 11-28).

Quick Review

- Chromatography is a means of separating and tentatively identifying the components of a mixture.
- Thin-layer chromatography (TLC) uses a solid stationary phase, usually coated onto a glass plate, and a mobile liquid phase to separate the components of the mixture.

- Gas chromatography (GC) separates mixtures on the basis of their distribution between a stationary liquid phase and a mobile gas phase.
- Spectrophotometry is the measurement of the absorption of light by chemical substances.
- Dispersion is the process of separating light into its component colors. Each component bends, or refracts, at a different angle as it emerges from the prism. The large family of radiation waves is known as the "electromagnetic spectrum."
- Most forensic laboratories use ultraviolet (UV) and infrared (IR) spectrophotometers to characterize chemical compounds.
- IR spectrophotometry provides a far more complex pattern than UV spectrophotometry. Because different materials have distinctively different infrared spectra, each IR spectrum is equivalent to a "fingerprint" of that substance.
- Mass spectrometry characterizes organic molecules by observing their fragmentation pattern after their collision with a beam of high-energy electrons.
- Infrared spectrophotometry and mass spectrophotometry typically are used to identify a specific drug substance.

FIGURE 11-28 A scientist injecting a sample into a research-grade mass spectrometer. *Geoff Tompkinson/Science Source*

CHAPTER REVIEW

- A drug is a natural or synthetic substance that is used to produce physiological or psychological effects in humans or other animals.

- Nondrug factors that play a part in drug dependence include the personal characteristics of the user, his or her expectations about the drug experience, society's attitudes toward and possible responses to the drug, and the setting in which the drug is used.

- Physical dependence is defined as a physiological need for a drug that has been brought about by its regular use. Psychological dependence is the conditioned use of a drug caused by underlying emotional needs.

- Narcotic drugs are analgesics, meaning that they relieve pain by depressing the central nervous system.

- The most common source for narcotic drugs is opium. Morphine is extracted from opium and used to synthesize heroin.

- Opiates are not derived from opium or morphine, but they have the same physiological effects on the body. Examples of opiates are methadone and OxyContin (i.e., oxycodone).

- Hallucinogens cause marked changes in normal thought processes, perceptions, and moods. Marijuana is the most well-known drug in this class. Other hallucinogens include LSD, mescaline, PCP, psilocybin, and MDMA (or Ecstasy).

- Depressants decrease the activity of the central nervous system, calm irritability and excitability, and produce sleep. Depressants include alcohol (i.e., ethanol), barbiturates, tranquilizers, and various substances that can be sniffed such as airplane glue and model cement.

- Stimulants increase the activity of the central nervous system and are taken to increase alertness and activity. Stimulants include amphetamines, sometimes known as "uppers" or "speed," and cocaine, which in its freebase form is known as "crack."

- Club drugs are synthetic drugs that are used at nightclubs, bars, and raves (i.e., all-night dance parties). Some club drugs act as stimulants; others have depressant effects.

- Anabolic steroids are synthetic compounds that are chemically related to the male sex hormone testosterone. Anabolic steroids are often abused by individuals who are interested in accelerating muscle growth.

- Federal law establishes five schedules of classification for controlled dangerous substances on the basis of a drug's potential for abuse, potential for physical and psychological dependence, and medical value.

- The packaging of drug evidence must prevent loss and/or cross-contamination of the contents, and often the original container in which the drug was seized is used. Specimens suspected of containing volatile solvents must be packaged in an airtight container to prevent evaporation.

- The investigator may help in the identification of the drug by supplying to the drug analyst any background information that may relate to the drug's identity.

- Analysts use screening tests to determine the identity of drugs present in a sample. These tests reduce the number of possible drugs to a small and manageable number.

- A series of color tests produce characteristic colors for the more commonly encountered illicit drugs. In a microcrystalline test, a drop of a chemical reagent added to a small quantity of drug on a microscope slide produces crystals highly characteristic of a drug.

- After preliminary testing, forensic chemists use more specific tests to identify a drug substance to the exclusion of all other known chemical substances.

- Chromatography is a means of separating and tentatively identifying the components of a mixture.

- Thin-layer chromatography (TLC) uses a solid stationary phase, usually coated onto a glass plate, and a mobile liquid phase to separate the components of the mixture.

- Gas chromatography (GC) separates mixtures on the basis of their distribution between a stationary liquid phase and a mobile gas phase.

- Spectrophotometry is the measurement of the absorption of light by chemical substances.

- Dispersion is the process of separating light into its component colors. Each component bends, or refracts, at a different angle as it emerges from the prism. The large family of radiation waves is known as the electromagnetic spectrum.

- Most forensic laboratories use ultraviolet (UV) and infrared (IR) spectrophotometers to characterize chemical compounds.

- IR spectrophotometry provides a far more complex pattern than UV spectrophotometry. Because different materials have distinctively different infrared spectra, each IR spectrum is equivalent to a "fingerprint" of that substance.

- Mass spectrometry characterizes organic molecules by observing their fragmentation pattern after their collision with a beam of high-energy electrons.

- Infrared spectrophotometry and mass spectrophotometry typically are used to identify a specific drug substance.

KEY TERMS

anabolic steroids, 267

analgesic, 257

chromatography, 274

confirmation, 272

depressant, 262

dispersion, 278

electromagnetic spectrum, 279

frequency, 280

hallucinogen, 258

infrared, 281

ion, 282

microcrystalline test, 273

narcotic, 256

physical dependence, 252

psychological dependence, 252

refraction, 278

screening test, 271

spectrophotometry, 278

stimulant, 264

ultraviolet, 280

visible light, 279

wavelength, 280

X-ray, 279

REVIEW QUESTIONS

1. A(n) _____ can be defined as a natural or synthetic substance that is used to produce physiological or psychological effects in humans or other animals.

2. True or False: Underlying emotional factors are the primary motives leading to the repeated use of a drug. _____

3. True or False: Drugs such as alcohol, heroin, amphetamines, barbiturates, and cocaine can lead to a low degree of psychological dependence with repeated use. _____

4. The development of _____ dependence on a drug is shown by withdrawal symptoms such as convulsions when the user stops taking the drug.

5. True or False: Abuse of barbiturates can lead to physical dependency. _____

6. True or False: Repeated use of LSD leads to physical dependency. _____

7. Physical dependency develops only when the drug user adheres to a(n) _____ schedule of drug intake.

8. Narcotic drugs are _____ that have _____ effects on the central nervous system.

9. _____ is a gummy, milky juice exuded from cuts made on the unripe pods of the Asian poppy.

10. _____ is a chemical derivative of morphine made by reacting morphine with acetic anhydride.

11. A legally available drug that is chemically related to heroin and heavily used is _____.

12. True or False: Methadone is classified as a narcotic drug, even though it is not derived from opium or morphine. _____

13. Drugs that cause marked alterations in mood, attitude, thought processes, and perceptions are called _____.

14. _____ is the sticky resin extracted from the marijuana plant.

15. The active ingredient of marijuana largely responsible for its hallucinogenic properties is _____.

16. True or False: The potency of a marijuana preparation depends on the proportion of the various plant parts in the mixture. _____

17. The marijuana preparation with the highest THC content is _____.

18. LSD is a chemical derivative of _____, a chemical obtained from the ergot fungus that grows on certain grasses and grains.

19. The drug phencyclidine is often manufactured for the illicit-drug market in _____ laboratories.

20. True or False: Alcohol depresses the central nervous system. _____

21. _____ are called "downers" because they depress the central nervous system.

22. True or False: Phenobarbital is an example of a long-acting barbiturate. _____

23. _____ is a powerful sedative and muscle relaxant that possesses many of the depressant properties of barbiturates.

24. _____ and _____ drugs are used to relieve anxiety and tension without inducing sleep.

25. True or False: Huffing volatile solvents stimulates the central nervous system. _____

26. _____ are a group of synthetic drugs that stimulate the central nervous system.

27. _____ is extracted from the leaf of the coca plant.

28. Traditionally, cocaine is _____ into the nostrils.

29. True or False: Cocaine is a powerful central nervous system depressant. _____

30. The two drugs usually associated with drug-facilitated sexual assaults are _____ and _____.

31. _____ steroids are designed to promote muscle growth but have harmful side effects.

32. Federal law establishes _____ schedules of classification for the control of dangerous drugs.

33. Drugs that have no accepted medical use are placed in schedule _____.

34. Librium and Valium are listed in schedule _____.

35. True or False: Color tests are used to identify drugs conclusively. _____

36. The _____ color-test reagent turns purple in the presence of heroin.

37. The Duquenois-Levine test is a valuable color test for _____.

38. The _____ test is a widely used color test for cocaine.

39. _____ tests tentatively identify drugs by the size and shape of crystals formed when the drug is mixed with specific reagents.

40. A technique that uses a moving liquid phase and a stationary solid phase to separate mixtures is _____.

41. True or False: Thin-layer chromatography yields the positive identification of a material. _____

42. The process of separating light into its component colors is called _____.

43. True or False: Color is an indication that substances selectively absorb light. _____

44. Visible light and X-rays are only part of the family of radiation waves known as the _____.

45. Red light is (higher, lower) in frequency than violet light.

46. The selective absorption of electromagnetic radiation by materials (can, cannot) be used as an aid for identification.

47. The pattern of a(n) _____ and _____ absorption spectrum suggests a probable identity of a drug.

48. An (infrared, ultraviolet) absorption spectrum provides a unique "fingerprint" of a chemical substance.

49. The study of the absorption of light by chemical substances is known as _____, and the instrument used to measure and record this absorption spectrum is the _____.

50. A mixture's components can be separated by the technique of _____, which separates mixtures on the basis of their distribution between a stationary liquid phase and a moving gas phase.

51. The gas chromatograph, in combination with the _____, can separate the components of a drug mixture and then unequivocally identify each substance present in the mixture.

52. The technique of _____ exposes molecules to a beam of high-energy electrons in order to fragment them.

53. True or False: A mass spectrum is normally considered a specific means for identifying a chemical substance. _____

APPLICATION AND CRITICAL THINKING

1. An individual who has been using a drug for an extended period of time suddenly finds himself unable to secure more of the drug. He acts nervous and irritable and is hyperactive. He seems almost desperate to find more of the drug but experiences no sickness, pain, or other outward physical discomfort. Based on his behavior, what drugs might he possibly have been using? Explain your answer.

2. Following are descriptions of behavior that are characteristic among users of certain classes of drugs. For each description, indicate the class of drug (narcotics, stimulants, etc.) for which the behavior is most characteristic. For each description, also name at least one drug that produces the described effects.

   a) Slurred speech, slow reaction time, impaired judgment, reduced coordination

   b) Intense emotional responses, anxiety, altered sensory perceptions

   c) Alertness, feelings of strength and confidence, rapid speech and movement, decreased appetite

   d) Drowsiness, intense feeling of well-being, relief from pain

3. Following are descriptions of four hypothetical drugs. According to the Controlled Substances Act, under which drug schedule would each substance be classified?

   a) This drug has a high potential for psychological dependence, it currently has accepted medical uses in the United States, and the distributor is not required to report to the U.S. Drug Enforcement Administration.

   b) This drug has medical use in the United States, is not limited by manufacturing quotas, and may be exported without a permit.

   c) This drug must be stored in a vault or safe, requires separate record keeping, and may be distributed with a prescription.

   d) This drug may not be imported or exported without a permit, is subject to manufacturing quotas, and currently has no medical use in the United States.

4. A police officer stops a motorist who is driving erratically and notices a bag of white powder that he suspects is heroin on the front seat of the car. The officer brings the bag to you, a forensic scientist in the local crime lab. Name one screening test that you might perform to determine the presence of heroin. Assuming the powder tests positive for heroin, what should you do next?

5. The figure below shows a chromatogram of a known mixture of barbiturates. Based on this figure, answer the following questions:

   a) What barbiturate detected by the chromatogram had the longest retention time?

   b) Which barbiturate had the shortest retention time?

   c) What is the approximate retention time of amobarbital?

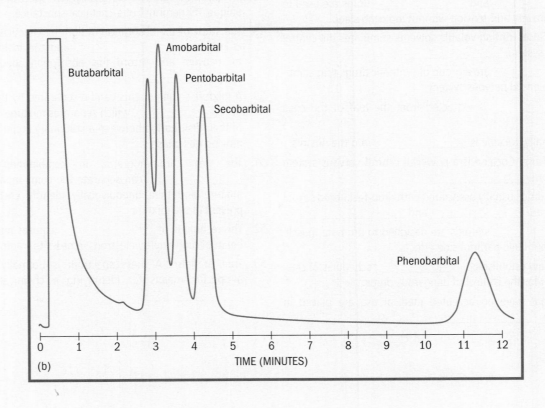

6. When investigating a warehouse for potentially storing illegal drugs, the police collected a variety of drugs. The drugs were tested with presumptive color tests for determining their possible identity. The test tubes shown in the following figure display the positive color tests. Match the drugs on the right with the color tests on the left and name the test.

SAFERSTEIN, RICHARD, Ph.D., CRIMINALISTICS: AN INTRODUCTION TO FORENSIC SCIENCE, 11th Ed., © 2015. Reprinted and Electronically reproduced by permission of Pearson Education, Inc., Upper Saddle River, New Jersey.

ENDNOTE

1. *Marijuana–A Signal of Misunderstanding.* (Washington, DC: U.S. Government Printing Office, 1972), p. 56.

12 Forensic Toxicology

LEARNING OBJECTIVES

After studying this chapter, you should be able to:

- Explain how alcohol is absorbed into the bloodstream, transported throughout the body, and eliminated by oxidation and excretion.
- Understand how alcohol is transported through the circulatory system.
- Understand the process by which alcohol is excreted in the breath via the lungs.
- Understand the concepts of infrared and fuel cell breath-testing devices for alcohol testing.
- Describe commonly employed field sobriety tests to assess alcohol impairment.
- List and contrast laboratory procedures for measuring the concentration of alcohol in the blood.
- Relate the precautions necessary to properly preserve blood in order to analyze its alcohol content.
- Understand the significance of implied-consent laws and the *Schmerber* v. *California* case to traffic enforcement.
- Understand the challenges forensic toxicologists face in their search for drugs and poisons in the human body.
- Describe the proper collection and preservation of toxicological evidence.
- Describe techniques that forensic toxicologists use to isolate and identify drugs and poisons.
- Appreciate the significance of finding a drug in human tissues and organs as it relates to assessing impairment.
- Describe how to coordinate the drug recognition expert (DRE) program with a forensic toxicology finding.

WHAT KILLED NAPOLEON?

Napoleon I, emperor of France, was sent into exile on the remote island of St. Helena by the British after his defeat at the Battle of Waterloo in 1815. St. Helena was hot, unsanitary, and rampant with disease. There, Napoleon was confined to a large, reconstructed, agricultural building known as Longwood House. Boredom and unhealthy living conditions gradually took their toll on Napoleon's mental and physical state. He began suffering from severe abdominal pains and experienced swelling of the ankles and general weakness of his limbs. From the fall of 1820, Napoleon's health began to deteriorate rapidly until he died on May 5, 1821. An autopsy concluded the cause of death was stomach cancer.

Because Napoleon died in British captivity, it was inevitable that numerous conspiratorial theories would develop to account for his death. One of the most fascinating inquiries was conducted by a Swedish dentist, Sven Forshufvud, who systematically correlated the clinical symptoms of Napoleon's last days to those of arsenic poisoning. He published a book in Swedish about this case in 1961. For Forshufvud, the key to unlocking the cause of Napoleon's death rested with Napoleon's hair. Forshufvud arranged to have Napoleon's hair measured for arsenic content by neutron activation analysis and found it consistent with arsenic poisoning. Nevertheless, the cause of Napoleon's demise is still a matter for debate and speculation. Other Napoleon hairs collected in 1805 and 1814 have also shown high concentrations of arsenic, giving rise to the speculation that Napoleon was innocently exposed to arsenic over a long period of time. Even hair collected from Napoleon's three sisters show significant levels of arsenic. Some scientists question whether Napoleon even had the clinical symptoms associated with arsenic poisoning. In truth, forensic science may never be able to answer the question, What killed Napoleon?

Role of Forensic Toxicology

Because the uncontrolled use of drugs has become a worldwide problem affecting all segments of society, the role of the **toxicologist** has taken on new and added significance. Toxicologists detect and identify drugs and poisons in body fluids, tissues, and organs. Their services are required not only in such legal institutions as crime laboratories and medical examiners' offices, but they also reach into hospital laboratories—where identifying a drug overdose may represent the difference between life and death—and into various health facilities that monitor the intake of drugs and other toxic substances. Primary examples include performing blood tests on children exposed to leaded paints and analyzing the urine of addicts enrolled in methadone maintenance programs.

The role of the forensic toxicologist is limited to matters that pertain to violations of criminal law. However, responsibility for performing toxicological services in a criminal justice system varies considerably throughout the United States. In systems with a crime laboratory independent of the medical examiner's office, this responsibility may reside with one or the other, or it may be shared by both. Some systems, however, take advantage of the expertise of government health department laboratories and assign this role to them. Nevertheless, whatever facility handles this work, its caseload will reflect the prevailing popularity of the drugs that are abused in the community. In most cases, this means that the forensic toxicologist handles numerous requests to determine the presence of alcohol in the body.

All of the statistical and medical evidence available shows that ethyl alcohol—a legal, over-the-counter substance—is the most heavily abused drug in Western countries. Forty percent of all traffic deaths in the United States—nearly 17,500 fatalities per year—are alcohol related, along with more than two million injuries that require hospital treatment each year. This highway death toll, as well as the untold damage to life, limb, and property, shows the dangerous consequences of alcohol abuse. Because of the prevalence of alcohol in the toxicologist's work, we will begin by taking a closer look at how the body processes and responds to alcohol.

toxicologist
An individual charged with the responsibility of detecting and identifying the presence of drugs and poisons in body fluids, tissues, and organs.

Quick Review

- Forensic toxicologists detect and identify drugs and poisons in body fluids, tissues, and organs in situations that involve violations of criminal laws.
- Ethyl alcohol is the most heavily abused drug in Western countries.

Toxicology of Alcohol

The subject of the alcohol analysis immediately confronts us with the primary objective of forensic toxicology: to detect and isolate drugs in the body so that their influence on human behavior can be determined. Knowing how the body metabolizes alcohol provides the key to understanding its effects on human behavior. This knowledge has also made possible the development of instruments that measure the presence and concentration of alcohol in individuals suspected of driving while under its influence.

METABOLISM OF ALCOHOL

All chemicals that enter the body are eventually broken down by chemicals within the body and transformed into other chemicals that are easier to eliminate. This process of transformation, called **metabolism**, consists of three basic steps: absorption, distribution, and elimination.

metabolism
The transformation of a chemical in the body to other chemicals for the purpose of facilitating its elimination from the body.

ABSORPTION AND DISTRIBUTION   Alcohol, or ethyl alcohol, is a colorless liquid normally diluted with water and consumed as a beverage. Alcohol appears in the blood within minutes after it has been consumed and slowly increases in concentration while it is being absorbed from the stomach and the small intestine into the bloodstream. During the **absorption** phase, alcohol slowly enters the body's bloodstream and is carried to all parts of the body. When the absorption period is completed, the alcohol becomes distributed uniformly throughout the watery portions of the body—that is, throughout about two-thirds of the body volume. Fat, bones, and hair are low in water content and therefore contain little alcohol, whereas alcohol concentration in the rest of the body is fairly uniform. After absorption is completed, a maximum alcohol level is reached in the blood, and the postabsorption period begins. Then the alcohol concentration slowly decreases until it reaches zero again.

Many factors determine the rate at which alcohol is absorbed into the bloodstream, including the total time taken to consume the drink, the alcohol content of the beverage, the amount consumed, and the quantity and type of food present in the stomach at the time of drinking. With so many variables, it is difficult to predict just how long the absorption process will require. For example, beer is absorbed more slowly than an equivalent concentration of alcohol in water, apparently because of the carbohydrates in beer. Also, alcohol consumed on an empty stomach is absorbed faster than an equivalent amount of alcohol taken when there is food in the stomach (see Figure 12-1).

absorption
The passage of substances such as alcohol across the wall of the stomach and small intestine into the bloodstream.

oxidation
The combination of oxygen with other substances to produce new products.

excretion
The elimination of substances such as alcohol from the body in an unchanged state, typically in breath and urine.

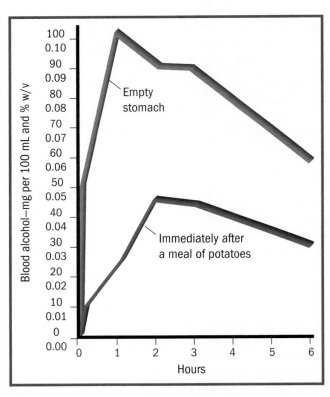

FIGURE 12-1   Blood-alcohol concentrations after ingestion of 2 ounces of pure alcohol mixed in 8 ounces of water (equivalent to about 5 ounces of 80-proof vodka). *Courtesy U.S. Department of Transportation, Washington, D.C.*

ELIMINATION   As the alcohol is circulated by the bloodstream, the body begins to eliminate it. Alcohol is eliminated through two mechanisms: **oxidation** and **excretion**. Nearly all of the alcohol consumed (95 to 98 percent) is eventually oxidized to carbon dioxide and water. Oxidation takes place almost entirely in the liver. There, in the presence of the enzyme "alcohol dehydrogenase," the alcohol is converted into acetaldehyde and then to acetic acid. The acetic acid is subsequently oxidized in practically all parts of the body, becoming carbon dioxide and water.

The remaining alcohol is excreted, unchanged, in the breath, urine, and perspiration. Most significant, the amount of alcohol exhaled in the breath is in direct proportion to the concentration of alcohol in the blood. This observation has had a tremendous impact on the technology and procedures used for blood-alcohol testing. The development of instruments to reliably measure breath for its alcohol content has made possible the testing of millions of people in a quick, safe, and convenient manner.

The fate of alcohol in the body is therefore relatively simple—namely, absorption into the bloodstream, distribution throughout the body's water, and finally, elimination by oxidation and excretion. The elimination, or "burn-off," rate of alcohol varies in different individuals; 0.015 percent w/v (weight per volume) per hour is the average rate after the absorption process is complete.[1] However, this figure is an average that varies by as much as 30 percent among individuals.

BLOOD-ALCOHOL CONCENTRATION   Logically, the most obvious measure of intoxication would be the amount of liquor a person has consumed. Unfortunately, most arrests are made after the fact, when such information is not available to legal authorities; furthermore, even if these data could be collected, numerous related factors, such as body weight and the rate of alcohol's absorption into the body, are so variable that it would be impossible to prescribe uniform standards that would yield reliable alcohol intoxication levels for all individuals.

Theoretically, for a true determination of the quantity of alcohol impairing an individual's normal body functions, it would be best to remove a portion of brain tissue and analyze it for alcohol content. For obvious reasons, this cannot be done on living subjects. Consequently, toxicologists concentrate on the blood, which provides the medium for circulating alcohol throughout the body, carrying it to all tissues including the brain. Fortunately, experimental evidence supports this approach and shows blood-alcohol concentration to be directly proportional to the concentration of alcohol in the brain. From the medicolegal point of view, blood-alcohol levels have become the accepted standard for relating alcohol intake to its effect on the body.

The longer the total time required for complete absorption to occur, the lower the peak alcohol concentration in the blood. Depending on a combination of factors, maximum blood-alcohol concentration may not be reached until two or three hours have elapsed from the time of consumption. However, under normal social drinking conditions, it takes anywhere from 30 to 90 minutes from the time of the final drink until the absorption process is completed.

As noted earlier, alcohol becomes concentrated evenly throughout the watery portions of the body. This knowledge can be useful for the toxicologist analyzing a body for the presence of alcohol. If blood is not available, as in some postmortem situations, a medical examiner can select a water-rich organ or fluid—for example, the brain, cerebrospinal fluid, or vitreous humor—to estimate the body's equivalent blood alcohol content to a reasonable degree of accuracy.

Quick Review

- Alcohol appears in the blood within minutes after it has been taken by mouth. It slowly increases in concentration while it is being absorbed from the stomach and the small intestine into the bloodstream.
- When all the alcohol has been absorbed, a maximum alcohol level is reached in the blood, and the postabsorption period begins. During postabsorption, the alcohol concentration slowly decreases until a zero level is reached.
- Elimination of alcohol throughout the body is accomplished through oxidation and excretion. Oxidation takes place almost entirely in the liver, whereas alcohol is excreted unchanged in the breath, urine, and perspiration.
- Breath-testing devices operate on the principle that the ratio between the concentration of alcohol in alveolar breath and its concentration in blood is fixed.

Testing for Intoxication

From a practical point of view, drawing blood from veins of motorists suspected of being under the influence of alcohol is simply not convenient. The need to transport each suspect to a location where a medically qualified person can draw blood would be costly and time consuming, considering the hundreds of suspects that the average police department must test every year. The methods used must be designed to test hundreds of thousands of motorists annually, without causing them undue physical harm or unreasonable inconvenience, and provide a reliable diagnosis that can be supported

CLOSER ANALYSIS
ALCOHOL IN THE CIRCULATORY SYSTEM

The extent to which an individual may be under the influence of alcohol is usually determined by measuring the quantity of alcohol present in the blood system. Normally, this is accomplished in one of two ways: (1) by analyzing the blood for its alcohol content or (2) by measuring the alcohol content of the breath. In either case, the significance and meaning of the results can better be understood when the movement of alcohol through the circulatory system is studied.

Humans, like all vertebrates, have a closed circulatory system, which consists basically of a heart and numerous arteries, capillaries, and veins. An **artery** is a blood vessel carrying blood away from the heart, and a **vein** is a vessel carrying blood back toward the heart. **Capillaries** are tiny blood vessels that connect the arteries with the veins. The exchange of materials between the blood and the other tissues takes place across the thin walls of the capillaries. A schematic diagram of the circulatory system is shown in Figure 1.

Ingestion and Distribution

Let us now trace the movement of alcohol through the human circulatory system. After alcohol is ingested, it moves down the esophagus

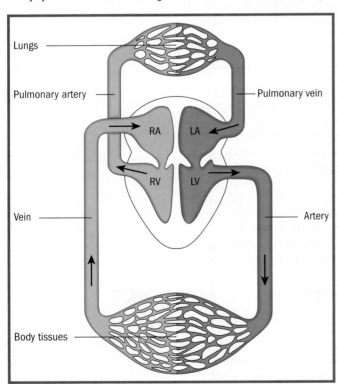

FIGURE 1 A simplified diagram of the human circulatory system. Vessels shown in red contain oxygenated blood; vessels shown in gray contain deoxygenated blood. *SAFERSTEIN, RICHARD, Ph.D., CRIMINALISTICS: AN INTRODUCTION TO FORENSIC SCIENCE, 11th Ed., © 2015. Reprinted and Electronically reproduced by permission of Pearson Education, Inc., Upper Saddle River, New Jersey.*

into the stomach. About 20 percent of the alcohol is absorbed through the stomach walls into the portal vein of the blood system. The remaining alcohol passes into the blood through the walls of the small intestine. Once in the blood, the alcohol is carried to the liver, where enzymes begin to break it down.

As the blood (still carrying the alcohol) leaves the liver, it moves up to the heart. The blood enters the upper-right chamber of the heart, called the "right atrium" (or "auricle"), and is forced into the lower-right chamber of the heart, known as the "right ventricle." Having returned to the heart from its circulation through the tissues, the blood at this time contains very little oxygen and much carbon dioxide. Consequently, the blood must be pumped up to the lungs, through the pulmonary artery, to be replenished with oxygen.

Aeration

In the lungs, the respiratory system bridges with the circulatory system so that oxygen can enter the blood and carbon dioxide can leave it. As shown in Figure 2, the pulmonary artery branches into capillaries lying close to tiny pear-shaped sacs called **alveoli**. The lungs contain about 250 million alveoli, all located at the ends of the bronchial tubes. The bronchial tubes connect to the windpipe (trachea), which leads up to the mouth and nose (see Figure 3). At the surface of the alveolar sacs, blood flowing through the capillaries comes into contact with fresh oxygenated air in the sacs.

A rapid exchange now takes place between the fresh air in the sacs and the spent air in the blood. Oxygen passes through the walls of the alveoli into the blood while carbon dioxide is discharged from the blood into the air. If, during this exchange, alcohol or any other volatile substance is in the blood, it too will pass into the alveoli. During breathing, the carbon dioxide and alcohol are expelled through the nose and mouth, and the alveoli are replenished with fresh oxygenated air breathed into the lungs, allowing the process to begin all over again.

The temperature at which the breath leaves the mouth is normally 34°C. At this temperature, the ratio of alcohol in the blood to alcohol in alveolar air is approximately 2,100 to 1. In other words, 1 milliliter of blood contains nearly the same amount of alcohol as 2,100 milliliters of alveolar breath.

Recirculation and Absorption

Now let's return to the circulating blood. After emerging from the lungs, the oxygenated blood is rushed back to the upper-left chamber of the heart (left atrium) by the pulmonary vein. When the left atrium contracts, it forces the blood through a valve into the left ventricle, which is the lower-left chamber of the heart. The left ventricle then pumps the freshly oxygenated blood into the arteries, which carry the blood to all parts of the body. Each of these

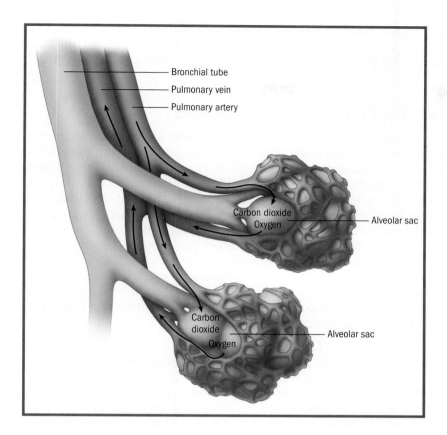

arteries, in turn, branches into smaller arteries, which eventually connect with the numerous tiny capillaries embedded in the tissues. Here the alcohol moves out of the blood and into the tissues. The blood then runs from the capillaries into tiny veins that fuse to form larger veins. These veins eventually lead back to the heart to complete the circuit.

During absorption, the concentration of alcohol in the arterial blood is considerably higher than the concentration of alcohol in the venous blood. One typical study revealed a subject's arterial blood-alcohol level to be 41 percent higher than the venous level 30 minutes after the subject's last drink.[2] This difference is thought to exist because of the rapid diffusion of alcohol into the body tissues from venous blood during the early phases of absorption. Because the administration of a blood test requires drawing venous blood from the arm, this test is clearly to the advantage of a subject who may still be in the absorption stage. However, once absorption is complete, the alcohol becomes equally distributed throughout the blood system.

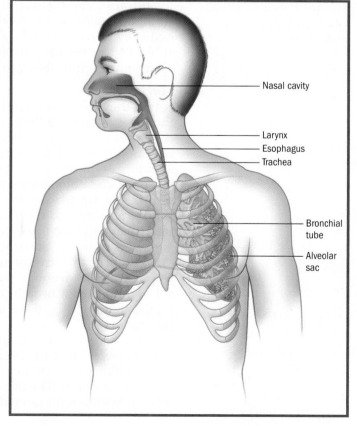

FIGURE 3   The respiratory system. The trachea connects the nose and mouth to the bronchial tubes. The bronchial tubes divide into numerous branches that terminate in the alveoli in the lungs. *SAFERSTEIN, RICHARD, Ph.D., CRIMINALISTICS: AN INTRODUCTION TO FORENSIC SCIENCE, 11th Ed., © 2015. Reprinted and Electronically reproduced by permission of Pearson Education, Inc., Upper Saddle River, New Jersey.*

artery
A blood vessel that carries blood away from the heart.

vein
A blood vessel that transports blood toward the heart.

capillary
A tiny blood vessel that receives blood from arteries and carries it to veins, and across whose walls the exchange of materials between the blood and the tissues takes place.

alveoli
Small sacs in the lungs through whose walls air and other vapors are exchanged between the breath and the blood.

fuel cell detector
A detector in which a chemical reaction involving alcohol produces electricity.

and defended within the framework of the legal system. This means that toxicologists have had to devise rapid and specific procedures for measuring a driver's degree of alcohol intoxication that can be easily administered in the field.

BREATH TESTING FOR ALCOHOL

The most widespread method for rapidly determining alcohol intoxication is breath testing. A breath tester is simply a device for collecting and measuring the alcohol content of alveolar breath. As we saw earlier, alcohol is expelled, unchanged, in the breath of a person who has been drinking. A breath test measures the alcohol concentration in the pulmonary artery by measuring its concentration in alveolar breath. Thus, breath analysis provides an easily obtainable specimen along with a rapid and accurate result.

Breath-test results obtained during the absorption phase may be higher than results obtained from a simultaneous analysis of venous blood. However, the former are more reflective of the concentration of alcohol reaching the brain and therefore more accurately reflect the effects of alcohol on the subject. Again, once absorption is complete, the difference between a blood test and a breath test should be minimal.

BREATH-TEST INSTRUMENTS   The first widely used instrument for measuring the alcohol content of alveolar breath was the "Breathalyzer," developed in 1954 by R. F. Borkenstein, who was a captain in the Indiana State Police. Starting in the 1970s, the Breathalyzer was phased out and replaced by other instruments. Like the Breathalyzer, they assume that the ratio of alcohol in the blood to alcohol in alveolar breath is 2,100 to 1 at a mouth temperature of 34°C. Unlike the Breathalyzer, modern breath testers are free of chemicals. These devices include infrared light–absorption devices (described in the Closer Analysis feature on page 296) and **fuel cell detectors**.

Infrared and fuel-cell-based breath testers are microprocessor controlled, so all an operator has to do is to press a start button; the instrument automatically moves through a sequence of steps and produces a readout of the subject's test results. These instruments also perform self-diagnostic tests to ascertain whether they are in proper operating condition.

CONSIDERATIONS IN BREATH TESTING   An important feature of these instruments is that they can be connected to an external alcohol standard or simulator in the form of either a liquid or a gas. The liquid simulator comprises a known concentration of alcohol in water. It is heated to a controlled temperature and the vapor formed above the liquid is pumped into the instrument. Dry-gas standards typically consist of a known concentration of alcohol mixed with an inert gas and compressed in cylinders. The external standard is automatically sampled by the breath-test instrument before and/or after the subject's breath sample is taken and recorded. Thus the operator can check the accuracy of the instrument against the known alcohol standard.

The key to the accuracy of a breath-testing device is to ensure that the unit captures the alcohol in the alveolar (i.e., deep-lung) breath of the subject. This is typically accomplished by programming the unit to accept no less than 1.1 to 1.5 liters of breath from the subject. Also, the subject must blow for a minimum time (e.g., 6 seconds) with a minimum breath flow rate (e.g., 3 liters per minute).

The breath-test instruments just described feature a "slope detector," which ensures that the breath sample is alveolar, or deep-lung, breath. As the subject blows into the instrument, the breath-alcohol concentration is continuously monitored. The instrument accepts a breath sample only when consecutive measurements fall within a predetermined rate of change. This approach ensures that the sample measurement is deep-lung breath and closely relates to the true blood-alcohol concentration of the subject being tested.

A breath-test operator must take other steps to ensure that the breath-test result truly reflects the actual blood-alcohol concentration within the subject. A major consideration is to avoid measuring "mouth alcohol" resulting from regurgitation, belching, or recent intake of an alcoholic beverage. Also, recent gargling with an alcohol-containing mouthwash can lead to the presence of mouth alcohol. As a result, the alcohol concentration detected in the exhaled breath is higher than the concentration in the alveolar breath. To avoid this possibility, the operator must not allow the subject to take any foreign material into his or her mouth for at least 15 minutes before the breath test. Likewise, the subject should be observed not to have belched or regurgitated during this period. Mouth alcohol has been shown to dissipate after 15 to 20 minutes from its inception.

Measurement of independent breath samples taken within a few minutes of each other is another extremely important check of the integrity of the breath test. Acceptable agreement between the two tests taken minutes apart significantly reduces the possibility of errors caused by the operator, mouth alcohol, instrument component failures, and spurious electric signals.

CLOSER ANALYSIS
INFRARED LIGHT ABSORPTION

In principle, infrared instruments operate no differently than the spectrophotometers described in Chapter 11. An evidential testing instrument that incorporates the principle of infrared light absorption is shown in Figure 1. Any alcohol present in the subject's breath flows into the instrument's breath chamber. As shown in Figure 2, a beam of infrared light is aimed through the chamber. A filter is used to select a wavelength of infrared light at which alcohol will absorb. As the infrared light passes through the chamber, it interacts with the alcohol and causes the light to decrease in intensity. The decrease in light intensity is measured by a photoelectric detector that gives a signal proportional to the concentration of alcohol present in the breath sample. This information is processed by an electronic microprocessor, and the percent blood-alcohol concentration is displayed on a digital readout. Also, the blood-alcohol level is printed on a card to produce a permanent record of the test result. Most infrared breath testers aim a second infrared beam into the same chamber to check for acetone or other chemical interferences on the breath. If the instrument detects differences in the relative response of the two infrared beams that does not conform to ethyl alcohol, the operator is immediately informed of the presence of an "interferant."

FIGURE 1   An infrared breath-testing instrument—the BAC Data Master. *Intoximeters, Inc.*

(continued)

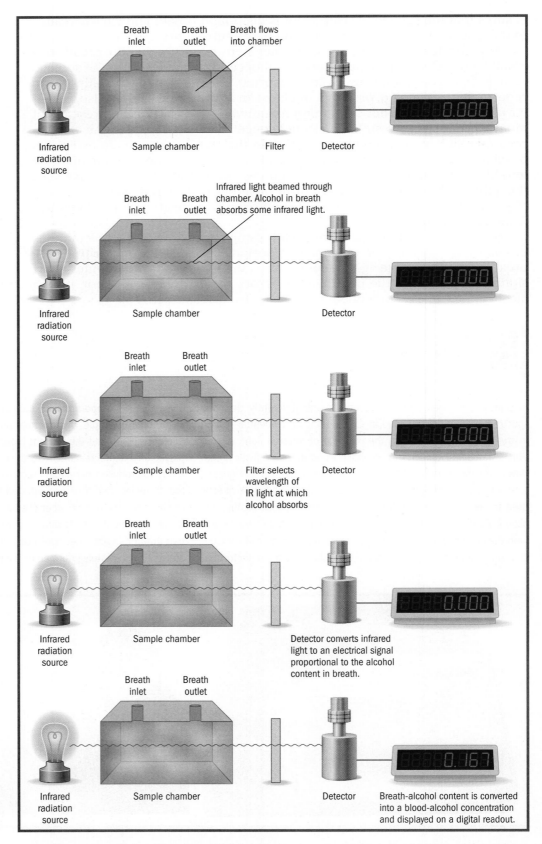

FIGURE 2 A schematic diagram of an infrared breath-testing instrument. *SAFERSTEIN, RICHARD, Ph. D., CRIMINALISTICS: AN INTRODUCTION TO FORENSIC SCIENCE, 11th Ed., © 2015. Reprinted and Electronically reproduced by permission of Pearson Education, Inc., Upper Saddle River, New Jersey.*

CLOSER ANALYSIS
THE FUEL CELL

A fuel cell converts energy arising from a chemical reaction into electro-chemical energy. A typical fuel cell consists of two platinum electrodes separated by an acid- or base-containing porous membrane. A platinum wire connects the electrodes and allows a current to flow between them. In the alcohol fuel cell, one of the electrodes is positioned to come into contact with a subject's breath sample. If alcohol is present in the breath, a reaction at the electrode's surface converts the alcohol to acetic acid. One by-product of this conversion is free electrons, which flow through the connecting wire to the opposite electrode, where they interact with atmospheric oxygen to form water (see figure). The fuel cell also requires the migration of hydrogen ions across the acidic porous membrane to complete the circuit. The strength of the current flow between the two electrodes is proportional to the concentration of alcohol in the breath.

A detector in which chemical reactions are used to produce electricity.
SAFERSTEIN, RICHARD, Ph.D., CRIMINALISTICS: AN INTRODUCTION TO FORENSIC SCIENCE, 11th Ed., © 2015. Reprinted and Electronically reproduced by permission of Pearson Education, Inc., Upper Saddle River, New Jersey.

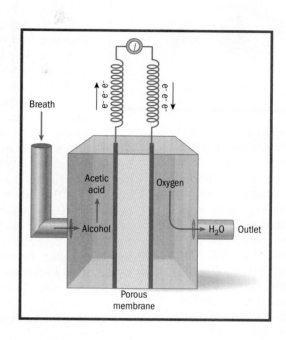

FIELD SOBRIETY TESTING

A police officer who suspects that an individual is under the influence of alcohol usually conducts a series of preliminary tests before ordering the suspect to submit to an evidential breath or blood test. These preliminary, or field, sobriety tests are normally performed to ascertain the degree of the suspect's physical impairment and whether an evidential test is justified.

Field sobriety tests usually consist of a series of psychophysical tests and a preliminary breath test (if such devices are authorized and available for use). A portable, handheld, roadside breath tester is shown in Figure 12-2. This

FIGURE 12-2   The Alco-Sensor IV. *Intoximeters, Inc.*

Eye looking straight ahead

45°

FIGURE 12-3 When a person's blood-alcohol level is in the vicinity of 0.10 percent, jerking of the eye during the horizontal-gaze nystagmus test will begin before the eyeball has moved 45 degrees to the side. *SAFERSTEIN, RICHARD, Ph.D., CRIMINALISTICS: AN INTRODUCTION TO FORENSIC SCIENCE, 11th Ed., © 2015. Reprinted and Electronically reproduced by permission of Pearson Education, Inc., Upper Saddle River, New Jersey.*

device, about the size of a pack of cigarettes, weighs 5 ounces and uses a fuel cell to measure the alcohol content of a breath sample. The fuel cell absorbs the alcohol from the breath sample, oxidizes it, and produces an electrical current proportional to the breath-alcohol content. This instrument can typically be used for three to five years before the fuel cell needs to be replaced. It has been approved for use as an evidential breath tester by the National Highway Traffic Safety Administration.

Horizontal-gaze nystagmus, "walk and turn," and the one-leg stand constitute a series of reliable and effective psychophysical tests. Horizontal-gaze nystagmus is an involuntary jerking of the eye as it moves to the side. A person experiencing nystagmus is usually unaware that the jerking is happening and is unable to stop or control it. The subject being tested is asked to follow a penlight or some other object with his or her eye as far to the side as the eye can go. The more intoxicated the person is, the less the eye has to move toward the side before jerking or nystagmus begins. Usually, when a person's blood-alcohol concentration is in the range of 0.10 percent, the jerking begins before the eyeball has moved 45 degrees to the side (see Figure 12-3). Higher blood-alcohol concentration causes jerking at smaller angles. Also, if the suspect has taken a drug that also causes nystagmus (such as phencyclidine, barbiturates, and other depressants), the nystagmus-onset angle may occur much earlier than would be expected from alcohol alone.

Walk and turn and the one-leg stand are divided-attention tasks, testing the subject's ability to comprehend and execute two or more simple instructions at one time. The ability to understand and simultaneously carry out more than two instructions is significantly affected by increasing blood-alcohol levels. Walk and turn requires the suspect to maintain balance while standing heel-to-toe and at the same time listening to and comprehending the test instructions. During the walking stage, the suspect must walk a straight line, touching heel-to-toe for nine steps, and then turn around on the line and repeat the process. The one-leg stand requires the suspect to maintain balance while standing with heels together listening to the instructions. During the balancing stage, the suspect must stand on one foot while holding the other foot several inches off the ground for 30 seconds; simultaneously, the suspect must count out loud during the 30-second time period.

Quick Review

- Modern breath testers are free of chemicals. They include infrared light absorption devices and fuel cell detectors.
- The key to the accuracy of a breath-testing device is to ensure that the unit captures the alcohol in the alveolar (deep-lung) breath of the subject.
- Many breath testers collect a set volume of breath and expose it to infrared light. The instrument measures the concentration of alcohol in the collected breath sample by measuring the degree of interaction between the light and the alcohol present.
- Law enforcement officers use field sobriety tests to estimate a motorist's degree of physical impairment from alcohol and to determine whether an evidential test for alcohol is justified.
- The horizontal-gaze nystagmus test, the walk and turn, and the one-leg stand are all considered reliable and effective psychophysical tests for alcohol impairment.

Analysis of Blood for Alcohol

Gas chromatography is the approach most widely used by forensic toxicologists for determining alcohol levels in blood. Under proper gas chromatographic conditions, alcohol can be separated from other volatile substances in the blood. By comparing the resultant alcohol peak area to ones obtained from known blood-alcohol standards, the investigator can calculate the alcohol level with a high degree of accuracy (see Figure 12-4).

Another procedure for alcohol analysis involves the oxidation of alcohol to acetaldehyde. This reaction is carried out in the presence of the enzyme alcohol dehydrogenase and the coenzyme nicotin-amide-adenine dinucleotide (NAD). As the oxidation proceeds, NAD is converted into another chemical species, NADH. The extent of this conversion is measured by a spectrophotometer and is related to alcohol concentration. This approach to blood-alcohol testing is normally associated with instruments used in clinical or hospital settings. Instead, forensic laboratories normally use gas chromatography for determining blood-alcohol content.

COLLECTION AND PRESERVATION OF BLOOD

Blood must always be drawn under medically acceptable conditions by a qualified individual. A nonalcoholic disinfectant should be applied before the suspect's skin is penetrated with a sterile needle or lancet. It is important to eliminate any possibility that an alcoholic disinfectant could inadvertently contribute to a falsely high blood-alcohol result. Nonalcoholic disinfectants such as aqueous benzalkonium chloride (Zepiran), aqueous mercuric chloride, or povidone-iodine (Betadine) are recommended for this purpose.

Once blood is removed from an individual, it is best preserved sealed in an airtight container after adding an anticoagulant and a preservative. The blood should be stored in a refrigerator until delivery to the toxicology laboratory. The addition of an **anticoagulant**, such as EDTA or potassium oxalate, prevents clotting; a **preservative**, such as sodium fluoride, inhibits the growth of microorganisms capable of destroying alcohol.

One study performed to determine the stability of alcohol in blood removed from living individuals found that the most significant factors affecting alcohol's stability in blood are storage temperature, the presence of a preservative, and the length of storage.[3] Not a single blood specimen examined showed an

anticoagulant
A substance that prevents coagulation or clotting of the blood.

preservative
A substance that stops the growth of microorganisms in blood.

FIGURE 12-4 A gas chromatograph showing ethyl alcohol (ethanol) in whole blood. *SAFERSTEIN, RICHARD, Ph.D., CRIMINALISTICS: AN INTRODUCTION TO FORENSIC SCIENCE, 11th Ed., © 2015. Reprinted and Electronically reproduced by permission of Pearson Education, Inc., Upper Saddle River, New Jersey.*

increase in alcohol level with time. Failure to keep the blood refrigerated or to add sodium fluoride resulted in a substantial decline in alcohol concentration. Longer storage times also reduced blood-alcohol levels. Hence, failure to adhere to any of the proper preservation requirements for blood works to the benefit of the suspect and to the detriment of society.

The collection of postmortem blood samples for alcohol-level determinations requires added precautions. Ethyl alcohol may be generated in the body of a deceased individual as a result of bacterial action. Therefore, it is best to collect a number of blood samples from different body sites. For example, blood may be removed from the heart and from the femoral vein (in the leg) and cubital vein (in the arm). Each sample should be placed in a clean, airtight container containing an anticoagulant and sodium fluoride preservative and should be refrigerated. Blood-alcohol levels can be attributed solely to alcohol consumption if they are nearly similar in all blood samples collected from the same person. As an alternative to blood collection, the collection of vitreous humor and urine is recommended. Vitreous humor and urine usually do not experience any significant postmortem ethyl alcohol production.

Quick Review

- Gas chromatography is the most widely used approach for determining blood-alcohol levels in forensic laboratories.
- An anticoagulant should be added to a blood sample to prevent clotting; a preservative should be added to inhibit the growth of microorganisms capable of destroying alcohol.

Alcohol and the Law

Constitutionally, every state in the United States must establish and administer statutes regulating the operation of motor vehicles. Although such an arrangement might encourage diverse laws defining permissible blood-alcohol levels, this has not been the case. Since the 1930s, both the American Medical Association and the National Safety Council have exerted considerable influence in persuading the states to establish uniform and reasonable blood-alcohol standards.

BLOOD-ALCOHOL LAWS

The American Medical Association and the National Safety Council initially recommended that a person with a blood-alcohol concentration in excess of 0.15 percent w/v was to be considered under the influence of alcohol.[4] However, subsequent experimental studies showed a clear correlation between drinking and driving impairment at blood-alcohol levels much below 0.15 percent w/v. These findings eventually led to a lowering of the blood-concentration standard for intoxication from 0.15 percent w/v to its current 0.08 percent w/v.

In 1992, the U.S. Department of Transportation (DOT) recommended that states adopt 0.08 percent blood-alcohol concentration as the legal measure of drunk driving. This recommendation was enacted into federal law in 2000. All fifty states have now established "per se laws," meaning that any individual meeting or exceeding a defined blood-alcohol level (usually 0.08 percent) shall be deemed intoxicated. No other proof of alcohol impairment is necessary. Starting in 2003, states that had not adopted the 0.08 percent per se level stood to lose part of their federal funds for highway construction. The 0.08 percent level applies only to noncommercial drivers, as the federal government has set the maximum allowable blood-alcohol concentration for commercial truck and bus drivers at 0.04 percent.

Several other Western countries have also set 0.08 percent w/v as the blood-alcohol level above which it is an offense to drive a motor vehicle, including Canada, Italy, Switzerland, and the United Kingdom. Finland, France, Germany, Ireland, Japan, the Netherlands, and Norway have a 0.05 percent limit, as do the Australian states. Sweden has lowered its blood-alcohol concentration limit to 0.02 percent.

As shown in Figure 12-5, a driver with a blood-alcohol level of 0.08 percent is about four times as likely to become involved in an automobile accident than a sober individual. At the 0.15 percent level, the chances of an automobile accident are twenty-five times higher than those for a sober driver. To estimate the relationship of blood-alcohol levels to body weight and the quantity of 80-proof liquor consumed, refer to Figure 12-6.

CONSTITUTIONAL ISSUES

The Fifth Amendment to the U.S. Constitution guarantees all citizens protection against self-incrimination—that is, against being forced to make an admission that would prove one's own guilt in a legal matter. Because consenting to a

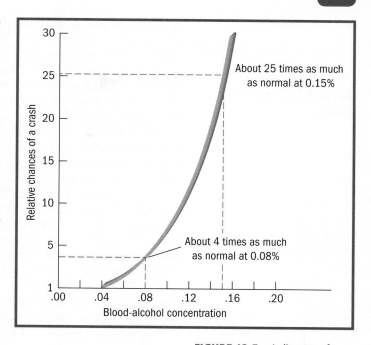

FIGURE 12-5   A diagram of increased driving risk in relation to blood-alcohol concentration. *U.S. Department of Transportation*

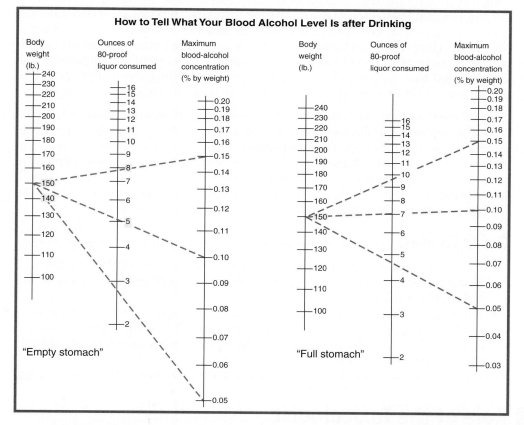

FIGURE 12-6   To use this diagram, lay a straight edge across your weight and the number of ounces of liquor you've consumed on an empty or full stomach. The point where the edge hits the right-hand column is your maximum blood-alcohol level. The rate of elimination of alcohol from the bloodstream is approximately 0.015 percent per hour. Therefore, to calculate your actual blood-alcohol level, subtract 0.015 from the number indicated in the right-hand column for each hour from the start of drinking. *U.S. Department of Transportation*

WebExtra 12.1

Calculate Your Blood-Alcohol Level

WebExtra 12.2

See How Alcohol Affects Your Behavior

breath test for alcohol might be considered a form of self-incrimination, the National Highway Traffic Safety Administration recommended an "implied-consent law" to prevent a person from refusing to take a test on those constitutional grounds. This law states that the operator of a motor vehicle on a public highway must either consent to a test for alcohol intoxication, if requested, or lose his or her license for some designated period—usually six months to one year.

In 1966, the Supreme Court, in *Schmerber* v. *California*,[5] addressed the constitutionality of collecting a blood specimen for alcohol testing, as well as for obtaining other types of physical evidence from a suspect without consent. While being treated at a Los Angeles hospital for injuries sustained in an automobile collision, Schmerber was arrested for driving under the influence of alcohol. A physician took a blood sample from Schmerber at the direction of the police, over the objection of the defendant. On appeal to the U.S. Supreme Court, the defendant argued that his privilege against self-incrimination had been violated by the introduction of the results of the blood test at his trial. The Court ruled against the defendant, reasoning that the Fifth Amendment prohibits only compelling a suspect to give "testimonial" evidence that may be self-incriminating; being compelled to furnish "physical" evidence, such as fingerprints, photographs, measurements, and blood samples, the Court ruled, was not protected by the Fifth Amendment.

The Court also addressed the question of whether Schmerber was subjected to an unreasonable search and seizure by the taking of a blood specimen without a search warrant. In the 1966 decision, the Court upheld the blood removal, reasoning that the natural body elimination of alcohol created an emergency situation allowing for a warrantless search. The Court revisited this issue once again forty-seven years after Schmerber in the case of *Missouri v. McNeely*.[6] Here, the Court addressed the issue as to whether the natural elimination of alcohol in blood categorically justifies a warrantless intrusion. The Court noted that advances in communication technology now allow police to obtain a warrant quickly by phone, e-mail, or teleconferencing.

> In those drunk-driving investigations where police officers can reasonably obtain a warrant before a blood sample can be drawn without significantly undermining the efficacy of the search, the Fourth Amendment mandates that they do so. . . . In short, while the natural dissipation of alcohol in the blood may support a finding of exigency in a specific case, as it did in Schmerber, it does not do so categorically. Whether a warrantless blood test of a drunk-driving suspect is reasonable must be determined case by case based on the totality of the circumstances.

Quick Review

- The current legal measure of drunk driving in the United States is a blood-alcohol concentration of 0.08 percent, or 0.08 grams of alcohol per 100 milliliters of blood.
- The implied-consent law states that the operator of a motor vehicle on a public highway must either consent to a test for alcohol intoxication, if requested, or lose his or her license for some designated period—usually six months to one year.

Role of the Toxicologist

Once the forensic toxicologist ventures beyond the analysis of alcohol, he or she encounters an encyclopedic maze of drugs and poisons. Even a cursory discussion of the problems and handicaps imposed on toxicologists is enough to engender an appreciation for their accomplishments and ingenuity.

CHALLENGES FACING THE TOXICOLOGIST

The toxicologist is presented with body fluids and/or organs and asked to examine them for drugs and poisons. When he or she is fortunate, which is not often, some clue about the type of toxic substance present may develop from the victim's symptoms, a postmortem pathological examination, an examination of the victim's personal effects, or the nearby presence of empty drug containers or household chemicals. Without such supportive information, the toxicologist must use general screening procedures with the hope of narrowing thousands of possibilities to one.

If this task does not seem monumental, consider that the toxicologist is not dealing with drugs at the concentration levels found in powders and pills. By the time a drug specimen reaches the toxicology laboratory, it has been dissipated and distributed throughout the body. The drug analyst may have gram or milligram quantities of material to work with, but the toxicologist must be satisfied with amounts in nanograms or, at best, micrograms, acquired only after being carefully extracted from body fluids and organs.

Furthermore, the body is an active chemistry laboratory, and no one can appreciate this observation more than a toxicologist. Few substances enter and completely leave the body in the same chemical state. The drug that is injected is not always the substance extracted from the body tissues. Therefore, a thorough understanding of how the body alters or metabolizes the chemical structure of a drug is essential in detecting its presence.

It would, for example, be futile and frustrating to search exhaustively for heroin in the human body. This drug is almost immediately metabolized to morphine on entering the bloodstream. Even with this information, the search may still prove impossible unless the examiner also knows that only a small percentage of morphine is excreted unchanged in urine. For the most part, morphine becomes chemically bonded to body carbohydrates before being eliminated in urine. Thus, successful detection of morphine requires that its extraction be planned in accordance with a knowledge of its chemical fate in the body.

Another example of why a toxicologist needs to know how different drugs metabolize in the body is provided by the investigation of the death of Anna Nicole Smith. In her case, the sedative chloral hydrate was a major contributor to her death, but its presence was confirmed by detecting its active metabolite, trichloroethanol (see the Case File on page 306).

Last, when and if the toxicologist has surmounted all of these obstacles and has finally detected, identified, and quantitated a drug or poison, he or she must assess the substance's toxicity. Fortunately, there is published information relating to the toxic levels of most drugs. However, even when such data are available, their interpretation must assume that the victim's physiological behavior agrees with that of subjects of previous studies. Such an assumption may not be entirely valid without knowing the subject's case history. No experienced toxicologist would be surprised to find an individual tolerating a toxic level of a drug that would have killed most other people.

COLLECTION AND PRESERVATION OF TOXICOLOGICAL EVIDENCE

The toxicologist's capabilities depend directly on input from the attending physician, medical examiner, and police investigator. It is a tribute to forensic toxicologists, who often must labor under conditions that do not afford such cooperation, that they can achieve the high level of proficiency that they do.

Generally, when questions about drug use involve a deceased person, the medical examiner decides what biological specimens must be shipped to the toxicology laboratory for analysis. However, a living person suspected of

■■■■ ■ CASEFILES ■■■■

CELEBRITY TOXICOLOGY:
MICHAEL JACKSON—THE DEMISE OF A SUPERSTAR

A call to 911 had the desperate tone of urgency. The voice of a young man implored an ambulance to hurry to the home of pop star Michael Jackson. The unconscious performer was in cardiac arrest and was not responding to CPR. The fifty-year-old Jackson was pronounced dead on arrival at a regional medical center. When the initial autopsy results revealed no signs of foul play, rumors immediately began to swirl around a drug-related death. News media coverage showed investigators carrying bags full of medical supplies out of the Jackson residence. Therefore, it came as no surprise when the forensic toxicology report accompanying Jackson's autopsy showed that the entertainer had died of a drug overdose.

Apparently, Jackson had become accustomed to receiving sedatives to help him sleep. On the morning of his death, his physician stated that he administered valium to Mr. Jackson. Further, at 2:00 a.m., he administered the sedative lorazepam, and at 3:00 a.m. the physician administered another sedative, midazolam. Those drugs were administered again at 5:00 a.m. and 7:30 a.m., but Mr. Jackson still was unable to sleep. Finally, at about 10:40 a.m., Jackson's doctor gave him 25 milligrams of propofol, at which point Mr. Jackson went to sleep. Propofol is a powerful sedative that is used principally for the maintenance of surgical anesthesia. All of the drugs administered to Jackson were sedatives that act in concert to depress the activities of the central nervous system, so it comes as no surprise that this drug cocktail resulted in cardiac arrest and death.

Michael Jackson. *Justin Sullivan/Pool/AP Images*

being under the influence of a drug presents a completely different problem, and few options are available. In this case, an entire urine void (i.e., urine sample) is collected and submitted for toxicological analysis. Preferably, two consecutive voids should be collected in separate specimen containers.

When a licensed physician or registered nurse is available, a sample of blood should also be collected. The amount of blood taken depends on the type of examination to be conducted. Comprehensive toxicological tests for drugs and poisons can conveniently be carried out on a minimum of 10 milliliters of blood. A determination solely for the presence of alcohol will require much less—approximately 5 milliliters of blood. However, many therapeutic drugs, such as tranquilizers and barbiturates, taken in combination with a small, non-intoxicating amount of alcohol, produce behavioral patterns resembling alcohol intoxication. For this reason, the toxicologist must be given enough blood to perform a comprehensive analysis for drugs in cases in which only low alcohol concentrations are discovered.

TECHNIQUES USED IN TOXICOLOGY

For the toxicologist, the upsurge in drug use and abuse has meant that the overwhelming majority of fatal and nonfatal toxic agents are drugs. Not surprisingly, a relatively small number of drugs—namely, those discussed

■■■■ CASEFILES ■■■■
ACCIDENTAL OVERDOSE:
THE TRAGEDY OF ANNA NICOLE SMITH

Rumors exploded in the media when former model, Playboy playmate, reality television star, and favorite tabloid subject Anna Nicole Smith was found unconscious at age 39 in her hotel room at the Seminole Hard Rock Hotel and Casino in Hollywood, Florida. She was taken to Memorial Legal Hospital, where she was declared dead. Postmortem analysis of Smith's blood revealed an array of prescribed medications. Most pronounced was a toxic level of a metabolite of the sedative chloral hydrate. Some of the contents of the toxicology report from Smith's autopsy are shown here.

Anna Nicole Smith. *Manuel Balce Cenet/Landov Media*

FINAL PATHOLOGICAL DIAGNOSES

I. ACUTE COMBINED DRUG INTOXICATION
   A. Toxic/legal drug: Chloral Hydrate (Noctec)

1. Trichloroethanol (TCE)	75 mg/L	(active metabolite)
2. Trichloroacetic acid (TCA)	85 mg/L	(inactive metabolite)

   B. Therapeutic drugs:

1. Diphenhydramine (Benadryl)	0.11 mg/L
2. Clonazepam (Klonopin)	0.04 mg/L
3. Diazepam (Valium)	0.21 mg/L
4. Nordiazepam (metabolite)	0.38 mg/L
5. Temazepam (metabolite)	0.09 mg/L
6. Oxazepam	0.09 mg/L
7. Lorazepam	0.022 mg/L

   C. Other noncontributory drugs present (atropine, topiramate, ciprofloxacin, acetaminophen)

Although many of the drugs present were detected at levels consistent with typical doses of the prescribed medications, it was their presence in combination with chloral hydrate that exacerbated the toxic level of chloral hydrate. The lethal combination of these prescription drugs caused failure of both her circulatory and respiratory systems and resulted in her death. The investigators determined that the overdose of chloral hydrate and other drugs was accidental and not a suicide. This was because of the nonexcessive levels of most of the prescription medications and the discovery of a significant amount of chloral hydrate still remaining in its original container; had she intended to kill herself, she probably would have ingested it all. Anna Nicole Smith was a victim of accidental overmedication.

in Chapter 11—compose nearly all the toxic agents encountered. Of these, alcohol, marijuana, and cocaine account for at least 90 percent of the drugs encountered by toxicologists in a typical toxicology laboratory.

ACIDS AND BASES Like the drug analyst, the toxicologist must devise an analytical scheme to detect, isolate, and identify a toxic substance. The first chore is to remove and isolate drugs and other toxic agents from the biological materials submitted as evidence. Because drugs constitute a large portion of the toxic materials found, a good deal of effort must be devoted to their extraction and detection. So many different procedures are used that a useful description of them would be too detailed for this text. We can best understand the underlying principle of drug extraction by observing that many drugs fall into the categories of **acids** and **bases**.

By controlling the acidity or basicity (i.e., **pH**) of a water solution into which blood, urine, or tissues are dissolved, the toxicologist can control the type of drug that is recovered. For example, acidic drugs are easily extracted

acid
A compound capable of donating a hydrogen ion (H^+) to another compound.

base
A compound capable of accepting a hydrogen ion (H^+).

pH
A symbol used to express the basicity or acidity of a substance. A pH of 7 is neutral; lower values are acidic, and higher values are basic.

from an acidified water solution (i.e., with a pH of less than 7) with organic solvents such as chloroform. Similarly, basic drugs are readily removed from a basic water solution (i.e., with a pH of greater than 7) with organic solvents. This simple approach gives the toxicologist a general technique for extracting and categorizing drugs. Some of the more commonly encountered drugs may be classified as follows:

Acid Drugs	**Basic Drugs**
Barbiturates	Phencyclidine
Acetylsalicylic acid (aspirin)	Methadone
	Amphetamines
	Cocaine

SCREENING AND CONFIRMATION   Once the specimen has been extracted and divided into acidic and basic fractions, the toxicologist can identify the drugs present. The strategy for identifying abused drugs entails a two-step approach: "screening" and "confirmation" (see Figure 12-7). A screening test normally gives quick insight into the likelihood that a specimen contains a drug substance. This test allows a toxicologist to examine a large number of specimens within a short period of time for a wide range of drugs. Any positive results from a screening test are tentative at best and must be verified with a confirmation test.

Screening Tests. The three most widely used screening tests are thin-layer chromatography (TLC), gas chromatography (GC), and immunoassay. The techniques of GC and TLC were described in Chapter 10. The third technique, immunoassay, has proved to be a useful screening tool in toxicology laboratories. Its principles are very different from any of the analytical techniques we have discussed so far. Basically, immunoassay is based on specific drug antibody reactions. We will learn about this concept in Chapter 15. The primary advantage of immunoassay is its ability to detect small concentrations of drugs in body fluids and organs. In fact, this technique provides the best approach for detecting the low drug levels normally associated with smoking marijuana.

Confirmation Tests. A positive screening test may be due to a substance's close chemical structure to an abused drug. For this reason, the toxicologist must follow up any positive screening test with a confirmation test. Because of the potential legal impact of the results of a drug finding on an individual, only the most conclusive confirmation procedures should be used.

Gas chromatography/mass spectrometry is generally accepted as the confirmation test of choice. As we learned in Chapter 11, the combination of gas chromatography and mass spectrometry provides a one-step confirmation test of unequaled sensitivity and specificity. Figure 12-8 illustrates the process. After being introduced to the gas chromatograph, the sample is separated into its components. When the separated sample component leaves the column of the gas chromatograph, it enters the mass spectrometer, where it is bombarded with high-energy electrons. This bombardment causes the sample to break up into fragments, producing a fragmentation pattern, or mass spectrum, for each sample. For most compounds, the mass spectrum represents a unique pattern that can be used for identification.

There is tremendous interest in drug-testing programs for use not only in criminal matters but in industry and government as well.

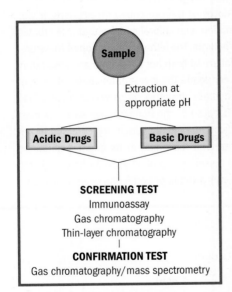

FIGURE 12-7 Biological fluids and tissues are extracted for acidic and basic drugs by controlling the pH of a water solution in which they are dissolved. Once this is accomplished, the toxicologist analyzes for drugs by using screening and confirmation test procedures. *SAFERSTEIN, RICHARD, Ph.D., CRIMINALISTICS: AN INTRODUCTION TO FORENSIC SCIENCE, 11th Ed., © 2015. Reprinted and Electronically reproduced by permission of Pearson Education, Inc., Upper Saddle River, New Jersey.*

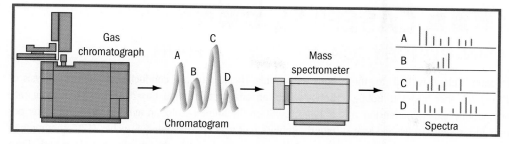

FIGURE 12-8 The combination of the gas chromatograph and the mass spectrometer enables forensic toxicologists to separate the components of a drug mixture and enables the specific identification of a drug substance. *SAFERSTEIN, RICHARD, Ph.D., CRIMINALISTICS: AN INTRODUCTION TO FORENSIC SCIENCE, 11th Ed., © 2015. Reprinted and Electronically reproduced by permission of Pearson Education, Inc., Upper Saddle River, New Jersey.*

Submitting job applicants and employees in the workplace to urine testing for drugs is becoming common practice. Likewise, the U.S. military has an extensive urine-testing program for its members. Many urine-testing programs rely on private laboratories to perform the required analyses. In any case, when the drug-test results may form the basis for taking action against an individual, both a screening and confirmation test must be incorporated into the testing protocol to ensure the integrity of the laboratory's conclusions.

DETECTING DRUGS IN HAIR When a forensic toxicological examination on a living person is required, the interests of speed and practicality limit the specimens taken to blood and urine. Most drugs remain in the bloodstream for about 24 hours; in urine, they normally are present for up to 72 hours. However, it may be necessary to go farther back in time to ascertain whether a subject has been abusing a drug. If so, the only viable alternative to blood and urine specimens is head hair.

Hair is nourished by blood flowing through capillaries located close to the hair root. Drugs present in blood diffuse through the capillary walls into the base of the hair and become permanently entrapped in the hair's hardening protein structure. As the hair continues to grow, the drug's location on the hair shaft becomes a historical marker for delineating the onset of drug intake. Given that the average human head hair grows at the rate of 1 centimeter per month, analyzing segments of hair for drug content may define the timeline of drug use, tracing it back over a period of weeks, months, or possibly years, depending on the hair's length.

However, caution is required in interpreting the timeline. The chronology of drug intake may be distorted by drugs that have penetrated the hair's surface as a result of environmental exposure or by drugs that have entered the hair's surface through sweat. Nevertheless, drug hair analysis is the only viable approach for measuring long-term abuse of a drug.

DETECTING NONDRUG POISONS Although forensic toxicologists devote most of their efforts to detecting drugs, they also test for a wide variety of other toxic substances. Some of these are rare elements, not widely or commercially available. Others are so common that virtually everyone is exposed to nontoxic amounts of them every day.

Heavy Metals. One group of poisons once commonly encountered in criminal cases of murder are known as "heavy metals." They include arsenic, bismuth, antimony, mercury, and thallium. These days, however, the forensic toxicologist only occasionally encounters heavy metals because severe environmental protection regulations restrict their availability to the general public. Nevertheless, as the following Case File makes clear, their use is by no means only a historical curiosity.

■■■■ CASEFILES ■■■■

JOANN CURLEY: CAUGHT BY A HAIR

A vibrant young woman named Joann Curley rushed to the Wilkes-Barre (Pennsylvania) General Hospital—her husband, Bobby, required immediate medical attention. Bobby was experiencing a burning sensation in his feet, numbness in his hands, a flushed face, and intense sweating. After being discharged, Bobby experienced another bout of debilitating pain and numbness. He was admitted to another hospital. There doctors observed extreme alopecia, or hair loss.

Test results of Bobby's urine showed high levels of the heavy metal thallium in his body. Thallium, a rare and highly toxic metal that was used decades ago in substances such as rat poison and to treat ringworm and gout, was found in sufficient quantities to cause Bobby's sickness. The use of thallium had been banned in the United States in 1984. Now, at least, Bobby could be treated. However, before Bobby's doctors could begin treating him for thallium poisoning, he experienced cardiac arrest and slipped into a coma. Joann Curley made the difficult decision to remove her husband of thirteen months from life-supporting equipment. He died shortly thereafter.

Investigators learned that Bobby had changed his life insurance to list his wife, Joann, as the beneficiary of his $300,000 policy. Based on this information, police consulted a forensic toxicologist in an effort to glean as much from the physical evidence in Bobby Curley's body as possible. The toxicologist conducted segmental analysis of Bobby's hair, an analytical method based on the predictable rate of hair growth on the human scalp: an average of 1 centimeter per month. Bobby's hair was approximately 5 inches (12.5 centimeters) long, which represents almost twelve months of hair growth. Each section tested represented a specific period of time in the final year of Bobby's life.

The hair analysis confirmed that Bobby Curley had been poisoned with thallium. The first few doses were small, which probably barely made him feel sick at the time. Gradually, over a year or more, Bobby was receiving more doses of thallium until he finally succumbed to a massive dose three or four days before his death. After careful scrutiny of the timeline, investigators concluded that only Joann Curley had access to Bobby during each of these intervals. She also had motive, in the amount of $300,000.

Presented with the timeline and the solid toxicological evidence against her, Joann Curley pleaded guilty to murder. As part of her plea agreement, she provided a forty-page written confession of how she haphazardly dosed Bobby with rat poison she had found in her basement. She admitted that she murdered him for the money she would receive from Bobby's life insurance policy.

FIGURE 12-9 Intentionally inhaling carbon monoxide fumes from an automobile is a common way to commit suicide.

To screen for many of these metals, the investigator may dissolve the suspect body fluid or tissue in a hydrochloric acid solution and insert a copper strip into the solution. This process is known as the "Reinsch test." The appearance of a silvery or dark coating on the copper indicates the presence of a heavy metal. Such a finding must be confirmed by analytical techniques suitable for inorganic analysis—namely, emission spectroscopy, or X-ray diffraction.

Carbon Monoxide. Unlike heavy metals, carbon monoxide is still one of the most common poisons encountered in a forensic laboratory. Inhaling the carbon monoxide from automobile exhaust fumes is a relatively common way to commit suicide (see Figure 12-9). The victim typically uses a garden or vacuum cleaner hose to connect the tailpipe with the vehicle's interior or allows the engine to run in a closed garage: A level of carbon monoxide sufficient to cause death accumulates in 5 to 10 minutes in a closed single-car garage.

When carbon monoxide enters the human body, it is primarily absorbed by the red blood cells, where it combines with hemoglobin to form carboxyhemoglobin. An average red blood cell contains about 280 million molecules of hemoglobin. Oxygen normally combines with hemoglobin, which transports the oxygen throughout the body. However, if a high percentage of the hemoglobin combines with carbon monoxide, not enough is left to carry sufficient oxygen to the tissues, and death by asphyxiation quickly follows.

There are two basic methods for measuring the concentration of carbon monoxide in the blood: Spectrophotometric methods examine the visible spectrum of blood to determine the amount of carboxyhemoglobin relative to oxyhemoglobin or total hemoglobin. Alternatively, a volume of blood can be treated with a reagent to liberate the carbon monoxide, which is then measured by gas chromatography.

The amount of carbon monoxide in blood is generally expressed as "percent saturation." This represents the extent to which the available hemoglobin has been converted to carboxyhemoglobin. The transition from normal or occupational levels of carbon monoxide to toxic levels is not sharply defined. It varies with, among other things, the age, health, and general fitness of each individual. In a healthy middle-age individual, a carbon monoxide blood saturation greater than 50 to 60 percent is considered fatal. However, in combination with alcohol or other depressants, fatal levels may be significantly lower. For instance, a carbon monoxide saturation of 35 to 40 percent may prove fatal in the presence of a blood-alcohol concentration of 0.20 percent w/v. Interestingly, chain smokers may have a constant carbon monoxide level of 8 to 10 percent in normal circumstances because of the carbon monoxide present in cigarette smoke.

The level of carbon monoxide in the blood of a victim found dead at the scene of a fire can help ascertain whether foul play has occurred. High levels of carbon monoxide in the blood prove that the victim breathed the combustion products of the fire and was therefore alive when the fire began. By contrast, low levels of carbon monoxide indicate that the victim was probably dead before the fire started, and may have been deliberately placed at the scene in order to destroy the body. Many attempts at covering up a murder by setting fire to a victim's house or car have been uncovered in this manner.

SIGNIFICANCE OF TOXICOLOGICAL FINDINGS

Once a drug is found and identified, the toxicologist assesses its influence on the behavior of the individual. Interpreting the results of a toxicology finding is one of the toxicologist's most difficult chores. Recall that many countries have designated a specific blood-alcohol level at which an individual is deemed to be under the influence of alcohol. These levels were established as a result of numerous studies conducted over several years to measure the effects of alcohol levels on driving performance. However, no such legal guidelines are available to the toxicologist who must judge how a drug other than alcohol affects an individual's performance or physical state.

For many drugs, blood concentration levels are readily determined and can be used to estimate the pharmacological effects of the drug on the individual. Often, when dealing with a living person, the toxicologist has the added benefit of knowing what a police officer may have observed about an individual's behavior and motor skills. For a deceased person, drug levels in various body organs and tissues provide additional information about the individual's state at the time of death. However, before drawing conclusions about drug-induced behavior, the analyst must consider other factors, including the age, physical condition, and tolerance of the drug user.

With prolonged use of a drug, an individual may become less responsive to a drug's effects and tolerate blood concentrations of the drug that would kill a casual drug user. Therefore, knowledge of an individual's history of drug use is important in evaluating drug concentrations. Another consideration is the additive or synergistic effects of the interaction of two or more drugs, which may produce a highly intoxicated or comatose state even though none of the drugs alone is present in high or toxic levels. The combination of alcohol with barbiturates or narcotics is a common example of a potentially lethal drug combination.

The amount of a drug in urine is a poor indicator of how extensively an individual's behavior or state is influenced by the drug. Urine is formed outside the body's circulatory system, and consequently drug levels can build up in it over a relatively long period of time. Some drugs are found in the urine one to three days after they have been taken and long after their effects on the user have disappeared. Nevertheless, the value of this information should not be discounted. Urine drug levels, like blood levels, are best used by law enforcement authorities and the courts to corroborate other investigative and medical findings regarding an individual's condition. Hence, for an individual arrested under suspicion of being under the influence of a drug, a toxicologist's determinations supplement the observations of the arresting officer, including the results of field sobriety tests and a drug influence evaluation (discussed in the following section).

For a deceased person, the medical examiner or coroner must establish a cause of death. However, before a conclusive determination is made, the examining physician depends on the forensic toxicologist to demonstrate the presence or absence of a drug or poison in the tissues or body fluids of the deceased. Only through the combined efforts of the toxicologist and the medical examiner or coroner can society be assured that death investigations achieve high professional and legal standards.

Drug Recognition Experts

Although recognizing alcohol-impaired performance is an expertise generally accorded to police officers by the courts, recognizing drug-induced intoxication is much more difficult and generally not part of police training. During the 1970s, the Los Angeles Police Department developed and tested a series of clinical and psychophysical examinations that a trained police officer can use to identify and differentiate among types of drug impairment. This program has evolved into a national program to train police as "drug recognition experts." Normally, a three- to five-month training program is required to certify an officer as a drug recognition expert (DRE).

The DRE program incorporates standardized methods for examining suspects to determine whether they have taken one or more drugs. The process is systematic and standard: To ensure that each subject has been tested in a routine fashion, each DRE must complete a standard Drug Influence Evaluation form (see Figure 12-10). The entire drug evaluation takes approximately 30 to 40 minutes. The components of the twelve-step process are summarized in Table 12.1.

The DRE evaluation process can suggest the presence of the following seven broad categories of drugs:

1. Central nervous system depressants
2. Central nervous system stimulants
3. Hallucinogens
4. Dissociative anesthetics (includes phencyclidine and its analogs)
5. Inhalants
6. Narcotic analgesics
7. Cannabis

■■■■ CASEFILES ■■■■
DEATH BY RADIATION POISONING

In November 2006, Alexander V. Litvinenko lay at death's doorstep in a London hospital. He was in excruciating pain and had symptoms that included hair loss, an inability to make blood cells, and gastrointestinal distress. His organs slowly failed as he lingered for three weeks before dying. British investigators soon confirmed that Litvinenko died from the intake of polonium 210, a radioactive element, in what appeared to be its first use as a murder weapon.

Litvinenko's death almost immediately set off an international uproar. Litvinenko, a former KBG operative, had become a vocal critic of the Russian spy agency FSB, the domestic successor to the KGB. In 2000, he fled to London, where he was granted asylum. Litvinenko had continued to voice his criticisms of the Russian president, Vladimir Putin. Just before his death, Litvinenko was believed to have compiled, on behalf of a British company looking to invest millions in a project in Russia, an incriminating report regarding the activities of senior Kremlin officials.

Suspicions immediately fell on Andrei Lugovoi and Dmitri Kovtun, business associates of Mr. Litvinenko. Lugovoi was himself a former KGB officer. On the day he fell ill, Litvinenko had met Lugovoi and Kovtun at the Pine Bar of the Millennium Hotel in London. At the meeting, Mr. Litvinenko drank tea out of a teapot later found to be highly radioactive. British officials have accused Lugovoi of poisoning Litvinenko. Although the precise nature of the evidence against him still has not been made clear, investigators have linked him and Mr. Kovtun to a trail of polonium 210 radioactivity in hotel rooms, restaurants, bars, and offices stretching from London to Hamburg, Germany, as well as in British Airways planes that had flown to Moscow. Each man has denied killing Mr. Litvinenko.

Polonium 210 is highly radioactive and very toxic. By weight, it is about 250 million times as toxic as cyanide, so a particle the size of a few grains of sand could be fatal. It emits a radioactive ray known as an "alpha particle." Because this form of radiation cannot penetrate the skin, polonium 210 can be effective as a poison only if it is swallowed, breathed in, or injected. The particles disperse through the body and first destroy fast-growing cells such as those in bone marrow, blood, hair, and the digestive tract. This is consistent with Mr. Litvinenko's symptoms. There is no antidote for polonium poisoning.

Polonium does have industrial uses and is produced by commercial or institutional nuclear reactors. Polonium 210 has been found to be ideal for making antistatic devices that remove dust from film and lenses, as well as from the atmosphere of paper and textile plants. Its non-body-penetrating rays produce an electric charge on nearby air. Bits of dust with static attract the charged air, which neutralizes them. Once free of static, the dust is easy to blow or brush away. Manufacturers of such antistatic devices take great pains to make the polonium hard to remove from their products.

Alexander Litvinenko, former KGB agent, before (left) and after he became sick (right).
Alistair Fuller/AP Images; Natasja Weitsz/Getty Images

DRUG INFLUENCE EVALUATION

PAGE _____ OF _____
DR NUMBER:
EVALUATOR:
CONTROL #:
BOOKING #:

ARRESTEE'S NAME (Last, First, MI) | AGE | SEX | RACE | ARRESTING OFFICER (Name, Badge, District)

DATE EXAMINED/TIME/LOCATION

BREATH RESULTS: ☐ Refused
RESULTS   Instrument ⬤

CHEMICAL TEST   ☐ Both Tests
☐ Urine   ☐ Blood   Refused

MIRANDA WARNING GIVEN: ☐ Yes ☐ No
Given by:

What have you eaten today?   When?

What have you been drinking? How much?

Time of last drink?

Time now?   When did you last sleep? How long?

Are you sick or injured? ☐ Yes ☐ No

Are you diabetic or epileptic? ☐ Yes ☐ No

Do you take insulin? ☐ Yes ☐ No

Do you have any physical defects? ☐ Yes ☐ No

Are you under the care of a doctor/dentist? ☐ Yes ☐ No

Are you taking any medication or drugs? ☐ Yes ☐ No

ATTITUDE

COORDINATION

SPEECH | BREATH | FACE

CORRECTIVE LENS: ☐ None
☐ Glasses ☐ Contacts, if so ☐ Hard ☐ Soft

Eyes: ☐ Normal ☐ Bloodshot ☐ Watery

Blindness: ☐ None ☐ R. Eye ☐ L. Eye

Tracking: ☐ Equal ☐ Unequal

PUPIL SIZE: ☐ Equal ☐ Unequal (explain)

HGN Present: ☐ Yes ☐ No

Able to follow stimulus: ☐ Yes ☐ No

Eyelids: ☐ Normal ☐ Droopy

PULSE & TIME
1. ____ / ____
2. ____ / ____
3. ____ / ____

HGN | Right Eye | Left Eye
Lack of Smooth Pursuit
Max. Deviation
Angle of Onset

Vertical Nystagmus? ☐ Yes ☐ No
Convergence   Right Eye   Left Eye

ONE LEG STAND:

BALANCE EYES CLOSED | WALK AND TURN TEST

Cannot keep balance _____
Starts too soon _____   1st Nine   2nd Nine
Stops Walking
Misses Heel-Toe
Steps off Line
Raises Arms
Actual Steps Taken

L R
☐ ☐ Sways while balancing.
☐ ☐ Uses arms to balance.
☐ ☐ Hopping.
☐ ☐ Puts foot down.

INTERNAL CLOCK: _____ Estimated as 30 sec.

Describe Turn

Cannot do Test (explain)

Type of Footwear

☐ Right △ Left
Draw lines to spots touched

PUPIL SIZE | Room Light | Darkness | Indirect | Direct
Left Eye
Right Eye

NASAL AREA

ORAL CAVITY

HIPPUS ☐ Yes ☐ No

REBOUND DILATION ☐ Yes ☐ No

Reaction to Light

② ④ ⑤   △1 △3 △6

RIGHT ARM   LEFT ARM

BLOOD PRESSURE: _____ / _____   TEMP _____°

MUSCLE TONE:
☐ Near Normal ☐ Flacid ☐ Rigid
Comments:

ATTACH PHOTOS OF FRESH PUNCTURE MARKS

What medicine or drug have you been using? | How much? | Time of use? | Where were the drugs used? (Location)

DATE/TIME OF ARREST | TIME DRE NOTIFIED | EVAL START TIME | TIME COMPLETED

OFFICER'S SIGNATURE | DISTRICT | ID NUMBER | REVIEWED BY

FIGURE 12-10 Drug Influence Evaluation form. *National Highway Traffic Safety Administration (NHTSA)*

The DRE program is not designed to be a substitute for toxicological testing. The toxicologist can often determine that a suspect has a particular drug in his or her body, but the toxicologist often cannot infer with reasonable certainty that the suspect was impaired at a specific time. On the other hand, the DRE can supply credible evidence that the suspect was impaired at a specific time and that the nature of the impairment was consistent with a particular family of drugs. However, the DRE program usually cannot determine which specific drug was ingested. Proving drug intoxication requires a coordinated effort and the production of competent data from both the DRE and the forensic toxicologist.

TABLE 12.1 Components of the Drug Recognition Process

1. *Breath-Alcohol Test.* By obtaining an accurate and immediate measurement of the suspect's blood-alcohol concentration, the drug recognition expert (DRE) can determine whether alcohol may be contributing to the suspect's observable impairment and whether the concentration of alcohol is sufficient to be the sole cause of that impairment.

2. *Interview with the Arresting Officer.* Spending a few minutes with the arresting officer often enables the DRE to determine the most promising areas of investigation.

3. *Preliminary Examination.* This structured series of questions, specific observations, and simple tests provides the first opportunity to examine the suspect closely. It is designed to determine whether the suspect is suffering from an injury or from another condition unrelated to drug consumption. It also affords an opportunity to begin assessing the suspect's appearance and behavior for signs of possible drug influence.

4. *Eye Examination.* Certain categories of drugs induce nystagmus, an involuntary, spasmodic motion of the eyeball. Nystagmus is an indicator of drug-induced impairment. The inability of the eyes to converge toward the bridge of the nose also indicates the possible presence of certain types of drugs.

5. *Divided-Attention Psychophysical Tests.* These tests check balance and physical orientation and include the walk and turn, the one-leg stand, the Romberg balance, and the finger-to-nose.

6. *Vital Signs Examinations.* Precise measurements of blood pressure, pulse rate, and body temperature are taken. Certain drugs elevate these signs; others depress them.

7. *Dark Room Examinations.* The size of the suspect's pupils in room light, near-total darkness, indirect light, and direct light is checked. Some drugs cause the pupils to either dilate or constrict.

8. *Examination for Muscle Rigidity.* Certain categories of drugs cause the muscles to become hypertense and quite rigid. Others may cause the muscles to relax and become flaccid.

9. *Examination for Injection Sites.* Users of certain categories of drugs routinely or occasionally inject their drugs. Evidence of needle use may be found on veins along the neck, arms, and hands.

10. *Suspect's Statements and Other Observations.* The next step is to attempt to interview the suspect concerning the drug or drugs he or she has ingested. Of course, the interview must be conducted in full compliance of the suspect's constitutional rights.

11. *Opinions of the Evaluator.* Using the information obtained in the previous ten steps, the DRE is able to make an informed decision about whether the suspect is impaired by drugs and, if so, what category or combination of categories is the probable cause of the impairment.

12. *Toxicological Examination.* The DRE should obtain a blood or urine sample from the suspect for laboratory analysis in order to secure scientific, admissible evidence to substantiate his or her conclusions.

Quick Review

- The forensic toxicologist must devise an analytical scheme to detect, isolate, and identify toxic drug substances extracted from biological fluids, tissues, and organs.
- A screening test gives quick insight into the likelihood that a specimen contains a drug substance. Positive results arising from a screening test are tentative at best and must be verified with a confirmation test.
- The most widely used screening tests are thin-layer chromatography, gas chromatography, and immunoassay. Gas chromatography/mass spectrometry is generally accepted as the confirmation test of choice.
- Once a drug is extracted and identified, a toxicologist may be required to judge the drug's effect on an individual's natural performance or physical state.
- A three- to five-month training program is required to certify an officer as a drug recognition expert (DRE). This training incorporates standardized methods for examining suspects to determine whether they have taken one or more drugs.

VIRTUAL LAB
BLOOD ALCOHOL ANALYSIS
To perform a virtual blood alcohol analysis, go to *www .pearsoncustom.com/us/vlm/*

CHAPTER REVIEW

- Forensic toxicologists detect and identify drugs and poisons in body fluids, tissues, and organs in situations that involve violations of criminal laws.

- Ethyl alcohol is the most heavily abused drug in Western countries.

- Alcohol appears in the blood within minutes after it has been taken by mouth. It slowly increases in concentration while it is being absorbed from the stomach and the small intestine into the bloodstream.

- When all the alcohol has been absorbed, a maximum alcohol level is reached in the blood, and the postabsorption period begins. During postabsorption, the alcohol concentration slowly decreases until a zero level is reached.

- Elimination of alcohol throughout the body is accomplished through oxidation and excretion. Oxidation takes place almost entirely in the liver, whereas alcohol is excreted unchanged in the breath, urine, and perspiration.

- Breath-testing devices operate on the principle that the ratio between the concentration of alcohol in alveolar breath and its concentration in blood is fixed.

- Modern breath testers are free of chemicals. They include infrared light absorption devices and fuel cell detectors.

- The key to the accuracy of a breath-testing device is to ensure that the unit captures the alcohol in the alveolar (deep-lung) breath of the subject.

- Many breath testers collect a set volume of breath and expose it to infrared light. The instrument measures the concentration of alcohol in the collected breath sample by measuring the degree of interaction between the light and the alcohol present.

- Law enforcement officers use field sobriety tests to estimate a motorist's degree of physical impairment from alcohol and to determine whether an evidential test for alcohol is justified.

- The horizontal-gaze nystagmus test, the walk and turn, and the one-leg stand are all considered reliable and effective psychophysical tests for alcohol impairment.

- Gas chromatography is the most widely used approach for determining blood-alcohol levels in forensic laboratories.

- An anticoagulant should be added to a blood sample to prevent clotting; a preservative should be added to inhibit the growth of microorganisms capable of destroying alcohol.

- The current legal measure of drunk driving in the United States is a blood-alcohol concentration of 0.08 percent, or 0.08 grams of alcohol per 100 milliliters of blood.

- The implied-consent law states that the operator of a motor vehicle on a public highway must either consent to a test for alcohol intoxication, if requested, or lose his or her license for some designated period—usually six months to one year.

- The forensic toxicologist must devise an analytical scheme to detect, isolate, and identify toxic drug substances extracted from biological fluids, tissues, and organs.

- A screening test gives quick insight into the likelihood that a specimen contains a drug substance. Positive results arising from a screening test are tentative at best and must be verified with a confirmation test.

- The most widely used screening tests are thin-layer chromatography, gas chromatography, and immunoassay. Gas chromatography/mass spectrometry is generally accepted as the confirmation test of choice.

- Once a drug is extracted and identified, a toxicologist may be required to judge the drug's effect on an individual's natural performance or physical state.

- A three- to five-month training program is required to certify an officer as a drug recognition expert (DRE). This training incorporates standardized methods for examining suspects to determine whether they have taken one or more drugs.

KEY TERMS

absorption, 292
acid, 307
alveoli, 294
anticoagulant, 301
artery, 294

base, 307
capillary, 294
excretion, 292
fuel cell detector, 296
metabolism, 291

oxidation, 292
pH, 307
preservative, 301
toxicologist, 291
vein, 294

■■■■ REVIEW QUESTIONS

1. The _____ studies body fluids, tissues, and organs to detect and identify drugs and poisons.

2. True or False: Toxicologists are employed only by crime laboratories. _____

3. The most heavily abused drug in the Western world is _____.

4. The transformation of chemicals introduced into the body into substances that are easier to eliminate is called _____.

5. Alcohol consumed on an empty stomach is absorbed (faster, slower) than an equivalent amount of alcohol taken when there is food in the stomach.

6. Alcohol is eliminated from the body by _____ and _____.

7. Approximately 98 percent of the ethyl alcohol consumed is oxidized to carbon dioxide and water in the _____.

8. The amount of alcohol exhaled in the _____ is directly proportional to the concentration of alcohol in the blood.

9. Alcohol is eliminated from the blood at an average rate of _____ percent w/v.

10. True or False: The amount of alcohol in the blood is not directly proportional to the concentration of alcohol in the brain. _____

11. True or False: Blood-alcohol levels have become the accepted standard for relating alcohol intake to its effect on the body. _____

12. Under normal drinking conditions, alcohol concentration in the blood peaks in _____ to _____ minutes.

13. A(n) _____ carries blood away from the heart; a(n) _____ carries blood back to the heart.

14. The _____ artery carries deoxygenated blood from the heart to the lungs.

15. Alcohol passes from the blood capillaries into the _____ sacs in the lungs.

16. One milliliter of blood contains the same amount of alcohol as approximately _____ milliliters of alveolar breath.

17. True or False: When alcohol is being absorbed into the blood, the alcohol concentration in venous blood is higher than that in arterial blood. _____

18. True or False: Portable, handheld, roadside breath testers for alcohol provide evidential test results. _____

19. Most modern breath testers use _____ radiation to detect and measure alcohol in the breath.

20. In an alcohol _____, two platinum electrodes are separated by an acid- or base-containing porous membrane, and one of the electrodes is positioned to come into contact with a subject's breath sample.

21. To avoid the possibility of testing "mouth alcohol," the operator of a breath tester must not allow the subject to take any foreign materials into the mouth for _____ to _____ minutes prior to the test.

22. True or False: A series of reliable and effective psychophysical tests are the horizontal-gaze nystagmus, the walk and turn, and the one-leg stand. _____

23. Alcohol can be separated from other volatiles in blood and measured by the technique of _____.

24. When drawing blood for alcohol testing, the breath-test operator must first wipe the suspect's skin with a(n) _____ disinfectant.

25. True or False: Failure to add a preservative, such as sodium fluoride, to blood removed from a living person may lead to a decline in alcohol concentration. _____

26. Most states have established _____ percent w/v as the impairment limit for blood-alcohol concentration in noncommercial drivers.

27. Studies show that an individual is about _____ times as likely to become involved in an automobile accident at the legal limit for blood alcohol as a sober individual.

28. In the case of _____, the Supreme Court ruled that taking nontestimonial evidence, such as a blood sample, did not violate a suspect's Fifth Amendment rights.

29. After entering the body, heroin is changed into _____.

30. The body fluids _____ and _____ are both desirable for the toxicological examination of a living person suspected of being under the influence of a drug.

31. A large number of drugs can be classified chemically as _____ or _____.

32. True or False: Water with a pH value of less than 7 is basic. _____

33. Drugs are extracted from body fluids and tissues by carefully controlling the _____ of the medium in which the sample has been dissolved.

34. Both _____ and _____ tests must be incorporated into the drug-testing protocol of a toxicology laboratory to ensure the correctness of the laboratory's conclusions.

35. The screening tests most widely used by toxicologists are _____, _____, and _____.

36. The preferred method for confirmation testing is a combination of _____ and _____, which creates a unique pattern that can be used for identification.

37. A toxicologist may be able to detect and identify a long-abused drug or poison because drugs present in blood diffuse through capillary walls into the base of a(n) _____ and become permanently entrapped in its hardening protein structure.

38. The gas _____ combines with hemoglobin in the blood to form carboxyhemoglobin, thus interfering with the transportation of oxygen in the blood.

39. True or False: Blood levels of drugs can be used alone to draw definitive conclusions about the effects of a drug on an individual. _____

40. True or False: The level of a drug present in the urine is by itself a poor indicator of how extensively an individual is affected by a drug. _____

41. Urine and blood drug levels are best used by law enforcement authorities and the courts to _____ other investigative and medical findings pertaining to an individual's condition.

42. A program to train police as _____ incorporates systematic and standardized methods for examining suspects to determine whether they have taken one or more drugs.

APPLICATION AND CRITICAL THINKING

1. Answer the following questions about driving risk associated with drinking and blood-alcohol concentrations:

   a) Randy is just barely legally intoxicated. How much more likely is he to have an accident than someone who is sober?

   b) Marissa, who has been drinking, is fifteen times as likely to have an accident as her sober friend, Christine. What is Marissa's approximate blood-alcohol concentration?

   c) After several drinks, Charles is ten times as likely to have an accident as a sober person. Is he more or less intoxicated than James, whose blood alcohol level is 0.10?

   d) Under the original blood-alcohol standards recommended by the National Highway Traffic Safety Administration, a person considered just barely legally intoxicated was how much more likely to have an accident than a sober individual?

2. Following are descriptions of four individuals who have been drinking. Rank them by blood-alcohol concentration, from highest to lowest:

   a) John, who weighs 200 pounds and has consumed eight 8-ounce drinks on a full stomach

   b) Frank, who weighs 170 pounds and has consumed four 8-ounce drinks on an empty stomach

   c) Gary, who weighs 240 pounds and has consumed six 8-ounce drinks on an empty stomach

   d) Stephen, who weighs 180 pounds and has consumed six 8-ounce drinks on a full stomach

3. Following are descriptions of four individuals who have been drinking. In which (if any) of the following countries would each be considered legally drunk: the United States, Australia, and/or Sweden?

   a) Bill, who weighs 150 pounds and has consumed three 8-ounce drinks on an empty stomach

   b) Sally, who weighs 110 pounds and has consumed three 8-ounce drinks on a full stomach

   c) Rich, who weighs 200 pounds and has consumed six 8-ounce drinks on an empty stomach

   d) Carrie, who weighs 140 pounds and has consumed four 8-ounce drinks on a full stomach

4. You are a forensic scientist who has been asked to test two blood samples. You know that one sample is suspected of containing barbiturates and the other contains no drugs; however, you cannot tell the two samples apart. Describe how you would use the concept of pH to determine which sample contains barbiturates. Explain your reasoning.

5. You are investigating an arson scene and you find a corpse in the rubble, but you suspect that the victim did not die as a result of the fire. Instead, you suspect that the victim was murdered earlier and that the blaze was intentionally started to cover up the murder. How would you go about determining whether the victim died before the fire?

ENDNOTES

1. In the United States, laws that define blood-alcohol levels almost exclusively use the unit *percent weight per volume*—% w/v. Hence, 0.015 percent w/v is equivalent to 0.015 gram of alcohol per 100 milliliters of blood, or 15 milligrams of alcohol per 100 milliliters.

2. R. B. Forney et al., "Alcohol Distribution in the Vascular System: Concentrations of Orally Administered Alcohol in Blood from Various Points in the Vascular System and in Rebreathed Air during Absorption," *Quarterly Journal of Studies on Alcohol* 25 (1964): 205.

3. G. A. Brown et al., "The Stability of Ethanol in Stored Blood," *Analytica Chemica Acta* 66 (1973): 271.

4. 0.15 percent w/v is equivalent to 0.15 grams of alcohol per 100 milliliters of blood, or 150 milligrams per 100 milliliters.

5. 384 U.S. 757 (1966)

6. 133 S. Ct. 932 (2013)

13 Trace Evidence I
Hairs and Fibers

Michael Williamson/ Getty Images

LEARNING OBJECTIVES
After studying this chapter, you should be able to:
- Recognize and understand the cuticle, cortex, and medulla areas of hair.
- List the three phases of hair growth.
- Appreciate the distinction between animal and human hairs.
- List hair features that are useful for microscopic comparisons of human hairs.
- Explain the proper collection of forensic hair evidence.
- Describe and understand the role of DNA typing in hair comparisons.
- Understand the differences between natural and manufactured fibers.
- List the properties of fibers that are most useful for forensic comparisons.
- Describe the proper collection of fiber evidence.

JEFFREY MACDONALD: FATAL VISION

The grisly murder scene that confronted police on February 17, 1970, is one that would not be wiped from memory. Summoned to the Fort Bragg residence of Captain Jeffrey MacDonald, a physician, police found the bludgeoned body of MacDonald's wife. She had been repeatedly knifed, and her face was smashed to a pulp. MacDonald's two children, ages 2 and 5, had been brutally and repeatedly knifed and battered to death.

Suspicion quickly fell on MacDonald. To the eyes of investigators, the murder scene had a staged appearance. MacDonald described a frantic effort to subdue four intruders who had slashed at him with an ice pick. However, the confrontation left MacDonald with minor wounds and no apparent defensive wounds on his arms. MacDonald then described how he had covered his slashed wife with his blue pajama top. Interestingly, when the body was removed, blue threads were observed under the body. In fact, blue threads matching the pajama top turned up throughout the house—nineteen in one child's bedroom, including one beneath her fingernail, and two in the other child's bedroom. Eighty-one blue fibers were recovered from the master bedroom, and two were located on a bloodstained piece of wood outside the house.

Forensic examination showed that the forty-eight ice pick holes in the pajama top were smooth and cylindrical, a sign that the top was stationary when it was slashed. Also, folding the pajama top demonstrated that the forty-eight holes actually could have been made by twenty-one thrusts of an ice pick. This coincided with the number of wounds that MacDonald's wife sustained. As described in the book *Fatal Vision*, which chronicles the murder investigation, when MacDonald was confronted with adulterous conduct, he replied, "You guys are more thorough than I thought." MacDonald is currently serving three consecutive life sentences.

The trace evidence transferred between individuals and objects during the commission of a crime, if recovered, often corroborates other evidence developed during the course of an investigation. Although in most cases physical evidence cannot by itself positively identify a suspect, laboratory examination may narrow the origin of such evidence to a group that includes the suspect. Using many of the instruments and techniques we have already examined, the crime laboratory has developed a variety of procedures for comparing and tracing the origins of physical evidence. This chapter will focus on the value of hairs and fibers as physical evidence.

Forensic Examination of Hair

Hair is encountered as physical evidence in a wide variety of crimes. However, any review of the forensic aspects of hair examination must start with the observation that it is not yet possible to individualize a human hair to any single head or body through its morphology, or structural characteristics. Over the years, criminalists have tried to isolate the physical and chemical properties of hair that could serve as individual characteristics of identity. Partial success has finally been achieved by isolating and characterizing the DNA present in hair.

The importance of hair as physical evidence cannot be overemphasized. Its removal from the body often denotes physical contact between a victim and perpetrator and hence a crime of a serious or violent nature. When hair is properly collected at the crime scene and submitted to the laboratory along with enough standard/reference samples, it can provide strong corroborative evidence for placing an individual at a crime site. The first step in the forensic examination of hair logically starts with its color and structure (i.e., morphology) and, if warranted, progresses to the more detailed DNA extraction, isolation, and characterization.

MORPHOLOGY OF HAIR

Hair is an appendage of the skin that grows out of an organ known as the "hair follicle." The length of a hair extends from its root, or bulb, which is embedded in the follicle, continues into the shaft, and terminates at the tip. The shaft, which is composed of three layers—the **cuticle**, **cortex**, and **medulla**—is most intensely examined by the forensic scientist (see Figure 13-1).

CUTICLE   Two features that make hair a good subject for establishing individual identity are its resistance to chemical decomposition and its ability to retain structural features over a long period of time. Much of this resistance and stability is attributed to the cuticle, a scale structure covering the exterior of the hair. The cuticle is formed by overlapping scales that always point toward the tip end of each hair. The scales form from specialized cells that have hardened (i.e., keratinized) and flattened in progressing from the follicle. Three basic patterns describe the appearance of the cuticle: cornal, spinous, and imbricate (see Figure 13-2).

Although the scale pattern is not a useful characteristic for individualizing human hair, the variety of patterns formed by animal hair makes it an important feature for species identification. Figure 13-3 shows the scale patterns of some animal hairs and of a human hair as viewed with a scanning electron microscope. Another method of studying the scale pattern of hair is to make a cast of its surface. This is done by embedding the hair in a soft medium, such as clear nail polish or softened vinyl. When the medium has hardened, the hair is removed, leaving a clear, distinct impression of the hair's cuticle, ideal for examination with a compound microscope.

cuticle
The scale structure covering the exterior of the hair.

cortex
The main body of the hair shaft.

medulla
A cellular column running through the center of the hair.

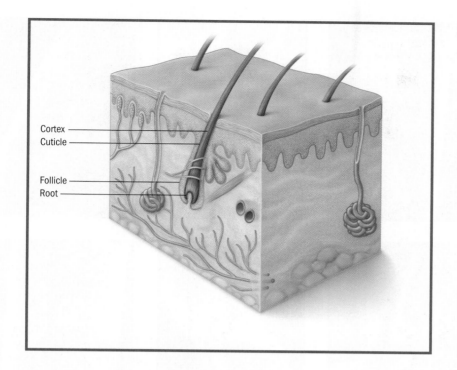

FIGURE 13-1 A cross-section of skin showing hair growing out of a tubelike structure called the follicle. *SAFERSTEIN, RICHARD, Ph.D., CRIMINALISTICS: AN INTRODUCTION TO FORENSIC SCIENCE, 11th Ed., © 2015. Reprinted and Electronically reproduced by permission of Pearson Education, Inc., Upper Saddle River, New Jersey.*

FIGURE 13-2 (a) The coronal, or crownlike, scale pattern resembles a stack of paper cups. (b) Spinous or petal-like scales are triangular in shape and protrude from the hair shaft. (c) The imbricate, or flattened-scale, type consists of overlapping scales with narrow margins.

CORTEX   Contained within the protective layer of the cuticle is the cortex, the main body of the hair shaft. The cortex is made up of spindle-shaped cortical cells aligned in a regular array, parallel to the length of the hair. The cortex derives its major forensic importance from the fact that it is embedded with the pigment granules that give hair its color. The color, shape, and distribution of these granules provide important points of comparison among the hairs of different individuals.

FIGURE 13-3 Scale patterns of various types of hair: (a) human head hair (600×), *New Jersey State Police* (b) dog (1350×), *New Jersey State Police* (c) deer (120×), *Richard Saferstein, Ph.D.* (d) rabbit (300×), *New Jersey State Police* (e) cat (2000×), *Richard Saferstein, Ph.D.* and (f) horse (450×). *Richard Saferstein, Ph.D.*

The structural features of the cortex are examined microscopically after the hair has been mounted in a liquid medium with a refractive index close to that of the hair. Under these conditions, the amount of light reflected off the hair's surface is minimized, and the amount of light penetrating the hair is optimized.

MEDULLA The medulla is a collection of cells that looks like a central canal running through a hair. In many animals, this canal is a predominant feature, occupying more than half of the hair's diameter. The "medullary index" measures the diameter of the medulla relative to the diameter of the hair shaft and is normally expressed as a fraction. For humans, the index is generally less than one-third; for most other animals, the index is one-half or greater.

The presence and appearance of the medulla vary from individual to individual and even among the hairs of a given individual. Not all hairs have medullae, and when they do exist, the degree of medullation can vary. In this respect, medullae may be classified as being either continuous, interrupted, fragmented, or absent (see Figure 13-4). Human head hairs generally exhibit no medullae or have fragmented ones; they rarely show continuous medullation. One noted exception is in people of the Mongoloid race, who usually

Continuous   Interrupted   Fragmented

FIGURE 13-4 Medulla patterns. *SAFERSTEIN, RICHARD, Ph.D., CRIMINALISTICS: AN INTRODUCTION TO FORENSIC SCIENCE, 11th Ed., © 2015. Reprinted and Electronically reproduced by permission of Pearson Education, Inc., Upper Saddle River, New Jersey.*

FIGURE 13-5 Medulla patterns for various types of hair: (a) human head hair (400×), (b) dog (400×), (c) deer (500×), (d) rabbit (450×), (e) cat (400×), and (f) mouse (500×). *Richard Saferstein, Ph.D.*

have head hairs with continuous medullae. Also, most animals have medullae that are either continuous or interrupted.

Another interesting feature of the medulla is its shape. Humans, as well as many animals, have medullae that give a nearly cylindrical appearance. Other animals exhibit medullae that have a patterned shape. For example, the medulla of a cat can best be described as resembling a string of pearls, whereas members of the deer family show a medullary structure consisting of spherical cells occupying the entire hair shaft. Figure 13-5 illustrates medullary sizes and forms for a number of common animal hairs and a human head hair.

A searchable database on CD-ROM of the thirty-five most common animal hairs encountered in forensic casework is commercially available.[1] This database allows an examiner to rapidly search for animal hairs based on scale patterns and/or medulla type using a PC. A typical screen presentation arising from such a data search is shown in Figure 13-6.

ROOT The root and other surrounding cells within the hair follicle provide the tools necessary to produce hair and continue its growth. Human head hair grows in three developmental stages, and the shape and size of the hair root is determined by the hair's current growth phase. The three phases of hair growth are the **anagen, catagen,** and **telogen phases.**

anagen phase
The initial growth phase during which the hair follicle actively produces hair.

catagen phase
A transition stage between the anagen and telogen phases of hair growth.

telogen phase
The final growth phase in which hair naturally falls out of the skin.

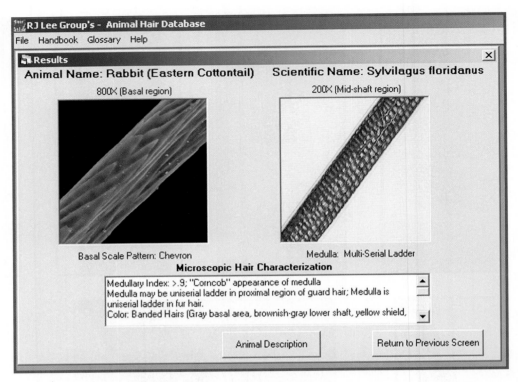

FIGURE 13-6 Information on rabbit hair contained within the *Forensic Animal Hair Atlas. RJ Lee Group*

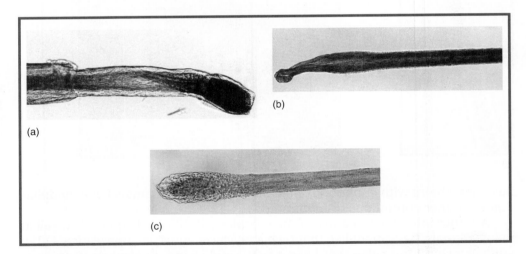

FIGURE 13-7 Hair roots in the (a) anagen phase, (b) catagen phase, and (c) telogen phase (100×). *Virginia Division of Forensic Science*

follicular tag
A translucent piece of tissue surrounding the hair's shaft near the root that contains the richest source of DNA associated with hair.

In the anagen phase (the initial growth phase), which may last up to six years, the root is attached to the follicle for continued growth, giving the root bulb a flame-shaped appearance (Figure 13-7[a]). When pulled from the root, some hairs in the anagen phase have a **follicular tag**. With the advent of DNA analysis, this follicular tag is important for individualizing hair.

Hair continues to grow, but at a decreasing rate, during the catagen phase, which can last anywhere from two to three weeks. In the catagen phase, roots typically take on an elongated appearance (Figure 13-7[b]) as the root bulb shrinks and is pushed out of the hair follicle. Once hair growth ends, the telogen phase begins and the root takes on a club-shaped appearance (Figure 13-7[c]). Over two to six months, the hair is pushed out of the follicle, causing the hair to be naturally shed.

IDENTIFICATION AND COMPARISON OF HAIR

Most often the prime purpose for examining hair evidence in a crime laboratory is either to establish whether the hair is human or animal in origin or to determine whether human hair retrieved at a crime scene compares with hair from a particular individual. A careful microscopic examination of hair reveals morphological features that can distinguish human hair from animal hair. The hair of various animals also differs enough in structure that the examiner can often identify the species. Before reaching such a conclusion, however, the examiner must have access to a comprehensive collection of reference standards and the accumulated experience of hundreds of prior hair examinations. Scale structure, medullary index, and medullary shape are particularly important in hair identification.

The most common request when hair is used as forensic evidence is to determine whether hair recovered at the crime scene compares to hair removed from a suspect. In most cases, such a comparison relates to hair obtained from the scalp or pubic area. Ultimately, the evidential value of the comparison depends on the degree of probability with which the examiner can associate the hair in question with a particular individual.

FACTORS IN COMPARISON OF HAIR Although animal hair normally can be distinguished from human hair with little difficulty, human hair comparisons must be undertaken with extreme caution. Hair tends to exhibit variable morphological characteristics, not only from one person to another but also within a single individual. In comparing hair, the criminalist is particularly interested in matching color, length, and diameter. Other important features are the presence or absence of a medulla and the distribution, shape, and color intensity of the pigment granules in the cortex. A microscopic examination may also distinguish dyed or bleached hair from natural hair. A dyed color is often present in the cuticle as well as throughout the cortex. Bleaching, on the other hand, tends to remove pigment from the hair and gives it a yellowish tint.

If hair has grown since it was last bleached or dyed, the natural-end portion will be quite distinct in color. An estimate of the time since dyeing or bleaching can be made because hair grows approximately 1 centimeter per month. Other significant but less frequent features may be observed in hair. For example, morphological abnormalities may be present as a result of certain diseases or nutrient deficiencies. Also, the presence of fungal and nit infections can further link a hair specimen to a particular individual.

MICROSCOPIC EXAMINATION OF HAIR A comparison microscope is an invaluable tool that allows the examiner to view the questioned and known hair together, side by side. Any variations in the microscopic characteristics will thus be readily observed. Because hair from any part of the body exhibits a range of characteristics, it is necessary to have an adequate number of known hairs that are representative of all its features when making a comparison.

Although the microscopic comparison of hairs has long been accepted as an appropriate approach for including and excluding questioned hairs against standard/reference hairs, many forensic scientists have long recognized that this approach is very subjective and is highly dependent on the skills and integrity of the analyst, as well as the hair morphology being examined. However, until the advent of DNA analysis, the forensic science community had no choice but to rely on the microscope to carry out hair comparisons.

Any lingering doubts about the necessity of augmenting microscopic hair examinations with DNA analysis evaporated with the publication of an FBI study describing significant error rates associated with microscopic comparison of hairs.[2] Hair evidence submitted to the FBI for DNA analysis between 1996 and 2000 was examined both microscopically and by DNA analysis.

Approximately 11 percent of the hairs (nine out of eighty) in which FBI hair examiners found a positive microscopic match between questioned and standard/reference hairs were found to be nonmatches when they were later subjected to DNA analysis. The course of events is clear: Microscopic hair comparisons must be regarded by police and courts as presumptive in nature, and all positive microscopic hair comparisons must be confirmed by DNA determinations.

QUESTIONS ABOUT HAIR EXAMINATION A number of questions may be asked to further ascertain the present status of forensic hair examinations. The answers to these questions can be of great significance to the investigator working with hair evidence.

Can the Body Area from Which a Hair Originated Be Determined? Normally it is easy to determine the body area from which a hair came. For example, scalp hairs generally show little diameter variation and have a more uniform distribution of pigment when compared to other body hairs. Pubic hairs are short and curly, with wide variations in shaft diameter, and usually have continuous medullae. Beard hairs are coarse, are normally triangular in cross-section, and have blunt tips acquired from cutting or shaving.

Can the Racial Origin of Hair Be Determined? In many instances, the examiner can distinguish hair originating from members of different races; this is especially true of Caucasian and Negroid head hair. Negroid hairs are normally kinky, containing dense, unevenly distributed pigments. Caucasian hairs are usually straight or wavy, with very fine to coarse pigments that are more evenly distributed when compared to Negroid hair. Mongoloid hairs often have a dense pigment distribution, but they normally don't exhibit the pigment clumping seen in Negroid hairs. Mongoloids also tend to have thicker hair shaft diameters when compared to the other two races.

Sometimes a cross-sectional examination of hair may help identify race. Cross-sections of hair from Caucasians are oval to round in shape; Mongoloid generally exhibit a round cross-sectional shape; and cross-sections of Negroid hair are flat to oval in shape. However, all of these observations are general, with many possible exceptions. The criminalist must approach the determination of race from hair with caution and a good deal of experience.

Can the Age and Sex of an Individual Be Determined from a Hair Sample? The age of an individual cannot be learned from a hair examination with any degree of certainty except in the case of infant hairs, which are fine and short and have fine pigmentation. Although the presence of dye or bleach on the hair may offer some clue to sex, present hairstyles make these characteristics less valuable than they were in the past. The recovery of nuclear DNA either from tissue adhering to a hair or from the root structure of the hair will allow a determination of whether the hair originated from a male or female.

Is It Possible to Determine Whether Hair Was Forcibly Removed from the Body? A microscopic examination of the hair root may establish whether the hair fell out or was pulled out of the skin. A hair root with follicular tissue (root sheath cells) adhering to it, as shown in Figure 13-8, indicates a hair that has been pulled out either by a person or by brushing or combing. Hair naturally falling off the body has a bulbous-shaped root free of any adhering tissue.

The absence of sheath cells cannot always be relied on for correctly judging whether hair has been forcibly pulled from the body. In some cases the root of a hair is devoid of any adhering tissue even when it has been pulled from the body. Apparently, an important consideration is how quickly the hair is pulled out of the head. Hairs pulled quickly from the head are much more likely to have sheath cells compared to hairs that have been removed slowly from the scalp.[3]

■■■■ CASEFILES ■■■■
CENTRAL PARK JOGGER CASE REVISITED

On April 19, 1989, a young woman left her apartment around 9:00 p.m. to jog in New York's Central Park. Nearly 5 hours later, she was found comatose lying in a puddle of mud in the park. She had been raped, her skull was fractured, and she had lost 75 percent of her blood. When the woman recovered, she had no memory of what happened to her. The brutality of the crime sent shock waves through the city and seemed to fuel a national perception that crime was running rampant and unchecked through the streets of New York.

Already in custody at the station house of the Central Park Precinct was a group of fourteen- and fifteen-year-old boys who had been rounded up leaving the park earlier in the night by police who suspected that they had been involved in a series of random attacks. Over the next two days, four of the teenagers gave videotaped statements, which they later recanted, admitting to participating in the attack. Ultimately, five of the teenagers were charged with the crime.

Interestingly, none of the semen collected from the victim could be linked to any of the defendants. However, according to the testimony of a forensic analyst, two head hairs collected from the clothing of one of the defendants microscopically compared to those of the victim, and a third hair collected from the same defendant's T-shirt microscopically compared to the victim's pubic hair. Besides these three hairs, a fourth hair was found to be microscopically similar to the victim's. This hair was recovered from the clothing of Steven Lopez, who was originally charged with rape but not prosecuted for the crime.

Hairs were the only pieces of physical evidence offered by the district attorney to directly link any of the teenagers to the crime. The hairs were cited by the district attorney as proof for the jury that the videotaped confessions of the teenagers were reliable.

The five defendants were convicted and ultimately served from nine to thirteen years.

In August 1989, more than three months after the jogger attack, New York police arrested a man named Matias Reyes, who pleaded guilty to murdering a pregnant woman, raping three other women, and committing a robbery. For these crimes Reyes was sentenced to thirty-three years to life. In January 2002, Reyes also confessed to the Central Park attack. Follow-up tests revealed that Reyes's DNA compared to semen recovered from the jogger's body and her sock. Other DNA tests showed that the hairs offered into evidence at the original trial did not come from the victim and so could not be used to link the teenagers to the crime as the district attorney had argued. After an eleven-month reinvestigation of the original charges, a New York State Supreme Court judge dismissed all the convictions against the five teenage suspects in the Central Park jogger case.

Paolo Omero/Shutterstock

FIGURE 13-8 Forcibly removed head hair with follicular tissue attached. *New Jersey State Police*

FIGURE 13-9   Hair and banded root. *Palenik, Dr. Chris*

200 μm

Is It Possible to Determine Whether Hair Came from a Deceased Individual?   During the murder trial of Casey Anthony (see page 1), witnesses testified that a human head hair was recovered from the trunk of Casey's automobile. Examination showed that the hair was microscopically similar to that of Casey's daughter, Caylee. The hair was microscopically distinguishable from Casey's head hair. Mitochondrial DNA sequence analysis revealed similarity between the trunk hair, Caylee's hair, and Casey's hair, as one would expect from maternally inherited mitochondrial DNA. An FBI analyst testified that the hair from the truck exhibited "root banding," a phenomenon consistent with hair from a deceased individual's head.

As exemplified by the Casey Anthony case, a forensic examiner may on occasion be confronted with situations where it's important to know whether hair was deposited after the donor was deceased. Studies have noted that postmortem decomposition may be accompanied by a darkening or banding around the root area of the hair (see Figure 13-9). Eventually, the hair will break off at the area of the dark hair, leaving a discolored hair end with a point or brushlike appearance. Recently, it has been confirmed that the onset of postmortem changes to the root portion of hair was observed only in anagenic and catagenic hairs, and specifically within a short area of the root where the hair would have been beneath the scalp. Root banding was slow to occur in cold weather and progressed at a faster rate in warmer temperatures. Significantly, hairs in the telogen stage showed no evidence of postmortem root banding.[4]

Are Efforts Being Made to Individualize Human Hair?   As we will see in Chapter 15, forensic scientists routinely isolate and characterize individual variations in DNA. Forensic hair examiners can link human hair to a particular individual by characterizing the **nuclear DNA** in the hair root or in follicular tissue adhering to the root (see Figure 13-8). Recall that the follicular tag is the richest source of DNA associated with hair. In the absence of follicular tissue, an examiner must extract DNA from the hair root.

The growth phase of hair is a useful predictor of the likelihood of successfully typing DNA in human hair.[5] Examiners have a higher success rate in extracting DNA from hair roots in the anagen phase or from anagen-phase hairs entering the catagen phase of growth. Telogen-phase hairs have an inadequate amount of DNA for typing. Because most hairs are naturally shed and are expected to be in the telogen stage, these observations do not portend well for hairs collected at crime scenes. However, some crime scenes are populated with forcibly removed hairs that are expected to be rich sources for nuclear DNA.

When a questioned hair does not have adhering tissue or a root structure amenable to isolation of nuclear DNA, there is an alternative source of information: **mitochondrial DNA**. Unlike the nuclear DNA described earlier, which is located in the nuclei of practically every cell in the body, mitochondrial DNA is found in cellular material outside the nucleus. Interestingly, unlike nuclear DNA, which is passed down from both parents, mitochondrial DNA is transmitted only from mother to child. Importantly, many more copies of mitochondrial DNA than nuclear DNA are located in the cells. For this reason, the success rate of finding and typing mitochondrial DNA is much greater from samples that have limited quantities of nuclear DNA, such as hair. Hairs 1 to 2 centimeters long can be subjected to mitochondrial analysis with extremely high odds of success. This subject is discussed in greater detail in Chapter 15.

nuclear DNA

DNA that is present in the nucleus of a cell and that is inherited from both parents.

mitochondrial DNA

DNA present in small structures (i.e., mitochondria) outside the nucleus of a cell. Mitochondria supply energy to the cell. This form of DNA is inherited maternally (from the mother).

■ ■■■ CASEFILES ■■■■

THE ENNIS COSBY HOMICIDE

Bill Cosby and his son Ennis Cosby. *Andrea Mohin/Redux Pictures*

The murder of Ennis Cosby, son of entertainer Bill Cosby, at first appeared unsolvable. It was a random act. When his car tire went flat, Ennis pulled off the road and called a friend on his cellular phone to ask for assistance. Shortly thereafter, an assailant demanded money and, when Cosby didn't respond quickly enough, shot him once in the temple. Acting on a tip from a friend of the assailant, police investigators later found a .38-caliber revolver wrapped in a blue cap miles from the crime scene. Mikail Markhasev was arrested and charged with murder.

At the trial, the district attorney introduced firearms evidence to show that the recovered gun had fired the bullet that killed Cosby. A single hair also recovered from the hat dramatically linked Markhasev to the crime: Los Angeles Police Department forensic analyst Harry Klann identified six DNA markers from the follicular tissue adhering to the hair root that matched Markhasev's DNA. This particular DNA profile is found in 1 out of 15,500 members of the general population. On hearing all the evidence, the jury deliberated and convicted Markhasev of murder.

Can DNA Individualize a Human Hair? In some cases, the answer is yes. As we will learn in Chapter 15, nuclear DNA produces frequencies of occurrence as low as one in billions or trillions. On the other hand, mitochondrial DNA cannot individualize human hair. However, its diversity within the human population often permits the exclusion of a significant portion of a population as potential contributors of a hair sample. Ideally, the combination of a positive microscopic comparison and an association through nuclear or mitochondrial DNA analysis strongly links a questioned hair and standard/reference hairs. However, a word of caution: Mitochondrial DNA cannot distinguish microscopically similar hairs from individuals who are maternally related.

COLLECTION AND PRESERVATION OF HAIR EVIDENCE

When questioned hairs are submitted to a forensic laboratory for examination, they must always be accompanied by an adequate number of standard/reference samples from the victim of the crime and from individuals suspected of having deposited hair at the crime scene. We have learned that hair from different parts of the body varies significantly in its physical characteristics. Likewise, hair from any one area of the body can also have a wide range of characteristics. For this reason, the questioned and standard/reference hairs must come from the same area of the body; one cannot, for instance, compare head hair to pubic hair. It is also important that the collection of standard/reference hair be carried out in a way that ensures a representative sampling of hair from any one area of the body.

Forensic hair comparisons generally involve either head hair or pubic hair. Collecting 25 full-length hairs from all areas of the scalp normally ensures a representative sampling of head hair. Likewise, a minimum collection of 25 full-length pubic hairs should cover the range of characteristics present in this type of hair. In rape cases, care must first be taken to comb the pubic area with a clean comb to remove all loose foreign hair present before the victim is sampled for standard/reference hair. The comb should then be packaged in a separate envelope.

Because a hair may vary in color and other morphological features over its entire length, the entire hair is collected. This requirement is best accomplished by either pulling the hair out of the skin or clipping it at the skin line. During an autopsy, hair samples are routinely collected from victims of suspicious deaths. Because the autopsy may occur early in an investigation, the need for hair standard/reference samples may not always be apparent. However, one should never rule out the possible involvement of hair evidence in subsequent investigative findings. Failure to make this simple collection may result in complicated legal problems later.

Quick Review

- The hair shaft is composed of three layers called the "cuticle," "cortex," and "medulla" and is the part of a hair most intensely examined by the forensic scientist.
- When comparing strands of hair, the criminalist is particularly interested in matching the color, length, and diameter. Other important features for comparing hair are the presence or absence of a medulla and the distribution, shape, and color intensity of pigment granules in the cortex.
- The likelihood of successfully detecting DNA in hair roots is higher in hair being examined in its anagen or early growth phase than in its catagen or telogen phases.
- The follicular tag, a translucent piece of tissue surrounding the hair's shaft near the root, is a rich source of DNA associated with hair. Mitochondrial DNA can also be extracted from the hair shaft.
- All positive microscopic hair comparisons must be confirmed by DNA analysis.

Forensic Examination of Fibers

Just as hair left at a crime scene can be used for identification, so can the fibers that compose fabrics and garments. Fibers may become important evidence in incidents that involve personal contact—such as homicide, assault, and sexual offenses—in which cross-transfers may occur between the clothing of suspect and victim. Similarly, the force of impact between a hit-and-run victim and a vehicle often leaves fibers, threads, or even whole pieces of clothing adhering to parts of the vehicle. Fibers may also become fixed in screens or on glass that is broken in the course of a breaking-and-entering attempt.

Regardless of where and under what conditions fibers are recovered, their ultimate value as forensic evidence depends on the criminalist's ability to narrow their origin to a limited number of sources or even to a single source. Unfortunately, mass production of garments and fabrics has limited the value of fiber evidence in this respect, and only rarely do fibers recovered at a crime scene provide individual identification with a high degree of certainty.

TYPES OF FIBERS

For centuries, humans depended on fibers derived from natural sources such as plants and animals. However, early in the twentieth century, the first manufactured fiber—rayon—became a practical reality, followed in the 1920s by the introduction of cellulose acetate. Since the late 1930s, scientists have produced dozens of new fibers. In fact, there have been greater advances in the development of fibers, fabrics, finishes, and other textile-processing techniques since

1900 than in the preceding five thousand years of recorded history. Today, such varied items as clothing, carpeting, drapes, wigs, and even artificial turf attest to the predominant role that manufactured fibers have come to play in our culture and environment. When discussing forensic examination of fibers, it is convenient to classify them into two broad groups: "natural" and "manufactured."

NATURAL FIBERS   Natural fibers are wholly derived from animal or plant sources. Natural fibers encountered in crime laboratory examinations come primarily from animals. These include hair coverings from such animals as sheep (wool), goats (mohair, cashmere), camels, llamas, alpacas, and vicuñas. Fur fibers include those obtained from animals such as mink, rabbit, beaver, and muskrat.

> **natural fibers**
> Fibers derived entirely from animal or plant sources.

The forensic examination of animal fibers uses the same procedures discussed in the previous section for the forensic examination of animal hairs. The identification and comparison of such fibers relies solely on a microscopic examination of color and morphological characteristics. Again, a sufficient number of standard/reference specimens must be examined to establish the range of fiber characteristics that make up the suspect fabric.

By far the most prevalent plant fiber is cotton. The wide use of undyed white cotton fibers in clothing and other fabrics has made its evidential value almost meaningless, but the presence of dyed cotton in a combination of colors has, in some cases, enhanced its evidential significance. The microscopic view of cotton fiber shown in Figure 13-10 reveals its most distinguishing feature—its ribbonlike shape with twists at irregular intervals.

MANUFACTURED FIBERS   Beginning with the introduction of rayon in 1911 and the development of nylon in 1939, **manufactured fibers** have increasingly replaced natural fibers in garments and fabrics. Such fibers are marketed under hundreds of trade names. To reduce consumer confusion, the U.S. Federal Trade Commission has approved "generic" or family names for the grouping of all manufactured fibers. Many of these generic classes are produced by several manufacturers and are sold under a confusing variety of trade names. For example, in the United States, polyesters are marketed under names that include Dacron, Fortrel, and Kodel. In England, polyesters are called Terylene. Table 13.1 lists major generic fibers, along with common trade names and their characteristics and applications.

> **manufactured fibers**
> Fibers derived from either natural or synthetic polymers.

The first machine-made fibers were manufactured from raw materials derived from cotton or wood pulp, and these are still being made. The raw materials are processed, and pure cellulose is extracted from them. Depending on the type of fiber desired, the cellulose may be chemically treated and dissolved in an appropriate solvent before it is forced through the small holes of a spinning jet, or spinneret, to produce the fiber. Fibers manufactured from natural raw materials in this manner are classified as "regenerated fibers" and commonly include rayon, acetate, and triacetate, all of which are produced from regenerated cellulose.

Most of the fibers currently manufactured are produced solely from synthetic chemicals and are therefore classified as "synthetic fibers." These include nylons, polyesters, and acrylics. The creation of synthetic fibers became a reality only when scientists developed a method of synthesizing long-chained molecules called polymers.

In 1930, chemists discovered an unusual characteristic of one of the polymers under investigation. When a glass rod in contact with viscous material in a beaker was slowly pulled away, the substance adhered to the rod and formed a fine filament that hardened as soon as it entered the cool air. Furthermore, the cold filaments could be stretched several times their

FIGURE 13-10   Photomicrograph of cotton fiber (450×). *Richard Saferstein, Ph.D.*

TABLE 13.1 Major Generic Fibers

MAJOR GENERIC FIBER	CHARACTERISTICS	MAJOR DOMESTIC AND INDUSTRIAL USES
Acetate	• Luxurious feel and appearance • Wide range of colors and lusters • Excellent drapability and softness • Relatively fast-drying • Shrink-, moth-, and mildew-resistant	*Apparel:* Blouses, dresses, foundation garments, lingerie, linings, shirts, slacks, sportswear *Fabrics:* Brocade, crepe, double knits, faille, knitted jerseys, lace, satin, taffeta, tricot *Home Furnishings:* Draperies, upholstery *Other:* Cigarette filters, fiberfill for pillows, quilted products
Acrylic	• Soft and warm • Wool-like • Retains shape • Resilient • Quick-drying • Resistant to moths, sunlight, oil, and chemicals	*Apparel:* Dresses, infant wear, knitted garments, skiwear, socks, sportswear, sweaters *Fabrics:* Fleece and pile fabrics, face fabrics in bonded fabrics, simulated furs, jerseys *Home Furnishings:* Blankets, carpets, draperies, upholstery *Other:* Auto tops, awnings, hand-knitting and craft yarns, industrial and geotextile fabrics
Aramid	• Does not melt • Highly flame-resistant • Great strength • Great resistance to stretch • Maintains shape and form at high temperatures	Hot-gas filtration fabrics, protective clothing, military helmets, protective vests, structural composites for aircraft and boats, sailcloth, tires, ropes and cables, mechanical rubber goods, marine and sporting goods
Bicomponent	• Thermal bonding • Self-bulking • Very fine fibers • Unique cross-sections • The functionality of special polymers or additives at reduced cost	Uniform distribution of adhesive; fiber remains a part of structure and adds integrity; customized sheath materials to bond various materials; wide range of bonding temperatures; cleaner, environmentally friendly (no effluent); recyclable; lamination/molding/densification of composites
Lyocell	• Soft, strong, absorbent • Good dyeability • Fibrillates during wet processing to produce special textures	Dresses, slacks, and coats
Melamine	• White and dyeable • Flame resistance and low thermal conductivity • High-heat dimensional stability • Processable on standard textile equipment	*Fire-Blocking Fabrics:* Aircraft seating, fire blockers for upholstered furniture in high-risk occupancies (e.g., to meet California TB 133 requirements) *Protective Clothing:* Firefighters' turnout gear, insulating thermal liners, knit hoods, molten metal splash apparel, heat-resistant gloves *Filter Media:* High-capacity, high-efficiency, high-temperature baghouse air filters
Modacrylic	• Soft • Resilient • Abrasion- and flame-resistant • Quick-drying • Resists acids and alkalies • Retains shape	*Apparel:* Deep-pile coats, trims, linings, simulated fur, wigs and hairpieces *Fabrics:* Fleece fabrics, industrial fabrics, knit-pile fabric backings, nonwoven fabrics *Home Furnishings:* Awnings, blankets, carpets, flame-resistant draperies and curtains, scatter rugs *Other:* Filters, paint rollers, stuffed toys

MAJOR GENERIC FIBER	CHARACTERISTICS	MAJOR DOMESTIC AND INDUSTRIAL USES
Nylon	• Exceptionally strong • Supple • Abrasion-resistant • Lustrous • Easy to wash • Resists damage from oil and many chemicals • Resilient • Low in moisture absorbency	*Apparel:* Blouses, dresses, foundation garments, hosiery, lingerie and underwear, raincoats, ski and snow apparel, suits, windbreakers *Home Furnishings:* Bedspreads, carpets, draperies, curtains, upholstery *Other:* Air hoses, conveyor and seat belts, parachutes, racket strings, ropes and nets, sleeping bags, tarpaulins, tents, thread, tire cord, geotextiles
Olefin	• Unique wicking properties that make it very comfortable • Abrasion-resistant • Quick-drying • Resistant to deterioration from chemicals, mildew, perspiration, rot, and weather • Sensitive to heat • Soil-resistant • Strong; very lightweight • Excellent colorfastness	*Apparel:* Pantyhose, underwear, knitted sports shirts, men's half-hose, men's knitted sportswear, sweaters *Home Furnishings:* Carpet and carpet backing, slipcovers, upholstery *Other:* Dye nets, filter fabrics, laundry bags, sandbags, geotextiles, automotive interiors, cordage, doll hair, industrial sewing thread
Polyester	• Strong • Resistant to stretching and shrinking • Resistant to most chemicals • Quick-drying • Crisp and resilient when wet or dry • Wrinkle- and abrasion-resistant • Retains heat-set pleats and creases • Easy to wash	*Apparel:* Blouses, shirts, career apparel, children's wear, dresses, half-hose, insulated garments, ties, lingerie and underwear, permanent press garments, slacks, suits *Home Furnishings:* Carpets, curtains, draperies, sheets and pillowcases *Other:* Fiberfill for various products, fire hoses, power belting, ropes and nets, tire cord, sail, V-belts
PBI	• Extremely flame-resistant • Outstanding comfort factor combined with thermal and chemical stability properties • Will not burn or melt • Low shrinkage when exposed to flame	Suitable for high-performance protective apparel such as firefighters' turnout coats, astronaut space suits, and applications in which fire resistance is important
Rayon	• Highly absorbent • Soft and comfortable • Easy to dye • Versatile • Good drapability	*Apparel:* Blouses, coats, dresses, jackets, lingerie, linings, millinery, rainwear, slacks, sports shirts, sportswear, suits, ties, work clothes *Home Furnishings:* Bedspreads, blankets, carpets, curtains, draperies, sheets, slipcovers, tablecloths, upholstery *Other:* Industrial products, medical-surgical products, nonwoven products, tire cord
Spandex	• Can be stretched 500 percent without breaking • Can be stretched repeatedly and recover original length • Lightweight • Stronger and more durable than rubber • Resistant to body oils	*Apparel* (articles in which stretch is desired): Athletic apparel, bathing suits, delicate laces, foundation garments, golf jackets, ski pants, slacks, support and surgical hose

Source: American Fiber Manufacturers Assoc. Inc., Washington, DC, www.fingersource.com Reprinted by permission.

extended length to produce a flexible, strong, and attractive fiber. This first synthetic fiber was improved and then marketed as nylon. Since then, fiber chemists have successfully synthesized new polymers and have developed more efficient methods for manufacturing them. These efforts have produced a multitude of synthetic fibers.

IDENTIFICATION AND COMPARISON OF MANUFACTURED FIBERS

The evidential value of fibers lies in the criminalist's ability to trace their origin. Obviously, if the examiner is presented with fabrics that can be exactly fitted together at their torn edges, the fabrics must be of common origin.

More often, however, the criminalist obtains a limited number of fibers for identification and comparison. Generally, in these situations obtaining a physical match is unlikely, and the examiner must resort to a side-by-side comparison of the standard/reference and crime-scene fibers.

MICROSCOPIC EXAMINATION OF FIBERS The first and most important step in the examination is a microscopic comparison for color and diameter using a comparison microscope. Unless these two characteristics agree, there is little reason to suspect a match. Other morphological features that may aid in the comparison are lengthwise striations (lined markings) on the surface of some fibers and the pitting of the fiber's surface with delustering particles (usually titanium dioxide) added in the manufacturing process to reduce shine (see Figure 13-11).

The cross-sectional shape of a fiber may also help characterize the fiber (see Figure 13-12).[6] In the early 1880s, Wayne Williams was charged and tried for the murder of two individuals in the Atlanta, Georgia, region. During the eight-week trial, evidence linking Williams to those murders and to the murder of ten other individuals was introduced. An essential part of the

FIGURE 13-11 Photomicrographs of synthetic fibers: (a) cellulose triacetate (450×) and (b) olefin fiber embedded with titanium dioxide particles (450×). *Richard Saferstein, Ph.D.*

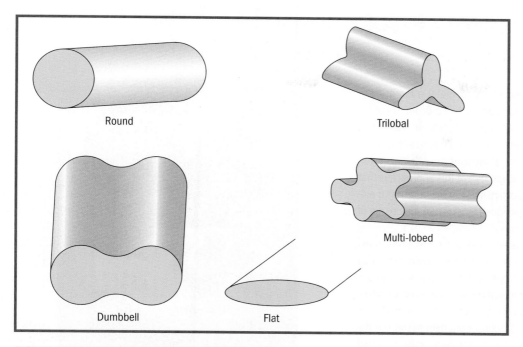

FIGURE 13-12 Cross-sectional shapes of fibers.

government's case was the numerous fibers linking Williams to the murders. Unusually shaped yellow-green fibers discovered on a number of the murder victims were linked to a carpet in the Williams home. This fiber was a key element in proving Williams's guilt. A photomicrograph of this unusually shaped fiber is shown in Figure 13-13.

Although two fibers may seem to have the same color when viewed under the microscope, compositional differences may actually exist in the dyes that were applied to them during their manufacture. In fact, most textile fibers are impregnated with a mixture of dyes selected to obtain a desired shade or color. The significance of a fiber comparison is enhanced when the forensic examiner can show that the questioned and standard/reference fibers have the same dye composition.

ANALYTICAL TECHNIQUES USED IN FIBER EXAMINATION In Chapter 11, we saw how a chemist can use selective absorption of light by materials to characterize them. In particular, light in the ultraviolet, visible, and infrared regions of the electromagnetic spectrum is most helpful for this purpose. Unfortunately, in the past, forensic chemists were unable to take full advantage of the capabilities of spectrophotometry for examining trace evidence because

FIGURE 13-13 A scanning electron photomicrograph of the cross-section of a nylon fiber removed from a sheet used to transport the body of a murder victim. The fiber, associated with a carpet in Wayne Williams's home, was manufactured in 1971 in relatively small quantities. *Federal Bureau of Investigation*

CLOSER ANALYSIS
THE MICROSPECTROPHOTOMETER

With the development of the microspectrophotometer, a forensic analyst can view a particle under a microscope while a beam of light is directed at the particle to obtain its absorption spectrum. Depending on the type of light employed, an examiner can acquire either a visible or an infrared (IR) spectral pattern of the substance being viewed under the microscope. The obvious advantage of this approach is that it provides added information to characterize trace quantities of evidence. A microspectrophotometer designed to measure the uptake of visible light by materials is shown here.

Visual comparison of color is usually one of the first steps in examining paint, fiber, and ink evidence. Such comparisons are easily obtained using a comparison microscope. A forensic scientist can use the microspectrophotometer to compare the color of materials visually while plotting an absorption spectrum for each item under examination. This displays the exact wavelengths at which each item absorbs in the visible-light spectrum. Occasionally, colors that appear similar by visual examination show significant differences in their absorption spectra.

Another emerging technique in forensic science is the use of the IR microspectrophotometer to examine fibers and paints. The "fingerprint" IR spectrum (see Figures 1 and 2 in the Case File on pages 338 and 339) is unique for each chemical substance. Therefore, obtaining such a spectrum from either a fiber or a paint chip allows the analyst to better identify and compare the type of chemicals from which these materials are manufactured. With a microspectrophotometer, a forensic analyst can view a substance through the microscope and at the same time have the instrument plot the infrared absorption spectrum for that material.

A visible-light microspectrophotometer. *CRAIC Technologies Inc.*

most spectrophotometers are not well suited for examining the very small particles frequently encountered as evidence. Recently, linking the microscope to a computerized spectrophotometer has added a new dimension to its capability. This combination has given rise to a new instrument called the microspectrophotometer. In many respects, this is an ideal marriage from the forensic scientist's viewpoint.

The visible-light microspectrophotometer is a convenient way for analysts to compare the colors of fibers through spectral patterns. This technique is not limited by sample size; a fiber as small as 1 millimeter long or less can be examined by this type of microscope. The examination is nondestructive and is carried out on fibers simply mounted on a microscope slide.

CHEMICAL COMPOSITION Before the forensic scientist can reach a conclusion that two or more fibers compare, it must be shown that the fibers in question have the same chemical composition. In this respect, tests are performed to confirm that all of the fibers involved belong to the same broad generic class. Additionally, the comparison will be substantially enhanced if it can be demonstrated that all of the fibers belong to the same subclassification within their generic class. For example, at least four types of nylon are available in commercial and consumer markets, including nylon 6, nylon 6-10, nylon 11, and nylon 6-6. Although all types of nylon have many properties in common, each may differ in physical shape, appearance, and dyeability because of modifications in their basic chemical structure.

Textile chemists have devised numerous tests for determining the class of a fiber. However, unlike the textile chemist, the criminalist frequently does not have the luxury of a substantial quantity of the fabric to work with and must therefore select tests that will yield the most information with the least amount of material. Only a single fiber may be available for analysis, and often this may amount to no more than a minute strand recovered, for example, from a fingernail scraping from a homicide or rape victim.

INFRARED ABSORPTION   The polymers that compose a manufactured fiber, like any organic substance, selectively absorb infrared light in a characteristic pattern. Infrared spectrophotometry thus provides a rapid and reliable method for identifying the generic class, and in some cases the subclass, of a fiber. The infrared microspectrophotometer combines a microscope with an infrared spectrophotometer. Such a combination makes possible the infrared analysis of a small, single-strand fiber while it is being viewed under a microscope.

SIGNIFICANCE OF FIBER EVIDENCE

Once a fiber match has been determined, the question of the significance of such a finding is bound to be raised. In reality, no analytical technique permits the criminalist to link a fiber strand definitively to any single garment. Furthermore, except in the most unusual circumstances, no statistical databases are available for determining the probability of a fiber's origin. Considering the mass distribution of synthetic fibers and the constantly changing fashion tastes of our society, it is highly unlikely that such data will be available in the foreseeable future.

Despite these limitations, an investigator should not discount or minimize the significance of a fiber association. An enormous variety of fibers exists in our society. By simply looking at the random individuals we meet every day, we can see how unlikely it is to find two people wearing identically colored fabrics (with the exception of blue denims or white cottons). There are thousands of different-colored fibers in our environment. Combine this with the fact that forensic scientists compare not only the color of fibers but also their size, shape, microscopic appearance, chemical composition, and dye content, and one can now begin to appreciate how unlikely it is to find two indistinguishable colored fibers on two randomly selected sources.

Furthermore, the significance of a fiber association increases dramatically when the analyst can link two or more distinctly different fibers to the same object. Likewise, the associative value of fiber evidence is dramatically enhanced if it is accompanied by other types of physical evidence linking a person or object to a crime. As with most class evidence, the significance of a fiber comparison is dictated by the circumstances of the case; by the location, number, and nature of the fibers examined; and, most important, by the judgment of an experienced examiner.

Collection and Preservation of Fiber Evidence

As criminal investigators have become more aware of the potential contribution of trace physical evidence to the success of their investigations, they have placed greater emphasis on conducting thorough crime-scene searches for evidence of forensic value. Their skill and determination at carrying out these tasks is tested in the collection of fiber-related evidence. Fiber evidence can

■■■■ CASEFILES ■■■■

FATAL VISION REVISITED

Dr. Jeffrey MacDonald, pictured here, was convicted in 1979 of murdering his wife and two young daughters. The events surrounding the crime and the subsequent trial were recounted in Joe McGinniss's best-selling book *Fatal Vision*. The focus of Dr. MacDonald's defense was that intruders entered his home and committed these violent acts. Eleven years after this conviction, Dr. MacDonald's attorneys filed a petition for a new trial, claiming the existence of "critical" new evidence.

The defense asserted that wig fibers found on a hairbrush in the MacDonald residence were evidence that an intruder dressed

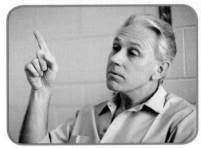

Jeffrey MacDonald in 1995 at Sheridan, Oregon, Federal Correctional Institution. *AP Images Inc.*

in a wig entered the MacDonald home on the day of the murder. Subsequent examination of this claim by the FBI Laboratory focused on a blond fall (a type of artificial hair extension) frequently worn by Dr. MacDonald's wife. Fibers removed from the fall were shown to clearly match fibers on the hairbrush. The examination included the use of infrared microspectrophotometry to demonstrate that the suspect wig fibers were chemically identical to fibers found in the composition of Mrs. MacDonald's fall (see Figure 1). Hence, although wig fibers were found at the crime scene, the source of these fibers could be accounted for: Mrs. MacDonald's fall.

Another piece of evidence cited by Dr. MacDonald's lawyers was a bluish-black woolen fiber found on the body of Mrs. MacDonald. They claimed that this fiber compared to a bluish-black woolen fiber recovered from the club used to assault her. These wool fibers were central to Dr. MacDonald's defense that the "intruders" wore dark-colored clothing. Initial examination showed that the fibers were microscopically indistinguishable. However, the FBI also compared the two wool fibers by visible-light microspectrophotometry. Comparison of their spectra clearly showed that their dye compositions differed, providing no evidence of outside intruders (see Figure 2). Ultimately, the U.S. Supreme Court denied the merits of Jeffrey MacDonald's petition for a new trial.

Source: Based on information contained in B. M. Murtagh and M. P. Malone, "Fatal Vision Revisited," *Police Chief* (June 1993): 15.

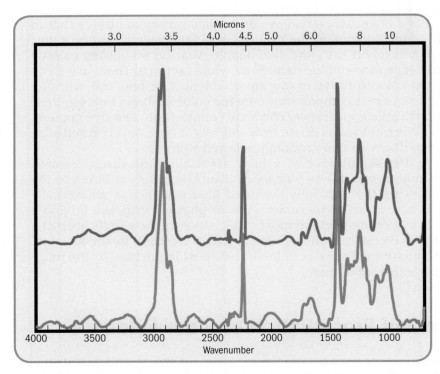

FIGURE 1   A fiber comparison made with an infrared spectrophotometer. The infrared spectrum of a fiber from Mrs. MacDonald's fall compares to a fiber recovered from a hairbrush in the MacDonald home. These fibers were identified as modacrylics, the most common type of synthetic fiber used in the manufacture of human hair goods. *Courtesy SA Michael Malone, FBI Laboratory, Washington, D.C.*

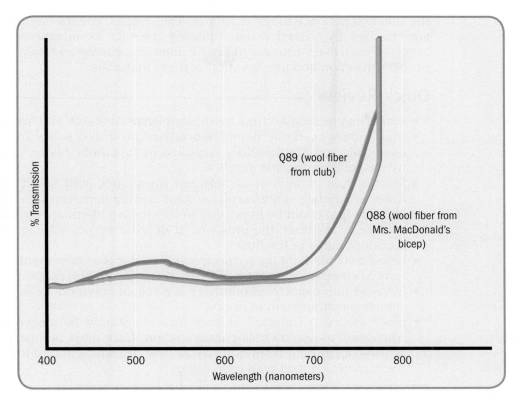

FIGURE 2   The visible-light spectrum for the woolen fiber recovered from Mrs. MacDonald's body is clearly different from that of the fiber recovered from the club used to assault her. *Federal Bureau of Investigation*

be associated with virtually any type of crime. It usually cannot be seen with the naked eye and thus can be easily overlooked by someone not specifically searching for it.

An investigator committed to optimizing the laboratory's chances for locating minute strands of fibers identifies and preserves potential "carriers" of fiber evidence. Relevant articles of clothing should be packaged carefully in paper bags. Each article must be placed in a separate bag to avoid cross-contamination of evidence. Scrupulous care must be taken to prevent articles of clothing from different people or from different locations from coming into contact. Such articles must not even be placed on the same surface prior to packaging. Likewise, carpets, rugs, and bedding are to be folded carefully to protect areas suspected of containing fibers. Car seats should be carefully covered with polyethylene sheets to protect fiber evidence, and knife blades should be covered to protect adhering fibers. If a body is thought to have been wrapped at one time in a blanket or carpet, adhesive tape lifts of exposed body areas may reveal fiber strands.

Occasionally the field investigator may need to remove a fiber from an object, particularly if loosely adhering fibrous material may be lost in transit to the laboratory. These fibers must be removed with a clean forceps and placed in a small sheet of paper, which, after folding and labeling, should be placed inside another container. Again, scrupulous care must be taken to prevent contact between fibers collected from different objects or from different locations.

In the laboratory, the search for fiber evidence on clothing and other relevant objects, as well as in debris, is time consuming and tedious and will test the skill and patience of the examiner. The crime-scene investigator can manage this task by collecting only relevant items for examination—pinpointing areas where a likely transfer of fiber evidence occurred and then ensuring the proper collection and preservation of these materials.

Quick Review

VIRTUAL LAB
FORENSIC HAIR ANALYSIS
To perform a virtual forensic hair analysis, go to *www.pearsoncustom.com/us/vlm/*

VIRTUAL LAB
EXAMINATION OF TEXTILE FIBERS BY MICROSCOPY
To perform a virtual fiber examination lab, go to *www.pearsoncustom.com/us/vlm/*

- Fibers may be classified into two broad groups: "natural" and "manufactured."
- Most fibers currently manufactured are produced solely from synthetic chemicals and are therefore classified as "synthetic fibers." They include nylons, polyesters, and acrylics.
- Microscopic comparisons between questioned and standard/reference fibers are initially undertaken for color and diameter characteristics. Other features that could be important in comparing fibers are striations on the surface of the fiber, the presence of delustering particles, and the cross-sectional shape of the fiber.
- Using a visible-light microspectrophotometer is a convenient way for analysts to compare the colors of fibers through spectral patterns.
- Infrared microspectrophotometry is a reliable method for identifying the chemical composition of fibers.
- Fiber evidence collected at each location should be placed in separate containers to avoid cross-contamination. Care must be taken to prevent articles of clothing from different people or from different locations from coming into contact with each other.

CHAPTER REVIEW

- The hair shaft is composed of three layers called the "cuticle," "cortex," and "medulla" and is the part of the hair most intensely examined by the forensic scientist.

- When comparing strands of hair, the criminalist is particularly interested in matching the color, length, and diameter. Other important features for comparing hair are the presence or absence of a medulla and the distribution, shape, and color intensity of pigment granules in the cortex.

- The likelihood of successfully detecting DNA in hair roots is higher in hair being examined in its anagen or early growth phase than in its catagen or telogen phases.

- The follicular tag, a translucent piece of tissue surrounding the hair's shaft near the root, is a rich source of DNA associated with hair. Mitochondrial DNA can also be extracted from the hair shaft.

- All positive microscopic hair comparisons must be confirmed by DNA analysis.

- Fibers may be classified into two broad groups: "natural" and "manufactured."

- Most fibers currently manufactured are produced solely from synthetic chemicals and are therefore classified as "synthetic fibers." They include nylons, polyesters, and acrylics.

- Microscopic comparisons between questioned and standard/reference fibers are initially undertaken for color and diameter characteristics. Other features that could be important in comparing fibers are striations on the surface of the fiber, the presence of delustering particles, and the cross-sectional shape of the fiber.

- Using a visible-light microspectrophotometer is a convenient way for analysts to compare the colors of fibers through spectral patterns.

- Infrared microspectrophotometry is a reliable method for identifying the chemical composition of fibers.

- Fiber evidence collected at each location should be placed in separate containers to avoid cross-contamination. Care must be taken to prevent articles of clothing from different people or from different locations from coming into contact with each other.

KEY TERMS

anagen phase, 323

catagen phase, 323

cortex, 320

cuticle, 320

follicular tag, 324

manufactured fibers, 331

medulla, 320

mitochondrial DNA, 328

natural fibers, 331

nuclear DNA, 328

telogen phase, 323

REVIEW QUESTIONS

1. Hair is an appendage of the skin, growing out of an organ known as the _____.

2. The three layers of the hair shaft are the _____, the _____, and the _____.

3. The scale pattern of hair's _____ can be observed by making a cast of its surface in clear nail polish or softened vinyl.

4. The _____ contains the pigment granules that impart color to hair.

5. The central canal running through many hairs is known as the _____.

6. The diameter of the medulla relative to the diameter of the hair shaft is the _____.

7. Human hair generally has a medullary index of less than _____; the hair of most animals has an index of _____ or greater.

8. True or False: Human head hairs generally exhibit no medullae. _____

9. True or False: If a medulla exhibits a pattern, the hair is animal in origin. _____

10. The three stages of hair growth are the _____, _____, and _____ phases.

11. True or False: Individual hairs can show variable morphological characteristics within a single individual. _____

12. True or False: A single hair cannot be individualized to one person by microscopic examination. _____

13. In making hair comparisons, it is best to view the hairs side by side under a(n) _____ microscope.

14. _____ hairs are short and curly, with wide variation in shaft diameter.

15. True or False: It is possible to estimate when hair was last bleached or dyed by microscopic examination. _____

16. True or False: The age and sex of the individual from whom a hair sample has been taken can be determined through an examination of the hair's morphological features. _____

17. True or False: Hair forcibly removed from the body sometimes has follicular tissue adhering to its root. _____

18. Microscopic hair comparisons must be regarded by police and courts as presumptive in nature, and all positive microscopic hair comparisons must be confirmed by _____ typing.

19. A hair root in the _____ or _____ growth phase is a likely candidate for DNA typing.

20. True or False: The onset of postmortem changes to the root portion of hair is observed only in anagenic and catagenic hairs. _____

21. A minimum collection of _____ full-length hairs normally ensures a representative sampling of head hair.

22. A minimum collection of _____ full-length pubic hairs is recommended to cover the range of characteristics present in this region of the body.

23. The ultimate value of fibers as forensic evidence depends on the ability to narrow their _____ to a limited number of sources or even to a single source.

24. _____ fibers are derived totally from animal or plant sources.

25. The most prevalent natural plant fiber is _____.

26. _____ fibers such as rayon, acetate, and triacetate are manufactured from natural raw materials such as cellulose.

27. Fibers manufactured solely from synthetic chemicals are classified as _____.

28. True or False: Polyester was the first synthetic fiber. _____

29. True or False: A first step in the forensic examination of fibers is to compare color and diameter. _____

30. The microspectrophotometer employing _____ light is a convenient way for analysts to compare the colors of fibers through spectral patterns.

31. The microspectrophotometer employing _____ light provides a rapid and reliable method for identifying the generic class of a single fiber.

32. True or False: Statistical databases are available for determining the probability of a fiber's origin. _____

33. True or False: Normally, fibers possess individual characteristics. _____

34. In order to preserve fiber evidence not originally apparent to the investigator, all _____ of possible fiber evidence should be carefully collected and packaged.

■■■■ APPLICATION AND CRITICAL THINKING

1. Indicate the phase of growth of each of the following hairs:
   a) The root is club shaped.
   b) The hair has a follicular tag.
   c) The root bulb is flame shaped.
   d) The root is elongated.

2. A criminalist studying a dyed sample hair notices that the dyed color ends about 1.5 centimeters from the tip of the hair. Approximately how many weeks before the examination was the hair dyed? Explain your answer.

3. Following are descriptions of several hairs. Based on these descriptions, indicate the likely race of the person from whom the hair originated.
   a) Evenly distributed, fine pigmentation.
   b) Continuous medullation.
   c) Dense, uneven pigmentation.
   d) Wavy with a round cross-section.

4. Criminalist Pete Evett is collecting fiber evidence from a murder scene. He notices fibers on the victim's shirt and trousers, so he places both of these items of clothing in a plastic bag. He also sees fibers on a sheet near the victim, so he balls up the sheet and places it in a separate plastic bag. Noticing fibers adhering to the windowsill from which the attacker gained entrance, Pete carefully removes it with his fingers and places it in a regular envelope. What mistakes, if any, did Pete make while collecting this evidence?

5. For each of the following human hair samples, indicate the medulla pattern present.

Richard Safestein, Ph.D.
a. _____

Richard Safestein, Ph.D.
b. _____

Richard Safestein, Ph.D.
c. _____

Richard Safestein, Ph.D.
d. _____

Richard Safestein, Ph.D.
e. _____

Richard Safestein, Ph.D.
f. _____

Richard Safestein, Ph.D.
g. _____

Richard Safestein, Ph.D.
h. _____

Richard Safestein, Ph.D.
i. _____

6. The most common scale patterns found on hairs are generally classified as coronal, spinous, and imbricate. Examine the scale casts of animal hairs shown here and indicate the scale pattern of each.

a. _____

b. _____

c. _____

d. _____

e. _____

f. _____

g. _____

h. _____

7. A young child is kidnapped from her school playground. Shown on the top is a reference sample of the kidnapped child's hair. The only cars that left the parking lot before the child was discovered to be missing were those of four cafeteria workers. The car of each worker was searched and hairs collected. These recovered hairs are shown below the victim's reference hair. Which recovered hair, if any, is consistent with that of the victim and warrants further investigation?

Reference Hair from Victim
Richard Safestein, Ph.D.

Hair from Car of Worker A
Richard Safestein, Ph.D.

Hair from Car of Worker B
Richard Safestein, Ph.D.

Hair from Car of Worker C
Richard Safestein, Ph.D.

Hair from Car of Worker D
Richard Safestein, Ph.D.

▪▪▪▪▪ ENDNOTES

1. J. D. Baker and D. L. Exline, Forensic Animal Hair -Atlas: A Searchable Database on CD-ROM (Version 1.3). (Monroeville, PA: RJ Lee Group, 1999).

2. M. M. Houk and B. Budowle, "Correlation of Microscopic and Mitochondrial DNA Hair Comparisons," *Journal of Forensic Sciences* 47 (2002): 964.

3. L. A. King, R. Wigmore, and J. M. Twibell, "The Morphology and Occurrence of Human Hair Sheath Cells," *Journal of the Forensic Science Society* 22 (1982): 267.

4. S. L. Koch, A. L. Michaud, and C. Mikell, "Taphonomy of Hair—A Study of Postmortem Root Banding," *Journal of Forensic Sciences* 58 (2013): S52.

5. C. A. Linch et al., "Evaluation of the Human Hair Root for DNA Typing Subsequent to Microscopic Comparison," *Journal of Forensic Sciences* 43 (1998): 305.

6. S. Palenki and C. Fitzsimmons, "Fiber Cross-Sections: Part I," *Microscope* 38 (1990): 187.

14 Trace Evidence II
Paint, Glass, and Soil

GREEN RIVER KILLER

This case takes its name from the Green River, which flows through Washington state and empties into Puget Sound in Seattle. In 1982, within six months the bodies of five females were discovered in or near the river. Most of the victims were known prostitutes who were strangled and apparently raped. As police focused their attention on an area known as Sea-Tac Strip, a haven for prostitutes, girls mysteriously disappeared with increasing frequency. By the end of 1986, the body count in the Seattle region rose to 40, all of whom were believed to have been murdered by the Green River Killer. As the investigation pressed on into 1987, the police renewed their interest in one suspect, Gary Ridgway, a local truck painter. Interestingly, in 1984 Ridgway had passed a lie detector test. Now with a search warrant in hand, police searched the Ridgway residence and also obtained hair and saliva samples from Ridgway. Again, insufficient evidence caused Ridgway to be released from custody. However, as the investigation proceeded, a DNA link between Ridgway and his victims eluded investigators. Ultimately, a careful microscopic search of Ridgway's clothing revealed the presence of paint spheres of various colors, which compared to spheres on the clothing of six of the victims. The paint was microscopically and chemically identified as Imron, a high-end specialty paint that was manufactured before 1984. This product had been used at the truck plant where Ridgway worked and was identified as dried paint spheres emanating from a spray paint. Two of the victims were further linked to Ridgway through DNA, further solidifying the case against Ridgway. Ridgway avoided the death penalty by confessing to the murders of 48 women.

LEARNING OBJECTIVES

After studying this chapter, you should be able to:

- Describe the composition of paint.
- List the most useful examinations for performing a forensic comparison of paint.
- Understand the applications of stereoscopic microscopes, pyrolysis gas chromatography, and infrared spectrophotometry in forensic paint comparison and examination.
- Describe the composition of glass.
- Define and understand the properties of density and refractive index.
- List and explain forensic methods for comparing glass fragments.
- Understand how to examine glass fractures to determine the direction of impact of a projectile.
- List the important forensic properties of soil.
- Describe the proper collection and preservation methods for forensic paint, glass, and soil evidence.

Forensic Examination of Paint

Our environment contains millions of objects whose surfaces are painted. Thus paint, in one form or another, is one of the most prevalent types of physical evidence received by the crime laboratory.

Paint as physical evidence is perhaps most frequently encountered in hit-and-run and burglary cases. For example, a chip of dried paint or a paint smear may be transferred to the clothing of a hit-and-run victim on impact with an automobile, or paint smears could be transferred onto a tool during a burglary. Obviously, in many situations a transfer of paint from one surface to another could impart an object with an identifiable forensic characteristic.

In most circumstances, the criminalist must compare two or more paints to establish their common origin. For example, such a comparison may associate an individual or a vehicle with the crime site. However, the criminalist need not be confined to comparisons alone. Crime laboratories often help identify the color, make, and model of an automobile by examining small quantities of paint recovered at an accident scene. Such requests, normally made in hit-and-run cases, can lead to the apprehension of the responsible vehicle.

COMPOSITION OF PAINT

Paint is composed of a binder and pigments, as well as other additives, all dissolved or dispersed in a suitable solvent. Pigments impart color and hiding (or opacity) to paint and are usually mixtures of various inorganic and organic compounds added to the paint by the manufacturer. The binder is a polymeric substance that provides the support medium for the pigments and additives. After paint has been applied to a surface, the solvent evaporates, leaving behind a hard polymeric binder and any pigments that are suspended in it.

The most common types of paint examined in the crime laboratory are finishes from automobiles. Manufacturers apply a variety of coatings to the body of an automobile; this adds significant diversity to automobile paint and contributes to the forensic significance of automobile paint comparisons. The automotive finishing system for steel usually consists of at least four organic coatings: electrocoat primer, primer surfacer, basecoat, and clearcoat.

ELECTROCOAT PRIMER   The first layer applied to the steel body of a car is the electrocoat primer. The primer, consisting of epoxy-based resins, is electroplated onto the steel body of the automobile to provide corrosion resistance. The resulting coating is uniform in appearance and thickness. The color of these primers ranges from black to gray.

PRIMER SURFACER   Originally responsible for corrosion control, the surfacer usually follows the electrocoat layer and is applied before the basecoat. Primer surfacers are epoxy-modified polyesters or urethanes. The function of this layer is to completely smooth out and hide any seams or imperfections because the basecoat will be applied on this surface. This layer is highly pigmented. Color pigments are used to minimize color contrast between primer and topcoats. For example, a light gray primer may be used under pastel shades of a colored topcoat; a red oxide may be used under a dark-colored topcoat.

BASECOAT   The next layer of paint on a car is the basecoat or colorcoat. This layer provides the color and aesthetics of the finish and represents the "eye appeal" of the finished automobile. The integrity of this layer depends on its ability to resist weather, UV radiation, and acid rain. Most commonly, an acrylic-based polymer composes the binder system of basecoats. Interestingly, the choice of automotive pigments is dictated by toxic and environmental concerns. Thus, the use of lead, chrome, and other heavy-metal pigments has been abandoned in favor of organic-based pigments. There is also a growing trend toward pearl luster, or mica, pigments. Mica pigments are coated with layers of metal oxide to generate interference colors. Also, the addition of aluminum flakes to automotive paint imparts a metallic look to the paint's finish.

CLEARCOAT   An unpigmented clearcoat is applied to improve gloss, durability, and appearance. Most clearcoats are acrylic based, but polyurethane clearcoats are increasing in popularity. These topcoats provide outstanding etch resistance and appearance.

MICROSCOPIC EXAMINATION OF PAINT

The microscope has traditionally been, and remains, the most important instrument for locating and comparing paint specimens. Considering the thousands of paint colors and shades, it is quite understandable that color, more than any other property, gives paint its most distinctive forensic characteristics. Questioned and known specimens are best compared side by side under a stereoscopic microscope for color, surface texture, and color layer sequence (see Figure 14-1).

The importance of layer structure for evaluating the evidential significance of paint evidence cannot be overemphasized. When paint specimens possess colored layers that match in number and sequence of colors, the examiner can begin to relate the paints to a common origin. How many layers must be matched before the criminalist can conclude that the paint specimens came from the same source? Much depends on the uniqueness of each layer's color and texture, as well as the frequency with which the particular combination of colors under investigation is observed. Because no books or journals have compiled this type of information, the criminalist is left to his or her own experience and knowledge when making this determination.

Unfortunately, most paint specimens do not have a layer structure of sufficient complexity to allow them to be individualized to a single source (see Figure 14-2). However, the diverse chemical composition of modern paints provides additional points of comparison between specimens. Specifically, a thorough comparison of paint must include a chemical analysis of the paint's pigments, its binder composition, or both.

ANALYTICAL TECHNIQUES USED IN PAINT COMPARISON

The wide variation in binder formulations in automobile finishes provides significant information. More important, paint manufacturers make automobile finishes in hundreds of varieties; this knowledge is most helpful to the criminalist who is trying to associate a paint chip with one car as distinguished from the thousands of similar models that have been produced in any one year. For instance, there are more than a hundred automobile production plants in the United States and Canada. Each can use one paint supplier for a particular color or vary suppliers during a model year. Although a paint supplier must maintain strict quality control over a paint's color, the batch formulation of any paint binder can vary, depending on the availability and cost of basic ingredients.

FIGURE 14-1 A stereoscopic microscope comparison of two automotive paints. The questioned paint on the left has a layer structure consistent with the control paint on the right.
Leica Microsystems Inc.

FIGURE 14-2   Red paint chips peeling off a wall revealing underlying layers.
Jack Hollingsworth/Getty Images

CHARACTERIZATION OF PAINT BINDERS An important extension of the application of gas chromatography to forensic science is the technique of pyrolysis gas chromatography. Many solid materials commonly encountered as physical evidence—for example, paint chips, fibers, and plastics—cannot be readily dissolved in a solvent for injection into the gas chromatograph. Thus, under normal conditions these substances cannot be subjected to gas chromatographic analysis. However, materials such as these can be heated to high temperatures (500°C–1000°C), or "pyrolyzed," so that they will decompose into numerous gaseous products. Pyrolyzers permit these gaseous products to enter the carrier gas stream, where they flow into and through the gas chromatography (GC) column. The pyrolyzed material can then be characterized by the pattern produced by its chromatogram, or "pyrogram."

Pyrolysis gas chromatography is particularly invaluable for distinguishing most paint formulations. In this process, paint chips as small as 20 micrograms are decomposed by heat into numerous gaseous products and are sent through a gas chromatograph.

As shown in Figure 14-3, the polymer chain is decomposed by a heated filament, and the resultant products are swept into and through a gas chromatograph column. The separated decomposition products of the polymer emerge and are recorded. The pattern of this chromatogram, or pyrogram, distinguishes one polymer from another. The result is a pyrogram that is sufficiently detailed to reflect the chemical makeup of the binder. Figure 14-4 illustrates how the patterns produced by paint pyrograms can differentiate acrylic enamel paints removed from two automobiles. Note the subtle differences between the minor peaks when comparing the two pyrograms.

Infrared spectrophotometry is still another analytical technique that provides information about the binder composition of paint. Binders selectively absorb infrared radiation to yield a spectrum that is highly characteristic of a paint specimen.

pyrolysis
The decomposition of organic matter by heat.

CLOSER ANALYSIS
THE STEREOSCOPIC MICROSCOPE

The details that characterize many types of physical evidence do not always require examination under very high magnifications. For such specimens, the stereoscopic microscope has proved quite adequate, providing magnifying powers from 10× to 125×. This microscope has the advantage of presenting a distinctive three-dimensional image of an object. Also, whereas the image formed by the compound microscope is inverted and reversed (upside-down and backward), the stereoscopic microscope is more convenient because prisms in its light path create a right-side-up image.

The stereoscopic microscope, shown in Figure 1, is actually two monocular compound microscopes properly spaced and aligned to present a three-dimensional image of a specimen to the viewer, who looks through both eyepiece lenses. The light path of a stereoscopic microscope is shown in Figure 2.

The stereoscopic microscope is undoubtedly the most frequently used and versatile microscope found in the crime laboratory. Its wide field of view (i.e., the area of the specimen that can be seen when magnified) and great depth of focus (i.e., the thickness of the specimen that is entirely in focus) make it an ideal instrument for locating trace evidence in debris, garments, weapons, and tools. Furthermore, its potentially large working distance (i.e., the distance between the objective lens and the specimen) makes it ideal for microscopic examination of big, bulky items. When fitted with vertical illumination, or a light source above the specimen, the stereoscopic microscope becomes the primary tool for viewing opaque specimens, to characterize physical evidence as diverse as paint, soil, gunpowder residues, and marijuana.

FIGURE 1   A stereoscopic microscope. *Chuck Rausin/ Shutterstock*

FIGURE 2   A schematic diagram of a stereoscopic microscope. This microscope is actually two separate monocular microscopes, each with its own set of lenses except for the lowest objective lens that is common to both microscopes. *SAFERSTEIN, RICHARD, Ph.D., CRIMINALISTICS: AN INTRODUCTION TO FORENSIC SCIENCE, 11th Ed., © 2015. Reprinted and Electronically reproduced by permission of Pearson Education, Inc., Upper Saddle River, New Jersey.*

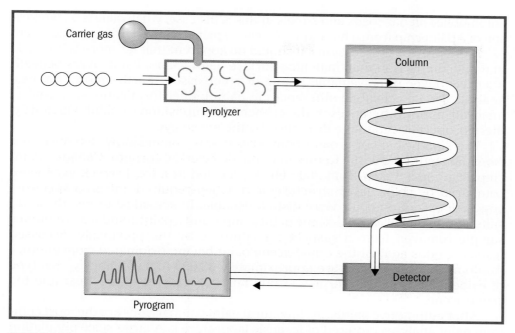

FIGURE 14-3 A schematic diagram of pyrolysis gas chromatography. *SAFERSTEIN, RICHARD, Ph.D., CRIMINALISTICS: AN INTRODUCTION TO FORENSIC SCIENCE, 11th Ed., © 2015. Reprinted and Electronically reproduced by permission of Pearson Education, Inc., Upper Saddle River, New Jersey.*

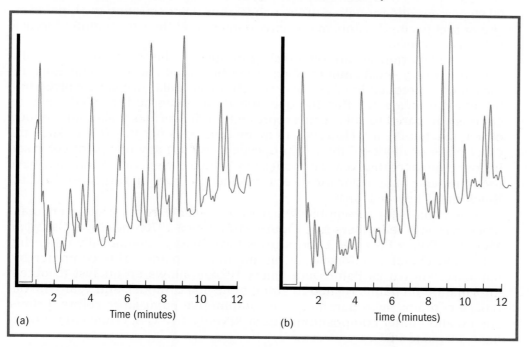

FIGURE 14-4 Paint pyrograms of acrylic enamel paints: (a) paint from a Ford model and (b) paint from a Chrysler model. *SAFERSTEIN, RICHARD, Ph.D., CRIMINALISTICS: AN INTRODUCTION TO FORENSIC SCIENCE, 11th Ed., © 2015. Reprinted and Electronically reproduced by permission of Pearson Education, Inc., Upper Saddle River, New Jersey.*

SIGNIFICANCE OF PAINT EVIDENCE

Once a paint comparison is completed, the task of assessing the significance of the finding begins. How certain can one be that two similar paints came from the same surface? For instance, a casual observer sees countless identically colored automobiles on our roads and streets. If this is the case, what value is a comparison of a paint chip from a hit-and-run scene to paint removed from a suspect car?

From previous discussions, it should be apparent that far more is involved in paint comparison than matching surface paint colors. Paint layers beneath a surface layer offer valuable points of comparison. Furthermore, forensic analysts can detect subtle differences in paint binder formulations, as well as major or minor differences in the elemental composition of paint. Obviously, these properties cannot be discerned by the naked eye.

The significance of a paint comparison was convincingly demonstrated from data gathered at the Centre of Forensic Science, Toronto, Canada.[1] Paint chips randomly taken from 260 vehicles located in a local wreck yard were compared by color; layer structure; and, when required, infrared spectroscopy. All except one pair were distinguishable. In statistical terms, these results signify that, if a crime-scene paint sample and a paint standard/-reference sample removed from a suspect car compare by the previously discussed tests, the odds against the crime-scene paint having originated from another randomly chosen vehicle are approximately 33,000 to 1. Obviously, this type of evidence is bound to forge a strong link between the suspect car and the crime scene.

After automotive paints, architectural paint comparisons are the most common paint analyses required of forensic laboratories. A large-scale population study of architectural paints collected throughout North America has been conducted for their forensic value.[2] Intercomparisons of nearly 960 randomly collected paints by visual, microscopic, and infrared technology resulted in a 99.99 percent differentiation of the paints, thus demonstrating the high diversity of architectural paints in our environment and their meaningful forensic value as class evidence.

Crime laboratories are often asked to identify the make and model of a car from a very small amount of paint left behind at a crime scene. Such information is frequently of use in a search for an unknown car involved in a hit-and-run incident. Often the questioned paint can be identified when its color is compared to color chips representing the various makes and models of manufactured cars. However, in many cases it is not possible to state the exact make or model of the car in question because any one paint color can be found on more than one car model. For instance, General Motors may have used the same paint color for several production years on cars in its Cadillac, Buick, and Chevrolet lines.

Color charts for automobile finishes are available from various paint manufacturers and refinishers (see Figure 14-5). Since 1975, the Royal Canadian Mounted Police Forensic Laboratories have been systematically gathering color and chemical information on automotive paints. This computerized database, known as Paint Data Query (PDQ), allows an analyst to obtain information on paints related to automobile make, model, and year. The database contains such parameters as automotive paint layer colors, primer colors, and binder composition. Nearly seventy-five U.S. crime laboratories have access to PDQ.

COLLECTION AND PRESERVATION OF PAINT EVIDENCE

As has already been noted, paint chips are most likely to be found on or near people or objects involved in hit-and-run incidents. The recovery of loose paint chips from a garment or from the road surface must be done with the utmost care to keep the paint chip intact. Paint chips may be picked up with tweezers or scooped up with a piece of paper. Paper made into druggist folds and glass and plastic vials make excellent containers for paint. If the paint is smeared on or embedded in garments or objects, the investigator should not attempt to remove it; instead, it is best to package the whole item carefully and send it to the laboratory for examination.

When a transfer of paint occurs in hit-and-run situations (such as to the clothing of a pedestrian victim), uncontaminated standard/reference paint must always be collected from an undamaged area of the vehicle for comparison in the laboratory. The collected paint must be close to the area of the car that is suspected to have come into contact with the victim. This is necessary because other portions of the car may have faded or been repainted.

Standard/reference samples are always removed in a way that includes all the paint layers down to the bare metal. This is best accomplished by removing a painted section with a disposable scalpel. Samples 1/4 inch square are sufficient for laboratory examination. Each paint sample should be separately packaged and marked with the exact location of its recovery.

When a cross-transfer of paint occurs between two vehicles, all of the layers, including the foreign as well as the underlying original paints, must be removed from each vehicle. A standard/reference sample from an adjacent undamaged area of each vehicle must also be taken in such cases. Before collecting each sample, an investigator must use a new disposable scalpel in order to prevent cross-contamination of paints.

FIGURE 14-5   An automotive color chart of various car models. *Damian Dovarganes/AP Images*

Quick Review

- Paint spread onto a surface dries into a hard film that is best described as consisting of pigments and additives suspended in a binder.
- Questioned and known paint specimens are best compared side by side under a stereoscopic microscope for color, surface texture, and color layer sequence.
- Pyrolysis gas chromatography and infrared spectrophotometry are used to distinguish most paint binder formulations.
- Paint Data Query (PDQ) is a computerized database that allows an analyst to obtain information on paints related to automobile make, model, and year.

Forensic Analysis of Glass

Glass that is broken and shattered into fragments and minute particles during the commission of a crime can be used to place a suspect at the crime scene. For example, chips of broken glass from a window may lodge in a suspect's shoes or garments during a burglary; particles of headlight glass found at the scene of a hit-and-run accident may confirm the identity of a suspect vehicle. All of these possibilities require the comparison of glass fragments found on the suspect, whether a person or vehicle, with the shattered glass remaining at the crime scene.

■■■■ CASEFILES ■■■■
THE PREDATOR

September in Arizona is usually hot and dry, much like the rest of the year—but September 1984 was a little different. Unusually heavy rains fell for two days, which must have seemed fitting to the friends and family of eight-year-old Vicki Lynn Hoskinson. Vicki went missing on September 17 of that year, and her disappearance was investigated as a kidnapping. A schoolteacher who knew Vicki remembered seeing a suspicious vehicle loitering near the school that day, and he happened to jot down the license plate number. This crucial tip led police to twenty-eight-year-old Frank Atwood, recently paroled from a California prison. Police soon learned that Atwood had been convicted for committing sex offenses and for kidnapping a boy. This galvanized the investigators, who realized Vicki could be at the mercy of a dangerous and perverse man.

The only evidence the police had to work with was Vicki's bike, which was found abandoned in the middle of the street a few blocks from her home. Police found scrapes from her bike pedal on the underside of the gravel pan on Atwood's car, as well as pink paint on Atwood's front bumper, apparently transferred from Vicki's bike. The police believed that Atwood deliberately struck Vicki while she was riding her bicycle, knocking her to the ground.

The pink paint on Atwood's bumper was first looked at microscopically and then examined by pyrolysis gas chromatography. This technique provides investigators with a "fingerprint" pattern of the paint sample, enabling them to compare this paint to any other paint evidence. In this case, the pink paint on Atwood's bumper matched the paint from Vicki's bicycle.

Vicki's skeletal remains were discovered in the desert, several miles away from her home, in the spring of 1985. Positive identification was made using dental records, but investigators wanted to see if the remains could help them determine how long she had been dead. Atwood had been jailed on an unrelated charge three days after Vicki disappeared, so the approximate date of death was very important to proving his guilt.

Investigators found adipocere, a white, fatty residue produced during decomposition, inside Vicki's skull. This provided evidence that moisture was present around Vicki's body after her death, which did not seem to make sense, considering her body was found in the Arizona desert! A check of weather records revealed that there had been an unusual amount of rainfall during only one period of time since Vicki was last seen alive: a mere 48 hours after her disappearance. This put Vicki's death squarely within Frank Atwood's three-day window of opportunity between her disappearance and his arrest. Frank Atwood was sentenced to death in 1987 for the murder of Vicki Lynn Hoskinson. He remains on death row awaiting execution.

COMPOSITION OF GLASS

tempered glass
Glass to which strength is added by introducing stress through rapid heating and cooling of the glass surface

laminated glass
Two sheets of ordinary glass bonded together with a plastic film.

density
The measurement of mass per unit of volume.

intensive property
A property that is not dependent on the size of an object.

Glass is a hard, brittle, amorphous substance composed of sand (specifically, silicon oxides) mixed with various metal oxides. When sand is mixed with metal oxides, melted at high temperatures, and then cooled to a rigid condition without crystallization, the product is glass. Soda (or sodium carbonate) is normally added to the sand to lower its melting point and make it easier to work with. Another necessary ingredient is lime (or calcium oxide), which is added to prevent the glass, known as "soda-lime" glass, from dissolving in water. Often the molten glass is cooled on top of a bath of molten tin. This manufacturing process produces flat glass typically used for windows. This type of glass is called "float glass." The forensic scientist is often asked to analyze soda-lime glass, which is used for manufacturing most windows and glass bottles.

The common metal oxides found in soda-lime glass are sodium, calcium, magnesium, and aluminum. In addition, a wide variety of special glasses can be made by partially or completely substituting other metal oxides for the silica, sodium, and calcium oxides. For example, automobile headlights and heat-resistant glass, such as Pyrex, are manufactured with boron oxide added to the oxide mix. These glasses are therefore known as "borosilicates."

Another type of glass that the reader may be familiar with is **tempered glass**. This glass is made stronger than ordinary window glass by introducing stress through rapid heating and cooling of the glass surfaces. When tempered glass breaks, it does not shatter but rather fragments into small squares, or "dices," with little splintering (see Figure 14-6). Because of this safety feature, tempered glass is used in the side and rear windows of automobiles sold in the United States. The windshields of all cars manufactured in the United States are constructed from **laminated glass**. This glass is given strength by sandwiching one layer of plastic between two pieces of ordinary window glass.

COMPARING GLASS FRAGMENTS

For the forensic scientist, comparing glass consists of finding and measuring the properties that will associate one glass fragment with another while minimizing or eliminating the possible existence of other sources. Considering the prevalence of glass in our society, it is easy to appreciate the magnitude of this analytical problem. Obviously, glass possesses its greatest evidential value when it can be individualized to one source. Such a determination, however, can be made only when the suspect and crime-scene fragments are assembled and physically fitted together. Comparisons of this type require piecing together irregular edges of broken glass as well as matching all irregularities and striations on the broken surfaces (see Figure 14-7). The possibility that two pieces of glass originating from different sources will fit together exactly is so unlikely as to exclude all other sources from practical consideration.

Unfortunately, most glass evidence is either too fragmentary or too minute to permit a comparison of this type. In such instances, the search for individual properties proves fruitless. For example, the general chemical composition of various window glasses has so far been found to be relatively uniform among various manufacturers and thus offers no basis for individualization within the capability of current analytical methods. However, as more sensitive analytical techniques are developed, trace elements present in glass may prove to be distinctive and measurable characteristics.

The physical properties of density and refractive index are used most successfully for characterizing glass particles. However, these properties are class characteristics, which cannot provide the sole criteria for individualizing glass to a common source. They do, however, give the analyst sufficient data to evaluate the significance of a glass comparison, and if the density and refractive index values are not comparable, this certainly excludes the possibility that the glass fragments originated from the same source.

MEASURING AND COMPARING DENSITY

Density is defined as mass per unit volume:

$$\text{Density} = \frac{\text{mass}}{\text{volume}}$$

Density is an **intensive property** of matter—that is, it remains the same regardless of the size of an object; thus, it is a characteristic property of a substance and can be used in identification. Solids tend to be more dense than liquids, and liquids are more dense than gases.

A simple procedure for determining the density of a solid is illustrated in Figure 14-8. First, the solid is weighed on a balance against standard gram weights to determine its mass. The solid's volume is then determined from

FIGURE 14-6   When tempered glass breaks, it usually holds together without splintering.
Xyno6/Thinkstock/Getty Images

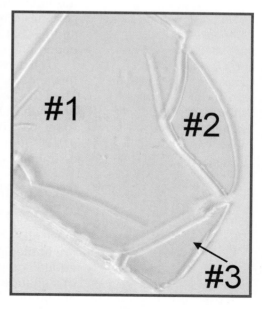

FIGURE 14-7   A match of broken glass. Note the physical fit of the edges.
Sirchie Finger Print Laboratories

Mass = 20 g

$$Density = \frac{Mass}{Volume\ (v_2 - v_1)}$$

$$Density = \frac{75g}{(50ml - 40ml)}$$

$$Density = \frac{75g}{10ml} = 7.5g/ml$$

Volume

FIGURE 14-8 A simple procedure for determining the density of a solid is first to measure its mass on a scale and then to measure its volume by noting the volume of water it displaces. *SAFERSTEIN, RICHARD, Ph.D., CRIMINALISTICS: AN INTRODUCTION TO FORENSIC SCIENCE, 11th Ed., © 2015. Reprinted and Electronically reproduced by permission of Pearson Education, Inc., Upper Saddle River, New Jersey.*

the volume of water it displaces. This is easily measured by filling a cylinder with a known volume of water (V_1), adding the object, and measuring the new water level (V_2). The difference ($V_2 - V_1$), expressed in milliliters, is equal to the volume of the solid. Density can now be calculated from the equation in grams per milliliter (i.e., mass per volume).

The fact that a solid object either sinks, floats, or remains suspended when immersed in a liquid can be accounted for by its density. For instance, if the density of a solid is greater than that of the liquid in which it is immersed, the object sinks; if the solid's density is less than that of the liquid, it floats; and when the solid and liquid have equal densities, the solid remains suspended in the liquid medium. This knowledge gives the criminalist a rather precise and rapid method for comparing densities of glass.

In a method known as "flotation," a standard/reference glass particle is immersed in a liquid, possibly a mixture of bromoform and bromobenzene. The composition of the liquid is carefully adjusted by adding small amounts of bromoform or bromobenzene until the glass chip remains suspended in the liquid medium. At this point, the standard/reference glass and liquid each have the same density. Glass chips of approximately the same size and shape as the standard/reference are now added to the liquid for comparison. If both the unknown and the standard/reference particles remain suspended in the liquid, their densities are equal to each other and to that of the liquid.[3] Particles of different densities either sink or float, depending on whether they are more or less dense than the liquid.

The density of a single sheet of window glass is not completely homogeneous throughout. It has a range of values that can differ by as much as 0.0003 g/mL. Therefore, in order to distinguish between the normal internal density variations of a single sheet of glass and those of glasses of different origins, it is advisable to let the comparative density approach but not exceed a sensitivity value of 0.0003 g/mL. The flotation method meets this requirement and can adequately distinguish glass particles that differ in density by 0.001 g/mL.

DETERMINING AND COMPARING REFRACTIVE INDEX

Once glass has been distinguished by a density determination, different origins are immediately concluded. Comparable density results, however, require the added comparison of refractive indices. The bending of a light wave because of a change in velocity is called "refraction." The phenomenon of refraction is apparent when we view an object that is immersed in a transparent medium such as water; because we are accustomed to thinking that light travels in a straight line, we often forget to account for refraction. For instance, suppose a ball is observed at the bottom of a swimming pool; the light rays reflected from the ball travel through the water and into the air to reach the eye. As the

refractive index
The ratio of the speed of light in a vacuum to its speed in a given medium.

rays leave the water and enter the air, their velocity suddenly increases, causing them to be refracted. However, because of our assumption that light travels in a straight line, our eyes deceive us and make us think we see an object lying at a higher point than is actually the case. This phenomenon is illustrated in Figure 14-9.

The ratio of the velocity of light in a vacuum to its velocity in any medium determines the **refractive index** of that medium and is expressed as follows:

$$\text{Refractive index} = \frac{\text{velocity of light in vacuum}}{\text{velocity of light in medium}}$$

For example, at 25°C the refractive index of water is 1.333. This means that light travels 1.333 times as fast in a vacuum as it does in water at this temperature.

Like density, the refractive index is an intensive physical property of matter and characterizes a substance. However, any procedure used to determine a substance's refractive index must be performed under carefully controlled temperature and lighting conditions because the refractive index of a substance varies with its temperature and the wavelength of light passing through it. Nearly all tabulated refractive indices are determined at a standard wavelength, usually 589.3 nanometers; this is the predominant wavelength emitted by sodium light and is commonly known as the "sodium D" light.

When a transparent solid is immersed in a liquid with a similar refractive index, light is not refracted as it passes from the liquid into the solid. For this reason, the eye cannot distinguish the liquid–solid boundary, and the solid seems to disappear from view. This observation, as we will see, offers the forensic scientist a rather simple method for comparing the refractive indices of transparent solids.

This determination is best accomplished by the "immersion method." For this, glass particles are immersed in a liquid medium whose refractive index is adjusted until it equals that of the glass particles. At this point, known as the "match point," the observer notes the disappearance of the **Becke line**, indicating minimum contrast between the glass and liquid medium. The Becke line is a bright halo observed near the border of a particle that is immersed in a liquid of a different refractive index. This halo disappears when the medium and fragment have similar refractive indices.

The refractive index of an immersion fluid is best adjusted by changing the temperature of the liquid. Temperature control is, of course, critical to the success of the procedure. One approach is to heat the liquid in a special apparatus known as a "hot-stage microscope" (see Figure 14-10). The glass fragments are immersed in a boiling immersion fluid, usually a silicone oil, and illuminated with sodium D light or another wavelength of light. The liquid is then heated at the rate of 0.2°C per minute until the match point is reached. This is the point at which the examiner observes the disappearance of the Becke line on the glass fragments. If all the glass fragments examined have similar match points, it can be concluded that they have comparable refractive indices (see Figure 14-11). Furthermore, the examiner can determine the refractive index value of the immersion fluid as it

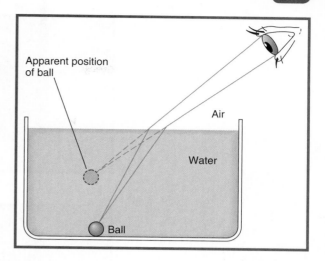

FIGURE 14-9 Light is refracted when it travels obliquely from one medium to another. *SAFERSTEIN, RICHARD, Ph.D., CRIMINALISTICS: AN INTRODUCTION TO FORENSIC SCIENCE, 11th Ed., © 2015. Reprinted and Electronically reproduced by permission of Pearson Education, Inc., Upper Saddle River, New Jersey.*

Becke line
A bright halo observed near the border of a particle immersed in a liquid of a different refractive index.

FIGURE 14-10 A hot-stage microscope used to view glass chips when determining their refractive index.
Chris Palenik

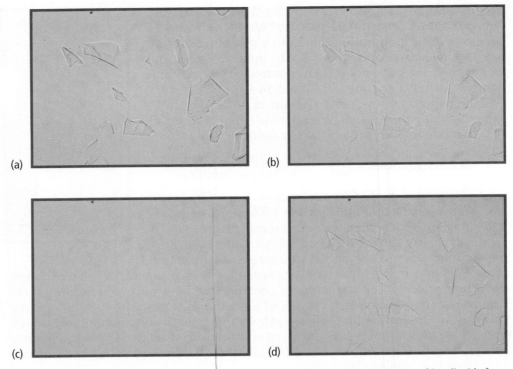

FIGURE 14-11 Determining the refractive index of glass. (a) Glass particles are immersed in a liquid of a much higher refractive index at a temperature of 20°C. (b) At 68°C the liquid still has a higher refractive index than the glass. (c) The refractive index of the liquid is closest to that of the glass at 100°C, as shown by the disappearance of the glass and the Becke lines. (d) At the higher temperature of 160°C, the liquid has a much lower index than the glass, resulting in significant edge contrast. The reference glass fragments shown here has a refractive index of 1.529. *Richard Saferstein, Ph.D.*

changes with temperature. With this information, the exact numerical value of the glass refractive index can be calculated at the match point temperature.

Along with varying in density, glass fragments removed from a single sheet of plate glass may not have a uniform refractive index; instead, these values may vary by as much as 0.0002. Hence, for comparison purposes, the difference in refractive index between a standard/reference and questioned glass must exceed this value. This allows the examiner to differentiate between the normal internal variations present in a sheet of glass and those present in glasses that originated from completely different sources.

CLASSIFICATION OF GLASS SAMPLES

A significant difference in either density or refractive index proves that the glass fragments examined do not have a common origin. But what if two pieces of glass exhibit comparable densities and comparable refractive indices? How certain can one be that they did, indeed, come from the same source? After all, there are untold millions of windows and other glass objects in this world.

To provide a reasonable answer to this question, the FBI Laboratory has collected density values and refractive indices from glass submitted to it for examination. What has emerged is a data bank correlating these values to their frequency of occurrence in the glass "population" of the United States. This collection is available to all forensic laboratories in the United States. This means that, once a criminalist has completed a comparison of glass fragments, he or she can correlate their density and refractive index values to their frequency

FIGURE 14-12 The frequency of occurrence of refractive index values (measured with sodium D light) in approximately 2,000 flat glass specimens analyzed by the FBI Laboratory. *Federal Bureau of Investigation*

of occurrence and assess the probability that the fragments came from the same source.

Figure 14-12 shows the distribution of refractive index values (measured with sodium D light) for approximately 2,000 glass specimens analyzed by the FBI. The wide distribution of values clearly demonstrates that the refractive index is a highly distinctive property of glass and is thus useful for defining its frequency of occurrence and hence its evidential value. For example, a glass fragment with a refractive index of 1.5290 is found in approximately only 1 out of 2,000 specimens, whereas glass with an index of 1.5180 occurs in approximately 22 specimens out of 2,000.

The distinction between tempered and nontempered glass particles can be made by slowly heating and then cooling the glass (a process known as "annealing"). The change in the refractive index of tempered glass upon annealing is significantly greater than that of nontempered glass and thus serves as a point of distinction.

GLASS FRACTURES

Glass bends in response to any force that is exerted on any one of its surfaces; when the limit of its elasticity is reached, the glass fractures. Frequently, fractured window glass reveals information about the force and direction of an impact; such knowledge may be useful for reconstructing events at a crime-scene investigation.

CLOSER ANALYSIS
GRIM 3

An automated approach for measuring the refractive index of glass fragments by the immersion method with a hot-stage microscope is to use the instrument known as GRIM 3 Glass Refractive Index Measurement (GRIM 3)* (see Figure 1). The GRIM 3 is a personal computer/video system designed to automatically measure the match temperature and refractive index of glass fragments. This instrument uses a video camera to view the glass fragments as they are being heated. As the immersion oil is heated or cooled, the contrast of the video image is measured continually until a minimum, the match point, is detected (see Figure 2). The match point temperature is then converted to a refractive index using stored calibration data.

*Foster and Freeman Limited, 25 Swan Lane, Evesham, Worcestershire WRII 4PE, UK

FIGURE 1 An automated system for glass fragment identification. *Photo courtesy of Foster & Freeman*

FIGURE 2 GRIM 3 identifies the refraction match point by monitoring a video image of the glass fragment immersed in an oil. As the immersion oil is heated or cooled, the contrast of the image is measured continuously until a minimum, the match point, is detected.

Photo courtesy of Foster & Freeman

FIGURE 14-13 Radial and concentric fracture lines in a sheet of glass.
Sirchie Finger Print Laboratories

FIGURE 14-14 A crater-shaped hole made by a projectile passing through glass. The upper surface is the side the projectile exited.
Don Farrall/Getty Images

The penetration of ordinary window glass by a projectile, whether a bullet or a stone, produces a familiar fracture pattern in which cracks both radiate outward and encircle the hole, as shown in Figure 14-13. The radiating lines are appropriately known as **radial fractures**, and the circular lines are termed **concentric fractures**.

Often it is difficult to determine just from the size and shape of a hole in glass whether it was made by a bullet or by some other projectile. For instance, a small stone thrown at a comparatively high speed against a pane of glass often produces a hole very similar to that produced by a bullet. On the other hand, a large stone can completely shatter a pane of glass in a manner closely resembling the result of a close-range shot. However, in the latter instance, the presence of gunpowder deposits on the shattered glass fragments signifies damage caused by a firearm.

When it penetrates glass, a high-velocity projectile such as a bullet often leaves a round, crater-shaped hole surrounded by a nearly symmetrical pattern of radial and concentric cracks. The hole is inevitably wider on the exit side (see Figure 14-14), and hence examining it is an important step in determining the direction of impact. However, as the velocity of the penetrating projectile decreases, the irregularity of the shape of the hole and of its surrounding cracks increases, so at some velocities the hole shape will not help determine the direction of impact. At this point, examining the radial and concentric fracture lines may help determine the direction of impact.

When a force pushes on one side of a pane of glass, the elasticity of the glass permits it to bend in the direction of the force applied. Once the elastic limit is exceeded, the glass begins to crack. As shown in Figure 14-15, the first fractures form on the surface opposite that of the penetrating force and develop into radial lines. The continued motion of the force places tension on the front surface of the glass, resulting in the formation of concentric cracks. An examination of the edges of the radial and concentric cracks frequently reveals stress markings ("Wallner lines"), whose shape can be related to the side on which the window first cracked.

radial fracture
A crack in a glass that extends outward, like a spoke of a wheel, from the point at which the glass was struck.

concentric fracture
A crack in a glass that forms a rough circle around the point of impact.

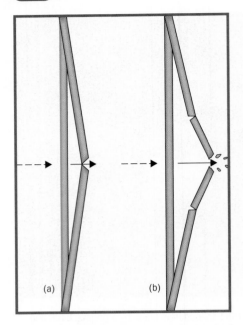

FIGURE 14-15 The production of radial and concentric fractures in glass. (a) Radial cracks are formed first, beginning on the side of the glass opposite the destructive force. (b) Concentric cracks occur outward, starting on the same side of the force. *SAFERSTEIN, RICHARD, Ph.D., CRIMINALISTICS: AN INTRODUCTION TO FORENSIC SCIENCE, 11th Ed., © 2015. Reprinted and Electronically reproduced by permission of Pearson Education, Inc., Upper Saddle River, New Jersey.*

FIGURE 14-16 Stress marks on the edge of a radial glass fracture. The arrow indicates the direction of force. *Richard Saferstein, Ph.D.*

Stress marks, shown in Figure 14-16, are shaped like arches that are perpendicular to one glass surface and curve to nearly parallel the opposite surface. The importance of stress marks stems from the observation that the perpendicular edge always faces the surface on which the crack originated. Thus, in examining the stress marks on the edge of a radial crack near the point of impact, the perpendicular end is always found opposite the side from which the force of impact was applied. For a concentric fracture, the perpendicular end always faces the surface on which the force originated. A convenient way for remembering these observations is the 3R rule: *R*adial cracks form a *r*ight angle on the *r*everse side of the force. These facts enable the examiner to determine which side of a broken window was impacted. Unfortunately, the absence of radial or concentric fracture lines prevents these observations from being applied to broken tempered glass.

When there have been successive penetrations of a piece of glass, it is frequently possible to determine the sequence of impact by observing the existing fracture lines and their points of termination. A fracture always terminates at an existing line of fracture. In Figure 14-17, the fracture on the left preceded that on the right; we know this because the latter's radial fracture lines terminate at the cracks of the former.

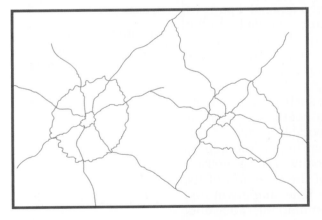

FIGURE 14-17 Two bullet holes in a piece of glass. The left hole preceded the right hole. *SAFERSTEIN, RICHARD, Ph.D., CRIMINALISTICS: AN INTRODUCTION TO FORENSIC SCIENCE, 11th Ed., © 2015. Reprinted and Electronically reproduced by permission of Pearson Education, Inc., Upper Saddle River, New Jersey.*

COLLECTION AND PRESERVATION OF GLASS EVIDENCE

The gathering of glass evidence at the crime scene and from the suspect must be thorough if the examiner is to have any chance at individualizing the fragments to a common source. If even the remotest possibility exists that fragments may be pieced together, every effort must be made to collect all the glass found. For example, evidence collection at hit-and-run scenes must include all the broken parts of the headlight and reflector lenses. This evidence may ultimately prove invaluable in placing a suspect vehicle at the accident scene, if the fragments can be matched with glass remaining in the headlight or reflector shell of the suspect vehicle. In addition, examining the headlight's filaments may reveal whether an automobile's headlights were on or off before the impact (see Figure 14-18).

When an individual fit is improbable, the evidence collector must submit all glass evidence found in the possession of the suspect along with a sample of broken glass remaining at the crime scene. This standard/reference glass should always be taken from any remaining glass in the window or door frames, as close as possible to the point of breakage. About one square inch of sample is usually adequate for this purpose. The glass fragments should be packaged in solid containers to avoid further breakage. If the suspect's shoes and/or clothing are to be examined for the presence of glass fragments, they should be individually wrapped in paper and transmitted to the laboratory. The field investigator should avoid removing such evidence from garments unless absolutely necessary for its preservation.

FIGURE 14-18 The presence of black tungsten oxide on the upper filament indicates that the filament was on when it was exposed to air. The lower filament was off, but its surface was coated with a yellow/white tungsten oxide, which was vaporized from the upper ("on") filament and condensed onto the lower filament. *Richard Saferstein, Ph.D.*

When a determination of the direction of impact is needed, all broken glass must be recovered and submitted for analysis. Wherever possible, the exterior and interior surfaces of the glass must be indicated. When this is not immediately apparent, the presence of dirt, paint, grease, or putty may indicate the exterior surface of the glass.

Quick Review

- To compare glass fragments, a forensic scientist evaluates density and refractive index.
- The "immersion method" is used to determine a glass fragment's refractive index. It involves immersing a glass particle in a liquid medium whose refractive index is adjusted by varying its temperature. At the refractive index match point, the visual contrast between the glass and liquid is at a minimum.
- The "flotation method" is used to determine a glass fragment's density. It involves immersing a glass particle in a liquid whose density is carefully adjusted by adding small amounts of an appropriate liquid until the glass chip suspends in the liquid medium.
- By analyzing the radial and concentric fracture patterns in glass, the forensic scientist can determine the side of impact by applying the 3R rule: *R*adial cracks form a *r*ight angle on the *r*everse side of the force.

Forensic Analysis of Soil

The term "soil" has many definitions; however, for forensic purposes, soil may be thought of as any disintegrated material, natural and/or artificial, that lies on or near the earth's surface. Therefore, forensic examination of soil is not only concerned with the analysis of naturally occurring rocks, minerals, vegetation, and animal matter; it also encompasses the detection of such manufactured objects as glass, paint chips, asphalt, brick fragments, and cinders, whose presence may impart soil with characteristics that make it unique to a particular location. When this material is collected accidentally or deliberately in a manner that associates it with a crime under investigation, it becomes valuable physical evidence.

SIGNIFICANCE OF SOIL EVIDENCE

The value of soil as evidence rests on its prevalence at crime scenes and its transferability between the scene and the criminal. Thus, soil or dried mud found adhering to a suspect's clothing or shoes or to an automobile, when compared to soil samples collected at the crime site, may link a suspect or object to the crime scene. As with most types of physical evidence, forensic soil analysis is comparative in nature; soil found in the possession of the suspect must be carefully collected and then compared to soil samplings from the crime scene and its vicinity.

However, one should not rule out the value of soil even if the site of the crime has not been ascertained. For instance, small amounts of soil may be found on a person or object far from the actual site of a crime. A geologist who knows the local geology may be able to use geological maps to direct police to the general vicinity where the soil was originally picked up and the crime committed.

FORENSIC EXAMINATION OF SOIL

Most soils can be differentiated by their gross appearance. A side-by-side visual comparison of the color and texture of soil specimens is easy to perform and provides a sensitive property for distinguishing soils that originate from different locations. Soil is darker when it is wet; therefore, color comparisons must always be made when all the samples are dried under identical laboratory conditions. It is estimated that there are nearly 1,100 distinguishable soil colors; hence, color offers a logical first step in a forensic soil comparison (see Figure 14-19).

Low-power microscopic examination of soil reveals the presence of plant and animal materials as well as artificial debris. Further high-power microscopic examination helps characterize minerals and rocks in earth materials. Although this approach to forensic soil identification requires the expertise of an investigator trained in geology, it can provide the most varied and significant points of comparison between soil samples. Only by carefully examining and comparing the minerals and rocks naturally present in soil can one take advantage of the large number of variations between soils and thus add to the evidential value of a positive comparison. A **mineral** is a naturally occurring crystal and, like any other crystal, its physical properties—for example, its color, geometric shape, density, and refractive index—are useful for identification. More than 2,200 minerals exist; however, most are so rare that forensic geologists usually encounter only about 20 of them. Rocks are composed of a combination of minerals and therefore exist in thousands of varieties on the earth's surface. They are usually identified by characterizing their mineral content and grain size (see Figure 14-20).

mineral
A naturally occurring crystalline solid.

FIGURE 14-19 A technician classifies a soil sample based on a soil color chart.
Daniel Wallace/ZUMA Press/Alamy

Considering the vast variety of minerals and rocks and the possible presence of artificial debris in soil, the forensic geologist is presented with many points of comparison between two or more specimens. The number

FIGURE 14-20   A mineral viewed under a microscope. *Chris Palenik*

of comparative points and their frequency of occurrence must be considered before concluding that specimens are similar and judging the probability of their common origin.

Rocks and minerals not only are present in earth materials but also are used to manufacture a wide variety of industrial and commercial products. For example, the tools and garments of an individual suspected of breaking into a safe often contain traces of safe insulation. Safe insulation may be made from a wide combination of mineral mixtures that provide significant points of identification. Similarly, building materials such as brick, plaster, and concrete blocks are combinations of minerals and rocks that can easily be recognized and compared microscopically to similar minerals found on the breaking-and-entering suspect.

VARIATIONS IN SOIL

The ultimate forensic value of soil evidence depends on its uniqueness at the crime scene. If, for example, soil composition is indistinguishable for miles surrounding the location of a crime, associating soil found on the suspect with that particular site will have limited value. Significant conclusions that link a suspect with a particular location through a soil comparison may be made when variations in soil composition occur within a 100-foot radius of the crime scene. However, even when such variations do exist, the forensic geologist usually cannot individualize soil to any one location unless it contains an unusual combination of rare minerals, rocks, or artificial debris.

No statistically valid forensic studies have examined the variability of soil evidence. A study conducted in southern Ontario, Canada, seems to indicate that soil in that part of Canada shows extensive diversity. It estimates a probability of less than one in fifty of finding two soils that are indistinguishable in both color and mineral properties but originate in two different locations separated by a distance of at least 1,000 feet. Based on these preliminary results, similar diversity may be expected in the northern United States, Canada, northern Europe, and eastern Europe. However, such probability values can only generally indicate the variation of soil within these geographical areas. Each crime scene must be evaluated separately to establish its own soil variation probabilities.

COLLECTION AND PRESERVATION OF SOIL EVIDENCE

When gathering soil specimens, the evidence collector must give primary consideration to establishing the variation of soil at the crime-scene area. For this reason, standard/reference soils should be collected at various intervals within a 100-yard radius of the crime scene, as well as at the site of the crime, for comparison to the questioned soil. Soil specimens also should be collected at all possible alibi locations that the suspect may have claimed.

All specimens gathered should be representative of the soil that was removed by the suspect. In most cases, only the top layer of soil is picked up during the commission of a crime. Thus, standard/reference specimens must be removed from the surface, without digging into the unrepresentative subsurface layers. Approximately a tablespoon or two of soil in each sample is all the laboratory needs for a thorough comparative analysis. All specimens collected should be packaged in individual containers, such as plastic vials. Each vial should be marked to indicate the location at which the sampling was made.

Soil found on a suspect must be carefully preserved for analysis. If it is found adhering to an object, as in the case of soil on a shoe, the investigator must not remove it. Instead, each object should be individually wrapped in paper, with the soil intact, and transmitted to the laboratory. Similarly, loose soil adhering to garments should not be removed; these items should be carefully and individually wrapped in paper bags and sent to the laboratory for analysis. Care must be taken that particles that may accidentally fall off the garment during transportation will remain in the paper bag.

When a lump of soil is found, it should be collected and preserved intact. For example, an automobile tends to collect and build up layers of soil under the fenders, body, and so on. The impact of an automobile with another object may jar some of this soil loose. Once the suspect car has been apprehended, a comparison of the soil left at the scene with soil remaining on the automobile may help establish that the car was present at the accident scene. In these situations, separate samples are collected from under all of the fender and frame areas of the vehicle; care is taken to remove the soil in clump form to preserve the order in which the particles of soil adhered to the car and to the other soils on the car. Undoubtedly, during the normal use of an automobile, soil will be picked up from numerous locations over a period of months and years. This layering effect may impart soil with greater variation, and hence greater evidential value, than that normally associated with loose soil.

Quick Review

- A side-by-side visual comparison of the color and texture of soil specimens provides a way to distinguish soils that originated from different locations.
- Minerals are naturally occurring crystalline solids found in soil. Their physical properties—for example, their color, geometric shape, density, and refractive index—are useful for characterizing soils.

VIRTUAL LAB
FORENSIC GLASS ANALYSIS
To perform a virtual forensic glass analysis, go to www
.pearsoncustom.com/us/vlm/

■■■■■ CASEFILES ■■■■

SOIL: THE SILENT WITNESS

Alice Redmond was reported missing by her husband on a Monday night in 1983. Police learned that she had been seen with a coworker, Mark Miller, after work that evening. When police questioned Miller, he stated that the two just "drove around" after work and then she dropped him off at home. Despite his statement, Miller was the prime suspect because he had a criminal record for burglary and theft.

Alice's car was recovered in town the following morning. The wheel wells were thickly coated in mud, which investigators hoped might provide a good lead. These hopes were dampened when police learned that Alice and her husband had attended a motorcycle race on Sunday, where her car was driven through deep mud.

After careful scrutiny, analysts found two colors of soil on the undercarriage of Alice's car. The thickest soil was brown; on top of the brown layer was a reddish soil that looked unlike anything in the county. Investigators hoped the reddish soil, which had to have been deposited sometime after the Sunday night motorcycle event and before the vehicle was discovered on Tuesday morning, could link the vehicle to the location of Alice Redmond.

An interview with Mark Miller's sister provided a break in the case. She told police that Mark had visited her on Monday evening. During that visit, he confessed that he had driven Alice in her car across the Alabama state line into Georgia, killed her, and buried her in a remote location. Now that investigators had a better idea where to look for Alice, forensic analysts took soil samples that would prove or disprove Miller's sister's story.

Each field sample was dried and compared for color and texture by eye and stereomicroscopy to the reddish-colored soil gathered from the car. Next, soils that compared to the car were passed through a series of mesh filters, each of a finer gauge than the last. In this way, the components of the soil samples were physically separated by size. Finally, each fraction was analyzed and compared for mineral composition with the aid of a polarizing light microscope.

Only samples collected from areas across the Alabama state line near the suspected dump site were consistent with the topmost reddish soil recovered from Alice's car. This finding supported Miller's sister's story and was instrumental in Mark Miller's being charged with murder and kidnapping. After pleading guilty, the defendant led the authorities to where he had buried the body. The burial site was within half a mile of the location where forensic analysts had collected a soil sample consistent with the soil removed from Alice's vehicle.

Source: Based on information contained in T. J. Hopen, "The Value of Soil Evidence," in *Trace Evidence Analysis: More Cases in Mute Witnesses*, M. M. Houck, ed. (Elsevier Academic Press, Burlington, MA: 2004), pp. 105–122.

■■■■ CHAPTER REVIEW

- Paint spread onto a surface dries into a hard film that is best described as consisting of pigments and additives suspended in a binder.

- Questioned and known paint specimens are best compared side by side under a stereoscopic microscope for color, surface texture, and color layer sequence.

- Pyrolysis gas chromatography and infrared spectrophotometry are used to distinguish most paint binder formulations.

- Paint Data Query (PDQ) is a computerized database that allows an analyst to obtain information on paints related to automobile make, model, and year.

- To compare glass fragments, a forensic scientist evaluates density and refractive index.

- The "immersion method" is used to determine a glass fragment's refractive index. It involves immersing a glass particle in a liquid medium whose refractive index is adjusted by varying its temperature. At the refractive index match point, the visual contrast between the glass and liquid is at a minimum.

- The "flotation method" is used to determine a glass fragment's density. It involves immersing a glass particle in a liquid whose density is carefully adjusted by adding small amounts of an appropriate liquid until the glass chip suspends in the liquid medium.

- By analyzing the radial and concentric fracture patterns in glass, the forensic scientist can determine the side of impact by applying the 3R rule: *R*adial cracks form a *r*ight angle on the *r*everse side of the force.

- A side-by-side visual comparison of the color and texture of soil specimens provides a way to distinguish soils that originated from different locations.

- Minerals are naturally occurring crystalline solids found in soil. Their physical properties—for example, their color, geometric shape, density, and refractive index—are useful for characterizing soils.

KEY TERMS

Becke line, 355

concentric fracture, 359

density, 353

intensive property, 353

laminated glass, 353

mineral, 362

pyrolysis, 347

radial fracture, 359

refractive index, 355

tempered glass, 352

REVIEW QUESTIONS

1. The _____ component of paint is commonly a mixture of inorganic and organic compounds and imparts color and hiding (or opacity).

2. The support within paint is provided by the _____ component, which is a polymeric substance.

3. True or False: Layers of paint are applied in the order of primer first, then surfacer, basecoat, and finally clearcoat. _____

4. The questioned and known paint specimens collected from a scene should be compared side by side under a(n) _____ microscope, which shows a three-dimensional image, to look at color, surface texture, and color layer sequence.

5. In a forensic comparison, the most important physical property of paint is _____.

6. Paints can be individualized to a single source only when they have a sufficiently detailed _____.

7. True or False: Pyrolysis gas chromatography is a particularly valuable technique for characterizing paint's binder. _____

8. Pyrolysis gas chromatography yields a(n) _____ to reflect the chemical makeup of the binder.

9. The Royal Canadian Mounted Police's computerized database, called _____, allows an analyst to obtain information on paints related to automobile make, model, and year.

10. True or False: Paint samples removed for examination must always include all of the paint layers. _____

11. _____ is defined as a hard, brittle, amorphous substance composed of sand (specifically, silicon oxides) mixed with various metal oxides.

12. True or False: Automobile headlights and heat-resistant glass, such as Pyrex, are manufactured with lime oxide added to the oxide mix. _____

13. _____ glass fragments into small squares, or "dices," with little splintering when broken.

14. _____ glass gains added strength from a layer of plastic inserted between two pieces of ordinary window glass; it is used in automobile windshields.

15. Broken glass that can be physically pieced together has _____ characteristics.

16. The two most useful physical properties of glass for forensic comparisons are _____ and _____.

17. Comparing the relative densities of glass fragments is readily accomplished by a method known as _____.

18. When glass is immersed in a liquid of similar refractive index, its _____ disappears and minimum contrast between the glass and liquid is observed.

19. The exact numerical density and refractive indices of glass can be correlated to their _____ in order to assess the evidential value of the comparison.

20. The fracture lines radiating outward from a crack in glass are known as _____ fractures.

21. Glass fracture lines that encircle the hole in the glass are known as _____ fractures.

22. True or False: A crater-shaped hole in glass is wider on the side where the projectile entered the glass. _____

23. True or False: It is easy to determine from the size and shape of a hole in glass whether it was made by a bullet or some other projectile. _____

24. When glass's elastic limit is exceeded, the first fractures develop into radial lines on the surface of the (same, opposite) side to that of the penetrating force.

25. True or False: Stress marks on the edge of a radial crack are always perpendicular to the edge of the surface on which the impact force originated. _____

26. A fracture line from a successive impact will always _____ at an existing line fracture.

27. Collected glass fragment evidence should be packaged in _____ containers to avoid further breakage.

28. Glass-containing shoes and/or clothing should be individually wrapped in _____ and transmitted to the laboratory.

29. True or False: Most soils have indistinguishable color and texture. _____

30. Color and texture comparisons cannot be made on samples until they are all _____ under identical laboratory conditions.

31. Naturally occurring crystals commonly found in soils are _____.

32. True or False: The ultimate value of soil as evidence depends on its uniqueness to the crime scene. _____

33. To develop an idea of the soil variation within the crime-scene area, standard/reference soils should be collected at various intervals within a(n) _____-foot radius of the crime scene.

34. True or False: Each object collected at the crime scene that contains soil evidence must be individually wrapped in plastic, with the soil intact, and transmitted to the laboratory. _____

■■■■■ APPLICATION AND CRITICAL THINKING

1. You are investigating a hit-and-run accident and have identified a suspect vehicle. Describe how you would collect paint to determine whether the suspect vehicle was involved in the accident. Be sure to indicate the tools you would use and the steps you would take to prevent cross-contamination.

2. An accident investigator arrives at the scene of a hit-and-run collision. The driver who remained at the scene reports that the windshield or a side window of the car that struck him shattered on impact. The investigator searches the accident site and collects a large number of fragments of tempered glass. This is the only type of glass recovered from the scene. How can the glass evidence help the investigator locate the vehicle that fled the scene?

3. Indicate the order in which the bullet holes were made in the glass depicted in the figure at the left below. Explain the reason for your answer.

Richard Saferstein, Ph.D.

4. The figure at the right on page 367 depicts stress marks on the edge of a glass fracture caused by the application of force. If this is a radial fracture, from which side of the glass (left or right) was the force applied? From which side was force applied if it is a concentric fracture? Explain the reason for your answers.

5. Criminalist Jared Heath responds to the scene of an assault, on an unpaved lane in a rural neighborhood. Rain had fallen steadily the night before, making the area quite muddy. A suspect with very muddy shoes was apprehended nearby but claims to have picked up the mud either from his garden or from the unpaved parking lot of a local restaurant. Jared uses a spade to remove several samples of soil, each about 2 inches deep, from the immediate crime scene and places each in a separate plastic vial. He collects the muddy shoes and wraps them in plastic as well. At the laboratory, he unpackages the soil samples and examines them carefully, one at a time. He then analyzes the soil on the shoes to see whether it matches the soil from the crime scene. What mistakes, if any, did Jared make in his investigation?

ENDNOTES

1. G. Edmondstone, J. Hellman, K. Legate, G. L. Vardy, and E. Lindsay, "An Assessment of the Evidential Value of Automotive Paint Comparisons," *Canadian Society of Forensic Science Journal* 37 (2004): 147.

2. D. W. Wright et al. "Analysis and Documentation of Architectural Paint Samples via a Population Study," *Forensic Science International* 209 (2011):86.

3. As an added step, the analyst can determine the exact numerical density value of the particles of glass by transferring the liquid to a density meter, which will electronically measure and calculate the liquid's density. See A. P. Beveridge and C. Semen, "Glass Density Measurement Using a Calculating Digital Density Meter," *Canadian Society of Forensic Science Journal* 12 (1979): 113.

15 Biological Stain Analysis
DNA

LEARNING OBJECTIVES

After studying this chapter, you should be able to:

- List the A-B-O antigens and antibodies found in each of the four blood types: A, B, AB, and O.
- Understand how immunoassay is used to test for drugs-of-abuse in urine.
- List and describe forensic tests used to characterize a stain as blood.
- List the laboratory tests necessary to characterize seminal stains.
- Explain how to properly preserve suspect blood and semen stains for laboratory examination.
- Contrast chromosomes and genes.
- Name the parts of a nucleotide and explain how they are linked together to form DNA.
- Understand the concept of base pairing as it relates to the double-helix structure of DNA.
- Explain the technology of polymerase chain reaction (PCR) and how it applies to forensic DNA typing.
- Understand the DNA-typing technique known as short tandem repeats (STRs).
- Describe the difference between nuclear and mitochondrial DNA.
- Understand the use of computerized DNA databases in criminal investigation.
- List the necessary procedures for the proper preservation of biological evidence for laboratory DNA analysis.

O. J. SIMPSON: A MOUNTAIN OF EVIDENCE

On June 12, 1994, police who arrived at the home of Nicole Simpson viewed a horrific scene. The bodies of O. J. Simpson's estranged wife and her friend Ron Goldman were found on the path leading to the front door of Nicole's home. Both bodies were covered in blood and had received deep knife wounds. Nicole's head was nearly severed from her body. This was not a well-planned murder. A trail of blood led away from the murder scene. Blood was found in O. J. Simpson's Bronco. Blood drops were found on O. J.'s driveway and in the foyer of his home. A blood-soaked sock was located in O. J. Simpson's bedroom, and a bloodstained glove rested on the ground outside his residence.

As DNA was extracted and profiled from each bloodstained article, a picture emerged that seemed to irrefutably link Simpson to the murders. A trail of DNA leaving the crime scene was consistent with O. J.'s profile, as was the DNA found in Simpson's home. Simpson's DNA profile was found in the Bronco along with that of both victims. The glove contained the DNA profiles of Nicole and Ron, and the sock had Nicole's DNA profile. At trial, the defense team valiantly fought back. Miscues in evidence collection were craftily exploited. The defense strategy was to paint a picture of not only an incompetent investigation but one that was tinged with dishonest police planting evidence. The strategy worked. O. J. Simpson was acquitted of murder.

In 1901, Karl Landsteiner announced one of the most significant discoveries of the twentieth century—the typing of blood—a finding that earned him a Nobel Prize twenty-nine years later. For years, physicians had attempted to transfuse blood from one individual to another. Their efforts often ended in failure because the transfused blood tended to coagulate, or clot, in the body of the recipient, causing instantaneous death. Landsteiner was the first to recognize that all human blood was not the same; instead, he found that blood is distinguishable by its group, or type.

Out of Landsteiner's work came the classification system that we call the "A-B-O system." Now physicians have the key for properly matching the blood of a donor to that of a recipient. Because one blood type cannot be mixed with a different blood type without disastrous consequences, this discovery, of course, had important implications for blood transfusion, and millions of lives have since been saved.

Meanwhile, Landsteiner's findings opened a new field of research in the biological sciences. Others began to pursue the identification of additional characteristics that could further differentiate blood. By 1937, the Rh factor in blood had been demonstrated, and shortly thereafter, numerous blood factors or groups were discovered. More than one hundred blood factors have been identified. However, the ones in the A-B-O system are still the most important for properly matching a donor and recipient for a transfusion.

Until the early 1990s, forensic scientists focused on blood factors, such as A-B-O, as offering the best means for linking blood to an individual. What made these factors so attractive was that, in theory, no two individuals, except for identical twins, could be expected to have the same combination of blood factors. In other words, blood factors are controlled genetically and have the potential of being a highly distinctive feature for personal identification. What makes this observation so relevant is the great frequency of bloodstains at crime scenes, especially crimes of the most serious nature: homicides, assaults, and sexual assaults. Consider, for example, a transfer of blood between the victim and assailant during a struggle, that is, the transfer of a victim's blood to the suspect's garment, or vice versa. If the criminalist could individualize human blood by identifying all of its known factors, the result would be strong evidence for linking the suspect to the crime.

The advent of DNA technology has dramatically altered the approach of forensic scientists toward the individualization of bloodstains and other biological evidence. The search for genetically controlled blood factors in bloodstains has been abandoned in favor of characterizing biological evidence by select regions of our **deoxyribonucleic acid (DNA)**, which carries the body's genetic information. As a result, the individuation of dried blood and other biological evidence has become a reality and has significantly altered the role that crime laboratories play in criminal investigations. In fact, the high sensitivity of DNA analysis and the resultant search for DNA evidence has even altered the types of materials collected from crime scenes.

deoxyribonucleic acid (DNA)
The molecules that carry the body's genetic information.

The Nature of Blood

plasma
The fluid portion of unclotted blood.

The word "blood" refers to a highly complex mixture of cells, enzymes, proteins, and inorganic substances. The fluid portion of blood is called **plasma**; it is composed principally of water and accounts for 55 percent of blood content. Suspended in the plasma are solid materials consisting chiefly of several types of cells: red blood cells (i.e., erythrocytes), white blood cells (i.e., leukocytes), and platelets. The solid portion of blood accounts for 45 percent of its content. Blood clots when a protein in the plasma known as "fibrin" traps and enmeshes the red blood cells. If the clotted material were removed from the blood, a pale yellowish liquid known as **serum** would be left.

Considering the complexity of blood, a full discussion of its function and chemistry would extend beyond the scope of this text. Instead, this chapter concentrates on the components of blood that are directly pertinent to the forensic aspects of blood identification: the red blood cells and the blood serum.

serum
The liquid that separates from the blood when a clot is formed.

ANTIGENS AND ANTIBODIES

Red blood cells transport oxygen from the lungs to the body tissues and remove carbon dioxide from tissues by transporting it back to the lungs, where it is exhaled. However, for reasons unrelated to the red blood cell's transporting mission, on the surface of each cell are millions of characteristic chemical structures called **antigens**. Antigens impart specific characteristics to the red blood cells. Blood antigens are grouped into systems depending on their relationship to one another. More than fifteen blood antigen systems have been identified to date; of these, the A-B-O and Rh systems are the most important.

antigen
A substance, usually a protein, that stimulates the body to produce antibodies against it.

If an individual has type A blood, this simply means that each red blood cell has A antigens on its surface; similarly, all type B individuals have B antigens, and the red blood cells of type AB individuals contain both A and B antigens. Type O individuals have neither A nor B antigens on their cells. Hence, the presence or absence of A and B antigens on the red blood cells determines a person's blood type in the A-B-O system.

Another important blood antigen has been named the "Rh factor," or D antigen. Those people who have the D antigen are said to be "Rh positive"; those without this antigen are "Rh negative." In routine blood banking, the presence or absence of the three antigens—A, B, and D—must be tested to determine the compatibility of the donor and recipient.

Serum is important because it contains proteins known as **antibodies**. The fundamental principle of blood typing is that, for every antigen, there exists a specific antibody. Each antibody symbol contains the prefix "anti-", followed by the name of the antigen for which it is specific. Hence, anti-A is specific only for the A antigen, anti-B for the B antigen, and anti-D for the D antigen. The antibody-containing serum is referred to as the **antiserum**, meaning a serum that reacts against something (i.e., antigens).

antibody
A protein in the blood serum that destroys or inactivates a specific antigen.

antiserum
Blood serum that contains specific antibodies.

An antibody reacts only with its specific antigen and no other. Thus, if serum containing anti-B is added to red blood cells carrying the B antigen, the two will combine, causing the antibody to attach itself to the cell. Antibodies are normally *bivalent*—that is, they have two reactive sites. This means that each antibody can simultaneously be attached to antigens located on two different red blood cells. This creates a vast network of cross-linked cells usually seen in the form of clumping, or **agglutination** (see Figure 15-1).

Let's look a little more closely at this phenomenon. In normal blood, shown in Figure 15-2(a), antigens on red blood cells and antibodies coexist without destroying each other because the antibodies present are not specific toward any of the antigens. However, suppose a foreign serum added to the blood introduces a new antibody. This results in a specific antigen–antibody reaction that immediately causes the red blood cells to link together, or agglutinate, as shown in Figure 15-2(b).

agglutination
The clumping together of red blood cells by the action of an antibody.

Evidently, nature has taken this situation into account, for when we examine the serum of type A blood, we find anti-B but no anti-A. Similarly, type B blood contains only anti-A, type O blood has both anti-A and anti-B, and

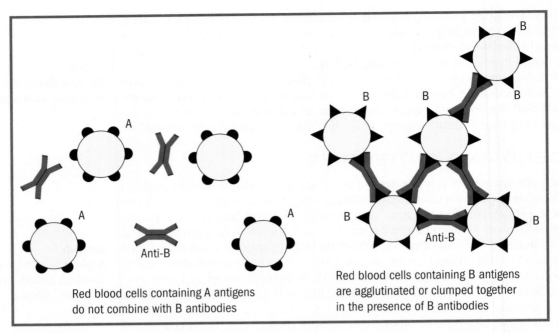

Red blood cells containing A antigens do not combine with B antibodies

Red blood cells containing B antigens are agglutinated or clumped together in the presence of B antibodies

FIGURE 15-1 Agglutination of blood cells. *SAFERSTEIN, RICHARD, Ph.D., CRIMINALISTICS: AN INTRODUCTION TO FORENSIC SCIENCE, 11th Ed., © 2015. Reprinted and Electronically reproduced by permission of Pearson Education, Inc., Upper Saddle River, New Jersey.*

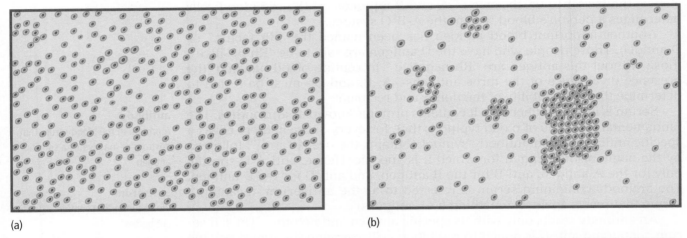

(a)

(b)

FIGURE 15-2 (a) A microscopic view of normal red blood cells (500x). (b) A microscopic view of agglutinated red blood cells (500x). *SAFERSTEIN, RICHARD, Ph.D., CRIMINALISTICS: AN INTRODUCTION TO FORENSIC SCIENCE, 11th Ed., © 2015. Reprinted and Electronically reproduced by permission of Pearson Education, Inc., Upper Saddle River, New Jersey.*

type AB blood contains neither anti-A nor anti-B. The antigen and antibody components of normal blood are summarized in the following table:

Blood Type	Antigens on Red Blood Cells	Antibodies in Serum
A	A	Anti-B
B	B	Anti-A
AB	AB	Neither anti-A nor anti-B
O	Neither A nor B	Both anti-A and anti-B

The reasons for the fatal consequences of mixing incompatible blood during a transfusion should now be quite obvious. For example, the transfusion of type A blood into a type B patient will cause the natural anti-A in the blood of the type B patient to react promptly with the incoming A antigens, resulting in agglutination. In addition, the incoming anti-B of the donor will react with the B antigens of the patient.

Immunoassay Techniques

The concept of a specific antigen–antibody reaction is being applied in other areas unrelated to blood typing. Most significant, similar reactions are being applied to the detection of drugs in blood and urine. Antibodies that react with drugs do not exist naturally; however, they can be produced in animals such as rabbits by first combining the drug with a protein and injecting this combination into the animal. This drug–protein complex acts as an antigen, stimulating the animal to produce antibodies (see Figure 15-3). The recovered blood serum of the animal now contains antibodies that are specific or nearly specific to the drug.

Currently, each day, thousands of individuals are voluntarily being subjected to urinalysis tests for the presence of commonly abused drugs. These individuals include military personnel, transportation industry employees, police and corrections personnel, and candidates undergoing preemployment drug screening. Immunoassay testing for drugs has proved quite suitable for handling the large volume of specimens that must be rapidly analyzed on a daily basis for drug content. Testing laboratories have available to them a variety of commercially prepared sera that were developed in animals injected with any one of a variety of drugs. Once a particular serum is added to a urine specimen, it's designed to interact with either opiates, cannabinoids, amphetamines, phencyclidine, barbiturates, methadone, or another type of drug that might be present. A word of caution: Immunoassay is only presumptive in nature, and its result must be confirmed by additional testing.

Quick Review

- An antibody reacts or agglutinates only with its specific antigen. The concept of specific antigen–antibody reactions has been applied to techniques for the detection of commonly abused drugs in blood and urine.
- Every red blood cell contains either an A antigen, a B antigen, both antigens, or no antigen (this is called "type O"). The type of antigen on one's red blood cells determines one's A-B-O blood type. Persons with type A blood have A antigens on their red blood cells, those with type B blood have B antigens, those with type AB blood have both antigens, and those with type O blood have no antigens on their red blood cells.

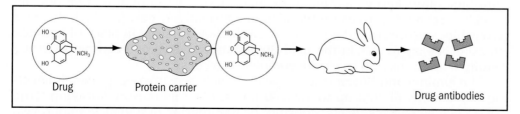

Drug   Protein carrier   Drug antibodies

FIGURE 15-3 Stimulating production of drug antibodies. *SAFERSTEIN, RICHARD, Ph.D., CRIMINALISTICS: AN INTRODUCTION TO FORENSIC SCIENCE, 11th Ed., © 2015. Reprinted and Electronically reproduced by permission of Pearson Education, Inc., Upper Saddle River, New Jersey.*

- To produce antibodies capable of reacting with drugs, a specific drug is combined with a protein, and this combination is injected into an animal such as a rabbit. This drug–protein complex acts as an antigen, stimulating the animal to produce antibodies. The recovered blood serum of the animal will now contain antibodies that are specific or nearly specific to the drug.

Forensic Characterization of Bloodstains

The criminalist must answer the following questions when examining dried blood: (1) Is it blood? (2) From what species did the blood originate? (3) If the blood is human, how closely can it be associated with a particular individual?

COLOR TESTS

The determination that a substance is blood is best made by means of a preliminary color test. For many years, the most common test was the "benzidine color test." However, because benzidine has been identified as a known carcinogen, its use has generally been discontinued, and the chemical phenolphthalein is usually substituted (this test is also known as the "Kastle-Meyer color test").

Both the benzidine and Kastle-Meyer color tests are based on the observation that blood *hemoglobin* possesses peroxidase-like activity. Peroxidases are enzymes that accelerate the oxidation of several classes of organic compounds when combined with peroxides. For example, when a bloodstain, phenolphthalein reagent, and hydrogen peroxide are mixed together, oxidation of the hemoglobin in the blood produces a deep pink color.

The Kastle-Meyer test is not a specific test for blood; some vegetable materials, for instance, may turn Kastle-Meyer pink. These substances include potatoes and horseradish. However, such materials will probably not be encountered in criminal situations, and thus, from a practical point of view, a positive Kastle-Meyer test is highly indicative of blood. Field investigators also have found Hemastix strips a useful presumptive field test for blood. Designed as a urine dipstick test for blood, the strip can be moistened with distilled water and placed in contact with a suspect bloodstain. The appearance of a green color indicates the presence of blood.

WebExtra 15.1

See a Color Test for Blood
www.mycrimekit.com

LUMINOL AND BLUESTAR

Another important presumptive identification test for blood is the "luminol" test.[1] Unlike the benzidine and Kastle-Meyer tests, the reaction of luminol with blood produces light rather than color. After spraying luminol reagent onto suspect items, agents darken the room; any bloodstains produce a faint blue glow, known as "luminescence." Using luminol, investigators can quickly screen large areas for bloodstains. A relatively new product, Bluestar (www.bluestar-forensic.com), is now available to be used in place of luminol. Bluestar is easy to mix in the field. Its reaction with blood can be observed readily without having to create complete darkness.

The luminol and Bluestar tests are extremely sensitive—capable of detecting bloodstains diluted up to 100,000 times. For this reason, spraying large areas such as carpets, walls, flooring, or the interior of a vehicle may reveal blood traces or patterns that would have gone unnoticed under normal lighting conditions (see Figure 15-4). Luminol and Bluestar will not interfere with any subsequent DNA testing.[2]

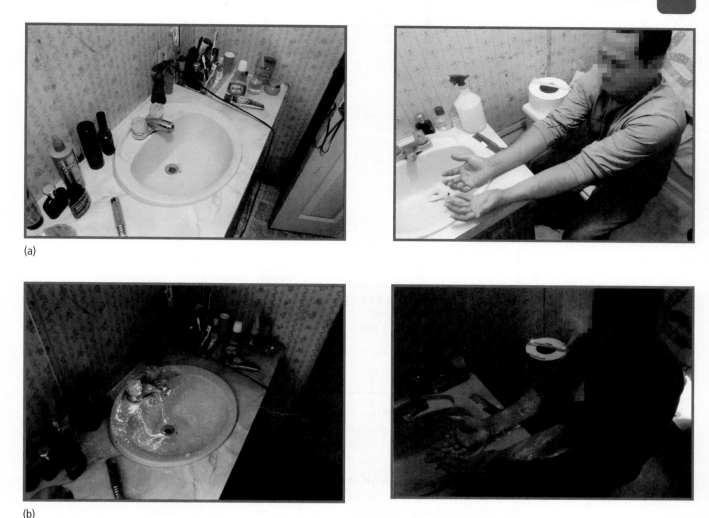

(a)

(b)

FIGURE 15-4 (a) Sink and arms before application of Bluestar reagent. (b) Bluestar applications reveal bloodstain patterns. *Johnnie Sutphin with BLUESTAR*

MICROCRYSTALLINE TESTS

The identification of blood can be made more specific if microcrystalline tests are performed on the material. Several tests are available; the two most popular ones are the "Takayama" and "Teichmann" tests. Both depend on the addition of specific chemicals to the blood to form characteristic crystals containing hemoglobin derivatives. Crystal tests are far less sensitive than color tests for blood identification and are more susceptible to interference from contaminants that may be present in the stain.

PRECIPITIN TEST

Once the stain has been characterized as blood, the serologist determines whether the blood is of human or animal origin. The standard test for this is the "precipitin" test. Precipitin tests are based on the fact that when animals (usually rabbits) are injected with human blood, antibodies form that react with the invading human blood to neutralize its presence. The investigator can recover these antibodies by bleeding the animal and isolating the blood serum, which contains antibodies that specifically react with human antigens. For this reason, the serum is known as "human antiserum." In the same manner,

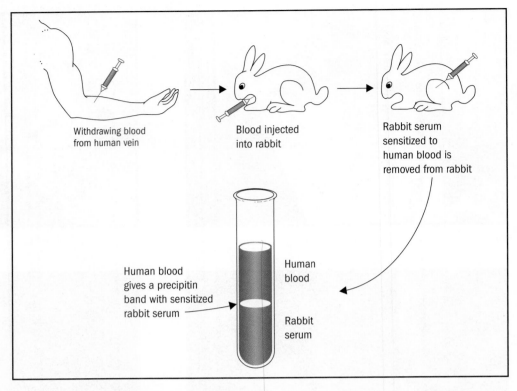

FIGURE 15-5 The precipitin test. *SAFERSTEIN, RICHARD, Ph.D., CRIMINALISTICS: AN INTRODUCTION TO FORENSIC SCIENCE, 11th Ed., © 2015. Reprinted and Electronically reproduced by permission of Pearson Education, Inc., Upper Saddle River, New Jersey.*

by injecting rabbits with the blood of other known animals, virtually any kind of animal antiserum can be produced. Antiserums are commercially available for human blood and for the blood of a variety of commonly encountered animals, such as dogs, cats, and deer.

Several techniques have been devised for performing precipitin tests on bloodstains. The classic method is to layer an extract of the bloodstain on top of the human antiserum in a capillary tube. Human blood—or, for that matter, any protein of human origin in the extract—reacts specifically with antibodies present in the antiserum, indicated by the formation of a cloudy ring or band at the interface of the two liquids (see Figure 15-5).

GEL DIFFUSION

Another precipitin method, called "gel diffusion," takes advantage of the fact that antibodies and antigens diffuse or move toward one another on a plate coated with a gel medium made from a natural polymer called "agar." The extracted bloodstain and the human antiserum are placed in separate holes opposite each other on the gel. If the blood is human, a line of precipitation forms where the antigens and antibodies meet.

The precipitin test is very sensitive and requires only a small amount of blood for testing. Human bloodstains that have been dry for ten to fifteen years and longer may still give a positive precipitin reaction. Even extracts of tissue from mummies four to five thousand years old have given positive reactions with this test. Furthermore, human bloodstains diluted by washing in water and left with only a faint color may still yield a positive precipitin reaction (see Figure 15-6).

Similarly, the antigens and antibodies can be induced to move toward one another under the influence of an electrical field. In the "electrophoretic

FIGURE 15-6 Results of the precipitin test of dilutions of human serum up to 1 in 4,096 against a human antiserum. A reaction is visible for blood dilutions up to 1 in 256. *SAFERSTEIN, RICHARD, Ph.D., CRIMINALISTICS: AN INTRODUCTION TO FORENSIC SCIENCE, 11th Ed., © 2015. Reprinted and Electronically reproduced by permission of Pearson Education, Inc., Upper Saddle River, New Jersey.*

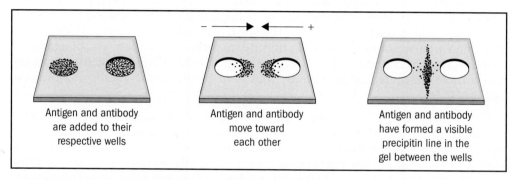

FIGURE 15-7 Antigens and antibodies moving toward one another under the influence of an electrical potential. *SAFERSTEIN, RICHARD, Ph.D., CRIMINALISTICS: AN INTRODUCTION TO FORENSIC SCIENCE, 11th Ed., © 2015. Reprinted and Electronically reproduced by permission of Pearson Education, Inc., Upper Saddle River, New Jersey.*

method," an electrical potential is applied to the gel medium; a specific antigen–antibody reaction is denoted by a line of precipitation formed between the hole containing the blood extract and the hole containing the human antiserum (see Figure 15-7).

Once it has been determined that the bloodstain is human, an effort must be made to associate the stain with or disassociate the stain from a particular individual. Until the mid-1990s, routine characterization of bloodstains included the determination of A-B-O types; however, the widespread use of DNA profiling, or typing, has relegated this subject to one of historical interest only.

Quick Review

- The criminalist must be prepared to answer the following questions when examining dried blood: (1) Is it blood? (2) From what species did the blood originate? (3) If the blood is of human origin, how closely can it be associated to a particular individual?
- The determination that a substance is blood is best made by means of a preliminary color test. A positive result from the Kastle-Meyer color test is highly indicative of blood.
- The luminol and Bluestar tests are used to search out trace amounts of blood located at crime scenes.
- The precipitin test uses antisera, normally derived from rabbits that have been injected with the blood of a known animal, to determine the species origin of a questioned bloodstain.

Forensic Characterization of Semen

Many cases encountered in a forensic laboratory involve sexual offenses, making it necessary to examine evidence for the presence of seminal stains. The forensic examination of articles for seminal stains can be considered a two-step process. First, before any tests can be conducted, the stain must be located. Considering the potential number and soiled condition of outer garments, undergarments, and possibly bed clothing submitted for examination, this can be an arduous task. Once located, stains must be subjected to tests that will prove their identity. A stain may even be tested for the blood type of the individual from whom it originated.

TESTING FOR SEMINAL STAINS

Often seminal stains are visible on a fabric because they exhibit a stiff, crusty appearance. However, reliance on such appearance for locating the stain is unreliable and is useful only when the stain is in an obvious area. If the fabric has been washed or contains only minute quantities of semen, visual examination offers little chance of detecting the stain. The best way to locate and at the same time characterize a seminal stain is to perform the "acid phosphatase color test."

acid phosphatase
An enzyme found in high concentrations in semen.

ACID PHOSPHATASE TEST   Acid phosphatase is an enzyme that is secreted by the prostate gland into seminal fluid. Its concentrations in seminal fluid are up to 400 times those found in any other body fluid. Its presence can easily be detected when it comes into contact with an acidic solution of sodium alpha naphthylphosphate and Fast Blue B dye. Also, 4-methylumbelliferyl phosphate (MUP) will fluoresce (i.e., emit light) under UV light when it comes into contact with acid phosphatase.

The utility of the acid phosphatase test is apparent when it becomes necessary to search many garments or large pieces of fabric for seminal stains. Simply moistening a filter paper with water and rubbing it lightly over the suspect area transfers any acid phosphatase present to the filter paper. Placing a drop or two of the sodium alpha naphthylphosphate and Fast Blue B solution on the paper produces a purple color that indicates the acid phosphatase enzyme. In this manner, any fabric or surface can be systematically searched for seminal stains.

If it is necessary to search extremely large areas—for example, a bedsheet or carpet—the article can be tested in sections, narrowing the location of the stain with each successive test. Alternatively, the garment can be pressed against a suitably sized piece of moistened filter paper. The paper is then sprayed with MUP solution. Semen stains appear as strongly fluorescent areas under UV light. A negative reaction can be interpreted as an absence of semen. Although some vegetable and fruit juices (such as cauliflower and watermelon), fungi, contraceptive creams, and vaginal secretions give a positive response to the acid phosphatase test, none of these substances normally reacts with the speed of seminal fluid. A reaction time of less than 30 seconds is considered a strong indication of semen.

MICROSCOPIC EXAMINATION OF SEMEN   Semen can be unequivocally identified by the presence of spermatozoa. When spermatozoa are located through a microscopic examination, the stain is definitely identified as having been derived from semen. Spermatozoa are slender, elongated structures 50 to 70 microns long, each with a head and a thin flagellate tail (see Figure 15-8). The criminalist can normally locate them by immersing the stained material in a small volume of water. Rapidly stirring the liquid transfers a small percentage of the spermatozoa present into the water. A drop of the water is dried onto

FIGURE 15-8 A photomicrograph of human spermatozoa (300×). *John Walsh/Photo Researchers, Inc.*

a microscope slide, and then stained and examined under a compound microscope at a magnification of approximately 400×.

Considering the extremely large number of spermatozoa found in seminal fluid (the normal male releases 250 to 600 million spermatozoa during ejaculation), the chance of locating one should be very good; however, this is not always true. One reason is that spermatozoa bind tightly to cloth materials.[3] Also, spermatozoa are extremely brittle when dry and easily disintegrate if the stain is washed or when the stain is rubbed against another object, as happens frequently in the handling and packaging of this type of evidence. Furthermore, sexual crimes may involve males who have an abnormally low sperm count, a condition known as **oligospermia**, or who have no spermatozoa at all in their seminal fluid (**aspermia**). Significantly, aspermatic individuals are increasing in numbers because of the growing popularity of vasectomies.

oligospermia
An abnormally low sperm count.

aspermia
The absence of sperm; sterility in males.

PROSTATE-SPECIFIC ANTIGEN (PSA)   Analysts often examine stains or swabs that they suspect contain semen (because of the presence of acid phosphatase), but that yield no detectable spermatozoa. How, then, can one reliably prove the presence of semen? The solution to this problem apparently came with the discovery in the 1970s of a protein called "p30" or "prostate-specific antigen (PSA)." At first, this protein was thought to be prostate specific and hence a unique identifier of semen. However, additional research has shown that low levels of p30 may be detectable in other human tissues. A more reasonable approach to the unequivocal identification of semen is to use a positive p30 test in combination with an acid phosphatase color test with a reaction time of less than 30 seconds.[4]

When p30 is isolated and injected into a rabbit, it stimulates the production of polyclonal antibodies (anti-p30). The serum collected from these immunized rabbits can then be used to test suspected semen stains. As shown in Figure 15-9, the stain extract is placed in one well of an electrophoretic plate and the anti-p30 in an opposite well. When an electric potential is applied, the antigens and antibodies move toward each other. The formation of a visible line midway between the two wells shows the presence of p30 in the stain and indicates that the stain originated from semen.

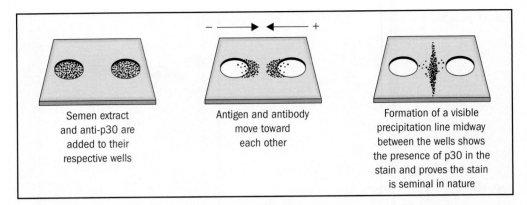

FIGURE 15-9 PSA testing by electrophoresis. *SAFERSTEIN, RICHARD, Ph.D., CRIMINALISTICS: AN INTRODUCTION TO FORENSIC SCIENCE, 11th Ed., © 2015. Reprinted and Electronically reproduced by permission of Pearson Education, Inc., Upper Saddle River, New Jersey.*

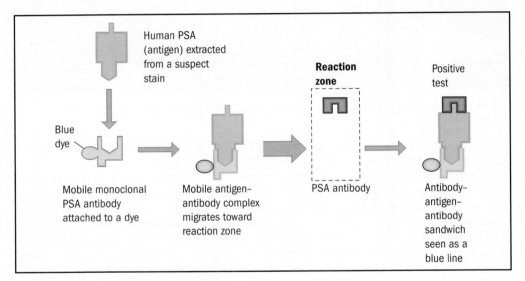

FIGURE 15-10 An antibody–antigen–antibody "sandwich," or complex, is seen as a colored band arising from the attached blue dye. This signifies the presence of PSA in the extract of a stain and positively identifies human semen. *SAFERSTEIN, RICHARD, Ph.D., CRIMINALISTICS: AN INTRODUCTION TO FORENSIC SCIENCE, 11th Ed., © 2015. Reprinted and Electronically reproduced by permission of Pearson Education, Inc., Upper Saddle River, New Jersey.*

A more elegant approach to identifying PSA (or p30) is shown in Figure 15-10. First, a monoclonal PSA antibody is attached to a dye and placed on a porous membrane. Monoclonal antibodies are specially designed to attack a single antigen site. Next, an extract from a sample suspected of containing PSA is placed on the membrane. If PSA is present in the extract, it combines with the monoclonal PSA antibody to form a PSA antigen–monoclonal PSA antibody complex. This complex migrates along the membrane, where it interacts with a PSA antibody imbedded in the membrane. The antibody–antigen–antibody "sandwich" that forms is apparent by the presence of a colored line (see Figure 15-10). This monoclonal antibody technique is about 100 times as sensitive as the electrophoretic method for detecting PSA.

Once the material is proved to be semen, the next task is to associate the semen as closely as possible with an individual. As we will learn, forensic scientists can link seminal material to one individual with DNA technology. Just as important is the fact that this technology can exonerate many of those wrongfully accused of sexual assault.

Quick Review

- The best way to locate and characterize a seminal stain is to perform the acid phosphatase color test.
- The presence of spermatozoa is a unique identifier of semen. Also, the protein called "prostate-specific antigen (PSA)," also known as "p30," is useful in combination with the acid phosphatase color test for characterizing a sample stain as semen.
- Forensic scientists can link seminal material to an individual by DNA typing.

Collection of Sexual Assault Evidence

Seminal constituents on a sexual assault victim are important evidence that sexual intercourse has taken place, but their absence does not necessarily mean that a sexual assault did not occur. Physical injuries such as bruises and bleeding tend to confirm that a violent assault occurred. Furthermore, the forceful physical contact between victim and assailant may result in a transfer of physical evidence such as blood, semen, hairs, and fibers. The presence of such evidence helps forge a vital link in the chain of circumstances surrounding a sexual crime.

To protect this kind of evidence, all the outer garments and undergarments from the victim should be carefully removed and packaged separately in paper (not plastic) bags. A clean bedsheet should be placed on the floor and a clean paper sheet placed over it. The victim must remove her shoes before standing on the paper. The person should disrobe while standing on the paper in order to collect any loose foreign material falling from the clothing. Each piece of clothing should be collected as it is removed and placed in a separate paper bag to avoid cross-contamination. The paper sheet should be folded carefully so that all foreign materials are contained inside. If appropriate, bedding or the object on which the assault took place should be submitted to the laboratory for processing.

Items suspected of containing seminal stains must be handled carefully. Folding an article at the location of a stain may cause it to flake off, as will rubbing the stained area against the surface of the packaging material. If, under unusual circumstances, it is not possible to transport the stained article to the laboratory, the stained area should be cut out and submitted along with a separately packaged unstained piece as a substrate control.

In the laboratory, analysts try to link seminal material to a source using DNA typing. Because an investigator may transfer his or her DNA types to a stain through perspiration, stained articles must be handled with care, minimizing direct personal contact. The evidence collector must wear disposable latex gloves when such evidence must be touched.

The sexual assault victim must undergo a medical examination as soon as possible after the assault. At this time, the appropriate items of physical evidence are collected by trained personnel. Evidence collectors should have an evidence-collection kit from the local crime laboratory (see Figures 15-11, 15-12, and 15-13).

The following procedure should be followed by a medical professional to collect items of physical evidence from the sexual assault victim:

1. *Pubic Combings.* Place a paper towel under the buttocks and comb the pubic area for loose or foreign hairs.
2. *Pubic Hair Standard/Reference Samples.* Cut approximately 25 full-length hairs from the pubic area at the skin line.

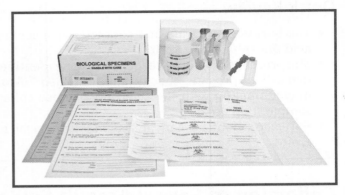

FIGURE 15-11   Victim rape collection kit with instructions, and forms for medical history and assault information. Envelope for foreign materials. Collection bags for outer clothing and underpants. Envelopes for debris, pubic hair combings. Envelope for pulled pubic hair. Envelopes for vaginal swabs and rectal swabs with swap boxes and microscope slides. Envelopes for oral swabs and smear with microscope and a swab box. Envelope for known saliva sample. Known blood sample envelope. Anatomical drawings. *Tri-Tech Inc.*

FIGURE 15-12   Drug-Facilitated Sexual Assault Evidence Toxicology Kit containing a blood tube and urine specimen bottle holder. *Tri-Tech, Inc.*

3. ***External Genital Dry-Skin Areas.***   Swab with at least one dry swab and one moistened swab.
4. ***Vaginal Swabs and Smear.***   Using two swabs simultaneously, carefully swab the vaginal area and let the swabs air-dry before packaging. Using two additional swabs, repeat the swabbing procedure and smear the swabs onto separate microscope slides, allowing them to air-dry before packaging.
5. ***Cervix Swabs.***   Using two swabs simultaneously, carefully swab the cervix area and let the swabs air-dry before packaging.
6. ***Rectal Swabs and Smear.***   To be taken when warranted by case history. Using two swabs simultaneously, swab the rectal canal, smearing one of the swabs onto a microscope slide. Allow both samples to air-dry before packaging.
7. ***Oral Swabs and Smear.***   To be taken if oral–genital contact occurred. Use two swabs simultaneously to swab the buccal area and gum line. Using both swabs, prepare one smear slide. Allow both swabs and the smear to air-dry before packaging.
8. ***Swabs of Body Areas, Such as Breasts,***   that are suspected of being in contact with DNA arising from touching or saliva.

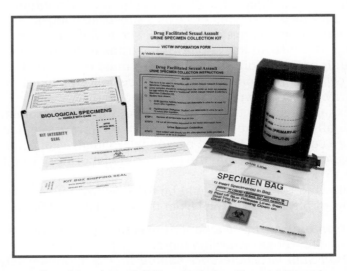

FIGURE 15-13   Drug-Facilitated Sexual Assault Evidence Toxicology Kit containing a urine specimen bottle. *Tri-Tech Inc.*

9. *Head Hairs.* Cut at skin line a minimum of five full-length hairs from each of the following scalp locations: center, front, back, left side, and right side. It is recommended that a total of at least 25 hairs be cut and submitted to the laboratory.

10. *Blood Sample.* Collect at least 20 milliliters in a vacuum tube containing the preservative EDTA. The blood sample can be used for suspected drug-facilitated sexual assaults (see pages 265–66).

11. *Collect Buccal Swab for DNA Typing.*

12. *Fingernail Scrapings.* Scrape the undersurface of the nails with a dull object over a piece of clean paper to collect debris. Use separate paper, one for each hand.

13. *All Clothing.* Package as described earlier.

14. *Urine Specimen.* Collect 30 milliliters or more of urine from the victim for the purpose of conducting a drug toxicological analysis for Rohypnol, GHB, and other substances associated with drug-facilitated sexual assaults (see pages 265–66).

Often, during the investigation of a sexual assault, the victim reports that a perpetrator engaged in biting, sucking, or licking areas of the victim's body. As we will learn in the next section, the tremendous sensitivity associated with DNA technology offers investigators the opportunity to identify a perpetrator DNA types from saliva residues collected off the skin. The most efficient way to recover saliva residues from the skin is to first swab the suspect area with a rotating motion using a cotton swab moistened with distilled water. A second, dry swab is then rotated over the skin to recover the moist remains on the skin's surface from the wet swab. The swabs are air-dried and packaged together as a single sample.

If a suspect is apprehended, the following items are routinely collected:

1. *All clothing* and any other items believed to have been worn at the time of assault

2. Pubic hair combings

3. Head and pubi*c hair standard/reference samples*

4. A *penile swab* taken within 24 hours of the assault, when appropriate to the case history

5. A *buccal swab* for DNA typing purposes

The advent of DNA profiling has forced investigators to rethink what items are evidential in a sexual assault. DNA levels in the range of one-billionth of a gram are now routinely characterized in crime laboratories. In the past, scant attention was paid to the underwear recovered from a male who was suspected of being involved in a sexual assault; seminal constituents on a man's underwear had little or no investigative value. Today, the sensitivity of DNA analysis has created new areas of investigation. It is possible to link a victim and an assailant by analyzing biological material recovered from the interior front surface of a male suspect's underwear. This is especially important when investigations have failed to yield the presence of the suspect's DNA on evidence recovered from the victim.

The persistence of seminal constituents in the vagina may help determine the time of an alleged sexual attack. Although spermatozoa in the vaginal cavity provide evidence of intercourse, important information regarding the time of sexual activity may be obtained from the knowledge that motile (living) sperm generally survive for up to six hours in the vaginal cavity of a living female. However, a successful search for motile sperm requires a microscopic examination of a vaginal smear immediately after it is taken from the victim. Some investigaters question the value of investing time into seeking out motile sperm. Noting that such findings may be expected to be found in a relatively small percentage of cases (about 5%).[5]

A more extensive examination of vaginal collections is later made at a forensic laboratory. Nonmotile sperm may be found in a living female for up

■■■■ CASEFILES ■■■■

A common mode of DNA transfer occurs when skin cells from the walls of a female victim's vagina are transferred onto the suspect during intercourse. Subsequent penile contact with the inner surface of the suspect's underwear often leads to the recovery of the female victim's DNA from the underwear's inner surface. The power of DNA is illustrated by a case in which the female victim of a sexual assault had consensual sexual intercourse with a male partner before being assaulted by a different male. DNA extracted from the inside front area of the suspect's underwear revealed a female DNA profile matching that of the victim. The added bonus to investigators in this case was finding male DNA on the same underwear that matched that of the consensual partner.

Source: Based on information contained in Gary G. Verret, "Sexual Assault Cases with No Primary Transfer of Biological Material from Suspect to Victim: Evidence of Secondary and Tertiary Transfer of Biological Material from Victim to Suspect's Undergarments," Proceedings of the Canadian Society of Forensic Science, Toronto, Ontario, November 2001.

to three days after intercourse and occasionally up to six days later. Intact sperm (i.e., sperm with tails) are not normally found more than 16 hours after intercourse, but they have been found as late as 72 hours later. The likelihood of finding seminal acid phosphatase in the vaginal cavity markedly decreases with time following intercourse, with little chance of identifying this substance 48 hours after intercourse.[4] Hence, with the possibility of prolonged persistence of both spermatozoa and acid phosphatase in the vaginal cavity after intercourse, investigators should determine if and when voluntary sexual activity last occurred before the sexual assault. This information will help in evaluating the significance of finding these seminal constituents in a female victim. Blood or buccal swabs for DNA analysis should be taken from any consensual partner who had sex with the victim within 72 hours of the assault.

Another significant indicator of recent sexual activity is PSA. This semen marker normally is not detected in the vaginal cavity beyond 72 hours following intercourse.[4]

Quick Review

- A sexual assault victim should undergo a medical examination as soon as possible after the assault. At that time clothing, hairs, and vaginal and rectal swabs can be collected for subsequent laboratory examination.
- The persistence of seminal constituents in the vagina may help determine the time of an alleged sexual attack.

■■■■

■ Understanding DNA

■
■
■
■

The discovery of deoxyribonucleic acid (DNA), the deciphering of its structure, and the decoding of its genetic information were turning points in our understanding of the underlying concepts of inheritance. Now, with incredible speed, as molecular biologists unravel the basic structure of genes, we can create new products through genetic engineering and develop diagnostic tools and treatments for genetic disorders.

For a number of years, these developments were of seemingly peripheral interest to forensic scientists. All that changed when, in 1985, what started out as a more or less routine investigation into the structure of a human gene led to the discovery that portions of the DNA structure of certain genes are as unique to each individual as fingerprints. Alec Jeffreys and his colleagues at Leicester University, England, who were responsible for these revelations, named the process for isolating and reading these DNA markers "DNA fingerprinting." As researchers uncovered new approaches and variations to

gene
The basic unit of heredity, consisting of a DNA segment located on a chromosome.

chromosome
A threadlike structure in the cell nucleus composed of DNA, along which the genes are located.

the original Jeffreys technique, the terms "DNA profiling" and "DNA typing" came to be applied to describe this relatively new technology.

This discovery caught the imagination of the forensic science community because forensic scientists have long searched for ways to definitively link biological evidence such as blood, semen, hair, and tissue to a single individual. Although conventional testing procedures had gone a long way toward narrowing the source of biological materials, individualization remained an elusive goal. DNA typing has allowed forensic scientists to accomplish this goal. Although the technique is still relatively new, DNA typing has become routine in public crime laboratories. It also has been made available to interested parties through the services of a number of skilled private laboratories. In the United States, courts have overwhelmingly admitted DNA evidence and accepted the reliability of its scientific underpinnings.

GENES AND CHROMOSOMES

Hereditary material is transmitted via microscopic units called **genes**. The gene is the basic unit of heredity. Each gene by itself or in concert with other genes controls the development of a specific characteristic in the new individual; the genes determine the nature and growth of virtually every body structure.

The genes are positioned on **chromosomes**, threadlike bodies that appear in the nucleus of every body cell (see Figure 15-14). Almost all human cells contain forty-six chromosomes, mated in twenty-three pairs. The only exceptions are the human reproductive cells, the **egg** and **sperm**, which contain twenty-three unmated chromosomes. During fertilization, a sperm and egg combine so that each contributes twenty-three chromosomes to form the new cell (**zygote**). Hence, the new individual begins life properly, with twenty-three mated chromosome pairs. Because the genes are positioned on the chromosomes, the new individual inherits genetic material from each parent.

Actually, two dissimilar chromosomes are involved in the determination of sex. The egg cell always contains a long chromosome known as the **X chromosome**; the sperm cell may contain either a long X chromosome or a short **Y chromosome**. When an X-carrying sperm fertilizes an egg, the new cell has two X chromosomes (i.e., XX) and develops into a female. A Y-carrying sperm produces an XY fertilized egg and develops into a male. Because the sperm cell determines the nature of the chromosome pair, we can say that the father biologically determines the sex of the child.

ALLELES Just as chromosomes come together in pairs, so do the genes they bear. The position a gene occupies on a chromosome is its **locus**. Genes that govern a given characteristic are similarly positioned on the chromosomes inherited from the mother and father. Thus, a gene for eye color on the mother's chromosome will be aligned with a gene for eye color on the corresponding chromosome inherited from the father. Alternative forms of genes that influence a given characteristic and are aligned with one another on a chromosome pair are known as **alleles**.

egg
The female reproductive cell.

sperm
The male reproductive cell.

zygote
The cell arising from the union of an egg and a sperm cell.

X chromosome
The female sex chromosome.

Y chromosome
The male sex chromosome.

locus
The physical location of a gene on a chromosome.

allele
Any of several alternative forms of a gene located at the same point on a particular pair of chromosomes.

FIGURE 15-14 A computer-enhanced photomicrograph image of human chromosomes. *Alfred Pasieka/Science Source*

homozygous
Having two identical allelic genes on two corresponding positions on a pair of chromosomes.

heterozygous
Having two different allelic genes on two corresponding positions on a pair of chromosomes.

Inheritance of blood type offers a simple example of allele genes in humans. An individual's blood type is determined by three genes, designated A, B, and O. A gene pair made up of two similar alleles—for example, AA and BB—is said to be **homozygous**. For example, if the chromosome inherited from the father carries the A gene and the chromosome inherited from the mother carries the same gene, the offspring will have an AA combination. Thus, when an individual inherits two similar genes from his or her parents, there is no problem in determining the blood type of that person. An individual with an AA combination will always be type A, a BB will be type B, and an OO will be type O.

A gene pair made up of two different alleles—AO, for example—is said to be **heterozygous**. For example, if the chromosome from one parent carries the A gene and the chromosome from the other parent carries the O gene, the genetic makeup of the offspring will be AO. When two different genes are inherited, one gene will be *dominant*—that is, the characteristic coded for by that gene is expressed. The other gene will be *recessive*—that is, its characteristics remain hidden. In the case of blood types, A and B genes are dominant, and the O gene is recessive. Thus, with an AO combination, A is always dominant over O, and the individual is typed as A. Similarly, a BO combination is typed as B. In the case of AB, the genes are *codominant*, and the individual's blood type will be AB. The recessive characteristics of O appear only when both recessive genes are present in combination OO, which is typed simply as O.

Quick Review

- The gene is the basic unit of heredity. A chromosome is a threadlike structure in the cell nucleus along which the genes are located.
- Most human cells contain forty-six chromosomes, arranged in twenty-three mated pairs. The only exceptions are the human reproductive cells, the egg and sperm, which contain twenty-three unmated chromosomes each.
- During fertilization, a sperm and an egg combine so that each contributes twenty-three chromosomes to form the new cell, or "zygote," that develops into the offspring.
- An allele is any of several alternative forms of genes that influence a given characteristic and that are aligned with one another on a chromosome pair.
- A heterozygous gene pair is made up of two different alleles; a homozygous gene pair is made up of two similar alleles.
- When two different genes are inherited, the characteristic in the dominant gene's code will be expressed. The characteristic in the recessive gene's code will remain hidden.

WebExtra 15.2
Learn About the Chromosomes as Present in Our Cells

WebExtra 15.3
Learn About the Structure of Our Genes

WebExtra 15.4
See How Genes Position Themselves on a Chromosome Pair

WebExtra 15.5
See How Genes Define Our Genetic Makeup

WHAT IS DNA?

Inside each of 60 trillion cells in the human body are strands of genetic material called "chromosomes." Arranged along the chromosomes, like beads on a thread, are nearly 25,000 genes. The gene is the fundamental unit of heredity. It instructs the body's cells to make proteins that determine everything from hair color to susceptibility to diseases. Each gene is composed of DNA designed to carry out a single body function.

Although DNA was first discovered in 1868, scientists were slow to understand and appreciate its fundamental role in inheritance. Painstakingly, researchers developed evidence that DNA was probably the substance by which genetic instructions are passed from one generation to the next. However, the first major breakthrough in comprehending how DNA works did not occur until the early 1950s, when two researchers, James Watson and Francis Crick, deduced the structure of DNA. It turns out that DNA is an extraordinary molecule skillfully designed to control the genetic traits of all living cells, plant and animal.

STRUCTURE OF DNA   Before examining the implications of Watson and Crick's discovery, let's see how DNA is constructed. DNA is a "polymer." A polymer is a very large molecule made by linking a series of repeating units, or monomers. In this case, the units are known as **nucleotides**.

NUCLEOTIDES   A nucleotide is composed of a sugar molecule, a phosphorus atom surrounded by four oxygen atoms, and a nitrogen-containing molecule called a "base." Figure 15-15 shows how nucleotides can be strung together to form a DNA strand. In this figure, *S* designates the sugar component, which is joined with a phosphate group to form the backbone of the DNA strand. Projecting from the backbone are the bases.

The key to understanding how DNA works is to appreciate the fact that only four types of bases are associated with DNA: adenine, cytosine, guanine, and thymine. To simplify our discussion of DNA, we will designate each of these bases by the first letter of their names. Hence, *A* will stand for adenine, *C* for cytosine, *G* for guanine, and *T* for thymine.

Again, notice in Figure 15-15 how the bases project from the backbone of DNA. Also, although this figure shows a DNA strand of four bases, keep in mind that in theory there is no limit to the length of the DNA strand; a DNA strand can be composed of a long chain with millions of bases. This information was well known to Watson and Crick by the time they started detailing the structure of DNA. Their efforts led them to discover that the DNA molecule is composed of two DNA strands coiled into a *double helix*. This can be thought of as resembling two wires twisted around each other.

As Watson and Crick manipulated scale models of DNA strands, they realized that the only way the bases on each strand could be properly aligned with each other in a double-helix configuration was to place base *A* opposite *T* and *G* opposite *C*. Watson and Crick had solved the puzzle of the double helix and presented the world with a simple but elegant picture of DNA (see Figure 15-16).

COMPLEMENTARY BASE PAIRING   The concept that the only arrangement possible in the double-helix configuration is the pairing of bases *A* to *T* and *G* to *C* is known as "complementary base pairing." Although *A–T* and *G–C* pairs are always required, there are no restrictions on how the bases are sequenced on a DNA strand. Thus, one can observe the sequences *T–A–T–T* or *G–T–A–A* or *G–T–C–A*. When these sequences are joined with their complements in a double-helix configuration, they pair as follows:

```
T A T T    G T A A    G T C A
| | | |    | | | |    | | | |
A T A A    C A T T    C A G T
```

Any base can follow another on a DNA strand, which means that the number of possible sequence combinations is staggering. Consider that the average human chromosome has DNA containing 100 million base pairs. All of the human chromosomes taken together contain about three billion base pairs. From these numbers, we can begin to appreciate the diversity of DNA and, hence, the diversity of living organisms. DNA is like a book of instructions. The alphabet used to create the book is simple enough: *A, T, G,* and *C*. The order in which these letters are arranged defines the role and function of a DNA molecule.

nucleotide
A repeating unit of DNA consisting of one of four bases—adenine, guanine, cytosine, or thymine—attached to a phosphate–sugar group.

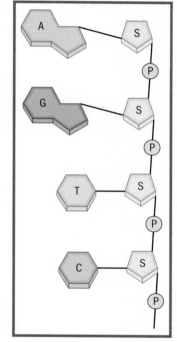

FIGURE 15-15   How nucleotides can be linked to form a DNA strand. *S* designates the sugar component, which is joined with phosphate groups (*P*) to form the backbone of DNA. Projecting from the backbone are four bases: *A*, adenine; *G*, guanine; *T*, thymine; and *C*, cytosine. *SAFERSTEIN, RICHARD, Ph.D., CRIMINALISTICS: AN INTRODUCTION TO FORENSIC SCIENCE, 11th Ed., © 2015. Reprinted and Electronically reproduced by permission of Pearson Education, Inc., Upper Saddle River, New Jersey.*

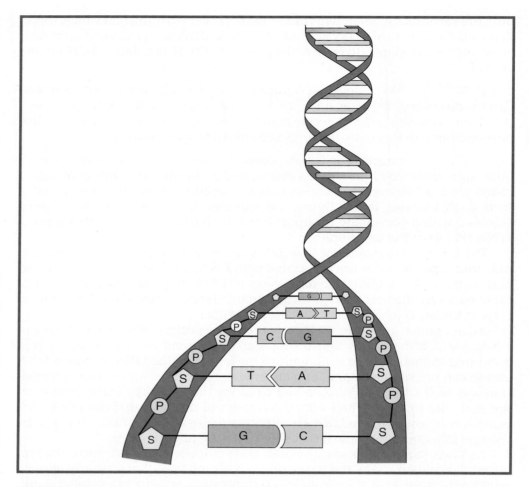

FIGURE 15-16 A representation of a DNA double helix. Notice how bases *G* and *C* pair with each other, as do bases *A* and *T*. This is the only arrangement in which two DNA strands can align with each other in a double-helix configuration. *SAFERSTEIN, RICHARD, Ph.D., CRIMINALISTICS: AN INTRODUCTION TO FORENSIC SCIENCE, 11th Ed., © 2015. Reprinted and Electronically reproduced by permission of Pearson Education, Inc., Upper Saddle River, New Jersey.*

Polymerase Chain Reaction (PCR)

Once the double-helix structure of DNA was discovered, how DNA duplicated itself prior to cell division became apparent. The concept of base pairing in DNA suggests the analogy of positive and negative photographic film. Each strand of DNA in the double helix has the same information; one can make a positive print from a negative or a negative from a positive.

PCR PROCESS

WebExtra 15.6

What Is DNA?

polymerase chain reaction (PCR)

A technique for replicating or copying a portion of a DNA strand outside a living cell.

The synthesis of new DNA from existing DNA begins with the unwinding of the DNA strands in the double helix. Each strand is then exposed to a collection of free nucleotides. Letter by letter, the double helix is re-created as the nucleotides are assembled in the proper order, as dictated by the principle of base pairing (*A* with *T* and *G* with *C*). The result is the emergence of two identical copies of DNA where before there was only one (see Figure 15-17). A cell can now pass on its genetic identity when it divides.

Many enzymes and proteins are involved in unwinding the DNA strands, keeping the two DNA strands apart, and assembling the new DNA strands. For example, DNA "polymerases" are enzymes that assemble a new DNA strand in the proper base sequence determined by the original, or parent, DNA strand. DNA polymerases also "proofread" the growing DNA double helices for mismatched base pairs, which are replaced with correct bases.

Until recently, the phenomenon of DNA replication appeared to be of only academic interest to forensic scientists interested in DNA for identification. However, this changed when researchers perfected the technology of using DNA polymerases to copy a DNA strand located outside a living cell. This laboratory technique is known as **polymerase chain reaction (PCR)**. Put simply, PCR is a technique designed to copy or multiply DNA strands.

In PCR, small quantities of DNA or broken pieces of DNA found in crime-scene evidence can be copied with the aid of a DNA polymerase. The copying process is highly temperature dependent and can be accomplished in an automated fashion using a DNA thermal cycler (see Figure 15-18). Each cycle of the PCR technique results in a doubling of the DNA, as shown in Figure 15-17. Within a few hours, thirty cycles can multiply DNA a billionfold. Once DNA copies are in hand, they can be analyzed by any of the methods of modern molecular biology. The ability to multiply small bits of DNA opens new and exciting avenues for forensic scientists to explore. It means that sample size is no longer a limitation in characterizing DNA recovered from crime-scene evidence.

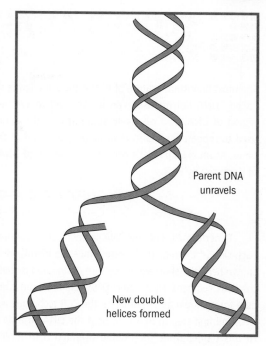

FIGURE 15-17 Replication of DNA. The strands of the original DNA molecule are separated, and two new strands are assembled. *SAFERSTEIN, RICHARD, Ph.D., CRIMINALISTICS: AN INTRODUCTION TO FORENSIC SCIENCE, 11th Ed., © 2015. Reprinted and Electronically reproduced by permission of Pearson Education, Inc., Upper Saddle River, New Jersey.*

Quick Review

- The gene is the fundamental unit of heredity. Each gene is composed of DNA specifically designed to control the genetic traits of our cells.
- DNA is constructed as a very large molecule made of a linked series of repeating units called "nucleotides."
- Four types of bases are associated with the DNA structure: adenine *(A)*, guanine *(G)*, cytosine *(C)*, and thymine *(T)*.
- The bases on each strand of DNA are aligned in a double-helix configuration so that adenine pairs with thymine and guanine pairs with cytosine. This concept is known as "complementary base pairing."
- The order in which the base pairs are arranged defines the role and function of a DNA molecule.
- DNA replication begins with the unwinding of the DNA strands in the double helix. The double helix is re-created as the nucleotides are assembled in the proper order (*A* with *T* and *G* with *C*). Two identical copies of DNA emerge from the process.
- PCR (polymerase chain reaction) is a technique for replicating, or copying, a portion of a DNA strand outside a living cell.

FIGURE 15-18 The DNA thermal cycler, an instrument that automates the rapid and precise temperature changes required to copy a DNA strand. Within a matter of hours, DNA can be multiplied a billionfold. *Applied Biosystems*

CLOSER ANALYSIS
POLYMERASE CHAIN REACTION

The most important feature of PCR is the knowledge that an enzyme called "DNA polymerase" can be directed to synthesize a specific region of DNA. In a relatively straightforward manner, PCR can be used to repeatedly duplicate or amplify a strand of DNA millions of times. As an example, let's consider a segment of DNA that we want to duplicate by PCR:

–G–T–C–T–C–A–G–C–T–T–**C–C–A–G**–
–**C–A–G–A**–G–T–C–G–A–A–G–G–T–C–

To perform PCR on this DNA segment, short sequences of DNA on each side of the region of interest must be identified. In the example shown here, the short sequences are designated by boldface letters in the DNA segment. These short DNA segments must be available in a pure form known as a "primer" if the PCR technique is going to work.

The first step in PCR is to heat the DNA strands to about 94°C. At this temperature, the double-stranded DNA molecules separate completely:

–G–T–C–T–C–A–G–C–T–T–C–C–A–G–

–C–A–G–A–G–T–C–G–A–A–G–G–T–C–

The second step is to add the primers to the separated strands and allow the primers to combine, or hybridize, with the strands by lowering the test-tube temperature to about 60°C.

–G–T–C–T–C–A–G–C–T–T–C–C–A–G–
C–A–G–A

C–C–A–G
–C–A–G–A–G–T–C–G–A–A–G–G–T–C–

The third step is to add the DNA polymerase and a mixture of free nucleotides (A, C, G, T) to the separated strands. When the test tube is heated to 72°C, the polymerase enzyme directs the rebuilding of a double-stranded DNA molecule, extending the primers by adding the appropriate bases, one at a time, resulting in the production of two complete pairs of double-stranded DNA segments:

–G–T–C–T–C–A–G–C–T–T–C–C–A–G–
C–A–G–A–G–T–C–G–A–A–G–G–T–C–

–G–T–C–T–C–A–G–C–T–T–C–C–A–G
–C–A–G–A–G–T–C–G–A–A–G–G–T–C–

This completes the first cycle of the PCR technique, which results in a doubling of the number of DNA molecules from one to two. The cycle of heating, cooling, and strand rebuilding is then repeated, resulting in a further doubling of the DNA molecules. On completion of the second cycle, four double-stranded DNA molecules have been created from the original double-stranded DNA sample. Typically, twenty-eight to thirty-two cycles are carried out to yield more than one billion copies of the original DNA molecule. Each cycle takes less than 2 minutes.

DNA Typing with Short Tandem Repeats

Geneticists have discovered that portions of the DNA molecule contain sequences of letters that are repeated numerous times. In fact, more than 30 percent of the human genome is composed of repeating segments of DNA. These repeating sequences, or "tandem repeats," seem to act as filler or spacers between the coding regions of DNA. Although these repeating segments do not seem to affect our outward appearance or control any other basic genetic function, they are nevertheless part of our genetic makeup, inherited from our parents. The origin and significance of these tandem repeats is a mystery, but to forensic scientists they offer a means of distinguishing one individual from another through DNA typing.

WebExtra 15.7

Polymerase Chain Reaction

SHORT TANDEM REPEATS (STRS)

short tandem repeat (STR)
A region of a DNA molecule that contains short segments of three to seven repeating base pairs.

Currently, **short tandem repeat (STR)** analysis has emerged as the most successful and widely used DNA-profiling procedure. STRs are locations (loci) on the chromosome that contain short sequence elements that repeat themselves within the DNA molecule. They serve as helpful markers for identification because they are found in great abundance throughout the human genome.

STRs normally consist of repeating sequences of three to seven bases; the entire strand of an STR is also very short, less than 450 bases long. These strands are significantly shorter than those encountered in other DNA typing procedures. This means that STRs are much less susceptible to degradation and are often recovered from bodies or stains that have been subject to extreme decomposition. Also, because of their shortness, STRs are an ideal candidate for multiplication by PCR, thus overcoming the limited-sample-size problem often associated with crime-scene evidence. Only the equivalent of eighteen DNA-containing cells is needed to obtain a DNA profile. For instance, STR profiles have been used to identify the origin of saliva residue on envelopes, stamps, soda cans, and cigarette butts.

To understand the utility of STRs in forensic science, let's look at one commonly used STR known as TH01. This DNA segment contains the repeating sequence *A–A–T–G*. Seven TH01 variants have been identified in the human genome. These variants contain five to eleven repeats of *A–A–T–G*. Figure 15-19 illustrates two such TH01 variants, one containing six repeats and the other containing eight repeats of *A–A–T–G*.

During a forensic examination, TH01 is extracted from biological materials and amplified by PCR as described earlier. The ability to copy an STR means that extremely small amounts of the molecule can be detected and analyzed. Once the STRs have been copied or amplified, they are separated by electrophoresis. Here, the STRs are forced to move across a gel-coated plate under the influence of an electrical potential. Smaller DNA fragments move along the plate faster than do larger DNA fragments. By examining the distance the STR has migrated on the electrophoretic plate, one can determine the number of *A–A–T–G* repeats in the STR. Every person has two STR types for TH01, one inherited from each parent. Thus, for example, one may find in a semen stain TH01 with six repeats and eight repeats. This combination of TH01 is found in approximately 3.5 percent of the population. It is important to understand that all humans have the same type of repeats, but there is tremendous variation in the number of repeats each of us has.

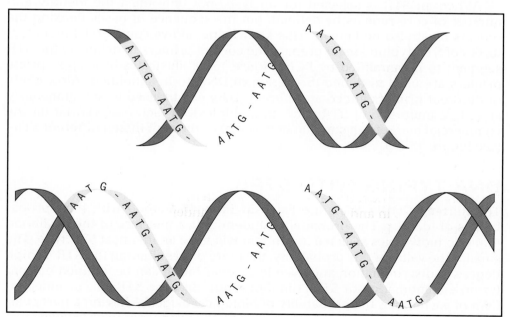

FIGURE 15-19 Variants of the short tandem repeat TH01. The upper DNA strand contains six repeats of the sequence *A–A–T–G*; the lower DNA strand contains eight repeats of the sequence *A–A–T–G*. This DNA type is known as TH01 6,8. *Variants of the Short Tandem Repeat TH01 Copyright © by Pearson Education. Reprinted and electronically reproduced by Pearson Education, Inc. Upper Saddle River, New Jersey.*

FIGURE 15-20 A DNA profile pattern of a suspect and its match to crime-scene DNA. From left to right, lane 1 is a DNA standard marker; lane 2 is the crime-scene DNA; and lanes 3 to 5 are control samples from suspects 1, 2, and 3, respectively. Crime-scene DNA matches suspect 2. *SAFERSTEIN, RICHARD, Ph.D., CRIMINALISTICS: AN INTRODUCTION TO FORENSIC SCIENCE, 11th Ed., © 2015. Reprinted and Electronically reproduced by permission of Pearson Education, Inc., Upper Saddle River, New Jersey.*

multiplexing
A technique that simultaneously detects more than one DNA marker in a single analysis.

WebExtra 15.8

See the Thirteen CODIS STRs and Their Chromosomal Positions

WebExtra 15.9

Calculate the Frequency of Occurrence of a DNA Profile

WebExtra 15.10

Understand the Operational Principles of Capillary Electrophoresis

When examining an STR DNA pattern, one merely needs to look for a match between band sets. For example, in Figure 15-20, DNA extracted from a crime-scene stain matches the DNA recovered from one of three suspects. When comparing only one STR, a limited number of people in a population would have the same STR fragment pattern as the suspect. However, by using additional STRs, a high degree of discrimination or complete individualization can be achieved.

MULTIPLEXING

What makes STRs so attractive to forensic scientists is that hundreds of types of STRs are found in human genes. The more STRs one can characterize, the smaller the percentage of the population from which these STRs can emanate. This gives rise to the concept of **multiplexing**. Using PCR technology, one can simultaneously extract and amplify a combination of different STRs.

One STR system on the commercial market is the STR Blue Kit. This kit provides the necessary materials for amplifying and detecting three STRs (a process called "triplexing"): D3S1358, vWA, and FGA. The design of the system ensures that the size of the STRs does not overlap, thereby allowing each marker to be viewed clearly on an electrophoretic gel, as shown in Figure 15-21. In the United States, the forensic science community has standardized thirteen STRs for entry into a national database known as the Combined DNA Index System (CODIS).

When an STR is selected for analysis, not only must the identity and number of core repeats be defined, but the sequence of bases flanking the repeats must also be known. This knowledge allows commercial manufacturers of STR typing kits to prepare the correct primers to delineate the STR segment to be amplified by PCR. Figure 15-22 illustrates how appropriate primers are used to define the region of DNA to be amplified. Also, a mix of different primers aimed at different STRs will be used to simultaneously amplify a multitude of STRs (i.e., to multiplex). In fact, one STR kit on the commercial market can simultaneously make copies of fifteen different STRs (see Figure 15-23).

DNA TYPING WITH STRS

The thirteen CODIS STRs are listed in Table 15.1 along with their probabilities of identity. The probability of identity is a measure of the likelihood that two individuals selected at random will have an identical STR type. The smaller the value of this probability, the more discriminating the STR. A high degree of discrimination and even individualization can be attained by analyzing a combination of STRs (multiplexing). Because STRs occur independent of each other, the probability of biological evidence having a particular combination of STR types is determined by the product of their frequency of occurrence in a population. This combination is referred to as the "product rule" (see p. 108). Hence, the greater the number of STRs characterized, the smaller the frequency of occurrence of the analyzed sample in the general population.

The combination of the first three STRs shown in Table 15.1 typically produces a frequency of occurrence of about 1 in 5,000. A combination of the first six STRs typically yields a frequency of occurrence in the range of 1 in 2 million for the Caucasian population, and if the top nine STRs are determined in combination, this frequency declines to about 1 in 1 billion. The combination of all thirteen STRs shown in Table 15.1 typically produces frequencies of occurrence that measure in the range of 1 in 575 trillion for Caucasian Americans and 1 in 900 trillion for African Americans. Several commercially available kits allow forensic scientists to profile STRs in the kinds of combinations cited here.

SEX IDENTIFICATION USING STRS

Manufacturers of commercial STR kits typically used by crime laboratories provide one additional piece of useful information along with STR types: the sex of the DNA contributor. The focus of attention here is the *amelogenin gene* located on both the X and Y chromosomes. This gene, which is actually the gene for tooth pulp, has an interesting characteristic in that it is shorter by six bases in the X chromosome than in the Y chromosome. Hence, when the amelogenin gene is amplified by PCR and separated by electrophoresis, males, who have an X and a Y chromosome, show two bands; females, who have two X chromosomes, have just one band. Typically, these results are obtained in conjunction with STR types.

Another tool in the arsenal of the DNA analyst is the ability to type STRs located on the Y chromosome. The Y chromosome is male specific and is always paired with an X chromosome. More than twenty **Y-STR** markers have been identified, and a commercial kit allows for the characterization of seventeen Y chromosome STRs. When is it advantageous to seek out Y-STR types? Generally, Y-STRs are useful for analyzing blood, saliva, or a vaginal swab that is a mix originating from more than one male. For example, Y-STRs prove useful when multiple males are involved in a sexual assault. Further simplifying the analysis is that any DNA in the mixture that originates from a female will not show.

Unlike a conventional STR analysis that is derived from two chromosomes and typically shows two bands or peaks, a Y-STR has only one band or peak for each STR type.

For example, the traditional STR DNA pattern may be overly complex when a vaginal swab contains the semen of two males. Each STR type would be

FIGURE 15-21 A triplex system containing three loci: FGA, vWA, and D3S1358, indicating a match between the questioned and the standard/reference stains. *SAFERSTEIN, RICHARD, Ph.D., CRIMINALISTICS: AN INTRODUCTION TO FORENSIC SCIENCE, 11th Ed., © 2015. Reprinted and Electronically reproduced by permission of Pearson Education, Inc., Upper Saddle River, New Jersey.*

Y-STRs

Short tandem repeats located on the human Y chromosome.

WebExtra 15.11

See the Electropherogram Record from One Individual's DNA

WebExtra 15.12

An Animation Depicting Y-STRs

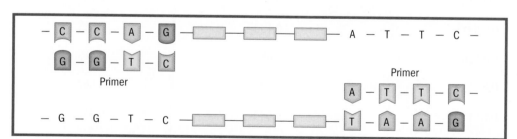

FIGURE 15-22 Appropriate primers flanking the repeat units of a DNA segment must be selected and put into place to initiate the PCR process. *SAFERSTEIN, RICHARD, Ph.D., CRIMINALISTICS: AN INTRODUCTION TO FORENSIC SCIENCE, 11th Ed., © 2015. Reprinted and Electronically reproduced by permission of Pearson Education, Inc., Upper Saddle River, New Jersey.*

FIGURE 15-23 STR profile for fifteen loci. *Richard Saferstein, Ph.D.*

expected to show four bands, two from each male. Also complicating the appearance of the DNA profile may be the presence of DNA from skin cells from the walls of the vagina. In this circumstance, homing in on the Y chromosome greatly simplifies the appearance and interpretation of the DNA profile. Thus, when presented with a DNA mixture of two males and one female, each STR type would be expected to show six bands. However, the same mixture subjected to Y-STR analysis would show only two bands (one band for each male) for each Y-STR type.

When gauging the significance of a Y-STR match between questioned and known specimens, one should take into consideration that all male paternal relatives (e.g., brothers, father, male offspring, and uncles) would be expected to have the same Y-STR profile. Another advantage of employing STR technology is to extend the success of detecting evidential DNA from vaginal swabs collected from rape victims. Casework experience has demonstrated significant difficulties in obtaining traditional STR DNA profiles for the male donor from vaginal swabs collected after three to four days after intercourse. However, the application of Y-STR technology often extends the routine postcoital detection time to five days for the male donor.

TABLE 15.1 Thirteen CODIS STRs and Their Probability of Identities

STR	AFRICAN AMERICAN	U.S. CAUCASIAN
D3S1358	0.094	0.075
vWA	0.063	0.062
FGA	0.033	0.036
TH01	0.109	0.081
TPOX	0.090	0.195
CSF1PO	0.081	0.112
D5S818	0.112	0.158
D13S317	0.136	0.085
D7S820	0.080	0.065
D8S1179	0.082	0.067
D21S11	0.034	0.039
D18S51	0.029	0.028
D16S539	0.070	0.089

Source: The Future of Forensic DNA Testing: Predictions of the Research and Development Working Group. (Washington, DC: National Institute of Justice, Department of Justice, 2000), p. 41.

■■■■ **CASE**FILES ■■■■

REOPENING THE BOSTON STRANGLER CASE

Albert DeSalvo's rape and murder of eleven women shocked the country in the early 1960's. Better known as the Boston Strangler, Desalvo would gain entry to primarily single female's apartments using disguises and tricks. Boston Police finally apprehended Desalvo through a witness sketch, and he confessed to the crimes through detailed descriptions. Despite his confession, Desalvo later recanted and forensic experts have contested his guilt. Desalvo was charged with life in prison for unrelated sexual assaults, but never was charged with the Boston Strangler killings. Albert Desalvo died in jail in 1973, further complicating the situation.

Through funding by the National Institute of Justice, the Boston Strangler case was reopened and examined with new DNA testing techniques. The Boston Police Department's cold case squad used DNA found on one of the Strangler's victims, Mary Sullivan, to link the crimes back to Desalvo. Forensic scientists focused their research on the (Y) chromosome, as it relates back to every male in a paternal lineage. Desalvo's nephew provided the key DNA used to tie Albert to the killings, and a positive match was made. Detectives confirmed these results by exhuming Desalvo's body; they concluded that the odds of someone else committing these crimes were 1 in 220 billion. The Boston Strangler Case has finally been resolved.

SIGNIFICANCE OF DNA TYPING

STR DNA typing has become an essential and basic investigative tool in the law enforcement community. The technology has progressed at a rapid rate and in only a few years has surmounted numerous legal challenges so that DNA typing is now vital evidence for resolving violent crimes and sex offenses. DNA evidence is impartial, implicating the guilty and exonerating the innocent.

In a number of well-publicized cases, DNA evidence has exonerated individuals who have been wrongly convicted and imprisoned. The importance of DNA analyses in criminal investigations has also placed added burdens on crime laboratories to improve their quality-assurance procedures and to ensure the correctness of their results. In fact, in several well-publicized instances, the accuracy of DNA tests conducted by government-funded laboratories has been called into question.

Quick Review

- Short tandem repeats (STRs) are locations on the chromosome that contain short sequences that repeat themselves within the DNA molecule. They serve as useful markers for identification because they are found in great abundance throughout the human genome.
- The entire strand of an STR is very short: less than 450 bases long. This makes STRs much less susceptible to degradation, and they are often recovered from bodies or stains that have been subjected to extreme decomposition.
- The more STRs one can characterize, the smaller the percentage of the population from which a particular combination of STRs can emanate. This gives rise to the concept of multiplexing, in which the forensic scientist can simultaneously extract and amplify a combination of STRs.
- With STRs, as few as eighteen DNA-containing cells are required for analysis.

Mitochondrial DNA

Typically, when one describes DNA in the context of a criminal investigation, the DNA is assumed to be the DNA in the nucleus of a cell. Actually, a human cell contains two types of DNA: nuclear and mitochondrial. The first constitutes the twenty-three pairs of chromosomes in the nuclei of our cells. Each

CLOSER ANALYSIS
CAPILLARY ELECTROPHORESIS

Capillary electrophoresis has emerged as the preferred technology for characterization of STRs. Capillary electrophoresis is carried out in a thin glass column. As illustrated in the figure, each end of the column is immersed in a reservoir of buffer liquid that also holds electrodes (coated with platinum) to supply high-voltage energy. The column is coated with a gel polymer, and the DNA-containing sample solution is injected into one end of the column with a syringe. The STR fragments then move through the column under the influence of an electrical potential at a speed that is related to the length of the STR fragments. The other end of the column is connected to a detector that tracks the separated STRs as they emerge from the column. As the DNA peaks pass through the detector, they are recorded on a display known as an "electropherogram."

(a) and (b) The separation of DNA segments is carried out on the interior wall of a glass capillary tube coated with a gel polymer and kept at a constant voltage. The size of the DNA fragments determines the speed at which they move through the column. This figure illustrates the separation of three sets of STRs (called "triplexing").

parent contributes to the genetic makeup of these chromosomes. Mitochondrial DNA (mtDNA), on the other hand, is found outside the nucleus of the cell and is inherited solely from the mother.

Mitochondria are cell structures found in all human cells. They are the power plants of the body, providing about 90 percent of the energy that the body needs to function. A single mitochondrion contains several loops of DNA, all of which are involved in energy generation. Further, because each cell in our bodies contains hundreds to thousands of mitochondria, there are hundreds to thousands of mtDNA copies in a human cell. This compares to just one set of nuclear DNA located in that same cell.

Forensic scientists rely on mtDNA to identify a subject when nuclear DNA is significantly degraded, as in the case of charred remains, or when nuclear DNA may be present in only very small quantities (e.g., in a hair shaft). Interestingly, when authorities cannot obtain a reference sample from an individual who may be long deceased or missing, an mtDNA reference sample can be obtained from any maternally related relative. However, this also means that all individuals of the same maternal lineage will be indistinguishable by mtDNA analysis.

Although mtDNA analysis is significantly more sensitive than nuclear DNA profiling, forensic analysis of mtDNA is more rigorous, time consuming, and costly than nuclear DNA profiling. For this reason, only a handful of public and private forensic laboratories receive evidence for mtDNA determination. The FBI Laboratory strictly limits the types of cases in which it will apply mtDNA technology.

One of the most publicized cases performed on human remains was the identification of the individual buried in the tomb of the Vietnam War's unknown soldier. The remains lying in the tomb were believed to belong to 1st Lt. Michael J. Blassie, whose A-37 warplane was shot down near An Loc, South Vietnam, in 1972. In 1984, the U.S. Army Central Identification Laboratory failed to identify the remains by physical characteristics, personal artifacts, or blood-typing results. The remains were subsequently placed in the tomb. In 1998, at the insistence of the Blassie family, the remains were disinterred for mtDNA analysis and the results were compared to references from seven families thought to be associated with the case. The remains in the tomb were subsequently analyzed and confirmed to be consistent with DNA from Lt. Blassie's family.

mitochondria
Small structures outside the nucleus that supply energy to a cell.

WebExtra 15.13

See How We Inherit Our Mitochondrial DNA

WebExtra 15.14

Look into the Structure of Mitochondrial DNA and See How It's Used for DNA Typing

Quick Review

- Mitochondrial DNA is located outside the cell's nucleus and is inherited from the mother.
- Mitochondria are cell structures found in all human cells. They provide most of the energy that the body needs to function.
- Mitochondrial DNA typing does not approach STR analysis in its discrimination power and thus is best reserved for analyzing samples, such as hair, for which STR analysis is not possible.

Combined DNA Index System (CODIS)

Perhaps the most significant investigative tool to arise from a DNA-typing program is the Combined DNA Index System (CODIS), a computer software program developed by the FBI that maintains local, state, and national databases of DNA profiles from convicted offenders, unsolved crime-scene evidence, and profiles of missing people. CODIS allows crime laboratories to compare DNA types recovered from crime-scene evidence to those of convicted sex offenders and other convicted criminals.

CLOSER ANALYSIS
FORENSIC ASPECTS OF MITOCHONDRIAL DNA

As discussed previously, nuclear DNA is composed of a continuous linear strand of nucleotides (*A, C, G,* and *T*). By contrast, mtDNA is constructed in a circular or loop configuration. Each loop contains enough *A, C, G,* and *T* (approximately 16,569 total nucleotides) to make up thirty-seven genes involved in mitochondrial energy generation.

Two regions of mtDNA have been found to be highly variable in the human population. These two regions have been designated hypervariable region I (HV1) and hypervariable region II (HV2), as shown in the figure. Again, the process for analyzing HV1 and HV2 is tedious. It involves generating many copies of these DNA hypervariable regions by PCR and then determining the order of the *A–T–C–G* bases constituting the hypervariable regions. This process is known as "sequencing." The FBI Laboratory, the Armed Forces DNA Identification Laboratory, and other laboratories have collaborated to compile an mtDNA population database containing the base sequences from HV1 and HV2.

Once the sequences of the hypervariable regions from a case sample are obtained, most laboratories simply report the number of times these sequences appear in the mtDNA database maintained by the FBI. The mtDNA database contains about five thousand sequences. This approach permits an assessment of how common or rare an observed mtDNA sequence is in the database.

Interestingly, many of the sequences that have been determined in casework are unique to the existing database, and many types are present at frequencies of no greater than 1 percent in the database. Thus, it is often possible to demonstrate how uncommon a particular mtDNA sequence is. However, even under the best circumstances, mtDNA typing does not approach STR analysis in its discrimination power. Thus, mtDNA analysis is best reserved for samples for which nuclear DNA typing is simply not possible.

The first time mtDNA was admitted as evidence in a U.S. court was in 1996 in the case of *State of Tennessee* v. *Paul Ware*. Here, mtDNA was used to link two hairs recovered from the crime scene to the defendant. Interestingly, in this case, blood and semen evidence were absent. Mitochondrial DNA analysis also plays a key role in the identification of human remains. An abundant amount of mtDNA is generally found in skeletal remains. Importantly, mtDNA reference samples are available from family members sharing the same mother, grandmother, great-grandmother, and so on.

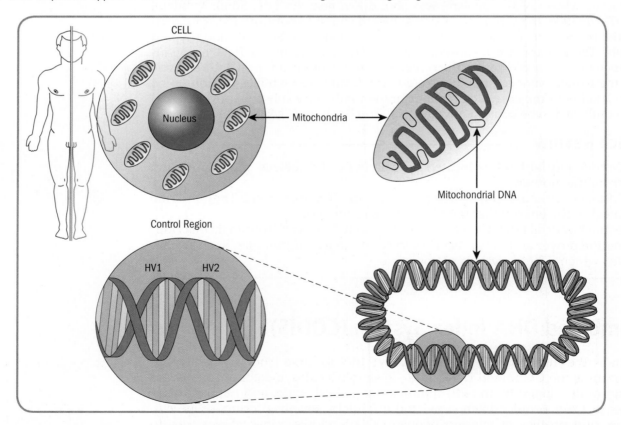

Every cell in the body contains hundreds of mitochondria, which provide energy to the cell. Each mitochondrion contains numerous copies of DNA shaped in the form of a loop. Distinctive differences between individuals in their mitochondrial DNA makeup are found in two specific segments of the control region on the DNA loop, known as "HV1" and "HV2."

■■■■ **CASE**FILES ■■■■

In the fall of 1979, a sixty-one-year-old patient wandered away from a U.S. Department of Veterans Affairs medical facility. Despite an extensive search, authorities never located the missing man. More than ten years later, a dog discovered a human skull in a wooded area near the facility. DNA Analysis Unit II of the FBI Laboratory received the case in the winter of 1999. The laboratory determined that the mitochondrial

DNA profile from the missing patient's brother matched the mitochondrial DNA profile from the recovered skull and provided the information to the local medical examiner. Subsequently, the remains were declared to be those of the missing patient and returned to the family for burial.

Source: *FBI Law Enforcement Bulletin* 78 (2002): 21.

Thousands of CODIS matches have linked serial crimes to each other and have solved crimes by allowing investigators to match crime-scene evidence to known convicted offenders. This capability is of tremendous value to investigators in cases in which the police have not been able to identify a suspect. The CODIS concept has already had a significant impact on police investigations in various states, as shown in the Case Files feature on page 105.

Quick Review

- CODIS is a computer software program developed by the FBI that maintains local, state, and national databases of DNA profiles from convicted offenders, unsolved crime-scene evidence, and profiles of missing people.

■■■■

Collection and Preservation of Biological Evidence for DNA Analysis

Since the early 1990s, the advent of DNA profiling has vaulted biological crime-scene evidence to a stature of importance that is eclipsed only by the fingerprint. In fact, the high sensitivity of DNA determinations has even changed the way police investigators define biological evidence.

Just how sensitive is STR profiling? Forensic analysts using currently accepted protocols can reach sensitivity levels as low as 125 **picograms**. Interestingly, a human cell has an estimated 7 picograms of DNA, which means that only eighteen DNA-bearing cells are needed to obtain an STR profile. However, modifications in the technology can readily extend the level of detection down to nine cells. A quantity of DNA that is below the normal level of detection is defined as a **low copy number**. (However, analysts must take extraordinary care in analyzing low-copy-number DNA and often may find that courts will not allow this data to be admissible in a criminal trial.) With this technology in hand, the horizon of the criminal investigator extends beyond the traditional dried blood or semen stain to include stamps and envelopes licked with saliva, a cup or can that has touched a person's lips, chewing gum, the sweat band of a hat, or a bedsheet containing dead skin cells. Likewise, skin or **epithelial cells** transferred onto the surface of a weapon, the interior of a glove, or a pen have yielded DNA results.[5] The phenomenon of transferring DNA via skin cells onto the surface of an object has come to be called **touch DNA**. Again, keep in mind that, in theory, only eighteen skin cells deposited on an object are required to obtain a DNA profile. However, before investigators become enamored with the wonders of DNA, they should first realize that the crime scene must be treated in the traditional manner. Before the collection of evidence begins, biological evidence should be photographed close up and its

picograms
One-trillionth of a gram or 0.000000000001 gram.

low copy number
Fewer than eighteen DNA-bearing cells.

epithelial cells
The outer layer of skin cells.

touch DNA
DNA from skin cells transferred onto the surface of an object by simple contact.

location relative to the entire crime scene recorded through notes, sketches, and photographs. If the shape and position of bloodstains may provide information about the circumstances of the crime, an expert must immediately conduct an on-the-spot evaluation of the blood evidence. The significance of the position and shape of bloodstains can best be ascertained when the expert has an on-site overview of the entire crime scene and can better reconstruct the movement of the individuals involved. No attempt should be made to disturb the blood pattern before this phase of the investigation is completed.

The evidence collector must handle all body fluids and biologically stained materials with a minimum amount of personal contact. All body fluids must be assumed to be infectious; hence, wearing disposable latex gloves while handling the evidence is required. Latex gloves also significantly reduce the possibility that the evidence collector will contaminate the evidence. These gloves should be changed frequently during the evidence-collection phase of the investigation. Safety considerations and avoidance of contamination also call for the wearing of face masks, a lab coat, eye protection, shoe covers, and possibly coveralls.

substrate control
An unstained object adjacent to an area on which biological material has been deposited.

The deposition of DNA onto crime-scene objects via saliva, sweat, skin, blood, and semen has created a vast array of forensic evidence that is quite different from the traditional evidence collected at crime scenes prior to the DNA era (see Table 15.2).

TABLE 15.2 Location and Sources of DNA at Crime Scenes

EVIDENCE	POSSIBLE LOCATION OF DNA ON THE EVIDENCE	SOURCE OF DNA
Baseball bat or similar weapon	Handle, end	Sweat, skin, blood, tissue
Hat, bandanna, or mask	Inside	Sweat, hair, dandruff
Eyeglasses	Nose or ear pieces, lens	Sweat, skin
Facial tissue, cotton swab	Surface area	Mucus, blood, sweat, semen, ear wax
Dirty laundry	Surface area	Blood, sweat, semen
Toothpick	Tips	Saliva
Used cigarette	Cigarette butt	Saliva
Stamp or envelope	Licked area	Saliva
Tape or ligature	Inside/outside surface	Skin, sweat
Bottle, can, or glass	Sides, mouthpiece	Saliva, sweat
Used condom	Inside/outside surface	Semen, vaginal and/or rectal cells
Blanket, pillow, sheet	Surface area	Sweat, hair, semen, urine, saliva
"Through and through" bullet	Outside surface	Blood, tissue
Bite mark	Person's skin or clothing	Saliva
Fingernail, partial fingernail	Scrapings	Blood, sweat, tissue

Source: National Institute of Justice, U.S. Department of Justice.

■■■■ CASEFILES ■■■■

In 1990, a series of attacks on elderly victims was committed in Goldsboro, North Carolina, by an unknown individual dubbed the Night Stalker. During one such attack in March, an elderly woman was brutally sexually assaulted and almost murdered. Her daughter's early arrival home saved the woman's life. The suspect fled, leaving behind materials intended to burn the residence and the victim in an attempt to conceal the crime.

In July 1990, another elderly woman was sexually assaulted and murdered in her home. Three months later, a third elderly woman was sexually assaulted and stabbed to death. Her husband was also murdered. Although their house was set alight in an attempt to cover up the crime, fire and rescue personnel pulled the bodies from the house before it was engulfed in flames. DNA analysis of biological evidence collected from vaginal swabs from the three sexual assault victims enabled authorities to conclude that the same perpetrator had committed all three crimes. However, there was no suspect.

More than ten years after these crimes were committed, law enforcement authorities retested the biological evidence from all three cases using newer DNA technology and entered the DNA profiles into North Carolina's DNA database. The DNA profile developed from the crime-scene evidence was compared to thousands of convicted-offender profiles already in the database.

In April 2001, a "cold hit" was made: The DNA profile was matched to that of an individual in the convicted-offender DNA database. The perpetrator had been convicted of shooting into an occupied dwelling, an offense that requires inclusion of the convict's DNA in the North Carolina DNA database. The suspect was brought into custody for questioning and was served with a search warrant to obtain a sample of his blood. That sample was analyzed and compared to the crime-scene evidence, confirming the DNA database match. When confronted with the DNA evidence, the suspect confessed to all three crimes.

Source: National Institute of Justice, "Using DNA to Solve Cold Cases" (NIJ Special Report), July 2002, www.ncjrs.gov/pdffiles1/nij/194197.pdf.

PACKAGING OF BIOLOGICAL EVIDENCE

Biological evidence should not be packaged in plastic or airtight containers because accumulation of residual moisture could contribute to the growth of DNA-destroying bacteria and fungi. **Each stained article should be packaged separately in a paper bag or a well-ventilated box.** A red-biohazard label must be attached to each container. If feasible, the entire stained article should be packaged and submitted for examination. If this is not possible, dried blood is best removed from a surface with a sterile cotton-tipped swab lightly moistened with distilled water from a dropper bottle. A portion of the unstained surface material near the recovered stain must likewise be removed or swabbed and placed in a separate package. This is known as a **substrate control**. The forensic examiner may use the substrate swab to confirm that the results of the tests performed were brought about by the stain and not by the material on which it was deposited. However, this practice is normally not necessary when DNA determinations are carried out in the laboratory. One point is critical, and that is that the collected swabs must not be packaged in a wet state. After the collection is made, the swab must be air-dried for approximately 5 to 10 minutes. Then it is best to place it in a swab box (see Figure 15-24), which has a circular hole to allow air circulation. The swab box can then be placed in a paper or manila envelope.

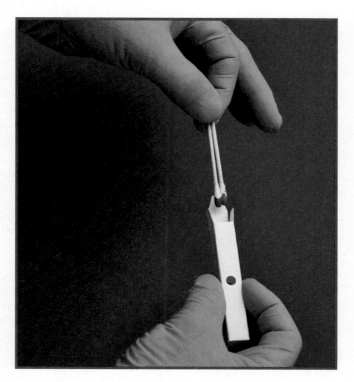

FIGURE 15-24 Air-dried swabs are placed in a swab box for delivery to the forensic laboratory. *Tri-Tech Inc.*

All packages containing biological evidence should be refrigerated or stored in a cool location out of direct sunlight until delivery to the laboratory. However, one common exception is blood mixed with soil. Microbes present in soil rapidly degrade DNA. Therefore, blood in soil must be stored in a clean glass or plastic container and immediately frozen.

OBTAINING DNA REFERENCE SPECIMENS

buccal swab
Cells from the inner cheek lining.

Biological evidence attains its full forensic value only when an analyst can compare each of its DNA types to known DNA samples collected from victims and suspects. The least intrusive method for obtaining a DNA standard/reference, one that nonmedical personnel can readily use, is the **buccal swab**. Cotton swabs are placed in the subject's mouth and the inside of the cheek is vigorously swabbed, resulting in the transfer of buccal cells onto the swab (see Figure 15-25).

If an individual is not available to give a DNA standard/reference sample, some interesting alternatives are available to evidence collectors, including a toothbrush, combs and hairbrushes, a razor, soiled laundry, used cigarette butts, and earplugs. Any of these items may contain a sufficient quantity of DNA for typing purposes. Interestingly, as investigators worked to identify the remains of victims of the World Trade Center attack on September 11, 2001, the families of the missing were requested to supply the New York City DNA Laboratory with these types of items in an effort to match recovered DNA with human remains.

CONTAMINATION OF DNA EVIDENCE

One key concern during the collection of a DNA-containing specimen is contamination. Contamination can occur by introducing foreign DNA through coughing or sneezing onto a stain during the collection process, or there can be a transfer of DNA when items of evidence are incorrectly placed in contact with each other during packaging. Fortunately, an examination of DNA band patterns in the laboratory readily reveals the presence of contamination. For example, with an STR, one will expect to see a two-band pattern. More than two bands suggest a mixture of DNA from more than one source.

Crime-scene investigators can take some relatively simple steps to minimize contamination of biological evidence:

1. Use disposable gloves.
2. Wear a face mask while collecting evidence, a lab coat, eye protection, as well as shoe covers.
3. Change gloves before handling each new piece of evidence.
4. Collect a substrate control for possible subsequent laboratory examination.
5. Pick up small items of evidence such as cigarette butts and stamps with clean forceps. Disposable forceps are to be used so that they can be discarded after a single evidence collection.
6. Always package each item of evidence in its own well-ventilated container.

A common occurrence at crime scenes is to suspect the presence of blood but not be able to observe any with the naked eye. In these situations, the common test of choice is luminol or Bluestar (see page 374). Interestingly, neither luminol nor Bluestar is expected to inhibit the ability to detect and characterize STRs.[2] Therefore, luminol and Bluestar can be used to locate traces of blood and areas that have been washed nearly free of blood without compromising the potential for DNA typing.

WebExtra 15.15

Step into the Role of the First Responding Officer at a Sexual Assault Scene

WebExtra 15.16

Assume the Duties of an Evidence-Collection Technician at a Sexual Assault Scene

VIRTUAL LAB
BLOODSTAIN ANALYSIS
To perform a virtual bloodstain analysis, go to *www.pearsoncustom.com/us/vlm/*

VIRTUAL LAB
DNA ANALYSIS
To perform a virtual DNA analysis, go to *www.pearsoncustom.com/us/vlm/*

FIGURE 15-25   A buccal swab collection kit is designed for use by nonmedical personnel. The cotton-tipped swabs are placed in the subject's mouth and the inside of the cheek is vigorously swabbed, resulting in the transfer of buccal cells onto the cotton bulb of the swab. The kit is then delivered to the forensic laboratory. *Tri-Tech Inc.*

Quick Review

- Packaging of bloodstained evidence in plastic or airtight containers must be avoided because the accumulation of residual moisture could contribute to the growth of DNA-destroying bacteria and fungi. Each stained article should be packaged separately in a paper bag or in a well-ventilated box.

■■■■ CASEFILES ■■■■

A woman alleged that she had been held in an apartment against her will and sexually assaulted by a male friend. During the course of the assault, a contact lens was knocked from the victim's eye. After the assault, she escaped, but out of fear from threats made by her attacker, she did not report the assault to the police for three days. When the police examined the apartment, they noted that it had been thoroughly cleaned. A vacuum cleaner bag was seized for examination, and several pieces of material resembling fragments of a contact lens were discovered within the bag.

In the laboratory, approximately 20 nanograms of human DNA were recovered from the contact lens fragments. Because cells from both a person's eyeballs and the interior of the eyelids are naturally replaced every 6 to 24 hours, both were potential sources for the DNA found. The DNA profile originating from the fragments matched the victim, thus corroborating the victim's account of the crime. The estimated frequency of occurrence in the population for the nine matching STRs is approximately 1 in 850 million. The suspect subsequently pleaded guilty to the offense.*

STR Locus	Victim's DNA Type	Contact Lens
D3S1358	15,18	15,18
FGA	24,25	24,25
vWA	17,17	17,17
THO1	6,7	6,7
F13A1	5,6	5,6
fes/fps	11,12	11,12
D5S818	11,12	11,12
D13S317	11,12	11,12
D7S820	10,12	10,12

*Based on information contained in R. A. Wickenheiser and R. M. Jobin, "Comparison of DNA Recovered from a Contact Lens Using PCR DNA Typing." *Canadian Society of Forensic Science Journal* 32 (1999): 67.

• The least intrusive method for obtaining a DNA standard/reference is the buccal swab. In this procedure, cotton swabs are inserted into the subject's mouth, and the inside of the cheek is vigorously swabbed, resulting in the transfer of cells from the inner cheek lining onto the swab. ■■■■

■■■■ CHAPTER REVIEW

• An antibody reacts or agglutinates only with its specific antigen. The concept of specific antigen–antibody reactions has been applied to techniques for the detection of commonly abused drugs in blood and urine.

• Every red blood cell contains either an A antigen, a B antigen, both antigens, or no antigen (this is called type O). The type of antigen on one's red blood cells determines one's A-B-O blood type. Persons with type A blood have A antigens on their red blood cells, those with type B blood have B antigens, those with type AB blood have both antigens, and those with type O blood have no antigens on their red blood cells.

• To produce antibodies capable of reacting with drugs, a specific drug is combined with a protein, and this combination is injected into an animal such as a rabbit. This drug–protein complex acts as an antigen, stimulating the animal to produce antibodies. The recovered blood serum of the animal will now contain antibodies that are specific or nearly specific to the drug.

• The criminalist must be prepared to answer the following questions when examining dried blood: (1) Is it blood? (2) From what species did the blood originate? (3) If the blood is of human origin, how closely can it be associated to a particular individual?

• The determination that a substance is blood is best made by means of a preliminary color test. A positive result from the Kastle-Meyer color test is highly indicative of blood.

• The luminol and Bluestar tests are used to search out trace amounts of blood located at crime scenes.

• The precipitin test uses antisera, normally derived from rabbits that have been injected with the blood of a known animal, to determine the species origin of a questioned bloodstain.

• The best way to locate and characterize a seminal stain is to perform the acid phosphatase color test.

• The presence of spermatozoa is a unique identifier of semen. Also, the protein called "prostate-specific antigen (PSA)," also known as "p30," is useful in combination with the acid phosphatase color test for characterizing a sample stain as semen.

- Forensic scientists can link seminal material to an individual by DNA typing.

- A sexual assault victim should undergo a medical examination as soon as possible after the assault. At that time clothing, hairs, and vaginal and rectal swabs can be collected for subsequent laboratory examination.

- The persistence of seminal constituents in the vagina may help determine the time of an alleged sexual attack.

- The gene is the basic unit of heredity. A chromosome is a threadlike structure in the cell nucleus along which the genes are located.

- Most human cells contain forty-six chromosomes, arranged in twenty-three mated pairs. The only exceptions are the human reproductive cells, the egg and sperm, which contain twenty-three unmated chromosomes each.

- During fertilization, a sperm and an egg combine so that each contributes twenty-three chromosomes to form the new cell, or "zygote," that develops into the offspring.

- An allele is any of several alternative forms of genes that influence a given characteristic and that are aligned with one another on a chromosome pair.

- A heterozygous gene pair is made up of two different alleles; a homozygous gene pair is made up of two similar alleles.

- When two different genes are inherited, the characteristic in the dominant gene's code will be expressed. The characteristic in the recessive gene's code will remain hidden.

- The gene is the fundamental unit of heredity. Each gene is composed of DNA specifically designed to control the genetic traits of our cells.

- DNA is constructed as a very large molecule made of a linked series of repeating units called "nucleotides."

- Four types of bases are associated with the DNA structure: adenine (A), guanine (G), cytosine (C), and thymine (T).

- The bases on each strand of DNA are aligned in a double-helix configuration so that adenine pairs with thymine and guanine pairs with cytosine. This concept is known as "complementary base pairing."

- The order in which the base pairs are arranged defines the role and function of a DNA molecule.

- DNA replication begins with the unwinding of the DNA strands in the double helix. The double helix is re-created as the nucleotides are assembled in the proper order (A with T and G with C). Two identical copies of DNA emerge from the process.

- PCR (polymerase chain reaction) is a technique for replicating or copying a portion of a DNA strand outside a living cell.

- Short tandem repeats (STRs) are locations on the chromosome that contain short sequences that repeat themselves within the DNA molecule. They serve as useful markers for identification because they are found in great abundance throughout the human genome.

- The entire strand of an STR is very short: less than 450 bases long. This makes STRs much less susceptible to degradation, and they are often recovered from bodies or stains that have been subjected to extreme decomposition.

- The more STRs one can characterize, the smaller the percentage of the population from which a particular combination of STRs can emanate. This gives rise to the concept of multiplexing, in which the forensic scientist can simultaneously extract and amplify a combination of STRs.

- With STRs, as few as eighteen DNA-containing cells are required for analysis.

- Mitochondrial DNA is located outside the cell's nucleus and is inherited from the mother.

- Mitochondria are cell structures found in all human cells. They provide most of the energy that the body needs to function.

- Mitochondrial DNA typing does not approach STR analysis in its discrimination power and thus is best reserved for analyzing samples, such as hair, for which STR analysis is not possible.

- CODIS is a computer software program developed by the FBI that maintains local, state, and national databases of DNA profiles from convicted offenders, unsolved crime-scene evidence, and profiles of missing people.

- Packaging of bloodstained evidence in plastic or airtight containers must be avoided because the accumulation of residual moisture could contribute to the growth of DNA-destroying bacteria and fungi. Each stained article should be packaged separately in a paper bag or in a well-ventilated box.

- The least intrusive method for obtaining a DNA standard/reference is the buccal swab. In this procedure, cotton swabs are inserted into the subject's mouth and the inside of the cheek is vigorously swabbed, resulting in the transfer of cells from the inner cheek lining onto the swab.

KEY TERMS

acid phosphatase, 378
agglutination, 371
allele, 385

antibody, 371
antigen, 371
antiserum, 371

aspermia, 379
buccal swab, 402
chromosome, 385

deoxyribonucleic acid (DNA), 370

egg, 385

epithelial cells, 399

gene, 385

heterozygous, 386

homozygous, 386

locus, 385

low copy number, 399

mitochondria, 397

multiplexing, 392

nucleotide, 387

oligospermia, 379

picogram, 399

plasma, 370

polymerase chain reaction (PCR), 389

serum, 371

short tandem repeat (STR), 390

sperm, 385

substrate control, 401

touch DNA, 399

X chromosome, 385

Y chromosome, 385

Y-STRs, 393

zygote, 385

■■■■■ REVIEW QUESTIONS

1. Karl Landsteiner discovered that blood can be classified by its _____.

2. True or False: No two individuals, except for identical twins, can be expected to have the same combination of blood types, or antigens. _____

3. _____ is the fluid portion of unclotted blood.

4. The liquid that separates from the blood when a clot is formed is called the _____.

5. _____ transport oxygen from the lungs to the body tissues and carry carbon dioxide back to the lungs.

6. On the surface of red blood cells are chemical substances called _____ that impart blood type characteristics to the cells.

7. Type A individuals have _____ antigens on the surface of their red blood cells.

8. True or False: Type O individuals have both A and B antigens on their red blood cells. _____

9. The presence or absence of the _____ and _____ antigens on the red blood cells determines a person's blood type in the A-B-O system.

10. The D antigen is also known as the _____ antigen.

11. Serum contains proteins known as _____, which destroy or inactivate antigens.

12. True or False: An antibody reacts with any antigen. _____

13. The term _____ describes the clumping together of red blood cells by the action of an antibody.

14. Type B blood contains _____ antigens and anti-_____ antibodies.

15. True or False: Type AB blood has neither anti-A nor anti-B. _____

16. Type B red blood cells agglutinate when added to type _____ blood.

17. Type A red blood cells agglutinate when added to type _____ blood.

18. A drug–protein complex can be injected into an animal to form specific _____ for that drug.

19. For many years, the most commonly used color test for identifying blood was the _____ color test.

20. The reagent in the _____ test turns pink if oxidation takes place. It is not a specific test for blood, however, because some vegetable materials may turn the reagent pink.

21. _____ reagent reacts with blood, causing it to luminesce.

22. Blood can be characterized as being of human origin by the _____ test.

23. The antigens of a human blood sample will move toward the well containing human antiserum in a process called _____.

24. The concentration of the enzyme _____ secreted by the prostate is up to 400 times higher in seminal fluid than other bodily fluids.

25. Semen is unequivocally identified by the microscopic appearance of _____.

26. True or False: Males with a low sperm count have a condition known as "oligospermia." _____

27. The protein _____ is useful for the identification of semen.

28. True or False: The collection of sexual assault evidence should include swabs, combings, and fingernail scrapings from the victim and the suspect. _____

29. True or False: Seminal constituents may remain in the vagina for up to six days after intercourse. _____

30. The basic unit of heredity is the _____.

31. Genes are positioned on threadlike bodies called _____.

32. All cells in the human body, except the reproductive cells, have _____ pairs of chromosomes.

33. Genes that influence a given characteristic and are aligned with one another on a chromosome pair are known as _____.

34. When a pair of allelic genes is identical, the genes are said to be _____.

35. A(n) _____ is composed of a sugar molecule, a phosphorus-containing group, and a nitrogen-containing molecule called a base.

36. _____ different bases are associated with the makeup of DNA.

37. Watson and Crick demonstrated that DNA is composed of two strands coiled into the shape of a(n) _____.

38. The base sequence T–G–C–A can be paired with the base sequence _____ in a double-helix configuration.

39. True or False: Enzymes known as DNA polymerases assemble new DNA strands into a proper base sequence during replication. _____

40. DNA evidence can be copied using DNA polymerases in a technique known as _____.

41. Used as markers for identification purposes, _____ are locations on the chromosome that contain short sequences that repeat themselves within the DNA molecule and in great abundance throughout the human genome.

42. True or False: The longer the DNA strand, the less susceptible it is to degradation. _____

43. The short length of STRs allows them to be replicated by _____.

44. The concept of _____ involves the simultaneous detection of more than one DNA marker.

45. STR fragments are preferably separated and identified by _____.

46. True or False: Y-STR typing is useful when one is confronted with a DNA mixture containing more than one male contributor. _____

47. Mitochondrial DNA is inherited only from the _____.

48. True or False: Mitochondrial DNA is less plentiful in the human cell than is nuclear DNA. _____

49. (CODIS, AFIS) maintains local, state, and national databases of DNA profiles from convicted offenders, unsolved crime-scene evidence, and profiles of missing people.

50. Amazingly, the sensitivity of STR profiling requires only _____ DNA-bearing cells to obtain an STR profile.

51. During evidence collection, all body fluids must be assumed to be _____ and handled with latex-gloved hands.

52. True or False: Airtight packages make the best containers for blood-containing evidence. _____

53. True or False: Small amounts of blood are best submitted to a crime laboratory in a wet condition. _____

54. The least intrusive method for obtaining a DNA standard/reference is the _____.

■■■■ APPLICATION AND CRITICAL THINKING

1. Police investigating the scene of a sexual assault recover a large blanket that they believe may contain useful physical evidence. They take it to the laboratory of forensic serologist Scott Alden, asking him to test it for the presence of semen. Noticing faint pink stains on the blanket, Scott asks the investigating detective if he is aware of anything that might recently have been spilled on the blanket. The detective reports that an overturned bowl of grapes and watermelon was found at the scene, as well as a broken glass that had contained wine. After the detective departs, Scott chooses and administers what he considers the best test for analyzing the piece of evidence in his possession. Three minutes after completion of the test, the blanket shows a positive reaction. What test did Scott choose, and what was his conclusion? Explain your answer.

2. Criminalist Cathy Richards is collecting evidence from the victim of a sexual assault. She places a sheet on the floor, asks the victim to disrobe, and places the clothing in a paper bag. After collecting pubic combings and pubic hair samples, she takes two vaginal swabs, which she allows to air-dry before packaging. Finally, Cathy collects blood, urine, and scalp hair samples from the victim. What mistakes, if any, did she make in collecting this evidence?

3. The following sequence of bases is located on one strand of a DNA molecule:

   C–G–A–A–T–C–G–C–A–A–T–C–G–A–C–C–T–G

   List the sequence of bases that will form complementary pairs on the other strand of the DNA molecule.

4. Police discover a badly decomposed body buried in an area where a man disappeared some years before. The case was never solved, nor was the victim's body ever recovered. As the lead investigator, you suspect that the newly discovered body is that of the man who disappeared. What is your main challenge in using DNA typing to determine whether your suspicion is correct? How would you go about using DNA technology to test your theory?

5. You are a forensic scientist performing DNA typing on a blood sample sent to your laboratory. While performing an STR analysis on the sample, you notice a four-band pattern. What conclusion should you draw? Why?

6. A woman reports being mugged by a masked assailant, whom she scratched on the arm during a brief struggle. The victim is not sure whether the attacker was male or female. DNA analysts extract and amplify the amelogenin gene from the epithelial cells under the victim's fingernails (allegedly belonging to the attacker) and from a buccal swab of the victim. The sample is separated by gel electrophoresis with the result shown here. The victim's amelogenin DNA is in lane 2, and the amelogenin DNA from the fingernail scraping is in lane 4. What conclusion can you draw about the attacker from this result? How did you reach this conclusion?

7. At a crime scene you encounter each of the following items. For each item, indicate the potential sources of DNA. The five possible choices are saliva, skin cells, sweat, blood, and semen.

Tarasyuk Igor/Shutterstock

g. _____

Africa Studio/Shutterstock

h. _____

donatas1205/Shutterstock

a. _____

Elena Elisseeva/Shutterstock

b. _____

Somchaiij/Shutterstock

c. _____

R-O-M-A/Shutterstock

d. _____

Birgit Reitz-Hofmann/Shutterstock

e. _____

Lim Yong Hian/Shutterstock

f. _____

8. The 15-STR locus DNA profile of a missing person, James Dittman, is shown in the following table.

STR Loci	Allele
D3S1358	15
THO1	6, 9.3
D21S11	27
D18S51	15, 16
PENTA E	10
D5S818	11
D13S807	10, 13
D7S820	9, 10
D16S539	11, 12
CSF1PO	13
PENTA D	12, 13
AMELOGENIN	XY
VWA	17, 19
D8S1170	10, 13
TPOX	8, 12
FGA	21

Decomposing remains were found deep in the woods near Dittman's house. DNA from these remains was extracted, amplified, and analyzed at 15 STR loci. Compare the resulting STR readout for Dittman (on the previous page) with the chart below to determine whether the remains could belong to James Dittman. If not, at which STR loci do the profiles differ?

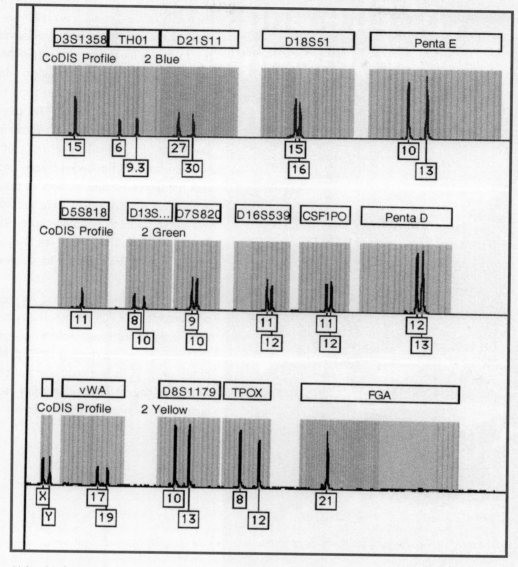

Richard Saferstein, Ph.D.

ENDNOTES

1. The luminol reagent is prepared by mixing 0.1 grams of 3-amino-phthalthydrazide and 5.0 grams sodium carbonate in 100 milliliters of distilled water. Before use, 0.7 grams of sodium perborate is added to the solution.

2. S. H. Tobe et al., "Evaluation of Six Presumptive Tests for Blood: Their Specificity, Sensitivity, and Effect on High Molecular-Weight DNA," *Journal of Forensic Sciences* 52 (2007): 102.

3. In one study, a maximum of only 4 sperm cells out of 1,000 could be extracted from a cotton patch and observed under the microscope. Edwin Jones (Ventura County Sheriff's Department, Ventura, CA), personal communication.

4. R. Dziak, et al., "Providing Evidence-Based Opinions on Time Since Intercourse (TSI) Based on Body Fluid Testing Results of Internal Samples," *Canadian Society of Forensic Science Journal* 44 (2011): 59.

5. S. Cavness et al. "Hospital Wet Mount Examination for the Presence of Sperm in Sexual Assault Case is of Questionable Value," *Journal of Forensic Sciences* 59 (2014):729.

6. R. A. Wickenheiser, "Trace DNA: A Review, Discussion of Theory, and Application of the Transfer of Trace Qualities through Skin Contact," *Journal of Forensic Sciences* 47 (2002): 442.

16

Forensic Aspects of Fire and Explosion Investigation

© Everett Collection Inc/Alamy

THE OKLAHOMA CITY BOMBING

It was the biggest act of mass murder in U.S. history. On a sunny spring morning in April 1995, a Ryder rental truck pulled into the parking area of the Alfred P. Murrah federal building in Oklahoma City. The driver stepped down from the truck's cab and casually walked away. Minutes later, the truck exploded into a fireball, unleashing enough energy to destroy the building and kill 138 people, including 19 children and infants in the building's day care center.

Later that morning, an Oklahoma Highway Patrol officer pulled over a beat-up 1977 Mercury Marquis being driven without a license plate. On further investigation of the car, the officer found the driver, Timothy McVeigh, to be in possession of a loaded firearm and charged him with transporting a firearm. Back at the explosion site, remnants of the Ryder truck were located and the truck was quickly traced to its renter—Robert Kling, an alias of Timothy McVeigh. On both the rental agreement and his driver's license, McVeigh used the address of his friend Terry Nichols.

Investigators later recovered McVeigh's fingerprint on a receipt for 2,000 pounds of ammonium nitrate, a basic explosive ingredient. Forensic analysts also located PETN residues on the clothing McVeigh wore on the day of his arrest. PETN is a component of detonating cord. After three days of deliberation, a jury declared McVeigh guilty of the bombing and sentenced him to die by lethal injection.

LEARNING OBJECTIVES

After studying this chapter, you should be able to:

- List the conditions necessary to initiate and sustain combustion.
- Recognize the telltale signs of an accelerant-initiated fire.
- Describe how to collect physical evidence at the scene of a suspected arson.
- Describe laboratory procedures used to detect and identify hydrocarbon residues.
- Understand the chemistry of explosives.
- Understand how explosives are classified.
- List some common commercial, homemade, and military explosives.
- Describe how to collect physical evidence at the scene of an explosion.
- Describe laboratory procedures used to detect and identify explosive residues.

Forensic Investigation of Arson

Arson often presents complex and difficult circumstances to investigate. Normally these incidents are committed at the convenience of a perpetrator who has thoroughly planned the criminal act and has left the crime scene long before any official investigation is launched. Furthermore, proving commission of the offense is more difficult because of the extensive destruction that frequently dominates the crime scene. The contribution of the criminalist is only one aspect of a comprehensive and difficult investigative process that must establish a motive, the **modus operandi**, and a suspect.

The criminalist's function is limited; usually he or she is expected only to detect and identify relevant chemical materials collected at the scene and to reconstruct and identify igniters. Although a chemist can identify trace amounts of gasoline or kerosene in debris, no scientific test can determine whether an arsonist used a pile of rubbish or paper to start a fire. Furthermore, a fire can have many accidental causes—including faulty wiring, overheated electric motors, improperly cleaned and regulated heating systems, and cigarette smoking—which usually leave no chemical traces. Thus, the final determination of the cause of a fire must take into consideration numerous factors and requires an extensive on-site investigation. The ultimate determination must be made by an investigator whose training and knowledge have been augmented by the practical experiences of fire investigation.

modus operandi
An offender's pattern of operation.

Chemistry of Fire

Humankind's early search to explain the physical concepts underlying the behavior of matter always bestowed a central and fundamental role on fire. To ancient Greek philosophers, fire was one of the four basic elements from which all matter was derived. The medieval alchemist thought of fire as an instrument of transformation, capable of changing one element into another. One ancient recipe expresses its mystical power as follows: "Now the substance of cinnabar is such that the more it is heated, the more exquisite are its sublimations. Cinnabar will become mercury, and passing through a series of other sublimations, it is again turned into cinnabar, and thus it enables man to enjoy eternal life."

Today, we know of fire not as an element of matter but as a transformation process during which oxygen is united with some other substance to produce noticeable quantities of heat and light (i.e., a flame). Therefore, any insight into why and how a fire is initiated and sustained must begin with the knowledge of the fundamental chemical reaction of fire: **oxidation**.

OXIDATION

In a simple description of oxidation, oxygen combines with other substances to produce new products. Thus, we may write the chemical equation for the burning of methane gas, a major component of natural gas, as follows:

$$CH_4 + 2O_2 \longrightarrow CO_2 + 2H_2O$$
methane   oxygen yields carbon dioxide   water

However, not all oxidation proceeds in the manner that one associates with fire. For example, oxygen combines with many metals to form oxides. Thus, iron forms a red-brown iron oxide, or rust, as follows (see Figure 16-1):

$$4Fe + 3O_2 \longrightarrow 2Fe_2O_3$$
iron   oxygen yields iron oxide

oxidation
The combination of oxygen with other substances to produce new substances.

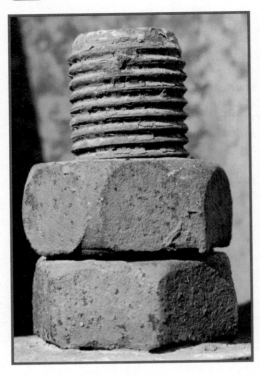

FIGURE 16-1 Rust forming on iron is an example of oxidation. *Wallenrock/Shutterstock*

energy
The ability or potential of a system or material to do work.

Yet chemical equations do not give us a complete insight into the oxidation process. We must consider other factors to understand all of the implications of oxidation or, for that matter, any other chemical reaction. Methane burns when it unites with oxygen, but merely mixing methane and oxygen does not produce a fire. Nor, for example, does gasoline burn when it is simply exposed to air. However, lighting a match in the presence of any one of these fuel–air mixtures (assuming proper proportions) produces an instant fire.

What are the reasons behind these differences? Why do some oxidations proceed with the outward appearances that we associate with a fire but others do not? Why do we need a match to initiate some oxidations but others proceed at room temperature? The explanation lies in a fundamental but abstract concept—energy.

ENERGY

Energy can be defined as the ability or potential of a system or material to do work. Energy takes many forms, such as heat energy, electrical energy, mechanical energy, nuclear energy, light energy, and chemical energy. For example, when methane is burned, the stored chemical energy in methane is converted to energy in the form of heat and light. This heat may be used to boil water or to provide high-pressure steam to turn a turbine. This is an example of converting chemical energy to heat energy to mechanical energy. The turbine can then be used to generate electricity, transforming mechanical energy to electrical energy. Electrical energy may then be used to turn a motor. In other words, energy can enable work to be done; heat is energy.

The quantity of heat from a chemical reaction comes from the breaking and formation of chemical bonds. Methane is a molecule composed of one carbon atom bonded with four hydrogen atoms:

$$\begin{array}{c} H \\ | \\ H - C - H \\ | \\ H \end{array}$$

An oxygen molecule forms when two atoms of the element oxygen bond:

$$O = O$$

In chemical changes, atoms are not lost but merely redistributed during the chemical reaction; thus, the products of methane's oxidation will be carbon dioxide:

$$O = C = O$$

and water:

$$H - O - H$$

This rearrangement, however, means that the chemical bonds holding the atoms together must be broken and new bonds formed. We now have arrived at a fundamental observation in our dissection of a chemical reaction—that molecules must absorb energy to break apart their chemical bonds, and that they liberate energy when their bonds are reformed.

The amount of energy needed to break a bond and the amount of energy liberated when a bond is formed are characteristic of the type of chemical bond involved. Hence, a chemical reaction involves a change in energy content; energy is going in and energy is given off. The quantities of energies involved are different for each reaction and are determined by the participants in the chemical reaction.

COMBUSTION

All oxidation reactions, including the **combustion** of methane, are examples of reactions in which more energy is liberated than is required to break the chemical bonds between atoms. The excess energy is liberated as heat, and often as light, and is known as the **heat of combustion**. Table 16.1 summarizes the heat of combustion of some important fuels in fire investigation.

Thus, all reactions require an energy input to start them. We can think of this requirement as an invisible energy barrier between the reactants and the products of a reaction (see Figure 16-2). The greater this barrier, the more energy required to initiate the reaction. Where does this initial energy come from? There are many sources of energy; however, for the purpose of this discussion, we need to look at only one: heat.

HEAT   The energy barrier in the conversion of iron to rust is relatively small, and it can be surmounted with the help of heat energy in the surrounding environment at normal outdoor temperatures. Not so for methane or gasoline; these energy barriers are quite high, and a high temperature must be applied to start the oxidation of these fuels. Hence, before any fire can result, the temperature of these fuels must be raised enough to exceed the energy barrier. Table 16.2 shows that this temperature, known as the **ignition temperature**, is quite high for common fuels.

Once combustion starts, enough heat is liberated to keep the reaction going by itself. In essence, the fire becomes a chain reaction, absorbing a portion of its own liberated heat to generate even more heat. The fire burns until either the oxygen or the fuel is exhausted.

Normally, a lighted match provides a convenient igniter of fuels. However, the fire investigator must also consider other potential sources of ignition—for example, electrical discharges, sparks, and chemicals—while reconstructing

combustion
The rapid combination of oxygen with another substance, accompanied by the production of noticeable heat and light.

heat of combustion
The heat liberated during combustion.

ignition temperature
The minimum temperature at which a fuel spontaneously ignites.

TABLE 16.1 Heat of Combustion of Fuels

FUEL	HEAT OF COMBUSTION*
Crude oil	19,650 Btu/gal
Diesel fuel	19,550 Btu/lb
Gasoline	19,250 Btu/lb
Methane	995 Btu/cu ft
Natural gas	128–1,868 Btu/cu ft
Octane	121,300 Btu/gal
Wood	7,500 Btu/lb
Coal, bituminous	11,000–14,000 Btu/lb
Anthracite	13,351 Btu/lb

*Btu (British thermal unit) is defined as the quantity of heat required to raise by 1°F the temperature of 1 pound of water that is at or near its point of maximum density.

$CH_4 + 2O_2$ $CO_2 + 2H_2O$

FIGURE 16-2 An energy barrier must be hurdled before reactants such as methane and oxygen can combine with one another to form the products of carbon dioxide and water. *SAFERSTEIN, RICHARD, Ph.D., CRIMINALISTICS: AN INTRODUCTION TO FORENSIC SCIENCE, 11th Ed., © 2015. Reprinted and Electronically reproduced by permission of Pearson Education, Inc., Upper Saddle River, New Jersey.*

flash point

The minimum temperature at which a liquid fuel produces enough vapor to burn.

the initiation of a fire. All of these sources have temperatures higher than the ignition temperature of most fuels.

SPEED OF REACTION   Although the liberation of energy explains many important features of oxidation, it does not explain all characteristics of the reaction. Obviously, although all oxidations liberate energy, not all are accompanied by a flame; witness the oxidation of iron to rust. Therefore, one other important consideration will make our understanding of oxidation and fire complete: the rate or speed at which the reaction takes place.

A chemical reaction, such as oxidation, takes place when molecules combine or collide with one another. The faster the molecules move, the greater the number of collisions between them and the faster the rate of reaction. Many factors influence the rate of these collisions. In our description of fire and oxidation, we consider only two: the physical state of the fuel and the temperature.

PHYSICAL STATE OF FUEL   A fuel achieves a reaction rate with oxygen sufficient to produce a flame only when it is in the gaseous state, for only in this state can molecules collide frequently enough to support a flaming fire. This remains true whether the fuel is a solid such as wood, paper, cloth, or plastic, or a liquid such as gasoline or kerosene.

For example, the conversion of iron to rust proceeds slowly because the iron atoms cannot achieve a gaseous state. The combination of oxygen with iron is thus restricted to the surface area of the metal exposed to air, a limitation that severely reduces the rate of reaction. On the other hand, the reaction of methane and oxygen proceeds rapidly because all the reactants are in the gaseous state. The speed of the reaction is reflected by the production of noticeable quantities of heat and light (i.e., flames).

FUEL TEMPERATURE   How then does a liquid or solid maintain a gaseous reaction? In the case of a liquid fuel, the temperature must be high enough to vaporize the fuel. The vapor that forms burns when it mixes with oxygen and combusts as a flame. The **flash point** is the *lowest* temperature at which a liquid gives off sufficient vapor to form a mixture with air that will support combustion. Once the flash point is reached, the fuel can be ignited by some outside source of temperature to start a fire. The ignition temperature of a fuel is always considerably higher than the flash point. For example, gasoline has

TABLE 16.2   Ignition Temperatures of Some Common Fuels

FUEL	IGNITION TEMPERATURE, °F
Acetone	869
Benzene	928
Fuel oil	495
Gasoline	495
Kerosene	410
n-Octane	428
Petroleum ether	550
Turpentine	488

FIGURE 16-3   Intense heat causes solid fuels such as wood to decompose into gaseous products, a process called "pyrolysis." *LiveMan/Shutterstock*

a flash point of –50°F; however, an ignition temperature of 495°F is needed to start a gasoline fire.

With a solid fuel such as wood, the process of generating vapor is more complex. A solid fuel burns only when exposed to heat intense enough to decompose the solid into gaseous products. This chemical breakdown of solid material is known as **pyrolysis**. The gaseous products of pyrolysis combine with oxygen to produce a fire (see Figure 16-3). Here again, fire can be described as a chain reaction. A match or other source of heat initiates the pyrolysis of the solid fuel, the gaseous products react with oxygen in the air to produce heat and light, and this heat in turn pyrolyzes more solid fuel into volatile gases.

Typically, the rate of a chemical reaction increases when the temperature is raised. The magnitude of the increase varies from one reaction to another and also from one temperature range to another. For most reactions, a 10°C (18°F) rise in temperature doubles or triples the reaction rate. This observation explains in part why burning is so rapid. As the fire spreads, it raises the temperature of the fuel–air mixture, thus increasing the rate of reaction; this in turn generates more heat, again increasing the rate of reaction. Only when the fuel or oxygen is depleted does this vicious cycle come to a halt.

FUEL–AIR MIX   As we have seen from our discussion about gaseous fuel, air (specifically, oxygen) and sufficient heat are the basic ingredients of a flaming fire. There is also one other consideration: the gas fuel–air mix. A mixture of gaseous fuel and air burns only if its composition lies within certain limits. If the fuel concentration is too low ("lean") or too great ("rich"), combustion does not occur. The concentration range between the upper and lower limits is called the **flammable range**. For example, the flammable range for gasoline is 1.3 to 6.0 percent. Thus, in order for a gasoline–air mix to burn, gasoline must make up at least 1.3 percent, but no more than 6 percent, of the mixture.

GLOWING COMBUSTION   Although a flaming fire can be supported only by a gaseous fuel, in some instances a fuel can burn without a flame. Witness a burning cigarette or the red glow of hot charcoals (see Figure 16-4). These

pyrolysis
The decomposition of solid organic matter by heat.

flammable range
The entire range of possible gas or vapor fuel concentrations in air that are capable of burning.

FIGURE 16-4   Red-hot charcoals are an example of glowing combustion. *Lev Kropotov/Shutterstock*

glowing combustion
Combustion on the surface of a solid fuel in the absence of heat high enough to pyrolyze the fuel.

are examples of **glowing combustion**, or "smoldering." Here combustion occurs on the surface of a solid fuel in the absence of heat high enough to pyrolyze the fuel. Interestingly, this phenomenon generally ensues long after the flames have gone out. Wood, for example, tends to burn with a flame until all of its pyrolyzable components have been expended; however, wood's carbonaceous residue continues to smolder long after the flame has extinguished itself.

SPONTANEOUS COMBUSTION   One interesting phenomenon often invoked by arson suspects to explain the cause of a fire is **spontaneous combustion**. Actually, the conditions under which spontaneous combustion can develop are rather limited and rarely account for the cause of a fire. Spontaneous combustion is the result of a natural heat-producing process in poorly ventilated containers or areas. For example, hay stored in barns provides an excellent growing medium for bacteria whose activities generate heat. If the hay is not properly ventilated, the heat builds to a level that supports other types of heat-producing chemical reactions in the hay. Eventually, as the heat rises, the ignition temperature of hay is reached, spontaneously setting off a fire.

spontaneous combustion
A fire caused by a natural heat-producing process in the presence of sufficient air and fuel.

Another example of spontaneous combustion involves the ignition of improperly ventilated containers containing rags soaked with certain types of highly unsaturated oils, such as linseed oil. Heat can build up to the point of ignition as a result of a slow, heat-producing chemical oxidation between the air and the oil. Of course, storage conditions must encourage the accumulation of the heat over a prolonged period of time. However, spontaneous combustion does not occur with hydrocarbon lubricating oils, and it is not expected to occur with most household fats and oils.

In summary, three requirements must be satisfied to initiate and sustain combustion:

1. A fuel must be present.
2. Oxygen must be available in sufficient quantity to combine with the fuel.
3. Heat must be applied to initiate the combustion, and sufficient heat must be generated to sustain the reaction.

Quick Review

- Oxidation is the combination of oxygen with other substances to produce new substances.
- Combustion is the rapid combination of oxygen with another substance, accompanied by the production of noticeable heat and light.
- Pyrolysis is the chemical breakdown of solid organic matter by heat. The gaseous products of pyrolysis combine with oxygen to produce a fire.
- Spontaneous combustion is fire caused by a natural heat-producing process in the presence of sufficient air and fuel.
- To initiate and sustain combustion, (1) a fuel must be present; (2) oxygen must be available in sufficient quantity to combine with the fuel; and (3) heat must be applied to initiate the combustion, and sufficient heat must be generated to sustain the reaction.

Searching the Fire Scene

The arson investigator should begin examining a fire scene for signs of arson as soon as the fire has been extinguished. Most arsons are started with petroleum-based **accelerants** such as gasoline or kerosene. Thus, the presence of containers capable of holding an accelerant arouses suspicions of arson. Discovery of an ignition device ranging in sophistication from a candle to a time-delay device is another indication of possible arson. A common telltale sign of arson may be an irregularly shaped pattern on a floor or on the ground (see Figure 16-5) resulting from accelerant having been poured onto the surface. In addition to these visual indicators, investigators should look for signs of breaking and entering and theft, and they should begin interviewing any eyewitnesses to the fire.

accelerant
Any material used to start or sustain a fire.

TIMELINESS OF INVESTIGATION

Time constantly works against the arson investigator. Any accelerant residues that remain after a fire is extinguished may evaporate within a few days or even hours. Furthermore, safety and health conditions may necessitate that cleanup and salvage operations begin as quickly as possible. Once this occurs, a meaningful investigation of the fire scene is impossible. Accelerants in soil and vegetation can be rapidly degraded by bacterial action. Freezing samples containing soil or vegetation is an effective way to prevent this degradation.

The need to begin an *immediate* investigation of the circumstances surrounding a fire takes precedence even over the requirement to obtain a search warrant to enter and search the premises. The Supreme Court, explaining its position on this issue, stated in part:

Fire officials are charged not only with extinguishing fires, but with finding their causes. Prompt determination of the fire's origin may be necessary to prevent its recurrence, as through the detection of continuing dangers such as faulty wiring or a defective furnace. Immediate investigation may also be necessary to preserve evidence from intentional or accidental destruction. And, of course, the sooner the officials complete their duties, the less will be their subsequent interference with the privacy and the recovery efforts of the victims. For these reasons, officials need no warrant to remain in a building for a reasonable time to investigate the cause of a blaze after it has been extinguished.

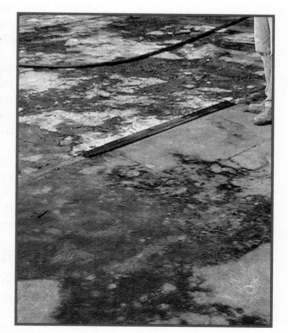

FIGURE 16-5 An irregularly shaped pattern on the ground resulting from a poured ignitable liquid.

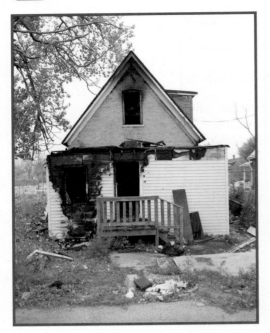

FIGURE 16-6 Typical V patterns illustrating the upward movement of the fire. *David Schalliol/Getty Images*

And if the warrantless entry to put out the fire and determine its cause is constitutional, the warrantless seizure of evidence while inspecting the premises for these purposes also is constitutional. . . .

In determining what constitutes a reasonable time to investigate, appropriate recognition must be given to the exigencies that confront officials serving under these conditions, as well as to individuals' reasonable expectations of privacy.[1]

LOCATING THE FIRE'S ORIGIN

A search of the fire scene must focus on finding the fire's origin, which will make any search for an accelerant or ignition device more productive. In searching for a fire's specific point of origin, the investigator may uncover telltale signs of arson such as evidence of separate and unconnected fires or the use of "streamers" to spread the fire from one area to another. For example, the arsonist may have spread a trail of gasoline or paper to cause the fire to move rapidly from one room to another.

There are no fast and simple rules for identifying a fire's origin. Normally a fire tends to move upward, and thus the origin is most likely to be located closest to the lowest point that shows the most intense characteristics of burning. Sometimes, as the fire burns upward, a V-shaped pattern forms against a vertical wall, as shown in Figure 16-6. Because flammable liquids always flow to the lowest point, more severe burning found on the floor than on the ceiling may indicate the presence of an accelerant. If a flammable liquid was used, charring is expected to be more intense on the bottom of furniture, shelves, and other items than on the top.

However, many factors can contribute to the deviation of a fire from normal behavior. Prevailing drafts and winds; secondary fires due to collapsed floors and roofs; the physical arrangement of the burning structure; the presence of stairways and elevator shafts; holes in the floor, wall, or roof; and the effects of the firefighter in suppressing the fire—these are all factors that the fire investigator must consider before determining conclusive findings. Using burn patterns, such as depth of char, a V-shaped pattern, or low intense burn area, as an indicators of a fire's origin can prove to be misleading; particularly, when a structural fire burns beyond flashover to full-room involvement. In these situations, air flow currents through the burning room can become a dominant factor in creating burn patterns.

Once located, the point of origin should be protected to permit careful investigation. As at any crime scene, nothing should be touched or moved before notes and photographs are taken and sketches are made. An examination must also be made for possible accidental causes, as well as for evidence of arson. The most common material used by an arsonist to ensure the rapid spread and intensity of a fire is gasoline or kerosene or, for that matter, any volatile flammable liquid.

SEARCHING FOR ACCELERANTS

Fortunately, only under the most ideal conditions will combustible liquids be entirely consumed during a fire. When the liquid is poured over a large area, a portion of it will often seep into a porous surface, such as upholstery, rags, plaster, wallboards, carpet, or cracks in the floor. Enough of the liquid may remain unchanged to permit its detection in the crime laboratory. In addition, when a fire is extinguished with water, the evaporation rate of volatile fluids may be slowed because water cools and covers materials through which the combustible liquid may have soaked. Fortunately, water does not interfere with laboratory methods used to detect and characterize flammable liquid residues.

FIGURE 16-7 A portable hydrocarbon detector. *Sirchie Finger Print Laboratories*

The search for traces of flammable liquid residues may be aided by the use of a sensitive portable vapor detector, or "sniffer" (see Figure 16-7). This device can rapidly screen suspect materials for volatile residues by sucking in the air surrounding the questioned sample. The air is passed over a heated filament; if a combustible vapor is present, it oxidizes and immediately increases the temperature of the filament. The rise in filament temperature is then registered on the detector's meter.

Of course, such a device is not a conclusive test for a flammable vapor, but it is an excellent screening device for checking suspect samples at the fire scene. Another approach is to use dogs that have been trained to recognize the odor of hydrocarbon accelerants.

Collection and Preservation of Arson Evidence

Two to three quarts of ash and soot debris must be collected at the point of origin of a fire when arson is suspected. The collection should include all porous materials and all other substances thought likely to contain flammable residues. These include such things as wood flooring, rugs, upholstery, and rags.

PACKAGING AND PRESERVATION OF EVIDENCE

Specimens should be packaged immediately in airtight containers so possible residues are not lost through evaporation. New, clean paint cans with friction lids are good containers because they are low cost, airtight, unbreakable, and available in a variety of sizes (see Figure 16-8). Wide-mouthed glass jars are also useful for packaging suspect specimens, provided that they have airtight lids. Cans and jars should be filled one-half to two-thirds full, leaving an air space in the container above the debris.

Large, bulky samples should be cut to size at the scene as needed so that they will fit into available containers. Plastic polyethylene bags are not suitable for packaging specimens because they react with hydrocarbons and permit volatile hydrocarbon vapors to be depleted. Fluids found in open bottles or cans must be collected and sealed. Even when such containers appear to be empty, the investigator is wise to seal and preserve them in case they contain trace amounts of liquids or vapors.

SUBSTRATE CONTROL

The collection of all materials suspected of containing volatile liquids must be accompanied by a thorough sampling of similar but uncontaminated control

FIGURE 16-8 Various sizes of paint cans suitable for collecting debris at fire scenes. *Sirchie Finger Print Laboratories*

specimens from another area of the fire scene. This is known as a "substrate control." For example, if an investigator collects carpeting at the point of origin, he or she must sample the same carpet from another part of the room, where it can be reasonably assumed that no flammable substance was placed.

In the laboratory, the criminalist checks the substrate control to be sure that it is free of any flammables. This procedure reduces the possibility (and subsequent argument) that the carpet was exposed to a flammable liquid such as a cleaning solution during normal maintenance. In addition, laboratory tests on the unburned control material may help analyze the breakdown products from the material's exposure to intense heat during the fire. Common materials such as plastic floor tiles, carpet, linoleum, and adhesives can produce volatile hydrocarbons when they are burned. These breakdown products can sometimes be mistaken for an accelerant.

IGNITERS AND OTHER EVIDENCE

The scene should also be thoroughly searched for igniters. The most common igniter is a match. Normally the match is completely consumed during a fire and is impossible to locate. However, there have been cases in which, by force of habit, matches have been extinguished and tossed aside only to be recovered later by the investigator. This evidence may prove valuable if the criminalist can fit the match to a book found in the possession of a suspect.

Arsonists can construct many other types of devices to start a fire. These include burning cigarettes, firearms, ammunition, a mechanical match striker, electrical sparking devices, and a "Molotov cocktail"—a glass bottle containing flammable liquid with a cloth rag stuffed into it and lit as a fuse. Relatively complex mechanical devices are much more likely to survive the fire for later discovery. The broken glass and wick of the Molotov cocktail, if recovered, must be preserved as well.

One important piece of evidence is the clothing of the suspect perpetrator. If this individual is arrested within a few hours of initiating the fire, residual quantities of the accelerant may still be present in the clothing. As we will see in the next section, the forensic laboratory can detect extremely small quantities of accelerants, making the examination of a suspect's clothing a feasible investigative approach. Each item of clothing should be placed in a separate airtight container, preferably a new, clean paint can.

Quick Review

- Telltale signs of arson include evidence of separate and unconnected fires, the use of "streamers" to spread the fire from one area to another, and evidence of severe burning found on the floor as opposed to the ceiling of a structure.
- Other common signs of arson at a fire scene are the presence of accelerants and the discovery of an ignition device.
- Porous materials at a fire's suspected point of origin should be collected and stored in airtight containers.

Analysis of Flammable Residues

Criminalists are nearly unanimous in judging the gas chromatograph to be the most sensitive and reliable instrument for detecting and characterizing flammable residues. Most arsons are initiated by petroleum distillates, such as gasoline and kerosene, that are composed of a complex mixture of **hydrocarbons**. The gas chromatograph separates the hydrocarbon components of these liquids and produces a chromatographic pattern characteristic of a particular petroleum product.

hydrocarbon
Any compound consisting of only carbon and hydrogen.

HEADSPACE TECHNIQUE

Before accelerant residues can be analyzed, they first must be recovered from the debris collected at the scene. The easiest way to recover accelerant residues from fire-scene debris is to heat the airtight container in which the sample has been sent to the laboratory. When the container is heated, any volatile residue in the debris is driven off and trapped in the container's enclosed airspace. The vapor, or "headspace," is then removed with a syringe, as shown in Figure 16-9.

When the vapor is injected into the gas chromatograph, it is separated into its components, and each peak is recorded on the chromatogram. The identity of the volatile residue is determined when the pattern of the resultant chromatogram is compared to patterns produced by known petroleum products. For example, in Figure 16-10, a gas chromatographic analysis of debris recovered from a fire site shows a chromatogram similar to a known gasoline standard, thus proving the presence of gasoline.

In the absence of any recognizable pattern, the individual peaks can be identified when the investigator compares their retention times to known hydrocarbon standards (e.g., hexane, benzene, toluene, and xylenes). The brand name of a gasoline sample cannot currently be determined by gas chromatography or any other technique. Fluctuating gasoline markets and exchange agreements among the various oil companies preclude this possibility.

FIGURE 16-9 The removal of vapor from an enclosed container for gas chromatographic analysis. *Richard Saferstein, Ph.D.*

VAPOR CONCENTRATION

One major disadvantage of the headspace technique is that the size of the syringe limits the volume of vapor that can be removed from the container and injected into the gas chromatograph. To overcome this deficiency, many crime laboratories augment the headspace technique with a method called "vapor concentration." One setup for this analysis is shown in Figure 16-11.

A charcoal-coated strip, similar to that used in environmental monitoring badges, is placed within the container holding the debris that has been collected from the fire scene.[2] The container is then heated to 60°C and held at this temperature for about one hour. At this temperature, a significant quantity of accelerant vaporizes into the container airspace. The charcoal absorbs the accelerant vapor with which it comes into contact. In this manner, over a short period of time a significant quantity of the accelerant will be trapped by and concentrated on the charcoal strip.

Once the heating procedure is complete, the analyst removes the charcoal strip from the container and recovers the accelerant from the strip by washing it with a small volume of solvent (e.g., carbon disulfide). The solvent is then injected into the gas chromatograph for analysis. The major advantage of using vapor concentration with gas chromatography is its sensitivity. By absorbing the accelerant into a charcoal strip, the forensic analyst can increase the sensitivity of accelerant detection at least a hundredfold over the conventional headspace technique.

An examination of Figure 16-10 shows that identifying an accelerant such as gasoline by gas chromatography is an exercise in pattern recognition. Typically a forensic analyst compares the pattern generated by the sample to chromatograms from accelerant standards obtained under the same conditions. The pattern of gasoline, as with many other accelerants, can easily be placed in a searchable library. An invaluable reference known as "The Ignitable Liquids Reference Collection" (ILRC) is available on the Internet at www.ilrc.ucf.edu. The ILRC is a useful collection showing chromatographic patterns for approximately 500 ignitable liquids.

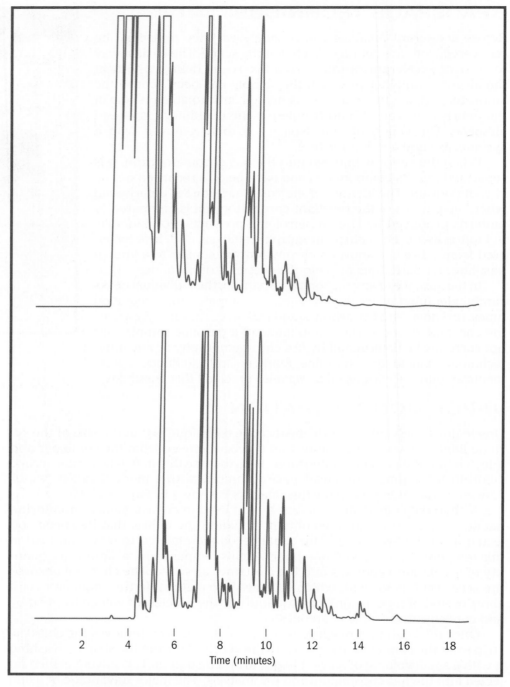

FIGURE 16-10 *(top)* A gas chromatogram of vapor from a genuine gasoline sample. *(bottom)* A gas chromatogram of vapor from debris recovered at a fire site. Note the similarity of the known gasoline to vapor removed from the debris.

GAS CHROMATOGRAPHY/ MASS SPECTROMETRY

On occasion, discernible patterns are not attainable by gas chromatography. This may be due to the presence of a combination of accelerants or to the mixing of accelerant residue with heat-generated breakdown products of materials burning at the fire scene. Under such conditions, a gas chromatographic pattern can be difficult, if not impossible, to interpret. In these cases, gas chromatography combined with mass spectrometry (discussed in Chapter 11) has proved valuable for solving difficult problems in the detection of accelerant residues.

Complex chromatographic patterns can be simplified by passing the separated components emerging from the gas chromatographic column through a mass spectrometer. As each component enters the mass spectrometer, it is fragmented into a collection of ions. The analyst can then control which ions will be detected and which will go unnoticed. In essence, the mass spectrometer acts as a filter allowing the analyst to see only the peaks associated with the ions selected for a particular accelerant. In this manner, the chromatographic pattern can be simplified by eliminating extraneous peaks that may obliterate the pattern.[3] The process is illustrated in Figure 16-12.

FIGURE 16-11   An apparatus for accelerant recovery by vapor concentration. The vapor in the enclosed container is exposed to charcoal, a chemical absorbent, where it is trapped for later analysis. *SAFERSTEIN, RICHARD, Ph.D., CRIMINALISTICS: AN INTRODUCTION TO FORENSIC SCIENCE, 11th Ed., © 2015. Reprinted and Electronically reproduced by permission of Pearson Education, Inc., Upper Saddle River, New Jersey.*

FIGURE 16-12   A chromatogram of a residue sample collected at a fire scene (a) shows a pattern somewhat like that of gasoline (b). However, a definitive conclusion that the unknown sample contained gasoline could be obtained only after extraneous peaks were eliminated from the chromatogram of the unknown by the use of GC/MS (c). *SAFERSTEIN, RICHARD, Ph.D., CRIMINALISTICS: AN INTRODUCTION TO FORENSIC SCIENCE, 11th Ed., © 2015. Reprinted and Electronically reproduced by permission of Pearson Education, Inc., Upper Saddle River, New Jersey.*

Quick Review

- Most arsons are initiated with petroleum distillates such as gasoline and kerosene.
- The gas chromatograph is the most sensitive and reliable instrument for detecting and characterizing flammable residues. A gas chromatograph separates the hydrocarbon components and produces a chromatographic pattern characteristic of a particular petroleum product.
- By comparing select gas chromatographic peaks recovered from fire-scene debris to known flammable liquids, a forensic analyst may be able to identify the accelerant used to initiate a fire.
- Complex chromatographic patterns can be simplified by passing the separated components emerging from the gas chromatographic column through a mass spectrometer.

Explosions and Explosives

The ready accessibility of potentially explosive laboratory chemicals; dynamite; and, in some countries, an assortment of military explosives has provided the criminal element of society with a lethal weapon. Unfortunately for society, explosives have become an attractive weapon to criminals bent on revenge, destruction of commercial operations, or just plain mischief.

Although politically motivated bombings have received considerable publicity worldwide, in the United States most bombing incidents are perpetrated by isolated individuals rather than by organized terrorists. These incidents typically involve homemade explosives and incendiary devices. The design of such weapons is limited only by the imagination and ingenuity of the bomber.

Like arson investigation, bomb investigation requires close cooperation among a group of highly specialized individuals trained and experienced in bomb disposal, bomb-site investigation, forensic analysis, and criminal investigation. The criminalist must detect and identify explosive chemicals recovered from the crime scene as well as identify the detonating mechanisms. This special responsibility is explored in the remainder of this chapter.

CHEMISTRY OF EXPLOSIONS

explosion
A chemical or mechanical action caused by combustion and accompanied by the creation of heat and the rapid expansion of gases.

Like fire, an **explosion** is the product of combustion accompanied by the creation of gases and heat. However, the distinguishing characteristic of an explosion is the rapid rate of the reaction. The sudden buildup of expanding gas pressure at the origin of the explosion produces the violent physical disruption of the surrounding environment.

Our previous discussion of the chemistry of fire referred only to oxidation reactions that rely on air as the sole source of oxygen. However, we need not restrict ourselves to this type of situation. For example, explosives are substances that undergo a rapid exothermic oxidation reaction, producing large quantities of gases. This sudden buildup of gas pressure constitutes an explosion. Detonation occurs so rapidly that oxygen in the air cannot participate in the reaction; thus, many explosives must have their own source of oxygen.

oxidizing agent
A substance that supplies oxygen to a chemical reaction.

Chemicals that supply oxygen are known as **oxidizing agents**. One such agent is found in black powder, a *low explosive*, which is composed of a mixture of the following chemical ingredients:

75 percent potassium nitrate (KNO_3)
15 percent charcoal (C)
10 percent sulfur (S)

In this combination, oxygen-containing potassium nitrate acts as an oxidizing agent for the charcoal and sulfur fuels. As heat is applied to black powder, oxygen is liberated from potassium nitrate and simultaneously combines with charcoal and sulfur to produce heat and gases (symbolized by ↑), as represented in the following chemical equation:

$$3C \quad + \quad S \quad + \quad 2KNO_3 \quad \longrightarrow$$

carbon   sulfur   potassium nitrate   yield

$$3CO_2 \uparrow \quad + \quad N_2 \uparrow \quad + \quad K_2S$$

carbon dioxide   nitrogen   potassium sulfide

Some explosives have their oxygen and fuel components combined within one molecule. For example, the chemical structure of nitroglycerin, the major constituent of dynamite, combines carbon, hydrogen, nitrogen, and oxygen:

$$
\begin{array}{ccccc}
\text{H} & & \text{H} & & \text{H} \\
| & & | & & | \\
\text{H} - \text{C} & - & \text{C} & - & \text{C} - \text{H} \\
| & & | & & | \\
NO_2 & & NO_2 & & NO_2
\end{array}
$$

When nitroglycerin detonates, large quantities of energy are released as the molecule decomposes, and the oxygen recombines to produce large volumes of carbon dioxide, nitrogen, and water.

Consider, for example, the effect of confining an explosive charge to a relatively small, closed container. On detonation, the explosive almost instantaneously produces large volumes of gases that exert enormously high pressures on the interior walls of the container. In addition, the heat energy released by the explosion expands the gases, causing them to push on the walls with an even greater force. If we could observe the effects of an exploding lead pipe in slow motion, we would first see the pipe's walls stretch and balloon under pressures as high as several hundred tons per square inch. Finally, the walls would fragment and fly outward in all directions. This flying debris, or shrapnel, constitutes a great danger to life and limb in the immediate vicinity.

On release from confinement, the gaseous products of the explosion suddenly expand and compress layers of surrounding air as they move outward from the origin of the explosion. This blast effect, or outward rush of gases, at a rate that may be as high as 7,000 miles per hour creates an artificial gale that can overthrow walls, collapse roofs, and disturb any object in its path. If a bomb is sufficiently powerful, more serious damage will be inflicted by the blast effect than by fragmentation debris (see Figure 16-13).

TYPES OF EXPLOSIVES

The speed at which explosives decompose varies greatly from one to another and permits their classification as "high" and "low" explosives. In a low explosive, this speed is called the speed of **deflagration** (i.e., burning). It is characterized by very rapid oxidation that produces heat, light, and a subsonic pressure wave. In a high explosive, it is called the speed of detonation. **Detonation** refers to the creation of a supersonic shock wave within the explosive charge. This shock wave breaks the chemical bonds of the explosive charge, leading to a new, instantaneous buildup of heat and gases.

deflagration
A very rapid oxidation reaction accompanied by the generation of a low-intensity pressure wave that can disrupt the surroundings.

detonation
An extremely rapid oxidation reaction accompanied by a violent disruptive effect and an intense, high-speed shock wave.

FIGURE 16-13 A violent explosion. *Stefan Zaklin/Corbis*

FIGURE 16-14 Samples of smokeless powders. *ATF Bureau of Alcohol, Tobacco, Firearms & Explosives*

low explosive
An explosive with a velocity of detonation less than 1,000 meters per second.

black powder
Normally, a mixture of potassium nitrate, carbon, and sulfur in the ratio 75/15/10.

safety fuse
A cord containing a core of black powder; used to carry a flame at a uniform rate to an explosive charge.

smokeless powder (single-base)
An explosive consisting of nitrocellulose.

LOW EXPLOSIVES Low explosives, such as black and smokeless powders, decompose relatively slowly, at rates of up to 1,000 meters per second. Because of their slow burning rates, they produce a propelling or throwing action that makes them suitable as propellants for ammunition or skyrockets. However, the danger of this group of explosives must not be underestimated because when any one of them is confined to a relatively small container, it can explode with a force as lethal as that of almost any known explosive.

Black Powder and Smokeless Powder. The most widely used explosives in the low-explosive group are black powder and smokeless powder. The popularity of these two explosives is enhanced by their accessibility to the public. Both are available in any gun store, and black powder can easily be made from ingredients purchased at any chemical supply house as well.

Black powder is a relatively stable mixture of potassium nitrate or sodium nitrate with charcoal and sulfur. Unconfined, it merely burns; thus it commonly is used in safety fuses that carry a flame to an explosive charge. A **safety fuse** usually consists of black powder wrapped in a fabric or plastic casing. When ignited, a sufficient length of fuse will burn at a rate slow enough to allow a person adequate time to leave the site of the pending explosion. Black powder, like any other low explosive, becomes explosive and lethal only when it is confined.

The safest and most powerful low explosive is **smokeless powder**. This explosive usually consists of nitrated cotton or nitrocellulose (i.e., **single-base powder**) or nitroglycerin mixed with nitrocellulose (i.e., **double-base powder**). The powder is manufactured in a variety of grain sizes and shapes, according to the intended applications (see Figure 16-14).

Chlorate Mixtures. The only ingredients required for a low explosive are fuel and a good oxidizing agent. The oxidizing agent potassium chlorate, for example, when mixed with sugar, produces a popular and accessible explosive mix. When confined to a small container—a lead pipe, for example—and ignited, this mixture can explode with a force equivalent to that of a stick of 40 percent dynamite.

■■■■■ CASEFILES ■■■■■
THE BOSTON MARATHON BOMBING

On April 15th 2013, Dzhokhar and Tamerlan Tsarnaev, two radicalized Chechen brothers, detonated two improvised explosive devices at the annual Boston Marathon. The blasts killed 3 people and wounded 264 others. Efforts made by the FBI procured images of the suspected bombers, and a manhunt ensued ending with a violent shoot-out with police. Tamerlan Tsarnaev sustained multiple gunshot wounds and succumbed to his injuries, while Dzhokhar was subsequently arrested and charged.

Moments after the blasts, FBI and police canvassed the scene for pieces of the explosives. The bombs were discovered to be pressure cooker bombs similar to many IEDs found in other extremist terrorist attacks. The Tsarnaev brothers used black powder from fireworks mixed with with nails and ball bearings packed in a 1.6 gallon regular kitchen pressure cooker. Fuses in the improvised explosive devise

(IEDs} were fashioned from ornamental Christmas lights, and the detonators were skillfully assembled from model car parts. Dzhokhar and Tamerlan left two bombs placed in a backpack and shopping bag among the onlookers of the Marathon. As they walked away, they triggered the explosions with a remote created from the parts of RC toy cars. The Tsarnaev brothers claimed to have acquired instructions on how to build these devices from an Al-Qaeda funded website

The key to these devices is the large amount of pressure they can withstand before rupturing and unleashing a blast effect accompanied by shrapnel flying in all directions. Explosive material is detonated by a remote electrical charge, and extreme pressure is built inside the chamber of the cooker, leading to a violent explosion. Ball bearings, nails, and various pieces of shrapnel are dispersed at extreme speeds, penetrating nearby objects and damaging and maiming tissue.

Some other commonly encountered ingredients that may be combined with chlorate to produce an explosive are carbon, sulfur, starch, phosphorus, and magnesium filings. Chlorate mixtures may also be ignited by the heat generated from a chemical reaction. For instance, sufficient heat can be generated to initiate combustion when concentrated sulfuric acid comes into contact with a sugar–chlorate mix.

Gas–Air Mixtures.   Another form of low explosive is created when a considerable quantity of natural gas escapes into a confined area and mixes with a sufficient amount of air. If ignited, this mixture results in simultaneous combustion and sudden production of large volumes of gases and heat. In a building, walls are forced outward by the expanding gases, causing the roof to fall into the interiors, and objects are thrown outward and scattered in erratic directions.

Mixtures of air and a gaseous fuel explode or burn only within a limited concentration range. For example, the concentration limits for methane in air range from 5.3 to 13.9 percent. In the presence of too much air, the fuel becomes too diluted and does not ignite. On the other hand, if the fuel becomes too concentrated, ignition is prevented because there is not enough oxygen to support the combustion.

Mixtures at or near the upper concentration limit (i.e., "rich" mixtures) explode; however, some gas remains unconsumed because there is not enough oxygen to complete the combustion. As air rushes back into the origin of the explosion, it combines with the residual hot gas, producing a fire that is characterized by a *whoosh* sound. This fire is often more destructive than the explosion that preceded it. Mixtures near the lower end of the limit (i.e., "lean" mixtures) generally cause an explosion without causing accompanying damage due to fire.

HIGH EXPLOSIVES High explosives include dynamite, TNT, PETN, and RDX. They detonate almost instantaneously at rates of 1,000 to 8,500 meters per second, producing a smashing or shattering effect on their target. High explosives are classified into two groups—primary and secondary explosives—based on their sensitivity to heat, shock, or friction.

Primary explosives are ultrasensitive to heat, shock, or friction and, under normal conditions, detonate violently instead of burning. For this reason, they are used to detonate other explosives through a chain reaction and are often referred to as "primers." Primary explosives provide the major ingredients of "blasting caps" (i.e., small explosive devices used to detonate larger explosives) and include lead azide, lead styphnate, and diazodinitrophenol (see Figure 16-15). Because of their extreme sensitivity, these explosives are rarely used as the main charge of a homemade bomb.

Secondary explosives are relatively insensitive to heat, shock, or friction, and normally burn rather than detonate when small quantities are ignited in open air. This group comprises most high explosives used for commercial and military blasting. Some common examples of secondary explosives are dynamite, TNT (trinitrotoluene), PETN (pentaerythritol tetranitrate), RDX (cyclotrimethylenetrinitramine), and tetryl (2,4,6-trinitrophenylmethylnitramine).

smokeless powder (double-base)
An explosive consisting of a mixture of nitrocellulose and nitroglycerin.

high explosive
An explosive with a velocity of detonation greater than 1,000 meters per second.

primary explosive
A high explosive that is easily detonated by heat, shock, or friction.

secondary explosive
A high explosive that is relatively insensitive to heat, shock, or friction.

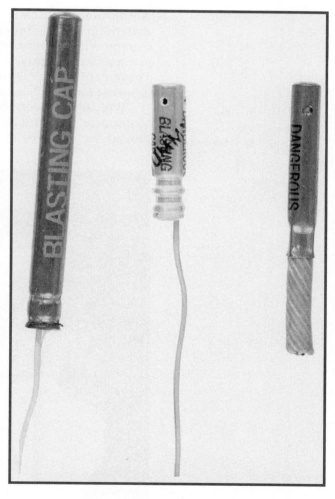

FIGURE 16-15 Blasting caps. The left and center caps are initiated by an electrical current; the right cap is initiated by a safety fuse. *Richard Saferstein, Ph.D.*

Dynamite. It is ironic that the prize most symbolic of humanity's search for peace—the Nobel Peace Prize—should bear the name of the developer of one of our most lethal discoveries: dynamite. In 1867, the Swedish chemist Alfred Nobel, searching for a method to desensitize nitroglycerin, found that when kieselguhr, a variety of diatomaceous earth, absorbed a large portion of nitroglycerin, it became far less sensitive but still retained its explosive force. Nobel later decided to use wood pulp as an absorbent instead because kieselguhr is a heat-absorbing material.

This so-called pulp dynamite was the beginning of what is now known as the "straight dynamite" series. These dynamites are used when a quick shattering action is desired. In addition to nitroglycerine and pulp, present-day straight dynamites also include sodium nitrate (which furnishes oxygen for complete combustion) and a small percentage of a stabilizer, such as calcium carbonate.

All straight dynamite is rated by strength; the strength rating is determined by the weight percentage of nitroglycerin in the formula. Thus, a 40 percent straight dynamite contains 40 percent nitroglycerin, a 60 percent grade contains 60 percent nitroglycerin, and so forth. However, the relative blasting power of various strengths of dynamite is not directly proportional to their strength ratings. A 60 percent straight dynamite, rather than being three times as strong as a 20 percent, is only one and a half times as strong (see Figure 16-16).

Ammonium Nitrate Explosives. In recent years, nitroglycerin-based dynamite has all but disappeared from the industrial explosives market. Commercially, these explosives have been replaced mainly by ammonium nitrate–based explosives—that is, water gels, emulsions, and ANFO explosives. These explosives mix oxygen-rich ammonium nitrate with a fuel to form a low-cost and very stable explosive.

Typically, water gels have a consistency resembling set gelatin or gel-type toothpaste. They are characterized by their water-resistant nature and are employed for all types of blasting under wet conditions. These explosives are

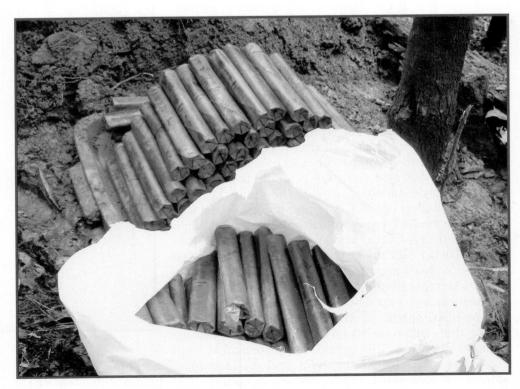

FIGURE 16-16 Sticks of dynamite. *U.S. Department of Justice/AP Images*

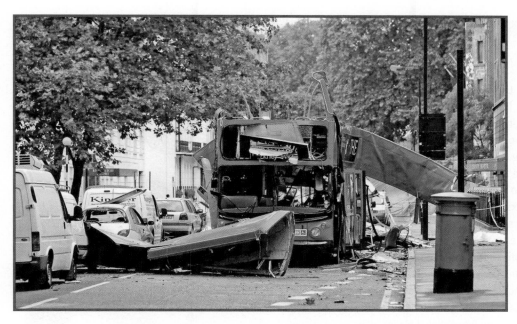

FIGURE 16-17   A London bus destroyed by a TATP-based bomb. *Peter Macdiarmid/Getty Images*

based on formulations of ammonium nitrate and sodium nitrate gelled with a natural polysaccharide such as guar gum. Commonly, a combustible material such as aluminum is mixed into the gel to serve as the explosive's fuel.

Emulsion explosives differ from gels in that they consist of two distinct phases, an oil phase and a water phase. In these emulsions, a droplet of a supersaturated solution of ammonium nitrate is surrounded by a hydrocarbon serving as a fuel. A typical emulsion consists of water, one or more inorganic nitrate oxidizers, oil, and emulsifying agents. Emulsions commonly contain micron-sized glass, resin, or ceramic spheres known as "microspheres" or "microballoons." The size of these spheres controls the explosive's sensitivity and detonation velocity.

Ammonium nitrate soaked in fuel oil is an explosive known as "ANFO." Such commercial explosives are inexpensive and safe to handle and have found wide applications in blasting operations in the mining industry. Ammonium nitrate in the form of fertilizer makes a readily obtainable ingredient for homemade explosives. Indeed, in an incident related to the 1993 bombing of New York City's World Trade Center, the FBI arrested five men during a raid on their hideout in New York City, where they were mixing a "witches' brew" of fuel oil and an ammonium nitrate-based fertilizer.

TATP. Triacetone triperoxide (TATP) is an improvised homemade explosive that has been used by terrorist organizations in Israel and other Middle Eastern countries. It is prepared by reacting the common ingredients of acetone and hydrogen peroxide in the presence of an acid catalyst such as hydrochloric acid.

TATP is a friction- and impact-sensitive explosive that is extremely potent when confined in a container such as a pipe. The 2005 London transit bombings were caused by TATP-based explosives and provide ample evidence that terrorist cells have moved TATP outside the Middle East. A London bus destroyed by one of the TATP bombs is shown in Figure 16-17.

A plot to use a "liquid explosive" to blow up ten planes on international flights from Britain to the United States apparently involved plans to smuggle the peroxide-based TATP explosive onto the planes. This plot has prompted authorities to prohibit airline passengers from carrying liquids and gels onto planes.

Military High Explosives. No discussion of high explosives would be complete without a mention of military high explosives. In many countries

■■■■ CASEFILES ■■■■

LIQUID EXPLOSIVES

In 2006, security agencies in the United States and Great Britain uncovered a terrorist plot to use liquid explosives to destroy ten commercial airplanes operating between the two countries. Of the hundreds of types of explosives, most are solid; only about a dozen are liquid. However, some of those liquid explosives can be readily purchased, and others can be made from hundreds of different kinds of chemicals that are not difficult to obtain.

After the September 11 attacks, worries about solid explosives had become the main concern for security specialists. Then, later in 2001, Richard Reid was arrested for attempting to destroy an American Airlines flight flying out of Paris. Authorities later found a high explosive with a TATP (triacetone triperoxide) detonator hidden in the lining of his shoe. Therefore it is perhaps not surprising that terrorists turned to liquids for this more recent plot. A memo issued by federal security officials about the plot to blow up the ten international planes highlighted a type of liquid explosive based on peroxide. The most common peroxide-based explosive is TATP, which can be used as a detonator or a primary explosive and has been used in terrorist-related bombings and by Palestinian suicide bombers.

In theory, scientists know how to detect peroxide-based explosives. The challenge is to design machines that can perform scans quickly and efficiently on thousands of passengers passing through airport security checks. Current scanning machines at airports are designed to detect nitrogen-containing chemicals and are not designed to detect peroxide-containing explosive ingredients. However, security experts are worried about the possibility of explosives in the form of liquids and gels getting onto airliners. Not having the luxury of waiting for newly designed scanning devices capable of ferreting out dangerous liquids to be in place at airports, authorities decided to use a commonsense approach: to restrict the types and quantities of liquids that passengers can carry onto a plane.

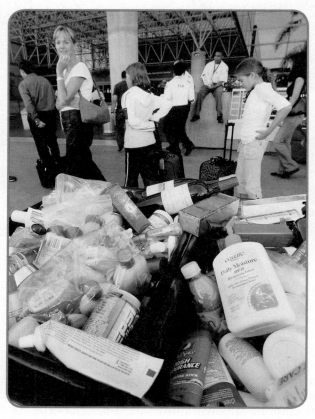

Gels and liquids discarded by airline passengers before boarding.
Stefano Paltera/AP Images

outside the United States, the accessibility of high explosives to terrorist organizations makes them very common constituents of homemade bombs. RDX, the most popular and powerful military explosive, is often encountered in the form of a pliable plastic of doughlike consistency known by the U.S. military's designation "composition C–4."

TNT was produced and used on an enormous scale during World War II and may be considered the most important military bursting-charge explosive. Alone or in combination with other explosives, it has found wide application in shells, bombs, grenades, demolition explosives, and propellant compositions. Interestingly, military "dynamite" contains no nitroglycerin but is actually composed of a mixture of RDX and TNT. Like other military explosives, TNT is rarely encountered in bombings in the United States.

PETN is used by the military in TNT mixtures for small-caliber projectiles and grenades. Commercially, the chemical is used as the explosive core in a **detonating cord** or "primacord." Instead of the slower-burning safety fuse, the detonating cord is often used to connect a series of explosive charges so that they will detonate simultaneously.

detonating cord

A cordlike explosive containing a core of high-explosive material, usually PETN; also called "primacord."

Detonators.   Unlike low explosives, bombs made of high explosives must be detonated by an initiating explosion. In most cases, detonators are blasting caps composed of copper or aluminum cases filled with lead azide as an initiating charge and PETN or RDX as a detonating charge. Blasting caps can be initiated by means of a burning safety fuse or by an electrical current.

Homemade bombs camouflaged in packages, suitcases, and the like, are usually initiated with an electrical blasting cap wired to a battery. An unlimited number of switching-mechanism designs have been devised for setting off these devices; clocks and mercury switches are the most common. Bombers sometimes prefer to employ outside electrical sources. For instance, most automobile bombs are detonated when the ignition switch of a car is turned on.

Quick Review

- Explosives are substances that undergo a rapid oxidation reaction, producing large quantities of gases. The sudden buildup of gas pressure leads to the explosion.
- The speed at which an explosive decomposes determines whether it is classified as a high or low explosive.
- The most widely used low explosives are black powder and smokeless powder. Common high explosives include ammonium nitrate–based explosives (e.g., water gels, emulsions, and ANFO explosives).
- Among the high explosives, primary explosives are ultrasensitive to heat, shock, or friction and provide the major ingredients found in blasting caps. Secondary explosives normally constitute the main charge of a high explosive.

Collection and Analysis of Evidence of Explosives

The most important step in the detection and analysis of explosive residues is the collection of appropriate samples from the explosion scene. Invariably, undetonated residues of the explosive remain at the site of the explosion. The detection and identification of these explosives in the laboratory depends on the bomb-scene investigator's skill and ability to recognize and sample the areas most likely to contain such materials.

DETECTING AND RECOVERING EVIDENCE OF EXPLOSIVES

The most obvious characteristic of a high or contained low explosive is the presence of a crater at the origin of the blast. Once the crater has been located, all loose soil and other debris must immediately be removed from the interior of the hole and preserved for laboratory analysis. Other good sources of explosive residues are objects located near the origin of detonation. Wood, insulation, rubber, and other soft materials that are readily penetrated often collect traces of the explosive. However, nonporous objects near the blast also must not be overlooked. For instance, residues can be found on the surfaces of metal objects near the site of an explosion. Material blown away from the blast's origin should also be recovered because it, too, may retain explosive residues.

The entire area must be systematically searched, with great care taken to recover any trace of a detonating mechanism or any other item foreign to the explosion site. Wire-mesh screens are best used for sifting through debris. All personnel involved in searching the bomb scene must take appropriate measures to avoid contaminating the scene, including dressing in disposable gloves, shoe covers, and coveralls.

FIGURE 16-18 Hardened MobileTrace®, a portable ion mobility spectrometer used to rapidly detect and tentatively identify trace quantities of explosives. *Morpho Detection, Inc.*

ION MOBILITY SPECTROMETER In pipe-bomb explosions, particles of the explosive are frequently found adhering to the pipe cap or to the pipe threads, as a result of either being impacted into the metal by the force of the explosion or being deposited in the threads during the construction of the bomb.

One approach for screening objects for the presence of explosive residues in the field or the laboratory is the ion mobility spectrometer (IMS).[4] A portable IMS is shown in Figure 16-18. This handheld detector uses a vacuum to collect explosive residues from suspect surfaces. Alternatively, the surface suspected of containing explosive residues is wiped down with a Teflon-coated fiberglass disc, and the collected residues are then drawn into the spectrometer off the disc. Once in the IMS, the explosive residues are vaporized by the application of heat. These vaporized substances are exposed to a beam of electrons or beta rays emitted by radioactive nickel and converted into electrically charged molecules or ions. The ions are then allowed to move through a tube, or drift region, under the influence of an electric field. A schematic diagram of an IMS is shown in Figure 16-19.

The preliminary identification of an explosive residue can be made by noting the time it takes the explosive to move through the tube. Because ions move at different speeds depending on their size and structure, they can be characterized by the speed at which they pass through the tube. Used as a screening tool, this method rapidly detects a full range of explosives, even at low levels. However, all results need to be verified through confirmatory tests.

The IMS can detect plastic explosives as well as commercial and military explosives. More than 10,000 portable and full-size IMS units are currently used at airport security checkpoints, and more than 50,000 handheld IMS analyzers have been deployed for chemical-weapons monitoring in various armed forces.

COLLECTION AND PACKAGING All materials collected for examination by the laboratory must be placed in airtight sealed containers and labeled with all pertinent information. Soil and other soft, loose materials are best stored in metal airtight containers such as clean paint cans. Debris and articles collected from different areas should be packaged in separate airtight containers. Plastic bags should not be used to store evidence suspected of containing explosive residues. Some explosives can actually escape through the plastic. Also, sharp-edged objects may pierce the sides of a plastic bag; it is best to place these types of items in metal containers.

Quick Review

- The entire bomb site must be systematically searched to recover any trace of a detonating mechanism or any other item foreign to the explosion site. Objects located at or near the origin of the explosion must be collected for laboratory examination.
- The most obvious characteristic of a high or contained low explosive is the presence of a crater at the origin of the blast.
- A device widely used to screen objects for the presence of explosive residues is the ion mobility spectrometer.
- All materials collected at bombing scenes must be placed in airtight containers such as clean paint cans.

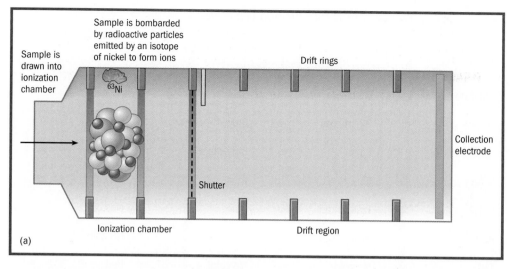

Sample is bombarded by radioactive particles emitted by an isotope of nickel to form ions

Sample is drawn into ionization chamber

^{63}Ni

Drift rings

Collection electrode

Shutter

Ionization chamber

Drift region

(a)

Sample is converted into ions of different sizes and structures

Drift rings

Collection electrode

Shutter

Ionization chamber

Drift region

(b)

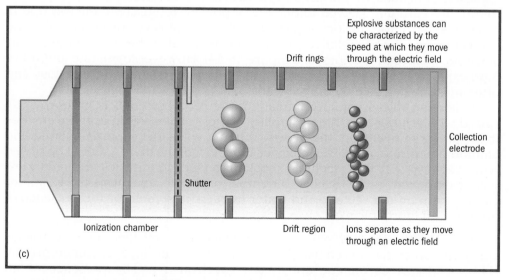

Explosive substances can be characterized by the speed at which they move through the electric field

Drift rings

Collection electrode

Shutter

Ionization chamber

Drift region

Ions separate as they move through an electric field

(c)

FIGURE 16-19 A schematic diagram of an ion mobility spectrometer. A sample is introduced into an ionization chamber, where bombardment with radioactive particles emitted by an isotope of nickel converts the sample to ions. The ions move into a drift region where ion separation occurs, based on the speed of the ions as they move through an electric field. *SAFERSTEIN, RICHARD, Ph.D., CRIMINALISTICS: AN INTRODUCTION TO FORENSIC SCIENCE, 11th Ed., © 2015. Reprinted and Electronically reproduced by permission of Pearson Education, Inc., Upper Saddle River, New Jersey.*

TABLE 16.3   Color Spot Tests for Common Explosives

SUBSTANCE	REAGENT		
	GRIESS[A]	DIPHENYLAMINE[B]	ALCOHOLIC KOH[C]
Chlorate	No color	Blue	No color
Nitrate	Pink to red	Blue	No color
Nitrocellulose	Pink	Blue-black	No color
Nitroglycerin	Pink to red	Blue	No color
PETN	Pink to red	Blue	No color
RDX	Pink to red	Blue	No color
TNT	No color	No color	Red
Tetryl	Pink to red	Blue	Red-violet

[A]Griess reagent: Solution 1—Dissolve 1 g sulfanilic acid in 100 mL 30% acetic acid. Solution 2—Dissolve 0.5 g *N*-(1-napthyl) ethylenediamine in 100 mL methyl alcohol. Add solutions 1 and 2 and a few milligrams of zinc dust to the suspect extract.
[B]Diphenylamine reagent: Dissolve 1 g diphenylamine in 100 mL concentrated sulfuric acid.
[C]Alcoholic KOH reagent: Dissolve 10 g of potassium hydroxide in 100 mL absolute alcohol.

ANALYSIS OF EVIDENCE OF EXPLOSIVES

When the bomb-scene debris and other materials arrive at the laboratory, everything is first examined microscopically to detect particles of unconsumed explosive. Portions of the recovered debris and detonating mechanism, if found, are carefully viewed under a low-power stereoscopic microscope in a painstaking effort to locate particles of the explosive. Black powder and smokeless powder are relatively easy to locate in debris because of their characteristic shapes and colors (see Figure 16-14). However, dynamite and other high explosives present the microscopist with a much more difficult task and often must be detected by other means.

Following microscopic examination, the recovered debris is thoroughly rinsed with acetone. The high solubility of most explosives in acetone ensures their quick removal from the debris. When a water-gel explosive containing ammonium nitrate or a low explosive is suspected, the debris should be rinsed with water so that water-soluble substances (such as nitrates and chlorates) will be extracted. Table 16.3 lists a number of simple color tests the examiner can perform on the acetone and water extracts to screen for the presence of organic and inorganic explosives, respectively.

SCREENING AND CONFIRMATION TESTS   Once collected, the acetone extract is concentrated and analyzed using color spot tests, thin-layer chromatography (TLC), and gas chromatography/mass spectrometry. The presence of an explosive is indicated by a well-defined spot on a TLC plate corresponding to a known explosive—for example, nitroglycerin, RDX, or PETN.

When sufficient quantities of explosives are recoverable, confirmatory tests may be performed by infrared spectrophotometry. The former produces a unique "fingerprint" pattern for an organic explosive, as shown by the IR spectrum of RDX in Figure 16-20.

VIRTUAL LAB
ARSON DETECTION—THE RECOVERY OF FLAMMABLE LIQUIDS
To perform a virtual arson detection analysis, go to www.pearsoncustom.com/us/vlm/

FIGURE 16-20   The infrared spectrum of RDX. *SAFERSTEIN, RICHARD, Ph.D., CRIMINALISTICS: AN INTRODUCTION TO FORENSIC SCIENCE, 11th Ed.,* © 2015. *Reprinted and Electronically reproduced by permission of Pearson Education, Inc., Upper Saddle River, New Jersey.*

Quick Review

- Debris collected at explosion scenes is examined microscopically for unconsumed explosive particles.
- Recovered debris may be thoroughly rinsed with organic solvents and analyzed by testing procedures that include color spot tests, thin-layer chromatography, and gas chromatography/mass spectrometry.
- Unconsumed explosives are identified by infrared spectrophotometry.

CHAPTER REVIEW

- Oxidation is the combination of oxygen with other substances to produce new substances.

- Combustion is the rapid combination of oxygen with another substance, accompanied by the production of noticeable heat and light.

- Pyrolysis is the chemical breakdown of solid organic matter by heat. The gaseous products of pyrolysis combine with oxygen to produce a fire.

- Spontaneous combustion is fire caused by a natural heat-producing process in the presence of sufficient air and fuel.

- To initiate and sustain combustion, (1) a fuel must be present; (2) oxygen must be available in sufficient quantity to combine with the fuel; and (3) heat must be applied to initiate the combustion, and sufficient heat must be generated to sustain the reaction.

- Telltale signs of arson include evidence of separate and unconnected fires, the use of "streamers" to spread the fire from one area to another, and evidence of severe burning found on the floor as opposed to the ceiling of a structure.

- Other common signs of arson at a fire scene are the presence of accelerants and the discovery of an ignition device.

- Porous materials found at a fire's suspected point of origin should be collected and stored in airtight containers.

- Most arsons are initiated with petroleum distillates such as gasoline and kerosene.

- The gas chromatograph is the most sensitive and reliable instrument for detecting and characterizing flammable residues. A gas chromatograph separates the hydrocarbon components and produces a chromatographic pattern characteristic of a particular petroleum product.

- By comparing select gas chromatographic peaks recovered from fire-scene debris to known flammable liquids, a forensic analyst may be able to identify the accelerant used to initiate a fire.

- Complex chromatographic patterns can be simplified by passing the separated components emerging from the gas chromatographic column through a mass spectrometer.

- Explosives are substances that undergo a rapid oxidation reaction, producing large quantities of gases. The sudden buildup of gas pressure leads to the explosion.

- The speed at which an explosive decomposes determines whether it is classified as a high or low explosive.

- The most widely used low explosives are black powder and smokeless powder. Common high explosives include ammonium nitrate–based explosives (e.g., water gels, emulsions, and ANFO explosives).

- Among the high explosives, primary explosives are ultrasensitive to heat, shock, or friction and provide the major ingredients found in blasting caps. Secondary explosives normally constitute the main charge of a high explosive.

- The entire bomb site must be systematically searched to recover any trace of a detonating mechanism or any other item foreign to the explosion site. Objects located at or near the origin of the explosion must be collected for laboratory examination.

- The most obvious characteristic of a high or contained low explosive is the presence of a crater at the origin of the blast.

- A device widely used to screen objects for the presence of explosive residues is the ion mobility spectrometer.

- All materials collected at bombing scenes must be placed in airtight containers such as clean paint cans.

- Debris collected at explosion scenes is examined microscopically for unconsumed explosive particles.

- Recovered debris may be thoroughly rinsed with organic solvents and analyzed by testing procedures that include color spot tests, thin-layer chromatography, and gas chromatography/mass spectrometry.

- Unconsumed explosives are identified by infrared spectrophotometry.

KEY TERMS

accelerant, 417
black powder, 426
combustion, 413
deflagration, 425
detonating cord, 430
detonation, 425
energy, 412
explosion, 424
flammable range, 415

flash point, 414
glowing combustion, 416
heat of combustion, 413
high explosive, 427
hydrocarbon, 420
ignition temperature, 413
low explosive, 426
modus operandi, 411
oxidation, 411

oxidizing agent, 424
primary explosive, 427
pyrolysis, 415
safety fuse, 426
secondary explosive, 427
smokeless powder (double-base), 426
smokeless powder (single-base), 426
spontaneous combustion, 416

REVIEW QUESTIONS

1. The combination of oxygen with other substances to produce new chemical products is called _____.

2. True or False: All oxidation reactions yield carbon dioxide and water as products. _____

3. _____ is the capacity for doing work.

4. Burning methane to heat water and thus produce steam for the purpose of driving a turbine is an example of converting _____ energy to _____ energy to _____ energy.

5. The quantity of heat evolved from a chemical reaction arises out of the _____ and _____ of chemical bonds.

6. Molecules must _____ energy to break their bonds and _____ energy when their bonds are reformed.

7. Excess heat energy liberated by an oxidation reaction is called the _____.

8. True or False: All reactions require an energy input to start them. _____

9. The minimum temperature at which a fuel burns is known as the _____ temperature.

10. A fuel achieves a sufficient reaction rate with oxygen to produce a flame only in the _____ state.

11. The lowest temperature at which a liquid fuel produces enough vapor to burn is the _____.

12. _____ is the chemical breakdown of a solid material to gaseous products.

13. The _____ defines the upper and lower limits between which a mixture of gaseous fuel and air burns.

14. _____ is a phenomenon in which a fuel burns without the presence of a flame.

15. True or False: The rate of a chemical reaction increases as the temperature rises. _____

16. _____ describes a fire caused by a natural heat-producing process in a poorly ventilated area.

17. True or False: An immediate search of a fire scene can commence without obtaining a search warrant. _____

18. A search of the fire scene must focus on finding the fire's _____.

19. True or False: The origin of a fire is most likely to be located closest to the lowest point that shows the most intense characteristics of burning. _____

20. A portable _____ detector can suck in the air surrounding a questioned sample to rapidly screen for the presence of volatile residues at fire scenes.

21. True or False: The collection of debris at the origin of a fire should include all nonporous materials. _____

22. _____ containers must be used to package all materials suspected of containing hydrocarbon residues.

23. True or False: Substrate controls should be collected at a fire scene from an area where it can be reasonably assumed that no flammable substance was placed. _____

24. A(n) _____ is a mechanism consisting of a glass bottle containing flammable liquid with a cloth rag stuffed into it and lit as a fuse.

25. The simplest way to recover accelerant residues from fire-scene debris for identification is to heat the airtight container in which the sample is packaged and remove the _____ with a syringe.

26. The most sensitive and reliable instrument for detecting and characterizing flammable residues is the _____.

27. Complex chromatographic patterns can be simplified by passing the components emerging from the gas chromatographic column through a(n) _____.

28. Rapid combustion accompanied by the creation of large volumes of gases describes a(n) _____.

29. True or False: Chemicals that supply oxygen are known as oxidizing agents. _____

30. Explosives that decompose at relatively slow rates are classified as _____ explosives.

31. The speed at which low explosives decompose is called the speed of _____.

32. Three ingredients of black powder are _____, _____, and _____.

33. _____ explosives detonate almost instantaneously to produce a smashing or shattering effect.

34. The most widely used low explosives are _____ and _____.

35. A low explosive becomes explosive and lethal only when it is _____.

36. True or False: Air and a gaseous fuel burn when mixed in any proportions. _____

37. High explosives can be classified as either _____ or _____ explosives.

38. The most widely used explosive in the military is _____.

39. The explosive core in detonating cord is _____.

40. A high explosive is normally detonated by a(n) _____ explosive contained within a blasting cap.

41. An obvious characteristic of a high explosive is the presence of a(n) _____ at the origin of the blast.

42. To screen objects for the presence of explosive residues in the field or the laboratory, the investigator may use a handheld _____.

43. Unconsumed explosive residues may be detected in the laboratory through a careful _____ examination of the debris.

44. True or False: Debris and articles at an explosion scene that are collected from different areas are to be packaged in separate airtight containers. _____

APPLICATION AND CRITICAL THINKING

1. It is late August in Houston, Texas, and you are investigating a fire that occurred at a facility that stores motor oils and other lubricating oils. A witness points out a man who allegedly ran from the structure around the same time that the fire started. You question the man, who turns out to be the owner of the facility. He tells you that he was checking his inventory when barrels of waste motor oil stored in an unventilated back room spontaneously burst into flames. The owner claims that the fire spread so rapidly that he had to flee the building before he could call 911. After speaking with several employees, you learn that the building has no air-conditioning and that the oil had been stored for almost a year in the cramped back room. You also learn from a detective assisting on the case that the owner increased his insurance coverage on the facility within the past three months. Should you believe the owner's story, or should you suspect arson? On what do you base your conclusion?

2. Criminalist Mick Mickelson is collecting evidence from a fire scene. He gathers about a quart of ash and soot debris from several rooms surrounding the point of origin. He stores the debris in a new, clean paint can, filled about three-quarters

full. Seeing several pieces of timber that he believes may contain accelerant residues, he cuts them and places them in airtight plastic bags. A short time later, a suspect is arrested and Mick searches him for any signs of an igniter or accelerants. He finds a cigarette lighter on the suspect and seizes it for evidence before turning the suspect over to the police. What mistakes, if any, did Mick make in collecting evidence?

3. The following pieces of evidence were found at separate explosion sites. For each item, indicate whether the explosion was more likely to have been caused by low or by high explosives, and explain your answers:

a) Lead azide residues

b) Nitrocellulose residues

c) Ammonium nitrate residues

d) Scraps of primacord

e) Potassium chlorate residues

4. Which color test or tests would you run first on a suspect sample to test for evidence of each of the following explosives? Explain your answers.

a) Tetryl

b) TNT

c) Chlorate

d) Nitrocellulose

5. Criminalist Matt Weir is collecting evidence from the site of an explosion. Arriving on the scene, he immediately proceeds to look for the crater caused by the blast. After finding the crater, he picks through the debris at the site by hand, looking for evidence of detonators or foreign materials. Matt collects loose soil and debris from the immediate area, placing the smaller bits into paper folded into a druggist fold. He stores larger items in plastic bags for transportation to the laboratory. What mistakes, if any, did Matt make in collecting and storing this evidence?

ENDNOTES

1. *Michigan* v. *Tyler*, 436 U.S. 499 (1978).

2. R. T. Newman et al., "The Use of Activated Charcoal Strips for Fire Debris Extractions by Passive Diffusion, Part 1: The Effects of Time, Temperature, Strip Size, and Sample Concentration," *Journal of Forensic Sciences* 41 (1996): 361.

3. M. W. Gilbert, "The Use of Individual Extracted Ion Profiles Versus Summed Extracted Ion Profiles in Fire Debris Analysis," *Journal of Forensic Sciences* 43 (1998): 871.

4. T. Keller et al., "Application of Ion Mobility Spectrometry in Cases of Forensic Interest," *Forensic Science International* 161 (2006): 130.

Document Examination

Luke Fraza/ Getty Images

LEARNING OBJECTIVES

After studying this chapter, you should be able to:
- Define "questioned document."
- Know what common individual characteristics are associated with handwriting.
- List some important guidelines for collecting known writings for comparison to a questioned document.
- Recognize some of the class and individual characteristics of printers and photocopiers.
- List some of the techniques document examiners use to uncover alterations, erasures, obliterations, and variations in pen inks.

THE UNABOMBER

In 1978, a parcel addressed to a Northwestern University professor exploded as it was being opened by a campus security officer. This was the start of a series of bomb-containing packages that were sent typically to universities and airlines. Considering the intended victims, the perpetrator was dubbed UN (university) A (airlines) BOM—hence, the Unabomber.

The explosives were usually housed in a pipe within a wooden box. The explosive ingredients generally were black powder, smokeless powder, or an ammonium nitrate mix. The box was filled with metal objects to create a shrapnel effect on explosion. The device typically had the initials "FC" punched into it.

The first Unabomber fatality came in 1985, when a computer store owner was killed after picking up a package left outside his business. The Unabomber emerged again in 1993 after a six-year hiatus when he mailed bombs to two university professors. Their injuries were not fatal, but his next two attacks did result in fatalities.

In 1995, the case took an unexpected turn when the Unabomber promised to end his mad spree if his 35,000-word typewritten "Manifesto," which he had sent to the *New York Times* and the *Washington Post*, were published by these newspapers. The manifesto turned out to be a long, rambling rant against technology, but it offered valuable clues that broke the case. David Kaczynski realized that the manifesto's writing style and the philosophy it espoused closely resembled that of his brother, Ted. His suspicions were confirmed by linguistics experts who carefully pored over the manifesto's content. Ted Kaczynski was arrested in Montana in 1996. Inside his ramshackle cabin were writings similar to the manifesto, three manual typewriters, and bomb-making materials. Forensic document examiners were able to match the typewritten manifesto to one of the typewriters recovered from the cabin.

Document Examiner

Ordinarily, the work of the document examiner involves examining handwriting and typescript to ascertain the source or authenticity of a questioned document. However, document examination is not restricted to a mere visual comparison of words and letters. The document examiner must know how to use microscopy, photography, and even such analytical methods as chromatography to uncover all efforts, both brazen and subtle, to change the content or meaning of a document.

Alterations of documents through overwriting, erasures, or the more obvious crossing out of words must be recognized and characterized as efforts to alter or obscure the original meaning of a document. The document examiner identifies such efforts and recovers the original contents of the writing. An examiner may even reconstruct writing on charred or burned papers, or uncover the meaning of indented writings found on a paper pad after the top sheet has been removed.

Any object that contains handwritten or typewritten markings whose source or authenticity is in doubt may be referred to as a **questioned document**. This broad term may be applied to any of the written and printed materials we normally encounter in our daily activities. Letters, checks, driver's licenses, contracts, wills, voter registrations, passports, petitions, and even lottery tickets are commonly examined in crime laboratories. However, we need not restrict our examples to paper documents. Questioned documents may include writings or other markings found on walls, windows, doors, or any other objects.

Document examiners possess no mystical powers or scientific formulas for identifying the authors of writings. They apply knowledge gathered through years of training and experience to recognize and compare the individual characteristics of questioned and known authentic writings. For this purpose, gathering documents of known authorship or origin is critical to the outcome of the examination. Collecting known writings may entail considerable time and effort and may be further hampered by uncooperative or missing witnesses. However, the uniqueness of handwriting makes this type of physical evidence, like fingerprints, one of few definitive individual characteristics available to the investigator, a fact that certainly justifies an extensive investigative effort.

questioned document
Any document about which some issue has been raised or that is the subject of an investigation.

Handwriting Comparisons

Document experts continually testify that no two individuals write exactly alike. This is not to say that there cannot be marked resemblances between two individuals' handwritings because many factors make up the total character of a person's writing.

GENERAL STYLE

Perhaps the most obvious feature of handwriting to the layperson is its general style. As children, we all learn to write by attempting to copy letters that match a standard form or style shown to us by our teachers. The style of writing acquired by the learner is that which is fashionable for the particular time and locale. In the United States, for example, the two most widely used systems of cursive writing are the Palmer method, first introduced in 1880, and the Zaner-Bloser method, introduced in about 1895 (see Figure 17-1). To some extent, both of these systems are taught in nearly all fifty states.

FIGURE 17-1 (*top*) An example of Zaner-Bloser handwriting; (*bottom*) an example of Palmer handwriting. *Courtesy Robert J. Phillips, Document Examiner, Audobon, New Jersey*

The early stages of learning and practicing handwriting are characterized by a conscious effort by the student to copy standard letter forms. Many pupils in a handwriting class tend at first to have writing styles that are similar to one another, with minor differences attributable to skill in copying. However, as initial writing skills improve, a child normally reaches the stage at which the nerve and motor responses associated with the act of writing become subconscious. The individual's writing now begins to take on innumerable habitual shapes and patterns that distinguish it from all others. The document examiner looks for these unique writing traits.

VARIATIONS IN HANDWRITING

The unconscious handwriting of two individuals can never be identical. Individual variations associated with mechanical, physical, and mental functions make it extremely unlikely that all of these factors can be exactly reproduced by any two people. Thus, variations are expected in angularity, slope, speed, pressure, letter and word spacings, relative dimensions of letters, connections between letters, pen movement, writing skill, and finger dexterity.

Furthermore, many other factors besides pure handwriting characteristics should be considered. The arrangement of the writing on the paper may be as distinctive as the writing itself. Margins, spacings, crowding, insertions, and alignment are all results of personal habits. Spelling, punctuation, phraseology, and grammar can be personal and, if so, combine to individualize the writer.

In a problem involving the authorship of handwriting, all characteristics of both the known and questioned documents must be considered and compared. Dissimilarities between the two writings strongly indicate two writers, unless these differences can logically be accounted for by the facts surrounding the preparation of the documents. Because any single characteristic, even the most distinctive one, may be found in the handwriting of other individuals, no single handwriting characteristic can, by itself, be taken as the basis for a positive comparison. The final conclusion of a match must be based on a sufficient number of common characteristics between the known and questioned writings to effectively preclude their having originated from two different sources.

What constitutes a sufficient number of personal characteristics? Here again, there are no hard-and-fast rules for making such a determination. The expert examiner can make this judgment only in the context of each particular case.

CHALLENGES TO HANDWRITING COMPARISON

When the examiner receives a reasonable amount of known handwriting for comparison, sufficient evidence to determine the source of a questioned document is usually easy to find. Frequently, however, circumstances prevent a positive conclusion or permit only the expression of a qualified opinion. Such situations usually develop when an insufficient number of known writings are available for comparison. Although nothing may be found that definitely points to the questioned and known handwriting being of different origin, not enough personal characteristics may be present in the known writings that are consistent with the questioned materials.

Difficulties may also arise when the examiner receives questioned writings containing only a few words, all deliberately written in a crude, unnatural form or all very carefully written and thought out to disguise the writer's natural style—a situation usually encountered in threatening or obscene letters. It is extremely difficult to compare handwriting that has been very carefully prepared to another document written with such little thought for structural details that it contains only the subconscious writing habits of the writer. However, although one's writing habits may be relatively easy to change for a few words or sentences, maintaining such an effort grows more difficult with each additional word.

When an adequate amount of writing is available, the attempt at total disguise may fail. This is illustrated by Clifford Irving's attempt to forge letters in the name of the late industrialist Howard Hughes in order to obtain lucrative publishing contracts for Hughes's life story. Figure 17-2 shows forged signatures of Howard Hughes along with Clifford Irving's known writings. By

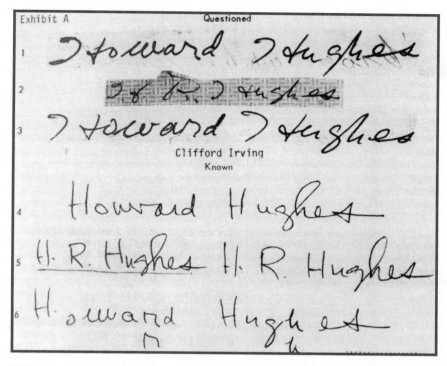

FIGURE 17-2   Forged signatures of Howard Hughes and examples of Clifford Irving's writing. *Reprinted with permission of the American Society for Testing and Materials from the* Journal of Forensic Sciences, *copyright 1975*

comparing these signatures, document examiner R. A. Cabbane of the U.S. Postal Inspection Service detected many examples of Irving's personal characteristics in the forged signatures.

For example, note the formation of the letter *r* in the word *Howard* on lines 1 and 3, compared with the composite on line 6. Observe the manner in which the terminal stroke of the letter *r* tends to terminate with a little curve at the baseline of Irving's writing and the forgery. Notice the way the bridge of the *w* drops in line 1 and also in line 6. Also, observe the similarity in the formation of the letter *g* as it appears on line 1 compared with the second signature on line 5.

The document examiner must also be aware that writing habits may be altered beyond recognition by the influence of drugs or alcohol. Under these circumstances, it may be impossible to obtain known writings of a suspect written under conditions comparable to those at the time the questioned document was prepared.

COLLECTION OF HANDWRITING EXEMPLARS

The collection of an adequate number of known writings, or **exemplars**, is critical for determining the outcome of a comparison. Generally, known writings of the suspect furnished to the examiner should be as similar as possible to the questioned document. This is especially true with respect to the writing implement and paper. Styles and habits may be somewhat altered if a person switches from a pencil to a ballpoint pen or to a fountain pen. The way the paper is ruled, or the fact that it is unruled, may also affect the handwriting of a person who has become particularly accustomed to one type or the other. Known writings should also contain some of the words and combinations of letters present in the questioned document.

exemplar
An authentic sample used for comparison purposes, such as a handwriting sample.

DATE	SIGNATURE
6/27/96	*Patrick williams*
6/28/96	*Patrick williams*
7/1/96	*Patrick williams*
7/3/96	*Patrick williams*
7/5/96	*Patrick williams*
7/8/96	*Patrick williams*
7/11/96	*Patrick williams*
7/12/96	*Patrick williams*
7/15/96	*Patrick williams*
7/17/96	*Patrick williams*
7/19/96	*Patrick williams*
7/22/96	*Patrick williams*
7/24/96	*Patrick williams*
7/26/96	*Patrick williams*
7/29/96	*Patrick williams*
7/31/96	*Patrick williams*
8/2/96	*Patrick williams*
8/5/96	*Patrick williams*
8/7/96	*Patrick williams*

FIGURE 17-3 Examples of handwriting from the same individual over an extended period of time.
Courtesy Robert J. Phillips, Document Examiner, Audobon, New Jersey

natural variations
Normal deviations found between repeated specimens of an individual's handwriting.

The known writings must be adequate in number to show the examiner the range of **natural variations** in a suspect's writing characteristics. No two specimens of writing prepared by one person are ever identical in every detail. Variation is an inherent part of natural writing. In fact, a signature forged by tracing an authentic signature can often be detected even if the original and tracing coincide exactly because no one ever signs two signatures exactly alike (see Figures 17-3 and 17-4).

Many sources are available to the investigator for establishing the authenticity of the writings of a suspect. An important consideration in selecting sample writings is the age of the genuine document relative to the questioned one. It is important to try to find standards that date closely to the questioned document. For most typical adults, basic writing changes are comparatively slow. Therefore, material written within two or three years of the disputed writing is usually satisfactory for comparison; as the time between the writing of the genuine and unknown specimens becomes greater, the standard tends to become less representative.

Despite the many potential sources of handwriting exemplars, obtaining an adequate set of collected standards may be difficult or impossible. In these

■■■■ CASEFILES ■■■■
HITLER'S DIARIES

In 1981, a spectacular manuscript attributed to Adolf Hitler was disclosed by the brother of an East German general. These documents included Hitler's twenty-seven-volume diary and an unknown third volume of his autobiography, *Mein Kampf*. The existence of these works was both culturally and politically significant to the millions who were affected by World War II.

Authentication of the diaries was undertaken by two world-renowned experts, one Swiss and one American. Both declared that the handwritten manuscripts were identical to the known samples of Adolf Hitler's handwriting that they were given. Bidding wars began for publishing rights, and a major national newspaper in the United States won with a price near $4 million.

The publishing company that originally released the documents to the world market undertook its own investigation, which ultimately revealed a clever but devious plot. The paper on which the diaries were written contained a whitener that didn't exist until 1954, long after Hitler committed suicide. The manuscript's binding threads contained viscose and polyester, neither of which was available until after World War II. Further, the inks used in the manuscript were all inconsistent with those in use during the year the pages were allegedly written.

Moreover, the exemplars sent to the Swiss and American experts as purportedly known examples of Hitler's handwriting were actually from the same source as the diaries. Thus, the experts were justified in proclaiming the documents were authentic because they were written by the same hand—it just wasn't Hitler's. Chemical analysis of the inks later determined that the "Hitler diaries" were in fact less than one year old—spectacular, but fake!

---

situations, handwriting may have to be obtained from the suspect either voluntarily or under court order. Ample case law supports the constitutionality of taking handwriting specimens. In *Gilbert* v. *California,* the Supreme Court upheld the taking of handwriting exemplars before the appointment of counsel.[1] The Court also reasoned that handwriting samples are identifying physical characteristics that lie outside the protection privileges of the Fifth Amendment. Furthermore, in *United States* v. *Mara,* the Supreme Court ruled that taking a handwriting sample did not constitute an unreasonable search and seizure of a person and hence did not violate Fourth Amendment rights.[2]

As opposed to "nonrequested specimens" (i.e., those written without the thought that they may someday be used in a police investigation), requested writing samples may be consciously altered by the writer. However, the investigator can take certain steps to minimize attempts at deception. The requirement of several pages of writing normally provides enough material that is free of nervousness or attempts at deliberate disguise for a valid comparison. In addition, writing from dictation yields exemplars that best represent the suspect's subconscious style and characteristics.

Other steps that can be taken to minimize a conscious writing effort, as well as to ensure conditions approximating those of the questioned writing, can be summarized as follows:

1. The writer should be allowed to write sitting comfortably at a desk or table and without distraction.
2. The suspect should not, under any conditions, be shown the questioned document or be told how to spell certain words or what punctuation to use.
3. The suspect should be furnished a pen and paper similar to those used in the questioned document.

FIGURE 17-4 Forged signature. The top signature is genuine. The bottom signature is a simulated forgery. The adaption to the space is incorrect; there are numerous pen lifts and over-writes. The forged signature is awkward and drawn. *Robin D. Williams*

4. The dictated text should be the same as the contents of the questioned document, or at least should contain many of the same words, phrases, and letter combinations found in the document. In handprinting cases, the suspect must not be told whether to use uppercase (capital) or lowercase (small) lettering. If, after writing several pages, the writer fails to use the desired type of lettering, he or she can then be instructed to include it. Altogether, the text must be no shorter than a page.

5. Dictation of the text should take place at least three times. If the writer is trying to disguise the writing, noticeable variations should appear among the three repetitions. Discovering this, the investigator must insist on continued repetitive dictation of the text.

6. Signature exemplars can best be obtained when the suspect is required to combine other writings with a signature. For example, instead of compiling a set of signatures alone, the writer might be asked to fill out completely twenty to thirty separate checks or receipts, each of which includes a signature.

7. Before requested exemplars are taken from the suspect, a document examiner should be consulted and shown the questioned specimens.

Quick Review

- Any object with handwriting or print whose source or authenticity is in doubt may be referred to as a "questioned document."
- Document examiners gather documents of known authorship or origin and compare them to the individual characteristics of questioned writings.
- Collecting an adequate number of known writings is critical for determining the outcome of a handwriting comparison. Known writing should contain some of the words and combinations of letters in the questioned document.
- The unconscious handwriting of two individuals can never be identical. However, the writing style of an individual may be altered beyond recognition by the influence of drugs or alcohol.

Typescript Comparisons

The document examiner analyzes not only handwritten documents but machine-created ones as well. Document-creating machines include a wide variety of devices; some examples are computer printers, photocopiers, fax machines, and typewriters.

PHOTOCOPIER, PRINTER, AND FAX EXAMINATION

With the emergence of digital technology, document examiners are confronted with a new array of machines capable of creating documents subject to alteration or fraudulent use. Personal computers use daisy wheel, dot-matrix, ink-jet, and laser printers. More and more, the document examiner encounters problems involving these machines, which often produce typed copies that have only inconspicuous defects.

In the cases of photocopiers, fax machines, and computer printers, an examiner may need to identify the make and model of the machine that may have been used in printing a document. Alternatively, the examiner may need to compare a questioned document with test samples printed from a suspect machine. Typically, the examiner generates approximately ten samples through each machine to obtain a sufficient representation of a machine's characteristics. A side-by-side comparison is then made between the questioned document and the printed exemplars to compare markings produced by the machine.

PHOTOCOPIERS   Transitory defect marks originating from random debris on the glass platen, inner cover, or mechanical portions of a copier produce images. These images are often irregularly shaped and sometimes form distinctive patterns. Thus, they become points of comparison as the document examiner attempts to link the document to suspect copiers. The gradual change, shift, or duplication of these marks may help the examiner date the document.

FAX MACHINES   Fax machines print a header known as the "transmitting terminal identifier (TTI)" at the top of each fax page. For the document examiner, the TTI is a very important point of comparison (see Figure 17-5). The header and the document's text should have different type styles. TTIs can be fraudulently prepared and placed in the appropriate position on a fax copy. However, a microscopic examination of the TTI's print quickly reveals significant characteristics that distinguish it from a genuine TTI.

In determining the fax machine's model type, the examiner usually begins by analyzing the TTI type style. The fonts of that line are determined by the sending machine. The number of characters, their style, and their position in the header are best evaluated through a collection of TTI fonts organized into a useful database. One such database is maintained by the American Society of Questioned Document Examiners.

COMPUTER PRINTERS   The determination of what model of computer printer has been used requires extensive analysis of the specific printer technology

FIGURE 17-5   A fax page showing a transmitting terminal identifier (TTI). *Pearson Education, Inc.*

and type of ink used. Visual and microscopic techniques help determine the technology and toner used. Generally printers are categorized as "impact" and "nonimpact" printers by the mechanism of their toner application. Nonimpact printers, such as ink-jet and laser printers, and impact printers, such as thermal and dot-matrix printers, all have characteristic ways of printing documents. Character shapes, toner differentiation, and toner application methods are easily determined with a low-power microscope and help the examiner narrow the possibilities of model type.

In analyzing computer printouts and faxes, examiners use the same approach for comparing the markings on a questioned document to exemplar documents generated by a suspect machine. These markings include all possible transitory patterns arising from debris and other extraneous materials. When the suspect machine is not available, the examiner may need to analyze the document's class characteristics to identify the make and model of the machine. It is important to identify the printing technology, the type of paper, the type of toner or ink used, the chemical composition of the toner, and the type of toner-to-paper fusing method used in producing the document.

Examination of the toner usually involves microscopic analysis to characterize its surface morphology, followed by identification of the inorganic and organic components of the toner. These results separate model types into categories based on their mechanical and printing characteristics. Typically, document examiners access databases to help identify the model type of machine used to prepare a questioned document. The resulting list of possibilities produced by the database hopefully reduces the number of potential machines to a manageable number. Obviously, once a suspect machine is identified, the examiner must perform a side-by-side comparison of questioned and exemplar printouts, as already described.

Quick Review

- The examiner compares the individual type character's style, shape, and size to a complete reference collection of past and present typefaces.
- Use of a printing device results in wear and damage to the machine's moving parts in a way that is both random and irregular, thereby imparting individual characteristics to it.
- Transitory defect marks originating from random debris on the glass platen, inner cover, or mechanical portions of a copier produce irregularly shaped images that may serve as points of comparison.
- A TTI, or transmitting terminal identifier, is a header at the top of each page of a fax document. It is useful in document comparison because it serves as a way to distinguish between a real and a fraudulently prepared fax document.

Alterations, Erasures, and Obliterations

Documents are often altered or changed after preparation, to hide their original intent or to perpetrate a forgery. Documents can be changed in several ways, and for each way, the application of a special discovery technique is necessary.

One of the most common ways to alter a document is to try to erase parts of it, using an India rubber eraser, sandpaper, a razor blade, or a knife to remove writing or type by abrading or scratching the paper's surface. All such attempts at **erasure** disturb the upper fibers of the paper. These changes are apparent when the suspect area is examined under a

erasure
The removal of writing, typewriting, or printing from a document, normally accomplished either by chemical means or by means of an abrasive instrument.

microscope using direct light or by allowing the light to strike the paper obliquely from one side (side lighting) (see Figure 17-6). Although microscopy may reveal whether an erasure has been made, it does not necessarily indicate the original letters or words present. Sometimes so much of the paper has been removed that identifying the original contents is impossible.

In addition to abrading the paper, the perpetrator may also choose to obliterate words with a chemical erasure. In this case, strong oxidizing agents are placed over the ink, producing a colorless reaction product. Although such an attempt may not be noticeable to the naked eye, examination under the microscope reveals a discoloration on the treated area of the paper. Sometimes examination of the document under ultraviolet or infrared lighting reveals the chemically treated portion of the paper. Interestingly, examination of documents under ultraviolet light may also reveal the presence of fluorescent ink markings that go unnoticed in room light, as seen in Figure 17-7.

FIGURE 17-6 Erasure in a checkbook deposit stub revealed by photography with the use of oblique lighting. The amount of cash deposited was changed and the difference was pocketed by the bookkeeper. *Robin D. Williams*

Another important application of infrared photography arises from the observation that inks differ in their ability to absorb infrared light. Thus, illuminating a document with infrared light and recording the light reflected off the document's surface with infrared-sensitive film enables the examiner to differentiate inks of a dissimilar chemical composition (see Figure 17-8).

Intentional **obliteration** of writing by overwriting or crossing out is seldom used for fraudulent purposes because of its obviousness. Nevertheless, such cases may be encountered in all types of documents. Success at permanently hiding the original writing depends on the material used to cover the writing. If it is done with the same ink as was used to write the original material, recovery will be difficult if not impossible. However, if the two inks are of a different chemical composition, photography with infrared-sensitive film

obliteration
Blotting out or smearing over writing or printing to make the original unreadable.

(a)

(b)

FIGURE 17-7   (a) A $20 bill as it appears under room light. (b) The bill illuminated with ultraviolet light reveals ink writing. *Sirchie Finger Print Laboratories*

(a)

(b)

FIGURE 17-8 This photograph, taken under normal illumination, shows the owner of an American Express check to be "Freda C. Brightly Jones." Actually, this signature was altered. The check initially bore the signature "Fred C. Brightly Jr." This photograph, taken under infrared illumination using infrared-sensitive film, clearly shows that the check was altered by adding *a* to *Fred* and *ones* to *Jr.* The ink used to make these changes is distinguishable because it absorbs infrared light, whereas the original ink does not. *Richard Saferstein, Ph.D.*

FIGURE 17-9 An order number was obliterated with magic marker to cover up a theft. Infrared photography was used to penetrate the covering ink to reveal the original writing. *Robin D. Williams*

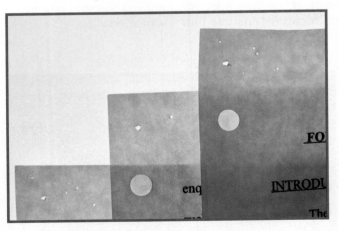

FIGURE 17-10 Staple hole exam. The middle sheet was substituted based on the evidence of staple hole pattern differences. *Jacqueline Joseph*

charred document

Any document that has become darkened and brittle through exposure to fire or excessive heat.

may reveal the original writing. Infrared radiation may pass through the upper layer of writing while being absorbed by the underlying area (see Figure 17-9).

Close examination of a questioned document sometimes reveals staple holes, crossing strokes or strokes across folds or perforations in the paper that are not in a sequence that is consistent with the natural preparation of the document. Again, these differences can be shown by microscopic or photographic scrutiny (see Figure 17-10).

Infrared photography sometimes reveals the contents of a document that has been accidentally or purposely charred in a fire. Another way to decipher **charred documents** involves reflecting light off the paper's surface at different angles in order to contrast the writing against the charred background (see Figure 17-11).

Digital image processing is the method by which the visual quality of digital pictures is improved or enhanced. "Digitizing" is the process by which the image is stored in memory. This is commonly done by scanning an image with a flatbed scanner or a digital camera and converting the image by computer into an array of digital intensity values called "pixels," or picture elements (see page 184). Once the image has been digitized, an image-editing program such as Adobe Photoshop is used to adjust the image. An image may be enhanced through lightening, darkening, and color and contrast controls. An example of how the technology is applied to forensic document examination is shown in Figures 17-12 and 17-13.

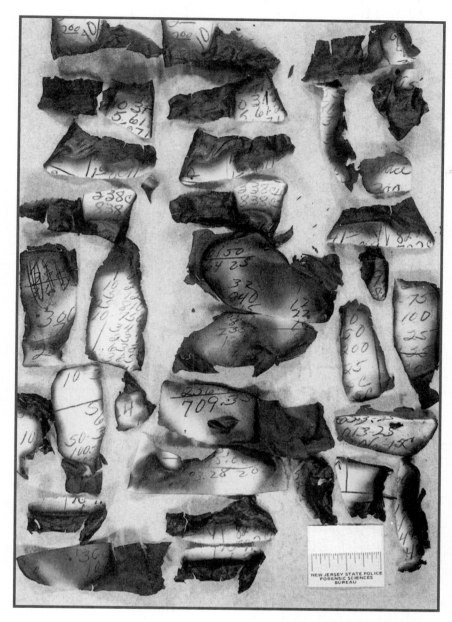

FIGURE 17-11 Decipherment of charred papers seized in the raid of a suspected bookmaking establishment. The charred documents were photographed with reflected light. *Richard Saferstein, Ph.D.*

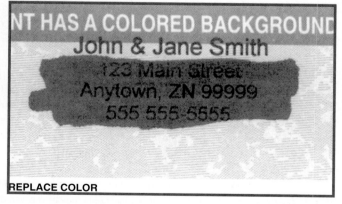

John & Jane Smith
123 Main Street
Anytown, ZN 99999
555 555-5555

LEVELS

NT HAS A COLORED BACKGROUND
John & Jane Smith
123 Main Street
Anytown, ZN 99999
555 555-5555

REPLACE COLOR

FIGURE 17-12 (a) This composite demonstrates the various changes that can be applied to a digitized image to reveal information that has been obscured. Using photo-editing software (in this case, Adobe Photoshop), the original was duplicated and pasted as a second layer. Colors were changed in selected areas of the image using the "screen" and "exclusion" options. "Replace color" allows the user to choose a specific color or range of colors and lighten, darken, or change the hue of the colors selected. "Level" and "curves" tools can adjust the lightest and darkest color ranges and optimize contrast, highlights, and shadow detail of the image for additional clarity. *Bob Garrett, IDMAN Forensics*

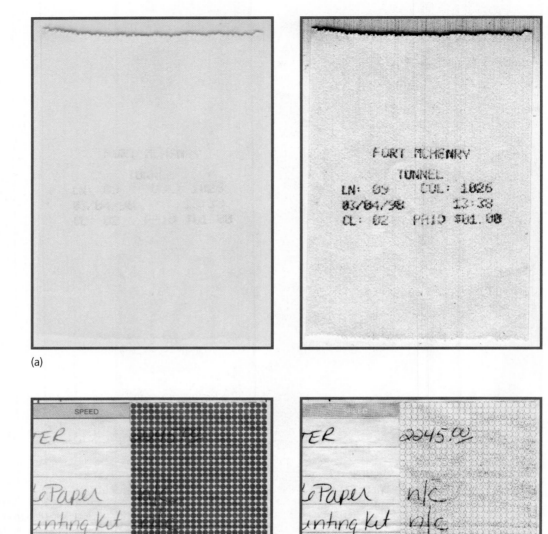

(a)

(b)

FIGURE 17-13 (a) Receipts are used in investigations to establish a victim's whereabouts, provide suspects with alibis, and substantiate a host of personal conduct. Unfortunately, because of wear, age, or poor printing by the register, receipts are often unreadable. This can be corrected using photo-editing software. In this example, the original toll receipt was scanned at the highest color resolution, which allows more than 17 million colors to be reproduced. The image was then manipulated, revealing the printed details, by adjusting the lightest and darkest levels and the color content of the image. (b) Invoices may contain details about a transaction that are important to an investigation. The copy that ships with the merchandise may have that information blocked out. This information may be recovered using digital imaging. The figure on the left shows the original shipping ticket. The figure on the right shows the information revealed after replacing the color of the blocking pattern.
Bob Garrett, IDMAN Forensics

Other Document Problems

Document examiners encounter other challenges when analyzing questioned documents, including visualizing writing pressed or indented into a surface and analyzing the inks and paper used in suspect documents.

INDENTED WRITINGS

Indented writings are the partially visible depressions on a sheet of paper that was underneath the one on which the visible writing appears while it was being written on. Such depressions form due to the application of pressure on the writing instrument during writing; for example, the indented writing would appear as a carbon copy of the top sheet if carbon paper had been inserted between the pages.

Indented writings have proved to be valuable evidence. For example, the top sheet of a bookmaker's records may have been removed and destroyed, but it still may be possible to determine what writing this sheet contained by the impressions left on the pad. These impressions may contain incriminating evidence supporting the charge of illegal gambling activities. When paper is studied under oblique or side lighting, its indented impressions are often readable.

An innovative approach to visualizing indented writings has been developed at the London College of Printing in close consultation with the Metropolitan Police Forensic Science Laboratory. The method involves applying an electrostatic charge to the surface of a polymer film that has been placed in contact with a questioned document, as shown in Figure 17-14. Indented impressions on the document are revealed by applying a toner powder to the charged film. For many documents examined by this process, clearly readable images have been produced from impressions that could not be seen or were barely visible under normal illumination. An instrument that develops indented writings by electrostatic detection is commercially available and is routinely used by document examiners.

indented writings
Impressions left on paper positioned under a piece of paper that has been written on.

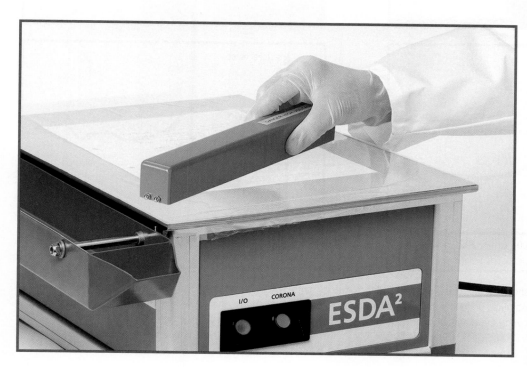

FIGURE 17-14 An electrostatic detection apparatus (ESDA) works by applying an electrostatic charge to a document suspected of containing indented writings. The indentations are then visualized by the application of charge-sensitive toner. *Foster and Freeman USA, Inc.*

INK AND PAPER COMPARISONS

An analysis of the chemical composition of writing ink present on documents may verify whether known and questioned documents were prepared by the same pen. A nondestructive approach to comparing ink lines is accomplished with a visible microspectrophotometer (see page 336). An example of this approach is shown in Figure 17-15, in which the microspectrophotometer is used to distinguish counterfeit and authentic currency by comparing the spectral

FIGURE 17-15 Two $50 bills are shown at top; one is genuine and the other is counterfeit. Below each bill is a micrograph of an inked line present on each bill. Each line was examined under a visible-light microspectrophotometer. As shown, the visible light absorption spectrum of each line is readily differentiated, thus allowing the examiner to distinguish the counterfeit bill from genuine currency. *Pfefferli, Dr. Peter W; SAFERSTEIN, RICHARD, Ph.D., CRIMINALISTICS: AN INTRODUCTION TO FORENSIC SCIENCE, 11th Ed., © 2015. Reprinted and Electronically reproduced by permission of Pearson Education, Inc., Upper Saddle River, New Jersey.*

patterns of inked lines on the paper. Thin-layer chromatography is also suitable for ink comparisons. Most commercial inks, especially ballpoint inks, are actually mixtures of several organic dyes. These dyes can be separated on a properly developed thin-layer chromatographic plate. The separation pattern of the component dyes is distinctly different for inks with different dye compositions and thus provides many points of comparison between a known and a questioned ink.

FIGURE 17-16 A chart demonstrating different TLC patterns of blue ballpoint inks. *U.S. Secret Service*

Ink can be removed from paper with a hypodermic needle with a blunted point used to punch out a small sample from a written line. About ten plugs, or microdots, of ink are sufficient for chromatographic analysis. The United States Secret Service and the Internal Revenue Service jointly maintain the United States International Ink Library. This collection includes more than 8,500 inks, some of which date back to the 1920s. Each year new pen and ink formulations are added to the reference collection. These inks have been systematically cataloged according to dye patterns developed by thin-layer chromatography (TLC; see Figure 17-16). On several occasions, this approach has been used to prove that a document has been fraudulently backdated. For example, in one instance, it was possible to establish that a document dated 1958 was backdated because a dye identified in the questioned ink had not been synthesized until 1959.

To further aid forensic chemists in ink-dating matters, several ink manufacturers, at the request of the U.S. Treasury Department, voluntarily tag their inks during the manufacturing process. The tagging program allows inks to be dated to the exact year of manufacture because the tags are changed annually.

Another area of inquiry for the document examiner is the paper on which a document is written or printed. Paper is often made from cellulose fibers found in wood and fibers recovered from recycled paper products. The most common features associated with a paper examination are general appearance, color, weight, and watermarks (see Figure 17-17). Other areas of examination include fiber identification and the characterization of additives, fillers, and pigments present in the paper product.

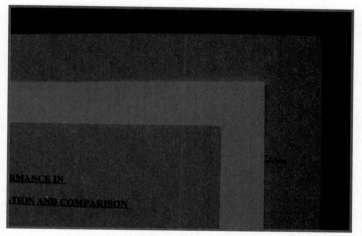

FIGURE 17-17 Ultra-violet light exam revealing a substituted document. The middle sheet was differentiated from the upper and lower sheets by exposure to UV light. *Jacqueline Joseph*

Quick Review

- Document examiners deal with evidence that has been changed in several ways, such as through alterations, erasures, and obliterations.
- A digitized image can be lightened or darkened, and its color and contrast adjusted, with appropriate software.
- It may be possible to read indented writing—the impressions left on a paper pad—by applying an electrostatic charge to the surface of a polymer film that has been placed in contact with a questioned document.
- Studying the chemical composition of writing ink present on documents may verify whether known and questioned documents were prepared by the same pen.

VIRTUAL LAB
THIN-LAYER CHROMATOGRAPHY OF INKS
To perform a virtual thin-layer chromatography analysis, go to *www.pearsoncustom.com/us/vlm/*

CHAPTER REVIEW

- Any object with handwriting or print whose source or authenticity is in doubt may be referred to as a "questioned document."

- Document examiners gather documents of known authorship or origin and compare them to the individual characteristics of questioned writings.

- Collecting an adequate number of known writings is critical for determining the outcome of a handwriting comparison. Known writing should contain some of the words and combinations of letters in the questioned document.

- The unconscious handwriting of two individuals can never be identical. However, the writing style of an individual may be altered beyond recognition by the influence of drugs or alcohol.

- The examiner compares the individual type character's style, shape, and size to a complete reference collection of past and present typefaces.

- Use of a printing device results in wear and damage to the machine's moving parts in a way that is both random and irregular, thereby imparting individual characteristics to it.

- Transitory defect marks originating from random debris on the glass platen, inner cover, or mechanical portions of a copier produce irregularly shaped images that may serve as points of comparison.

- A TTI, or transmitting terminal identifier, is a header at the top of each page of a fax document. It is useful in document comparison because it serves as a way to distinguish between a real and a fraudulently prepared fax document.

- Document examiners deal with evidence that has been changed in several ways, such as through alterations, erasures, and obliterations.

- A digitized image can be lightened or darkened, and its color and contrast adjusted, with appropriate software.

- It may be possible to read indented writing—the impressions left on a paper pad—by applying an electrostatic charge to the surface of a polymer film that has been placed in contact with a questioned document.

- Studying the chemical composition of writing ink present on documents may verify whether known and questioned documents were prepared by the same pen.

KEY TERMS

charred document, 450

erasure, 448

exemplar, 443

indented writings, 453

natural variations, 444

obliteration, 449

questioned document, 440

REVIEW QUESTIONS

1. Any object that contains handwriting or typescript and whose source or authenticity is in doubt is referred to as a(n) _____.

2. True or False: Our general style of handwriting develops as a result of our attempts in childhood to copy letters that match a standard form or style shown to us by our teachers. _____

3. True or False: Variations in mechanical, physical, and mental functions make it unlikely that the writing of two individuals can be distinguished. _____

4. In a problem involving the authorship of handwriting, all characteristics of both the _____ and _____ documents must be considered and compared.

5. True or False: A single handwriting characteristic can by itself be taken as a basis for a positive comparison. _____

6. Handwriting examples may have a crude, unnatural form or be written very carefully to disguise the writer's natural _____.

7. Known examples of writings, called _____, must be collected in order to determine the outcome of a comparison.

8. As the age difference between genuine and unknown specimens becomes greater, the standard tends to become _____ representative of the unknown.

9. True or False: Two or more specimens of writing prepared by one person are identical in every detail. _____

10. In the Supreme Court case of _____, the Court upheld the taking of handwriting exemplars before the appointment of counsel and determined handwriting to be nontestimonial evidence not protected by Fifth Amendment privileges.

11. True or False: Normally, known writings need not contain words and combinations of letters present in the questioned document. _____

12. When requested writing is being given by a suspect, care must be taken to minimize a(n) _____ writing effort.

13. An examiner should generate approximately _____ samples through a questioned photocopier, printer, or fax machine to obtain a sufficient representation of a machine's characteristics.

14. A fax machine prints a kind of header known as a _____ at the top of each page it prints, which can be used for comparison and authentication purposes.

15. Examination of a printer's _____ involves microscopic analysis and the identification of organic and inorganic components.

16. Examination of a document under _____ or _____ lighting may reveal chemical erasures of words or numbers.

17. Handwriting containing inks of different chemical compositions may be distinguished by photography with _____ film.

18. True or False: If obliteration of writing is carried out with the same ink as was used to write the original material, recovery will be difficult if not impossible. _____

19. Infrared photography can also be used to visualize writing on paper that has been accidentally or purposely _____ in a fire.

20. _____ writings are partially visible impressions that appear on a sheet of paper that, at the time of writing, was underneath the one on which the visible writing was done.

21. When comparing the chemical composition of ink lines on a questioned document, a(n) _____ can be used without destroying the document.

22. Many ink dyes can be separated by the technique of _____ chromatography.

23. True or False: Examination of the paper of a questioned document is based on general appearance, color, weight, and watermarks. _____

APPLICATION AND CRITICAL THINKING

1. Criminalist Julie Sandel is investigating a series of threatening notes written in pencil and sent to a local politician. A suspect is arrested, and Julie directs the suspect to prepare writing samples to compare to the writing on the notes. She has the suspect sit at a desk in an empty office and gives him a pen and a piece of paper. She begins to read one of the notes and asks the suspect to write the words she dictates. After reading about half a page, she stops, then dictates the same part of the note a second time for the suspect. At one point, the suspect indicates that he does not know how to spell one of the words, so Julie spells it for him. After completing the task, Julie takes the original notes and the dictated writing from the suspect to a document examiner. What mistakes, if any, did Julie make?

2. In each of the following situations, indicate how you would go about recovering original writing that is not visible to the naked eye.
   a) The original words have been obliterated with a different ink than was used to compose the original.
   b) The original words have been obliterated by chemical erasure.
   c) The original writing was made with fluorescent ink.
   d) The original documents have been charred or burned.

3. You have been asked to determine whether a handwritten will, supposedly prepared thirty years ago, is authentic or a modern forgery. What aspects of the document would you examine to make this determination? Explain how you would use thin-layer chromatography to help you come to your conclusion.

ENDNOTES

1. 388 U.S. 263 (1967).

2. 410 U.S. 19 (1973).

18 Computer Forensics

Andrew W. Donofrio

LEARNING OBJECTIVES

After studying this chapter, you should be able to:

- List and describe the hardware and software components of a computer.
- Understand the difference between read-only memory and random-access memory.
- Describe how a hard disk drive is partitioned.
- Describe the proper procedure for preserving computer evidence at a crime scene.
- Understand the difference between and location of visible and latent data.
- List the areas of the computer that will be examined to retrieve forensic data.
- Relate various areas found on the computer where a user's Internet activities can be investigated.
- Describe how e-mails, chat, and instant messages on the Internet can be traced and recovered.
- List and describe three locations where investigators may pinpoint the origin of a hacker.
- Describe the types of services offered by modern mobile devices, such as cell phones, and the potential investigative value they have.

THE BTK KILLER

Dennis Rader was arrested in February 2005 and charged with committing ten murders since 1974 in the area around Wichita, Kansas. The BTK killer, whose nickname stands for "bind, torture, kill," hadn't murdered since 1991, but resurfaced in early 2004 when he sent a letter to a local newspaper taking credit for a 1986 slaying. Included with the letter were a photocopy of the victim's driver's license and three photos of her body. The BTK killer was back to his old habit of taunting the police. Three months later, another letter surfaced. This time the letter detailed some of the events surrounding BTK's first murder victims. In 1974, he had strangled Joseph and Julie Otero along with two of their children. Shortly after committing those murders, BTK had also sent a letter to a local newspaper in which he gave himself the name "BTK." In December 2004, a package found in a park contained the driver's license of another BTK victim along with a doll whose hands were bound with pantyhose and covered with a plastic bag.

The major break in the case came when BTK sent a message on a floppy disk to a local TV station. "Erased" information on the disk was recovered and restored by forensic computer specialists, and the disk was traced to the Christ Lutheran Church in Wichita. The disk was then quickly linked to Dennis Rader, the church council president. The long odyssey of searching for the BTK killer was finally over.

Since the 1990s, few fields have progressed as rapidly as computer technology. Computers are no longer a luxury, nor are they in the hands of just a select few. Technology and electronic data are a part of everyday life and permeate all aspects of society. Consequently, computers have become increasingly important as sources of evidence in an ever-widening spectrum of criminal activities. Moreover, on the corporate side, issues of regulatory compliance, such as HIPAA and Sarbanes-Oxley, and problems of employee misconduct have made IT investigations and data forensics a necessary component of a company's security program.

Police investigators frequently encounter computers and other digital devices in all types of cases. As homicide investigators sift for clues, they may inquire, for example, whether the method for a murder was researched on the Internet, whether signs of an extramarital affair can be found in e-mails or remnants of instant messages (which may provide a motive for a spouse killing or murder for hire), or whether threats were communicated to the victim before a murder by an obsessed stalker. Arson investigators may want to know whether financial records on a computer show a motive for an arson-for-profit fire. A burglary investigation would certainly be aided if law enforcement could show that the proceeds from a theft were being sold online—perhaps through eBay or a similar online auction site.

In addition, the use of computers poses some threats of its own. The accessibility of computers to children and the perception of anonymity in online interactions have given sexual predators a way to seek out child victims online. The vulnerability of computers to hacker attacks is a constant reminder of security issues surrounding digitally stored data. Finally, the fact that computers control most of our critical infrastructure makes technology an appetizing target for would-be terrorists.

Computer forensics involves the preservation, acquisition, extraction, analysis, and interpretation of computer data. Although this is a simple definition, it gets a bit more complicated. Part of this complication arises from technology itself. More and more devices are capable of storing electronic data: cell phones, personal digital assistants (PDAs), iPods, digital cameras, flash memory cards, smart cards, jump drives, and many others. Further complicating matters is the cross-pollination of devices. Cell phones now have the same capabilities as personal computers, and personal computers are often used to facilitate communications. Methods for extracting data from each of these devices present unique challenges. However, sound forensic practices apply to all these devices. The most logical place to start to examine these practices is with the most common form of electronic data: the personal computer.

From Input to Output:
How Does the Computer Work?

HARDWARE VERSUS SOFTWARE

Before we get into the nuts and bolts of computers, we must establish the important distinction between hardware and software. **Hardware** comprises

hardware
The physical components of a computer: case, keyboard, monitor, motherboard, RAM, HDD, mouse, and so on; generally speaking, if it is a computer component you can touch, it is hardware.

Andrew W. Donofrio is a retired detective lieutenant from the prosecutor's office in Bergen County, New Jersey, and is a leading computer forensics examiner for Bergen County, with more than twenty-three years of experience in the field of law enforcement. He has conducted hundreds of forensic examinations of computer evidence and frequently lectures on the subject throughout the state, as well as teaching multiday courses on computer forensics and investigative topics at police academies, colleges, and corporations throughout the United States. Mr. Donofrio now owns Cyberology Consultants, which provides IT investigation, computer and network forensics, and business continuity and disaster recovery planning services.

Computer case/chassis CPU External drive

RAM

Expansion bus
with expansion card

ROM

Power supply

CD/DVD drive

Floppy disk drive

Hard disk drive

FIGURE 18-1 Cutaway diagram of a personal computer showing the tangible hardware components of a computer system. *SAFERSTEIN, RICHARD, Ph.D., CRIMINALISTICS: AN INTRODUCTION TO FORENSIC SCIENCE, 11th Ed., ©2015. Reprinted and Electronically reproduced by permission of Pearson Education, Inc., Upper Saddle River, New Jersey*

software
A set of instructions compiled into a program that performs a particular task; software consists of programs and applications that carry out a set of instructions on the hardware.

the physical components of the computer: the computer chassis, monitor, keyboard, mouse, hard disk drive, random-access memory (RAM), central processing unit (CPU), and so on (see Figure 18-1). The list is extensive, but, generally speaking, if it is a computer component or peripheral that you can see, feel, and touch, then it is hardware.

Software, conversely, is a set of instructions compiled into a program that performs a particular task. Software consists of programs and applications that carry out a set of instructions on the hardware. Operating systems (e.g., Windows, Mac OS, Linux, Unix), word-processing programs (e.g., Microsoft Word, WordPerfect), Web-browsing applications (e.g., Internet Explorer, Safari, Firefox), and accounting applications (e.g., Quicken, QuickBooks, Microsoft Money) are all examples of software.

It is important not to confuse software with the physical media that it comes on. When you buy an application such as Microsoft Office, it comes on a compact disc (CD). The CD containing this suite of applications is typically referred to as software, but this is technically wrong. The CD is external computer media that contains the software; it is a container for a set of instructions and a medium from which to load the instructions onto the hard disk drive (i.e., the hardware).

HARDWARE COMPONENTS

COMPUTER CASE/CHASSIS The case is the physical box holding the fixed internal computer components in place. Cases come in many shapes and sizes: a full upright tower chassis, a slim model sitting on a desktop, or an all-in-one monitor/computer case like the iMac. For our purposes, the term "system unit" is probably most appropriate when describing a chassis seized as evidence. The term "system unit" accurately references the chassis, including the motherboard and other internal components.

POWER SUPPLY   The term "power supply" is actually a misnomer because it doesn't actually supply power—the power company does that. Rather, a computer's power supply converts power from the wall outlet to a usable format for the computer and its components. Different power supplies have different wattage ratings. The use or, more specifically, the components of the computer dictate the appropriate power supply.

MOTHERBOARD   The main circuit board in a computer (or other electronic device) is referred to as the **motherboard**. Motherboards contain sockets for chips and slots for add-on cards. Examples of add-on cards are the video card to connect the computer to the monitor, a network card or modem to connect to an internal network or the Internet, and a sound card to connect to speakers. Sockets on the motherboard typically accept things like random-access memory (RAM) or the central processing unit (CPU). The keyboard, mouse, CD-ROM drives, floppy disk drives, monitor, and other peripherals or components connect to the motherboard in some fashion through a wired or wireless connection.

motherboard
The main system board of a computer (and many other electronic devices), which delivers power, data, and instructions to the computer's components; every component in the computer connects to the motherboard, either directly or indirectly.

SYSTEM BUS   Contained on the motherboard, the "system bus" is a vast, complex network of wires that carry data from one hardware device to another. This network is analogous to a complex highway. Data is sent along the bus in the form of ones and zeros (or, to be accurate, as electrical impulses representing an "on" or "off" state); this two-state form of data is known as "binary computing."

READ-ONLY MEMORY (ROM)   This rather generic term describes special chips on the motherboard. ROM chips store programs called "firmware," used to start the boot process and configure a computer's components. Today's ROM chips, termed "flash ROM," are a combination of two types of chips used in past motherboard technologies. The first was known as the "system ROM," which was responsible for booting the system and handling the "assumed" system hardware present in the computer. As the system ROM, generally speaking, could not be altered, and because as technology matured changes to the "assumed" hardware were more common, a different type of chip was introduced. The "complementary metal-oxide semiconductor (CMOS)" was a separate chip that allowed the user to exercise setup control over several system components. Regardless of how this technology is present on the motherboard, it can be referred to as the BIOS, for "basic input-output system." The operation of the BIOS is relevant to several computer forensic procedures, particularly the boot sequence. It is the set of routines associated with the BIOS in ROM that initiates the booting process and enables the computer to communicate with various devices in the system such as disk drives, keyboard, monitor, and printer. As this chapter will make clear, it is important not to boot the actual computer under investigation to the original hard disk drive. This would cause changes to the data, thus compromising the integrity of evidence. The BIOS allows investigators to control the boot process to some degree.

CENTRAL PROCESSING UNIT (CPU)   The **central processing unit (CPU)**, also referred to as a "processor," is essentially the "brain" of the computer. It is the main (and typically the largest) chip that plugs into a socket on the motherboard. The CPU is the part of the computer that actually computes. Basically, all operations performed by the computer are run through the CPU.

central processing unit (CPU)
The main chip within the computer, also referred to as the "brain" of the computer, which handles most of the operations (i.e., code and instructions) of the computer.

The CPU carries out the program steps to perform a requested task. That task can range from opening and working in a Microsoft Word document to performing advanced mathematical algorithms. CPUs come in various shapes, sizes, and types. Intel Pentium chips and Advanced Micro Devices (AMD) chips are among the most common.

RANDOM-ACCESS MEMORY (RAM)   This is one of the most widely mentioned types of computer memory. **Random-access memory (RAM)** takes the burden off the computer's processor and hard disk drive (HDD). If the computer had to access the HDD each time it wanted data, it would run slowly and inefficiently. Instead the computer, aware that it may need certain data at a moment's notice, stores the data in RAM. It is helpful to envision RAM as chips that create a large spreadsheet, with each cell representing a memory address that the CPU can use as a reference to retrieve data. RAM is referred to as "volatile memory" because it is not permanent; its contents undergo constant change and are lost once power is taken away from the computer. RAM takes the physical form of chips that plug into the motherboard; SIMMs (single inline memory modules), DIMMs (dual inline memory modules), and SDRAM (synchronous dynamic random-access memory) are just a few of the types of chips. Today's computers come with varying amounts of RAM: 2 to 4 GB (gigabytes) is the most common capacity.[1]

INPUT DEVICES   Input devices are used to get data into the computer or to give the computer instructions. Input devices constitute part of the "user" side of the computer. Examples include the keyboard, mouse, joystick, and scanner.

OUTPUT DEVICES   Output devices are equipment through which data is obtained from the computer. Output devices are also part of the "user" side of the computer, and provide the results of the user's tasks. They include the monitor, printer, and speakers.

HARD DISK DRIVE (HDD)   Generally speaking, the **hard disk drive (HDD)** is the primary component of storage in the personal computer (see Figure 18-2). It typically stores the operating system (e.g., Windows, Mac OS, Linux, or Unix), the programs (e.g., Microsoft Word, Internet Explorer, Open Office for Linux) and data files created by the user (i.e., documents, spreadsheets, accounting information, the company database, etc.). Unlike RAM, the HDD is permanent storage and retains its information even after the power is turned off. HDDs work off a controller that is typically part of the motherboard, but sometimes take the form of an add-on (expansion) card plugged into the motherboard. The most common types of HDD controllers are integrated drive electronics (IDE), small computer system interface (SCSI), and serial ATA (SATA). Each HDD type has a different interface that connects it to the controller. Regardless of the type of controller, the data is stored in basically the same fashion. HDDs are mapped, or formatted, and have a defined layout. They are logically divided into sectors, clusters, tracks, and cylinders (see the section "Storing and Retrieving Data").

PUTTING IT ALL TOGETHER

A person approaches the computer, sits down, and presses the power button. The power supply wakes up and delivers power to the motherboard and all of the hardware connected to the computer. At this point the flash ROM chip on the motherboard (the one that contains the BIOS) conducts a power-on self test (POST) to make sure everything is working properly.

The flash ROM also polls the motherboard to check the hardware that is attached and follows its programmed boot order, thus determining from what device it should boot. Typically the boot device is the HDD, but it can also be a CD or USB drive. If it is the HDD, the HDD is then given control. It locates the first sector of its disk (known as the "master boot record"), determines its

---

random-access memory (RAM)
The volatile memory of a computer, where programs and instructions that are in use are stored; when power is turned off, its contents are lost.

hard disk drive (HDD)
Typically the main storage location within the computer, which consists of magnetic platters contained in a case (usually 3.5" long in a desktop computer and 2.5" in a laptop) and is usually where the operating system, applications, and user data are stored.

FIGURE 18-2 An inside view of the platter and read/write head of a hard disk drive. *Corbis*

layout (i.e., (partition[s]), and boots an operating system (e.g., Windows, Mac OS, Linux, or Unix). The person is then presented with a computer work environment, commonly referred to as a "desktop."

Now ready to work, the user double-clicks an icon on the desktop, such as a Microsoft Word shortcut, to open the program and begins to type a document. The CPU processes this request, locates the Microsoft Word program on the HDD (using a predefined map of the drive called a "file system table"), carries out the programming instructions associated with the application, loads Microsoft Word into RAM via the system bus, and sends the output to the monitor by way of the video controller, which is either located on or attached to the motherboard.

The user then begins to type, transferring data from the keyboard into RAM. When finished, the user may print the document or simply save it to the HDD for later retrieval. If printed, the data is taken from RAM, processed by the CPU, placed in a format suitable for printing, and sent through the system bus to the external port where the printer is connected. If the document is saved, the data is taken from RAM, processed by the CPU, passed to the HDD controller (i.e., IDE, SCSI, or SATA) by way of the system bus, and written to a portion of the HDD. The HDD's file system table is updated so it knows where to retrieve that data later. In actuality, the boot process is more complex than this, and the forensic examiner must possess an in-depth knowledge of the process.

The preceding example illustrates how three components perform most of the work: the CPU, RAM, and system bus. The example can get even more complicated as the user opens more applications and performs multiple tasks simultaneously (i.e., "multitasks"). Several tasks can be loaded into RAM at once, and the CPU is capable of juggling them all. This allows for a multitasking environment and the ability to switch back and forth between applications. All of this is orchestrated by the operating system and is written in the language of the computer—ones and zeros. The only detail missing, one that is important from a forensic standpoint, is a better understanding of how data is stored on the hard disk drive. This is discussed next.

CLOSER ANALYSIS
OTHER COMMON STORAGE DEVICES

Although the HDD is the most common storage device for the personal computer, many others exist. Methods for storing data and the layout of that data can vary from device to device. A CD-ROM, for example, uses a different technology and format for writing data than a smart media card or USB thumb drive. Fortunately, regardless of the differences among devices, the same basic forensic principles apply for acquiring the data. Common storage devices include the following:

CD-R/RW (Compact Disc—Record/Rewrite) and DVD-R/RW (DVD— Record/Rewrite)   Compact discs (CDs) and digital video discs (DVDs) are two of the most common forms of external data storage. They are used to store a wide variety of information, such as music, video, and data files. They are discs made largely of plastic, with an aluminum layer that is read by laser light in a CD/DVD reader. Blu-Ray discs have also emerged in the market offering larger storage capacity than their predecessor optical media. In addition to larger storage capacities, Blu-Ray discs are read by a blue laser light instead of the red laser that reads CDs and DVDs. Different optical media are encoded in different ways, making the job of the forensic examiner difficult at times.

USB Thumb Drives and Smart Media Cards   These devices can store a large amount of data—some as much as 64 GB. They are known as "solid-state storage devices" because they have no moving parts. Smart media cards are typically found in digital cameras, mobile devices, and PDAs, but USB thumb drives come in many shapes, sizes, and storage capacities.

Tapes   Tapes come in many different formats and storage capacities. Each typically comes with its own hardware reader and, sometimes, a proprietary application to read and write its contents. Tapes and thumb drives are typically used for backup purposes and consequently have great forensic potential.

Network Interface Card (NIC)   Very rarely does one encounter a computer today that doesn't have a NIC. Whether they are on a local network or the Internet, when computers need to communicate with each other, they typically do so through a NIC. NICs come in many different forms: add-on cards that plug into the motherboard, hard-wired devices on the motherboard, add-on cards (PCMCIA) for laptops, and universal serial bus (USB) plug-in cards, to name a few. Some are wired cards, meaning they need a physical wired connection to participate on the network, and others are wireless, meaning they receive their data via radio waves.

Quick Review

- Computer forensics involves preserving, acquiring, extracting, and interpreting computer data.
- Software programs are applications that carry out a set of instructions.
- The central processing unit (CPU) is the "brain" of the computer—the main chip responsible for doing the actual computing.
- The motherboard is the main circuit board within a computer.
- Read-only memory (ROM) chips store programs that control the boot (startup) process and configure a computer's components.
- Random-access memory (RAM) is volatile memory, which is frequently lost when power is turned off. Programs are loaded into RAM because of its faster read speed.
- The hard disk drive (HDD) is typically the primary location of data storage within the computer.

operating system (OS)
The software that provides the bridge between the system hardware and the user; the OS lets the user interact with the hardware and manages the file system and applications. Some examples are Windows (XP, Vista, and Windows 7), Linux, and Mac OS.

Storing and Retrieving Data

Before beginning to understand how data is stored on a hard disk drive (HDD), it is first important to understand the role of the **operating system (OS)**. An OS, such as Windows, Mac OS, Linux, or Unix, is the bridge between the human user and the computer's electronic components. It provides the user with a working environment and facilitates interaction with the system's components. Each OS supports certain types of file systems that store data in different ways.

FORMATTING AND PARTITIONING THE HDD

Generally speaking, before an OS can write to an HDD, it must first be formatted. But even before it can be formatted, a partition must be defined. A **partition** is nothing more than a contiguous set of blocks that are defined and treated as an independent disk. This means that a hard disk drive can hold several partitions, making a single HDD appear as several disks.

Partitioning a drive can be thought of as dividing a container that begins as nothing more than six sides. We then cut a hole in the front of the container and insert two drawers and the hardware required to open and close them. We have just created a two-drawer filing cabinet and defined each drawer as contiguous blocks of storage. A partitioning utility such as Disk Manager or fdisk defines the drawer or drawers (i.e., partitions) that will later hold the data on the HDD. Just as the style, size, and shape of filing cabinet drawers can vary, so too can partitions.

After a hard drive is partitioned, typically it is formatted. (At this point this would be high-level formatting, not to be confused with low-level formatting, which is generally done by the manufacturer of the HDD.) The formatting process initializes portions of the HDD and creates the structure of the file system. The file system can be thought of as the system for storing and locating data on a storage device. Some of the file system types are FAT12 (typically on floppy disks), FAT16 (older DOS and older Windows partitions), FAT32 (Windows file systems), NTFS (most current Windows systems—2008 Windows 7, and XP), EXT2 and EXT3 (Linux systems), and HPFS (some Macintosh systems).

Each of these file systems has a different way of storing, retrieving, and allocating data. In summary, a drive is prepared in three processes: low-level formatting (typically done by the manufacturer, dividing the platters into tracks and sectors), partitioning (accomplished through a utility such as fdisk or Disk Manager, defining a contiguous set of blocks), and formatting (i.e., initializing portions of the disk and creating the file system structure). The process is a bit more technical and detailed than this, but at the conclusion of these basic steps, the drive is logically defined. (We say "logically" because no real divisions are made. That is, if you were to crack open the HDD before or after partitioning and formatting, to your naked eye the platters would look the same.)

MAPPING THE HDD

As shown in Figure 18-3, HDDs contain several platters stacked vertically that are logically divided into sectors, clusters, tracks, and cylinders. **Sectors** are typically 512 bytes in size (a **byte** is eight bits; a **bit** is a single one or zero). (Currently, work is being done on hard disk drives with increased minimum sector sizes, in an effort to increase drive performance. However, at this time, 512 bytes is still the standard for most hard disk drives.) **Clusters** are groups of sectors; their size is defined by the file system, but they are always in sector multiples of two. (Although an NTFS partition does permit a one-sector-per-cluster scenario, such a scenario is not usually chosen.) A cluster, therefore, consists of two, four, six, or eight sectors, and so on. (With modern file systems, the user can exercise some control over the number of sectors per cluster.) "Tracks" are concentric circles that are defined around the platter. "Cylinders" are groups of tracks that reside directly above and below each other.

Additionally, the HDD has a file system table, or map, of the layout of the defined space in that partition. FAT file systems use a "file allocation table" (which is where the acronym "FAT" comes from) to track the location of files and folders

partition
A contiguous set of blocks that are defined and treated as an independent disk.

sector
The smallest addressable unit of data by a hard disk drive; generally consists of 512 bytes.

byte
A group of eight bits.

bit
Short for "binary digit"; taking the form of either a one or a zero, it is the smallest unit of information on a machine.

cluster
A group of sectors in multiples of two; cluster size varies from file system to file system and is typically the minimum space allocated to a file.

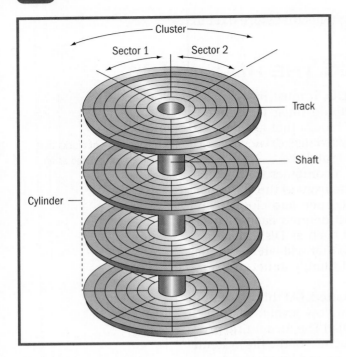

FIGURE 18-3 Partitions of a hard disk drive. *SAFERSTEIN, RICHARD, Ph.D., CRIMINALISTICS: AN INTRODUCTION TO FORENSIC SCIENCE, 11th Ed., ©2015. Reprinted and Electronically reproduced by permission of Pearson Education, Inc., Upper Saddle River, New Jersey*

(i.e., data) on the HDD, whereas NTFS file systems (used by most current Windows systems—Vista, XP, and Windows 7) use, among other things, a "master file table (MFT)." Each file system table tracks data in different ways, and computer forensic examiners should be versed in the technical nuances of the HDDs they examine. It is sufficient for our purposes here, however, to merely visualize the file system table as a map where the data is located. This map uses the numbering of sectors, clusters, tracks, and cylinders to keep track of the data.

One way to envision a partition and file system is as a room full of safe-deposit boxes. The room itself symbolizes the entire partition, and the boxes symbolize clusters of data. In order to determine who rented which box, and where each renter's property is, a central database is needed. This would be especially necessary if a person rented two boxes located in opposite ends of the room (this would be noncontiguous data on the HDD). The database tracking the locations of the safe-deposit boxes is much like a file system table tracking the location of data within the clusters.

This example is also useful for understanding the concept of reformatting an HDD. If the database managing the locations of the safe-deposit boxes were wiped out, the property in them would still remain; we just wouldn't know what was where. It is the same with the hard disk drive. If a user were to wipe the file system table clean—for example, by reformatting it—the data itself would not be gone. Both the database tracking the locations of the safe-deposit boxes and the file system table tracking the location of the data in the cluster are maps—they are not actual contents. (Exceptions exist with some file systems, such as an NTFS file system, which stores data for very small files right in its file system table, known as the "master file table").

Quick Review

- The computer's operating system (OS) is the bridge between the human user and the computer's electronic components. It provides the user with a working environment and facilitates interaction with the system's components.
- Formatting is the process of preparing a hard disk drive to store and retrieve data in its current form.
- A sector is the smallest unit of data that a hard drive can address. A cluster usually is the minimum space allocated to a file. Clusters are groups of sectors.
- A FAT is a file allocation table. It tracks the location of files and folders on the hard disk drive.

Processing the Electronic Crime Scene

Processing the electronic crime scene has a lot in common with processing a traditional crime scene. The investigator must first ensure that the proper legal requirements (e.g., search warrant, consent) have been met so that the scene can be searched and the evidence seized. The investigator should then devise a plan of approach based on the facts of the case and the physical location. The scene should be documented in as much detail as possible before disturbing any evidence and before the investigator lays a finger on any computer components. Of course, there are circumstances in which an investigator may have to act quickly and pull a plug before documenting the scene, such as when data is in the process of being deleted.

DOCUMENTING THE CRIME SCENE

Typical crime-scene documentation is accomplished through two actions: sketching and photographing. The electronic crime scene is no different. First, the scene should be sketched in the style of a floor plan (see Figure 18-4), and then overall photographs of the location should be taken. In the case of a network, a technical network sketch should also be included, if possible.

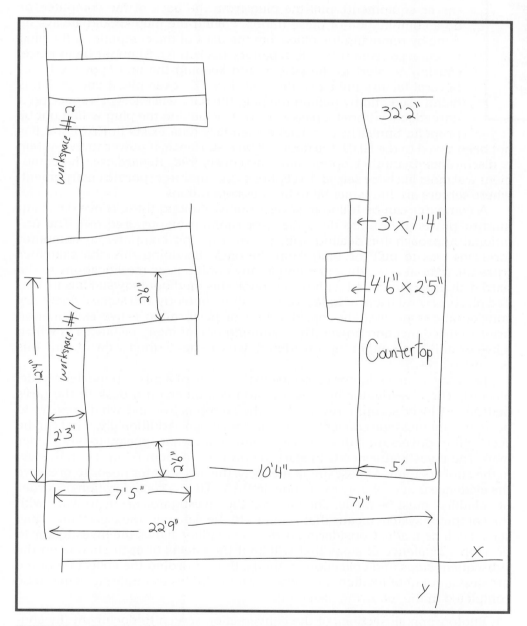

FIGURE 18-4   Rough sketch made at a crime scene with necessary measurements included. *SAFERSTEIN, RICHARD, Ph.D., CRIMINALISTICS: AN INTRODUCTION TO FORENSIC SCIENCE, 11th Ed., ©2015. Reprinted and Electronically reproduced by permission of Pearson Education, Inc., Upper Saddle River, New Jersey*

FIGURE 18-5 Back of a computer showing all connections. *SAFERSTEIN, RICHARD, Ph.D., CRIMINALISTICS: AN INTRODUCTION TO FORENSIC SCIENCE, 11th Ed., ©2015. Reprinted and Electronically reproduced by permission of Pearson Education, Inc., Upper Saddle River, New Jersey*

After photographs have been taken of the overall layout, close-up photographs should be shot. A close-up photograph of any running computer monitor should be taken. All the connections to the main system unit, such as peripheral devices (i.e., keyboard, monitor, speakers, mouse, etc.), should be photographed. If necessary, system units should be moved delicately and carefully to facilitate the connections photograph (see Figure 18-5). Close-up photographs of equipment serial numbers should be taken, if practical.

LIVE COMPUTER ACQUISITION

At this point, investigators must decide whether to perform a live acquisition of the data, perform a system shutdown (as in the case of server equipment), pull the plug from the back of the computer, or do a combination of these things. Pulling the plug should always be done by removing the plug from the back of the computer. If the plug is removed from the wall, a battery backup (UPS) might be in place, causing an alert to the system and keeping the unit "powered on." Several factors influence this decision. For example, if encryption is being used and by pulling the plug the data will encrypt, rendering it unreadable without a password or key, pulling the plug would not be prudent. Similarly, if crucial evidentiary data exists in RAM and has not been saved to the HDD, the data will be lost. Hence, if power to the system is discontinued, another option must be considered. Regardless, the equipment will most likely be seized. Exceptions exist in the corporate environment, where servers are fundamental to business operations.

A computer can be found in several states. Among these is live (i.e., running or powered on) and dead (i.e., not running or powered off). The traditional approach for dealing with a live, running computer in computer forensics was to pull the plug from the back. By doing this, the examiner froze the data in time, thus preventing any additions or modifications to the hard disk drive contained within. Although this methodology still has its limited place, several traits of today's computer technology and some evidentiary considerations necessitate consideration of performing a live examination prior to disconnecting power. By examining one of many instances in which a live examination might be considered, we can get a good view of how this process works.

Let's say an investigator responds to the scene of a missing fourteen-year-old girl. The investigator notices a laptop computer on a desk in the girl's bedroom. Closer scrutiny reveals that the laptop is live and what appears to be an instant message conversation is on the screen. Additionally, what can be seen of the conversation discusses a meeting with what appears to be an older man. The investigator needs to start the process of identifying the individual in the conversation. Almost simultaneously, the investigator needs to preserve the evidence that probably exists only in RAM. Here a consideration of "order of volatility" must be made. The fact that the investigator needs to work with the computer system means that changes to the data (i.e., the electronic crime scene) will be made. Considering order of volatility allows the investigator to develop a sequence of steps that will limit the effects of each change on the subsequent steps and collection methods, thus affording the collection of the greatest amount of unaltered evidentiary data. In this example steps might be completed in the following order:

1. Photograph all sections of the conversation screen to document the conversation in the same form the user sees. Merely scrolling through the conversation to afford photographing the entire conversation is minimally intrusive and limited (and arguably inconsequential) changes will occur.

2. Depending on his or her own skill level, the investigator may want to acquire the contents of RAM at this point. This would be accomplished by running a controlled application that the investigator already possesses and that is designed for such a purpose. Of course, the resulting content needs to be written somewhere, and it should not be written to the computer's hard drive. Rather, the examiner should use a clean piece of media that can handle the size of the output. There are several options for this.

3. Next, the investigator may want to consider copying the text and pasting it to a new document or utilizing a save command in the chat application to save the conversation in text format. Again, this conversation should not be saved to the hard dive of the system being examined.

4. If the investigator feels that encryption is being used, he or she may consider imaging the entire hard drive in this live environment. Because shutting the computer with an encryption in place renders the hard drive's contents unreadable without a password, it may be a good idea to get an image of the hard drive while it is still decrypted. This requires special response tools and external media that can handle the large image size.

This is just one way to approach this and other live examinations. The order of steps can also be debated among forensic examiners. The following questions are important for the forensic examiner to consider:

1. What is the type of case I am investigating?
2. What is the evidence I seek?
3. How best can I completely acquire that evidence without contaminating other aspects of the "electronic crime scene"?
4. In what order (order of volatility) should I take those steps?
5. Do I have the training, education, experience, equipment, and tools to accomplish this, or do I need assistance?

Finally, the only perfect crime scene is one that has not been entered. The minute investigators enter a crime scene, there will be changes to the environment, but obviously, entering the physical crime scene is a necessary function of evidence collection. Processing it should be done in a certain order so that, for example, the collection of fingerprints won't prevent the proper collection of blood, hair, fiber, and so on. The same applies to the electronic crime scene.

After the photographs and sketches are complete and, if appropriate, the live examination has been performed, but before disconnecting the peripherals from the computer, a label should be placed on the cord of each peripheral, with a corresponding label placed on the port to which it is connected. A numbering scheme should be devised to further identify each system unit if several computers are at the scene (Figure 18-6). The combination of sketching, photographing, and labeling should adequately document the scene, prevent future confusion about which component went with which system unit, and facilitate reconstruction if necessary for lab or courtroom purposes.

FIGURE 18-6 Back of a computer with each component correlated with its port through the use of a labeling scheme. *SAFERSTEIN, RICHARD, Ph.D., CRIMINALISTICS: AN INTRODUCTION TO FORENSIC SCIENCE, 11th Ed., ©2015. Reprinted and Electronically reproduced by permission of Pearson Education, Inc., Upper Saddle River, New Jersey*

FORENSIC IMAGE ACQUISITION

Now that the items have been seized, the data needs to be obtained for analysis. The number of electronic items that potentially store evidentiary data are too vast to cover in this section. The hard disk drive will be used as an example, but the same "best practices" principles apply for other electronic devices as well.

Throughout the entire process, the computer forensic examiner must use the least intrusive method. The goal in obtaining data from an HDD is to do so without altering even one bit of data. Because booting an HDD to its operating system changes many files and could potentially destroy evidentiary data, obtaining data is generally accomplished by removing the HDD from the system and placing it in a laboratory forensic computer so that a forensic image can be created. However, the BIOS of the seized computer sometimes interprets the geometry of the HDD differently than the forensic computer does. In these instances, the image of the HDD must be obtained using the seized computer. Regardless, the examiner must ensure that the drive to be analyzed is in a "write-blocked," or read-only, state when creating the forensic image. Furthermore, the examiner needs to be able to prove that the forensic image he or she obtained includes every bit of data and caused no changes, or writes, to the HDD.

To this end, a sort of fingerprint of the drive is taken before and after imaging. This fingerprint is taken through the use of a **Message Digest 5 (MD5)/ Secure Hash Algorithm (SHA)**, or similar validated algorithm. Before imaging the drive, the algorithm is run and a 32-character alphanumeric string is produced based on the drive's contents. The algorithm is then run against the resulting forensic image; if nothing changed, the same alphanumeric string is produced, thus demonstrating that the image is all-inclusive of the original contents and that nothing was altered in the process.

A forensic image of the data on an HDD (as well as on floppy disks, CDs, DVDs, tapes, flash memory devices, and any other storage medium) is merely an exact duplicate of the entire contents of the drive. In other words, all portions of the drive are copied, from the first bit (i.e., one or zero) to the last. Why would investigators want to copy what appears to be blank or unused portions of the HDD? The answer is simple: to preserve latent data, which is discussed later in the chapter. It suffices to say here that data exists in areas of the drive that are, generally speaking, unknown and inaccessible to most end users. This data can be valuable as evidence. Therefore, a forensic image—one that copies every single bit of information on the drive—is necessary. A forensic image differs from a backup or standard copy in that it takes the entire contents, not only data the operating system is aware of.

Many forensic software packages come equipped with a method for obtaining the forensic image. The most popular software forensic tools— EnCase, Forensic Toolkit (FTK), Forensic Autopsy (Linux-based freeware), and SMART (Linux-based software by ASR Data)—all include a method for obtaining a forensic image. All produce self-contained image files that can then be interpreted and analyzed. They also allow image compression to conserve storage. The fact that forensic imaging results in self-contained, compressed files allows many images from different cases to be stored on the same forensic storage drive. This makes case management and storage much easier (see Figure 18-7).

Message Digest 5 (MD5)/ Secure Hash Algorithm (SHA)
A software algorithm used to "fingerprint" a file or contents of a disk; used to verify the integrity of data. In forensic analysis it is typically used to verify that an acquired image of suspect data was not altered during the process of imaging.

Quick Review

- Aspects of a computer that should be photographed close up at an electronic crime scene include (1) the screen of any running computer monitor; (2) all the connections to the main system unit, such as peripheral devices (i.e., keyboard, monitor, speakers, mouse, etc.); and (3) equipment serial numbers.
- Evidentiary considerations may require the investigator to perform a live examination prior to disconnecting power.
- Two situations in which an investigator would not unplug a computer at an electronic crime scene are (1) if encryption is suspected, and thus pulling the plug would re-encrypt the data, rendering it unreadable without a password or key, and (2) if data exists in RAM that has not been saved to the HDD and will thus be lost if power to the system is discontinued.

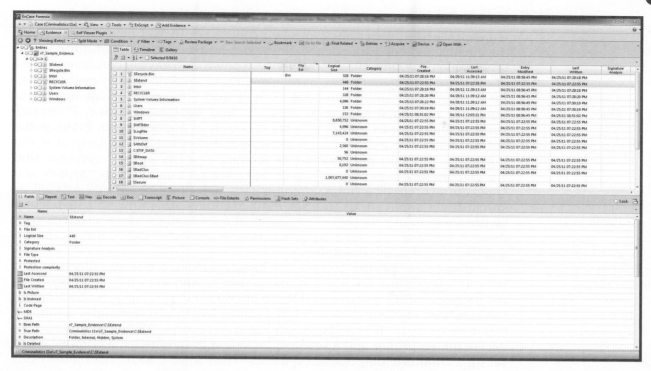

FIGURE 18-7   Screen shot of EnCase software. EnCase is a common forensic software application capable of imaging and assisting in the analysis of data. *Guidance Software, Inc.*

- The primary goal in obtaining data from an HDD is to do so without altering even one bit of data. To this end, a Message Digest 5 (MD5)/Secure Hash Algorithm (SHA) takes a "fingerprint" of a hard disk drive (HDD) before and after forensic imaging.

Analysis of Electronic Data

Analysis of electronic data is virtually limitless and bound only to the level of skill of the examiner. The more familiar an examiner is with computers, operating systems, application software, data storage, and a host of other disciplines, the more prepared he or she will be to look for evidentiary data.

Because computers are vast and complex, discussing each area, file, directory, log, or computer process that could potentially contain evidentiary data is beyond the scope of one chapter—and may be beyond the scope of an entire book. What follows are some of the more common areas of analysis. While reading this section, reflect on your own knowledge of computers and consider what other data might be of evidentiary value and where it might be found.

VISIBLE DATA

The category of **visible data** includes all information that the operating system is presently aware of and thus is readily accessible to the user. Here we present several common types of visible data considered in many investigations. This list is by no means exhaustive and can include any information that has value as evidence.

DATA/WORK PRODUCT FILES   One place to find evidence is in documents or files produced by the suspect. This category is extremely broad and can include

visible data
All data that the operating system is presently aware of and thus is readily accessible to the user.

data from just about any software program. Microsoft Word and WordPerfect word-processing programs typically produce text-based files such as typed documents and correspondence. These programs, and a host of other word-processing programs, have replaced the typewriter. They are common sources of evidence in criminal cases, particularly those involving white-collar crime.

Also relevant in white-collar crime and similar financial investigations are any data related to personal and business finance. Programs such as QuickBooks and Peachtree accounting packages can manage the entire financial portion of a small to midsize business. Similarly, it is not uncommon to find personal bank account records in the computer that are managed with personal finance software such as Microsoft Money and Quicken. Moreover, criminals sometimes use these programs as well as spreadsheet applications to track bank accounts stolen from unsuspecting victims. Computer forensic examiners should familiarize themselves with these programs, the ways in which they store data, and methods for extracting and reading the data.

Advances in printer technology have made high-quality color printing both affordable and common in many homes. Although this is a huge benefit for home office workers and those interested in graphic arts, the technology has been used for criminal gain. Counterfeiting and check and document fraud are easily perpetrated on most home computers. All that is required is a decent ink-jet printer and a scanner. Including the computer, a criminal could set up a counterfeiting operation for less than $1,500. Examiners must learn the graphics and photo-editing applications used for nefarious purposes. Being able to recognize the data produced by these applications and knowing how to display the images is key to identifying this type of evidence.

SWAP FILE DATA   When an application is running, the program and the data being accessed are loaded into RAM. A computer's RAM is much faster than the "read" speed of the hard disk drive, and that's why the programs are loaded here—for fast access and functioning. RAM, however, has its limits. Some computers have a gigabyte or two of RAM, and still others as much as four to eight gigabytes. Regardless of the amount, though, most operating systems (Windows, Linux, etc.) are programmed to conserve RAM when possible. This is where the **swap file** comes in. The operating system attempts to keep only data and applications that are presently being used in RAM. Other applications that were started, but are currently waiting for user attention, may be swapped out of RAM and written to the swap space on the hard disk drive.[2]

swap file
A file or defined space on the HDD used to conserve RAM; data is swapped, or paged, to this file or space to free RAM for applications that are in use.

For example, a manager of a retail store may want to type a quarterly report based on sales. The manager starts up Microsoft Word and begins his report. Needing to incorporate sales figures from a particular spreadsheet, he opens Microsoft Excel. Depending on what is running on the computer, the original Word document may be swapped from RAM to the swap space on the HDD to free up space for Excel. As the manager goes back and forth between the programs (and maybe checks his e-mail in between) this swapping continues. Data that is swapped back and forth is sometimes left behind in the swap space. Even as this area is constantly changed, some of the data is orphaned in unallocated space, an area of the HDD discussed later in this chapter.

A "swap file" or "space" can be defined as a particular file or even a separate HDD partition, depending on the operating system and file system type (e.g., FAT, NTFS, EXT2). For Windows systems, either the swap file "Win386.sys" or "pagefile.sys" is used, depending on the specific Windows version and file system type. Linux and current Mac OS systems can create partitions just for swapping data in and out of RAM. Data in the swap space can be read by examining the HDD through forensic software or a utility that provides a binary view, such as Norton Disk Editor or WinHex (see Figure 18-8).

FIGURE 18-8 As a user switches between applications and performs multiple tasks, data is swapped back and forth between RAM and the computer's hard drive. This area on the hard drive is referred to as either "swap space" or a "paging file." *SAFERSTEIN, RICHARD, Ph.D., CRIMINALISTICS: AN INTRODUCTION TO FORENSIC SCIENCE, 11th Ed., ©2015. Reprinted and Electronically reproduced by permission of Pearson Education, Inc., Upper Saddle River, New Jersey*

TEMPORARY FILES Any user who has suffered a sudden loss of power in the middle of typing a document can attest to the value of a **temporary file**. Most programs automatically save a copy of the file being worked on in a temporary file. After typing a document, working on a spreadsheet, or working on a slide presentation, the user can save the changes, thus promoting the temporary copy to actual file status. Temporary files are created as a sort of backup on the fly. If the computer experiences a sudden loss of power or other catastrophic failure, the temporary file can be recovered, limiting the amount of data lost. The loss is limited, but not altogether prevented, because the temporary file is not updated in real time. Rather, it is updated periodically, depending on the application's settings. The default interval in most programs is every ten minutes.

Temporary files can sometimes be recovered during a forensic examination. Additionally, some of the data that may have been orphaned from a previous version may be recoverable, if not the complete file. This is true even when a document has been typed and printed but never saved. The creation of the temporary file makes it possible for some of this "unsaved" data to be recovered during analysis.

Another type of temporary file valuable to the computer investigator is the print spool file. When a print job is sent to the printer, a spooling process delays the sending of the data to the printer. This happens so the application can continue to work while the printing takes place in the background. To facilitate this, a temporary print spool file is created; this file typically includes the data to be printed and information specific to the printer. There are different methods for accomplishing this, and thus the files created as a result of this process vary. It is sometimes possible to view the data in a readable format from the files created during the spooling process.

LATENT DATA

The term **latent data** includes data that is obfuscated (not necessarily intentionally) from a user's view. It includes areas of files and disks that are typically

temporary files
Files temporarily written by an application to perform a function or to provide a "backup" copy of a work product should the computer experience a catastrophic failure.

latent data
Areas of files and disks that are typically not apparent to the computer user (and often not to the operating system) but contain data nonetheless.

not apparent to the computer user but that contain data nonetheless. Latent data is one of the reasons a forensic image of the media is created. If a standard copy were all that is produced, only the logical data (i.e., that which the operating system is aware of) would be captured. Getting every bit of data ensures that potentially valuable evidence in latent data is not missed.

Once the all-inclusive forensic image is produced, how is the latent data viewed? Utilities that allow a user to examine a hard disk drive on a binary (ones and zeros) level are the answer. Applications such as Norton Disk Editor and WinHex provide this type of access to a hard disk drive or other computer media. Thus these applications, sometimes also referred to as "hex editors" (for the hexadecimal shorthand of computer language), allow all data to be read on the binary level independent of the operating system's file system table. Utilities such as these can write to the media under examination, thus changing data. Consequently, a software or hardware write-blocker should be used.

A more common option in data forensics is to use specialized forensic examination software. EnCase and Forensic Toolkit for Windows and SMART and Forensic Autopsy for Linux are examples of forensic software. Each allows a search for evidence on the binary level and provides automated tools for performing common forensic processing techniques. Examiners should be cautious, however, about relying too heavily on automated tools. To merely use an automated tool without understanding what is happening in the background and why evidentiary data may exist in particular locations would severely impede the investigator's ability to testify to the findings.

SLACK SPACE   Slack space is empty space on a hard disk drive created because of the way the HDD stores files. Recall that, although the smallest unit of data is one bit (either a one or a zero), an HDD cannot address or deal with such a small unit. In fact, not even a byte (eight bits) can be addressed. Rather, the smallest unit of addressable space by an HDD is the sector. HDDs typically assign sectors in 512-byte increments, whereas CD-ROMs allocate 2,048 bytes per sector.

If the minimum addressable unit of the HDD is 512 bytes, what happens if the file is only 100 bytes? In this instance, there are 412 bytes of slack space. It does not end here, however, because there is also minimum cluster requirement. As you may recall, clusters are groups of sectors used to store files and folders. The cluster is the minimum storage unit defined and used by the logical partition. It is because of the minimum addressable sector of the HDD and the minimum unit of storage requirement of the volume that we have slack space.

Minimum cluster allocation must be defined in sectors in multiples of two. Thus, a cluster includes two, four, six, or eight sectors or more. Returning to our initial example of the 100-byte file, suppose an HDD has a two-sectors-per-cluster volume requirement. This means that the HDD will allocate a minimum of two 512-byte sectors (a total of 1,024 bytes) of storage space for that 100-byte file. The remaining 924 bytes would be slack space (see Figure 18-9).

To illustrate this point, let us expand on the previous example of safe-deposit boxes. The bank offers safe-deposit boxes of a particular size. This is the equivalent of the HDD's clusters. A person wanting to place only a deed to a house in the box gets the same size box as a person who wants to stuff it full of cash. The former would have empty space should he or she desire to place additional items in the box. This empty space is the equivalent of slack space. But what if the box becomes full and the person needs more space? That person must then get a second box. Similarly, if a file grows to fill one cluster and beyond, a second cluster is allocated. The remaining space in the second cluster is slack space. This continues as more and more clusters are allocated to accommodate the size of the growing file.

FIGURE 18-9 Slack space illustrated in a two-sector cluster. Cluster sizes are typically greater than two sectors, but two sectors are displayed here for simplicity. *SAFERSTEIN, RICHARD, Ph.D., CRIMINALISTICS: AN INTRODUCTION TO FORENSIC SCIENCE, 11th Ed., ©2015. Reprinted and Electronically reproduced by permission of Pearson Education, Inc., Upper Saddle River, New Jersey*

There are actually two types of slack space: "RAM slack" and "file slack." Ram slack occupies the space from where the actual (i.e., logical) data portion of the file ends to where the first allocated sector in the cluster terminates. **File slack**, therefore, occupies the remaining space of the cluster. RAM slack is a concept that was more relevant in older operating systems. Remember that the minimum amount of space the HDD can address is the 512-byte sector. Therefore, if the file size is only 100 bytes, the remaining space must be padded. Some older operating systems pad this area with data contained in RAM. This could include Web pages, passwords, data files, or other data that existed in RAM when the file was written. Modern Windows operating systems pad this space with zeros, but some examinations may still yield valuable data in this area.

Let us go back to the 100-byte file with the two-sectors-per-cluster minimum requirement. Following the end of the logical data (i.e., beyond the 100 bytes), the remaining 412 bytes of that sector is RAM slack; the additional 512 bytes completing the cluster is then file slack. See Figure 18-10 for a visual depiction. The question now becomes: What can I expect to find in slack space, and why is this important? The answer: Junk—valuable junk.

File slack, on the other hand, can contain a lot of orphaned data. To illustrate this point, let's take the 100-byte file example a bit further. Let's say that before the 100-byte file was written to the HDD, occupying one cluster (two sectors totaling 1,024 bytes), a 1,000-byte file occupied this space but was deleted by the user. When a file is "deleted," the data still remains behind, so it is probably a safe bet that data from the original 1,000-byte file remain in the slack space of the new 100-byte file now occupying this cluster. This is just one example of why data exists in file slack and why file slack may be valuable as evidence.

In one final attempt to illustrate this point, let us again build on our safe-deposit box analogy. Suppose a person rents two safe-deposit boxes, each box representing a sector and the two combined representing a cluster. If that person places the deed to a house in the first box, the remaining space in that box would be analogous to RAM slack. The space in the second box would be

file slack

The area that begins at the end of the last sector that contains logical data and terminates at the end of the cluster.

FIGURE 18-10 File slack. *SAFERSTEIN, RICHARD, Ph.D., CRIMINALISTICS: AN INTRODUCTION TO FORENSIC SCIENCE, 11th Ed., ©2015. Reprinted and Electronically reproduced by permission of Pearson Education, Inc., Upper Saddle River, New Jersey*

the equivalent of file slack. The only difference is that, unlike the empty spaces of the safe-deposit box, the slack space of the file probably contains data that may be valuable as evidence.

The data contained in RAM and file slack is not really the concern of the operating system. As far as the OS is concerned, this space is empty and therefore ready to be used. Until that happens, however, an examination with one of the aforementioned tools will allow a look into these areas, thus revealing the orphaned data. The same is true for unallocated space.

unallocated space
The unused area of the HDD that the operating system file system table sees as empty (i.e., containing no logical files) but that may contain old data.

UNALLOCATED SPACE Latent evidentiary data also resides in **unallocated space**. What is unallocated space, how does data get in there, and what is done to access this space? If we have an 80 GB hard drive and only half of the hard drive is filled with data, then the other half, or 40 GB, is unallocated space (see Figure 18-11). Returning to our safe-deposit box analogy, if the entire bank of safe-deposit boxes contains 100 boxes, but only 50 are currently in use, then the other 50 would be the equivalent of unallocated space. The HDD's unallocated space typically contains a lot of useful data. The constant shuffling of files on the HDD causes data to become orphaned in unallocated space as the logical portion of the file is rewritten to other places. Some examples of ways in which data can become orphaned are through fragmentation, during the creation of swap files or swap space, or in the process of deleting files.

DEFRAGMENTING Defragmenting an HDD involves moving noncontiguous data back together. Remember that the HDD has minimum space reservation requirements. Again, if the file requires only 100 bytes of space, the operating system may allocate much more than that. If the file grows past what has been allocated for it, another cluster is required. If, however, a different file occupies the next cluster in line, then the operating system will have to find another place for that additional data on the drive. In this scenario, the file is said to be "fragmented" because data for the same file is contained in noncontiguous clusters. In the case of the HDD, the shuffling of files causes data to be orphaned in unallocated space.

Ultimately, fragmentation of numerous files can degrade the performance of an HDD, causing the read/write heads to have to traverse the platters to

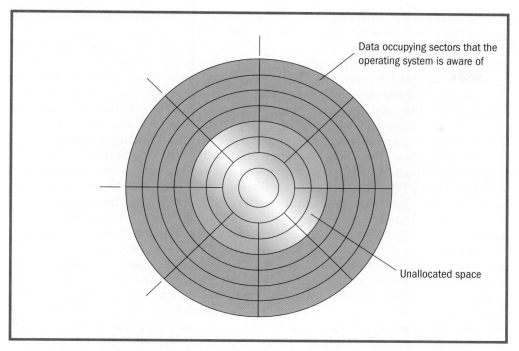

Data occupying sectors that the operating system is aware of

Unallocated space

FIGURE 18-11 A simplistic view of a hard drive platter demonstrating the concept of unallocated space.
SAFERSTEIN, RICHARD, Ph.D., CRIMINALISTICS: AN INTRODUCTION TO FORENSIC SCIENCE, 11th Ed., ©2015.
Reprinted and Electronically reproduced by permission of Pearson Education, Inc., Upper Saddle River, New Jersey

locate the data. Defragmenting the HDD rearranges noncontiguous data into contiguous clusters. Building yet again on our safe-deposit box analogy—If our renter eventually needs to store more property than the original box can hold, the bank will rent the person a second box. If, however, all the boxes around the original are occupied and the only free one is in another section of the room, then the renter's property is "fragmented." The bank would have to "defrag" the safe-deposit boxes to get the property of users with more than one box into adjacent boxes.

SWAP FILE/SWAP SPACE Recall that a computer uses the HDD to maximize its amount of RAM by constantly swapping data in and out of RAM to a predetermined location on the HDD, thus freeing valuable RAM. The constant read and write operations of RAM cause a constant change in the swap file—WIN386.swp or pagefile.sys—in Windows or in the swap space on a Linux system. Data can become orphaned in unallocated space from this constant swapping to and from the HDD.

DELETED FILES The deletion of files is another way that data becomes orphaned in unallocated space. Data from deleted files can manifest itself in different ways during a forensic examination. The actions that occur when a file is deleted vary among file systems. What is fairly consistent, though, is that generally the data is not truly removed. For example, consider what happens when a user or program deletes a file in a Windows operating system with a FAT file system. When a file is deleted, the first character in the file's directory entry (i.e., in its name) is replaced with the Greek letter sigma. When the sigma replaces the first character, the file is no longer viewable through conventional methods and the operating system views the space previously occupied by the file as available. The data, however, is still there.

This example doesn't account for the actions of the Windows Recycle Bin. When the Windows operating system is set up to merely place the deleted file in the Recycle Bin, the original directory entry is deleted and one is created in the Recycle folder for that particular user. The new Recycle folder entry is linked to another file, the "info" or "info2" file, which includes some additional data, such as the location of the file before its deletion should the user wish to restore it to that location. Detailed discussions of the function of the Recycle Bin are beyond the scope of this chapter, but suffice it to say that, even when the Recycle Bin has been "emptied," the data usually remains behind until overwritten. Although Windows NTFS partitions and Linux EXT partitions handle deleted files differently, in both cases the data typically remains.

What if a new file writes data to the location of the original file? Generally speaking, the data is overwritten. This is, of course, unless the new file only partially overwrites the original: If a file that occupied two clusters is deleted, and a new file overwrites one of the clusters, then the data in the second cluster is orphaned in unallocated space. Of course, yet a third file can overwrite the second cluster entirely, but until then the data remains in unallocated space.

Let us once again look to our safe-deposit box analogy. If, for example, the owner of two safe-deposit boxes stopped renting them, the bank would list them as available. If the owner didn't clean them out, the contents would remain unchanged. If a new owner rented one of the boxes, the contents from the former owner would be replaced with the new owner's possessions. The second box would therefore still contain orphaned contents from its previous owner. The contents would remain in this "unallocated box" until another renter occupies it.

Quick Review

- The types of computer evidence can be grouped under two major subheadings: visible and latent data.
- Visible data is data that the operating system is aware of, and thus is easily accessible to the user. It includes any type of user-created data, such as word-processing documents, spreadsheets, accounting records, databases, and pictures.
- Temporary files created by programs as a sort of on-the-fly backup can prove valuable as evidence. Data in the swap space used to conserve valuable RAM within the computer system can also yield evidentiary data.
- Latent data is data that the operating system is not aware of. The constant shuffling of data through deletion, defragmentation, swapping, and so on, is one of the reasons data is stored in latent areas.
- Latent data can exist in both RAM slack and file slack. RAM slack is the area from the end of the logical file to the end of the sector. File slack is the remaining area from the end of the final sector containing data to the end of the cluster.
- Latent data might be found in unallocated space—space on an HDD that the operating system sees as empty and ready for data.
- When a user deletes files, the data typically remains behind, so deleted files are another source of latent data.

Forensic Analysis of Internet Data

It's important from the investigative standpoint to be familiar with the evidence left behind regarding a user's Internet activity. A forensic examination of a computer system reveals quite a bit of data about a user's Internet activity. The data described next would be accessed and examined using the forensic techniques outlined in the previous sections of this chapter.

INTERNET CACHE

Evidence of Web browsing typically exists in abundance on the user's computer. Most Web browsers (e.g, Internet Explorer and Firefox) use a caching system to expedite Web browsing and make it more efficient. This was particularly true in the days of dial-up Internet access. When a user accesses a website, such as the *New York Times* home page, the data is fed from that server (in this example, that of the *New York Times*), via the Internet service provider and over whatever type of connection the user has, to his or her computer. If that computer is accessing the Internet via a dial-up connection, the transfer of the *New York Times* home page may take a while because the data transfer rate and capabilities (bandwidth) of the telephone system is limited. Even with the high-speed access of a fiber or cable connection, conservation of bandwidth is always a consideration. Taking that into account, Web browsers store, or cache, portions of the pages visited on the local hard disk drive. This way, if the page is revisited, portions of it can be reconstructed more quickly from this saved data, rather than having to use precious bandwidth to pull it yet again from the Internet.

This **Internet cache** is a potential source of evidence for the computer investigator. Portions of, or in some cases entire, visited Web pages can be reconstructed. For security purposes, modern Internet browsers take steps to clear out, or erase, the Web cache. But in some cases, even after having been deleted, these cached files can be recovered (see the section on deleted data). Investigators must know how to search for this data within the particular Web browser used by a suspect.

Internet cache
Portions of visited Web pages placed on the local hard disk drive to facilitate quicker retrieval when the Web page is revisited.

INTERNET COOKIES

Cookies provide another area where potential evidence can be found. To appreciate the value of cookies, you must first understand how they get onto the computer and their intended purpose. **Cookies** are placed on the local hard disk drive by websites the user has visited, if the user's Web browser (such as Internet Explorer) is set to allow this to happen. Microsoft Internet Explorer places cookies in a dedicated directory. Websites use cookies to track certain information about its visitors. This information can be anything, such as history of visits, purchasing habits, passwords, and personal information used to recognize the user for later visits.

cookies
Files placed on a computer from a visited website that are used to track visits to and usage of that site.

Consider a user who registers for an account at the Barnes and Noble bookstore website, then returns to the same site from the same computer a few days later. The site will then display "Welcome, [*User Name*]." This data was retrieved from the cookie file placed on the user's hard disk drive by the website during the initial visit and registration with the site.

It is helpful to think of cookies almost like a caller ID for websites. The site recognizes and retrieves information about the visitor, as when a salesperson recognizes a caller from a caller ID display and quickly pulls the client's file. Cookie files can be a valuable source of evidence. In Internet Explorer, they take the form of plain text files, which can typically be opened with a standard text viewer or word-processing program. The existence of the files themselves, regardless of the information contained within, can be of evidentiary value to show a history of Web visits. A typical cookie may resemble the following: rsaferstein@forensicscience.txt. From this we can surmise that someone using the local computer login "rsaferstein" accessed the forensic science website. It is possible that the cookie was placed there by an annoying pop-up ad, not a website the user visited, but considered against

FIGURE 18-12 The Internet history displays more than just Web-browsing activity. Here we see Microsoft Word documents and a picture accessed on the current day. *"The Internet History Displays More Than Just Web-Browsing Activity. Here We See Microsoft Word Documents and a Picture Accessed on the Current Day" from Screenshot of Microsoft Internet Explorer. Copyright © Microsoft Corporation. Used by permission of Microsoft Corporation*

Internet history
An accounting of websites visited; different browsers store this information in different ways.

bookmark
A feature that enables the user to designate favorite sites for fast and easy access.

other evidence in the computer data, the presence of a particular cookie may have corroborative value.

INTERNET HISTORY

Most Web browsers track the history of Web page visits for the computer user. This is probably done merely for convenience. Like the "recent calls" list on a cell phone, the **Internet history** provides an accounting of sites most recently visited, with some storing weeks' worth of visits. Users can go back and access sites they recently visited just by going through the browser's history. Most Web browsers store this information in one particular file; Internet Explorer uses the "index.dat" file. On a Windows system, an "index.dat" file is created for each login user name on the computer.

The history file can be located and read with most popular computer forensic software packages. It displays the uniform resource locator (URL) of each website, along with the date and time the site was accessed. An investigation involving Internet use almost always includes an examination of Internet history data.

In some respects, the term "Internet history" is wrong because it doesn't encompass all of these files' functions. Several browsers—Internet Explorer, for one—store other valuable evidence independent of Internet access. It is not uncommon to see files accessed over a network listed in the history. Similarly, files accessed on external media, such as CDs or thumb drives, may also appear in the history. Regardless, the Internet history data is a valuable source of evidence worthy of examination (see Figure 18-12).

BOOKMARKS AND FAVORITE PLACES

Another way users can access websites quickly is to store them in their **bookmarks** or Favorite Places. Like presetting radio stations, Web browsers allow users to bookmark websites for future visits (see Figure 18-13). A lot can be learned from a user's bookmarked sites. You may learn what online news a person is interested in or what type of hobbies he or she has. You may also see that person's favorite child pornography or computer-hacking sites bookmarked.

In Internet Explorer, the favorite places are kept in a folder with link files, or shortcuts, to particular URLs. They can be organized in subfolders or grouped by type. The same is true for the Firefox Web browser, except that Firefox bookmarks are stored in a document written in hypertext markup language (HTML), the same language interpreted by the Web browsers themselves.

Quick Review

- Places where a forensic computer examiner might look to determine what websites a computer user has visited recently are the Internet cache, cookies, and the Internet history.
- The history file can be located and read with a forensic software package. Another way to access websites that have been visited is by examining bookmarks and favorite places

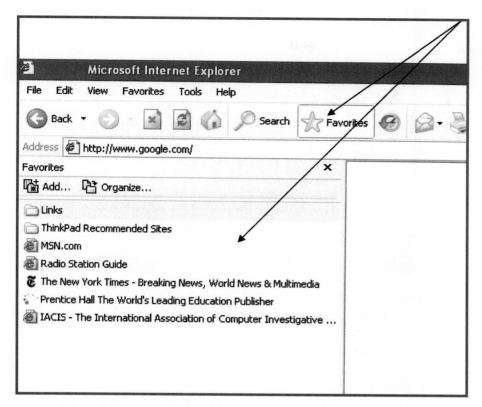

FIGURE 18-13 Bookmarks or favorite places can be saved for quick access in most Web browsers.
Screenshot of Microsoft Internet Explorer. Copyright © Microsoft Corporation. Used by permission of Microsoft Corporation

Forensic Investigation of Internet Communications

Computer investigations often begin with or are centered on Internet communication. Whether it is a chat conversation among many people, an instant message conversation between two individuals, or the back-and-forth of an e-mail exchange, human communication has long been a source of evidentiary material. Regardless of the type, investigators are typically interested in communication.

ROLE OF THE IP

With all of the computer manufacturers and software developers out there, some common rules are necessary for computers to be able to communicate on a global network. Just as any human language needs rules for communication to be successful, so does the language of computers. Computers that participate on the Internet, therefore, must be provided with an address known as an Internet protocol (IP) address from the Internet service provider to which they connect.

IP addresses take the form ###.###.###.###, in which, generally speaking, ### can be any number from 0 to 255. A typical IP address might look like this: 66.94.234.13. Not only do IP addresses provide the means by which data can be routed to the appropriate location, but they also provide the means by which most Internet investigations are conducted (see Figure 18-14). Thus the

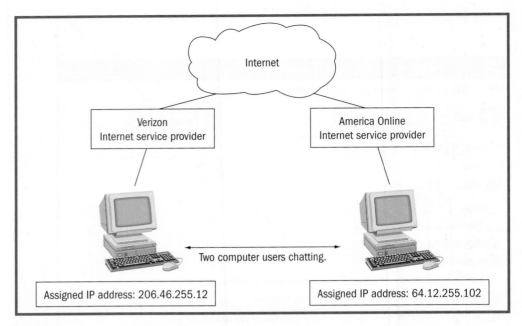

FIGURE 18-14 Two computers communicating by sending data to each other's IP address via the Internet. An IP address is assigned to each computer by its respective Internet service provider. *SAFERSTEIN, RICHARD, Ph.D., CRIMINALISTICS: AN INTRODUCTION TO FORENSIC SCIENCE, 11th Ed., ©2015. Reprinted and Electronically reproduced by permission of Pearson Education, Inc., Upper Saddle River, New Jersey*

IP address may lead to the identity of a real person. If an IP address is the link to the identity of a real person, then it is quite obviously valuable for identifying someone on the Internet.

To illustrate, let's assume that a user of the Internet, fictitiously named John Smith, connects to the Internet from his home by way of a Verizon FIOS connection. Verizon in this case would be responsible for providing Smith with his IP address. Verizon was issued a bank of IP addresses with which to service its customers from a regulatory body designed to track the usage of IP addresses (obviously, so no one address is used by two different users at the same time).

Suppose that Smith, while connected to the Internet, decides to threaten an ex-girlfriend by sending her an e-mail telling her he is going to kill her. That e-mail must first pass through Smith's Internet service provider's routers (in this case, Verizon's) on its way to its destination—Smith's girlfriend. The e-mail would be stamped by the servers that it passes through, and this stamp would include the IP address given to Smith by Verizon for his session on the Internet.

An investigator responsible for tracking that e-mail would locate the originating IP address stamped in the e-mail header. That IP address could be researched using one of many Internet sites (e.g., www.centralops.net) to determine which Internet service provider was given this IP as part of the block it was assigned for serving its customers. The investigator then files a subpoena with the Internet service provider (i.e., Verizon), asking which of its customers was using that IP address on that date and time.

IP addresses are located in different places for different methods of Internet communications. E-mail has the IP address in the header portion of the mail. This may not be readily apparent and may require a bit of configuration to reveal. Each e-mail client is different and needs to be evaluated on a case-by-case basis. For an instant message or chat session, the provider of the chat mechanism—AOL, Yahoo!, and so on—would be contacted to provide the user's IP address.

E-MAIL, CHAT, AND INSTANT MESSAGING

E-mail files can be read by a number of "clients," or software programs. Two of the most popular ways to access, read, and store e-mail in today's Internet environment, however, are Microsoft Outlook and through an Internet browser. Some people even use a combination of the two.

If an e-mail account is linked through Microsoft Outlook, then the e-mail is stored in a compound file (i.e., a file with several layers). Typically, compound files exist for received e-mail (i.e., the inbox), sent e-mail, and deleted e-mail. Users can also create new categories (shown as folders in Outlook) and categorize saved e-mail there. Most computer forensic software applications can view, or mount, these compound files so that the e-mail can be seen, including any file attachments. These files can also be imported into a clean copy of Microsoft Outlook (i.e., one not attached to an account), and the e-mail can be viewed there. Investigators must also be aware that, in a computer network environment, the user's Outlook files may not reside on his or her workstation computer but rather on a central mail or file server.

Most accounts offer the ability to access e-mail through a Web-based interface as well. This way, users can access their e-mail remotely from other computers. For e-mail accessed through a Web browser, the information presented earlier on Internet-based evidence applies. The Web interface converts the e-mail into a document suitable for reading in a Web browser. Consequently, Web-based e-mail is sometimes found in the Internet cache. This is particularly true of free Internet e-mail providers such as Hotmail and Yahoo!.

Much of the evidence from Internet communication is also derived from chat and instant-message technology. This is particularly true in the world of child sexual exploitation over the Internet. Various technologies provide chat and instant-messaging services. Most chat and instant-message conversations are not saved by the parties involved. Although most of the software does allow for conversation archiving, it is typically turned off by default. Therefore, conversations of this nature typically exist in the volatile memory space of random-access memory (RAM).

Recall that RAM is termed "volatile" because it holds data only while the computer has power. Unplugging the computer will cause the data located in RAM to be lost. If, however, chat or instant-message conversations occurred that are relevant as evidence, even if the computer was turned off, thus erasing the data in RAM, all may not be lost. Remember that there is an interaction between the computer system's RAM and the hard disk drive. RAM is a commodity, and therefore the computer's operating system makes an effort to conserve it as much as possible. This is done by swapping/paging that information back and forth into the swap space or paging file. Therefore, remnants of chat conversations are often found in the swap space or paging file during a forensic examination of the hard disk drive. These remnants, however, are typically fragmented, disconnected, and incomplete. Therefore, if the chat or instant message is still present on the screen (and thus probably still in RAM), the investigator needs a method by which to preserve and collect it.

A detailed discussion of capturing volatile data from RAM is beyond the scope of this chapter, but considerations for dealing with a live (running) computer have been discussed in the section "Live Computer Acquisition" in this chapter. Note that several commercial forensic software packages can capture this data. Similarly, Linux-based tools can accomplish this as well. The examiner may even be able to export the data remotely to another device. Regardless of the method, the data must be acquired.

Furthermore, many programs such as AOL Instant Messenger, Yahoo Messenger, and mIRC (Internet Relay Chat) create files regarding the rooms or channels a user chatted in or the screen names with which a user sent instant

WebExtra 18.1

Follow the Trail of an E-mail as It Travels Through the Internet

hacking

Frequently used as a slang term for performing an unauthorized computer or network intrusion.

firewall

Hardware or software designed to protect intrusions into an Internet network.

messages. Each application should be researched, and the computer forensic examination should be guided by an understanding of how each functions.

HACKING

Unauthorized computer intrusion, more commonly referred to as **hacking**, is the concern of every computer administrator. Hackers penetrate computer systems for a number of reasons. Sometimes the motive is corporate espionage; other times it is merely for bragging rights within the hacker community. Most commonly, though, a rogue or disgruntled employee with some knowledge of the computer network is looking to cause damage. Whatever the motivation, corporate America frequently turns to law enforcement to investigate and prosecute these cases.

Generally speaking, when investigating an unauthorized computer intrusion, investigators concentrate their efforts in three locations: "log files," "volatile memory," and "network traffic." Logs typically document the IP address of the computer that made the connection. Logs can be located in several locations on a computer network. Most servers on the Internet track connections made to them through the use of logs. Additionally, the router (i.e., the device responsible for directing data) may contain log files detailing connections.

Similarly, devices known as **firewalls** may contain log files listing computers that were allowed (or that merely attempted) access to the network or an individual system. Firewalls are devices (taking the form of either hardware or software) that permit only requested traffic to enter a computer system or, more appropriately, a network. In other words, if a user didn't send out a request for Internet traffic from a specific system, the firewall should block its entry unless previously configured to allow that traffic through. If the log files have captured the IP address of the intruder, then revealing the user behind the IP is the same process as for e-mail. Investigating a computer intrusion, however, does get a bit more complicated.

Frequently, in cases of unlawful access to a computer network, the perpetrator attempts to cover the tracks of his or her IP address. In these instances, advanced investigative techniques may be necessary to discover the hacker's true identity. When an intrusion is in progress, the investigator may have to capture volatile data, or data in RAM. The data in RAM at the time of an intrusion may provide valuable clues to the identity of the intruder or, at least, about his or her method or tools of attack. As in the case of an instant message or chat conversation, the data in RAM needs to be acquired.

Another standard tactic for investigating intrusion cases is to document all programs installed and running on a system in order to discover any additional malicious software installed by the perpetrator to facilitate entry. The investigator uses specialized software to document running processes, registry entries, open ports, and any installed files.

Additionally, the investigator may want to capture live network traffic as part of the evidence-collection and investigation process. Traffic that travels the network does so in the form of data packets. In addition to data, these packets also contain source and destination IP addresses. If the attack requires two-way communication, as in the case of a hacker stealing data, then data needs to be transmitted back to the hacker's computer using the destination IP address. Once this is learned, the investigation can focus on that system. However, care must be taken to ensure that the destination IP address does not belong to an unwitting and previously compromised computer under the control of the hacker. Moreover, the type of data that is being transmitted on the network may be a clue to what type of attack is being launched; whether any important data is being stolen; or what types of malicious software, if any, are involved in the attack.

Quick Review

- IP addresses take the form ###.###.###.###, in which, generally speaking, ### can be any number from 0 to 255.
- IP addresses provide the means by which data can be routed to the appropriate location, and they also provide the means by which most Internet investigations are conducted.
- An investigator tracking the origin of an e-mail seeks out the sender's IP address in the e-mail's header. Chat and instant messages are typically located in a computer's random-access memory (RAM).
- Tracking the origin of unauthorized computer intrusions, or hacking, requires investigating a computer's log file, RAM, and network traffic.
- A firewall is a device designed to protect against intrusions into a computer network.

Mobile Forensics

This section could just as well be titled Cell Phone Forensics, but because of the technological advances in mobile technology, handheld devices are much more than just phones. There truly has been cross-pollination between traditional computers and cell phones. In addition to traditional cell phone services, mobile devices offer many services that are offered by computers and other devices. These devices can provide a vast amount of useful and evidentiary data in an investigation.

The list of services available for mobile devices, although comprehensive, is certainly not exhaustive. It should be apparent, however, that aside from size and structure, little distinction can be made between the services offered by a computer system and those of a mobile device. As such, forensic examinations of mobile devices have much in common with computer forensics, at least in principle. Although there is a great deal of standardization in the computer market, the same is not true in the world of mobile devices. The operating systems that run mobile devices vary from manufacturer to manufacturer and device to device. Moreover, their inherent remote capabilities and constant connection and communication with service providers make collection and preservation difficult.

Recall from our early discussion that one of the principal goals in electronic evidence collection and analysis is to avoid alteration of data. With mobile devices, which are constantly registering their location with the service provider and potentially receiving GPS location updates, protecting against alteration is challenging. Compounded by the fact that many mobile devices offer remote kill and clear capabilities, investigators have their hands full. It may seem logical to merely shut the mobile device off to preserve data, but this is typically not recommended because it can clear out unsaved data existing in volatile memory (much like a computer's RAM contents).

Leaving the mobile device running but placing it in something that will block its communication is the preferred method. A "Faraday shield" is frequently used for mobile device evidence collection. Such a shield, often designed by mobile forensics manufacturers, will prevent the device from communicating (in or out) with the service provider. It has also been observed that other devices, such as the type of unlined paint can typically used for collecting arson-related evidence, can work as well. However, the effectiveness of alternatives should be tested in advance.

Another consideration in the collection of these devices is maintaining power so that the device can be transported, stored, and ultimately analyzed.

▦ CLOSER ANALYSIS

The following is a list of the more common services available on today's mobile devices, along with several examples of the potential evidentiary value they hold:

1. **Short Message Service (SMS)—Text Messaging** Text messages are another form of communication. They can be used to establish a link between two people simply by showing they have "messaged" each other. There have been cases where a person has entered a business to commit robbery while a lookout remains in a vehicle parked outside, and text messages were used to communicate between the two.

2. **Multimedia Message Service (MMS)** This can be thought of as text messaging with attachments such as video clips, sound files, or pictures. In one particular case, an individual took a video of himself sexually assaulting an incapacitated girl, and then sent the video clip to friends via MMS.

3. **Contact Lists and Call History** The names, phone numbers, addresses, and/or e-mail addresses of people who are associated with the owner of the mobile device and the log of recent contacts he or she has had are generally available and are of use in an investigation.

4. **Calendars, Appointments, and Tasks** This information may provide evidence of a suspect's actions on a particular date.

5. **Internet Access / Internet History / Internet Communication** Much like a traditional computer, Internet activity can be of great evidentiary value. For example, it may link a suspect to a specific social networking site or screen name in a child sexual exploitation case. Often, mobile devices contain the same Internet artifacts as computers, such as cookies, browser history, and bookmarks.

6. **Digital Camera / Video** There have been numerous cases where individuals have exploited this technology to take surreptitious, candid photographs of unsuspecting women in malls and stores.

7. **E-mail** Full e-mail access and clients (i.e., e-mail software) are available on most mobile devices, offering another source of potential evidence.

8. **Global Positioning System (GPS) and Map Data** Many devices, such as the Droid and iPhone, offer full GPS capabilities. The information in these applications can be extremely valuable in documenting the travel history of a suspect.

Mobile forensics manufacturers provide battery devices that can be used to keep a unit running while it is being transported to the lab. The investigator, if possible, should always seize the mobile device's charger and any associated cables. Because of the lack of standardization mentioned earlier, chargers and cables vary greatly between devices, and it is nearly impossible for examiners to stock every one.

Ultimately, data from the mobile device must be extracted and analyzed. Unlike computer forensics, however, the approach to mobile devices is more complicated. This complication arises because of the divergent ways that different devices store and manage data. Moreover, manufacturers vary in the type of memory used to store data, involving a combination of expansion cards and internal memory structures (RAM/ROM). Similarly, operating systems vary between devices. The Motorola Droid, for example, uses the Google's Android Operating System, while today's iPhone uses Apple's iPhone operating systems, typically referred to as iOS. The two vary in their partition, file, and directory structure. These are just two of the overwhelming number of devices on the market and thus encountered by investigators. Consequently, mobile device examiners need a multitude of equipment and a significant amount of knowledge.

There are numerous approaches to mobile forensics data extraction and analysis. Extraction of data can be done on the physical level, generally affording the greatest amount of total data collection but also, at times, presenting challenges in analysis. Extraction can also be done on a logical level, which limits the data acquired, but the data is often easier to analyze. The examiner generally makes these determinations based on the type of case, evidence sought, his or her own training, and the technological limitations of the mobile device or the tools available for analysis. It is the experience of most mobile forensic examiners that a lab needs to be equipped with several varied tools for acquisition and analysis.

Quick Review

- Mobile devices offer many of the services that are offered by computers and other devices. These devices can provide a vast amount of useful and evidentiary data in an investigation.
- Leaving a mobile device running but placing it in something that will block its communication is the preferred method for preserving data on a mobile device.
- Complications arise in extracting and evaluating data from mobile devices because of the variety of ways that different devices store and manage data.

CHAPTER REVIEW

- Computer forensics involves preserving, acquiring, extracting, and interpreting computer data.
- Software programs are applications that carry out a set of instructions.
- The central processing unit (CPU) is the "brain" of the computer—the main chip responsible for doing the actual computing.
- The motherboard is the main circuit board within a computer.
- Read-only memory (ROM) chips store programs that control the boot (startup) process and configure a computer's components.
- Random-access memory (RAM) is volatile memory, which is lost when power is turned off. Programs are loaded into RAM because of its faster read speed.
- The hard disk drive (HDD) is typically the primary location of data storage within the computer.
- The computer's operating system (OS) is the bridge between the human user and the computer's electronic components. It provides the user with a working environment and facilitates interaction with the system's components.
- Formatting is the process of preparing a hard disk drive to store and retrieve data in its current form.
- A sector is the smallest unit of data that a hard drive can address. A cluster usually is the minimum space allocated to a file. Clusters are groups of sectors.
- A FAT is a file allocation table. It tracks the location of files and folders on the hard disk drive.

- Aspects of a computer that should be photographed close up at an electronic crime scene include (1) the screen of any running computer monitor; (2) all the connections to the main system unit, such as peripheral devices (i.e., keyboard, monitor, speakers, mouse, etc.); and (3) equipment serial numbers.
- Evidentiary considerations may require the investigator to perform a live examination prior to disconnecting power.
- Two situations in which an investigator would not unplug a computer at an electronic crime scene are (1) if encryption is suspected, and thus pulling the plug would re-encrypt the data, rendering it unreadable without a password or key, and (2) if data exists in RAM that has not been saved to the HDD and will thus be lost if power to the system is discontinued.
- The primary goal in obtaining data from an HDD is to do so without altering even one bit of data. To this end, a Message Digest 5 (MD5)/Secure Hash Algorithm (SHA) takes a "fingerprint" of a hard disk drive (HDD) before and after forensic imaging.
- The types of computer evidence can be grouped under two major subheadings: visible and latent data.
- Visible data is data that the operating system is aware of and thus is easily accessible to the user. It includes any type of user-created data, such as word-processing documents, spreadsheets, accounting records, databases, and pictures.
- Temporary files created by programs as a sort of on-the-fly backup can prove valuable as evidence. Data in the swap space used to conserve the valuable RAM within the computer system can also yield evidentiary data.

- Latent data is data that the operating system is not aware of. The constant shuffling of data through deletion, defragmentation, swapping, and so on, is one of the reasons data is stored in latent areas.

- Latent data can exist in both RAM slack and file slack. RAM slack is the area from the end of the logical file to the end of the sector. File slack is the remaining area from the end of the final sector containing data to the end of the cluster.

- Latent data might be found in unallocated space—space on an HDD that the operating system sees as empty and ready for data.

- When a user deletes files, the data typically remains behind, so deleted files are another source of latent data.

- Places where a forensic computer examiner might look to determine what websites a computer user has visited recently are the Internet cache, cookies, and the Internet history.

- The history file can be located and read with a forensic software package. Another way to access websites that have been visited is by examining bookmarks and favorite places.

- IP addresses take the form ###.###.###.###, in which, generally speaking, ### can be any number from 0 to 255.

- IP addresses provide the means by which data can be routed to the appropriate location, and they also provide the means by which most Internet investigations are conducted.

- An investigator tracking the origin of an e-mail seeks out the sender's IP address in the e-mail's header. Chat and instant messages are typically located in a computer's random-access memory (RAM).

- Tracking the origin of unauthorized computer intrusions, or hacking, requires investigating a computer's log file, RAM, and network traffic.

- A firewall is a device designed to protect against intrusions into a computer network.

- Mobile devices offer many of the services that are offered by computers and other devices. These devices can provide a vast amount of useful and evidentiary data in an investigation.

- Leaving a mobile device running but placing it in something that will block its communication is the preferred method of choice for preserving data on a mobile device.

- Complications arise in extracting and evaluating data from mobile devices because of the variety of ways that different devices store and manage data.

KEY TERMS

bit, 465

bookmark, 480

byte, 465

central processing unit (CPU), 461

cluster, 465

cookies, 479

file slack, 475

firewall, 484

hacking, 484

hard disk drive (HDD), 462

hardware, 459

Internet cache, 479

Internet history, 480

latent data, 473

Message Digest 5 (MD5)/Secure Hash Algorithm (SHA), 470

motherboard, 461

operating system (OS), 464

partition, 465

random-access memory (RAM), 462

sector, 465

software, 460

swap file, 472

temporary files, 473

unallocated space, 476

visible data, 471

REVIEW QUESTIONS

1. Computer forensics involves the, _____, _____, _____, _____, and _____ of computer data.

2. True or False: Hardware comprises the physical components of the computer. _____

3. _____ is a set of instructions compiled into a program that performs a particular task.

4. (ROM, RAM) chips store programs used to start the boot process.

5. The term used to describe the chassis, including the motherboard and any other internal components of a personal computer, is _____.

6. True or False: The motherboard is a complex network of wires that carry data from one hardware device to another. _____

7. True or False: The first thing you should do when you encounter a computer system in a forensic investigation is to connect the power supply and boot the system. _____

8. RAM is referred to as "volatile memory" because it is not _____.

9. The "brain" of the computer is referred to as the _____.

10. The _____ is the primary component of storage in a personal computer.

11. Personal computers typically communicate with each other through a(n) _____.

12. The computer's _____ permits the user to manage files and applications.

13. A hard drive's partitions are typically divided into _____, _____, _____, and _____.

14. A(n) _____ is a single one or zero in the binary system and the smallest term in the language of computers.

15. A(n) _____ is a group of eight bits.

16. A group of sectors, always units in multiples of two, is called a(n) _____.

17. An exact duplicate of the entire contents of a hard disk drive is known as a(n) _____.

18. All data readily available to a computer user is known as _____ data.

19. A(n) _____ file is created when data is moved from RAM to the hard disk drive to conserve space.

20. Most programs automatically save a copy of a file being worked on into a(n) _____ file.

21. The existence of _____ data is why a forensic image of the media is created.

22. The smallest unit of addressable space on a hard disk drive is the _____.

23. The two types of slack space are _____ slack and _____ slack.

24. _____ slack is the area from the end of the data portion of the file to the end of the sector.

25. The portion of a disk that does not contain stored data is called _____.

26. True or False: Defragmenting a hard disk drive involves moving noncontiguous data back together. _____

27. True or False: A portion of a "deleted" file may be found in a computer's unallocated space. _____

28. A(n) _____ takes the form of a series of numbers to route data to an appropriate location on the Internet.

29. A user's hard disk drive will _____ portions of Web pages that have been visited.

30. A(n) _____ is placed on a hard disk drive by a website to track certain information about its visitors.

31. E-mails have the _____ address of the sender in the header portion of the e-mail.

32. True or False: Chat and instant messages conducted over the Internet are typically stored in RAM storage. _____

33. When investigating a hacking incident, investigators concentrate their efforts on three locations: _____, _____, and _____.

34. Devices that permit only requested traffic to enter a computer system are known as _____.

35. A(n) _____ is a device that can prevent a mobile phone from communicating with a service provider.

36. True or False: Extracting and analyzing data from mobile devices is complicated because manufacturers of these devices store and manage data in a variety of ways. _____

▪▪▪▪▪ APPLICATION AND CRITICAL THINKING

1. If a file system defines a cluster as six sectors, how many bits of information can be stored on each cluster? Explain your answer.

2. Criminalist Tom Parauda is investigating the scene of a crime involving a computer. After he arrives, he photographs the overall scene and takes close-up shots of all the connections to the single computer involved, as well as photos of the serial numbers of the computer and all peripheral devices. Tom then labels the cord to each peripheral device, then disconnects them from the computer. After making sure that all data in RAM has been saved to the hard disk drive, he unplugs the computer from the wall. What mistakes, if any, did Tom make?

3. You are investigating a case in which an accountant is accused of keeping fraudulent books for a firm. Upon examining his computer, you notice that the suspect uses two different accounting programs that are capable of reading the same types of files. Given this information, where would you probably begin to search for latent data on the computer and why?

4. You are examining two computers to determine the IP address from which several threatening e-mails were sent. The first computer uses Microsoft Outlook as an e-mail client and the second uses a Web-based e-mail client. Where would you probably look first for the IP addresses in each of these computers?

▪▪▪▪▪ ENDNOTES

1. A megabyte (MB) is approximately one million bytes; a gigabyte (GB) is approximately one billion bytes, or 1,000 megabytes.

2. Actually, the more appropriate term is probably "paging" as opposed to "swapping." This is because entire programs are typically not swapped in and out of memory to the swap space; rather, pages of memory are placed there.

19

Mobile Device Forensics

Peter Stephenson

THE KILLING OF SYLVESTER EDDINGS

Christopher Pullman's cell phone gave him away. In November of 2008, according to a jury, he murdered Sylvester Eddings in Scott County, Iowa. Unfortunately for Pullman, his cell phone was communicating with cell towers that put him in the vicinity of the murder. Pullman placed a phone call from his cell phone at 4:20 p.m. and it activated a nearby cell tower. The victim, Eddings, had been receiving text messages on his cell phone all day and had been responding. At 6:56 p.m., Eddings received a text message that was recorded on the same cell tower but he did not reply. Eddings's last cell call was made at 3:47 p.m., suggesting that he was killed sometime between 3:47 p.m. and 6:56 p.m. The cell tower "pings" (communications between cell towers and cell phones that establish connections) placed both Pullman and Eddings in the same vicinity when Eddings was killed. The jury agreed and found Pullman guilty.

LEARNING OBJECTIVES

After studying this chapter you should be able to:
- Identify the types of computing devices categorized as "mobile devices."
- Describe the different file systems typical in a mobile device.
- Describe different storage methods found in mobile devices.
- Describe the different types of operating systems used in mobile devices and their impact upon evidence collection and analysis.
- Describe the procedure for preserving evidence on a mobile device.
- Differentiate between logical and physical forensic images of mobile devices.
- Describe the procedure for seizing mobile devices.
- Describe the types of evidence that can be found on mobile devices including cell tower location evidence.
- Describe how to correlate evidence on a mobile device with evidence on a computer.
- Identify the types of forensic tools used to examine mobile devices.
- Describe techniques that may be used to extract data from older mobile devices.

O f all of the areas of digital forensics, mobile device forensics may be the most complicated. It is complicated for several reasons. First, there is a great number—and growing daily—of mobile devices. Second, these devices often have little in common, even those from the same manufacturer. Additionally, the proliferation of mobile devices as substitutes for full-size or laptop computers is significant and increasing rapidly. Finally, these devices are an amalgam of radio and computing technologies and may in some cases be treated differently under the law. The forensics involved certainly is complicated by this paradigm.

Mobile devices began as an outgrowth of ship-to-shore radios in the Second World War. Additionally, handheld radio transceivers, or walkie-talkies, were available then and they evolved into mobile phones for cars in the 1940s. The real explosion in mobile devices came much later. Before that, we saw the Motorola handheld phone debuting in 1973. From that point on, advances in cellular technology enabled the mobile phone boom that followed. Early mobile phone systems were **analog** (1G). They were followed by digital networks (2G).

When mobile **broadband** networks (3G) arrived on the scene in Japan in 2001, the mobile device landscape changed forever. Now it was possible to do much more than talk on a cell phone. Now the cell phone had the possibility of behaving like a small computer and could transfer data at near-Internet speeds. The smart phone was born. When native IP networks arrived (4G), the smart phone became a node on the Internet just like any other computing device. With the proliferation of **WiFi** networking, smart phones evolved into tablets, and products such as the iPad became viable substitutes for small computers.

analog
The traditional method of modulating radio signals so that they can carry information.

broadband
Communication channel that can provide higher-speed data communication than a standard telephone circuit.

WiFi
A term describing a wireless Local Area Network.

The Mobile Device Neighborhood

WHAT MAKES A MOBILE DEVICE "MOBILE"?

We start with the notion of "cellular systems." A cellular system is a network of relatively short-distance transceivers that are spaced strategically so that low-power transmitters can reach the phones in their coverage areas and the very-low-power transmitters in the cell phones can reach the cell tower. Since the 1960s, the concepts of handoff and frequency reuse allowed users to move between cells without dropping a call. Usually. As we will see, 1G networks suffered from this problem much to the consternation of their users. Figure 19-1 shows the layout of cell towers and their coverage areas. Although there is overlap as indicated by the red circles, the transmitting patterns are hexagonal due to the transmission patterns of the tower's antenna array.

Returning to the early 1G analog phones, we have several issues that laid the groundwork for modern mobile devices. Some of these are still with us and can bedevil the forensic examiner. 1G networks are "analog." That means that they behave in exactly the same way as older radio stations behave. A mobile

---

Dr. Peter Stephenson a cyber-criminologist and educator with fifty years of technology experience, has written, edited, or contributed to eighteen books and several hundred articles in major national and international trade, technical, and scientific publications. He is an associate professor teaching network attack and defense, digital forensics, and cyber investigation on both the graduate and undergraduate levels at Norwich University in Vermont; is the chief information security officer for the university; and is the director of the Center for Advanced Computing and Digital Forensics. He holds one of the first PhDs in the world in digital investigation and was one of the first recipients of the prestigious Certified Cyber Forensic Professional designation from (ISC). In addition, he holds the CISSP and CISM designations and is a member of the American Academy of Forensic Sciences and the Vidocq Society. He holds a master's degree in diplomacy with a concentration in terrorism.

FIGURE 19-1 Cell tower geographic configuration. *SAFERSTEIN, RICHARD, Ph.D., CRIMINALISTICS: AN INTRODUCTION TO FORENSIC SCIENCE, 11th Ed., ©2015. Reprinted and Electronically reproduced by permission of Pearson Education, Inc., Upper Saddle River, New Jersey*

GSM (Global System for Mobile Communication)
A set of standards for second generation cellular networks.

CDMA (Code Division Multiple Access)
A spread spectrum technology for cellular networks.

device is made up of a computer and one or more radios. The computer may be quite primitive and the radios may communicate with a network of some type. Since cellular networks are much different from WiFi networks, devices that communicate with both need two radios. 1G devices usually could communicate with only the cellular system.

2G, or digital cellular networks, appeared in the 1990s using two standards: **GSM (Global System for Mobile Communications)** and **CDMA (Code Division with Multiple Access)**. This new generation moved phones into the small, handheld form factor and, because they were digital, the new networks opened the door for practical data communications and the beginning of what was referred to as "feature phones." These phones had more features than simply being able to make and receive phone calls, hence the name. Feature phones could send and receive SMS (text) messages, synchronize with e-mail, and had other features that were heading the mobile device genre in the direction of smart phones and tablets.

Communications were slow, however, and such things as surfing the Web and transferring photos were not particularly practical. Smaller radios were practical, however, because of the increased density of cell tower installations that saved battery life, further reducing the physical size of the phones.

3G, or mobile broadband data, opened the floodgates for mobile communications and, thus, the explosion of mobile devices on the market. The architectural functionality that distinguishes 2G from 3G is that 2G systems were circuit switched and 3G systems are packet switched. Without delving too deeply into the technical differences between the two, we may say that, fundamentally, circuit switching is similar to landline telephone systems and packet switching is like the Internet. Indeed, one of the benefits of packet switching is the ability to connect more readily to the Internet.

The advent of packet-switched mobile phone networks allowed virtually any kind of data to be accessed by the mobile device and, so, the smart phone was born. Moving photos over the network, streaming video and television, video chat, and other advanced services now could be supported. 3G was launched in Japan in 2001.

4G, or native IP networks, differ technologically from 3G networks in that they access the Internet directly, increasing speed and bandwidth dramatically. With 4G, virtually any form of communication possible with a PC was now possible from a smart phone or tablet. The age of the mobile device was now in full swing.

Quick Review

- A "cellular system" is a network of relatively short-distance transceivers that are spaced strategically so that low-power transmitters can reach the phones in their coverage areas and the very-low-power transmitters in the cell phones can reach the cell.
- Digital (2G) cellular networks moved phones into the small, handheld form, and, because they were digital, the new networks opened the door for practical data communications and the beginning of what was referred to as "feature phones."

- The architectural functionality that distinguishes 2G from 3G is that 2G systems were circuit switched and 3G systems are packet switched.
- The advent of packet-switched mobile phone networks allowed virtually any kind of data to be accessed by the mobile device, and the smart phone was born.
- Native IP (4G) networks differ technologically from 3G networks in that they access the Internet directly, increasing speed and bandwidth dramatically.

Forensic Challenges

MOBILE DEVICES AS SMALL COMPUTERS—SORT OF

Modern mobile devices are, in many respects, little more than small PCs. However, they do have some unique aspects that complicate the digital forensic process a bit. Let's begin by going back to those 1G devices. They still exist in some parts of the world and even with die-hard users in the United States in regions where 1G networks still exist. While those are extremely rare, the more common occurrence is getting a 1G phone tied to a fifteen-year-old crime. The problem with these old devices is that they do not have the capabilities that we are used to with a computer. Virtually none have what we would classify as an **operating system**, and about the most you can hope to get off of them is the phone directory. Some may keep a call log, but the number of calls retained is fairly small. Anything that has been deleted is no longer available. Unlike many operating systems, we are unable to recover deleted material.

operating system
A custom-designed program that controls the components of mobile devices and facilitates how they function.

When we get to 2G, the ball game changes considerably. These phones still exist, mostly with people who are satisfied with their limited capabilities and who live in a 2G network area. The capabilities of these phones, while considerably fewer than smart phones, are well ahead of 1G phones; most of the 2G devices have real operating systems. Mostly these operating systems are custom designed for the phones—such as Palm and Blackberry—but in some cases they are the forerunners of smart phone operating systems.

Some 2G phones, such as feature phones, come closer to smart phones than others. However, the ability to recover deleted messages, for example, varies significantly from phone model to model. However, just because a phone has an operating system (OS) does not mean that the operating system is the same as a PC's. While the OS performs many of the same functions as that of a PC, it does not necessarily follow that it performs them in the same way or, in many cases, even as well. The most popular operating systems for mobile devices—including phones and tablets—are Apple iOS, Google Android, and Microsoft Windows Phone OS. Primitive versions of these were widely available for 2G devices.

Some had other features, but, the higher the bandwidth requirement, the poorer these devices performed. From a forensic perspective, it is a toss-up as to how much data you will be able to extract from a 2G device. More important, during this time the manufacturers of mobile devices started to go wild with new product releases. The problem was—and still is—that even if two phones looked a lot alike, had the same functionality, and used the same OS, there was no guarantee that they were the same; and if your mobile device forensic tool did not have a driver specifically designed for that particular phone, you were out of luck forensically. This continues to be the single most difficult issue plaguing mobile device forensics: it is nearly impossible to stay current with the available mobile device models.

3G and 4G phones are the closest in **architecture** and design to a PC. They behave the same way—especially 4G devices—and they have the ability

architecture
Defines the basic components of a mobile device.

FIGURE 19-2 Representation of geolocation using a mobile device. *Joel Shawn/Shutterstock*

geolocation
Assessment of actual geographical location of a mobile device.

GPS (Global Positioning System)
A system for determining position by comparing radio signals from several satellites.

SD card
Storage expansion card for a mobile device.

to download and install applications ("apps") the same as any PC or Mac. They are the same in architectural issues such as processors and file systems, but the nature of those architectures is different between mobile devices and computers. This is because mobile devices have special requirements such as multiple radios (e.g., WiFi and 4G), size restrictions, storage space, and so forth. Apps are both a boon and a devilment to the forensic examiner. Apps each have their own specific operating parameters, and how they communicate with the outside—*if* they communicate—is inconsistent from app to app. Apple has taken major steps to standardize the development of apps for its iPad and iPhone, but Android apps are far less constrained. Furthermore, just because an app is written for the iOS operating system does not mean that it runs equally well or behaves the same on an iPad and iPhone. In that regard, Android apps are a bit less forgiving.

For the forensic analyst, understanding what is running on the mobile device under examination is a key—and not trivial to figure out—issue. Once the examiner understands what is running, it is equally difficult to figure out what the app is doing and how it is interacting with the user and the outside. One interesting aspect of mobile device forensics is **geolocation**. Some devices and many apps report the geographical location of the device (see Figure 19-2). That can make it much easier to track the owner's movements.

Additionally, mobile devices that offer geolocation include not just smart phones and tablets, but we also can analyze **GPS (Global Positioning System)** devices such as Garmin or TomTom. However, special tools and drivers are required, as with other mobile devices, and GPS units are becoming as prolific and ever-changing as smart phones and tablets.

Another forensic challenge, particularly with phones, is the chipset used to build the phone. This adds another variable to the mix along with OS, model, manufacturer, and apps. The "chipset" is the hardware that makes the device work. Today, there is quite a large number of chipsets, and the most difficult to deal with are knockoffs of American chips manufactured in China. Not all of these behave the same as American chips, and special driver sets for mobile device forensic tools are required.

The big problem, of course, is that, even though some of these devices are really small computers with computer-like operating systems, they usually cannot be examined using typical computer forensic tools. Each device has its own quirks and each device needs special connectors and special device drivers on the tool that is examining it to decipher what is on the device's storage. Device storage also takes several forms from on-board nonvolatile memory to mini-**SD cards** that add storage in a modern smart phone or tablet. This does not include those devices that predate the computer-like architectures. They need special drivers and connectors as well, but the amount of information that can be gleaned from them is much less because the amount of information they store is much less.

Quick Review

- The most popular operating systems for mobile devices—including phones and tablets—are Apple iOS, Google Android, and Microsoft Windows Phone OS.
- 3G and 4G phones are the closest in architecture and design to a PC. They behave the same way—especially 4G devices—and they have the ability to download and install applications ("apps") the same as any PC or Mac.

- One interesting aspect of mobile device forensics is geolocation. The GPS can locate the user's activities and, when used with a timeline, can place the user in the vicinity of a crime. That can make it much easier to track the owner's movements.
- Each device has its own quirks, and each device needs special connectors and special device drivers on the tool that is examining it to decipher what is on the device's storage. Device storage also takes several forms, such as on-board nonvolatile memory and mini-SD cards that add storage in a modern smart phone or tablet.

Extracting Useful Data

THE DIFFERENCES IN VARIOUS TYPES OF MOBILE DEVICES

When working on a mobile device, there are several sources of information available to the investigator. Probably the most useful is Web searching. Doing a search on the phone model often gets you a wealth of information such as other investigators' experiences, battery-charging techniques, what can and cannot be recovered if it was deleted, and so on. Some phones and tablets are fairly modern and rather straightforward. With those, connection to the forensic tool and extraction is fairly simple to do. But some devices—and these include both very old and very new—are not so obvious. Some research before connecting is important. All mobile devices should be kept in a "Faraday" bag or box. This prevents changes from being made to the device remotely. These changes might be initiated by the owner of the device—remote wipe to preserve a picture of innocence by destroying evidence—or unintentional—changes made by the device's carrier that could overwrite evidence. The efficacy of Faraday enclosures has been debated by experts but the consensus still is to use them.

So, our first step is to determine with what we are working. Is it a very old feature phone, a typical iPad or iPhone, or is it a state-of-the-art, just-announced-last-week smart phone? Do a little research, select your tool, and then make your next decision: physical or **logical extraction** (or both)? Just as with computers, **physical extraction** is the best bet. Physical forensic images are bit-by-bit copies of the file system including deleted data. Logical extraction is a snapshot of the file system showing what the file system wants you to see. Here you get the same view that the user gets.

Some tools, such as Cellebrite's UFED Touch, are quite clear about which devices support physical extraction. If you have a device that supports physical extraction, that is the way to image the device. Logical extractions are useful only when the physical option is not available because of the device itself. The author has worked on a cell phone where an exchange of text messages may hold evidence in a murder. However, one side of the exchange is missing—obviously someone deleted it—and, because of the architecture of the phone, retrieving the deleted messages is not possible. The only solution is to acquire the other phone in the conversation and extract it from that phone. If that phone is not available, you are left with a tantalizing snippet that may or may not include evidence.

YouTube has a remarkable number of videos that show detailed step-by-step procedures for device disassembly. Special tools may be required. Working on a carpeted surface often raises the danger of static electricity. That can damage the chips in a device. It may be wise to wear a grounded antistatic wristband when working on a mobile device, especially if disassembly will be required.

When you have identified your device and the procedures to extract its data, run your tools and take your forensic image. Examiners make it a practice

logical extraction
A snapshot of the file system of a mobile device.

physical extraction
A duplicate of data located on a mobile device.

to run the imager twice, taking one of the images and treating it as evidence. The other is your working image. This ensures that, if necessary, you can make another copy of the evidence original as a new work copy should you inadvertently damage the one you are using.

Logical images are fairly fast for most devices, depending upon how much memory the device has and how much of the memory is full. Physical images can take a very long time to make because, on a large storage device, even if the storage is not full, the imager must look at the entire memory footprint, not just that part that has something saved to it. The examiner should decide, based upon what can be done with the particular device, whether to obtain a physical or logical extraction or both. The logical extraction is fairly fast and one might want to examine it for obvious evidence while the tool is making a physical image of the target.

It's important to select the proper connector—or "pigtail"—for your device from your tool kit.

Quick Review

- All mobile devices should be kept in a "Faraday" bag or box. This prevents changes from being made to the device remotely.
- Physical forensic images are bit-by-bit copies of the file system, including deleted data. Logical extraction is a snapshot of the file system showing what the file system wants the user to see.
- Mobile device forensic analysis can provide an overlay to physical evidence and timelines as well as computer forensic timelines to give a clearer picture of the events preceding and following a crime event.
- Examiners make it a practice to run the forensic image twice, taking one of the images and treating it as evidence.
- The examiner should decide, based on what can be done with the particular device, whether to obtain a physical or logical extraction or both.

Mobile Device Architecture

WHAT IS INSIDE THE DEVICE AND FOR WHAT IS IT USED?

All mobile devices have an "architecture." Just like computers, the architecture defines the basic components of the device. How and where is data stored? What kind of processor is used? What does the file system look like? Is there a formal file system? These and other questions form the basis of the analysis. Extraction is affected only if there is additional storage—such as an extra plug-in SD card—that must be analyzed. Most analysis tools acquire these add-in storage modules, but it is helpful to know which do so that data wasn't be missed.

SIMS AND SDS

SIM (Subscriber Identification Module) card
The smart card that is inserted into a mobile device that identifies the user account to the network, handles authentication, and provides storage for basic user data and network information.

Secure Digital (SD) cards are storage expansion cards that many mobile devices can accept. The SD adds memory for storing such things as photos and music. SD cards are "nonvolatile," meaning that, even if the power is turned off on the device, you won't lose your favorite tunes or your pictures of Great Aunt Susie just as she was going down the water slide at the local swimming pool (see Figure 19-3).

SIM cards are different. SIM means "subscriber identity (or identification) module." Each SIM has an international mobile subscriber identity (IMSI) number that associates the phone with the subscriber's mobile network. In

FIGURE 19-3 32 GB SD Card (right) and adapter. *Krisda Chamchuen/Alamy*

FIGURE 19-4 A SIM inserted in a cell phone.[1] *Brian Jackson/Alamy*

many cases, you can keep all of your subscriber information when you change mobile phones simply by switching the SIM to the new phone. SIMs may also store text messages and other user data, as well as the user's phone book and the phone number of the device. Not all mobile devices use SIMs. The information on the SIM may be stored in the device itself. However, for forensic purposes, you must be able to access that information because it is your way of identifying the target device unambiguously when a form of forensic analysis is performed.

Also on each SIM is the integrated circuit card identifier (ICCID). That number also is printed on the SIM. The ICCID contains the issuer identification number (IIN), the individual account identification, and a check digit. The forensic image of the mobile device is acquired and the tool will extract and record the ICCID. That is usually the way one identifies the phone, but if it is a SIM and not embedded in the mobile device, you must bear in mind that you are seeing only the SIM and not, necessarily, the device itself. Figure 19-4 shows the SIM ready for placement in the cell phone.

Often it is desirable to clone the SIM in much the same way as one would take a physical image of the mobile device or a computer. By cloning the SIM, the investigator retains a perfect copy for evidentiary purposes. Some mobile device forensics vendors, such as AccessData, developer of the MPE +, provide forensic SIMs for use as targets to which the investigator may clone the evidence SIM for preservation.

In addition to memory, the typical mobile device contains a digital signal processor, a microprocessor, radio frequency transmitter/receiver, audio components, and a power supply that takes battery power to run the device as well as providing for the ability to charge the battery. Thus, the mobile device is a simple radio transceiver with a few digital twists and turns that make it more like a computer in some regards.

This hybrid construction—a radio and a computer—means that, as forensic investigators, we must focus on the laws that cover both. In some regards, thinking from the computer side, we must be concerned about such things as privacy. From the radio side, there also are protections of which one must be aware that vary greatly from jurisdiction to jurisdiction.

FILE SYSTEMS—OR NOT

To say that every mobile device has a **file system** is both correct and incorrect. Certainly there needs to be a way to keep track of such things as phone books, but in some cases we simply are looking at a flat file database. A "flat file database," as we are using the term here, refers to a single file, usually

file system
A software mechanism that defines the way files are named, stored, organized, and accessed.

TABLE 19.1 Example Mobile Device File Systems (not exhaustive)

Blackberry	SQLite or MS exFAT
Android	Ext4, YAFFS, or vendor proprietary
iOS	HFSX

human-readable, that contains some collection of data, in this case names and phone numbers. The earliest, most primitive mobile devices had such a file structure.

When we think of a file system, though, we usually think of some organized method of collecting files of various types and keeping track of them. In computers, we have file tables that track both the files in the file system and their physical location on the computer's hard drive. A real file system must be able to do those two things: track the logical location of the files on the device and tie that to the files' physical locations. More modern mobile devices do both of those things, sometimes with a proprietary file system and occasionally with a more open one.

Tracking the locations of files, both physically and logically, is done with some sort of database. Sometimes the database is proprietary and tied to the file structure itself and sometimes it is a standard database such as SQL Lite (SQLite). In either case, the analysis tool must know what file system structure the device uses and it must know how to address files on the device both physically and logically. Extracting file information from such a data structure is critical to the analysis of mobile devices just as it is on computers. And the extraction and analysis are quite similar.

One important aspect of file system analysis is accessibility. Can you access deleted files, for example? Is there some indication, as is the case with the Windows operating system on a computer, that a file existed even if it has been deleted?[2] The answer, unfortunately, is "maybe." As shown in Table 19-1, different types of operating systems have different types of file systems, some more recoverable than others.

It may not be possible to recover deleted file items such as e-mails, texts, and photos from a mobile device. For example, Blackberries cannot be recovered directly. To recover deleted files one must go to the backup—usually on a PC somewhere—and recover from that. One can also recover from the Blackberry server if available. iOS devices are somewhat easier and tools such as Cellebrite's UFED can do that with a physical extraction. Androids are usually recoverable as well since they are, at heart, a form of Linux.

Analyzing Mobile Devices

FINDING FORENSICALLY VALUABLE ARTIFACTS

The detailed analysis of mobile devices is a book in itself. There are so many different devices (between 50,000 and 100,000 by some counts) and multiple generations of devices that a full discussion of analysis that would address all of these possibilities is not attainable in a single chapter. As well, a detailed understanding of computer and mobile device architecture is necessary to grasp many of the finer points of analysis. It suffices here to discuss process and give some examples that are at opposite ends of the mobile device spectrum. We have introduced the Apple iPad and the Samsung SCH R350. Let's start with our Samsung phone. The R350 is a feature phone popular around 2009. It had a lot of features but some, such as its music player, required an optional memory card. Overall, the R350 was a very good stepping stone to today's smart phones if you deployed all of its features. The file system is EFS (encrypting file system). By looking at the Project Tree on the UFED extraction report it's possible to find out if the user browsed the web and the history of web browsing.

Further, by browsing down the Project Tree on the UFED extraction report, one may find folders associated with a phone book and calendar.

The iPhone is replete with data for one's perusal. The calendar is referred to as *Calendar* rather than *task list*. That is because *Calendar* is the phone's terminology and the UFED simply uses it for consistency.

In addition to the calendar, we can follow the project tree in the UFED report and see several other resources that our iPhone gives up to our analysis.

There is a call log with details, chats including deleted messages, contacts including recently contacted, cookies, **SMS messages** (texts), voicemails, and more. This is a veritable treasure trove of data on the phone's user and his/her behavior. But there is much more if we look a bit deeper. For example, it would be nice to take all of the phone's activities and place them on a timeline. Digital forensic investigations depend upon time lines for their success. Indeed, when overlaid on the timelines of a physical crime, the timelines from mobile devices and computers provide an excellent yardstick by which to measure the play of events surrounding the crime itself. Because of the vast amount of data the iPhone 4S smart phone offers, we can create just such a timeline.

The UFED also provides us with the ability to analyze phone activity by caller giving us incoming, outgoing, missed, and SMS (text) calls.

Another very useful type of mobile device is the GPS. GPSs can locate the user's activities and, when used with a timeline, can place the user in the vicinity of a crime. Timelines are the meat and potatoes of digital forensic investigations. Because we have access to a fairly accurate clock on computers and mobile devices, we can match the activities on these devices to physical crime activities to do a precrime, pericrime (during the crime event), and postcrime analysis of a suspect's behavior.

For example with the Garmin nuvi 40 GPS, the UFED provides a timeline, but since there is a GPS the timeline is associated with a specific location. In addition to the timeline graph, there are specific entries noting where the GPS was located at a particular latitude and longitude at a particular time.

Following the track of locations using Google Maps and these coordinates is a straightforward way to track the progress of the GPS during some particular period of time. To make the tracking easier, the GPS provides a list of journeys, each with the coordinates of waypoints over the course of the trip. That can be correlated back to the timeline view for devices that have been used heavily, simplifying the tracking of the GPS on specific dates of interest.

Additionally, the GPS provides a list of favorite destinations with their coordinates.

SMS messages (Short Message Service) A cellular network facility that allows users to send and receive text messages.

Quick Review

- Secure Digital (SD) cards are storage expansion cards that many mobile devices can accept. The SD card adds memory for storing such things as photos and music. SD cards are nonvolatile.
- Subscriber Identification Module (SIM) cards have an international mobile subscriber identity (IMSI) number that associates the phone with the subscriber's mobile network.
- Each SIM is the integrated circuit card identifier (ICCID). The ICCID contains the issuer identification number (IIN), the individual account identification, and a check digit.
- In addition to memory, the typical mobile device contains a digital signal processor, a microprocessor, a radio frequency transmitter/receiver, audio components, and a power supply that takes battery power to run the device as well as providing the ability to charge the battery.

Hybrid Crime Assessment

FITTING THE MOBILE DEVICE INTO THE DIGITAL FORENSIC INVESTIGATION

Now that we've gotten a look at how digital forensics is performed on mobile devices, it would be useful to fit that process into the investigative process as a whole. In any investigation, chain of evidence is very important. *Chain of evidence,*[3] as opposed *to chain of custody* describes the events and concomitant evidence that make up the events of the crime. There are two types of chains of evidence. *Temporal chains* show events in the order in which they occurred. This commonly is called a "timeline" and is the easiest way for lay people, such as triers of fact, to visualize a crime, especially a complicated one.

Causal chains of evidence describe the events of a crime in terms of cause and effect. The links in the chain are the pieces of evidence and they are tied together based upon how one link affects one or more other links. We could say that our first link causes the next link to occur which in turn causes two other links—events—to happen and so on until the events of the crime describe, fully, the crime itself. For our purposes—and to keep this manageable—we will stick with the temporal chain. This is where a technique called *hybrid crime assessment* enters the picture.

Hybrid crime assessment is a technique that you can use when you are faced with a physical crime—murder, rape, robbery, and so on—and there is a digital element to it—a computer, cell phone, or other mobile device. The idea is to tie all of these elements together into a single crime scene and use the timelines to build a picture and describe the events, and supporting evidence, of the crime. This works very well. So well, in fact, that the author has used it to describe the last few minutes of a shooting victim's life when the closest physical event that could be corroborated occurred over a half hour prior to the shooting and had nothing to do with the crime itself.

In that regard, it is important to recognize that there are events in the timeline that have little or nothing to do with the actual crime but can act as markers—rather like quarter-hour chimes on a clock that simply happen but do not play any role beyond marking time. In the case of the shooting, the activities of the victim on his computer ended moments before he was murdered. Given the physical crime scene and the position of the body, the activities surrounding his use of the computer were very important. They placed, with little question, the time of the event within an eight-minute period which corroborated a witness account. They also allowed some level of description of the events immediately following the event since the computer was turned back on after it had been shut down briefly.

This is a simplistic example of correlating the events of a physical crime with a timeline of events on a computer. In this case, the period of inactivity on the computer could be measured and that timeline—very accurate since it was based upon the computer's clock—could be laid against the physical timeline to fill in gaps and corroborate witness accounts. When we add the dimension of a mobile device, which works in essentially the same manner as the computer for our purposes, we have a layered view of the timeline of an event and the pre-event and post-event elements/evidence that make up the layers. The mobile device is one of the layers, and, in most cases, the most accurate one.

Mobile devices may be synchronized to the network clock. That means that the network provider—AT&T, Verizon, T-Mobile, and so on—are sending the clock signal to the mobile device. Since the network provider is likely to use a time standard such as the U.S. Naval Observatory to obtain time ticks, it is likely that the mobile device is extremely accurate as a yardstick for measuring when events happen. How the user behaves with the mobile device can be measured precisely against that yardstick.

Mobile devices, like most computers, perform various types of housekeeping. That means that the device is constantly doing things on its own to maintain its own operation. For example, it must continue to stay in contact with the mobile network (or the WiFi network if it is set up to connect to one). It must make sure that all of its internal functions are working properly; so it is constantly testing parts of itself. When the device is in use, it does more. When it is in standby, it does less. When it is off, obviously, it does nothing. There are variations on that as well. For example, if you put the device in "airplane mode," the radio is off but the rest of the computer (in the phone) still is working. By checking logs, when they are present, we can see when the radio was turned off or on.

As we have seen, the amount of information that we can get from a mobile device varies greatly with the device. Unfortunately, most books that deal with mobile device forensics make the assumption that the digital investigator will invariably encounter a fairly recent device. That means that the oldest devices are likely to be feature phones. That, as it turns out, is not a practical position to take. Feature phones of widely varying capabilities are generally available and there are mobile phones that are little more than that: mobile phones. These and older phones often have very little to offer in the way of establishing timelines but should be examined in any event.

However, when a mobile device has information to give up it can be extremely useful. For example, when a mobile device is set to use WiFi, it will recognize any WiFi network in its range. It may not be able to join the network because of the security settings on the WiFi access point, but the mobile device will see it and note that it exists. When that happens, the device takes note of the network and logs it. This is a function of today's mobile devices such as smart phones. In our iPhone 4S, we can look at its timeline, expand it to get maximum resolution, and we can see, for example, that at 15:42:30 on 6/12/2012 the phone was in a Best Buy store. We see that because the timeline shows that it joined the Best Buy network at that time.

Taken with other evidence, such as GPS information, witness interviews, or the individual's own timeline as reported during an interview/interrogation, this evidence becomes a good corroborator and may, in some cases, provide an alibi for an individual. Also, however, it might place the individual near the crime scene. If one opts to take a bit more complicated look, the mobile device can be examined for everything going on on it at a particular time. Then the investigator can put all of the pieces together from both the mobile device logs—which are quite precise—and the physical evidence, which may not be as precise.

Quick Review

- Temporal chains show events in the order in time in which they occurred. This commonly is called a timeline.
- "Causal" chains of evidence describe the events of a crime in terms of cause and effect. The links in the chain are the pieces of evidence, and they are tied together based upon how one link affects one or more other links.
- "Hybrid crime assessment" is a technique that investigators can use when faced with a physical crime—such as murder, rape, or robbery—that has a digital element to it—a computer, a cell phone, or some other mobile device.
- The amount of information that one can get from a mobile device varies greatly with the device.

■■■■ CHAPTER SUMMARY

- A "cellular system" is a network of relatively short-distance transceivers that are spaced strategically so that low-power transmitters can reach the phones in their coverage areas and the very-low-power transmitters in the cell phones can reach the cell.

- Digital (2G) cellular networks moved phones into the small, handheld form, and, because they were digital, the new networks opened the door for practical data communications and the beginning of what was referred to as "feature phones."

- The architectural functionality that distinguishes 2G from 3G is that 2G systems were circuit switched and 3G systems are packet switched.

- The advent of packet-switched mobile phone networks allowed virtually any kind of data to be accessed by the mobile device, and, so, the smart phone was born.

- Native IP (4G) networks differ technologically from 3G networks in that they access the Internet directly, increasing speed and bandwidth dramatically.

- The most popular operating systems for mobile devices—including phones and tablets—are Apple iOS, Google Android, and Microsoft Windows Phone OS.

- 3G and 4G phones are the closest in architecture and design to a PC. They behave the same way—especially 4G devices—and they have the ability to download and install applications ("apps") the same as any PC or Mac.

- One interesting aspect of mobile device forensics is geolocation. The GPS can locate the user's activities and, when used with a timeline, can place the user in the vicinity of a crime. That can make it much easier to track the owner's movements.

- Each device has its own quirks, and each device needs special connectors and special device drivers on the tool that is examining it to decipher what is on the device's storage. Device storage also takes several forms, such as onboard nonvolatile memory and mini-SD cards that add storage in a modern smart phone or tablet.

- All mobile devices should be kept in a "Faraday" bag or box. This prevents changes from being made to the device remotely.

- Physical forensic images are bit-by-bit copies of the file system, including deleted data. Logical extraction is a snapshot of the file system showing what the file system wants the user to see.

- Mobile device forensic analysis can provide an overlay to physical evidence, and timelines (as well as computer forensic timelines) can give a clearer picture of the events preceding and following a crime event.

- Examiners make it a practice to run the forensic image twice, taking one of the images and treating it as evidence.

- The examiner should decide, based on what can be done with the particular device, whether to obtain a physical or logical extraction or both.

- Secure Digital (SD) cards are storage expansion cards that many mobile devices can accept. The SD card adds memory for storing such things as photos and music. SD cards are nonvolatile.

- Subscriber Identification Module (SIM) cards have an international mobile subscriber identity (IMSI) number that associates the phone with the subscriber's mobile network.

- Each SIM is the integrated circuit card identifier (ICCID). The ICCID contains the issuer identification number (IIN), the individual account identification, and a check digit.

- In addition to memory, the typical mobile device contains a digital signal processor, a microprocessor, a radio frequency transmitter/receiver, audio components, and a power supply that takes battery power to run the device as well as providing the ability to charge the battery.

- Temporal chains show events in the order in time in which they occurred. This commonly is called a timeline.

- "Causal" chains of evidence describe the events of a crime in terms of cause and effect. The links in the chain are the pieces of evidence, and they are tied together based upon how one link affects one or more other links.

- "Hybrid crime assessment" is a technique that investigators can use when faced with a physical crime—such as murder, rape, or robbery—that has a digital element to it: a computer, a cell phone, or some other mobile device.

- The amount of information that one can get from a mobile device varies greatly with the device.

KEY TERMS

analog, 491

architecture, 493

broadband, 491

CDMA (Code Division Multiple Access), 492

file system, 497

geolocation, 494

GSM (Global System for Mobile Communication), 492

GPS (Global Positioning System), 494

logical extraction, 495

operating system, 493

physical extraction, 495

SIM (Subscriber Identification Module) card, 496

SD card, 494

SMS messages (Short Message Service), 499

WiFi, 491

REVIEW QUESTIONS

1. Early mobile phone systems were followed by digital _____ networks.

2. True or False: The architectural functionality that distinguishes 2G from 3G is that 2G systems were circuit switched and 3G systems are packet switched. _____

3. True or False: One of the benefits of packet switching is the ability to connect more readily to the Internet. _____

4. It's (easy, difficult) to stay current with the available mobile device models.

5. Apple has taken major steps to standardize the development of apps for its _____ and _____.

6. Some devices and many apps report the _____ of the device. That can make it much easier to track the owner's movements.

7. When working on a mobile device, there are several sources of information available to the investigator. Probably the most useful source of information available to an investigator is _____.

8. An examiner should decide whether to obtain a _____ extraction or _____ extraction or both of a mobile device.

9. True or False: If you have a device that supports physical extraction, that is the way to image the device. Logical extractions are useful only when the physical option is not available because of the device itself. _____

10. True or False: Logical extractions are bit-by-bit copies of the file system including deleted data. _____

11. Examiners make it a practice to run an extracted image (once, twice).

12. The _____ extraction is fairly fast and one might want to examine it for obvious evidence while a tool is making a physical image of the target.

13. Just like computers, the _____ defines the basic components of the mobile device.

14. _____ are storage expansion cards that many mobile devices can accept.

15. True or False: SD cards are "nonvolatile," meaning that even if the power is turned off on the device, you won't lose your favorite tunes or your picture. _____

16. In many cases, you can keep your subscriber information when you change mobile phones by simply switching the _____ card to the new phone.

17. Often it is desirable to _____ the SIM in much the same way as one would take a physical image of the mobile device or a computer in order to retain a copy for evidentiary purposes.

18. True or False: It's always possible to recover deleted file items such as e-mails, texts, and photos from a mobile device. _____

19. _____ describes the events and concomitant evidence that make up the events of the crime.

20. _____ chains show events in the order in which they occurred.

21. _____ chains of evidence describe the events of a crime in terms of cause and effect.

22. _____ crime assessment attempts to tie elements of a crime together into a single crime scene and use the timelines to build a picture and describe the events and supporting evidence of the crime.

23. It is likely that the mobile device is extremely accurate as a yardstick for measuring when events happen as the device may be synchronized to a _____ clock.

24. When a mobile device is set to use _____, it will recognize any _____ network in its range.

25. True or False: Mobile device forensic analysis can provide an overlay to physical evidence, and timelines (as well as computer forensic timelines) can give a clearer picture of the events preceding and following a crime event. _____

APPLICATION AND CRITICAL THINKING

Here are some questions to focus your thinking about the digital forensic process and digital forensic investigation as they apply to mobile devices.

1. What precautions should one take when seizing/analyzing a live, turned-on mobile device?

2. Differentiate chain of evidence and chain of custody and give examples of both in the context of an investigation where mobile devices play an important part.

3. How can law enforcement make use of the locations of cell phone towers?

4. How are today's generations of mobile devices different from and the same as personal computers?

5. What are SIMs and SDs and why does a mobile device need them? Do all mobile devices have one or both of these? If not, what substitutes?

6. What is the IMSI; where might it reside; and for what is it used? How would the digital forensic investigator use it?

7. If there is a GPS capability on a smart phone, how might the investigator make use of it? Is it useful for correlation? What kind would it be and how would it be accomplished?

FURTHER REFERENCES

Digital Evidence and Forensics, 2010.
www.nij.gov/topics/forensics/evidence/digital/welcome.htm

Electronic Crime Scene Investigation: A Guide for First Responders, 2nd ed., 2008
www.nij.gov/pubs-sum/219941.htm

Guidelines on Cell Phone Forensics, 2007.
www.csrc.nist.gov/publications/nistpubs/800-101/SP800-101.pdf

ENDNOTES

1. www.flickr.com/photos/71390254@N04/6740223177/in/photostream/ accessed May 26, 2013.

2. The link or .lnk files on a MS Windows computer.

3. As opposed to chain of custody that describes access to evidence.

::APPENDIXES

The *Handbook of Forensic Services* provides guidance and procedures for the safe and efficient methods of collecting, preserving, packaging, and shipping evidence and describes the forensic examinations performed by the FBI's Laboratory Division and Operational Technology Division.

The contents of the *Handbook* are to be found by the reader on either the iPhone app entitled "FBI Handbook" or the Android app entitled "Handbook of Forensic Services."

APPENDIX II
INSTRUCTIONS FOR COLLECTING GUNSHOT RESIDUE (GSR)

INSTRUCTIONS FOR COLLECTING GUNSHOT RESIDUE (GSR)
for Scanning Electron Microscopy and Atomic Absorption Analysis

— NOTE —

In control test firings, it has been shown that the concentration of gunshot residue significantly declines on living subjects after approximately 4 hours. In view of these findings, if more than 4 hours have passed since the shooting, it is recommended that you check with your crime laboratory before submitting samples for analysis.

— S.E.M. COLLECTION PROCEDURE —

(A) When the covering is removed from the metal stubs, the adhesive collecting surface is exposed and care must be used to not drop the stub or contaminate the collecting surface by allowing this exposed surface to come in contact with an object other than the area that is to be sampled. (See Figure 1.)

(B) *Do not* return paper stub cover to stubs after collection. (*Discard stub covers.*)

(C) Heavily soiled or bloody areas should be avoided if possible.

(D) When pressing the stubs on the questioned areas, use enough pressure to cause a mild indentation on the surface of the subject's hand.

STEP 1 Fill out all information requested on the enclosed Gunshot Residue Analysis Information Form.

STEP 2 Put on the disposable plastic gloves provided in this kit. *Do not substitute with other gloves!*

> NOTE: If there is blood on the subject's hands or clothing, the investigating officer should put on latex or other approved barrier gloves to protect him/her from bloodborne pathogens, then put on the plastic gloves provided in this kit.

STEP 3 <u>RIGHT BACK:</u>

(A) Carefully remove the cap from the vial labeled RIGHT BACK, then remove the paper covering from the metal sample stub.

(B) While holding the vial cap, press the collecting surface of the stub onto the back of the subject's right hand until the area shown below in Figure 2 has been covered.

(C) After sampling the back of the subject's right hand, return the cap, with metal stub, to the RIGHT BACK vial. *Do not return paper covering to metal stub!*

VIAL CAP
METAL STUB
COLLECTING SURFACE

Fig. 1

STEP 4 <u>RIGHT PALM:</u>

Repeat the procedure described in Step 3, using the metal stub in the vial marked RIGHT PALM. Make sure to sample the area shown below in Figure 3.

STEP 5 <u>LEFT BACK and LEFT PALM:</u>

For collection from the left hand, repeat Steps 3 and 4 using the vials labeled LEFT BACK and LEFT PALM.

STEP 6 After sampling all four areas, return capped vials to kit envelope.

Fig. 2 (BACK)

Fig. 3 (PALM)

Source: Courtesy of Tri-Tech Forensics, Inc., Southport, NC

A.A. COLLECTION PROCEDURE

NOTE: (A) This second part of the GSR collection is *ONLY* to be performed *AFTER* sampling with the SEM stubs.

(B) If you feel that during the SEM collection procedure you have contaminated the gloves, discard contaminated gloves, then thoroughly wash your hands with soap and water and dry with a clean towel. At no time during the collection process should your hands (with or without gloves) come into contact with the cotton tip of the swab.

(C) When dispensing nitric acid, use 2 - 3 drops of 5% nitric acid solution to moisten each swab (do not over-moisten). In order to dispense an appropriate amount of the nitric acid solution, hold the acid dispenser in a horizontal position above and *almost* touching the top of the swab, and squeeze gently.

(D) To swab the subject's hands, the investigator should grasp the subject's arm above the wrist with one hand and swab with the other. The subject's hand should be in a "spread" position. Thorough swabbing of the hands is carried out by using moderate pressure while swabbing. The swab should be rotated during this procedure to insure that all of the surface of the cotton tip is utilized. At least 30 seconds per swab is required.

(E) When placing swabs in tubes, always place cotton tips *FACE DOWN*.

STEP 7   <u>CONTROL SWABS</u>: Remove *two* of the swabs from the unmarked ziplock bag. Moisten both swabs with 2 - 3 drops of the 5% nitric acid solution supplied in kit (do not substitute). Place both swabs in the tube labeled CONTROL. Then recap tube and set it aside.

STEP 8   <u>RIGHT BACK</u>:

(A) Moisten the tip of *ONE* swab with 2 - 3 drops of nitric acid solution, then thoroughly swab the back of the subject's right hand including the back of the fingers and all of the web area which would be exposed while holding a weapon. Fig. 4 illustrates the area of hand for swabbing. Place swab used in the tube labeled RIGHT BACK.

Fig. 4 (BACK)

(B) Repeat the above procedure using a *SECOND* swab. Place the second swab used in the RIGHT BACK tube, then recap tube and set it aside.

STEP 9   <u>RIGHT PALM</u>:

(A) Moisten the tip of *ONE* swab with 2 - 3 drops of nitric acid solution, then thoroughly swab the palm of the subject's right hand as shown in Fig. 5. Place swab used in the tube labeled RIGHT PALM.

(B) Repeat the above procedure using a *SECOND* swab. Place the second swab used in the RIGHT PALM tube, then recap tube and set it aside.

Fig. 5 (PALM)

STEP 10   <u>LEFT BACK/LEFT PALM</u>: Follow the same procedures described in Steps 8 and 9, but swabbing the subject's left hand.

STEP 11   <u>CARTRIDGE CASE</u>:

NOTE: For .22 cal and foreign manufactured ammunition, it is necessary that either Steps A and B described below be completed <u>OR</u> the casings be submitted to the laboratory. If latent prints are required on the expended casing(s), Steps A and B should be omitted and the casings should be submitted for latent print processing. If for any reason the CARTRIDGE CASE swabs are not used, mark the tube "*NOT USED*".

(A) Moisten the tip of *ONE* swab with 2 - 3 drops of nitric acid solution, then thoroughly swab the inside of the cartridge case. Place swab used in the tube labeled CARTRIDGE CASE.

(B) Repeat the above procedure using a *SECOND* swab. Place second swab used in the CARTRIDGE CASE tube, and then recap tube and set it aside.

FINAL INSTRUCTIONS

(A) Fill out all information requested on the front of the kit envelope.

(B) With the exception of the 5% nitric acid dispenser and the disposable gloves, return all other kit components, used or unused, to kit envelope.

(C) Moisten kit envelope flap, then seal envelope. Affix Police Evidence Seal where indicated, then initial seal.

(D) Mail or hand deliver sealed kit to the crime laboratory for analysis. (If mailed, package kit in a cardboard box to prevent damage in transit.)

Iodine Spray Reagent

1. Prepare the following stock solutions:

Solution A	Solution B
Dissolve gram of Iodine in 1 liter of Cyclohexane	Dissolve 5 grams of a-Naphthoflavone in 40 ml of Methylene Chloride (Dichloramethane)

2. Add 2 ml of Solution B to 100 ml of Solution A. Using a magnetic stirrer, mix thoroughly for 5 minutes.

3. Filter the solution through a facial tissue, paper towel, filter paper, etc., into a beaker. The solution should be lightly sprayed on the specimen using an aerosol spray unit or a mini spray gun powered with compressed air.

4. Lightly spray the suspect area with several applications until latent prints sufficiently develop.

Remarks

- Solution A may be stored at room temperature. Shelf life is in excess of 30 days.
- Solution B must be refrigerated. Shelf life is in excess of 30 days.
- The combined working solution (A and B) should be used within 24 hours after mixing.
- The Iodine Spray solution is effective on most surfaces (porous and nonporous).
- A fine spray mist is the most effective form of application.
- The Cyanoacrylate (Super Glue) process cannot be used prior to the Iodine Spray Reagent Process. Cyanoacrylate may be used, however, after the Iodine Spray Reagent.
- On porous surfaces, DFO and/or Ninhydrin may be used after the Iodine Spray.
- Propanol may be used to remove the staining of the Iodine Spray Reagent.
- 1,1,2 Trichlorotrifluoroethane may be substituted for Cyclohexane.

1,8-Diazafluoren-9-one (DFO)

Step 1: Stock solution: Dissolve 1 gram DFO in 200 ml Methanol, 200 ml Ethyl Acetate, and 40 ml Acetic Acid.

Step 2: Working solution (make as needed): Start with stock solution and dilute to 2 liters with Petroleum Ether (40° to 60° boiling point fraction). Pentane can also be used. Solution should be clear.

Dip the paper document into the working solution and allow to dry. Dip again and allow to dry. When completely dry, apply heat (200° for 10 to 20 minutes). An oven, hair dryer, or dry iron can be used.

Visualize with an alternate light source at 450, 485, 525, and 530 nm and observe through orange goggles. If the surface paper is yellow, such as legal paper, it may be necessary to visualize the paper at 570 nm and view it through red goggles.

Source: In part from *Processing Guide for Developing Latent Prints,* Revised 2000. Washington, D.C.: FBI; http://www.fbi.gov/about-us/lab/forensic-science-communications/fsc/jan2001/lpu.pdf

1,2-indanedione

2.0 g 1,2-indanedione

70 ml ethyl acetate

930 ml HFE 7100 (3M Company)

Ninhydrin

20 grams Ninhydrin

3,300 ml Acetone

Shelf life is approximately one month

or

5 grams Ninhydrin

30 ml Methanol

40 ml 2-Propanol

930 ml Petroleum Ether

Shelf life is approximately one year

Dip the paper document in the working solution and allow to dry. Dip again and allow to dry. When completely dry, heat may be applied. A steam iron should be used on the steam setting. Do not touch the iron directly to the paper. Rather, hold the iron above the paper and allow the steam to heat it.

Zinc Chloride Solution (Post-Ninhydrin Treatment)

5 grams of Zinc Chloride crystals

2 ml of Glacial Acetic Acid

100 ml of Methyl Alcohol

Add 400 ml of 1,1,2 Trichlorotrifluoroethane to the mixture and stir.

Add 2 ml of 5 percent Sodium Hypochlorite solution (commercially available liquid bleach such as Clorox, Purex, and others).

Lightly spray the paper with the Zinc solution. Repeat the spraying as needed. Do not overdo the spraying.

The ninhydrin-developed prints treated with this solution may fluoresce at room temperature with an alternate light source. For maximum fluorescence, place the paper in a bath of liquid nitrogen and examine again with an alternate light source.

Physical Developer

When mixing and using these solutions, make sure the glassware, processing trays, stirring rods, and stirring magnets are absolutely clean. Do not use metal trays or tweezers.

Stock Detergent Solution: 3 grams of *N*-Dodecylamine Acetate are combined with 4 grams of Synperonic-*N* mixed in 1 liter of distilled water.

Silver Nitrate Solution: 20 grams of Silver Nitrate crystals are mixed in 100 milliliters of distilled water.

Redox Solution: 60 grams of Ferric Nitrate are mixed in 1,800 milliliters of distilled water. After this solution is thoroughly mixed, add 160 grams of Ferrous Ammonium Sulfate, mix thoroughly and add 40 grams of Citric Acid, mix thoroughly.

Maleic Acid Solution: Put 50 grams of Maleic Acid into 2 liters of distilled water.

Physical Developer Working Solution: Begin with 2,125 milliliters of the Redox Solution and add 80 milliliters of the Stock Detergent Solution, mix well, then add 100 milliliters of the Silver Nitrate Solution and mix well. Appropriate divisions can be used if smaller amounts of the working solution are desired.

Immerse specimen in Maleic Acid Solution for 10 minutes. Incubate item in physical developer (PD) working solution for 15–20 minutes. Thoroughly rinse specimen in tap water for 20 minutes. Air-dry and photograph.

Cyanoacrylate Fluorescent Enhancement Reagents

Rhodamine 6G

Stock Solution
100 mg Rhodamine 6G
100 ml Methanol (Stir until thoroughly dissolved.)

Working Solution
3 ml Rhodamine 6G Stock Solution
15 ml Acetone
10 ml Acetonitrile
15 ml Methanol
32 ml 2-Propanol
925 ml Petroleum Ether (Combine in order listed.)

Ardrox

2 ml Ardrox P-133D
10 ml Acetone
25 ml Methanol
10 ml 2-Propanol
8 ml Acetonitrile
945 ml Petroleum Ether

MBD

7-(p-methoxybenzylaminol)-4-nitrobenz-2-oxa-1,3-diazole

Stock Solution
100 mg MBD
100 ml Acetone

Working Solution
10 ml MBD Stock Solution
30 ml Methanol
10 ml 2-Propanol
950 ml Petroleum Ether (Combine in order listed.)

Basic Yellow 40

2 grams Basic Yellow 40
1 liter Methanol

RAM Combination Enhancer*

3 ml Rhodamine 6G Stock Solution
2 ml Ardrox P-133D
7 ml MBD Stock Solution
20 ml Methanol
10 ml 2-Propanol
8 ml Acetonitrile
950 ml Petroleum Ether
(Combine in order listed.)

*Source: John H. Olenik, Freemont, Ohio.

RAY Combination Enhancer*

To 940 ml of either isopropyl alcohol or denatured ethyl alcohol add:

1.0 gram of Basic Yellow 40

0.1 gram of Rhodamine 6G

8 ml of Arodrox P-133D

50 ml of Acetonitrile (optional, but dye stain of prints will appear more brilliant)

MRM 10 Combination Enhancer

3 ml Rhodamine 6G Stock Solution

3 ml Basic Yellow 40 Stock Solution

7 ml MBD Stock Solution

20 ml Methanol

10 ml 2-Propanol

8 ml Acetonitrile

950 ml Petroleum Ether

(Combine in order listed.)

The above solutions are used on evidence that has been treated with cyanoacrylate (Super Glue) fumes. These solutions dye the cyanoacrylate residue adhering to the latent print residue. Wash the dye over the evidence. It may be necessary to rinse the surface with a solvent, such as Petroleum Ether, to remove the excess stain.

CAUTION: These solutions contain solvents that may be respiratory irritants, so they should be mixed and used in a fume hood or while wearing a full-face breathing apparatus. Also, these solvents may damage some plastics, cloth, wood, and painted surfaces.

Because of the respiratory irritation possible and the general inefficiency of spraying, it is *not* recommended to spray these solutions. To obtain the maximum benefit and coverage, it is recommended that evidence be soaked, submerged, or washed with these types of solutions.

*Source: John H. Olenik, Freemont, Ohio.

Amido Black

Staining Solution:

0.2 g Napthalene 12B or Napthol Blue Black

10 ml Glacial Acetic Acid

90 ml Methanol

Rinsing Solution:

90 ml Methanol

10 ml Glacial Acetic Acid

Stain the impression by spraying or immersing the item in the staining solution for approximately one minute. Next, treat with the rinsing solution to remove stain from nonimpression area. Then rinse well with distilled water.

Coomassie Blue

Staining Solution (add in this order):

0.44 g Coomassie Brilliant Blue

200 ml Methanol

40 ml Glacial Acetic Acid

200 ml Distilled Water

Rinsing Solution:

40 ml Glacial Acetic Acid

200 ml Methanol

200 ml Distilled Water

Spray object with the staining solution, completely covering the area of interest. Then spray the object with rinsing solution, clearing the background. Then rinse with distilled water.

Crowle's Double Stain

Developer:

2.5 grams Crocein Scarlet 7B

150 mg Coomassie Brilliant Blue R

50 ml Glacial Acetic Acid

30 ml Trichloroacetic Acid

Combine the above ingredients, then dilute to one liter with distilled water. Place the solution on a stirring device until all the Crocein Scarlet 7B and Coomassie Brilliant Blue R are dissolved.

Rinse:

30 ml Glacial Acetic Acid

970 ml Distilled Water

Apply the developer to the item(s) by dipping. Completely cover the target area, leaving the developer on for approximately 30 to 90 seconds, and then rinse. Finally, rinse well with distilled water.

Diaminobenzidine (DAB)

Solution A (Fixer Solution):

20 g 5-Sulphosalicylic Acid

Dissolved in 1 L Distilled Water

Solution B:

100 ml 1M Phosphate Buffer (pH 7.4)

800 ml Distilled Water

Solution C:

1 g Diaminobenzidine

Dissolved in 100 ml Distilled Water

Working Solution (Mix Just Prior to Use):

900 ml solution B

100 ml solution C

5 ml 30% Hydrogen Peroxide

Immerse impression area in fixer solution A for approximately 4 minutes. Remove and rinse in distilled water. Immerse impression area for approximately 4 minutes in the working solution or until print is fully developed. Remove and rinse in distilled water.

Fuchsin Acid

20 g Sulfosalicylic Acid

2 g Fuchsin Acid

Dissolved in 1 L Distilled Water

Stain the impression by spraying or immersing the item in the dye solution for approximately one minute. Rinse well with distilled water.

Hungarian Red

This product is available from: www.forensicssource.com

Leucocrystal Violet

10 g 5-Sulfosalicylic Acid

500 ml 3% Hydrogen Peroxide

3.7 g Sodium Acetate

1 g Leucocrystal Violet

If Leucocrystal Violet crystals are yellow instead of white, do not use. This indicates crystals are old and solution will not work.

Spray the object until completely covered. Then allow object to air-dry. Development of impressions will occur within 30 seconds. Store the solution in amber glassware and refrigerate.

Leucocrystal Violet Field Kit*

When the reagents are separated in the listed manner below, a "field kit" can be prepared. The field kit separation will allow for an extended shelf life.

Bottle A:

10 grams 5-Sulfosalicylic Acid

500 ml Hydrogen Peroxide 3%

Bottle B:

1.1 grams Leucocrystal Violet

Weigh out reagent and place in an amber 60 ml (2 ounce) bottle.

Bottle C:

4.4 grams Sodium Acetate

Weigh out reagent and place in an amber 60 ml (2 ounce) bottle.

Add approximately 30 ml of Bottle A reagent to Bottle B. Secure cap and shake Bottle B for two (2) to three (3) minutes. Pour contents of Bottle B back into Bottle A.

Add approximately 30 ml of Bottle A reagent to Bottle C. Secure cap and shake Bottle C for approximately two (2) to three (3) minutes. Pour contents of Bottle C into Bottle A. Secure Bottle A's cap and shake thoroughly.

Spray the target area; development will occur within thirty (30) seconds. After spraying, blot the area with a tissue or paper towel. Then allow object to air-dry.

Patent Blue

20 g Sulfosalicylic Acid

2 g Patent Blue V (VF)

Dissolved in 1 L Distilled Water

Stain object by spraying or immersing the item in the dye solution for approximately one minute. Rinse well with distilled water.

Tartrazine

20 g Sulfosalicylic Acid

2 g Tartrazine

Dissolved in 1 L Distilled Water

Stain object by spraying or immersing the item in the dye solution for approximately one minute. Rinse well with distilled water.

*Source: John Fisher, Forensic Research & Supply Corp., Gotha, Fla.

ANSWERS TO END-OF-CHAPTER QUESTIONS

Chapter 1
Review Questions

1. forensic science
2. Mathieu Orfila
3. Alphonse Bertillon; anthropometry
4. Sherlock Holmes
5. Edmond Locard; Locard's exchange principle
6. Hans Gross
7. True
8. Dr. Leone Lattes
9. Albert S. Osborn
10. Sir Alec Jeffreys
11. True
12. Los Angeles
13. California
14. federal; state; county; municipal
15. regional
16. FBI; Drug Enforcement Administration; Bureau of Alcohol, Tobacco, Firearms, and Explosives; U.S. Postal Inspection Service
17. Physical science
18. biological
19. firearms
20. document examination unit
21. toxicology
22. crime-scene investigation
23. False
24. *Frye* v. *United States*
25. *Daubert* v. *Merrell Dow Pharmaceuticals, Inc.*
26. False
27. *Coppolino* v. *State*
28. expert witness
29. True
30. True
31. True
32. *Melendez-Diaz* v. *Massachusetts*
33. training

Application and Critical Thinking

1. There are a range of possible answers to this question. Under the British fee-for-service model, government budgets might limit the number and type of laboratory tests police and prosecutors may request. On the other hand, if they must pay fees for crime lab services, police and prosecutors may be more careful about the types of evidence they submit. The fact that the U.S. model allows investigators to submit a theoretically unlimited amount of evidence for examination means that it might encourage police to spend more time and resources than necessary to investigate a case. Under a fee-for-service model, police must be more efficient in their investigations. However, this can be a drawback in cases in which initial tests prove inconclusive and more extensive methods of examination are needed.

2. The note would be examined by the document examination unit; the revolver would be examined by both the firearms unit and the latent fingerprint unit; the traces of skin and blood would be examined by the biology unit.

3. Again, this question could have several answers, which might include greater expertise in crime-scene investigation, using the skills of experts in several areas of criminalistics, and reducing the workload of patrol officers.

4. On appeal, the defense raised the question of whether a new test that has not been generally accepted by the scientific community is admissible as evidence in court. The court rejected the appeal, arguing that "general acceptance," as stated in *Frye* v. *United States*, is not an absolute prerequisite to the admissibility of scientific evidence.

5. C, A, G, E, B, F, D

6. A = Toxicology, B = Drugs, C = Biology, D = Computer and Digital, E = Biology, F = Criminalistics, G = Anthropology, H = Document Examination, I = Computer and Digital, J = Toxicology, K = Fingerprint, L = Criminalistics, M = Firearms

Chapter 2
Review Questions

1. True
2. first officer
3. medical assistance
4. excluded

5. False

6. log

7. False

8. primary; secondary

9. command center

10. systematic

11. physical evidence

12. False

13. fingerprints

14. True

15. False

16. final survey

17. False

Application and Critical Thinking

1. While waiting for backup, you should summon medical assistance for the victim, take a statement from the victim, detain any suspects at the scene, establish the boundaries of the crime scene, and ensure no unauthorized personnel enter the crime scene.

2. a. grid or line search

   b. quadrant (zone) search

   c. spiral or line search

3. Officer Walter made a mistake by opening the window and airing out the house. He should have kept the window closed until an investigation team arrived. From the lack of blood or evidence of a struggle, he concluded that the murder occurred somewhere else and that the room containing the body was a secondary scene.

Case Analysis

1. The first challenge investigators faced was destruction of evidence. Mexican authorities autopsied the bodies twice before the corpses had been inspected, which likely destroyed potentially helpful evidence. Authorities also prevented forensic scientists from examining the corpses until the bodies had decomposed significantly. Mexican police removed all of the obvious evidence from the residence where the victims were held before allowing the FBI forensic team to enter the scene. Mexican authorities later seized a license plate hidden at the scene and would not allow FBI agents to examine it or to conduct any further searches of the property. In addition, for "health reasons," Mexican authorities destroyed much of the evidence that had been collected from the crime scene.

   The second challenge was contamination of crime scenes linked to the murders. The location where the bodies were discovered was not sealed by police, thus allowing both police officers and onlookers to contaminate the scene. Also, the residence at 881 Lope De Vega, where the victims were believed to have been killed, was cleaned and painted before forensics experts had an opportunity

to examine it. In addition, Mexican federal police officers had been living in the residence since shortly after the time of the murders, further contaminating the scene.

2. Investigators collected reference samples of carpeting from the victims' bodies, as well as bits of the victims' clothing and the sheets in which the bodies were buried. The carpet samples matched samples taken from the residence at 881 Lope De Vega, where investigators suspected the victims were killed. The samples of the burial sheet matched pillowcases found at the residence, and bits of clothing matching that worn by the victims were also found at the residence. In addition, hair and blood samples matching those of the victims were found in the residence at 881 Lope De Vega.

3. Investigators found that soil samples from the victims' bodies did not match the soil from the area where the bodies were found. They also found no significant bodily fluids in the area where the bodies were found. This evidence suggested that the bodies had originally been buried elsewhere and later transported to the location where they were found. Investigators later compared soil samples from the victims' bodies to samples taken from a park where the bodies of two Americans killed by drug traffickers had been discovered. Soil samples from the bodies of Camarena and Zavala exactly matched the soil found at the location where the Americans' bodies were found.

Chapter 3
Review Questions

1. notes; photography; sketches

2. True

3. first responding officer

4. False

5. notes

6. False

7. False

8. single lens reflex (DSLR)

9. True

10. standard operating procedures

11. aperture

12. shutter speed

13. depth of field

14. False

15. electronic strobe flash

16. microchip

17. False

18. barrier

19. photography log

20. unaltered

21. True
22. overview; medium range; close-up
23. False
24. 90°
25. painting with light
26. True
27. arson
28. True
29. False
30. videotaping
31. rough
32. rectangular; triangulation; baseline; polar coordinates
33. False
34. finished sketch
35. computer-aided drafting

Application and Critical Thinking

1. a. macro lens
   b. normal lens
   c. wide-angle lens
2. a. bypass filter
   b. complementary color filter
   c. barrier filter
3. a. sports setting
   b. setting exposure compensation toward a negative value
   c. portrait mode
   d. white balance
   e. center-weighted metering
4. Missing elements are the time, a description of the type of crime, and measurements of the scene.

Chapter 4
Review Questions

1. physical evidence
2. True
3. mobile crime laboratories
4. carriers
5. True
6. fingernail
7. True
8. False
9. separate
10. False
11. False
12. False
13. druggist fold

14. disposable
15. paper
16. contamination
17. air-dried
18. chain of custody
19. True
20. standard/reference
21. buccal swabs
22. substrate controls
23. True
24. evidence submission
25. infectious
26. biohazard
27. False
28. warrantless
29. arson

Application and Critical Thinking

1. Officer Guajardo should not have removed the scrap of cloth until the photographer had arrived and taken a picture of the evidence. He also should have put on latex gloves or used a forceps or other tool to remove the scrap of cloth. Finally, he should have placed the cloth in a paper bag or other container in which air could circulate, rather than in a sealed plastic bag where moisture could accumulate and cause mold to grow on the cloth.

2. Officer Gurney should have recorded his initials on the original seal, along with the date on which the evidence was sealed. A red biohazard label should have been placed on the container delivered to the laboratory. The forensic scientist should have avoided breaking the old seal. The forensic scientist also should not have discarded the old seal.

Chapter 5
Review Questions

1. identification
2. exclude
3. comparative
4. probability
5. individual
6. class
7. True
8. personal experience
9. eyewitness
10. corroborate
11. weight
12. True
13. False

14. False

15. natural variations

16. experience

17. False

18. Combined DNA Index System (CODIS)

19. True

20. False

Application and Critical Thinking

1. Determining whether an unknown substance contains heroin (c) would require the least extensive testing because the investigator can select only procedures that are designed to identify the presence of heroin. Determining whether an unknown substance contains an illicit drug (a) would require the next most extensive testing regimen because the investigator must select as many procedures as necessary to test for all types of illicit drugs. Determining the composition of an unknown substance (b) would likely require the most extensive testing because of the extremely large number of possible substances to test for.

2. From most common to least common, the order would be a, c, and b.

3. a. class characteristic

   b. individual characteristic

   c. individual characteristic

   d. class characteristic

   e. individual characteristic

   f. class characteristic

   g. individual characteristic

   h. individual characteristic

4. PDQ and SICAR contain information that relates primarily to evidence exhibiting class characteristics. The paint finishes and sole prints in these databases can identify the manufacturer of a shoe or paint mixture but cannot determine the exact source of evidence that matches the samples stored in the database. CODIS, IAFIS, and NIBIN, on the other hand, contain information that relates primarily to evidence exhibiting individual characteristics. The DNA profiles, fingerprints, and striation markings stored in these databases are unique, and thus can be used to link specific individuals or weapons with a crime scene.

5. An investigator would likely collect standard/reference samples of hair, fibers, and blood because these items are most likely to have been transferred from the perpetrator to the victim, and vice-versa, during a long struggle.

Chapter 6

Review Questions

1. coroner; medical examiner

2. False

3. pathologist

4. False

5. cause of death

6. False

7. blunt

8. False

9. defensive

10. True

11. oxygen

12. True

13. hemoglobin

14. False

15. False

16. alive

17. petechiae

18. capillaries

19. False

20. True

21. False

22. True

23. autopsy

24. True

25. external; internal

26. stippling or tattooing

27. True

28. edema

29. False

30. False

31. Postmortem redistribution

32. True

33. carbon monoxide

34. False

35. algor mortis

36. livor mortis

37. True

38. potassium

39. autolysis; putrefaction

40. pelvis

41. False

42. True

43. forensic anthropology

44. forensic entomology

45. postmortem

46. True

Application and Critical Thinking

1. Rigor mortis would be an unsuitable method if the victim had been dead longer than 36 hours because the condition disappears after this time. Livor mortis ceases 16 hours after death, so it would be of limited value in estimating the time of death after this period has elapsed. Algor mortis would not be an accurate method for estimating the time of death if the body was stored in a particularly hot or cold environment because extreme temperatures would affect the rate at which the body lost heat.

2. a. a forensic entomologist
   b. a forensic odontologist
   c. a forensic anthropologist

3. a. homicide
   b. accidental
   c. homicide
   d. accidental
   e. homicide
   f. natural causes

4. Gender = Female
   Ancestry = Negroid
   Age Range = 24–32 years
   Height = 160.308 cm to 161.998 cm (approximately 63 inches, or 5 feet 3 inches)

5. D, B, F, C, A, E

Chapter 7
Review Questions

1. crime-scene reconstruction
2. criminalists
3. objectivity
4. False
5. False
6. inductive; deductive
7. circumstantial evidence
8. falsifiability
9. bifurcation
10. False
11. false linkage
12. True
13. physical evidence
14. direct physical evidence
15. testimonial evidence
16. reenactment
17. chain of custody
18. True

19. False
20. theories
21. True
22. event timeline

Application and Critical Thinking

1. a. generalization
   b. false linkage
   c. bifurcation

2. The only direct physical evidence that connects the acquaintance to the crime scene is his fingerprint on the knife. The ticket stub constitutes circumstantial evidence to connect the acquaintance to the scene; there is no proof that it belonged to the acquaintance. Based on direct physical evidence and deductive reasoning only, you can conclude that the acquaintance had at some time handled the knife found at the crime scene. Using circumstantial evidence and inductive reasoning, you might conclude that there is a probability that the acquaintance murdered the victim with the knife, but there also exists a probability that the acquaintance touched the knife at another time. You also might conclude that there is a probability that the acquaintance bought a ticket to the movie to give himself an alibi for his whereabouts at the time of the crime and dropped the stub at the crime scene. You may also conclude that there is a probability that the victim or another individual purchased the ticket.

Chapter 8
Review Questions

1. Alphonse Bertillon
2. anthropometry
3. Sir Francis Galton
4. Sir Edward Richard Henry
5. True
6. Federal Bureau of Investigation (FBI)
7. 64 billion
8. False
9. ridge characteristics/minutiae
10. fingerprints
11. dermal papillae
12. latent
13. dermal papillae
14. True
15. loops; whorls; arches
16. loop
17. arch
18. radial
19. plain arch

20. analysis; comparison; evaluation; verification
21. True
22. whorl
23. 1/1
24. False
25. True
26. minutiae
27. livescan
28. visible fingerprint
29. plastic
30. powder
31. chemical
32. iodine
33. ninhydrin
34. Physical Developer
35. False
36. Super Glue fuming
37. fluorescence
38. alternate light sources
39. photography
40. lifting

Application and Critical Thinking

1. a. whorl
   b. arch
   c. loop
   d. whorl
   e. whorl
   f. arch
2. The primary classification for this individual would be as follows:
$$\frac{0 + 8 + 4 + 0 + 1 + 1}{16 + 8 + 0 + 2 + 1 + 1}$$
   Thus, the classification would be 14/28.
3. a. chemicals
   b. powder
   c. powder
   d. chemicals
   e. chemicals
4. a. scaling and resizing
   b. spatial filtering
   c. frequency analysis, or frequency Fourier transform (FFT)
5. Tented arch = Ivan
   Accidental whorl = Charlie
   Double-loop whorl = KJ
   Plain loop = Lisa

6. 11
7. None of the suspects' fingerprints match.

Chapter 9
Review Questions

1. handguns; long
2. single-shot; revolver; semi-automatic
3. revolver
4. shot
5. choke
6. land
7. caliber
8. True
9. individual
10. comparison microscope
11. striations
12. False
13. smooth
14. gauge
15. False
16. True
17. NIBIN
18. True
19. False
20. 12; 18
21. bullet wipe
22. yard
23. infrared
24. True
25. primer
26. barium; antimony
27. False
28. scanning electron microscope
29. True
30. False
31. base; nose
32. False
33. False
34. gunpowder residue
35. tool mark
36. striations
37. cast
38. electrostatic lifting device
39. photography; casting
40. individual

Application and Critical Thinking

1. The most popular approach to collecting gunshot residues from a shooter's hands involves applying adhesive tape or adhesive to the surface of the hands to remove any adhering particles of residue. Another approach is to remove residues by swabbing both the firing and nonfiring hands with cotton that has been moistened with 5 percent nitric acid. The most specific method is to analyze the adhesive tape with SEM coupled with an X-ray analyzer to determine particle morphology and elemental composition.

2. The correct answer is (a), 18 yards. A 12-gauge shotgun with no choke would be expected to produce a spread of about 1 inch for each yard from the shooter to the target. Thus, a spread of 12 inches would represent a distance of about 12 yards. A moderately high choke, however, would narrow the spread of the pattern somewhat. This means that, at a distance of 12 yards, the spread would be less than 12 inches. At a distance of 6 yards, the spread would be much less than 12 inches. Answers (b) and (c), therefore, are incorrect. The distance in answer (d), 30 yards, is probably too far. Although the choke would narrow the spread of the pellets, it would probably not narrow it to such a great extent.

3. Ben made several errors. Before unloading the revolver, Ben should have indicated the chamber position in line with the barrel by scratching a mark on the cylinder. He then should have made a diagram of the gun, designating each chamber with a number. As he removed each cartridge, he should have marked it to correspond to the numbered chambers in the diagram. Ben also should have placed each cartridge in a separate envelope, and he should have put the tag on the trigger guard, not the grip. Instead of using pliers to grab the bullet and pull it from the wall, Ben should have carefully broken away the surrounding wall material while avoiding direct contact with the bullet. Finally, he should have wrapped the bullet in tissue paper before placing it in an envelope.

4. a. Photograph the print.
   b. Photograph the tool mark, and then make a cast of it.
   c. Photograph the tire marks, and then make a cast of them.
   d. Photograph the shoe print, and then bring the tile bearing the print to the laboratory.
   e. Photograph the print, and then use an electrostatic lifting device to lift it off the surface.

5. A = 6 inches; B = 1 inch; C = contact; D = 18 inches

Chapter 10
Review Questions

1. bloodstain patterns
2. control experiments
3. victims; suspects
4. True

5. increases
6. directionality; angle of impact
7. circular
8. width; length
9. impact spatter
10. False
11. low velocity; medium velocity; high velocity
12. False
13. area of convergence
14. area of origin
15. string
16. transfer pattern
17. lightens
18. True
19. True
20. pool
21. skeletonize
22. castoff
23. False
24. arterial spray spatter
25. trail
26. expirated blood
27. void
28. True
29. grid method
30. perimeter ruler method
31. True

Application and Critical Thinking

1. a. Drops 1, 5, and 8 struck the surface closest to a 90-degree angle; they are the most nearly circular in shape.
   b. Drops 3, 4, and 9 struck the surface farthest from a 90-degree angle; their shapes are the most elongated.
   c. Drop 2 was traveling right to left and drop 7 was traveling from bottom to top when they struck the surface. The tails of the drops point in the direction of travel.

2. Investigator Wright should conclude that the bullet did not exit the body.

3. The tiny droplets and linear pattern suggest that the weapon used in the assault was likely a small, pointed instrument, such as a knife.

Chapter 11
Review Questions

1. drug
2. True

3. False
4. physical
5. True
6. False
7. regular
8. analgesics; depressive
9. opium
10. heroin
11. OxyContin
12. True
13. hallucinogens
14. hashish
15. THC
16. True
17. liquid hashish
18. lysergic acid
19. clandestine
20. True
21. barbiturates
22. True
23. methaqualone
24. antipsychotic; antianxiety
25. False
26. stimulants
27. cocaine
28. sniffed/snorted
29. False
30. GHB; Rohypnol
31. anabolic
32. five
33. I
34. IV
35. False
36. Marquis
37. marijuana
38. Scott
39. microcrystalline
40. thin-layer chromatography
41. False
42. dispersion
43. True
44. electromagnetic spectrum
45. lower
46. can
47. ultraviolet; visible

48. infrared
49. spectrophotometry; spectrophotometer
50. gas chromatography
51. mass spectrometer
52. mass spectrometry
53. True

Application and Critical Thinking

1. The drug used by the individual was probably amphetamine, cocaine, or phencyclidine. All of these drugs produce psychological dependence, which would explain the individual's behavior, but none are known to produce physical dependence that would cause sickness or physical discomfort.

2. a. depressants; examples include alcohol, barbiturates, and tranquilizers
   b. hallucinogens; examples include marijuana, LSD, PCP, and MDMA (Ecstasy)
   c. stimulants; examples include amphetamines, methamphetamine, and cocaine
   d. narcotics; examples include heroin, morphine, codeine, and synthetic opiates such as OxyContin and methadone

3. a. schedule III
   b. schedule V
   c. schedule II
   d. schedule I

4. A screening test performed for heroin is the Marquis color test. If the powder tests positive for heroin, you would conduct confirmation tests, including mass spectrometry or IR spectrophotometry.

5. a. phenobarbital
   b. butabarbital
   c. three minutes

6. cocaine = B (Scott Test)
   barbiturates = D (Dillie-Koppanyi Test)
   heroin = A (Marquis Test)
   amphetamine = E (Marquis Test)
   marijuana = C (Duquenois-Levine Test)

Chapter 12
Review Questions

1. toxicologist
2. False
3. ethyl alcohol
4. metabolism
5. faster
6. oxidation; excretion
7. liver

8. breath
9. 0.015
10. False
11. True
12. 30; 90
13. artery; vein
14. pulmonary
15. alveoli
16. 2,100
17. False
18. False
19. infrared
20. fuel cell
21. 15; 20
22. True
23. gas chromatography
24. nonalcoholic
25. True
26. 0.08
27. four
28. *Schmerber* v. *California*
29. morphine
30. blood; urine
31. acids; bases
32. False
33. pH
34. screening; confirmation
35. thin-layer chromatography; gas chromatography; immunoassay
36. gas chromatography; mass spectrometry
37. hair
38. carbon monoxide
39. False
40. True
41. corroborate
42. drug recognition expert

Application and Critical Thinking

1. a. Randy is four times as likely to have an accident as a sober person.

   b. Marissa's blood-alcohol concentration is approximately 0.13.

   c. Charles is more intoxicated; his blood-alcohol concentration is approximately 0.11.

   d. At the original NHTSA standard of 0.15, an individual is about 25 times more likely to have an accident than is a sober person.

2. John (a), Gary (c), Frank (b), Stephen (d)

3. Bill (a) and Carrie (d) are both legally drunk in Australia and Sweden. Sally (b) is legally drunk in Sweden. Rich (c) is legally drunk in all three countries.

4. Barbiturates are acidic drugs, which means they have a pH of less than 7. You can use this knowledge to devise a simple test to determine which blood sample contains barbiturates. First, dissolve blood from each sample into separate containers of water. To each container add an acidic substance such as hydrochloric acid (to make the water more acidic). Then add an organic solvent such as chloroform to the water in each container. The blood sample containing barbiturates will be easily identified because acidic drugs are readily removed from an acidic solution with an organic solvent.

5. To determine whether the victim died before or as the result of the fire, measure the level of carbon monoxide in the victim's blood. High levels of carbon monoxide in the victim's blood indicate that he or she breathed the combustion products of the fire and was therefore alive when the fire started. Low levels of carbon monoxide indicate that the victim did not breathe the combustion products of the fire and was therefore dead before the fire started.

Chapter 13
Review Questions

1. hair follicle
2. cuticle; cortex; medulla
3. cuticle
4. cortex
5. medulla
6. medullary index
7. one-third; one-half
8. True
9. True
10. anagen; catagen; telogen
11. True
12. True
13. comparison
14. pubic
15. True
16. False
17. True
18. DNA
19. anagen; catagen
20. True
21. 25
22. 25
23. origin

24. natural fibers

25. cotton

26. regenerated

27. synthetic

28. False

29. True

30. visible

31. infrared

32. False

33. False

34. carriers

Application and Critical Thinking

1. a. telogen phase

   b. anagen phase

   c. anagen phase

   d. catagen phase

2. Because hair grows at a rate of about 1 centimeter per month, we know that the hair was dyed approximately six weeks earlier.

3. a. Caucasian

   b. Mongoloid

   c. Negroid

   d. Caucasian

4. Pete made several mistakes. First, he should have packaged all items of clothing containing fiber evidence in paper, not plastic. Second, he should have placed each individual piece of fiber evidence in a separate container. Third, he should have carefully folded the sheet before packaging it, rather than simply balling it up. Fourth, he should have used forceps, rather than his fingers, to collect fibers from the windowsill. Finally, he should have folded the fibers from the windowsill inside a piece of paper and then placed it in another container, not into a regular envelope

5. A = interrupted, B = absent, C = fragmented, D = continuous, E = interrupted, F = continuous, G = absent, H = absent, I = absent

6. Human = imbricate

   Mink = spinous

   Muscrat = imbricate

   Rabbit = spinous

   Goat = imbricate

   Sea otter = spinous

   Hamster = coronal

   Seal = spinous

7. Hair from car of worker C is consistent with victim's hair in width, color, and medulla pattern. This warrants further investigation.

Chapter 14
Review Questions

1. pigment

2. binder

3. True

4. stereoscopic

5. layer structure

6. layer structure

7. True

8. pyrogram

9. Paint Data Query (PDQ)

10. True

11. glass

12. False

13. tempered

14. laminated

15. individual

16. density; refractive index

17. floatation

18. Becke line

19. frequency of occurrence

20. radial

21. concentric

22. False

23. False

24. opposite

25. False

26. terminate

27. solid

28. paper

29. False

30. dried

31. minerals

32. True

33. 100

34. False

Application and Critical Thinking

1. In a hit-and-run situation, you would collect from each vehicle standard/reference samples that include all the paint layers down to the bare metal. This is best accomplished by removing a painted section with a clean scalpel or knife blade. Standard/reference samples should be collected from an undamaged area of each vehicle because other portions of the car may have faded or been repainted. To avoid cross-contamination of paints, carefully wipe the blade of any knife or scraping tool used before collecting each sample.

2. Windows on U.S.-built cars use laminated glass in their windshields and tempered glass for all other windows. From this evidence, the investigator knows that the other car involved in the accident has a broken side window, with its windshield intact.

3. Because the cracks from bullet holes A and C both terminate at the cracks from bullet hole B, bullet hole B was made first. Because the cracks from bullet hole C also terminate at the cracks from bullet hole A, bullet hole A was made second. Thus, bullet hole C was the last one made.

4. If this is a radial fracture, the force was applied from the left side of the glass. If it is a concentric fracture, the force was applied from the right side of the glass. The 3R rule states that *R*adial cracks form a *R*ight angle on the *R*everse side of the force. The cracks in the picture form a right angle on the right side of the glass, so if it is a radial fracture, the force was applied to the reverse (left) side of the glass.

5. Jared made several mistakes. First, the samples he removed from the scene should have included only the top layer of soil. Second, he should have collected soil samples from both alibi locations—the garden and the parking lot. Third, he should have packaged the shoes in paper, not plastic. Finally, he should have dried all of the soil samples under identical laboratory conditions before examining any of them.

Chapter 15
Review Questions

1. type
2. True
3. plasma
4. serum
5. red blood cells
6. antigens
7. A
8. False
9. A; B
10. Rh
11. antibodies
12. False
13. agglutination
14. B; A
15. True
16. A
17. B
18. antibodies
19. benzidine
20. Kastle-Meyer
21. luminol
22. precipitin
23. gel diffusion
24. acid phosphatase
25. spermatozoa
26. True
27. prostate specific antigen (PSA)/ p30
28. True
29. true
30. gene
31. chromosome
32. twenty-three
33. alleles
34. homozygous
35. nucleotide
36. four
37. double helix
38. A-C-G-T
39. True
40. polymerase chain reaction (PCR)
41. short tandem repeats (STRs)
42. False
43. polymerase chain reaction (PCR)
44. multiplexing
45. capillary electrophoresis
46. True
47. mother
48. False
49. CODIS (Combined DNA Index System)
50. eighteen
51. infectious
52. False
53. False
54. buccal swab

Application and Critical Thinking

1. Scott chose the acid phosphatase test because it is extremely useful in searching for semen on large areas of fabric, such as a blanket. He concluded that the blanket did not contain evidence of semen. First, he knew that certain fruit juices, including watermelon, can generate a positive reaction with acid phosphatase testing. However, these juices react much more slowly to the test than does semen. A reaction time of less than 30 seconds is considered a strong indication of semen. Because it took 3 minutes to obtain a positive reaction, Scott concluded that the positive reaction was caused by the watermelon.

2. Cathy made four mistakes in collecting evidence. First, she should have placed a paper sheet over the sheet on which the victim disrobed in order to collect any loose material

that may have fallen from the victim or the clothing. Second, she should have placed each item of clothing in a separate bag instead of placing all of them in the same bag. Third, she should have taken two additional vaginal swabs, smearing them onto microscope slides. Finally, she should have collected fingernail scrapings from the victim.

3. G–C–T–T–A–G–C–G–T–T–A–G–C–T–G–G–A–C

4. Investigators use mtDNA to determine whether the body is that of the victim of the unsolved murder. To do so, you would collect mtDNA from one of the victim's maternal relatives and compare it to the mtDNA recovered from the body. If the samples match, the body is that of the victim.

5. With an STR, you should expect to see a two-band pattern. The presence of more than two bands suggests a mixture of DNA from more than one source.

6. The attacker is a male, shown by the presence of two bands, one for the X chromosome and one for the Y chromosome.

7. A. saliva

   B. skin cells and sweat

   C. saliva, sweat, and skin cells

   D. saliva and skin cells

   E. sweat, skin cells, and blood

   F. sweat, semen, and skin cells

   G. saliva

   H. sweat and skin cells

8. The profile and read-out do not match. The remains are NOT those of James Dittman. They differ at D21S11, PENTA E, D13S807, CSF1PO.

Chapter 16
Review Questions

1. oxidation
2. False
3. energy
4. chemical; heat; mechanical
5. breaking; formation
6. absorb; liberate
7. heat of combustion
8. True
9. ignition
10. gaseous
11. flash point
12. pyrolysis
13. flammable range
14. glowing combustion
15. True
16. spontaneous combustion
17. True
18. origin
19. True
20. vapor
21. False
22. airtight
23. True
24. Molotov cocktail
25. headspace
26. gas chromatograph
27. mass spectrometer
28. explosion
29. True
30. low
31. deflagration
32. potassium nitrate; charcoal; sulfur
33. high
34. black powder; smokeless powder
35. confined
36. False
37. primary; secondary
38. RDX
39. PETN
40. initiating
41. crater
42. ion mobility spectrometer
43. microscopic
44. True

Application and Critical Thinking

1. You should suspect arson. Although the conditions in which the oil was stored—high heat and lack of ventilation—may lead to spontaneous combustion with some materials, spontaneous combustion does not occur with hydrocarbon lubricating oils such as motor oil. The owner is lying about the oil igniting spontaneously; he may have deliberately set the fire to collect on the increased insurance.

2. Mick made several mistakes. First, he should have used separate containers for each location where debris was collected. Debris should have come from the point of origin of the fire, not from the surrounding rooms. He should not have placed the timbers in plastic bags, which react with hydrocarbons and permit volatile hydrocarbon vapors to be depleted. Finally, Mick should have collected the suspect's clothes to undergo laboratory analysis for the presence of accelerant residues.

3. a. High explosives. Lead azide is a common component of blasting caps, which are used to detonate high explosives.

b. Low explosives. Nitrocellulose is an ingredient in smoke-less powder, one of the most common low explosives.

c. High explosives. Ammonium nitrate is the primary ingredient in a number of high explosives that have replaced dynamite for industrial uses.

d. High explosives. Primacord is used as a detonator to ignite several high-explosive charges simultaneously.

e. Low explosives. Potassium chlorate mixed with sugar is a popular low explosive.

4. a. Alcoholic KOH. Tetryl is the only explosive that produces a red-violet color in response to this test.

b. Alcoholic KOH. TNT produces a distinctive red color in response to the alcoholic KOH test.

c. Diphenylamine produces a blue color. No color is produced in response to the Greiss test or to the alcoholic KOH test.

d. Diphenylamine. Nitrocellulose produces a distinctive blue-black color in response to this test.

5. Matt made several mistakes. First, to avoid contaminating the scene, Matt should have put on disposable gloves, shoe covers, and overalls before beginning his search. Second, he should have used a wire mesh screen to sift through the debris instead of picking through it by hand. Third, he should have stored all explosive evidence in airtight metal containers, not plastic or paper bags. Fourth, Matt should have collected material not only from the immediate area of the blast but also from materials blown away from the blast's origin.

Chapter 17
Review Questions

1. questioned document
2. True
3. False
4. known; questioned
5. False
6. style
7. exemplars
8. less
9. False
10. *Gilbert* v. *California*
11. False
12. conscious
13. ten
14. transmitting terminal identifier (TTI)
15. toner
16. ultraviolet; infrared
17. infrared
18. True
19. charred
20. indented
21. microspectrophotometer
22. thin-layer
23. True

Application and Critical Thinking

1. Julie made several mistakes. She should have given the suspect a pencil, not a pen, because the original notes were written in pencil. She should have had the suspect prepare at least a full page of writing, and she should have had him write the material at least three times. Also, she should not have spelled any words for the suspect. Finally, Julie should have shown the original threatening notes to a document examiner before taking exemplars from the suspect, not afterward.

2. a. Photograph the document with infrared-sensitive film.

b. Examine the document under infrared or ultraviolet lighting.

c. Examine the document under ultraviolet lighting.

d. Photograph the document with infrared-sensitive film, or reflect light off the paper's surface at different angles in order to contrast the writing against the charred background.

3. The aspects of the document you would examine to determine whether the document was authentic would be the paper and the ink. You would use thin-layer chromatography to characterize the dye used in the ink and thus determine whether that particular ink was in use when the original document was prepared.

Chapter 18
Review Questions

1. preserving; acquiring; extracting; analyzing; interpreting
2. True
3. software
4. ROM
5. system unit
6. True
7. False
8. permanent
9. central processing unit (CPU)
10. hard disc drive (HDD)
11. network interface card
12. operating system
13. sectors; clusters; tracks; cylinders
14. bit
15. byte
16. cluster

17. forensic image
18. visible
19. swap
20. temporary
21. latent
22. sector
23. RAM; file
24. RAM
25. unallocated space
26. True
27. True
28. IP address
29. cache
30. cookie
31. IP
32. True
33. log files; volatile memory; network traffic
34. firewalls
35. Faraday shield
36. True

Application and Critical Thinking

1. Because each sector is 512 bytes, a cluster consisting of 6 sectors would hold 3,072 bytes of data. Because each byte equals 8 bits, each cluster would hold 24,576 bits of data.

2. Tom made several mistakes. When he arrived, he should have sketched the overall layout as well as photographing it. He also should have photographed any running monitors. In addition to labeling the cord of each peripheral, Tom should have placed a corresponding label on the port to which each cord was connected. Before unplugging the computer, he should have checked to ensure that the computer was not using encryption. Finally, he should have removed the plug from the back of the computer, not from the wall.

3. You probably would begin to search for latent data in the swap space on the hard disk drive. If the accountant was keeping fraudulent records, he may have been transferring data from one accounting program to another. Data from those operations will be left behind in the swap space, where it can be retrieved later.

4. On the first computer you probably would look first at the compound files created by Microsoft Outlook. On the second computer you probably would look first in the Internet cache.

Chapter 19
Review Questions

1. 2G
2. True
3. True
4. difficult
5. iPad; iPhone
6. geolocation
7. Web searching
8. physical; logical
9. True
10. False
11. twice
12. logical
13. architecture
14. SD or secure digital cards
15. True
16. SIM
17. clone
18. False
19. chain of evidence
20. temporal
21. casual
22. hybrid
23. network
24. WiFi, WiFi
25. True

Application and Critical Thinking

1. Place the phone in a Faraday box or bag to prevent it from communicating with the outside. When you analyze the device, be sure to follow the recommendations of the tool you are using for analysis. Do an Internet search to learn as much about the device's make and model as you can before attempting acquisition and analysis if you are unfamiliar with the specific device.

2. Chain of evidence describes the events leading up to the crime and the supporting evidence. Chain of custody describes the measures taken to control access to evidence from the time it is collected to the time it is used in court or another tribunal.

3. Since mobile devices "ping" (query) the cell towers that support them in whatever location they are at the time, those pings are logged and, by comparing the logs of cell

towers in the area of a crime, a pattern of mobile device use associated with those towers can be extracted and individual mobile devices can be traced as they move from tower to tower.

4. They are the same in architectural issues such as processors and file systems but the nature of those architectures are different between mobile devices and computers. This is because mobile devices have special requirements such as multiple radios (e.g., WiFi and 4G), size restrictions, storage space, and so on.

5. SD cards add storage to the device while SIMs contain critical information about the device such as its subscriber identification information. Not all mobile devices have these. If the device does not have a SIM, the contents of the SIM will be embedded in the device's system board on an on-board chip. If it does not have the ability to add an SD card, the device will be limited to the amount of on-board storage that comes with the device.

6. This is the international mobile subscriber identity (IMSI) number that associates the phone with the subscriber's mobile network. It is on the SIM or what substitutes for the SIM and it can be used for tracking the device.

7. GPS, if turned on, allows geolocation of the device. GPS information residing in the device can be correlated with the physically reported actions of the user to verify truthfulness. It also can be used to track the device's location in real time. Real-time tracking requires special tools, however.

:: INDEX